Contemporary Arab

CONTEMPORARY ARAB THOUGHT

Studies in Post-1967 Arab Intellectual History

Ibrahim M. Abu-Rabi‘

Pluto Press
LONDON • STERLING, VIRGINIA

First published 2004 by Pluto Press
345 Archway Road, London N6 5AA
and 22883 Quicksilver Drive, Sterling, VA 20166–2012, USA

www.plutobooks.com

British Library Cataloguing in Publication Data
A catalogue record for this book is available from the British Library

ISBN 0-7453-2170-4 hardback
ISBN 0-7453-2169-0 paperback

Library of Congress Cataloging-in-Publication Data

Abu-Rabi‘, Ibrahim M.
Contemporary Arab thought: studies in post-1967 Arab intellectual history / Ibrahim M. Abu-Rabi‘.
p. cm.
Includes bibliographical references and index.
ISBN 0-7453-2170-4—ISBN 0-7453-2169-0 (pbk.)
1. Arab countries—Intellectual life—20th century. 2. Arab nationalism. 3. Secularism—Arab countries. 4. Islamic renewal. 5. Islam and politics—Arab countries. 6. Globalization. I. Title.
DS36.88.A275 2004
909′.09749270825—dc21
2003010260

10 9 8 7 6 5 4 3 2 1

Designed and produced for Pluto Press by
Chase Publishing Services, Fortescue, Sidmouth, EX10 9QG, England
Typeset from disk by Newgen Imaging Systems, India
Printed and bound in Canada by
Transcontinental Printing

To Jasmine, Adam, and Jad:
Three Flowers from the Garden of Paradise

Contents

Acknowledgments

I spent eight years researching and writing this book. Over these years, a number of institutions and people made it possible for me to complete this project. In this regard, I would like to thank the Fulbright Foundation for its generous financial help which enabled me to live in three different Arab countries in 1997: Morocco, Egypt, and Syria. I had the benefit of meeting with a number of prominent Arab thinkers in those countries, among whom were Muḥammad ʻĀbid al-Jābīrī in Morocco, Ḥassan Ḥanafī, the late Muḥammad al-Ghazālī, Fahmī Huwaydī, and Muḥammad ʻImārah in Egypt, Ṣādiq Jalāl al-ʻAzm and Muḥammad Shaḥrūr in Syria, to mention but a few.

My thanks also go to Ms. Valerie Vick, Assistant Editor of *The Muslim World*, for copyediting the entire text. I did benefit a lot from her.

Finally, I should like to thank my colleagues at Hartford Seminary for their understanding and encouragement.

Foreword
The Travails of the Arab Intellectual

Ghada Talhami
D. K. Pearsons Professor of Politics
Lake Forest College, Illinois, USA

The war which the United States waged on Iraq eliminated the last bastion of Arab nationalism in the region, heralding a new age. This was painful and reminiscent of the past when Britain occupied the position of the world's great hegemon. Memories of the ignominious departure of that power from the region did little to dissuade the new overlords who quickly proceeded to secure their physical and cultural space. The result was hastening the process of globalization, economically as well as intellectually. Moreover, this much maligned term, which referred to the regularization of all economic relationships in favor of the super-capitalist powers of the world, alienated the poor masses of the underdeveloped segment of the globe. It is one of the contradictions of globalization that the more world markets are integrated, the more unequal becomes the distribution of wealth. Unable to perform the desired role of consumers of manufactured goods, the poor become a burden on the world economic system and its most visible victims.

This is the story of the Arab world today, especially as it moves from crisis to crisis and from economic loss to greater intellectual decline. But who speaks for the Arab world? Who speaks for its devastated and impoverished classes, as well as for its defeated intelligentsia? This is the main theme of this study, which, while definitely focused on the contemporary period, also takes the long view of the crisis of the Arab intellectual. In the long run, the Iraqi defeat may prove to be more devastating for the region than that other seismic event, namely the 1967 Arab-Israeli war, which the author correctly identifies as the great divide separating the Arab age of the *nakbah* and its accompanying sense of bereavement and shock from the age of despondency and deepening crisis. But since no comprehensive analysis of the intellectual confusion resulting from the events of 1967 exists, the task at hand becomes the necessary prelude to greater understanding.

It is also important to note the author's choice of the Arab world as the metaphor for the hegemonic consequences of globalization and his reference to the area's deep cultural wounds as but one of the most egregious examples of the human cost of this phenomenon. The Arab world, in a very colonial sense, remains vital to the survival of world capitalism both economically and strategically. No global power can afford to overlook its geographic location or its riches as long as the world continues to live under one hegemon. The Arab world, as the core of the Middle East, has the capacity to create a unified regional system capable of genuine autonomous rule based on its homogenous culture, past political experience and the existence of vast natural resources. The determination of the United States and others before it to annex it to the global world markets, is, therefore, neither novel nor surprising.

The author builds his case around the inevitable collusion between economics, religion and culture in order to maintain world leadership and control. For him, as for Antonio Gramsci in his prison notes, hegemony is elusive unless serviced by a class of intellectuals. The Gramscian world of the intellectual

> speaks of the non-neutrality of ideas and knowledge, of the partiality, that is, of the producers and disseminators of knowledge, of the political role of the intellectual as part of a system of relations that is inscribed by power and domination.[1]

Only the intellectuals, hence, are capable of acting as legitimators of power and its system of values. What Gramsci calls the "organic intellectuals," accompany the rise of every historical phase of human development. Hegemony often results in counter-hegemony which can only be legitimized by the intellectuals. But this study is not only an exposé of the work of Gramsci, the great Western Marxist, it is also a thoughtful recall of Samir Amin's contribution to our understanding of economics and intellectual dominance in the modern world. Amin not only heightened our understanding of the effects of hegemonic capitalism on the underdeveloped world, he also amplified the relationship between colonialism, capitalism and religion.

The author thus makes a concerted effort to distinguish various class formations and strands of social thought which reflect the dilemmas of each age. This gets him into the "problematic" of religion and changes in the Arab educational system, which diminished the power and influence of the traditional religious intelligentsia. The decline of the Muslim intelligentsia due to the spread of Western or modern education, first witnessed in Egypt, is one of his major themes. He then asks whether or not it would be appropriate to consider the Islamic intellectuals the "organic intellectuals" of Gramsci's definition.

The book poses additional crucial questions to students of Middle East history. Did Islam mandate the creation of a state, or was it intended to be a social system of values? Why is democracy absent from the debates of the intellectuals both before and after 1967? Or should we be satisfied with issues that could only be described as the preconditions of democracy and which were always the subject of debate? Despite the absence of the modern language of democracy, according to the contentions of Bernard Lewis, the ideas of what could be termed civil society, pluralism, and justice, both in its political and economic sense, were always emphasized. Did not constitutionalism occupy the attention of late nineteenth century intellectuals to such an extent that Shaykh Muḥammad 'Abduh, the Mufti of Egypt and its greatest Muslim reformer criticized Aḥmad 'Urābī's military solution for Egypt's colonial oppression?

Only this author, additionally, examines the Arab intellectuals' common experience of migration and imprisonment. These were two salient features of the life

[1] Renate Holub, *Antonio Gramsci: Beyond Marxism and Postmodernism* (London: Routledge, 1992), 24.

of the Arab intelligentsia, an experience which crept into their work but was hardly noted by scholars of Arab social thought. Indeed, one cannot overestimate the significance or meaning of the physical migration of Sayyid Quṭb or the spiritual migration of Munīr Shafīq. Neither can one ignore the prison experience of Nawal El-Saadawi or Rāshid al-Ghannūshī. The author also does not overlook the impact of oil and the oil economy on generations of writers, fueling the careers of traditional scholars, salafis, and sycophants, as well as erstwhile critics of the ideology of pan-Arabism. He keenly analyzes the superficial and technical types of modernization overtaking the Arab Gulf countries today as the work of the "Bedouin bourgeoisie" whose absorption of Western ideas rarely exceeded adaptation to consumerism and the material culture of industrialized societies. He describes their role today as the class which dominates the lives of naive Muslim believers flocking to their hallowed shrines and a multinational Muslim Asian workforce drawn to the Gulf countries by dreams of piety and prosperity.

It should be pointed out that the author possesses encyclopedic knowledge of modern intellectual life and social thought in the Arab World. He examines the work of crucial Arab writers who are still unknown to the Western reader. For the first time, the ideas and influence of such ideological figures as the Lebanese Marxist Mahdī 'Āmil, the Maghrebi liberal etatist Abdallah Laroui, and the Tunisian Islamist Rāshid al-Ghannūshī are brought to light. The work of these three alone illustrates not only the fecundity of modern Arab social thought but also the courage of that same intellectual class who challenge the forces of capitalist domination, sterile traditionalism and strict dogmatism.

Finally, the book provides new insights into the travails of the Arab intellectual by situating the author's own life journey within the narrative of the Arab intelligentsia. Abu-Rabi''s journey epitomizes the social and ideological alienation of the Arab intellectual, who, as in Albert Camus' *The Stranger*, develops the courage to rebel against his own environment. In a very genuine way, the author represents the final metamorphosis of the alienated intellectual into the social critic simply because, as in this case, he stands astride Israel, the place of his birth, and the Arab World, the embodiment of his cultural and civilizational universe. That experience alone has prepared him well for the writing of this book.

Preface

Of the many audiences I had in mind when writing this book, it is primarily addressed to the Muslim intelligentsia – professionals, teachers, students, and political activists – residing in the West, both indigenous and immigrant. They need to ask themselves the following questions: first, why have they failed to produce a critical and constructive Islamic theory of knowledge that will enable them to wrestle with the multitude of problems facing Muslims in the West, or, to be more precise, in any of the world's advanced capitalist societies? Second, why have they been unable to reinterpret and reactivate the "revolutionary heritage" of Islam that appears in the lives and thought of such people as Abū Dhar al-Ghifārī, 'Alī bin Abī Tālib, and 'Umar 'Abd al-'Azīz in the past, 'Abd al-Qādir al-Jazāi'rī, Jamāl al-Dīn al-Afghānī, 'Abd al-Karīm al-Khaṭṭābī, Sayyid Quṭb, Muḥammad Ḥussain Faḍlallah, the early Elijah Muḥammad, and Malcolm X in the modern era? Third, why have they failed to learn from the tradition of liberation theology, as practiced in Latin America, North America, Africa, and the Philippines?

The disheartening fact is that the Muslim community in the West is in a state of intellectual and religious disarray. This became glaringly apparent after the tragic attacks on the United States on September 11, 2001. The old methods and ways of thinking from "back home" have not translated well here, and the "Islamization of knowledge," adopted by some supposedly independent Muslim intellectuals in the West, seems to be a hopeless case of mere theorization. Some who espouse the underlying themes of the modernity paradigm have also failed to inform us as to how to become both "Muslim" and "modern." It is only by appealing to the long and established critical tradition in Islamic thought and practice and adopting reflective criticism that the Muslim intelligentsia will be able to rid itself of its complacent attitude toward what it calls "Islam," find ways to break out of its current historical impasse, in the Muslim world or in the West, and become a leading light to the downtrodden Muslim masses.

A simple detour to the revolutionary heritage of Islam is not a simple matter, especially in light of the world's tremendous intellectual and scientific achievements of the past two centuries. To be effective, any Islamic revolutionary discourse must take into account the numerous modern intellectual breakthroughs in the fields of the social sciences and humanities. An amalgamation of the Islamic radical discourse with the Western critical method is critical. Before we can begin the process of recentering ourselves, we must first decenter ourselves. Critical theory, in its various expressions and representations, from George Hegel to Karl Marx and down to Hannah Arendt, Max Horkheimer and Jürgen Habermas, forms a central force in Western critical tradition. Muslim intellectuals cannot keep on ignoring this important factor. Critical theory must play a leading role if theorization is to gain any validity. Modern critical theory, which must be wedded to the vast revolutionary Islamic tradition, has mainly been a product of critical reflection on the profound economic, cultural, and social transformations brought about by capitalism, which has since its appearance as a social system in the eighteenth century never ceased revolutionizing its means of production and universalizing its economic interests.

No Muslim or Third World intellectual can derive the necessary lessons from the predicaments of his/her society without first having a deep appreciation and critical understanding of capitalism. Capitalism has been the dominant economic, social, cultural, and political system in the Muslim and Arab worlds in the past two centuries. In this instance, critical theory in its different variations provides the necessary intellectual tools to grasp the problematic of capitalism.

It is only by seeking a rapprochement between the critical Islamic perspective and Western critical theory that the Muslim intelligentsia can reassert itself in its role of thorough consciousness and radical critique. The Arab and Muslim intelligentsia in both the West and the Arab and Muslim worlds must avoid sterilization of thought if they are to develop a mature consciousness of the multitude of problems affecting their world. As the Ecuadorian novelist Eduardo Galeano says, "The best way to colonize consciousness is to suppress it."

Some Arab and Muslim thinkers argue that accepting any form of Western knowledge is antithetical to Arab or Muslim cultural identity. This contentious and unproductive position prohibits us from grasping the nature of the most significant processes taking place in the Third World since the dawn of colonialism. It is inconceivable to articulate a credible Islamic/Arab/Third World critique of contemporary thought and life without having a background in the central arguments of Western critical theory, including Marxism. I hope that this book will encourage educated Muslims to take critical theory seriously.

Besides targeting the Muslim intelligentsia in the West, this book addresses those Arab intellectuals who have long been searching for the best methods of liberating their societies from internal exploitation and external domination. Although Western academia has dramatically increased our knowledge about the Arab world, the main contemporary Arab intellectuals, who write primarily in Arabic, have sadly been forgotten. This book is a reflection on the state of Arab thought and ideology since the debacle of 1967. One may divide thought into "official thought" and "popular thought." This book is sympathetic to the popular discourse and attempts to reveal the grandiose pretensions of "official thought" and its incompatibility with the demands of the contemporary age.

This book deals with post-1967 Arab intellectual history from the perspective of critical social thought and philosophy. Before 1967, some Arab countries launched an optimistic program of modernization; however, many hopes were dashed after the 1967 Arab defeat with Israel. The conservative Gulf states in the 1970s launched an ambitious program of modernization that was, alas, bereft of critical modernism, of a consciousness of being modern. In one sense, this book is about the Arab world's aborted modernity of the past several decades.

Apart from following a rigorous social and philosophical analysis, this book deals with such pertinent issues as the Sharīʿah and human rights questions, civil society, secularism, and globalization in the modern Arab world. To bring some focus to these crucial issues, I present the theories of a number of distinguished Arab thinkers who represent the most established trends of thought in the Arab world such as Muḥammad ʿĀbid al-Jābirī, Abdallah Laroui,

Muḥammad al-Ghazālī, Rāshid al-Ghannūshī, Costantine Zurayk, Mahdī ‘Āmil, and many others.

The following 14 theses more or less summarize the arguments presented in this book.

First thesis: "Modern Arab thought" is a complex term that encompasses a constellation of social/political/religious/ideological ideas that have evolved, more or less, over the past 200 years and that represent the leading positions of the social classes in Arab societies. Even if we were to reduce, for the sake of simplicity and clarification, modern Arab thought to "fixed" and "changing" variables, both "fixity" and "change" would have to be appraised against the changing historical and political context of the above period.

Second thesis: Modern Arab thought has matured against two solid historical backgrounds: first is the historical setting of the Arab world, which began with the rise of Islam and which has gone through many profound changes in its long history, and the second is the Western setting, which became an integral part of the modern history of the Arab world after the immense expansion of capitalism there in the nineteenth century. These settings are by no means equivalent. The Arab world, in its long evolution since the beginning of Islam, had failed to produce its capitalist mode of production on the eve of its encounter with the European capitalist mode of production. Western capitalist civilization, mushrooming around the world in the nineteenth century, has been double-edged: it has brought both exploitation and progress to the Arab world. This civilization was a direct consequence of the Western modernity project that began after the European discovery, or stumbling upon, of the New World after 1492. That is to say, modern world history is only around 500 years old: this is considered the age of modernity. It began after the European discovery of the new world in reaction to Muslim dominance in North Africa and the East. From its beginning, modernity has been double-edged: it contained within it both creative, scientific, and exploitative dimensions. In addition to representing rationalism, discovery, and the systematization of disciplines, modernity represents encounter, domination, and exploitation. Of course, modernity has gone through some major transformations in 500 years. Current globalization is a direct consequence of double-edged modernity.

Third thesis: The capitalist mode of production has significantly changed since the nineteenth century. Although it is incorrect to equate capitalism with Europeanization or Americanization, the capitalist mode of production enabled Europe in the colonial era, and the United States in the post-colonial era, to spread their hegemony around the globe. Since the nineteenth century, both the capitalist mode of production and European/American hegemony have to a large extent shaped the Arab world. It is therefore quite impossible to understand the significant political, economic, and religious movements of the modern Arab world without taking these two factors into account. Also, the fate of the Arab bourgeoisie has been intrinsically linked to that of international capitalism.

Fourth thesis: Due to the insatiable capitalist demand for cheap commodities (oil is a major current example) and the pressure of hegemonic powers, direct military interventions or conquests have been unavoidable in the modern world. Japan provides a major example of military conquest in Southeast Asia before and during World War Two and the United States is another example of military presence in the Gulf states after the end of the second Gulf War in 1991.

Fifth thesis: Capitalist civilization is the only dominant and transnational civilization in the contemporary world. Its evolution has been both painful and ecstatic. It is both constructive and destructive, promising and disappointing. A clashing of civilizations is a myth in the contemporary age. What exists is a clash of cultures, languages, or ideologies in the context of the domination of the capitalist civilization.

Sixth thesis: In the same vein, it is fallacious to speak of a clash between "Islam" or "the Muslim world" and capitalist civilization. One may speak of a clash between the Muslim world or certain countries in the Muslim world and the West. While Islam is a major component of the Arab culture and worldview and while Muslim forces have played a leading role in fighting against colonial powers, there is no "Islamic civilization" as such, and no conclusive proof that "Islam and capitalism" are incompatible. It is true that there are dominant or competing Muslim cultures or perspectives, but they must be understood only against the context of the dominant capitalist civilization. What is crucial to underline here is that the dominant mode of production in the world today is essentially capitalist. The Muslim world too has fallen to the capitalist mode of production, although in certain parts feudal elements still languish.

Seventh thesis: Although the most basic questions of modern Arab thought were raised by the nineteenth century Arab intelligentsia in their painful burgeoning awareness of the clash between their societies and the imperialist West, the questions they raised at the beginning of the twenty-first century are much more complex and wide ranging. In the course of one century or so, the Arab world has moved from being dominated by colonial modernity to being dominated by global capitalism. This transition has engendered many political, social, economic, and ideological movements within the Arab world that were either pro- or anti-Western hegemony. Political and economic structures, with the blessings of some intelligentsia, are there to support the domination of global capitalism.

Eighth thesis: One can speak of one Arab culture, distinguished by language, religion, and destiny. However, in the final analysis, what underlies Arab culture is a constellation of competing ideologies, or "cultural blocs," each of which struggles to enforce its worldview and project on society at large. The most dominant ideology in the Arab world represents the alliance of various social groups who will continue their hegemony by all sorts of means, including the manipulation of religious sentiment. These ideologies reflect different contending political, social, economic, and religious forces in society. The interplay between the sum of these forces is different from one Arab country to another and might also be different over time.

Ninth thesis: The crisis of culture in the contemporary Arab world is not so much due to the "loss of religious values" or a "doctrinal conflict between Islam and the West" or "cultural invasion" as much as it is due to the structural economic and, to a certain extent, political hegemony of the Arab world by the Western world. The Arab ruling classes have not as of yet figured out how to remove their economies from this dependency.

Tenth thesis: Because of the uniqueness of modern Arab history (in the sense that it has been an amalgamation of two sets of conditions or backgrounds), it is inaccurate to assume that modern political or social phenomena in the Arab world are carbon copies of those in the West. What this means is that the terms used should be qualified and linked to their socio-economic conditions. Take the example of nationalism. While European nationalisms and colonialism were wed in the nineteenth and twentieth centuries, Arab nationalism grew in opposition to Ottoman decline in the Middle East, and later fought European colonialism. However, that does not mean that twentieth century Arab nationalism was opposed in principle to capitalist modernization. Many Arab states or social forces within Arab societies have sought to apply their versions of capitalist or socialist modernization.

Eleventh thesis: Official Arab ideology, although dominant, is not the only source of modern Arab thought. Official ideology reflects, in large measure, the consensus reached by the Arab political elite on a number of issues. However, more often than not, official ideology is at odds with popular culture and competing intellectual ideologies in society. Furthermore, some official ideologies in the Arab world are not necessarily anti-religious or pro-secular.

Twelfth thesis: Over the past two centuries, the Arab intelligentsia has become very diversified. There are no consistent characteristics of the contemporary Arab intelligentsia. In other words, it is fallacious to argue, for example, that the religious intelligentsia is the only class of intelligentsia in Arab society. Furthermore, the current religious intelligentsia in the Arab world is much more complex and varied than its predecessor of the eighteenth or nineteenth centuries. Since the rise of the nation-state, the religious intelligentsia has faced tremendous changes and challenges. Some religious intellectuals have opted to work for the state, while others have worked to oppose it.

Thirteenth thesis: The preceding point begs the question of the articulation of Islam in contemporary Arab society. While one may argue that normative Islam is distinguised by a high sense of religious and intellectual integrity, the articulation of Islam or Islamic ideas is diverse, competitive, and ideological in nature. This articulation can be both pacifist or revolutionary.

Fourteenth thesis: Over the past century, modernization (urbanization) has affected a large segment of the Arab people; however, that does not mean that modernism has been as pervasive. Modernization is the practical application of a modernistic consciousness in a society. While it is possible to import modernization from abroad, it would be extremely difficult to import modernism.

Introduction

"Millions of people cheering and waving flags for joy in Manhattan. Have they forgotten the Corridors of Death that gave them such victory? Will another hundred thousand desert deaths across the world be cause for the next rejoicing?" Allen Ginsberg, "After the Big Parade," in *Cosmopolitan Greetings: Poems 1986–1992* (New York: Harper Perennial, 1995), 68.

"In the imperialist epoch a philosophy of power became the philosophy of the elite, who quickly discovered it and were quite ready to admit that the thirst for power could be quenched only through destruction." Hannah Arendt, *The Origins of Totalitarianism* (New York: Meridian Books, 1963), 144.

"My study of the World will have been barren and irresponsible if it has not equipped me and spurred me to do what I can – infinitesimal though the effect of my action may be – to help mankind to cure itself of some of the evil that, in my lifetime, I have seen human beings inflict on each other." Arnold Toynbee, *Experiences* (London: Oxford University Press, 1969), 81.

"One of the central themes of American historiography is that there is no American Empire. Most historians will admit, if pressed, that the United States once had an empire. They then promptly insist that it was given away. But they also speak persistently of America as a World Power." William Appleman William, "The Frontier Thesis and American Foreign Policy." *Pacific Historical Review* 24, November 1955, 379.

"To my knowledge there is no institute or major academic department in the Arab world whose main purpose is the study of America, although the United States is by far the largest outside force in the Arab world." Edward W. Said, "Ignorant Armies Clash by Night," in *The Politics of Dispossession* (New York: Vintage Books, 1995), 229.

"Most of what I learned in philosophy has come to seem to me erroneous, and I spent many subsequent years in gradually unlearning the habits of thought, which I had then acquired. The one habit of thought of real value that I acquired there was intellectual honesty." Bertrand Russell, *The Autobiography of Bertrand Russell, 1872–1914* (Boston: Little, Brown & Co., 1967), 99–100.

"The Philosophers have only interpreted the world, in various ways; the point, however, is to change it." Karl Marx, "Theses on Feuerbach," in Karl Marx and Friedrich Engels, *On Religion* (New York: Schocken Books, 1965), 72.

"We [liberals] are continually tempted by the urge to sit back and grasp our time in thought rather than continuing to change it." Richard Rorty, *Essays on Heidegger and Others: Philosophical Papers*, volume 2 (Cambridge: Cambridge University Press, 1991), 184.

"Intellectuals must interpret the world, not simply change or even explain it." Jeffrey Alexander, *Fin de Siècle Social Theory: Relativism, Reductionism, and the Problem of Reason* (London: Verso, 1995), 13.

"Finally, there is always the possibility of a 'social imperialism' that strives to unify people at home by displacing internal conflicts upon an external enemy, with tangible gains accruing to the members of the 'master race' from the domination of multitudes of 'wogs'." Eric Wolf, *Europe and the People Without History*, 2nd edition (Berkeley: University of California Press, 1997), 302.

"The East is languishing for want of a Revolution." The Earl of Cromer, *Modern Egypt*, volume 1 (New York: Macmillan Co., 1908), 151.

I researched and wrote most of this book in the 1990s, that is to say, in a decade that embodied, on the surface at least, the triumph of the neo-liberal philosophy of capitalism and its spread throughout the world without any serious universal contender.[1] This was the decade of the demise of the Left *par excellence*, at least the institutionalized Left that was represented by the Soviet system. More often than not, Francis Fukuyama's *The End of History and the Last Man*,[2] Samuel Huntington's *The Clash of Civilizations*,[3] and Anthony Giddens' *The Third Way: The Renewal of Social Democracy*[4] were on point when they represented the mood of a triumphant neo-liberalism that was, at heart, oblivious to issues of social justice and the persistence of poverty. Neo-liberalist-engineered globalization has broken down barriers, altered relationships, and been the cause of major structural change in the Third World. Neo-liberalism has offered the world an ideology of false hope while driving toward reconstructing the world in its own image. It was and remains a process intent on changing the former economic and social relations of the world, and creating a new cultural and intellectual order, in addition to an economic and political one. In the wise words of Pierre Bourdieu, "It is by arming itself with mathematics (and power over the media) that neo-liberalism has become the supreme form of conservative sociodicy, which started to appear some thirty years ago as 'the end of ideology', or more recently, as 'the end of history'."[5]

The decade began in earnest with two tectonic events in contemporary world history. First was the actual collapse of the Soviet system, and the second was the defeat of Iraq, the last bastion of Arab nationalism, by United Nations troops under the command of the United States. Beneath these two major events, however, a very subtle and dangerous process had been in the making: the globalization of the world led by the economic interest groups of the United States, Europe, and, to a lesser degree, Japan.[6] It is important to note that the recent globalization of capitalism has been accomplished against the background of three major phenomena: first, the exhaustion of the decolonization project in the Third World which began around the middle of the twentieth century; second, the defeat of the nationalist and socialist struggle in many Third World countries by the end of the 1980s; and, third, the great technological revolution achieved by world capitalism, which made globalization in its current form possible.[7]

What is important to underline at the outset is that neither the intellectual nor social nor economic history of the modern Arab world can be understood in isolation from the totality of world processes in the economic, political, and intellectual fields.[8] The interconnection of the world, as Eric Wolf points out in his masterpiece, *Europe and the People Without History*, is a fact, although "We have been taught…that there exists an entity called the West, and that one can think of this West as a society and civilization independent of and in opposition to other societies and civilizations."[9] In the same vein, it is quite impossible and indeed unrealistic to grasp the social and intellectual dynamics of the modern Arab world in isolation from other world factors. It is important to appreciate both the internal and external factors that have coalesced to make the contemporary political, social, economic, intellectual, and religious reality of the Arab world.

As I show in Chapter 7 of this book, globalization, far from being a recent phenomenon, has quickened to an unprecedented pace in the wake of the New World Order in the early 1990s. It comes on the heels of significant economic and technological transformations taking place in the capitalist world, especially in the United States and Western Europe since World War Two. Neo-liberal globalization has reveled in the collapse of the Soviet system, which meant the collapse of its ideological, political, and economic foundations. This major loss of meaning, an outcome of the Cold War, has created a vacuum of significant proportion in the Third World.[10] To be sure, globalization is a multilayered phenomenon that is not confined only to the economic, but that is bent on changing the cultural and consumption habits of the world at large. It purports to revolutionize the world in a way that is conducive to the further spread of capitalism's culture of gain. By doing so, neo-liberal capitalist globalization tends to multiply its domestic fault line worldwide: it relegates the poor who make up the majority of the world's population to a marginal status because of their inability to consume its products. What this globalization concerns itself with is a minority of worldwide consumers who share its ethic and capitalist system of domination. The Third World faces the enormous challenge of globalization, just as it faced the challenge of colonization and its aftermath about fifty years ago.

Globalization of the 1990s had been the direct result of the tremendous economic changes and breakthroughs achieved by the capitalist system since the end of World War Two. Contemporary capitalism, similar to that Marx described so eloquently in the nineteenth century, is still subject to "constant revolutionizing of production, and uninterrupted disturbance of all social relations." As Aijaz Ahmad rightly notes, world capitalism, especially American capitalism, had been able to make a transition from extensive industrialization to intensive technological revolution after World War Two.[11] This fact enabled the United States to become the leading hegemonic power with a level of accumulation outpacing what both France and Britain "had even enjoyed even at the height of the colonial period."[12] In the words of Noam Chomsky, the United States with its immense economic resources was able to "execute a global vision" after World War Two.[13] This global vision was based on an expanded military and economic power.[14] The unfolding of the technological revolution of post-World War Two capitalism coincided with another significant process taking place in the world at large: the deep crisis and later failure of the socialist project, which so far has had a tremendous impact on the Third World. The decade of the 1990s saw both a recession in the socialist project and a concerted effort to absorb China, the only remaining socialist country of any significant power, into the world capitalist market.[15]

In addition to these two major changes, the Third World, and especially the Arab world, which began a vibrant decolonization process in the name of nationalism in the 1950s and 1960s, faced a major impasse. The nationalist project in many Third World countries seems to have lost its energy by the end of the 1970s and the Islamist project, especially in Iran, began to pose a major challenge to Western, especially American, hegemony. However, it is important to note that as the twentieth century drew to a close, the Arab world became entangled in what Eric Hobsbawm calls "the global fog"[16] surrounding the world economic and political system in general.

One may point out the following challenges facing the Arab world: first, it became more entangled with the capitalist system than ever before. Second, in the wake of the collapse of the Arab nationalist project in the 1970s and in the absence of any organized political effort, the Arab world became more dependent on the West, especially on the United States; third, the conservative Arab regimes of the Gulf began to play very important political and social roles in the Arab world, which was due mainly to the influx of petroleum money and the collapse of the Arab national project. Fourth, with the gradual capitulation of the Arab state system to American hegemony, the Zionist/Israeli project achieved another breakthrough in terms of official Arab recognition of the state of Israel. As Aijaz Ahmad notes, in this period, "Zionism has succeeded in becoming one of the most powerful idéologies of the advanced capitalist countries, and the Zionist state has been the main beneficiary of the global sympathies generated by the Nazi concentration camps."[17] Fifth, the actual process of decolonization was derailed by a practical dilemma after the defeat of Iraq in the second Gulf War. In addition to destroying the Iraqi economy, the United States ended up having a *de facto* military presence in the Gulf, reminiscent of a similar military presence in Southeast Asia, especially in South Korea and Thailand. How is it possible to now revive decolonization, when the wealthiest portion of the Arab world has been recolonized by the United States? How is it possible to resist the United States' hegemony when many voices on the Right in the United States celebrate the return of a benevolent American Empire to the Third World?[18] Empire, for sure, is not a major theme in American studies, as Amy Kaplan shows in her important study.[19] Since 1898, however, the United States has acted as a major world power.

It is important to take a deep look at the Arab political system and its emergence in the context of the Arab League in the 1940s. This system is comprised of numerous, highly contentious nation-states that suffer from an unequal distribution of wealth within and among them.[20] Besides the Palestine issue, the Arab political system has faced a number of challenges: inter-Arab wars, the failure of Arab unity, regionalism, and Iraq in the 1990s. The Iraqi invasion of Kuwait on August 2, 1990, led to a major breach in the Arab state system. The Arab world emerged even more bruised from the crisis than it was before and was forced to accept American military presence in the area because of the perceived Iraqi threat to the security of the Gulf. The situation has not changed much over a decade after the expulsion of Iraq from Kuwait. On the contrary, *Pax Americana* seems to be a *de facto* system of hegemony that no one in the area dares challenge.[21] The Arab state system failed to give Kuwait security in its time of need, and since 1990, Gulf security has been in the firm hands of the United States and its allies.[22]

Whether invited or not, American troops will remain in the Gulf as long as that area is defined as one that meets the strategic interests of the United States. However, the question facing us is this: will American military presence solidify authoritarianism or open the way toward democratic practices in the area? This question is the more valid in view of the fact that within the United States, large numbers of people are led to believe that the United States acts with good intentions in the international arena. In the words of Edward Said, "Thus the notion that American military power might be used for malevolent purposes is relatively unthinkable within the consensus, just as the idea that America is a force for good in the world is routine and normal."[23] Some sophisticated liberal political theoreticians, such as Mark Lilla of the Committee on Social Thought at the University of Chicago, do not see much connection between the rise of new tyrannies in the post-Cold War era and American foreign policy. All Lilla can do is bemoan the inadequacy of American political language in dealing with what he terms the "new geography of tyranny" forming in the Arab and Muslim world lately.[24] The United States is a truly hegemonic power in the Arab world. Besides its military and economic prowess, the United States, through its advanced educational institutions, has begun to write the history of the Arab world in a scientific way. Military and economic hegemony is thus supported by intellectual power.

One can only speak of the Arab state system in theoretical terms. In reality, we have different state systems and economic blocs, which because of their economic power, have been led by the conservative Arab states. The Arab world lacks economic integration; it consists of different power blocs that are sometimes at odds with each other. Most of the Arab world, especially the Gulf area, has been integrated into the world capitalist system, and it is impossible to envision an independent course of development without this integration.

Both Europe and the United States have played major roles in the integration of the Arab world into advanced capitalism. That is why the Arab world has had to contend with these two major powers in the modern era. Because of the importance of the Arab world to the world capitalist market, Arab economic and political unity has been anathema to the advanced center. Europe and the United States have preferred a disunited Arab world to a united and powerful Arab entity. This was true even before Israel appeared on the political scene. Because of the lack of unity, the Arab world is not able to bargain with one voice in international economic and political matters, and this has hurt its interests considerably.

Because of its unequal incorporation into the world capitalist system, the social composition of the Arab world in the past five decades or so has changed dramatically. New social classes have emerged and, consequently, new social forces began to compete over power. However, it is important to study the old social classes in the Arab world and their persistence into the new social system created after the incorporation of a large number of Arab countries in the capitalist market. Here one has to ponder the insights of Arno Mayer's magisterial work, *The Persistence of the Old Regime: Europe to the Great War.*[25] Mayer argues that the old regime in Europe persisted all the way to World War One and that one of the major reasons for the war was the old establishment's fear of losing its privileged status in European societies. Even after the War, the *ancien régime* tried to reproduce itself by forging new alliances with the bourgeoisie and the new capitalist classes. In the Arab world, the pre-independence social *ancien régime* did not disappear after independence; on the contrary, its power was enhanced by all sorts of internal and external factors. In this regard, it would be interesting to examine the new social classes that came into existence after independence in the Arab countries and their persistence or lack thereof to the present time. One can look at the interesting case of Egypt after Sadat came to power in 1970. The old feudal classes that were supposedly crushed by the Nasserization of Egypt (1952–70) reincarnated themselves after Nasser's death.

The social map of the Arab world differs from one country to another. In reading the social map, one has to take account of demography as well as other factors. In many Arab countries, most of the population is very young, born only after 1975.[26] With rising social expectations that many Arab regimes have not yet been able to fulfill, "brain-drain" has become a significant problem. For example, it is estimated that 5 million Moroccans live in Europe, most notably in France, Spain, Italy, Holland, and Germany. Young people dissatisfied with the economic or political conditions of their countries find an easy escape in emigration. This human hemorrhage will have drastic repercussions on the political and economic state of the Arab world.

The "brain-drain" has not been as big a problem in many conservative Gulf countries for the simple reason that the power elite there have been able to financially co-opt the population. Therefore, it is important to examine the formation of the new political and social elite in the Arab world after independence. In the Gulf states, these elite have no aristocratic pretensions, as did the old European elite described by Mayer. However, they gained prominence after capitalist modes of production were thrust upon their societies in the twentieth century. In many cases, we have capitalism without democracy or a long tradition of economic evolution. Capitalism is not homegrown as much as it is imported. The Gulf is an example of deformed capitalism that lacks a broad base of societal power sharing.

One of the main questions I am interested in addressing in this study is the social, cultural, and religious rationales for political domination in the modern Arab world. In addition to being an "archeological" question in the sense of deconstructing the complex web of relationships between the social, cultural, religious, and political, this question is historical, as well. This complex web of relationships has changed somewhat since 1967. To unravel the question of political domination and its foundations is one of the main objectives of this study.

I began research for this work in 1996, immediately after I finished my book *Intellectual Origins of Islamic Resurgence in the Modern Arab World.* I am obliged to say that the field of contemporary Arab thought is still virgin territory, unmapped by studies in English. This lack of attention may have some legitimate justification. However, one thing remains clear: as a field of academic enquiry, contemporary Arab thought is fascinating, and in spite of the absence of real democracy in most, if not in all, Arab states, new patterns of critical and creative thinking, representing different trends of thought, have flourished since 1967. The interplay between the cultural and the political has been interesting in that creativity, in spite of the fact that authoritarianism, rather than subsiding under the New World Order and the blessings of "humanistic capitalism," has found new sources of nourishment. The principal trends of post-1967 Arab thought have been conditioned by the post-independence milieu of the Arab world. However, one must also consider older forms of conditioning. Although the thickest roots of the contemporary Arab world have been primarily nourished by the soil of the post-independence phase, some of their most critical tentacles appeared on the scene in the nineteenth century under the impact of the reform movement sweeping the entire Arab world as a result of its painful encounter with colonialism.

It is cliché to say that the student of contemporary Arab intellectual history, in addition to knowing Arabic and a handful of Western languages, must be familiar with the intellectual, cultural, social, and economic background of the contemporary Arab world, and its position vis-à-vis the modern capitalist West. Arab thought of the nineteenth century offers at the first instance a plethora of opinions and subjects that are, more or less, still debated by contemporary thinkers.[27] No one can speak about modern/contemporary Arab thought with any degree of confidence without carefully and systematically studying the origin and development of the encounter between the Arab world and the capitalist West, the gradual proliferation in the Arab world of the capitalist mode of production with its full social, cultural and intellectual implications and the serious derailment of traditional Muslim thought (the dominant system of thought in the pre-capitalist Arab world), faced since the encounter with the advanced West. It is against this background of derailment that such questions as tradition versus modernity, authenticity versus new forms of belonging, and cultural polarization in general become important.

It is correct to assume that since the nineteenth century, Arab intellectuals have grappled with such notions as tradition, modernity, reform, and progress. On the other hand, contemporary Arab thought is also occupied with such notions as democracy, civil society, religion, nationalism, class, social conditions, and hegemony. It is impossible to ignore the fact that almost every Arab thinker, be he/she from the Left or Right, thinks that the older visions of rebuilding society have been exhausted and that there is a long-standing crisis in Arab society that awaits a solution. Everyone seems to be talking about renewal, critique, and alternative. Although methods of diagnosis and the cure or cures given vary from one intellectual camp to another, there is an underlying assumption that something must be done to break the deadlock in the current situation. It is in this context of ongoing debate that I highlight in this book the intellectual contributions of contemporary Islamist, Marxist, nationalist, and liberal thinking about these questions. It is important to note, however, that it is difficult to fully appreciate each tendency apart from other dominant tendencies in contemporary Arab thought. This is why in the first chapter of this work I attempt to give a thorough treatment of the different dominant trends in contemporary Arab thought.

In addition, this book deals with a number of problematics in modern Arab and Muslim thought that have developed over time without yet taking definite shape. I discuss such issues as Sharī'ah implementation, civil society, secularism, globalization, and religious pluralism in the modern Arab world. To bring some focus to these crucial issues, I have chosen to dwell at length on the writings of some prominent post-independence Arab thinkers representing the various tendencies of contemporary Arab thought: Rāshid al-Ghannūshī, Muḥammad al-Ghazālī, Muḥammad 'Ābid al-Jābirī, Abdallah Laroui, Costantine Zurayk, Mahdī 'Āmil, and others.

How is it possible to conceptualize post-1967 Arab thought? The easiest way to answer this question is to propose the study of the modern history of the Arab world with a distinct social science perspective.[28] In modern Arab thought, a great number of epistemological formations have taken place that cannot be understood apart from their historical and social meanings. Arab intellectuals, coming as they have from various intellectual and cultural backgrounds and formations, have in various ways posed the following essential questions that reflect these often painful transitions. First, defeat: what are the reasons for defeat? What steps must be taken to fix the damage? Second, state: what state is to be established? A nationalist state, a liberal state, or an Islamic state? Third, elite: what is the nature of the political elite in the Arab world after 1967, and fourth, the West. The Arab intelligentsia still considers the West to be a major problematic. Most consider the Israeli victory as a Western victory over the Arab world.

What is the relationship between religion and society in the post-1967 Arab world? Here, I pose this question in the most general of terms for one major reason: this has been the most irksome question the Arab intelligentsia has faced and is still facing since the dawn of the Nahḍah. Numerous intellectuals have attacked this problematic. Some have concluded that religion and the attachment to the past is one of the principal reasons behind Arab defeat and their historical, cultural, and intellectual stagnation. Others have postulated that the reason for defeat was the absence of religious '*aṣṣabiyyah* (that is, spirit) from Arab society on the eve of the war and that the only sure option for overcoming defeat and building Arab society anew is to accept the basic religious and intellectual principles of Islam and model society according to the precepts of Qur'ānic revelation.

As shall be discussed in the third chapter of this book, the question of "religion and society" as an academic topic is almost taboo in most Arab universities. It is true that contemporary Arab political elite are on the whole non-religious; however, they have shown a marvelous tendency to co-opt and neutralize religious discourse. Religion is always taught as dogma, as a profession of faith in such leading universities as Imām 'Abd al-Wahāb in Saudi Arabia, Qarawiyyīn and Dār al-Ḥadīth al-Ḥassaniyah in Morocco and al-Azhar in Egypt. It is rare that students in these traditional Islamic institutions are acquainted with the methods and perspectives of modern social sciences, or even the huge tradition of Islamic criticism. Very often, these students and their professors have not been accustomed to thinking about the rapport between religion and society, but are taught to think instead about how to impose faith or dogma upon society. Their thought is more textual than historical or social. The textual method, although having its own logic and intellectual references, misses one crucial dimension: the social dimensions of Islam in the contemporary Arab world and the way religion is manipulated or used by a plethora of social, political, and religious forces to achieve specific goals and objectives. Few graduates from the traditional system can answer the following question: how has the status of the religious intelligentsia changed in the Arab world since independence?

Throughout this work, I deal with religion as a major social and historical factor in the modern and contemporary Arab world, while not neglecting the centrality of religion in the contemporary Arab-Muslim discourse as belief and metaphysics. It is important to underline the fact that almost throughout the modern Arab world, there has been a poignant and sometimes slow process of social, economic, and political reconstruction, which took the form of the Arab nation-state after independence. In the minds of the political elite in the Arab world, religion played a significant role either as a means of support (that is, the traditional official intelligentsia) or as a form of political opposition, especially with the Muslim Brotherhood movement (the Ikhwān). As shall be amply illustrated in upcoming chapters, the Muslim Brotherhood, which saw itself as an outgrowth of nineteenth century Islamic reform, adopted a clear-cut political program for the reconstruction of Islam in the modern period. It fought tirelessly to establish an Islamic political regime as a prelude toward the full "revival" of Islam in the modern period. However, one must note that since 1967, many Islamist discourses have emerged in the Arab world in addition to that of the Ikhwān.

In this book, I will focus on some salient features of contemporary Ikhwān discourse, especially in the thought of Tunisian Islamist Rāshid al-Ghannūshī and Egyptian Islamist Muḥammad al-Ghazālī. We must always bear in mind that Islamist discourse has largely failed, due to all sorts of factors, in implementing its vision of building an Islamic political system. We must also raise the following questions when dealing with contemporary Islamism: first, is the call to implement the Sharī'ah, so widely heard in Islamist circles nowadays, modern or as old as Islam itself? Second, is the call to establish an Islamic state a modern cry, as Talal Asad argues in one of his major articles,[29] or is it as old as Islam itself?

DEFEAT AND TRANSITION

While one might argue that the 1967 Arab defeat was primarily a defeat of the Arab nationalist project exemplified by Nasserism and Ba'thism, Arab nationalism did not receive a deathblow in 1967. It is true that the Sadat regime was successful at dismantling Nasserism after 1970. However, nationalism as the search for unity among the Arab people in facing the challenges of world capitalism and Zionism has not subsided.

One may argue that the 1967 defeat was a blessing in disguise for a number of ideological forces in Arab society. Islamists, the major political and ideological opponents of Nasserism and Ba'thism, welcomed defeat in the hopes that an Islamic alternative would be implemented.[30] Liberals hoped that defeat would lead to more democratization and the upholding of the rights of the individual in Arab society, and the Marxists thought defeat symbolized the crisis of Arab nationalism and the incomplete application of socialism. In their confusion, the Arab masses channeled their energies toward thwarting this defeat without paying sufficient attention to the internal reasons that caused it and the necessity of an overall change in the structure of Arab society and the intellectual and social foundations of the Arab personality. All sought change, transformation, and a new climate. Even the state was behind a certain type of change: it was for rebuilding the foundations of a shattered society in a new climate of the triumph of the West, capitalism, and Israel in 1967.[31]

Thus, the collective burden of defeat transforms itself into a "collective critique" of society, individual, tradition, socialism, and so on. One striking characteristic of such critique is that it lacks homogeneity in both method and alternative. It is heterogeneous in nature, and perhaps the positive side of this is that the Arab intellectual scene is still unfolding in "pockets" of criticism here and there. For the first time, in the 1970s and 1980s, one begins to hear of Islamist self-criticism or Marxist self-criticism. It is true that in one sense all of this had come under the impact of defeat, but it is also an indication of the level of maturity of the Arab intellectual scene in the 1970s and 1980s. For years and even decades, Arab intellectuals on the Left and Right had been speaking about "crisis" (*azmah*), its meaning, causes, and ways to overcome it. It is in the juxtaposition between these formulations of tradition versus modernity, ummah versus nation, secularism versus divine sovereignty, democracy versus dictatorship, criticism versus quietism, that the story of contemporary Arab thought lies.

The defeat of the Arab world by Israel in 1967 ushered in a series of important political, social, ideological, and intellectual transformations that are still evolving.[32] In the wake of 1967, a new type of writing (Islamist, Marxist, and liberal) has emerged, distinguished by sharp criticism on certain issues. Although one may argue that 1967 created many ruptures, including the ideological and epistemological, it is inaccurate to assume that 1967 was a brand new phase in the intellectual history of contemporary Arab thought. For example, one distinguishing mark of contemporary Arab thought is its focus on the issue of Arab unity versus regionalism and the position of religion in society. These issues were by no means the creation of the 1967 defeat. They had existed and been debated earlier by a number of Arab intellectuals and thinkers. That is to say, that although we must see 1967 as a rupture that initiated a series of important transitions in the life of the Arab world, it represented as well a continuation of the concepts and ideas that had already been debated. Perhaps the seriousness with which the issues were debated became intensified as a result of the urgency created by the defeat and the real unmasking of crisis of the Arab nationalist state.

Contemporary Arab thinkers are convinced that modern Arab thought, as a philosophical outlook and historical process, begins with European intervention in the Arab world (Middle East and North Africa) in the nineteenth century. In one sense, Europeans, through a direct military occupation of many Arab countries, took the opportunity to impose their brand of modernity on at least certain segments of Arab social forces. What that meant was that the Arab world ceased to exist as a self-contained and somewhat autonomous ideological and religious system. It had to face head-on the problematic of Westernization and the economic and political weight of Western colonization. Consequently, Western modernity, translated into modernization at the economic and political levels, and into modernism at the level of consciousness and general education, could not escape its colonialist essence. The colonized Arabs and their intellectual elite were bewildered by the progress of their colonizers and at the same time were alerted to their own outdated modes of structure and thought.[33] This dialectical situation, over the years, created many interesting Arab reactions, whose common denominator was dualism in thought and in solution to the problems facing Arab societies.

It is true that pre-colonial Arab thinkers of the eighteenth century did not seek out colonial modernity and the European *Weltanschauung*. However, a century later, a new generation of Arab intellectuals, educated and bred in the West and representing various tendencies, accepted the tenets of Western modernity with little or no reservation. In other words, at the speculative and philosophical levels, the new school of Arab thought was more synthetic than purely creative and faced the challenges of two distinct epistemological, philosophical, and ideological models. The amalgamation of two major historical "traditions" – the Arabo-Islamic and the European – was a process of enormous complexity. In a sense, modern Arab thought has dealt with two central traditions and many sub-traditions in between.

Because of the onslaught of European modernity in the guise of colonialism, modern Arab thought, in its different tendencies and various expressions, was from its inception an ideological discourse. It had to be ideological in order to find answers to the problems of stagnation, as in the writings of Muḥammad 'Abduh, Rashīd Riḍa, and Shakīb Arslān, and in order to theorize on progress, science, and the project of liberalism, in general, as a possible solution, as in the writings of Faraḥ Anṭūn,[34] Shiblī Shumayl,[35] Luṭfī al-Sayyid,[36] Salāma Mūsa,[37] Ṭāhā Ḥussain,[38] and 'Alī 'Abd al-Rāziq. In the writings of these authors, the political discourse of liberalism takes precedence over any other issue. Even 'Alī 'Abd al-Rāziq, an Azharite shaykh, argues on behalf of the separation of religion and state. Secularism as an Arab political concept is born.[39]

What the preceding means is that the process of synthesis referred to earlier ushered modern Arab thought to a new creative mode, which was unique itself as a result of the unusual and specific questions it had to tackle. The view that modern Arab thought was a carbon copy of Western thought or that it was not adequately creative, in the same way that European thought was, is irrelevant.[40] These singular questions, as I will illustrate in the following chapters, are defined by three major factors: (1) the presence of Islam as a religion and philosophy of life for the majority of Arabs in the nineteenth century; (2) the backward socio-economic conditions of the Arab world in the nineteenth century, and (3) colonialism as an historical fact. Modern Arab thought had to deal with these three major factors, which were always in a state of flux. Contemporary Arab thought, on the other hand, inherited these same factors with their evolving shape. Colonialism itself went through a process of metamorphosis and in the past three decades has been spearheaded by the United States as a neo-colonial power. Second, religion itself has undergone major changes in relation to both society and state. Although no religious revolution similar to the one in Iran has yet taken place in the Arab world, the fact that religion could assume such a powerful political presence in the contemporary Middle East has shocked the contemporary Arab political elite.

In addition to neo-colonialism, the new religious threat to the state and the backward economic and social conditions in many Arab countries have meant that contemporary Arab thought has dealt with issues of regionalism (the rise of the Gulf region into prominence as a result of oil and other international alliances [the defeat of Iraq in the second Gulf War], the failure of Arab unity, the rise of the military state, the Open Door policy, the disintegration of the Soviet system, issues of democracy, human rights and social justice, and the New World Order, and finally, the acceptance by some Arab thinkers (who were once radical) of the state of Israel as a regional fact.

The dualistic nature of the Arab intelligentsia, one modern and the other Salafī, gave rise to the problematic of traditionalism and contemporariness in modern Arab thought. Dualism in thought, action, outlook, and even institutions, seems to be the mark of the day in the contemporary Arab world. This deep-seated polarization meant on the one hand a movement toward modernization initiated by colonialism and encouraged by the nascent nation-state in the 1950s and 1960s, and, on the other, the rediscovery of tradition, the collective self and authenticity as a means to both protect and preserve. A large segment of Arab people who were challenged to the heart by colonial modernity found in their complex Islamic tradition not only a refuge but also an answer to the new questions that beset them. In one simple sense, traditional answers were given to the problematics of modernity.

Colonialism, which enabled modernity to assault the traditional roots and mentality of the colonized countries, did not spare time to plant its intellectual seeds wherever it went. It was successful in uprooting many traditional cultures, such as those in Africa and Latin America. The Arab world was no exception, although some thinkers speak of the tenacious presence of tradition, supported by an Islamic epistemology and the Arab language. Of course, the intellectual elite was most affected by the assault of modernity. Many of its members chose the language(s) of the West, its rules and even gods. Even with the aid of this bilingual and lonely indigenous intelligentsia, trained in the best schools of the West, the colonial state failed to cause a permanent epistemological and cultural rupture with the Islamic worldview. Therefore, it was but normal for some segments of Arab society, after waging the battle to rediscover their collective self and preserve tradition, to employ tradition as an ideological weapon in order to fight a dynamic new enemy – colonialism. The Ikhwān, as a traditional political and religious movement in the twentieth century Arab world, did employ tradition against the "Other" and did express its worries and concerns in a traditional language. What is fascinating about the progress of thought in the modern Arab world is that both tradition and the "Other" have become highly intertwined. In a sense, they are born in each other's shadow. It would be somewhat naive and historically inaccurate to assume the tradition in modern Arab thought was born in isolation or that modernity evolved away from the traditional domain. That is to say that the liberation of the modern Arab does not mean emancipation from the "shackles of tradition," nor does it mean emancipation from the burdens of colonial modernity, but means finding a formula that enables him or her to treat both tradition and modernity in a critical fashion: to be open to the achievements of the past while not neglecting the prospects of progress inherent in modernity, however that concept is defined.

AMERICAN PRAGMATISM AND CONTEMPORARY ISLAM

Modern Arab thought has always struggled with the notion of authenticity versus dependency. Out of the complex encounter between the Arab world and the advanced capitalist West in the nineteenth century, a distinct trend that I would like to call Arab Third-Worldism emerged. In contemporary Arab thought, this trend is best represented by such thinkers as the Moroccans Muḥammad Aziz Lahbabi,[41] and Mahdi Elmandjra;[42] in Egypt by Ḥassan Ḥanafī and Galāl Amīn;[43] and in Lebanon by René Ḥabashī. Arab Third-Worldism is a movement of intellectual resistance which aims first to betray the cultural Western designs on the Arab world and, second, stress an autonomous and modern Arab culture. It stresses to the native Arab intelligentsia the need to be authentic and free from the cultural shackles of the West. But what is authenticity? How is it possible to escape from the cultural influences of the West in an increasingly interdependent world where the West seems to be the most dominant player? In that sense, Arab Third-Worldism faces a torturous dilemma. On the one hand, it has embarked on a comprehensive process to interpret the West to the Arab world while, on the other, it has become painfully aware of the dependency of the Arab political and military elite, and the Arab economic system, on the West and their lack of patience vis-à-vis issues of understanding and dialogue with the intelligentsia. Interpreting the West is only getting half the job done; the other half is to change conditions in the Arab world.

With the emergence of the United States as a leading superpower in the wake of the defeat of Nazi Germany in World War Two, the creation of the state of Israel in the heart of the Arab world, shifting alliances in the Middle East after the 1973 war and the Open Door policy pursued by the Egyptian state in the 1970s and 1980s, several Arab voices critical of American influence emerged. On the Islamist side, Sayyid Quṭb in the late 1940s and early 1950s paved the way toward a major critique of the cultural and intellectual influences of "the white man" and "Americanized Islam" on Islamic authenticity. These same issues were taken up anew in the 1980s and 1990s by a significant number of Islamist thinkers who were convinced that Arabs and Muslims suffer a malicious pragmatic invasion of American modernity whose main goal is to exploit, impoverish, demean, and defeat contemporary Arabs and Muslims. American pragmatism has appropriated European secular ideas and offered them in an aggressive new form. The center of the Arab world, especially Egypt, follows an Open Door policy and permits a new culture: that of consumerism and individualism. This culture reflects the triumph of the *nouveaux riches* as a new consumerist class whose main aim is to enrich itself in the fastest and most corrupt way possible. On the other hand, the consumerist culture is the antithesis of the masses' aspirations. The masses' tolerance gets tested by the ordeals created by the Open Door policy culture.[44]

To some, the main goal of American style pragmatism is to ensure American economic and cultural hegemony in the Third World. In order to achieve this fundamental goal, American-owned multinational corporations have ensured their hegemony in three important arenas: mass media, politics, and economics. According to this view, the indigenous mass media have fallen under the influence of American ideas that promote leisure, consumerism, and amorality. The end result of all of this is that Islamic authenticity, self, civilization, and religious values are obliterated. At the economic level, the capitalist economy has invaded the Third World, created debt-ridden economies, and increased the level of poverty. The most dangerous result of pragmatic economics in Arab lands has been the creation of an indigenous pragmatic elite that serves the interests of American capitalism. The indigenous elite does not aim to modernize society as much as to serve the interests of its American master. In addition, this economic dependency plays in the hands of Israel. Since a country like Egypt cannot wage war against Israel, a new form of political dependency is created.

RELIGION AND ITS HAZARDS

In a seminal essay written in 1946 entitled "Politics and the English Language," British novelist George Orwell bemoaned the deterioration of post-World War Two English prose by pointing out that what was troublesome about some major English writing was lack of precision, sheer incompetence, and vagueness. This criticism is also applicable to many Arab and Western writings on Islam. Is Islam subject to theorization? Or is it a matter of belief that resists any form of conceptual scrutiny? One thing is clear: Islam has taken center stage in the contemporary Arab debate, and after the terrorist attacks on the United States on September 11, 2001, has become a matter of intense controversy.[45] An escape from the "Islamic problematic" is not just futile but is perhaps unnecessary in an environment of interdependence between the cultural and the religious. Arab thinkers have offered different if not exciting formulations of the Islamic problematic, the meaning and relevance of religious tradition, the connection of religion to the state, the changing status of the traditional religious intelligentsia, the creation of a new religious intelligentsia, and the nature of the current Islamic resurgence. While some Arab Marxist thinkers speak of religion as a superstructure that can be easily manipulated by the dominant elite, other Marxists have found great intellectual value in the Islamic tradition and have sought to revitalize those aspects of Islam that lend themselves to revolutionary, socialist, and universal meanings.[46]

In this work, I discuss religion under three broad headings or categories: (1) religion as doctrine; (2) religion as an historical and living tradition; and (3) religion as politics. One might subdivide the latter category into: (a) official religion, which takes the side of the state or the elite in power, and (b) as oppositional religion, which takes an anti-statist position. It is clear that religion and especially Islam has provided both the Arab intelligentsia and masses with a worldview and a high level of consciousness. This situation has prompted a leading Marxist thinker to postulate that, "Islam in specific, and religion in general, are a major source of my knowledge, as an Arab Marxist, of the history of my country, society and region...Religion is an essential tool of construction."[47] Other Marxist thinkers are less positive in their assessments of religion in Arab society.

There is no doubt that a great difference of opinion exists concerning the status of religion in society. Arab thinkers portray three broad opinions about the position of religion in contemporary Arab society: first, the Marxists believe that religion is the creation of man's imagination and that God, the central idea in Islam, is false consciousness. Therefore, any social expression of religion is, by definition, an idealist-utopian vision. The ruling elite have used this concept of religion as a tool of legitimation. Such thinkers as Ṣādiq Jalāl al-'Azm, Halim Barakat, and Rif'at al-Saī'd represent this view. Second is the liberal secular position that refuses to delve into metaphysical matters, nor will it discuss theological issues unless they have sociological dimensions. The proponents of this trend believe that religion is at best a mere subjective relationship between man and God. Third is the Islamist position that believes that religion is not just a collection of ideas and rites but rather has something fundamental to say about the nature of life, including government and society.

In addition to the three positions mentioned above, the state has something to say about religion. Traditionally, the state has never been disconnected from religion. The traditional ulama class legitimized the state with the leverage it had with the masses. Historically, "official Islam" enjoyed the protection and patronage of the ruling elite in Muslim society. Aside from its theological core, Islam grew from an urban environment and is "marked by an urban bourgeoisie outlook."[48] In the formative period and due to Islamic expansion, Islam was able to envision a universal community of believers who could transcend ethnic, linguistic, and geographic boundaries. However, in spite of the central role of the ulama in providing a universal vision to the Muslim ummah, no corporate "Church" body has ever existed in the Muslim world. The ulama, especially in the Sunni world, have more or less stood with the *status quo* by refusing to support opposition to existing political authority. The mainstream Muslim ulama, providing legitimacy, put their weight behind an Islamic tradition that was pro-*status quo* and enforced their notion of orthodoxy, often with the support of the political authorities. "The Sunni ulama have almost never acted in an organized fashion as if they constituted an institutionally distinct, hierarchically arranged body."[49] In the wake of independence from colonialism, many Muslim countries created Ministries of Religious and Islamic Affairs and encouraged a class of ulama to become official spokespersons of Islam. Very often, the official Islamic discourse shies away from dealing with the immediate issues facing the Arab and Muslim World. This discourse does not deal with such issues as poverty, illiteracy, and oppression within Muslim societies.

Today this role is being challenged, of course, by the rise of Islamism and its attractive formulation of the religious problematic. The concept of Islamic resurgence will be discussed fully within. Therefore, one can distinguish four discourses on religion in the contemporary Arab world: (1) Islamic; (2) Marxist; (3) liberal, and (4) statist. The Marxist, liberal, and statist intellectuals have something in common: they agree on the need to prevent Islamists from controlling power and the state. In a sense, all agree to preserve the *status quo* although some see major loopholes therein. Here, the state feels challenged at the core by the rise of resurgence, and in some sense a military confrontation is inevitable, such as that in Syria in the early 1980s and in Algeria in the 1990s. The nationalist state in the 1950s and 1960s seemed to have more than one enemy: both Marxists and Islamists were imprisoned. The post-nationalist and post-1967 Arab state seems to have one enemy: the Islamists. Even "at the cultural and ideological planes, the ruling elite imposed the state's ideology on all and barred all free expression, dialogue, and argument."[50] Many an Arab government treats Islamism, including moderate Islamism, "as a security threat," to borrow the words of Egyptian thinker Aḥmad Kamāl Abū'l Majd.[51] The major Islamist movements in the Arab world were born in the age of imperialism, and the Islamist movements' relationship with the nation-state has been troubled, at best. The absence of democracy in the Arab nation-states has forced a number of small Islamist movements to resort to violence to express the unhealthy conditions of Islamism in the contemporary period.[52]

Since September 11, 2001,[53] the Western world has more or less placed all Islamic movements in one category, that of extremism and terrorism.[54] Some have gone as far as equating Islamism with fascism and totalitarianism and others have considered Islamism to be a threat to the new world order.[55] Few scholars care to study the intellectual and social origins of Islamic resurgence, and even fewer point out that the majority of Islamic movements, although barred from politics, have not resorted to violence against the state. Resurgence has become a refuge to those segments of Arab society that have been alienated by the state and its economic and political policies. The Islamic tradition as a historical and religious depository of ideas and experience has given rise to a new mode of thought, one capable of protecting the alienated and giving them a new meaning in a meaningless society.

Although Arab thought, generally speaking, has always dealt with the question of religion in theological, philosophical, and critical fashions, contemporary Arab thought finds itself compelled to answer the following basic questions about Islam: first, how can one identify the main contents or the nature of post-1967 Arab religious discourse? Second, what is meant by religious resurgence? Do we mean only political Islam or resurgence in the larger social, religious, and popular senses? Third, what is the connection between Islam and violence?

The last question has received much attention in the West and not just since September 11, 2001. What is troubling here is the absence of a clear method with which to treat Islam or Islamism and violence. It is erroneous to assume that

Islamism, by and large, is just a political movement and therefore violent by nature.[56]

In order to understand Islamism, it seems to me that one needs to state the following:

1. Far from monolithic, Islamism (or fundamentalism) is a multi-layered phenomenon in the Muslim world. It is not a purely religious phenomenon.
2. It is possible to delineate several phases of Islamism: pre-colonial; colonial; and post-colonial.
3. Islamism is the product of the major factors affecting the Muslim world in the past two centuries or so.
4. Islamism in large measure is the product of modern European colonialism in the Muslim world and the failure of the modern nation-state to accommodate protest movements in their political systems.
5. The relationship between Islamism and the state in the Muslim world has been complex. In the case of Wahabiyyah, Islamism and the state have been allied, whereas in other cases, Islamism and the state have been at odds. The state in the modern Muslim world is a nineteenth century creation prompted by European colonialism.
6. As such, Islamism has never been a static phenomenon. It has invented a powerful religious discourse to legitimize itself in the eyes of the masses and gain political and economic support.
7. Islamism has been in crisis for the last four decades for many complex reasons: first because the whole of Muslim tradition has been in crisis; and second, because the new guard of Islamism is not satisfied with the achievements or lack thereof on the part of the old guard. This is true in the case of Wahabiyyah, and bin Laden is an example.

Islamism has built on a large reservoir of the Sacred – the nebulous Sacred, which has a powerful hold on people's imaginations and absorbs their fears of death and the afterlife. With economic modernization and Westernization of certain classes in Arab society, the religious Sacred, instead of becoming less important, has gained new ground. It is not unusual to hear of wealthy dancers and artists who turn to wearing the veil, expressing new forms of religiosity unknown in the modern Arab world. The world of Westernized art and cinema, a notorious bastion of individualism, has given way in the Arab world to the Sacred. Famous singers and artists are gripped by strange dreams that only preachers can interpret. It is the dawn of a new era.

Having said all of this, one must not underestimate the economic base of Islamism in the modern and contemporary Arab world. From its initial construction more or less at the end of the nineteenth century, Islamism was challenged to the core by imperialist economic and political hegemony in the Arab world. In response to imperialism, Islamism sought to construct not just a modernist ethical Islamic order but also an economic one. The rise of the Ikhwān movement in Egypt at the end of the 1920s and in the rest of the Arab world by the end of the 1940s gave the Ikhwān a strong Arab global base that allowed it to compete for the same resources and goals, that is, economic resources and the control of political power. This was true in Syria and Jordan in the 1950s, as it was true in Egypt in the 1940s.

The exile of a substantial number of the Ikhwān's leaders to the Gulf states in the 1960s after the Nasserite repression of the movement in Egypt and the subsequent migration of hundreds of thousands of Egyptian workers and professionals to the Gulf states in the 1970s and 1980s gave the Ikhwān a new opportunity to construct its financial base in "Arab exile," so to speak. By and large, Islamist groups were banned from competing in the economic field in many Arab countries in the 1980s and 1990s, precisely because of their newly gained power in the Gulf. Many were demonized and pushed to the extreme by the ruling elite in the Arab world. As an economic phenomenon, Islamism has been thinly studied. However, the ban on Islamist politics is at the heart of a ban on Islamist economics, as well.

Contemporary Arab religious discourse is ideological in nature. The *takfīr* of some major authors such as Salman Rushdie, Ḥāmid Abū Zayd, Muḥammad Saī'd al-'Ashmāwī and Ḥassan Ḥanafī are concrete examples of the ideological dimensions of religious discourse.[57] Preaching, as a medium of reaching the masses, is rarely bereft of ideology. There is so much talk about not just heaven and hell but women, poverty, morality, the West, and so on.

Islamism is an obvious phenomenon, but has it provided practical solutions to the numerous dilemmas besetting the Arab world? A consideration of the reasons behind resurgence may bring light to this question:

1. resurgence is simply a new cycle in the history of the Muslim world. It reflects continuity and change in Arab and Muslim thought;
2. resurgence is a natural result of the failure of the nation/state of the 1950s and 1960s. The modernizing Arab nationalist state of the 1950s and 1960s failed to solve society's economic and social problems, and with the defeat with Israel in 1967, their modernity project came to a standstill;
3. resurgence has resulted from the failure of Arab modernity to meet the needs of the marginalized. The result is continued marginalization, alienation, bitterness, and the radicalization of a social segment in society. One opinion goes as far as to characterize resurgence as a fascist movement that attempts to take Arab society back to pristine nomadism, "It is a movement against civilization and against modernity which began in the sixteenth century in the West and in the nineteenth century in the Arab world."[58] Fascism arises in the wake of economic crisis and military defeat, and its distinguishing characteristic is "radical mental terrorism" that can lead to complete intellectual hegemony. It also resorts to assassination as a means of intimidating its enemies;
4. the Arab Marxist opinion stipulates that only objective economic and political reasons can explain "fundamentalism."

According to Maḥmūd Amīn al-'Ālim, Samir Amin, Ṭayyib Tizīnī and Ṣādiq Jalāl al-'Azm, there are four major structural shifts in contemporary Arab societies:

(a) the rise of the military state (or security state, in the words of Tizīnī) in the Arab world whose oppressive policies preclude any real measure of democracy, human rights or freedom of thought. In other words, the real absence of a civil society. These trends have recently been aided by the rise of the United States to the position of sole superpower in the world;

(b) as a result of the disintegration of the socialist system and the ensuing of the New World Order, the Arab world is more connected to the world capitalist system than it has ever been before. The ruling Arab elite (military men, politicians, and top businessmen) are busy safeguarding their interests in the context of the New World Order by serving the interests of world capitalism in their countries;

(c) the expansion of poverty, wherein the poor and newly-impoverished (the middle class of yesteryear) share one thing in common: poverty and alienation from the state;

(d) this wide social arena is open to all sorts of ideologies from radical Islamism to superstition to radical Marxism. In one sense, they lack a homogeneous ideological or cultural outlook. They best represent the "poverty of thought and the thought of poverty" in the words of noted Egyptian novelist Yūsuf Idrīs. The Marxist position, therefore, believes that it is the economic and social contradictions, more than doctrinal or ideological changes within Arab societies, that have led to the rise of fundamentalism.

Some Arab thinkers propose a strong connection between the failure of Arab civil society and the emergence of fundamentalism. In other words, they hold on to the implicit assumption that had conditions in the Arab world been "normal," resurgence would not have emerged so powerfully in the last two decades. It is clear that most opponents of Islamic resurgence object on the premise that its main aim is to control the state. It is interesting to note that only a few serious (and objective) studies exist on religion and its present manifestations in the Arab world. Except for the recent efforts of the Center for Arab Studies in Beirut and a few studies here and there by a number of Arab social scientists and philosophers, the study of religion as an academic exercise in the Arab world has been rare. The lack of scholarly studies of religion is based on the notion that religion belongs to the incomprehensible domain of the Sacred and the mythical, and does not warrant academic treatment except when invoked by the oppressed or by a political movement such as the Ikhwān. This attitude is held by Arab secularists who believe that if religion is confined to the subjective domain, religious movements would wither away. The position of the state, which is often secular and Western-oriented, is not much different. If the state fails to gain legitimacy through its traditional allies – the ulama – it usually resorts to power as the only solution to political Islam. In other words, the state refuses to treat religion as an evolving reality that is deeply connected with the collective subconscious of the modern Arab people and subject to the ebbs and flows of political, economic, and social conditions. Religion becomes a security threat and in the view of the state requires "a security response, which is a military, political, and intellectual stamping out (*qam*')."[59] This position has been considerably strengthened since the tragic attacks on the United States on September 11, 2001.

It is important to underline one major point concerning the rise of religious fanaticism in the Arab world in the decades of the 1980s and 1990s.[60] With the opening of the Gulf states to millions of migrant Arab laborers from different Arab countries, some of these migrant laborers returned to their countries with the religious and cultural ideas of the Gulf. As a leading Egyptian thinker notes, Gulf culture is more or less one-dimensional in its ethnic, religious, and political composition and less tolerant than more culturally and religiously diverse Arab countries.[61]

THE ELITE AND THE MASSES

Most political elite in the Arab world, besides being authoritarian in character, are of minority extraction. They are either tribal or sectarian in nature, and this must be examined in the context of colonization in the modern Arab world.[62] The Gulf states may have a smaller population than the rest of the Arab world but are equipped with advanced technology and foreign troops with which they can confront their enemies, especially in the realm of the domestic. Islamic forces, by virtue of their entrenched presence in Saudi society, both traditional and Westernized, have become disillusioned with the state and thus pose a threat to it and its sources of legitimacy.

As pointed out earlier, the expansion of capitalism into the Gulf after 1945 was made possible by a number of factors, one of which was the internationalization of American capital, which followed on the heels of the collapse of the industrial European nations during World War Two. The American-sponsored Marshall Plan to rebuild Western Europe after World War Two was complemented by an American-sponsored modernization plan for the Arab Gulf states, which included Iran at the time.[63] Europe was then too weak to offer any plan for the Arab world.[64] By seeking the cooperation of a tiny but affluent indigenous elite, international capital made it possible for the elite to reproduce itself on a larger scale and accumulate more wealth and power in a few hands. Gradually, this elite became the main benefactor of capitalist largesse and defender of Western interests in the Middle East.

This alliance between American capital and the indigenous elite in the Gulf states encouraged the latter to appropriate the central tenets and features of American modernization, which focused on growth and expansion. Prosperity in the Gulf was tied to the world's need for oil, state spending on arms, welfare, and education, and the ability of the rich classes in the Gulf to spend more money than ever before on consumer goods. This is not to argue that the Gulf elite were themselves capable of producing their own unique theory of modernization or even of digesting the complex philosophy of modernization as it had evolved in the industrial West. The ruling classes in the Gulf strongly object to developing indigenous forms of modernism, since modernism has the potential of cultivating democratic ideals and practices, anathema in the view of the ruling elite in the Gulf and almost every Arab country.[65] Benedict Anderson's comment about "rich weak states" is very apt here: "On the other hand, as a result of the oil crisis of 1973, the world saw for the first time immensely *rich* weak, agrarian states, such as Saudi Arabia, Iran, and Iraq, which had the purchasing power to acquire first-class arms from the industrial core."[66] What is significant to note here is that the local elite bought into the American project of modernization, which promised them development and growth without having to relinquish political authority. On the contrary, with the passage of time, the tribal authority of many Gulf states seems to be stronger year after year. No wonder then, that with the aid of international capital, Gulf society since the 1950s has been able to launch a complex process of modernization, increase its population by at least 50 percent, and build impressive educational and industrial institutions. However, the broadening social and economic base of Gulf society has not translated into parallel political change at the top. Political authoritarianism in the Gulf is even more powerful and assertive today than it was half a century ago. How long can the Gulf elite go on appeasing their population with this faulty modernization without losing control?

The international need for oil has made all of this possible.[67] This process has naturally resulted in an increase in consumerism, the export of foreign labor, and the participation of women in the educational sphere. As far as I know, no scholar has studied the cultural and psychological consequences of such a rapid modernization program in the conservative Gulf society, where certain Islamic values have been utilized to defend the achievements of the affluent indigenous elite. One thing is very clear: the ruling classes, using a combination of religious propaganda and the pacification of all social classes, deny any class conflict or tension in their societies. In order to prove their point, they have imported a large class of foreign workers at the expense of an emerging indigenous working class.

Although Saudi society, for example, experienced an industrial breakthrough with the help of the capitalist West, it has tended to impose certain political and moral constraints in order to keep the political *status quo*. The tribal political elite of the Gulf and their capitalist sponsors in the West have launched an aggressive modernization program in their countries.[68] Colossal change in all aspects of society has taken place in the Gulf in the past few decades. However, is it possible to introduce such massive economic change on a vast scale without cultural, intellectual, and political consequences? Is it possible to introduce modernization without its cultural package, modernism? Therefore, it is appropriate to ask: what ideology drives the current political elite in a country like Saudi Arabia?[69] The most inaccurate answer one often receives is Islam. It is true that the ruling elite in the Gulf, coming as it did from traditional tribal classes or families, have never dissociated themselves from Islam in the public sphere. As Roger Owen rightly notes, although religion did not prove to be an obstacle to the control of the Arab political elite, "No regime felt able to abandon Islam entirely, for this would have been to cut the most important single ideological and cultural link between it and the bulk of the population."[70] Some Arab regimes go as far as to make the claim that they truly implement the Sharīʻah in their homeland. However, this claim has been weakened by the wholesale imposition of capitalism on these tribal societies in the past 50 years, thanks to consumer demand for petroleum. Perhaps the correct answer as to the ideology that drives the ruling elite in the Gulf rests in these changes.

Recent social and economic change in Saudi Arabia has been driven by the principle of capitalist expansion, which became possible with the high prices of oil and has been justified in certain Islamic terms that revere economic competition and private property. Besides being a capitalist monarchy of the highest order, Saudi Arabia is an American protectorate.[71] In essence, Islam was used as a cover for the engineering of new social forces in Saudi society, forces that were required to adhere to the political game of the ruling elite in the Gulf of one-family, one-country mentality. In other words, domination takes a new form: social classes begin to emerge and the middle class establishes deep commercial and financial roots while being denied access to the political base of society. Criticism of the state comes from two different directions: from the commercial middle class that seeks more liberalization in the political and public spheres, and Islamic forces, both traditional and modern, that criticize the state for its use of Islam in its new adventure of social and economic engineering. However, to be realistic, the transition the Arab world made has been at best to a shallow democracy. Most Arab states have experienced more not less authoritarianism since 1967.

The political elite in the Gulf did not hesitate to invite foreign troops to destroy Iraq and its economy for the sake of safeguarding their political interests – preserving power in the same hands. The ruling families in the Gulf, supported by a huge influx of money and the most advanced technology that money can buy, have found effective ways to increase their authority. They have been willing, for various reasons, to accommodate social change; however, they still refuse to broaden their political base and include the new forces in society produced by the modernization of the state.[72] It is to the disadvantage of the Western world to introduce true democratic reforms in these countries, "The family dictatorships...are considered appropriate partners, managing their resources in conformity to basic U.S. interests."[73] Therefore, real democratic change is not possible within the foreseeable future. In spite of the drastic economic and social changes wrought in the Gulf in the past few decades, the newly created social system subscribes to the whims of the political system, which is usually controlled by one family. In the words of Egyptian thinker Ghālī Shukrī, "dictatorship in the Arab world is a reflection of a deformed relationship between the political and social systems."[74]

A similar process took place under the Sadat regime in Egypt. Egyptian journalist Nabīl 'Abd al-Fattāḥ notes that one of the main characteristics of the Sadat regime was the impoverishment of culture and the withdrawal of the state from "cultural engineering," as had been the case under Nasser. The state under Sadat "drew its revolver against culture," which resulted in two important trends: (1) mediocre intellectual and semi-educated officials dominated the cultural scene and the press, and (2) the most talented intellectuals, representing a variety of trends, joined the increasing market of the "brain-drain" to the Gulf, Europe or North America. The modernization project of the Gulf states was bearing fruit by attracting some of the most sophisticated thinkers from poor Arab countries. Modernity is equated here with material luxury, and democracy the concern of a tiny committed intellectual minority. The phenomenon of the mercenary intellectual was born in earnest. The highest bidder could secure the best intellectual in its attack against the Sadat regime. A declared contract between some secular intellectuals and the state is signed in the 1980s. As long as these intellectuals attack the Islamic movement and do not raise issues of democracy or human rights or criticize the state, they are secured jobs and positions in the highest levels of society and the press.

Under these circumstances, official cultural production has come to a grinding halt. It is not encouraged at the state level and no critique of the state is tolerated.

The press is far from serious and few Arab countries publish important intellectual journals. Most of the important journals are published either in Lebanon or overseas. The intellectual scene is bleak. The most capable intellectuals have accepted low-paying jobs, emigrated or been coerced into silence. To conclude, although economic modernization has achieved tremendous success in certain parts of the Arab world, it is doubtful that modernism as an emancipatory intellectual project has gained the same level of success. Whereas economic modernization can be exported, modernism, to be effective, must be home-made.

The social and economic transformation of Arab societies since 1967 cannot be understood without examining the nature and extent of capitalist penetration into those societies. It is cliché to argue that economic means of production are owned by a minority in contemporary Arab society, and that class conflict abounds in the Arab world. It is hard to escape the conclusion drawn by Edward Said over two decades ago that there is an "Arab Right Wing," which lacks a mass base and which has "a state of mind, and, alas, a very large appetite."[75] Besides being schizophrenic, undemocratic, and brutal, the Arab Right wing represents the new rich classes that are "totally dependent on the Western market economy."[76] What is more important to note is that the increase in the margin of poverty in many Arab states is a direct consequence of the increasing prosperity of the rich. The rich are the dominant economic and political elite with access to a wide net of intellectual information and production, such as state television, newspapers, publications houses, and so on, and they use an umbrella or a complex net of ideologies, religious, secular or a combination of both, in order to preserve the *status quo* and enhance their power and control. The hegemony of the elite is solid and only a piercing counter-ideology can overcome this state of affairs.

The international financial system and in the main the need of the world market for oil has led to the formation of a transnational Arab capitalist class, especially in the Gulf, with a distinct economic and social philosophy. The consciousness of this class has been shaped by both domestic and international factors. Globalization is not a new phenomenon in the Arab world, since it is often associated with the rise of Islam in the seventh century CE. However, the new transnational capitalist classes possess a new globalization consciousness shaped solely by modern economic and political factors.[77] One of the major challenges this class faces is how to secure its hegemony both nationally and internationally. Domestically, the expansion of the oil trade has enabled this transnational class to create a new social bloc by co-opting many classes into its new vision of society.

In the process of securing its hegemony over the state apparatus, the Arab bourgeoisie, which is dependent on international capitalism, has resorted to various methods to uphold its authority and prestige, one of which, as mentioned above, is religion. I think what is significant about this bourgeoisie is that under both external and internal pressure, it has opted to modernize its societies without having a true underlying philosophy of indigenous modernization. One must admit that the Arab bourgeoisie had inherited backward Arab societies that lacked elaborate class differentiation. As a result of the modernization program, new social classes vying for power have been created in the Arab world. The Arab working class grows larger and larger, although there has been some concerted effort in the

Gulf states to circumscribe its power by depending almost entirely on cheap (and disposable) migrant labor. The vast scale of modernization in many Arab countries has created new wealth that is primarily enjoyed by the elite. However, the rapid pace of modernization has created a nervous class of ruling elite, people who cannot relax and who often resort to using military power in times of crisis. In addition, the vast wealth accumulated in the Gulf states, especially before the second Gulf War, made it possible for the tribal leadership in the grand style of the ancestors to distribute some of the booty to the masses. The net result of this distribution has been the creation of a very servile (obedient) class of people who dare not criticize the ruling elite. Furthermore, the enormous wealth created a false consciousness of distinctness between the Gulf Arabs and all other Arabs. In other words, to protect the sources of wealth, Gulf Arabs no longer supported Arab masses in their struggles against domestic dictatorship and international imperialism. This is one the major factors leading to the recession of the idea of Arab unity, and to the rise of the idea of the regional state in the Arab world. Also, one major feature of cultural production in the Arab world is that it faced a serious crisis linked to the political crisis of the Arab state in 1967. In the 1970s, with the rise of the Gulf states to power in the Arab world, a major shift took place in cultural production – what happened was the commodification of culture. Culture became a "product" for two reasons: petro-dollar diplomacy and the boycott of Egypt after the signing of the Camp David Accords.[78]

Different factors accounted for the rise of the Gulf states to religious and economic prominence after 1967, mainly in the 1970s and 1980s: first, the success of Arab nationalism, for a short period at least, in challenging the hegemony of the capitalist West in the Middle East and its impact on producing a true sense of Arab nationalism among people of the Middle East and North Africa, including people of the Gulf. This fact forced tribal regimes in the Gulf to push for nationalization under the pretext of fulfilling nationalist demands. Second was the increased demand of the capitalist market for petroleum and the gradual industrialization of the Gulf states. Those states moved from a simple production of oil for world consumption to the creation of capitalist relations in society where capitalism, as defined by Eric Wolf, *does not simply mean the accumulation of capital but wealth that enables its holders to control the means of production*, buy labor power, and put it out to work, thus, "continuously expanding surpluses by intensifying productivity through an ever-rising curve of technological inputs."[79] Third, the new capitalist mode of production dominant in the Gulf after 1967 made it possible for these states to establish well-endowed educational institutions. In others words, it enabled them to create new means of religious and intellectual production (that is, colleges and universities) that hitherto had not existed, at least on such a large scale in the Gulf. This fact produced many outstanding results: as mentioned previously, Gulf society was able to achieve modernization without a clear philosophy of modernism. On the surface, the pedagogical philosophy of the Saudi or Omani states was not opposed to traditional Islamic forces. However, in a significant way, the state's modernization program put these forces on the defensive by forcing them to work through the system. Also, because of the missionary nature of traditional forces in the Gulf, especially in Saudi Arabia, the modernization program, although initially opposed, was wholeheartedly embraced, since it was perceived in the final analysis as useful to the spread of Islam all over the world. Fourth, the new means of intellectual production began to compete with the old centers of Islamic learning, especially in Egypt, Tunisia, and Morocco. Students from all over the Muslim world, especially from poor regions in Africa, South Asia, and Southeast Asia (mainly Indonesia), began to flock to the Gulf, which was made possible by the huge grants many of these students received. When they returned to their countries, most carried back home with them the traditional ideology of the Gulf. That means that most of these people did not just carry an ideology that was anti-Marxist in nature, but also anti-nationalist and anti-socialist on the premise that both nationalism and socialism were foreign tools used to subvert the Muslim world.

THE THEORETICAL AND THE PROBLEMATIC

Perhaps the most difficult job facing a writer is constructing a meaningful theoretical framework that can bring enough light to the problems selected for discussion. The boundaries of this work are somewhat flexible and cut across many theoretical and thematic lines. This is because it is impossible to treat an intellectual discourse outside of its social and political contexts. No discourse can claim complete autonomy, even at the subconscious level.

Since this work discusses a plethora of themes from the political to the theological, it is important to follow some theoretical guidelines developed by other specialists in the following areas: political economy, culture and intelligentsia, ideology and pedagogy, and globalization and Eurocentrism. These and other themes will be developed in this book at length. However, it is important to point out at this stage that one must narrow the scope of the theoretical treatment of these subjects by focusing on the work of one individual in each case. Time and space do not allow us to enter into a detailed discussion of all the theories that deal with one particular problematic or issue.

Samir Amin's work stands out as especially relevant to my treatment of the political economy of the modern Arab world, its dependency on the world capitalist system since the nineteenth century, and the interplay between nation, class, culture, and religion in the post-independence era.[80] This choice becomes more pertinent when one realizes that out of the most prominent world theoreticians on these issues, Amin is the only one who has devoted special attention to the Arab world, both Mashreq and Maghreb.[81] Antonio Gramsci's insights into the domain of culture and the intelligentsia will guide this work as well. In no way do I mean to dismiss the important contributions in this area of such scholars as Edward Shils, Raymond Aron, Louis Althusser, and Abdelkabir al-Khatibi. Also, it is impossible to neglect the important work of Pierre Bourdieu in the area of ideology and pedagogy. While a full treatment of his ideas is untenable, I think he has a lot to offer concerning the interplay between ideology and education in the post-1967 Arab world and the increasing privatization of education that caters to the needs of the elite in the contemporary Arab world.

Samir Amin has written extensively on the subject of the political economy of the modern Arab world with an eye on the production of culture and ideas, their permutations, and present status. It is important to reflect on Amin's major conclusions. First, the interplay between the economic, on the one hand, and the political and cultural, on the other, defines the dynamics of world history. In other words, the mode of production is linked to the political/cultural/religious construct of any society. Second, the capitalist mode of production came to maturity in the eighteenth century after a long and sophisticated process of permutation spanning at least three centuries, which directly resulted in the eradication of outmoded pre-capitalist modes of production, most notably, the tributary, and defining a new relationship with culture and ideas.[82] In pre-capitalist societies, political authority is the source of wealth, whereas in capitalism, political authority is derived from wealth.[83]

Being the dominant mode of production, capitalism "has produced a decisive break in world history"[84] and facilitated the rise of new cultural modes of behavior and thinking that were not necessarily attached to religious metaphysics. In pre-capitalist societies, one can speak of such religious cultures as Islam, Confucianism, or Christianity, whereas after the eighteenth century, the culture of capitalism dominates. This underlines one of Amin's major points, that the intellectual history of the modern Arab world must be sought in the encounter between the capitalist and the Muslim cultures, formed against the background of the long Islamic centuries that were distinguished by long-distance trade. In this encounter, one can discern the intellectual/cultural/religious responses of the Arab world to issues ranging from capitalist domination to state formation and religious change. According to Amin, "Medieval scholastic metaphysics in its four successive forms: Hellenistic, Eastern Christian, Islamic, and Western Christian – constitutes the ideology *par excellence* of the tributary mode of production,"[85] that is, the pre-capitalist mode of production. Metaphysics sought to achieve a rapprochement between revelation and reason or between divine mystery and deductive human reason in order to offer an answer about "the final causes of the world."[86] Capitalist thought broke away from both the process and ideology of metaphysics by adopting Renaissance rationalism, which came to fruition during the Enlightenment of the eighteenth century, as the absolute measure of progress.[87] Therefore, the birth of contemporary capitalist modernity is based on the abandonment of the central question distinguishing the pre-capitalist tributary cultures, namely, the reconciliation between faith and reason.[88] The shift in relationship between capitalism and metaphysics does not cancel out religion, but places it in a new cultural and intellectual framework that is dependent on the capitalist mode of production. The shift engendered by capitalism has had grave consequences on the production of ideas, the domination of religious ideology, and the position of traditional religious intelligentsia. In pre-capitalist societies, religious ideas were the main source of legitimizing political authority and creating social order; under capitalism, the dominant culture creates new forms of ideas and ideology that play this role.[89] The religious domain is put to a severe test by the expansion of capitalism and, in fact, becomes subservient to the dominant culture. In the pre-capitalist Arab world, both Arabization and Islamization, under the pressure of economic and political unity, created the Arab nation with distinguished cultural and religious characteristics.

One has to agree with Amin, though, that the dominant capitalist culture does not *suppress* religious needs. Actually, it gives religion a new role, as in the case of missionary Christianity in the age of European imperialism. Mission and imperialism went hand in hand, as V. Y. Mudimbe contends.[90] One may conclude on the basis of Amin's discussion that as far as the Third World is concerned (a world that fell under the direct domination of the capitalist mode of production at the end of the eighteenth century), religion does not disappear under capitalism but acquires new functions and characteristics by adapting itself to the exigencies of the capitalist order. This formulation enables us to raise the following interrelated questions:

1. What happens to Third World religious institutions under the impact of capitalist expansion in the periphery?
2. How does the pre-capitalist Muslim intelligentsia respond to the challenges and dangers of imperialism/capitalism?
3. How does Muslim culture respond to the advancing capitalist culture?
4. What interaction is there between Muslim thought and liberal thought in the age of imperialism (1882–1950)?
5. How does Arab nationalism treat religious institutions and intelligentsia?
6. Is it correct to assume that the Arab world in the twentieth century has applied both socialism and capitalism, which have failed, and is it time to apply "Islam" in the twenty-first century?

These are significant questions, some of which are not addressed by Amin. Nevertheless, he provides an adequate theoretical outline with which to deal with these issues as they relate to the mutation of Arab thought in the twentieth century. I think that under the impact of capitalism and the creation of a dependent political elite from the nineteenth century until the time of independence, indigenous religion plays a double-edged role. On the one hand, it is used by the power elite to support capitalist expansion, on the other, it resists capitalism in the guise of fighting Westernization and missionary activities. The former tendency is represented by the official hierarchy and the latter by the Ikhwān. Actually, the Arab power elite's use of Islam as a means of legitimation and justification of political, economic, and social policies is an essential characteristic of most regimes, including the most "secularized," such as those in Syria, Iraq, and Tunisia.

This duality of modern religious discourse in the Third World has been explicit in the Arab world since the nineteenth century. As a matter of fact, modern Arab culture, under the impact of capitalism, has been characterized by a severe split: returning to its roots (that is, achieving authenticity) or appropriating *en masse* the cultural and scientific achievements of the capitalist West. In other words, the modern Arab world has not merely suffered from the absence of authenticity or modernity but has been caught unaware by the severe structural and intellectual changes engendered by the advances of an aggressive capitalist mode of production that laid its foundations in the Arab world under the threat of imperialism.

Perhaps the most significant question discussed by Amin is that in spite of appearances, it is capitalist and not Islamic culture that has been dominant in the

Arab world since the nineteenth century.[91] Although it is a distorted form of peripheral capitalism, it nevertheless carries with it capitalist ideas and modes of cultural behavior. Under the pressure of imperialism, the Arab world lost the political and cultural unity it had once achieved by virtue of long-distance trade during the Islamic centuries.[92] In Amin's words, imperialism was to accentuate these divisions in the Arab world and bring about the rebirth of its unity.

However controversial the above theses might be, I think they help us understand the notion that modern Muslim culture in the Arab world has been on the defensive since the nineteenth century, and that this defensiveness has taken a variety of forms in the contemporary era, one of which is revivalism. One can construe revivalism as a multifaceted response to the shock of capitalist penetration in the economic and cultural fields. This response is primarily a modern phenomenon and while it has taken different forms, especially after 1967, it is reflective of the deep crises in the Arab world created by the rise of capitalism to a hegemonic position.

To characterize Islamism as modern is to allude to the fact that the central preoccupation of Muslim thought in the modern Arab world has been the West–Islam dichotomy (or rapprochement), rather than the reconciliation between faith and reason, which had characterized pre-capitalist Muslim and Arab cultures. Islamic revivalism has not been able to surmount the problems this dichotomy presents. This might explain the festering crisis in contemporary Arab Muslim thought and its failure to either transcend or come to grips with capitalist modernity. In one significant sense, this is a catch-22 game and a form of cultural schizophrenia. To transcend capitalism, contemporary Muslim thought must offer a reliable economic and social alternative, and to come to grips with capitalism, it must abandon its metaphysical logic.[93] It is important to underline the fact, which is often emphasized by Amin, that Islamic revivalism was more of a response to the penetration of capitalism into the Arab world than the failure of capitalism in this world. Capitalism, Amin argues, has not failed at all, either at the international or Arab levels.[94] After 1967, it enhanced its position in the Arab world in the wake of the defeat of Nasserism and with the Center's increasing need for oil. The Gulf region, after the defeat of nationalism, becomes more powerful and important than the rest of the Middle East. The Center begins to gradually cut it off from the rest of the Arab world, until it falls under the occupation of the American military in the wake of the defeat of Iraq in the second Gulf War.[95]

Amin argues convincingly that the "gradual integration of the Arab world into the capitalist system was…initiated on the basis of inequality, even before the system became imperialist."[96] To push this statement to its logical conclusions, it is possible to say that the West began to impose its newly-formed capitalist culture on the Arab world through various means, one of which was the training of indigenous intelligentsia who are faithful to the precepts of capitalist modernity. The development of this class of intelligentsia underlined two basic facts: one economic and the other cultural. On the economic side, this class of intelligentsia was an outgrowth of a dependent indigenous bourgeoisie that was denied access to industrialization. On the cultural front, this class collided with the traditional religious class that refused to forsake its metaphysical worldview. That collision lies at the heart of the secularism and modernity discourse in modern Arab thought. The new Arab bourgeois intelligentsia adopted the philosophy of secularism as the criterion of progress and "catching up" with the West. This is what defined the Arab liberal project that was born in peripheral capitalism. From the start, this project was fragile, and its failure at the end of the imperialist hegemony (around the 1950s) opened the way for Nasserism as a pan-Arab project to achieve political unity and economic integration in the Arab world in order to face both Western imperialism and international Zionism. In the words of Amin, "The Arab world did not really wake up until imperialism installed itself in the heart of the region by creating the state of Israel."[97]

Amin goes on to argue that the period from 1947 to 1967 is characterized by the following: (1) the bankruptcy of the Arab national bourgeoisie; (2) the end of British influence and the beginning of the Cold War, and (3) the affirmation of the expansionist character of Zionism. The interaction between these factors came to determine the post-1967 period in the Arab world. In a sense, the unequal base of the relationship between the Arab world and the capitalist West beginning in the nineteenth century, has produced a very complex situation wherein the Arab world has been dependent on the West. Arab nationalism was the only organized Arab political movement that attempted to challenge the West's hegemony. Internationally, this was possible with the existence of a bipolar world system. The 1990s, however, "resulted in the collapse of the equilibria characteristic of the postwar world system."[98] Zionism played a significant role in deepening the relationship of inequality between the Arab world and the capitalist West.

I think that it is important to point out that Amin, in the final analysis, proposes Arab unity as the only model to achieve total Arab independence from capitalism. The road to Arab unity since the nineteenth century has been fraught with hurdles. The rise of the peripheral bourgeoisie, the establishment of Israel, the emergence of the Gulf as a conglomerate of states dependent on world capitalism; all of these factors impeded the process of political and economic unity in the Arab world.[99] Nasserism was an ambitious project that sought to achieve the political unity of the Arab world as a necessary step to accomplish economic integration and thus free the Arab world from dependency on the Center. However, Nasserism was deeply aware of the historical backwardness of the Arab world and felt it was too late, perhaps, to cause a radical break with political disunity and economic dependency on the West.[100] One sees a grim picture indeed in Amin's analysis about the future of the Arab world, especially as capitalism has renewed itself since the collapse of the Soviet project, entered into a new phase of globalization under the leadership of the United States with the industrialization of the periphery, and spread its neo-liberal philosophy under the threat of military and food embargos.[101] Amin characterizes the present state of affairs as the "empire of chaos," where polarization is the rule of the day between South and North. Because of its propensity toward perpetual expansion, capitalism has created a "savage order." He argues that "Liberal globalization will lead only to greater polarization, and by this act will summon up from the people of the periphery resistance movements which can only be massive and violent."[102]

Clearly Amin is obsessed with political economy to the extent that he preserves his rivals' main assumptions about the state of society. However, this obsession must not be understood as his way of devaluing culture or reducing it to the exigencies of the economic. I read Amin's project as an attempt to come to terms with the encounter between the economic and the cultural, and to extract the proper lessons from this interaction. What he says in the case of the Arab world is that this interaction has been fierce and that the victory of the capitalist mode of production with its implicit and explicit cultural assumptions has been overwhelming in the modern Arab world. In the same vein, one must see the Muslim reaction as overwhelming as well. In a sense, Amin does claim that political economy can explain all the intricate cultural and intellectual issues; however, without a real appreciation of political economy and the economic transformations of the modern world at large, the other aspects cannot be fathomed. Amin's major conclusion that the dominant culture in the Arab world is capitalist is intriguing and at odds with many views about the nature of culture in the modern Arab world. This observation begs many questions about culture itself, intelligentsia, and the state in the modern Arab world. For that reason, I will briefly treat the ideas of Antonio Gramsci on this matter.

Gramsci's theory of the intelligentsia, culture, and the state, it seems to me, can give us insights about the following questions in modern Arab thought:

1. How does one describe the contemporary culture of the Arab world, and what is the connection between the capitalist culture (of Arab peripheral capitalism) and the pre-capitalist Muslim culture?
2. What is the nature of the intelligentsia and their role in the modern Arab state?
3. How do we interpret Gramsci's notions of organic and ecclesiastic intellectuals in relation to the Arab world?

Even if one is to agree with Amin that the dominant culture in the Arab world since the dawn of imperialism has been capitalist in nature, that is, centered around the accumulation of cultural goods, competitiveness, individualism, and so on, one must notice the resilience of pre-capitalist Islamic culture. What that means is that capitalist culture, perhaps due to its deformed nature as peripheral capitalism in the Arab world, has not succeeded in stemming the tide of Islamic culture, which had formed against the background of early Islam and the formative phase of the Islamic empire in the first five centuries. However, one can argue that post-nineteenth century Muslim culture ceased to be self-propelling and new components went into the making of this culture ever since its encounter with capitalism. A new social formation was introduced in the Arab world as a result of the expansion of capitalism in the guise of imperialism.

With the onset of the independent Arab state in the 1950s, culture is subsumed under the authority of the state and many intellectuals find themselves at the economic mercy of the state.[103] As the state casts its centralization web wider and wider, the bureaucracy grows larger, and new fields of specialization are created.[104] The Arab state, more or less, has given some intelligentsia some type of political, religious or educational role. The state in the Gulf or the Middle East or North Africa is no exception. In Egypt, for example, the decline of the liberal state and the emergence of nationalism undermined the traditional liberal intelligentsia and created a new type that conformed to the state's vision of economic and political centralization. Undoubtedly, the economic program launched by many Arab states after independence was ambitious in that it created many new areas of specialization that reflected the growth of either state capitalism or bourgeois capitalism in society.

Where does all of this lead us in relation to organized religion and religious intelligentsia? One might argue that the Muslim hierarchy at the beginning of the twentieth century was not as powerful as the Catholic Church in Italy during Gramsci's time. According to Gramsci, the church was primarily interested in achieving doctrinal unity of both the masses and the intellectuals by preventing a new class of intelligentsia, which may prevent the masses from forming a higher level of consciousness.[105] Therefore, the ecclesiastical intelligentsia as conceived by Gramsci played a "backward" role in that it was not in their best interest to lead the masses into higher forms of cultural and religious expression congruent with the demands of contemporary life.

On the basis of the above discussion, one can make the following points:

1. Muslim culture had been dominant in the Arab world for at least 1,300 years and is distinguished by a conspicuous religious worldview;
2. this culture, in spite of its promotion of economic and social objectives in this life, did not succeed in developing capitalism as the main mode of economic behavior. Its commercial character did not translate into a higher mode of economic activity;
3. with the onslaught of capitalism under the guise of imperialism in the nineteenth century, Arab-Muslim culture was challenged to the core by a more aggressive culture. It is within this context that new religious and intellectual movements emerged to express the crisis of Arab culture and to find ways to transcend this crisis.

On the whole, one might say that in spite of the long relationship between the indigenous Arab-Muslim culture and the capitalist one (over 150 years by now), Arab culture is still in the mode of reaction to capitalism. In other words, it is imperative to understand religious, cultural, intellectual, and social responses to the crisis of modern Islamic culture in the wider context of the hegemony of modern capitalism in the Arab world.

It is difficult to come up with one succinct definition of the term "culture,"[106] especially when we consider that culture has had a rather long history in the Arab world. However, one can speak about the variables of cultures and how they change over time. In the modern context, the religious reaction, for example, to imperialism and capitalism has been a distinctive mode of Arab-Muslim culture. Another variable has been the role of the state, as we have seen. The modern Arab state, in a generic sense, has been powerful, and let us say more complex than the medieval state in Islam. From that angle, it has challenged pre-capitalist Islamic culture, as well. The state (tribal, nationalist, religious) created many new modernized institutions, some of which challenge the basic views of Islamic culture. For example, consider the concepts of *nation* versus *ummah*. Almost every state in the contemporary Arab world speaks of the nation as opposed to the ummah.

There do exist some Muslim groups here and there that speak in terms of ummah and some states that invoke the ummah. However, the nation has taken precedence over the ummah in even the most revolutionary Islamic regimes in the modern Muslim world, such as in the case of Iran.

One of the main consequences of the intervention of capitalism in the modern Arab world has been the diversification of the means of intellectual production, that is, schools, colleges, and universities. I think this is an important point to follow from the perspective of the modern intellectual history of the Arab world and the production of culture and intelligentsia. One of the byproducts of the capitalist expansion has been the diversification of the intellectual means of production at the expense of a homogeneous means of production supported by Islamic culture over the centuries and carried out in such institutions as the Azhar, Qarawiyyīn, and Zaytūna. The classical Muslim model was distinguished by a certain level of differentiation, a direct consequence of the diversity of the schools of Fiqh in Islam. However, this internal Islamic diversity was challenged by new systems of knowledge that did not originate from the Islamic core as understood by these schools of Fiqh but from the Western core of knowledge that is basically capitalist and secular in nature, although allowing religion (that is, Christianity) to spread under its supervision.

The capitalist intervention that gave rise to the colonial and post-colonial states in the Arab world accelerated the differentiation of culture, intellectual sources and worldviews, and produced new intelligentsia. It even forced a good number of the traditional intelligentsia to tow the line of the state, which is the case at present in the Arab world. Here, I think it is helpful to examine Gramsci's ideas about the two main types of intelligentsia: the organic intellectual and the ecclesiastical intellectual. Gramsci argues that the capitalist class coming to power on the basis of the new mode of production creates "one or more groups of intellectuals" to represent it in society.[107] This idea is best stated by Ernesto Laclau, who argues that, "A class is hegemonic not so much to the extent that it is able to impose a uniform conception of the world on the rest of society, but to the extent that it can articulate different visions of the world in such a way that their potential antagonism is neutralized."[108] But in its emergence, the new class comes into contact with the traditional classes from the vestiges of the old order. Gramsci defines the ecclesiastical class as a monopolist "of the religious ideology, the philosophy, and the science of the era, together with the school, education, morality, justice, charity, assistance, etc."[109] However, most traditional intellectuals tend "to effect a compromise with the new organic intellectuals and the values they express, usually because of institutional pressures."[110] Gramsci argues that all persons are intellectuals, although not all carry out the function of intellectuals in society.

The main point here is that the traditional Muslim class was challenged by the rise of modern intellectual classes in Arab society, a fact made possible by the advance of capitalism in Arab society and the diversification in the functions of the state, especially after independence. The state of which I speak is not just Nasser's nationalist petty bourgeois state but all states in the Arab world, including the most "backward." Second, the capitalist penetration created a major backlash from the Muslim culture that had been dominant up to the point of Western intervention. This backlash came on the heels of the failure of reform Islam to offer an acceptable synthesis to the crisis of Arab/Muslim society and culture under imperialism. This backlash was an Islamist backlash of the highest order carried out by lay Muslim intellectuals who were not absorbed by the dominant capitalist culture of Arab liberalism. Moreover, this backlash has taken different forms since its inception at the beginning of the twentieth century and has been persistent in challenging the state and its economic and cultural organization.

Pierre Bourdieu, one of the most fascinating of contemporary social theorists, to my mind, continues in a significant way Gramsci's cultural deconstruction by probing the proper connections between culture, power, and economics in contemporary French society.[111] His reflection on the state of education in French society and the relationship between power, culture, and elite provides an exceptional theoretical map with which one can examine the state of power/culture formation in the post-1967 Arab world, which was rapidly dominated by the Western capitalist mode of production after the decline of state socialism and Nasserism in the Arab world.[112] It is fair to argue that the Arab world has gone through rapid and dramatic changes in the past four decades that are distinguished by an unprecedented demographic explosion as well as by a gradual dependency of almost the entire Arab world on the capitalist system.

Under the patronage of state capitalism in Egypt, mainly between 1952 and 1970, and that of the quasi-capitalism of the Gulf states that generated a lot of hard currency because of the international need for oil, an ambitious process of modernizing educational systems took place. This allowed new segments of the population to enjoy the privileges of nationalized or modernized education, especially women and members of the working class. However, with the demise of Nasserism in the 1970s and the total dependence of the Gulf on the West, the number of private educational institutions has increased dramatically. Even in a country that has been dominated by the French such as Morocco, American education is gaining popularity. The privatization and Americanization of the educational institutions increases the power of the Arab elite on a grand scale by providing them with American degrees and rationales.[113]

At the expense of simplifying Bourdieu's complex thought and without committing "symbolic violence" against his intricate epistemological system, I would like to point out the following ideas that underlie his *oeuvre*: first, the dominant classes use education to reproduce their influence in society as well as to create new modes of domination, mostly subtle, as the society becomes more complex. Second, political and social order is maintained through two broad means: material and symbolic force. Material force is represented in the physical capacity of the state, the police or the military, for example. On the other hand, symbolic force is traditionally perpetuated in the field of religion, as discussed by Gramsci. Third, in modern industrial societies, schooling has taken the place of religion.[114] In a sense, both religion and education can be analyzed as systems of symbolic violence. Here, Bourdieu's argument is reminiscent of Althusser's famous analysis of ideological state apparatuses. Through schooling, the dominant elite in society reproduce themselves, obtain access to multiple fields of power, and reassert their authority. Fourth, the relationship between the dominant elite in society and cultural production is very intricate. Dominant elite acquire the social habit of distinction and differentiation on the basis of their access to education, defined in the broadest sense, and with their acquired educational power and the relationships that it implies, they acquire the ability to differentiate themselves from other classes. Differentiation means the ability to be distant and controlling at the same time. In Bourdieu's terms, "an elite is not only distinct and separate, but also recognized by others and by itself as worthy of being so."[115] In that sense, Bourdieu notes that "Taste is an acquired disposition to 'differentiate' and 'appreciate'."[116] Fifth, social distinction or recognition is the final objective of the dominant classes. In the words of David Swartz, Bourdieu's American interpreter, Bourdieu "advances the bold claim that all cultural symbols and practices, ranging from artistic tastes, style in dress, and habits to religion, science, and philosophy – indeed to language itself – embody interests and function to enhance social distinctions."[117]

The mushrooming of private educational institutions (that is, high schools, colleges, and universities) in most Arab countries since 1967, except perhaps in Syria and Algeria, is a concrete expression of the power of the dominant Arab elite. Those elite, a tiny minority of society, represent different ideologies of hegemony that are related by the structure of power to one legitimizing force. The main principle of domination in the Arab world is usually personified in the king, president or prince. However, under this personification, there are many agents of power that represent the multiplicity of economic and social elite in society. Bourdieu, for example, points out the tension between two kinds of elite: the bourgeois elite that owe their power to education, and the aristocratic elite that derive their power from its inherited forms of cultural and material power.[118] One may assume that a similar type of tension exists among the elite in the Arab world, between the new elite that has acquired Western knowledge and the old that had inherited power.

The recent privatization efforts in the field of education in many Arab countries does not negate the fact that many private schools and universities were established in the Middle East over a century ago. Most of these institutions were established by Christian missionaries whose goal was to produce an indigenous class of Christian intellectuals to help with the mission of the church. By sheer historical coincidence, perhaps, many of these schools educated the most nationalist of Arab leaders who fought against imperialist domination at home. It is doubtful that current private institutions in the Arab world are fulfilling this function.

The elite do incorporate in their structure some high members of the religious intelligentsia who ally their interests with those of the state. However, a good number of this traditional intelligentsia are not properly incorporated in the symbolic field of power of the ruling elite. Very often, either economic pressure or some other form of coercion is practiced against this intelligentsia if they step out of line. It seems to me that Islamists are the only ones who refuse to play the game of the power elite. Because of this fact, they have been easy to marginalize.

In addition to the sources of legitimacy the elite possess in Arab society, both material and symbolic, one must not forget their external sources of legitimacy. Politically, they aspire to the moral support of the ruling elites in the Western world. In a symbolic sense, they send their sons mainly to Western institutions to receive their educations. Usually, an Oxbridge or an Ivy League degree is worth much more than an Azhar degree. Very often, women are not permitted to compete with men in this area but are married at a young age, which reflects Bourdieu's point that "marriage strategies and economic strategies are [usually] interwoven."[119]

AN IMAGINED JOURNEY

In spite of the tribal origins of the ruling royal family in Saudi Arabia, the country went through an ambitious modernization program in the 1960s and 1970s.[120] Saudi Arabia adopted modernization without cultivating indigenous forms of modernism. The question arises as to the far-reaching religious and cultural consequences of imposing such a modernization program from above. It is the opinion of Talal Asad that the dramatic changes brought about by modernization in Saudi Arabia began to challenge the meaning of "orthodox Islam" in the minds of many Saudi Muslims.[121] To my mind, this is only one part of the story. Modernization has indeed created a new generation of wealthy Saudis who stand aloof from the tremendous social and political problems of the Arab and Muslim worlds. A new form of Saudi nationalism has evolved over the past several decades. The following imagined journey encapsulates some of the principal challenges facing Saudi Arabia and the larger Arab world.

I would like to share with the reader a fictitious jouney I imagined I had taken to Mecca, one of Islam's holiest places. Here in this journey, I imagine myself "flying like a bat into a narrowing tunnel, of driving alone without luggage into an open-ended highway," as the American poet Theodore Roethke said.[122] When I cross borders in this journey, I am often stopped by police of the nation-state asking me to reveal my identity. Modernity in the Arab world, imported from the Western masters of Arab rulers, is so organized that nobody can escape its clutches. Bureaucracy uses the latest models of information technology to keep everyone in line. Everyone has a number, photo, and passport. In this poor Arab world, the center seems to hold pretty well by sheer force, contrary to the poet W. B. Yeats' maxim, "Things fall apart, the center cannot hold; mere anarchy is loosed upon the world." Any citizen contemplating anarchy will be visited at night and snatched away from his loved ones. Modernity in the Arab world is not "a mode of vital experience…shared by men and women," as American thinker Marshall Berman would say. Modernity is organization, discipline, and control.[123]

In this travel, I am saved, thanks be to God, by my powerful American passport. The police of the Arab rulers handle American passports with extra care since they are intimidated from harassing their holders. However, I think of all the poor people in the Middle East, Latin America, and Africa who are continually harrassed; who are not respected as citizens by their own governments. I think of the many destitute killed in Guatemala, of the missing in Argentina, and the street children in Brazil.

I travel from Turkey to Syria, to Jordan and on to Saudi Arabia. In the good old days, 100 years ago or so, these regions constituted the center of the world of Islam. The Ottoman Empire based in Istanbul was strong and healthy. Any caravan of *ḥajj* or pilgrimage used to travel from Albania to Istanbul and on to the holy sites in Western Arabia without necessity of passport, without hindrance. The world of Islam was united then under the hegemony of Muslims. In traveling between Turkey and the holy places today, you'll get stopped at least twice. Officials check passports and condescend to their holders, trying to make them feel like nonentities.

I enter Jedda, which is only 60 miles north of Mecca, looking for any trace of my identity, my Islamic identity. Modernity is said to have been a revolt against the old tradition, the old identity. Modernity has transformed Jedda from a traditional Muslim city into a Westernized version of itself. The stubborn and authentic Muslim culture of generosity and hospitality seems to progressively give way to the "throwaway culture" of the future, so impressively discussed by Alvin Toffler in *Future Shock*.[124] The people of Jedda speak of the old part of town with faint voices. They are proud of their new space, their post-modern airport, and of Saudi Airlines which hold the most modern "fleeting" airplanes in the modern aviation industry. "Modernity is the transient, the fleeting, the contingent; it is the one half of art," says the French poet Baudelaire. The modern city of Jedda drives this sentiment home again and again. In Jedda, I see big shopping malls, highrises, and highways. Oh my God, am I in New York or San Francisco? What happened to Islamic space? This is alien to me; it is huge, unfriendly, and ephemeral. I see more cars in Jedda than human beings. In my past journey 200 years ago, I saw many people, men and women, Arab and *'ajam* (actually more *'ajam* than Arab) and their animals, all marching toward Mecca humbling themselves before Allah. I wonder now, who owns all these buildings? Who makes all the major decisions? Deeper yet, who owns the petroleum wells in the grand Arabian desert? Five years ago, in the blessed desert of Arabia (*wā subḥāna alladhī yuhyī al-arḍa ba'da mawtihah*), they discovered a huge oil lake 300 miles in length by 200 miles in width, an enormous ocean of oil deposited inside the whale, inside the desert. Is this a new gift from God to the world of capitalism? Who controls all this wealth? Is it the Muslim poor of Nigeria, Pakistan, Indonesia, and Egypt? I receive different answers to my questions: one voice tells me that it is controlled by the King of Saudi Arabia and members of his family, 500 strong men in all. This is the reason why many members of the royal family are able to build and maintain 300-room palaces with over 500 servants in each palace, 600 telephones and 300 television sets. Another voice tells me, it is the multinational companies, American, British, and German, that own the petroleum of Saudi Arabia, who benefit from this. After all, Americans have stationed themselves in Saudi Arabia since the end of the Gulf War. Over 60,000 Yankee soldiers have been placed in the desert protecting their petroleum, which God deposited for them since time immemorial. As a token of thanks to Ṣaddām Ḥussain, who gave them the golden opportunity to remain in the Gulf after 1990, Americans send every year, just before Christmas, Tomahawk and Cruise missiles to Baghdad, just to humiliate the Iraqi population.

I set out traveling alone toward Mecca on foot, imitating Muslim travelers of the past, remembering the great traveler Ibn Baṭṭūṭa who went from Morocco to India in the fourteenth century, mostly on foot, and recorded all that he saw on the way in minute detail.[125] He described not only buildings and people but also plants, changes in temperature and hurricanes. I rely heavily on the *collective memory* of my grand ancestors; it is the only thing that nourishes me spiritually through the hardship of travel and the heat of the desert. It takes me a whole day to reach Mecca; Oh, Mecca, what a sight and what a feeling! I had seen Mecca before only on television. What I see now is nothing compared to what I saw then. Modern technology has failed to communicate the depth of the feelings and the prayers of millions of women and men I see prostrating themselves, asking God to forgive and bless them and their families. I stare at the faces of these humble servants of God, trying to find my center. I have been center-less for many years. I have been aimlessly treading the path of modernity and post-modernity without full spiritual satisfaction. I try to recover my center by invoking the supplications and prayers of the millions of people, known and unknown, dead and alive, who have come to this Holy Place over the centuries. I go back fourteen centuries with my memory, back to the early period of Islam when the Prophet and his disciples were still alive. I listen to the Prophet's Ḥadīth, "Islam began in exile [*gharīban*] and it will be exiled again as in the beginning. Happy are the expatriates of the community of Muḥammad, for they live in solitude, alone with their religion."[126] I contemplate his other Ḥadīth, "Be in this world as if you were a stranger or an '*ābir sabīl* or passer-by," and feel secure in my alienation.

How many people have come here in fourteen centuries? Surely, the number is in the millions. They come from all walks of life, all corners of the earth, admitting their senses of finitude and clamoring for divine mercy. The early Muslims worshipped in these pristine places with no fanfare, or arrogance, but rather with utter humility. I feel totally redeemed in this Sacred place. People *do* worship God deeply. For the first time in many years, I feel a sense of triumph over fleeting modernity. Here, modernity seems to have failed to plant roots; it gives way to the piety of the millions of people who inhabit the place, devoting themselves to worship and only to worship. Here, modernity is washed away in the sea of eternity. In this sanctuary, people prefer silence to noise, meditation to music, and contemplation to making money. People do not seem to be rushed, they do not seem to sleep, they are awake all night long enjoying the fleeting moments of their lives. The moving supplications of the people strike me as a defense against the terror of loneliness, uncertainty, and death. Oh, what a sight, what a feeling! I see many gentle people, sobbing because they have spent a great deal of their lives, like Faust, making money and falling in love, for nothing.

In Mecca, I meet a variety of people from India, Tajikistan, America, China, and Latin America.[127] I meet a new breed of people I had never met before in my journeys: they are called "guest workers" by the Saudis. In their rush to make a living in the Gulf, guest workers carry with them not just their bodies but also their food and music, memories and cultures. I enjoy stopping at the little Afghani bakery in town that sells the best bread for a few cents. I have my hair cut by an Indian barber and wash my clothes with an old Javanese lady who had come all the way from Indonesia to eke out a living in the blessed desert. All of these guest workers are brought to the Gulf states by their sponsors; they perform all sorts of duties that the arrogant contemporary "Bedouin Bourgeoisie" refuse to perform. They do the menial jobs, take care of all the services, do whatever they have to do to send a few dollars to their families back home who are eager to hear their news. Most of these people are considered fortunate by the relatives they left behind. Relatives think all Arabs are wealthy. They associate Arabs today less with Islam and morality and more with money, television sets and music boxes. In their eyes, the true Arabs are the Gulf Arabs. The rest are an accretion.

I visit the enclaves where guest workers stay in Mecca. For a while, I feel I am in little Karachi or Delhi or Colombo or some unnamed village in Tamil Nadu. Most tell me that under better circumstances, they would have come to Mecca just to perform pilgrimage and not to make money. Many, although illiterate and simple folk, are not happy with their lot.

I have never seen so many races assembled in one small place. All seem to be intimate, confirming the ancient notion of one Muslim ummah bound by religious doctrine rather than ethnic or linguistic background. Harmony seems to be the rule of the day. However, I look around searching for Bedouins, the indigenous people of the land, nomads, known for their fortitude and perseverance who have proudly inhabited the environs of Mecca all these centuries, and who have imprinted meaning and authenticity on the place. The Bedouin culture has produced a great deal of wonderful poetry celebrating hospitality and generosity.[128] Alas, no Bedouins are in sight. The proud and true Bedouin race seems to have completely disappeared from Mecca. The fringes of the desert have become strewn with magnificent urban centers. The desert is truly empty without the Bedouins. I look around, I see fewer Arabs and more non-Arab Muslims. The venerable Bedouin sense of *'aṣṣabiyyah* has been entirely appropriated by these non-Arab Muslims, who refuse to accept ephemerality, fragmentation, and discontinuity.[129] What happened to the Arabian race? Are the desert Arabs reveling in luxury and corruption? One voice tells me that the Arabs, who grew tired of the desert heat after many centuries, *had decided to migrate* en masse *to London, Paris, and Tel Aviv, where the weather is cooler, the food tastier, and the women prettier*. This voice went on, informing me that this was possible with the influx of money after the discovery of huge oil reservoirs in the desert. Another voice told me, no, the true Bedouins migrated to the big cities, to modern Jedda and Riyadh, which are even more modern than New York. They inhabit all these highrises now. This voice went on, saying that initially the Bedouins were accompanied by their animals, especially their authentic Arabian horses, to the highrises but when they discovered this was impractical, they abandoned the idea. Some of them actually acquired horses in the pastures of Scotland, Kentucky, and Vermont. Whatever the case, the post-modern Bedouin race of Arabia, propelled to the international scene only twice in its long history (in the first instance by Islam in the seventh century and in the second by petroleum in the twentieth),[130] now prefer a Western type of space to the vast expanse of the boundary-less desert.[131] Because of Islam and petroleum, the Bedouin are sought after by almost every nation in the world, including the powerful and mighty. In his magisterial *The Muqaddimah*, Ibn Khaldūn notes that "Islam cemented the leadership of the Arabs with the religious laws,"[132] and modern oil resurrected them from the dead after they had lost the leadership of Islam to non-Arab Muslims, notably the Turks. Now you can find many Bedouin investing in the stock markets in Tokyo, London, and New York. The humble Bedouin of yesteryear negotiated their new style of life with their powerful tribal leaders and in exchange for political loyalty, were financially remunerated by the *status quo.*[133] In the past, they suffered from want and deprivation. They looked with envy upon the sedentary people in town.[134] Nowadays, a great number of people from foreign lands flock to their pitched tents in the Hilton and Sheraton hotels in the capitals of the world, begging them for donations to build this mosque or that Islamic school. In the desert of the old days, the indigenous people of the place were in direct and daily communication with God Almighty. They were free from urban or social constraints. They owned their destiny. At present, they worship God only once a week, as modern Europeans have done for two centuries. They are on the government dole. Their extreme independence has been lost in a matter of a few years.[135]

The change in space terrified me greatly. In Mecca, in the holy sanctuary, people were very close to each other, all praying and reading the Qur'ān, signs of contentment planted deeply on their foreheads. I imagine them to be the real *ghurabā'*,[136] or strangers, mentioned in the famous Ḥadīth of the Prophet of Islam, narrated above.

A PERSONAL NOTE

After sharing this fictitious journey with the reader, I would like to say that this work has grown out of my long reflection, oddly enough, on the specific situation of the Palestinian minority inside the Green Line after the creation of Israel in 1948. This minority was cut off from its larger social and political context in the Arab world after 1948, which led to a painful state of alienation and lost identity. Ironically enough, the Israeli occupation of the West Bank, Gaza, Sinai, and the Golan Heights in 1967 allowed this community to re-enter the Arab world through the back door, so to speak. It opened the way to new venues that had been firmly blocked and enabled it to regain some of its cultural, nationalist, and religious balance under occupation.[137] As a Palestinian with an Israeli passport, I was not able to visit the Arab world before I came to the United States in 1980. I was able to visit some Arab countries only after I became a naturalized American citizen in 1989. My goal was simply to get acquainted with the Arab world, meet some interesting people and get a feel for what it means to be an Arab in the contemporary world. Although Nasser passed away when I was barely 14 years old, he had a profound influence on my generation. At that time, Egypt seemed to me to be as fascinating as it was distant.

This work, therefore, is a reflection on the pain and dilemmas of the contemporary Arab world. Although the Palestine question still remains one of the most critical problems in the contemporary Arab world, there are other significant issues as well. To reflect on these issues is to consider the social, economic, and political realities and contradictions of the Arab world. Taking into account the collapse of Soviet communism and the great chaos in the world political system, the Arab world is faced with a host of uncertainties and anxieties. Because a new political order has been long overdue in the Arab world, the persistence of the old is alarming and unsettling. The crisis in the Arab political system is reflective of deep social, cultural, and religious crises in contemporary Arab societies. The very precariousness of the Arab political system has so far prevented the birth of a new order.

In reflecting on the inner problems of the Arab world, I have gained deeper insight into the Israeli state and society. While it is unconventional for scholars of Islamic studies to deal with Judaism, Zionism, and the state of Israel, this work on post-1967 Arab intellectual history has made me take the question of Israel more seriously than before. A lot can be said about the birth and evolution of the Israeli state and the challenges it has posed to the Arab world since 1948. However, it suffices to mention at this stage that Israel is the only state in the Middle East that possesses a nuclear arsenal and a huge conventional army. Have these two qualities made it a regional power in the Middle East? The answer is both yes and no. Yes, in the sense that Israeli military power is formidable and has gone unchallenged for a long while. However, Israel lacks the basic characteristics of a hegemon: that is, it lacks a strong economy, and has major competitors in the area, especially the United States and Europe. In addition, Israel lacks soft power, which is the ability to turn its cultural values into widely accepted norms in the Middle East.[138] Israel began to speak about a common Middle Eastern economic market that will be dominated by Israeli technology and scientific vision. However, this kind of talk collapsed as soon as the Aqsa Intifada began in 2000. However, the fundamental state of hostility between the Arab world and Israel has made its cultural and economic hegemony in the area tenuous. In this sense, Israel is a second-rate regional power with a strong military foundation.

Part One

Themes

1
The Scope and Limitation of Post-1967 Arab Thought

> "The writing of history requires numerous sources and greatly varied knowledge. It also requires a good speculative mind and thoroughness. Possession of these two qualities leads the historian to the truth and keeps him from slips and errors." Ibn Khaldūn, *The Muqaddimah: An Introduction to History*, volume 1, trans. Franz Rosenthal (New York: Pantheon, 1958), 15.
>
> "The progress of opinion is fluid and indefinite; it does not easily lend itself to any system of dates and clear-cut chronological divisions." D. C. Somervell, *English Thought in the Nineteenth Century* (London: Methuen & Co., 1929), 1.
>
> "Facts require explanations, and all explanations, even bad ones, presume a configuration of concepts, which we provisionally call 'theory'. In other words, theory is not simply a desirable but a *necessary* relation between facts and their explanations." Aijaz Ahmad, *In Theory: Classes, Nations, Literatures* (New Delhi: Oxford University Press, 1994), 34.
>
> "Critical theory [is] the intellectual equivalent of crack." Terry Eagleton, "The Crisis of Contemporary Culture." *New Left Review*, number 196, November/December 1992, p. 30.
>
> "No; defeat has more than one father. In politics, it hasn't been the modern Arab tradition to punish the leader for a defeat. He will go to the masses for sympathy, and they will console him by begging him to stay on the throne to outwit the enemy. For what does the enemy want but to bring down the leader and rescue us from the blessing of his presence? Let us therefore defeat the enemy and win a victory over ourselves as well by keeping the defeated leader as our executioner." Mahmoud Darwish, *Memory for Forgetfulness: August, Beirut, 1982*, trans. Ibrahim Muhawi (Berkeley: University of California Press, 1995), 103–4.

"The progress of thought is associated with situations of confrontation and disequilibrium," writes Samir Amin, and "periods of stable equilibrium are periods of stagnation in thought."[1] Contemporary Arab thought, just like nineteenth century Arab thought, is primarily an historical product of several decades of enormous changes in all spheres of life, and which is distinguished at heart by a number of philosophical orientations which advocate renewal at all levels of thought and society. In another sense, contemporary Arab thought has been a product of defeat, civil strife, disequilibrium, and confrontation with the "Other." It is in the face of this confrontation with the "Other" that the contemporary Arab world has been in search of its identity, roots, and foundations.[2] Generally speaking, Arab thought of the past four decades has been embedded in various ideals, from the renaissance of the Arab people to the restoration of a democratic environment or the establishment of the Sharī'ah as the main legal foundation of a new Arab civil society. However, the dominant trends of contemporary Arab thought agree that intellectual progress can be achieved only if Arab intellectuals have access to an unfettered exercise of thought and are able to freely criticize that which has gone wrong in the lives of the Arab people in the twentieth and now the twenty-first century.[3] In its painful exercise of criticism and its anguished and perhaps desperate attempts to rebel against the existing social, economic, and political realities, Arab thought stands apart as a truly engaged entity bounced about in a roiling sea of conflicting waves subject to the aching muscles of an aging military state.

Any intellectual historian attempting even a mere survey of the huge corpus of Arab intellectual production since 1967 will find this task daunting. Four general reasons make it quite challenging to discuss the intellectual and cultural climate of the period under consideration in a reasonable manner. The first is the fact that in the past four decades the Arab world has seen an explosion in writings on all aspects of Arab society, and that only a handful of Western scholars have attempted to follow in the footsteps of Hamilton Gibb, Anouar Abdel Malek, Albert Hourani, and Hishām Sharābī in writing down the general parameters of contemporary Arab thought.[4] A number of prominent research centers have emerged in the past several decades, most notably the Center for the Study of Arab Unity (Markaz Dirāsāt al-Wiḥdah al-'Arabīyyah) in Beirut, the Center for Palestinian Studies in Cyprus, formerly based in Beirut, and the Ahram Strategic Center in Cairo. These and other smaller centers of research have published important works on the political, economic, cultural, literary, and religious conditions of the Arab world since 1967. In addition to these publications, migrant Arab intellectuals, especially in Europe, have published a number of important books on the Arab world that cannot be easily bought in certain Arab capitals.[5]

The second difficulty is linked directly with the first. There is an unfortunate absence of critical studies in English on contemporary Arab thought. Compared with studies in the English language on contemporary African, Latin American or European thought, the scholarly consideration of contemporary Arab thought has barely begun.

The third reason that has rendered this discussion so difficult is the fact that there are two relatively different centers of intellectual production in the modern Arab world: one is in the Mashreq and the other in the Maghreb. There are historical as well as linguistic underpinnings for the Mashreq–Maghreb dichotomy in modern Arab intellectual history.[6] The fact that most of the Maghreb[7] (except Libya, if one considers it part of the Maghreb) fell under French colonialism in the nineteenth century made it necessary for a great number of distinguished Maghrebian thinkers to write and even think in French. Post-independence Arabization in such countries as Algeria, Tunisia, and Morocco has not stemmed the desire of influential authors to write in French. Some of these, well aware of the colonial implications of French in their native countries, consider it a language of emancipation that enables them to reach a wider audience in the world at large.[8] The translation into Arabic of the writings of the most distinguished Maghrebian thinkers who write in French has only very recently been accomplished. The writings of Muḥammad Lahbabi,[9] Taher Benjelloun, Mohammed Arkoun,[10] Hichem Djaït,[11] Fatima Mernissi, Assia Djebar, Kateb Yacine, Abdelkabir al-Khatibi, and Abdallah Laroui[12] have been in Arabic circulation for less than 20 years.[13]

The fourth reason relates to the explosion of information technology, made possible by the transition capitalism has been able to make since World War Two, from extensive industrialization to an intense technological revolution. In one sense, the globalization of information technology has something to do with the origins of ideas. Ideas are not insular by nature and with advanced technology tend to move quickly from one culture/nation to another or from one social formation to another. Although the process of assimilating ideas is very complex and varies from one situation to another, the fact remains that with the colossal advances made by the capitalist civilization in recent years, the contemporary transfer of ideas is a much more accessible process than before. However, one must note that the transfer of ideas in the information age is subject to ideology and is therefore selective by nature. This has a direct bearing on our topic in the sense that far from being insular, modern Arab intellectual history has been open to new ideas from a variety of cultures. That is to say, modern Arab intellectual history is indebted to indigenous as well as external epistemological formations that are essentially the reflection of a multitude of social formations under way in the post-1967 Arab world.

Attempting to survey, analyze, and critique the tremendous output of Arab writings requires a familiarity with the main original sources (most but not all written in Arabic), as well as the (few) secondary sources appearing on modern Arab thought, especially in Western languages.[14] The original sources are numerous and widespread. Most published material has appeared in the Arab world, but a significant number has appeared in Europe as well, especially in France and England. Also, against the tremendous output in recent Arab writing, it is important to fathom the different methodological approaches and worldviews, which underpin contemporary Arab thought. Arab thought has been subject to various interpretations, each belonging to a distinct intellectual and epistemological tradition.

AN EXERCISE IN CONTEMPORARY ARAB INTELLECTUAL HISTORY[15]

It is only by using a well-thought-out critical theory that one can understand the complexity of contemporary Arab intellectual history, its constituent trends, social/economic/political origins, and interrelatedness. My intention is to apply critical theory to post-1967 Arab intellectual history, a theory that must be guided by the insights gained from the most advanced theories developed by both Western and Eastern intellectuals in the fields of the social sciences and humanities.[16] Modernization theory is in itself too feeble to offer us significant insights and globalization theory, used recently as a means of spreading neo-liberal ideas, is too arrogant to offer us any constructive insights.[17] As shall be amply illustrated in this chapter, contemporary Arab intellectual history is interwoven with the complex cultural and economic processes of Arab society and their historical transformations since the advent of capitalism to the Middle East in the nineteenth century. As such, Arab intellectual history has accurately registered the cultural, religious, and intellectual responses to this encounter and documented the rise of new classes and new blocs of power in society. It has also highlighted the intersection of power, culture, and religion in the course of modern history.

Bearing this in mind, this chapter offers a preliminary reading of the post-1967 intellectual map with an attempt at some systematic analysis of the ideas of the main representatives of these trends, their historical and social origins, their present predicament and their future hope. However, this book is far from exhaustive on the matter. It cannot claim to cover every credible intellectual voice in the contemporary Arab world. Although the book is not Egypt-centered, I have failed to cover many voices in the Gulf states, Iraq, and Algeria. By implication, this work is a study of the post-defeat, perhaps post-nationalist, phase of the Arab world. It is the study of neo-colonialism in an age that has witnessed the defeat of the Arab nationalist project, the rise of Islamic resurgence, the re-tribalization of the Arab world, the strengthening of authoritarian regimes under the aegis of Western (including American) democracies, the demise of the Soviet Union, the emergence of the United States as the only superpower in the world, the creation of a new world order after the military defeat of Iraq in the second Gulf War, and the expansion of the Israeli Zionist project.[18]

Modern Western (both European and American) strategic political and economic interest in the Arab world (and the Third World for that matter) has been a blessing in disguise to Western academia: institutional money has poured in creating new academic jobs in order to come to grips with new movements of Arab and Muslim politics and thought. Specialization has underscored the need to study in as much detail as possible all manifestations of Arab and Muslim societies. This is perhaps the age of Orientalism triumphant. Different disciplines have coalesced to more or less produce a general history of the Arab world. In the political area, many journalists and political scientists have written the general outlines, at least, of the political history of the modern Arab world. In a more specialized way, due to academic division of labor, a number of scholars have written the social and political histories of each Arab country. Undoubtedly, Western academic interest in the Arab world, which has impinged on political factors and matters of national interest, has taken new forms in recent decades, either for internal or external reasons.

In general, one may propose three broad rationales for the current American interest in the fields of Arab and Islamic studies:[19]

1. The complexity of the Arab and Muslim world and the consequent American entanglement in this world since inheriting the classical colonial positions of mainly France and England.[20]
2. The recent eclipse of the Soviet bloc and the official end of the Cold War, which necessitated the creation of an outside entity, that is, an antagonistic "Other."

The Soviet Union and communism, as the antagonistic "Other" during the Cold War, created a substantial academic and political industry in American and Western societies. In the same vein, Islam and Muslims as the "Other" have been a blessing in disguise to academicians and politicians who owe their employment to this recent shift of interest in the world. This factor has become more significant since the tragic attacks on the United States on September 11, 2001.

3. The increasing presence of Muslims in America.[21]

These factors have more or less described the burgeoning American interest toward the Islamic factor.

As a scholar of contemporary Arab intellectual history, I am indebted to two particular types of work. The first is the important Western writing on the Arab world in different fields of specialization, most of which can be defined as an outside and professional type of writing where the scholar usually (except in a few cases) does not make a living in the Arab world and develops his/her research interests in the Arab world from his/her academic post in the West. The second type of work is the intellectual production of a vast array of Arab intellectuals, most of whom have lived mainly in the Arab world. Of course, a good number of professional Arab intellectuals and thinkers have held important positions in Western academia. In this regard, one may mention such people as 'Abdel Latif al-Tibawi, Ismā'īl Raji al-Faruqi, Mohammed Arkoun, Afaf Marsot, Ghada Talhami, Leila Ahmad, Samir Amin, Edward Said, Ibrahim Abu-Lughod, Naseer Aruri, Hishām Sharābī, Aziz Azmeh, and Halim Barakat, to mention but a few.

Although some reference will be made to the contributions of migrant Arab intellectuals, my main interest in this particular work is to wrestle with the huge subject of post-1967 intellectual history in the Arab world. Modern Arab intellectual history has been distinguished by a variety of trends – Islamic, Arab nationalist, liberal, and Leftist – which will be explained in greater detail in the second chapter of this book. One must be careful not to confuse modern Arab intellectual history with Muslim intellectual history. These are two somewhat different domains. Arab intellectual history is written mainly in Arabic, whereas Muslim intellectual history, if such a category exists, is basically written in other Islamic languages in addition to Arabic. However, in Arab intellectual history, the Islamic trend is distinguished and multifaceted. Herein lies the complexity. Each subcurrent that makes up post-1967 Arab intellectual history is very diverse, extremely complex, and is the product of various vital political, philosophical, religious, social, and historical conditions and formations.

The first question one must raise concerns the meaning and nature of the discipline of intellectual history. As Perry Anderson correctly notes, intellectual history "is not a Darwinian process. Major systems of thought rarely disappear, as if they were so many species become extinct."[22] What are the salient features of contemporary Arab intellectual history? What are its central problematics? A simple definition of intellectual history is impossible; however, one may discern different and often conflicting interpretations of this important term. Some scholars, mostly notably A. O. Lovejoy and George Boas, argue that intellectual history is an autonomous discipline since one may trace the influence of an idea of a group of ideas from one particular historical phase to another, or from one country to another.[23] This position, articulated in the first half of the twentieth century in American academia and represented in the main by the *Journal of the History of Ideas*, was an outgrowth of the "Great Texts" approach, still adopted by departments of philosophy and religious studies, which stipulates that intellectual history is the product of a few geniuses, especially men, who reflect on the human condition in full isolation from their surroundings and who usually end up writing coherent and complete thought systems.[24] Lovejoy's idea-centered method was a great improvement on the "Texts" approach. For example, he enumerates twelve different categories by which Western academia, to his mind, has studied ideas:

1. the history of philosophy;
2. the history of science;
3. folklore;
4. semantics;
5. literary history;
6. history of religious beliefs;
7. comparative literature;
8. the history of the arts;
9. economic history;
10. the history of education;
11. political and social history;
12. historical sociology.[25]

Lovejoy challenged the classical assumptions of writing or thinking about intellectual history and articulated the notion that if ideas are examined over a long period of time, they often have different meanings. Reification of meaning is not possible. However, some scholars have cast doubt on Lovejoy's notion of the autonomy of the discipline of intellectual history. One scholar argues that "The problem of intellectual history, epitomized in the current disputes about the social relations of ideas, is that it has too many methods, that this plurality reflects the diversity of its objects, and that this diversity has raised serious doubts about its integrity as a distinct and autonomous field of history."[26] Put more simply, various worldviews constitute any people's intellectual history and as such intellectual history is multidisciplinarian by nature. It cuts across different fields of specialization, especially philosophy, theology, history, politics, and political economy.[27] And it is guided by different philosophical and ideological positions. Ideology is at the heart of intellectual history. In other words, even a careful reading of any particular worldview constituting intellectual history will not render a purely objective picture of that trend. Intellectual history is ideological by nature.

Being ideological, one must read the constituent elements of intellectual history against their social, economic, and political background and context. What this means is that,

> Intellectual history cannot claim to be the true or only history...It exists only in connection with, and in relation to, the surrounding political, economic, and

> social forces. The investigation of subjects of intellectual history leads beyond the purely intellectual world, and intellectual history per se does not exist.[28]

Because of the different worldviews they represent, intellectual historians do not work on the assumption of a shared specific method. This justifies the notion that intellectual history lacks one "governing problematique,"[29] which makes it difficult to establish a single *Zeitgeist* of the epoch I am studying. It might be justifiable to claim that modern Arab thought is characterized by a number of *Zeitgeists*. In effect, contemporary Arab intellectual history, far from being reduced to one problematic, is distinguished at the core by a variety of conceptual approaches and questions with varying degrees of intensity and interrelationship. It is fair to say that this book wrestles with the works of those Arab intellectuals who represent various social and intellectual positions; therefore it can offer but a modest assessment of the core ideas discussed by the main intellectuals of the period under consideration.

Intellectual history as presented above reflects the ideas of the intelligentsia or the intellectual elite of Arab society. In this sense, it does not attempt to reflect amorphous opinions, unspoken assumptions, or even the ideas of the Arab masses. It is true that some of the intellectuals I treat in this work claim to represent the masses, but this work is by no means an elaboration of popular ideas on formal issues. The relationship of the intellectuals with the masses is very complex in modern Arab society. The religious intelligentsia, usually with the help of mosques or religious events, has always enjoyed the privileges of great access and contact with the masses. It is important to be guided, though not limited, by Antonio Gramsci's ideas on the meaning of the intellectual and power, culture and politics, exile and creativity, civil society and religion.[30] The distinction made by Gramsci between ecclesiastical and organic intellectuals might be helpful in dispelling some ambiguity about the role of the intellectual in contemporary Arab society. What prevents us from postulating that the most organic intellectual in the Arab world of late has been the ecclesiastical activist, he or she speaks the language of the masses and identifies with their suffering and predicament? The Leftists seem to speak a language that is not understood by the larger masses. Who prevents us from considering Sayyid Quṭb, Muḥammad al-Ghazālī, and Rāshid al-Ghannūshī as true organic intellectuals? It is true that one must interpret Gramsci's theses in light of the specific situation in the Arab world.[31] Every major trend in contemporary Arab intellectual history claims to have its own organic intellectuals, those who reflect the anguish and hope of the masses in their speeches and writings.

I do not claim that the masses have no philosophy or worldview of their own. They do indeed have their worldview as amply illustrated by Paulo Freire in *Pedagogy of the Oppressed*,[32] Ali Shari'āti in *On the Sociology of Islam*,[33] and Pierre Bourdieu in *Acts of Resistance: Against the Tyranny of the Market*.[34] However, the role of the intellectual historian must reconstruct the various discourses of the intellectual elite by highlighting their main epistemological and philosophical principles and ideological orientations. Thus, a movement is effected from the abstract plane of thought to the practical realm of life. As explained above, ideas on their own lack meaning unless connected to or understood against a certain historical and social context or background. Some understanding of the connection between intellectual and social/political history must be achieved. This point was well illustrated by the philosophers of the nineteenth century, most notably Karl Marx. The concern of intellectual history must not be purely with identifying "texts" or "languages" or "paradigms" or opinions, but it should be with establishing links between all of these and our suggested historical context (1967–2003).

In this work, intellectual history means a broad mental reconstruction of tangible historical events that possess and exhibit intrinsic moral and philosophical values. The abstract dimension of intellectual history underlies its universal and ever-changing expression. As such, intellectual history possesses many components that are anchored in many traditions and aspire to realize new futures. As mentioned above, intellectual history is inspired by many problematics that reflect the agonies behind the various transitions that a nation or a society usually undergoes. Intellectual history does not aspire to change as much as to interpret reality.

The political history of the post-1967 Arab world has been characterized by a number of grandiose events: the 1967 Arab defeat, the 1970 civil war in Jordan, the 1973 Arab–Israeli war, the 1975–76 civil war in Lebanon, the 1982 Israeli invasion of Lebanon, the 1977 Sadat visit to Israel, the first and second Palestinian Intifadas, and the first and second Gulf Wars.[35] These are some of the major political events that overshadow what seems to be a fixed pattern of Arab political life: the stunning stability of most Arab regimes, which is mainly due to narrow social bases, a military background that is often weary of cries for democracy, and the support most of these regimes have consistently received from the Western world.[36] However, one must not forget that for one reason or another, the political elite in most Arab countries, especially in recent years, have been nurtured in the main by the European powers and the United States.

It is perhaps a cliché to state that, at this moment in history, Western powers advocate democracy and mass representation at home but support the most dictatorial regimes abroad.[37] The second Gulf War betrayed the complicity of the Arab regimes, including Syria, with the West. The Gulf War is the single-most mind-boggling political phenomenon in the Arab world in the 1990s. This conflict restructured the whole area both militarily and politically, exposed as false many myths about Arab brotherhood and unity, enabled the West to station troops in the Gulf without help from Israel, and drove the economies of the area into bankruptcy. The Iraqi invasion of Kuwait in 1990 may have been the last bold Arab nationalist attempt to resist the West on Arab soil.[38] The Ba'th regime, in spite of its repressive nature, had launched an ambitious campaign of modernizing the country, giving the Kurds a degree of cultural autonomy that they lacked in both Iran and Iraq and of incorporating women into the economy.[39] The rise of the United States to the position of the world's only superpower after the demise of the Soviet Union has added more fuel to political authoritarianism in the Arab world. Rupture and then stability characterize the oscillatory nature of politics in the Arab world.[40]

Nor is this phenomenon of oscillation foreign to the intellectual scene. The rise of Arab nationalist thought in the 1950s and 1960s, due in part to Nasserism, was followed by its rapid decline after 1967. The Islamist project claimed to hold the keys of success for the Arab world. So far, this has not materialized in any significant way, not even in the Sudan where the Islamists came to power in alliance with the army. In the same vein, a serious wave or current of self-criticism in various Arab intellectual circles followed the 1967 defeat. This oscillation has exposed another major intellectual phenomenon in the modern Arab world, which can be referred to as the "migration" of some intellectuals from one ideological or intellectual commitment in the field of thought and practice to an opposing one. I have in mind the intellectual "conversion" of the Palestinian thinker Munir Shafiq from Maoism to Islamism, and the Egyptian 'Abd al-Wahāb al-Masīrī from critical Marxism to Islamic criticism, and on the international scale, the conversion of Roger Garaudy from Marxist humanism to Islamism. This oscillation has also been conspicuous in the political and economic arenas: a movement from being friend to the Soviet Union to being friend to the United States. This was very clear during the Sadat regime, which also instituted new laws to shift the economy from the public sector to the private sector.[41]

In order to give this huge and complex topic its due, one must begin with abstractions, posing questions in a general way and moving from the general to the more specific. The Arab thinkers surveyed and analyzed in this work do not constitute one homogeneous coalition of intellectual forces, nor do they invoke the aid of the same intellectual authority, paradigm, or worldview. In a sense, these intellectuals bring to the table different agendas and are in the habit of elaborating different cures for the common ills of contemporary Arab society. Lacking a common sense of loyalty and worldview has generated heated debate about the many aspects of society, the role of religion in the Arab world, and the meaning of the West in contemporary Arab intellectual discourse. When the imagination of the state becomes so narrow as to prevent such debate, many an Arab intellectual migrates. Migration has been an important phenomenon in contemporary Arab thought.[42] It has been a factor in the most important critical work in existence about Arab society. Aside from dealing with the theoretical work of such prominent Arab intellectuals as Aḥmad Bahā' al-Dīn, Mohammed Arkoun, Muḥammad 'Ābid al-Jābīrī, Abdallah Laroui, Costantine Zurayk, Ṣādiq Jalāl al-'Aẓm, Nawal El Saadawi, Safinaz Kazim, Ḥassan Ḥanafī, Galāl Amīn, Maḥmūd Darwīsh, Emīl Habīby, Gamāl al-Ghitānī, Maḥmūd Amīn al-'Ālim, Yūsuf al-Qaraḍāwī, Muḥammad al-Ghazālī, Fahmī Huwaydī, Muḥammad 'Imārah, Ṣalāh 'Īsa, Ghālī Shukrī, Muḥammad Ḥassanīn Haykal, Lewis 'Awad, Nabīl 'Abd al-Fattāḥ, Rajā' al-Naqqāsh, Burhān Ghalyūn and numerous others, this work deals with some important themes and issues that characterize the modern intellectual climate of the post-1967 Arab world and with the principal trends of thought that are currently in play.

Since the end of the Cold War, the military defeat of Iraq in the second Gulf War, the imposition of the New World Order in both its economic and political dimensions, the retreat of socialist and nationalist projects in some Arab countries – especially in Egypt, Algeria, and Syria – the signing of a fragile peace treaty between the Palestine Liberation Organization and Israel, which led to the Aqsa Intifada, and between Jordan and Israel, the deep cultural and societal (but not necessarily political) changes in some Arab countries in the 1970s and 1980s, and the increasing social and economic differences between rich and poor within and between many Arab societies, the Arab world has seen an unsettling cultural and intellectual scene that is characterized by polarization, tension, and an unpredictable future.

THREE QUESTIONS, THREE BURDENS

As I look at the Arab world at the beginning of this century, I realize the many challenges ahead. Broadly speaking, one can discern the following challenges: the first is demographic. There are around 300 million people in the Arab world, most of whom are young (under the age of 25) and were born after 1967. The second major challenge is political. Since its establishment in 1945, the Arab League has acted, more or less, as the embodiment of the Arab political entity. The Iraqi occupation of Kuwait in 1990 dealt a shattering blow to the Arab political entity that the League had been trying to nurture since 1945. This occupation was much more devastating than the Egyptian signing of a peace treaty with Israel in 1979. The third challenge is economic. The fourth is technological/scientific, and the fifth is made up of identity challenges.

In general terms, one may propose that contemporary Arab thought, in its different trends and representations, remains ambivalent about four major issues: first are the profound social and economic changes taking place in the Arab world since independence. Aside from a few publications about the state of the Arab social classes and social change, which are mainly written for the experts in the field, the average Arab does not possess enough knowledge about this important area, the rise and fall of classes in Arab societies, and the role of the state in promoting certain classes at the expense of others. For example, in examining the social and economic ramifications of the second Gulf War, one can easily see that the destruction of the Iraqi economic infrastructure during the war, and the subsequent economic blockade instituted by the United Nations drastically impacted the social lives of almost every Iraqi citizen. In addition, the war itself affected the lives of millions of guest workers in the Gulf states, including those in Iraq itself, who were forced to leave. These displaced guest workers were mainly the Palestinians forced out from Kuwait or Yemenis from Saudi Arabia. Yet, there is another social and economic dimension of this war; the weakening financial base of the state in the Gulf after the war, which has since 1991 curtailed the power of the authoritarian states in the Gulf from engaging in free spending on local projects in the same way as before the war. As John Waterbury astutely observes, these regimes, as most Arab regimes, "pledged welfare benefits in exchange for political discipline and quiescence."[43] Here, social classes within the Gulf are beginning to feel the effects of the Gulf War, which are not all negative. Some are beginning to criticize the state for the absence of democracy.

The second ambivalence pertains to the major transformations in the world in general and Eastern Europe in particular since the end of the Cold War. In the main, Arab thought has not been able to focus on these important events in a systematic way and derive from them the necessary lessons.

Third is the issue of Israel. Before 1967, most Arab and Muslim theoretical product on the problem of Israel and Zionism was either propagandist in nature, such as in the writings of post-1948 Arab nationalists, or marked by complete naivety; and riddled with clichés that were not helpful for the average citizen. Arab scientific studies on Zionism and Israel were rare, if non-existent. Therefore, Arab intellectuals in general were not able to understand the class composition of Israeli society, the nature of the Israeli political and military elite, the major differences between Ashkenazi and Sephardic immigrants, the ideological and intellectual orientation and contents of Zionism, Israel's strong relationship with the Center in Western Europe and the United States, and the military origins of the Israeli state.[44]

It is only after 1967 that Arab thought slowly began to wake up to the real nature of the state of Israel. The Center for Palestinian Studies and leading Arab thinkers began to devote their energies to scientifically study Israeli society. The leading multi-volume work written by the Egyptian Islamist scholar 'Abd al-Wahāb al-Masīrī is an example of Arab and Muslim reawakening to the importance of understanding Zionism and Israeli society.[45] In the United States, Edward Said became a leading authority on matters of Israel and Zionism.[46] However, there is still much to be desired from Arab writings on the Israeli problematic. Most of the contemporary Arab theoretical products on Israel, even after concluding several peace treaties between Israel and some Arab countries, still suffer from major theoretical loopholes and ill-informed social analysis.

Fourth, religion, and in particular, Islam and Christianity. These constitute some of the most complex and controversial issues in modern Arab thought. Contemporary Arab thought reflects a major polarization regarding "the religious problematic." On the one hand is a group of religious intellectuals who employ the logic of the Sacred and the textual without paying sufficient attention to the sociological, political, and historical manifestations of religion in contemporary Arab society. On the other is a group of Arab intellectuals raising the banner of religious terrorism and even fascism when speaking of the religious camp.[47] I think that both positions are insensitive to "a contemporary sociology of religion" in Arab society. The Arab library lacks scientific sociological studies informed by the large reservoir of Western social sciences in this area. Insufficient works exist on the social dimension of religion, the connection between religion and contemporary knowledge, the social functions of the ulama and the shaykhs, the role of women in religion, and the like.[48]

One major manifestation of such polarization is the ongoing debate, begun in the early 1980s, between the secularist and Islamic camps. To take just one problematic as an example, belief and unbelief in modern Arab thought, the meaning of the West and modernity, the role of reason and religion in society, besides reflecting polarization and tension is also an indication of the strength of the "traditionalist/Islamic" intelligentsia, which usually lacks a formal representation at the state level, and its desire, not just to compete with the secular intelligentsia, but to use the Sacred and its ability to influence people's emotions and minds in order to have a say in the intellectual, cultural, and religious matters. The debate about religion in contemporary Arab society is more than merely theological or metaphysical controversy. It is about all things that have gone wrong in contemporary Arab society; it is, in fact, about the identity of an Arab society that fell under the impact of the humanistic/capitalist/post-Enlightenment West of the nineteenth century. The battles that revolve around religion must be understood as a true reflection of the entire major social, economic, and cultural transitions taking place in Arab society since the last century. In the same vein, it is impossible to understand the Islamist trend in the contemporary Arab world except as a response to the complex project of modernity that has evolved since the early days of colonialism into a number of both subtle and concrete movements in the Arab world. Islamism in the contemporary Arab world took its mature form after the defeat of the modernization project of several Arab states, a defeat that was so stark in 1967, and in the inability of the state to deliver on its promises of modernization.

Islamism has proposed a new form of Islamic reason in order to counteract the main claims of Western rationalism in Arab society. Reason is a sacred venture, argue the Islamists, and thus an indigenous form of reason is appealed to in order to overcome the brutal presence of Western rationalism in Arab thought and practice. The Islamists have unleashed the power and mystery of the Sacred in order to recapture an historical moment that was thoroughly permeated by the project of a failed modernity. The Sacred is reproduced at the cultural, religious, social, and behavioral levels in various ways and leaps forward as a major force harnessing the power of religion and its hold over the Arab subconscious. All this said, it is simply impossible to fully appreciate the influence of the Sacred on the masses in the Arab world.

The project of modernity, although imposed on Arab society from the outside by colonialism in the nineteenth century, was absorbed by the end of the last century by a small, but significant number of Arab intellectuals who were fascinated by its seemingly progressive nature and infinite potential. To a large number of non-Islamist Arab thinkers, modernity still holds the answer to the predicaments of Arab society; modernity is a source of hope, vitality, and progress. According to this Arab view, secularism lies at the heart of the quest for modernity. To be modern is to erect a wall of separation between the Sacred and the secular or between religion and politics in Arab society.[49]

There are deep disagreements between both camps about the nature of civil society, the meaning of citizenship and nationhood, the position of religious minorities, especially Christians in Arab society, and the meaning of values in a changing atmosphere. All of this, in one way or another, is derivative of two different and antagonistic interpretations of religion, that is, the position of both Christianity and Islam in contemporary Arab society, its stable elements and those elements subject to interpretation and new understanding.

This polarization also reflects the painful and anguished relationship between the contemporary Arab world and its past. As much as there is disagreement on the role of religion in contemporary Arab society, Arab thinkers and intellectual leaders portray different images and formulations of the past. To some, the past is a way of life, a model to which the contemporary Arab world must aspire; to others, the past is a reflection of underdevelopment, backwardness, and stagnation that must be overcome. Different "pasts" or "heritages" are invoked, and in them only bits and pieces of Arab and Islamic history are discussed. The past, however, is employed by each ideological camp as a means to interpret and influence the present and a vehicle for shedding light on the future.

Equally so, the Arab intellectual scene is polarized over the notion of the West. One view, best represented by Ṭāhā Ḥussain,[50] Zakī Najīb Maḥmūd,[51] and to a lesser extent Lewis ʻAwad,[52] sees the West as a source of inspiration, an abode of salvation from the problems of Arab society. Another viewpoint, best represented by Muḥammad Ḥussain Faḍlallah, Muḥammad ʻImārah, Ṭāriq al-Bishrī, and Maḥmūd Muḥammad Shākir,[53] sees the West as a political and cultural project whose aim is to subordinate and colonize the Arab and Muslim world and render the average citizen culturally and religiously helpless vis-à-vis the advancing West. The former view identifies the "Self" with the "Other," while the latter identifies the "Self" against the "Other." Yet a third view, represented by the Arab Left, takes a different approach, that of analyzing the genesis and development of capitalism in the Center and its impact on the periphery, especially in its most recent manifestation, that of globalization.[54]

However, the views enumerated above, especially the first two, do not reject the technological and scientific product of the West. Modernization, the objective progress of society, seems to be a common bond between them. How is it possible to accept modernization without the total package, which includes both modernity and modernism? This is an issue into which Arab thought delves in different ways. These are two archetypal and extremist views that contain in between them a multitude of positions about the West and Israel and the nature of progress and modernization in Arab society.

The contemporary Arab intellectual scene is unsettling, very disturbing, but at the same time fascinating for the complex questions it raises and the many answers it attempts to find. It is heir to a long intellectual history that was marked in the early nineteenth century by a rupture, a fissure in the cultural and religious foundations of society and an encounter with aggressive capitalism. Broadly speaking, this encounter was the frying pan of all major ideas erupting on the scene ever since. Those who dominated the intellectual scene from the nineteenth century on – from Ḥassan al-ʻAṭṭār to Jamāl al-Dīn Afghānī,[55] Rashīd Riḍa, Ḥasan al-Banna, Ṭāhā Ḥussain, Bin Badīs, to Muḥammad ʻĀbid al-Jābirī, and so on – represent cultural and intellectual phenomena possessing a certain measure of connection to the past and an aspiration toward the future. Their projects, in various ways, are of survival either through connection to the past or attachment to the future. They grapple with those issues that have a concrete presence in the Arab world. These intellectual projects have been the product of complex social, political, and religious conditions and environments.

It is clear that the contemporary Arab intellectual scene is more complex than it was a century ago. New people, new circumstances, and new forces have given rise to more questions, challenges, and more issues. However, in spite of this dramatic change, some central questions still haunt the contemporary "historical imagination" of the Arab intelligentsia: how to achieve renaissance? How to cure social and economic problems? How to deal appropriately with the issues of women and society? What strategies are there to face the West, either the classical nineteenth century bourgeois West or the contemporary aggressive capitalist West under the leadership of the United States?

The relationship between knowledge and power or the intelligentsia and the state in the Arab world is marked, on the whole, by severe tension and a rejection of the role of the intellectual in the decision-making process. Intellectuals are treated as suspects and are subjects of fear by the political authorities. In several Arab countries, intellectuals need a special permit to leave. This situation begs the whole question of the relationship between culture and politics and cultural creativity in a politically oppressive society.[56] On the whole, creative intellectual production has flourished in recent decades as an expression of the dissatisfaction of the Arab intelligentsia with their state of affairs.[57]

Only in a few cases does one find that intellectuals are extremely close to the decision-making process. This is true in the case of the well-known Egyptian journalist, Muḥammad H. Haykal, who was very close to both Nasser and Sadat.[58] But this closeness did not prevent Sadat from having Haykal arrested along with hundreds of Egyptian intellectuals a few months before the assassination of the former in 1981. Therefore, one important phenomenon in the relationship between knowledge and politics is the prison experience of a large number of influential Arab thinkers – it is an experience that no one, to my knowledge, has analyzed and discussed systematically. The prison experience looms large in the works of such thinkers as Muḥammad Ḥassanīn Haykal,[59] Nawal El Saadawi,[60] Ghālī Shukrī,[61] Farīdah al-Naqqāsh,[62] Latīfah al-Zayyāt, Fathī ‘Abd al-Fattāh, ‘Abbās Madanī, Ḥassan al-Turābī and many others. The prison experience has produced a unique genre of Arab thought and literature that is marked by reflection, criticism, and alienation. It is a personal diagnosis of collective problems and a reflection of hope in desperation. This genre of writings is illuminating not so much for the questions raised but for its ability to present in a deep and sensitive manner the different layers of Arab sensation, their humanistic nature, and their anguish over the present and hope for a better future.

This book attempts to document and analyze the most significant theoretical output of the post-1967 Arab intelligentsia. One can define the nature of this output in political, religious, philosophical, and intellectual terms. It has grown out of years of interest in the Arab intellectual scene, a scene that extends from Morocco in the West to Iraq and Syria in the East. In a number of his books, Haykal brilliantly wrote the political history of the Arab world, especially the Middle East and the Arab-Israeli conflict. Haykal, who is known to house many of his personal archives in Europe, has put out tremendous material on the subject that can be best termed authoritative and encyclopedic. I am indeed indebted to many of his political judgments and insights in some of my political analyses of the Middle East.

The Arabic library contains a significant number of original works on contemporary Arab intellectual history and the central questions debated by the Arab intelligentsia, especially the meaning, nature, and methods of Nahḍah or renaissance, the meaning of the 1967 defeat, the nature of the state, the position of religion in society, the nature of popular culture, social and economic change and its impact on the Arab personality, the role of the Arab intelligentsia and other important issues related to civil society, human rights, and democracy. The English library, although gaining momentum in numerous studies on "political Islam," the social and economic history of the modern Arab world, Arabic literature, especially in the wake of Naguib Mahfouz's winning the Nobel Prize for literature in 1988, and Arab feminism, still lacks comprehensive and systematic studies on contemporary Arab thought and philosophical expressions. This work is not just a systematic presentation of some of the central issues besetting contemporary Arab consciousness, but is an attempt to relate these issues to the concerns of the English-language reader, especially the American.

Major studies in English of contemporary Arab thought are unfortunately rare. This is one reason why the average student of the Arab world, who studies this world from a distant corner in the United States or Europe, may not be in a position to appreciate the great intellectual and cultural dynamics of this world. He or she fails to find any common thread between this world and his, and is unable as a result to relate the great issues facing the Arab world to his own.

It is important to warn the reader from the outset that this work is by no means a comprehensive study of post-1967 Arab intellectual history. A team of researchers would be needed to accomplish such a task. This present work is an attempt to raise some critical questions about contemporary Arab thought by analyzing the individual works of a selected number of important Arab thinkers and discussing some of the major problematics that promise to remain for many years to come. With the few studies in English on the subject, this work aims to give a clearer picture of the various concerns of the Arab intelligentsia, both secular and religious, in the wider sense of the term.

1967 AS A STARTING POINT

To do justice to such a complex topic and for the sake of simplicity, I take 1967 as a point of departure in my treatment of contemporary Arab thought. What is the origin of contemporary Arab thought? Is 1967 the beginning of contemporary Arab thought? These two questions are pertinent indeed when one raises the larger questions about the origin(s) of modern Arab thought, that is, that thought which since the nineteenth century has unleashed a barrage of important questions about tradition, being, ontology, and future.

Although 1967 was an earth-shattering experience that forced a great number of Arab intellectuals, representing different social and cultural forces in society, to reflect on the meaning of disaster and raise critical questions about the state of the individual, in addition to the state of the economy and technology in the Arab world, it does not constitute the beginning of contemporary Arab thought. Contemporary Arab thought falls within the epistemological boundaries set by modern Arab thinkers, which originated from the painful encounter with the capitalist and imperialist West and the Arab world of the nineteenth century. Imperialist modernity has painfully coexisted with the crux of Arab being since that time, and the important transformation this modernity has undergone, from a symbol of progress to a direct military presence or to an Americanized presence in the contemporary Arab society (that is, American globalization, as I show in

Chapter 7 of this work), betray the tense foundations of modern Arab thought. This thought finds itself in an irreconcilable position. On the one hand, it desires to overcome the sense of loss the modern Arab consciousness had experienced for centuries; on the other, it finds itself oppressed at the core by the very modernity that has offered it a sense of hope and liberation. As a result of all of this, Arab thought finds itself trying to give answers to more complex questions than ever before.

As previously stated, it would be disingenuous to trace the beginning of contemporary Arab thought, as a collective entity, to one particular year or event. Historically, one may trace the origins of contemporary Arab thought to the vital debates taking place among the Arab intelligentsia of the nineteenth century. These debates resulted from the following major factors:

1. the Western intervention in the Arab world (in both the Middle East and North Africa) begun by the French invasion of Egypt in 1798 and the French occupation of Algeria in 1839;
2. this intervention introduced a more advanced system of capitalism into the area than the various modes of production coexisting in the pre-imperialist Middle East.[63] The result was that the economic systems of the Arab world became dependent on European capitalism;
3. as a result of the deep transformations in the Arab socio-economic structure and cultural realities, new forces, representing different trends of thought, began to articulate the first serious movement of renaissance in the modern Arab world, commonly referred to as Nahḍah;
4. the Nahḍah failed to form Arab national or religious entities and these feelings remained dormant, more or less, until the creation of Israel in 1948;
5. the Arab world began to wake up to the new realities of a different world and began to express feelings of dismay at imperialism;
6. the failure of the ruling classes to prevent the creation of Israel in 1948 led to a number of political and social upheavals, one of which was the Free Officers' revolution in Egypt, and another was the short-lived communist take-over in Iraq in 1958 under the leadership of 'Abd al-Karīm Qāsim;
7. the post-1948 period saw the *de facto* end of British and French colonialism in the Arab world and the rise of both the United States and the Soviet Union to world prominence in what is termed the Cold War era;
8. this period also saw the expansion of the Israeli-Zionist project and the occupation of more Arab land in the aftermath of the 1967 war.

The above factors reflect some of the major political, economic, and social changes in Arab society from the nineteenth century up to the 1967 war. It seems to me that it is impossible to understand the nature of contemporary Arab thought without coming to grips with the historical and intellectual conditions of the last century. Taking 1967 as a starting point is one way of simplifying matters in our pursuit to present a convincing picture of post-1967 thought.

Aside from seeing the Arab military defeat in 1967 in the context of international alliances in the 1950s and the 1960s, Western support for Israel, and the "inter-Arab cold war," to use a favorite term of Malcolm Kerr, it was also a reflection of a deeper organizational, social, religious, moral, and linguistic crisis in modern Arab society. Further, it was an indication of the lack of familiarity of the "Other" – Israeli society, Zionism, and the threat that a state like Israel would pose to the Arab world and its political and military strategies.[64] If 1948 – the year of the establishment of the state of Israel – posed a major shock to Arab consciousness, the 1967 defeat, which resulted in the defeat of the "Arab progressive project" of Nasserism and the project of Arab nationalism begun in the nineteenth century, signaled the beginning of a slow and deep awakening of the Arab world to the painful realities, the expansionist project of the Israeli state, and the concrete steps that must be taken in order to strike a balance between this painful reality and Arab potential. For a while, during the painful days of the defeat, the Arab world showed a strange paralysis of thinking. No one knew what to do. In the words of the Palestinian thinker, Ghassān Kanafānī, the Arab world was intellectually immobile to the extent it employed "blind language" in expressing its predicament.[65] The leadership lost its vision and ability to maneuver. Nasser offered his resignation and 'Abd al-Ḥakīm 'Āmir committed suicide. All felt a great need to transform Arab society and the Arab person in a real and democratic way.[66] The 1967 defeat proved beyond any shadow of doubt the necessity of a new leadership as well as creating a new Arab individual in a democratic and open atmosphere.

Also, 1967 signaled the outpouring of a number of critical Arab writings on the Arab situation. These writings range from the political to the philosophical and literary production. Many contemporary Arab thinkers were forced by the 1967 defeat to reconsider a great number of issues that had been taken for granted, and even question the relevance of the Sacred in Arab thought. The Arab Left, the Islamic trend, and the nationalist trend were all perturbed by the reasons behind defeat and sought in their different ways to diagnose and remedy the situation. The Arab intelligentsia was anxious to produce a new intellectual project of self-criticism and rejuvenation. The Arab Left shouldered the responsibility of self-criticism and analysis, and defeat gave the Islamic tendency its best historical moments in decades. In short, a mixture of critical traditions stalked like specters across the wounded paths of Arab consciousness. From the Leftist side, Yāssin al-Ḥāfiz wrote *Ideology and Defeated-ideology*;[67] Ṣādiq Jalāl al-'Azm wrote *Self-Criticism After Defeat*[68] and *Criticism of Religious Thought*,[69] and Abdallah Laroui wrote *L'idéologie arabe contemporaine*.[70] Islamist thinker Yūsuf al-Qaraḍāwī wrote *The Islamic Solution*,[71] and Costantine Zurayk of the nationalist trend wrote *Revisiting the Meaning of Disaster*.[72] These thinkers and others who followed suit posed the question in various ways, "Why have we been defeated and what steps must be taken to remedy the situation?"[73]

Defeat creates shock and bewilderment and is responsible for the emergence of critical consciousness and writing. Defeat makes the encounter with the "Self" much more painful than the encounter with the "Other." Defeat wounds the spirit and may lead to either death or permanent paralysis – paralysis of the soul, imagination, and an inability to act clearly and forcefully. However, in spite of the alienation it produces, defeat may inculcate in the soul a new potential, a will to survive, and a desire to prove the "Self." 1967 was painful for the mere fact that it was the first time in the Arab world since the beginning of the Arab-Israeli conflict that the entire Arab world, from Morocco in the West to Iraq in the East, felt the depth of the tragedy. By the standards that the Arab world applied before 1967, the creation of Israel in 1948 and the beginning of the Palestinian refugee problem was just a temporary setback that would be corrected in a matter of a few years. It was merely a loss of land. 1967 proved that it was far more than just a loss of land, but was also a loss of soul and a vision.

Contemporary Arab writings are still delving into the meaning of defeat and are still obsessed with finding solutions to the state of affairs. A slew of critical Arab writings in all fields has opened up the great intellectual potential of the Arab world. Thinkers have begun to criticize the classical discourse of the Arabic language and how it has been used to numb the feelings and poison the imagination. Adonis, Abdallah Laroui, Zakī Najīb Maḥmūd, Maḥmūd Darwīsh and others have attacked that rhetorical language of incantation that miserably fails to give a precise and scientific reading of the situation and that escapes into the ornate past. To some Arab thinkers, creating a revolutionary language is the key to creating a revolutionary intelligentsia and conditions.

On the surface, the question asked by the Arab intelligentsia after the 1967 defeat, "Why have we been defeated?" appears similar to the one asked by the nineteenth century Arab intelligentsia, "Why have we (Muslims and Arabs) declined?"[74] These two questions reflect two perplexing situations and deep configurations in the modern Arab world. However, because of the shock of defeat, its concreteness, its impact on all aspects of contemporary Arab society, that is, the alienation of youth, the great devaluation in traditional, social and cultural values, and the loss of correspondence or harmony between values and the social system, the first question seems to be more agonizing, specific, and meaningful. The 1967 Arab world is not the same as that of the nineteenth century. Things have changed dramatically. 1967 is the age of the nation-states, national independence, and the formation of cultural and national unity and identity.

However, according to the leading Arab intelligentsia, regardless of their ideological orientation, Israel still represents the stumbling block toward the development and progress of Arab society and is, in fact, a colonial implant inside the Arab world. Those Arab intellectuals who have accepted the existence of the state of Israel, especially the signers of the Copenhagen agreement, do believe that the best way to secure progress in the Arab world and serve the Arab national interest is by living peacefully with Israel, that is, isolating "aggressive Israel" and accepting "peace-loving Israel." However, the recent Intifada in the Occupied West Bank and Gaza once more reveals to the Arab world the painful reality of the Arab-Israeli conflict. The creation and expansion of Israel are a reflection of the collective weaknesses of the Arab world, the loss of direction in common cultural and political matters, and an indication that new and vital values and mental attitudes are needed in the Arab world in order to rectify the situation. What is more significant than the Israeli power is perhaps the resilience of the Arab regimes in the Middle East. Edward Said is correct to argue that the persistence of the old regime in the Arab world is a disturbing fact, "The great irony is that every Arab regime of consequence is still essentially unchanged today, thirty years after the collective defeat in Arab history."[75]

In addition to dealing with these central questions, one may raise other significant questions about particular countries or regions in the Arab world. For example, in North Africa questions are raised about cultural decolonization, the nature of the state, privatization, unemployment and its impact on the youth, the loss of traditional Islamic values and the rise of Islamism, the sacred and violence. In the context of Lebanon, one can raise the following: the disintegration of the state in the wake of the successive civil wars and the Palestinian, Syrian, Israeli and American military presence, the rebuilding of the state, and the emergence of sectarianism and its impact on Lebanese identity. In Egypt, a number of questions emerged before 1982: the question of peace and war with Israel, the national character of Egypt (that is, whether or not it belongs to the Arab world)[76] and the new economic Open Door policy of the Sadat regime. After 1982, other issues were raised: rapid economic and social change in society, the relationship between Muslims and Christians, and the position of the Copts in Egyptian society (*fitnah ṭā'fiyyah*); the rise of Islamic terrorism; the rise of the *nouveux riches* and connection with the Gulf states.

Therefore, I take 1967 as a starting point for the following reasons:

1. Arab defeat with Israel had a dual effect: it made the Arab world compare its social, economic, and military state of affairs to one more superior, the Israeli, which in turn resulted in a deep retrospection and self-criticism that has been the landmark of the most important trends of contemporary Arab thought;
2. the Arab world was forced to re-examine its own identity and connection to the "Other" or the West/Israel. This has been a thorough re-examination at the level of modernity, ideas, and relationships. The 1990 Gulf War and the defeat of Iraq did heighten the intensity of various debates in the Arab world about the "Self" and the "Other";
3. the 1967 defeat resulted in the radical failure of the nationalist/socialist Arab project (especially Nasserism) that attempted to escape from the clutches of Western economic and ideological hegemony, and inaugurated a new phase in the relationship of Arab dependency on the capitalist West. The class composition that Nasserism in Egypt and Ba'thism in Syria had been erecting did not prove to be solid enough to prevent defeat. Arab economic thought began to deal with the major social and economic loopholes that defeat portrayed;
4. 1967, although it did not lead to major political changes or the toppling of regimes usually implicated in defeat, did nevertheless lead to a very significant orientation in the relationship between religion and state or society in the Arab world. The pre-1967 secular/socialist/royalist Arab world did succeed in reducing the scope of the religious sphere and depoliticizing religion by all sorts of methods. The defeat of 1967 was a blessing in disguise for the Islamic movement and its different offshoots. The defeat touched the most sensitive emotional and psychological foundations of the Arab people. The "return" of religion was a response to certain concrete needs and an impulse toward new social and political action, the kinds of which had either been absent or barred from occurring in Arab society;
5. 1967 reignited the debate about the meaning of the contemporary ruling state and whether or not a new constellation of forces was needed to impact new political changes;

6. the meaning of the Arab nation in light of the consequences of 1967. This is perhaps one of the most complex notions dealt with in this work. In this regard, we are invited to examine the following relevant notions: (a) ummah or nation? Is it an Arab Muslim ummah that we discuss, or (b) a secular Arab nation that relegates religion to the personal sphere and that does not distinguish between followers of the different religions? (c) Post-nomadic, post-tribal, highly modern, highly affluent petro-dollar and Islamo-sacred state?;
7. the 1967 defeat gave a new breath to the "counter-revolutionary elements," especially in Egypt, those classes and individuals whose economic and political fortunes were adversely affected by the 1952 revolution. The roots of the economic Infitāḥ encouraged by the Egyptian state in the mid 1970s, and the revolution against the public sector, began to emerge in the wake of the defeat.

On the whole, the 1967 defeat more so than the second Gulf crisis forced the Arab intelligentsia to be self-critical and retrospective, a fact that led to creative writing in all fields of intellectual production. Although the intellectual market in many Arab countries is replete with obsolete and meaningless works, a better quality material is produced in the arts, literature, philosophy, and religious studies. The creative margin in the Arab intellectual market is making its presence a reality in spite of many political and conservative odds. It is impossible to pin down the exact number of writings in the Arab world since 1967, but this area has seen more quality work that underlines the need of Arab society for a more concrete and realistic treatment, not just a mystical or theological treatment of its state of affairs.

One salient feature of contemporary Arab thought is its dual, eclectic, and, consequently, confused and confusing nature. Dualism is defined here as the domination of two worldviews, philosophies, and epistemological models in the thought and writings of many Arab authors. In one article or book, for instance, can often be found two worldviews, one Islamic and the other liberal, without a clear delineation of the concepts used or their epistemological history and evolution.

2
Contemporary Arab Intellectual Trends

"The battle over [our Arabo-Islamic] identity has enabled the West to plant – not only in Western countries but in ours as well – intellectual trends, parties, associations, universities, and research institutions whose underlying aim is to manufacture our minds along Western models and methods. The final objective of the West is to secure the dissipation of our collective identity so that we give up resistance easily. Once the West achieves this goal, the dependency of world of Islam on the West is promoted and, in a sense, made permanent." Muḥammad ʻImārah, *al-Jadīd fī'l mukhaṭaṭ al-gharbī tijāh al-muslimīn* [*The Novel Side of Western Plans about Muslims*] (Cairo: International Institute of Islamic Thought, 1993), 33.

"Far from consisting of a monolithic essence, Western Tradition is multi-dimensional and multi-directional in nature. It has been produced by a multitude of classes, powers, and trends against a background of conflict and contradiction. In addition to the Western capitalist and socialist traditions, a dominating, hegemonic and conquering Western tradition exists side by side with a conquered, dominated, and submissive one [such as in Latin America]." Ḥassan Ḥanafī, *Muqadimmah fī ʻilm al-istighrāb* (Cairo: al-Dār al-Faniyyah li'l Nashr wa'l Tawzīʻ, 1991), 102.

"There are in the Middle East today two challenging ideas: old and new. The old ideas will vanish because they are weak and exhausted. There is in the Middle East an awakening that defies slumber. This awakening will conquer because the sun is its leader and the dawn is its army." Gibran Khalil Gibran, *The Treasured Writings of Khalil Gibran* (Secaucus, N.J.: Castle Books, 1985), 861.

"One of the main factors in the ideological repertoire of the Iranian intelligentsia is what they call the 'intellectual element' (*ʻonsor-e rowshan-fekri*), referring to the perspective, or the ideological attribute, through which the intelligentsia view the world and view themselves as a distinct type." Ali Gheissari, *Iranian Intellectuals in the 20th Century* (Austin: University of Texas Press, 1998), 69.

In studying Arab thought, it is important to define exactly what "Arab thought" is, the origin and nature of Arab intellectual production, and its expression. One may simply posit that Arab thought is a complex "epistemological and philosophical construct" that comprehends all those intellectual tendencies or movements that describe, analyze, critique, and deconstruct the socio-economic, religious, political, and intellectual spheres in contemporary Arab society. In this sense, Arab thought is much more comprehensive than Muslim thought in the Arab world, as mentioned above. In other words, Muslim thought in the Arab world, as will be explained shortly, represents only one major trend among many competing trends in contemporary Arab thought. In addition to the Islamic current, Arab thought reflects a number of secular approaches to the issues that face the Arab world. In other words, contemporary Arab thought is the product of a complex intellectual formation that is, simply stated, both traditional and modern. One may easily agree with Ḥassan Ḥanafī's general classification that contemporary Arab thought is based on three foundations: (1) classical Islamic heritage; (2) modern Western heritage; and (3) the present realities of the Arab world.[1] As stated previously, my starting point in treating contemporary Arab thought is the 1967 Arab defeat. However, one can trace contemporary Arab thought to the nineteenth century and the efforts of the Arab intelligentsia of the time to grapple with the major problems of their societies.

Arab thought is historical, interchangeable, and reflective of the deep social, political, and religious questions from which it was born. In other words, it is impossible to define the intellectual content of Arab thought in its generality without considering its underlying preoccupation with colonialism and the problematic of the West, or the meaning of the Sacred in the modern world. All major Arab thinkers, from Left and Right, have dealt with these issues from various perspectives. Colonialism as an historical process does indeed unveil the modern process of Arab thought and the debates of modern Arab intelligentsia about this issue reflects both a diagnosis and solution that imply, in turn, a certain direction for Arab societies, be it Islamic or Marxist or liberal.

Modern Arab intellectuals dealt with such issues as the regeneration of their societies, securing independence from colonialism and building a strong national state. Unlike American intellectuals of the 1940s, Arab intellectuals of the same period were less concerned about the Cold War and more about achieving independence from various European powers. In the 1940s and 1950s, the American intellectual scene was subject to the conversion of a good number of intellectuals from Marxism to liberalism or socialism. Such names as Sidney Hook, Irving Howe, Daniel Bell, Dwight Macdonald, and Richard Hofstadter come to mind.[2]

In addition, I take Arab thought to mean also this form of intellectual writings that is written in languages other than Arabic. What prohibits us, for instance, from considering the work of Hishām Sharābī,[3] Edward Said, Abdallah Laroui, and Mohammed Arkoun[4] as part of Arab thought, though most of their work was written in Western languages. Arab thought is the product of Arab thinkers who live both in the Arab world and overseas.

Generally speaking, one may discern four major intellectual currents (categories of thought) in contemporary Arab thought:

1. the Islamic current;
2. the nationalist current;

3. the liberal current;
4. the Marxist/Leftist currents.[5]

In addition, one may add "regionalism" as a current in contemporary Arab thought. "Regionalism" is defined as an affiliation to a particular region in the Arab world, such as the Gulf states, that goes against the spirit of Arab unity. "Regionalism" has been a dominant force in the Arab world since 1967.[6]

ISLAMIC CURRENT

In his assessment of the post-1967 Arab intellectual scene, Laroui argues that "Arab intellectuals think according to two rationales. Most of them profess the traditional rationale (salafī); the rest profess an eclecticism."[7] Whether or not the Salafī trend has succeeded in abolishing the historical dimension, as Laroui maintains, is a matter of dispute. The contemporary Islamic current, which is Salafī in nature, is in the main an historical product. It has read the past in a manner that is congruous with the conditions/challenges of the present. It is true that the Salafī *Weltanschauung* is rooted in the Islamic past, in the model of the Prophet and his early disciples, especially the Rightly Guided caliphs. This model was canonized in theological terms by a number of distinguished jurists, Kalām philosophers, mystics, exegetes and traditionists. In a sense, the distinct Salafī orientation of the Islamic trend in contemporary Arab thought is very complex indeed; it is historical in nature and has gone through a number of challenges and mutations without losing sight of the importance of the past Prophetic model as the criterion against which contemporary Islamic tradition, authenticity, and identity are defined.

As a religious movement with distinct normative values, one may speak of different types of Salafīyyah throughout Islamic history, both classical and modern. The first type is classical Salafīyyah, which is best represented by Ahmad bin Ḥanbal of the third Islamic century and Ahmad bin Taymiyya of the eighth Islamic century. This school bases its philosophy on imitating the thought and methods of the ancestors, especially the Prophet and his companions, and on rejecting any innovation in theological principles. It advocates the notion that all the general principles about this life and the afterworld are contained in the Qur'an and discussed by the Prophet in many of his sayings and practices.[8] According to Fahmī Jad'ān, as a theological doctrine, classical Salafīyyah is based first on a discursive notion of acceptance, submission, and imitation, which avoids advocating an overt rational position. Second, classical Salafīyyah is humanist in the most ethical meaning of the term. It advocates a merciful position toward human beings. Third, in the political realm, classical Salafīyyah is pacifist since it advocates full submission to the *status quo*, and, fourth, it considers history to evolve negatively and not positively.[9]

The second form of Salafīyyah is pre-colonial and is best represented by the Wahabiyyah of the eighteenth and nineteenth centuries.[10] One may consider the Wahabiyyah a great revolutionary movement in its initial thrust since it relied on a comprehensive ideology of radical social and political change. It intended to purify society of superstitions and negative social practices. The third is the colonial Salafīyyah represented by such scholars as 'Abd al-Qādir al-Jazā'irī, Aḥmad al-Mahdī, al-Sanūsī, Ḥassan al-'Aṭṭār, al-Saffār, Jamāl al-Dīn Afghānī, Muḥammad 'Abduh and Rashīd Riḍa. Fourth, the post-colonial Salafīyyah represented by 'Abd al-Qādir 'Awdah, Yūsuf al-Sibaī', 'Allāl al-Fāsī, Sayyid Quṭb and Muḥammad Quṭb, and fifth, the post-1967 Salafīyyah as represented by Yūsuf al-Qaraḍāwī, Muḥammad al-Ghazālī, Fahmī Huwaydī, Ṭāriq al-Bishrī from Egypt, Ḥassan al-Turābī from the Sudan, 'Abd al-Salām Yāssīn from Morocco, Muḥammad Bāqir al-Ṣadr, Muḥammad al-Rāshid, and Ṭāhā Jābīr al-'Alwānī from Iraq, 'Abd al-Majīd al-Zandānī from Yemen, Muḥammad Sa'īd Ramaḍān al-Būṭī, 'Abd al-Fattāh Abū Ghuda from Syria, and Muḥammad Ḥussain Faḍlallah and Fatḥī Yakan from Lebanon, Rāshid al-Ghannūshī from Tunisia, Takīy al-Dīn al-Nabahānī, and Munīr Shafīq from Palestine, and also with many others. In the same token, the main Islamic movements in the Arab world such as the Ikhwān in Egypt and many Arab countries, the National Salvation Front in Algeria, the Islamic Liberation Party (Hizb al-Taḥrīr), the Hizb al-'Amal in Jordan, Hizb al-Nahḍah of Tunisia, and al-Jabhat al-Islāmiyyah al-Qawmiyyah in the Sudan all represent Salafī trends of thought.[11] One must not forget the several militant Salafī movements, such as the Jihad and Jamā'ah al-Islāmiyyah in Egypt. Unlike the major Salafī trends, these movements seek to establish the Islamic polity through a military take-over of the state.

In addition to its strong and complex Salafī orientation, the Islamic trend in contemporary Arab thought is distinguished by the pre-eminence of the Sacred as ideal at its root. The religious text, the Qur'an, and to a lesser extent, the Ḥadīth, form the heart of its intellectual tradition. To many Muslim thinkers, the Muslim intellectual tradition has been the product of a dialogue between the Sacred, as defined above, and the changing historical and political conditions in the Muslim world.

Thus, one may argue that Salafīyyah is a broad term that encompasses all of those Islamic perspectives, trends, and positions that take Islamic revelation as the main criterion of truth. As a movement, the Salafīyyah can be both anti-colonialist, as in the case of 'Abd al-Qādir al-Jazā'irī, 'Abd al-Karīm al-Khaṭṭābī, Bin Badīs and 'Allāl al-Fāsī in North Africa,[12] or pacifist as in the case of the Wahabiyyah in twentieth century Saudi Arabia. Also, one can argue that the modern Salafīyyah movement was born in the nineteenth century in reaction to both the modernity of Western imperialism and Muslim decline.[13] Modernity was distinguished by its capitalist origins and its drive toward global expansion and profit making. Globalized capitalism of the nineteenth century introduced drastic changes in the relationship between political authority and economic wealth. In pre-capitalist societies, political authority was the main source of wealth; whereas in capitalism, wealth is the source of political authority.[14] The new and dominant culture of capitalism placed the Salafīyyah on the defensive. Muslim metaphysics and a certain reading of the past produced a more or less coherent brand of Salafīyyah. However, the encounter with capitalism placed the nineteenth century Salafīyyah on shaky grounds. Many Salafī thinkers, including Muḥammad 'Abduh, were not sure whether they were dealing with Christianity, modernity or capitalism. For a while, the concept of the West was somewhat amorphous in their minds.

In its enlightened form, the Salafīyyah resurrected the classical Kalām motif of the compatibility of reason and faith, best expressed by such leading Muslim philosophers as Ibn Sīna, Ibn Rushd, and al-Fārābī.[15] In the nineteenth century, the Salafīyyah revisited this motif as a means of coming to grips with the challenges of capitalism. However, as Samir Amin forcefully argues, capitalism had already made a break with this motif and elevated rationalism to a higher level than metaphysics. This was a qualitative break. Reason was no longer attached to matters of faith.[16] It is only in the twentieth century that Salafī thinkers began to contemplate the disastrous implications of capitalist culture and philosophy toward Islamic metaphysics and ethics. The West meant imperialism, capitalism, and exploitation in the thought of such people as Sayyid Quṭb, Muḥammad Bāqir al-Ṣadr, and Muḥammad Ḥussain Faḍlallah. Because of its aggressive nature, capitalist modernity forced Salafī thinkers to seriously consider the capitalist mode of production and its impact on modern Muslim societies.

The best representative of the Salafīyyah in the nineteenth and early part of the twentieth centuries in Shaykh Muḥammad 'Abduh, who was almost aloof in his endeavors to search for proper concepts with which to analyze the reasons for decline in his society and ways of reform.[17] In this sense, he stands on par with such nineteenth century European philosophers and thinkers, also aloof in their conceptual formulations, as Freud and Nietzsche.[18] Another major Salafī thinker who somewhat followed in the footsteps of 'Abduh is Ḥassan al-Banna and the rest of the Ikhwān thinkers of the twentieth century.

In reacting to both decline and modernity, the Salafīyyah sought to modernize the modern Muslim world. The Islamic movement in the Arab world, in a number of its main positions, never let go of this vision to the point that in many Arab countries, Islamism and mysticism are considered opposites. This is clear in the intellectual legacy of the Ikhwān in a Sufi-oriented society, such as in the Sudan and Northern Nigeria. The Ikhwān, through the efforts of Ḥassan al-Turābī, sought to modernize the country by ridding it of Sufi thinking and by introducing new and rational criteria to interpret *fiqh*. In the same way that modern Islamic thought was a response to severe tensions in nineteenth century Arab society, these tensions became more pronounced in the high age of imperialism in the first half of the twentieth century.

Islamism was, therefore, the natural outgrowth of the nineteenth century Salafīyyah, especially in its 'Abduh and Afghānī formulations. Islamism can be summarized both as a response to triumphant imperialism and the deep sense of political, religious, and intellectual malaise enveloping Arab society in the interwar period, especially after the abolition of the Ottoman caliphate in 1924. Being a response to the penetration of the modernity of imperialism in the different corners of the Arab world has always defined Islamist identity as intricately linked to that of the West. In a sense, this aggressive modernity has forced Islamism to be an avid observer of things Western and has led it to present a comprehensive critique of the Western worldview and strategies in the Muslim world. This important dimension characterizes the thought of such people as Banna, Quṭb, Faḍlallah and many others.

Although critical of imperialist modernity, both nineteenth century Salafīyyah and interwar Salafīyyah adopted one key idea of Western modernity: the notion of reform and progress. However, one must draw an important distinction between the notion of progress as espoused by modernity and that as understood by the Islamic Salafīyyah. The Salafīyyah espousal of progress is not at all divorced from its appreciation of the centrality of the Islamic intellectual tradition and its modern intellectual positions.

In addition, the interwar Salafīyyah, especially in North Africa, was wedded to an anti-colonial struggle. That is to say, the North African Salafīyyah, represented in the main by the ideas of 'Allāl al-Fāsī in Morocco and Bin Badīs in Algeria, was an ally to the nationalist movement in seeking independence from the French.[19] According to a contemporary Moroccan historian, "Moroccan Salafīyyah was not only militant in the sense of playing an active role against corrupt Islam; it was also militant in its resistance to the colonizer…Religion and nationalism in Morocco went hand in hand."[20] However, after independence a divergence takes place between nationalism and Salafīyyah in most Arab countries. The Salafīyyah, which considers Islam and politics to be one, is not allowed by the new nation-state to develop into an instrument of power. It is relegated to a secondary status.

Egyptian thinker Ghālī Shukrī offers a different classification of the Salafīyyah movement in the contemporary Arab world. He argues that four forms of Salafīyyah coexist in Arab societies:

1. "folk" Salafīyyah that forms a significant part of popular culture in the Arab world and that depends on oral culture;
2. institutionalized Salafīyyah or "Official Islam," which has been at the service of the power elite;
3. reform Salafīyyah, which is best represented by the reform tradition of Muḥammad 'Abduh in Egypt and Shaykh bin Badīs in Algeria;
4. Ikhwān Salafīyyah, which advocates the establishment of an Islamic state following the model laid in early Islam by the Rightly Guided caliphate.[21]

This classification is indeed helpful in elaborating the dynamics, or lack thereof, of Islam in contemporary Arab society. One must note that the second form of Salafīyyah mentioned by Shukrī exists all over the Arab world, including Lebanon, but its strength varies from one country to another.

Salafīyyah literature is replete with references to the state of Christianity in modern Western societies. Modern Salafī thinkers assume without sufficient scholarly evidence that Christianity lives on the margins of modern European societies, which have lost touch with the origins of the religion. Thus, one common feature of the thought of the Muslim Salafīyyah from the nineteenth century forward is the lament of the sad state of affairs of Christianity in the Western world and the gradual materialization of Christian thought and practice. In a sense, the Salafī discourse, conscious as it was of its immense responsibility in highlighting the Sacred in a progressively profane/secular world, expressed pity over the position of Christianity in the West; a position, according to the Salafīyyah, of that perpetual decline and defeat.

In other words, the Salafīyyah arguments on behalf of uplifting the status of Christianity in modern Western society can be viewed as another direct attack on a key component of Western modernity: secularism. The Salafīyyah critique of secularism is anchored in the notion that Christianity, like Islam, ought to be religion and state combined and that there must not be any compromise on this significant point. Thus, the Salafīyyah places its finger on one of the most irksome problems in modern Muslim and Western thought: the separation of religion and state. This separation has forced a number of Muslim scholars to take the issue of secularism quite seriously.

This does not mean that the Salafīyyah presented a comprehensive view of the relationship between religion and society in the modern and contemporary West. Many Muslim scholars are satisfied with the yet unproven premise that religion in the West, especially Christianity, is totally marginalized. Because of its occupation with the notion of highlighting the Sacred in contemporary Muslim life, the Salafīyyah arguments are far from conclusive or convincing when it comes to the position of Christianity in contemporary Western societies.[22] One can argue that there has not been a Muslim critique of the revival of religion in the West or any exhaustive study of Christian thought in the modern world. This is quite apparent in the fragmented Islamic writings on this topic.

Because of the historical conditions that led to its birth and the challenges it has faced in the twentieth century, the Salafīyyah movement has understood progress in terms of a return to the sublime past. Thus, in the post-independence era, with the rise of the national bourgeoisie to power in many Arab countries, the Salafīyyah found itself in a state of confrontation with Arab nationalism, a major political and intellectual movement in the modern Arab world. Arab nationalism aimed to revitalize the Arab world in its fight against imperialism and for a secular Arab society. In theological terms, the Salafīyyah was not able to relate to the constructed or invented worldview of nationalism, which, in essence, refused to subscribe to the importance of the sacred in its ideological and intellectual discourse. Although some "moderate" Salafīyyah thinkers were able to appreciate the anti-imperialist feelings and underpinnings of Arab nationalism, complete sympathy with it was quite impossible. The breach between Salafīyyah and nationalism became more apparent at the height of the nationalist rise in certain Arab countries in the 1950s and the 1960s, when nationalism pushed for the substitution of the Salafīyyah notion of the Muslim ummah with the nationalist notion of the Arab nation. The major theoreticians of nationalism, both in the pre- and post-independence eras, sought to invent an Arab nation in quite different terms than the Salafīyyah. At best, Islam has its place as part of the cultural heritage of the Arab people. To use Benedict Anderson's celebrated study, the social imaginaire of Arab nationalism was distinctly different from that of the Salafīyyah.

In addition to marginalizing Islam in the thought of Arab nationalism, an attack was launched on the Muslim ulama, that is, the traditional religious leadership, for the purpose of weakening their position and pushing them out of the social imaginaire of nationalism. To be sure, the Salafīyyah movement was also critical of the ulama, although it did not strive to deprive them of their basic function, the preservation and propagation of the Sacred Text. The purpose of Salafīyyah was to reform and strengthen their position in Arab society.

In pre-1967 Arab society, especially in the Middle East, the Salafīyyah was on the defensive and Arab nationalism was on the offensive. The 1967 defeat drastically changed this formula in a drastic way: it weakened and even paralyzed nationalism and forced it to revert to Islamic themes in its public pronouncements. In the words of the Egyptian thinker Ghālī Shukrī, the Salafīyyah "mushroomed" after the 1967 defeat.[23] This happened in such countries as Syria, Egypt, and Jordan. A similar phenomenon took place in Iraq, especially after the second Gulf War.

This condition led to a gradual resurgence and regrouping of the Salafīyyah as a movement seeking to counter Western/Israeli imperialism in the area by offering authenticity as a salvation from the malaise striking Arab society.[24] The Salafīyyah critique of nationalism centered on the failure of the nationalist project of modernity to provide satisfactory answers for the Arab and Muslim decline. The Salafīyyah offered authenticity as a criterion of progress against this decline. Thus, the Salafīyyah refuses to accept secularism as the answer.

In its quest for progress, the Salafīyyah espouses modernization (*taḥdīth*), that is, the adoption of the scientific techniques and even ideas of the West without Westernization (*taghrīb*), the cultural environment in which Western modernity was born. This is one of the major outlines of the thought of Shaykh Muḥammad al-Ghazālī, which will be discussed in detail in Chapter 10 of this book. The Salafīyyah sought to revive Fiqh as a means of attaining its intellectual and ideological goals. The following thinkers stand out in this regard: ʿAbd al-Qādir ʿAwdah, Yūsuf al-Qaraḍāwī, Muḥammad al-Ghazālī, Ḥassan al-Turābī, and Rāshid al-Ghannūshī. At the height of the struggle between Arab nationalism and the Salafīyyah movement, some thinkers, especially Sayyid Quṭb and his brother Muḥammad Quṭb, went as far as condemning all Muslim societies, individuals, and practices in the name of *Jāhiliyyah*. This condemnation gained new momentum with the 1967 defeat.

After considering this historical sketch of the religious permutations of Salafīyyah, one must remember that the Salafīyyah movement in the Middle East was responding to a different set of circumstances than that in the Gulf states, especially the Wahabiyyah Salafīyyah in Saudi Arabia.[25] In several Gulf states and most notably in Saudi Arabia, the Salafīyyah was intimately wed to the state to the extent that only an astute observer could distinguish the subtle difference between the state and the Wahabiyyah. The state claimed adherence to Islamic identity and the modernization of society. While the Salafīyyah in such countries as Syria and Egypt was on the defensive in the pre- and even post-1967 era, this was not the case in the Gulf states. The tribal Gulf state needed the Salafīyyah in order to boost its imported modernization programs in the 1960s and the 1980s and it needed it once again to attack Iraq in the second Gulf War. Furthermore, one may argue that the official Salafīyyah in most countries in the Gulf took the side of the state against Iraq after its occupation of Kuwait. The fact that this official Salafīyyah sanctioned the intervention of the foreign troops against an Arab and Muslim country shows how far it will go in order to safeguard its interests, which have mainly been wedded to the state in the modern era.[26] However, it is important to note that in the past several decades, a new revolutionary Salafīyyah movement has arisen in many Gulf countries, most notably in Saudi Arabia, which is critical of the alliance between the traditional Salafīyyah and the political *status quo*.[27]

It is important to note that one must place under the Salafīyyah banner a number of distinguished Shī'ī thinkers in the Arab world, most notably Muḥammad Bāqir al-Ṣadr of Iraq and Muḥammad Ḥussain Faḍlallah of Lebanon. These two thinkers, in particular, have had a major impact not just on Shī'ī youth but Sunni youth as well. In addition, one must not forget the major impact of the 1979 Iranian revolution on Arab consciousness in general and the Salafī outlook in particular. The success of the Iranian revolution was seen as the concrete embodiment of genuine Islam in an Islamic society. A number of Salafī thinkers began to publicize the ideas of such figures as Ali Shari'āti and Imām Khomeini.

In treating the Salafī trend with its complex components in contemporary Arab thought, it is important to invoke the famous distinction drawn by Maxime Rodinson between "Official Islam" and "Popular Islam."[28] To begin with, this is more than an academic sociological distinction about the nature of religion in contemporary Arab society. "Official Islam" represents the position of the state on religion and its various mechanisms, both subtle and concrete, to define a manageable relationship between the two. The constitution of almost every Arab state proclaims that Islam is the official religion of the country and that the Sharī'ah is the main source of legislation. Besides raising questions about non-Muslims in Arab societies where the Sharī'ah is the main source of legislation, this official position raises the fundamental question about the religious elite that enjoy the support of the state. This religious elite, dispersed as it is in different corners of the country, gains the official patronage of the state through the creation of a ministry for endowment and religious affairs, whose function becomes to keep those rebellious young preachers who may not heed the call of official reason in check.

The official religious elite are also popular in nature. Since the beginning of Islam, a small class of religious leaders remained aloof from the muddy world of politics. Others favored a more activist approach. Over the centuries, the religious elite has distinguished itself by defining Islam in a certain way and carrying the banner of the Sacred in society. A good number of the members of this elite proclaim their support to the sultan, to the *status quo*, and it finds enough rationale from within the Islamic legal system and history to do so. If the state decides to modernize society, or a part thereof, the official religious elite lends its unequivocal support in the name of progress and rationalism.

The official elite in contemporary Arab society is in no position to condemn the economic and social practices of the state and the widening margin of between rich and poor in many Arab countries. In its public pronouncements, it remains oblivious to the economic structure of the state, the transformation in the world economy and its impact on local economies, the widening gap between rich and poor, the emigration of the professional elite, whose fortunes have declined over the past two decades, and the state of privatization that affects every sector of society.

It is perhaps not surprising to discover the poverty of this elite when it comes to social and economic analysis and criticism. The religious discourse it offers, although shrouded in the mystery of the Sacred and the sublime rhetoric of the Arab language, is devoid of any real political, social, or economic insight. This class has learned the simple lesson that to keep itself in business, it must not delve into these "worldly" matters. Abstract theology and Arabic grammar are preferred to social and political analysis.

The activist Salafī trend is preoccupied with realizing the meaning of Islam and the state in real life. Because it is the product of both local and international historical factors, this trend has carried the banner of the Sharī'ah application in a state that already claims to have applied the Sharī'ah and which is supported in its claim by the official religious elite. However, since the death of Sayyid Quṭb in 1966, or rather his execution by the Egyptian state, a number of subdivisions have emerged within the body of Islamic activist Salafīyyah. One may classify these divisions under two broad categories: one seeks to control political authority as a means of fully applying Islam, through political and peaceful means, and another that uses Jihad as the only means to realize its objectives. The first is true of the Ikhwān in Egypt and the other is true of the Jihad movement in the same country. The above two trends in Salafī Islamism are complemented by a powerful academic/intellectual/journalistic trend represented by such people as Aḥmad Kamāl Abū'l Majd, Fahmī Huwaydī, Munīr Shafīq, Muḥammad 'Imārah, Ṭāriq al-Bishrī, 'Ādil Ḥussain, and many others.[29]

It is impossible to fathom the importance of modern Salafīyyah in its different mutations and offshoots without appreciating the religious, historical, and intellectual circumstances and conditions that led to its birth.[30] In that sense, Salafīyyah is historical in nature. It is erroneous to assume, as does the contemporary Sudanese thinker Ḥaydar Ibrahim 'Alī, that the Salafīyyah in the contemporary Arab world is the product of crisis.[31] The modern Salafīyyah is the product of the encounter between the advanced/aggressive/imperialist West and the Arab world. The Salafīyyah can not ignore this historical condition. As mentioned previously, the Salafīyyah is based on the primacy of the Sacred Text in Muslim life. Real life must imitate the ideal. An offshoot of Salafīyyah is what has been termed "political Islam," that is, those Islamic movements that advocate the notion that state and religion are one and that seek to apply this notion in real life. Salafīyyah is not to be equated to political Islam as such, since there are tendencies in Salafīyyah such as the Wahabiyyah that are satisfied with the relationship of state and religion in their society.

The Salafīyyah represents a broad coalition of religious and social forces, some of which have risen to prominence due to the unceasing need of the contemporary industrial societies for oil. However, one major underlying cause of the prominence of the Salafīyyah in its different offshoots is the strong religious component of popular Arab culture. Religion is always appealed to in times of crisis.

THE LIBERAL DISCOURSE

As with the above discourse, the liberal discourse in contemporary Arab thought traces its origin to the reform movement of the nineteenth century, especially in applying the Western notions of progress to Arab society. To the liberal, neither Christianity nor Islam is the criterion of progress; rather, it is modern Western civilization with its scientific and material achievements. From the start, Arab liberalism has sought a qualitative break with religion, a position that has attracted to it the wrath of the religious intelligentsia.

Liberalism in Western thought refers to a broad coalition of economic, political, and philosophical forces emerging in the sixteenth century and achieving its goals in the nineteenth century, which is the age of liberalism triumphant in the world. In Europe, liberalism represented the economic and cultural aspirations of the nascent bourgeoisie. It "is the bourgeois as capitalist that has been the centerpiece of modern politico-economic discourse."[32] In its different economic and political activities, liberalism prides itself on the notion of liberty, which is "built, after all, upon the simple consideration that the world is likely to be more happy if it refuses to build its institutions upon injustice."[33] Democracy looms large in the thought of liberalism. However, it is possible to argue that bourgeois democracy remains "a façade behind which the capitalist class continue[s] to rule and dominate society."[34] Liberalism posited progress as the landmark of the happiness desired.[35]

As a complex bourgeois movement, liberalism sought to achieve a number of things: philosophically, it sought to introduce a radical break between metaphysics and rationalism or between faith and reason. Liberalism no longer considered metaphysics to be the queen of sciences; an unfettered exercise of thought was considered the new criterion for progress. To be sure, the progress of science in the nineteenth century gave liberalism an edge over all religious philosophies. Economically, liberalism sought to achieve the unfettered movement of goods. *Laissez-faire* capitalism was its natural expression in the eighteenth and nineteenth centuries. Socially, liberalism was for constituting a new social and work ethic that was not defined by either religion or tradition,[36] or where religious philosophies occupy a marginal position. Educationally, liberalism preaches a new type of liberal education that rejects the control of religious reason and institutions. Politically, liberalism was against the state interference in economic activity and saw the state as a matter of contract between the citizen and political authority. It represented the aspirations of the rising bourgeoisie against the interests of the *ancien régime*.

According to Harold Laski, the foremost historian of European liberalism in the twentieth century, several objective reasons gave rise to the social and economic movement called liberalism: "There are the geographical discoveries. There is the breakdown of feudal economic relations. There is the establishment of new churches which no longer recognize the supremacy of Rome. There is a scientific revolution which altogether alters the perspective of men's thought. There is a growing volume of technological invention which leads to new wealth and increased population."[37]

Liberalism was, then, the product of historical conditions in Europe. Its rise coincided with that of the Reformation in sixteenth century Germany. The Reformation purported to break down both the economic and mental monopolies Rome enjoyed over the believers of Christendom by retrieving what was considered to be the original message of Christianity: to achieve goodness on the basis of the Bible without any ecclesiastical mediation. Therefore, liberalism gave new meaning to the Reformation by assisting it in breaking down the fetters of the church. The product of this alliance was the rise of the secular state, which advances mercantilism as its commercial philosophy. "Mercantilism, in the first stage, therefore simply transfers the idea of social control from the church to the state in the economic realm."[38] The state, therefore, finds itself compelled to develop its own sense of conduct and rejects the interference of religious authority. Nineteenth century European bourgeoisie held to heart the notion that liberalism is "a belief that progress, leading to final perfection, could be achieved by means to free institutions."[39] In other words, liberalism was not satisfied with just economic activity but had as its goal the reconstruction of the state and molding it according to its own economic philosophy.[40]

Liberalism's appealing philosophy did not escape the attention of some leading Arab thinkers in the early part of the twentieth century who had already been critical of the stagnant spirit of their societies. European notions of progress, science and freedom galvanized the minds of Arab thinkers who were able to envision a new Arab civil society to be based on rationalism, democracy, and secularism. In his classical work on Arabic thought in the liberal age, Hourani analyzes Arab liberalism in detail. It suffices to mention here that in the interwar period, liberalism was able to attract to its ranks such leading Arab thinkers as Ṭāha Ḥussain,[41] 'Alī 'Abd al-Rāziq, Rāfiq al-'Azm, Salīm al-Bustānī, and Khālid Muḥammad Khālid. At present, some distinguished contemporary thinkers as 'Alī al-Dīn Hilāl,[42] Saī'd al-Najjār and Ḥāzem al-Bablāwī, and Sayyid Yāssīn represent this trend.

The transfer of liberalism into the Arab world was not a simple process of cultural or political exchange across national lines. The globalization of capitalism in the nineteenth century created the necessary conditions for the spread of liberalism into pre-industrial societies, which had suffered from economic and structural stagnation for a long while. As suggested earlier, liberalism was the culmination of a long and painful process of political, economic, and religious transition in the life of Europe since the sixteenth century, which pitted the bourgeoisie against the feudal class. Arab liberalism, on the other hand, was not in such a fortunate position; it was on the receiving end of things under the most adverse conditions facing the Arab world at the time. In a significant way, Arab liberalism was a poor version of European liberalism, a cheap imitation copy, for it lacked the objective conditions that made European liberalism viable. One is tempted to agree with Fanon's contention that, "The national middle class which takes over power at the end of the colonial regime is an underdeveloped class. It has practically no economic power, and in any case it is in no way commensurate with the bourgeoisies of the mother country which it hopes to replace."[43] This, in part, explains the rise of Arab liberalism under the protection of European capitalism in the interwar period, and its tragic failure after national independence.[44] A strong Arab bourgeoisie failed to rise in the interwar period for two main reasons: first, the advanced capitalist system of the colonial power in the Arab world blocked any independent emergence of the Arab bourgeoisie, and second, the feudal system in many Arab countries was too entrenched to allow any flourishing of the bourgeoisie.[45] The decline of the social and economic systems of the Arab world on the eve of Western intervention created the perfect conditions for Western liberalism to spread into the Arab world. Al-ʻĀlim is quite correct to note that in the eighteenth and nineteenth centuries, the liberal culture of the West was the most viable and creative in the world. It was the only way out of the social and economic stagnation of Arab societies in that period. In addition,

> the nascent Arab bourgeoisie [of the eighteenth and nineteenth centuries] found in the rational culture of liberalism positive values it identified with and considered to be an extension of its ancient Islamic tradition, especially in its mercantilist, productive and creative phase, before it was crushed by the crusades and the internal schisms.[46]

In an insightful piece on the crisis of liberalism in modern Arab thought, Egyptian political scientist ʻAlī al-Dīn Hilāl, argues that the transfer of Western liberal ideas to the nineteenth century Arab world was historically necessary and was initially made possible by the students' missions overseas. In certain Arab countries, most notably Egypt and Iraq, constitutional liberalism was the norm in the first half of the twentieth century. However, with the rise of Nasserism and the Baʻth Party in both Iraq and Syria, liberalism was on the defensive. In the mind of Hilāl, liberalism has been the only plausible political and intellectual discourse in the world since the collapse of the Soviet Union in 1989. Hilāl does not raise any questions about the weak foundations of Arab liberalism, in that it was the creation of an unequal relation of power between the capitalist center and peripheral Arab world.[47] However, he argues that conditions in the Arab world are again ripe for the resurgence of liberalism, especially after the collapse of the Soviet system, the privatization of the Third World economies, and the need for civil and religious liberties in the Arab world.

Hilāl believes that Arab nationalism, Marxism, and Islamism have failed to come to grips with the consequences of the New World Order and the specific conditions of the Arab world. He advocates the resurrection of a contemporary version of Arab liberalism, which embraces such issues as constitutionalism and parliamentary democracy; the freedom to establish parties and labor unions; the emancipation of women; equality before the law regardless of gender or religion; the meaning of nationhood and citizenship; political and economic freedoms; receptivity to Western ideas, and giving value to science and reason with the aid of education and learning.[48] He further argues that under the new conditions in the Arab world, the Arab bourgeoisie can play the active role that was somewhat aborted under colonialism. The Arab bourgeoisie then could not keep pace with the European bourgeoisie and was thus unable to lead a constitutional state. Other hurdles faced the nascent Arab bourgeoisie: increased urbanization, demographic explosion, and widening gaps between rich and poor.[49] Hilāl argues that since the collapse of the Soviet Union, the liberal discourse has been the only viable one and that the Arab world has a great opportunity to carry out constitutional reform and establish a strong civil society. However, is the liberal discourse in the Arab world tenable in view of American hegemony? Egyptian thinker Ghālī Shukrī thinks not. He argues that,

> Over its modern history, the West has not permitted any Arab liberal [and democratic] experiment to succeed, since, to start with, it has not allowed an Arab

> bourgeoisie to grow independent of its control. This is the reason why the West has always sought the explicit alliance of patriarchal and theocratic societies which vehemently oppose secularism.[50]

It is true that the Arab bourgeoisies has been indicted by many a corner. In the words of Robert Springborg, the old Arab bourgeoisie "was written off by Washington as too weak to conclude peace treaties with Israel or to counter the growing communist threat."[51]

The Arab world has been in the throes of major change since the demise of the old bourgeoisie. A resurgence of neo-bourgeoisie has been under way in the past several decades. However, the question is, does the neo-Arab bourgeoisie rule the state? The military elite in the contemporary Arab world hail from either tribal or military backgrounds and most of them show no tolerance for constitutions and democracies. In addition, the advanced capitalist West has no interest in the development of a strong Arab bourgeoisie. Its interests are better served by the existing ruling regimes in the Arab world.

It is doubtful that the Arab world is ready to embrace the central tenets of liberalism for the simple reason that comparable conditions that gave rise to European liberalism are not yet to be found in the Arab world. In addition, the Arab world suffers from pernicious authoritarianism that is supported both morally and militarily by the capitalist "Center." Lastly, Arab liberalism seems to have failed to understand the persistence and resurgence of the religious phenomenon in Arab society. At best, Arab liberalism shies away from advocating the modernization of Islam.

Having said all the above, it is clear that the Arab economic system follows capitalist criteria and logic. With the collapse of the socialist experiment in those Arab countries that had advocated socialism, the neo-liberal bourgeoisie has been running the show. In Egypt, for example, Nasserism could not completely stamp out the old bourgeois classes.[52] After the death of Nasser in 1970 and the liberalization of the Egyptian economy under Sadat in 1974, this class reverted to its old position without much difficulty. Three groups of people make up the neo-liberal class in Egypt: (1) the pre-revolutionary bourgeoisie; (2) the top bureaucrats of the state; and (3) the new merchants and representatives of foreign companies who have recently acquired wealth.[53] In its move to again dominate society, the neo-liberal forces in Egyptian society launched a major attack on the economic and cultural achievements of Nasserism and accused the Nasser regime of impoverishing the country, spreading socialist and atheist ideas, stamping out democracy, and planting in the minds of the poor and the peasants such ideas as social justice, equality, and distribution of wealth.[54] One has to agree with Mansī's assessment that the neo-liberal discourse is the most hegemonic in Egypt, and even the Arab world, and that individualism is a dominant behavioral trend. However, it is hegemonic only with the support of the army and the ruling political elite. The bourgeoisie is no longer maligned in the contemporary Arab world. It has even found a place in Ba'thist Syria.[55] The liberalization of such countries as Egypt is characterized by a Right-wing ideology, more interested in preserving the economic and social interests of the Egyptian bourgeoisie than in securing political freedom for all citizens. The liberal intellectuals claim to defend freedom while defending the control of the Egyptian capitalist class over all sensitive positions in society.[56]

THE NATIONALIST TREND

Arab nationalism is dead at the beginning of the twenty first century, although the Arab nation is still alive.[57] Technology has made the 22 states of the Arab nation more culturally and linguistically interdependent. The Arab intelligentsia from Morocco in the west to Iraq in the east understand that they more or less face the same challenges and perhaps the same enemies.

There isn't as much media discussion about Arab nationalism lately as there is about "Political Islam" or "Islamic fundamentalism" or "Islamic terrorism." Some even assume that with the debacle of Nasserism after the June 1967 war and the defeat of nationalist Iraq in the second Gulf War in 1991, Arab nationalism has been relegated to the dustbin of history. Capitalist globalization has exerted much time and effort to dispense with Arab nationalism as one of the most serious contenders to its economic and political hegemony in the Arab world. 1967 was the first major blow to Arab nationalism, followed by another severe hit in the second Gulf War, which resulted in the defeat of Iraq, a direct occupation of the Gulf by American troops, and the strengthening of authoritarianism in the Arab world in general. It is to the advantage of globalist forces to deal with the Arab world as disparate entities rather than as one cohesive political unit. The Zionist movement was astute enough to discover this axiom many years before the creation of Israel in 1948.[58]

Arab nationalism began as a vigorous movement of liberation fighting for the cultural sovereignty of the Arabs beside their economic and political independence. In its long history, Arab nationalism had gone through much change. One may distinguish four major phases in the Arab nationalist movement in the Mashreq: (1) Ottoman; (2) the interwar period; (3) the 1948–70 phase; and (4) 1970 to the present.[59] The first phase was the product of the broad Tanzimat period begun by the empire at the beginning of the nineteenth century and which sought to place the empire on par with Europe.[60] Ottoman nationalism, whether Arab or Turkish, sought to create a new civil society to be bound by new constitutional rules.[61] The best representatives of this trend were 'Abd al-Raḥmān al-Kawākibī (1848–1902) and Ṣāṭi' al-Ḥuṣrī.[62] With the military defeat of the Ottoman caliphate during World War One and inevitable Western conquest (both British and French) of the Arab East, the Arab nationalist movement entered a new phase. A number of prominent Arab nationalist thinkers carried the banner of Arab nationalism, the most distinguished of whom were Muḥammad 'Izzat Darwaza,[63] and Costantine Zurayk who, until his death in 2000, played a major role in shaping the intellectual foundations of contemporary Arab nationalism. The post-1948 phase witnessed three distinct Arab nationalist subcurrents: (1) the Ba'th Party, best represented by Michel 'Aflaq and Ṣalāḥ al-Biṭār;[64] (2) Nasserism;[65] and (3) the Arab Nationalists' Movement or Ḥarakat al-Qawmiyyīn al-'Arab, best represented by George Habbash and Nāyif Ḥawātima.[66]

Even before the formation of the Arab nationalist order in the 1950s, Arab nationalist thinkers promoted the idea of the fight against imperialism and the achievement of Arab unity. Afterward, the Arab nationalist order began to incorporate the main outlines of nationalist philosophy with regard to nation-building and the attempt to liberate Palestine from the enemy. In short, the Arab nationalist order sought to change power relations in the Arab world by promoting a pan-Arab ideology capable of withstanding the challenges of post-colonial capitalism.

It is clear that Egypt was at the heart of the Arab nationalist struggle in the 1950s and 1960s. Its quest for nationalist independence went a long way. However, in the process of building its independent institutions and achieving a certain form of Arab unity, the Egyptian state faced some major hurdles in the 1960s that concluded with the 1967 defeat. Three decades later, Egypt, although still a major player in Arab politics and culture, has abandoned the quest for Arab unity and signed a peace agreement with Israel. Institutionally, the drive toward Arab unity and the "liberation of Palestine" have been immensely weakened if not completely discarded.[67] Anouar Abdel-Malek refers to the whole process as the "occultation" of Egypt; that is, the total reversal experienced by the Egyptian political elite in the 1970s when Egypt signed the Camp David Accords with Israel and abdicated its nationalist Arab responsibilities. The Camp David Accords constitute "the second foundation of the state of Israel."[68]

In a reflective piece originally written in 1972 on the reasons behind defeat in 1967, the late Egyptian nationalist thinker Aḥmad Bahā' al-Dīn (d. 1993) predicts the dismemberment of Egypt from the Arab nationalist body. He argues that the strategy of the United States after the 1967 war was to isolate Egypt from the Arab world and to focus on the oil wealth of the Gulf states while keeping them politically fragmented.[69] In other words, it was not in the interest of either the United States or Israel to keep the Arab nationalist system intact. The United States' policy toward the Arab world since 1967 betrays its great desire on the side of the USA to keep the Arab world divided.

It is important to point out that in the colonial stage, Arab nationalism fought very hard to liberate itself from imperialism, French or British, in two important domains: the spiritual and the institutional. On the spiritual level, as Partha Chatterjee ably shows, nationalism seeks to ensure its sovereignty on the personality of the nation, its past, and cultural identity. On the institutional level, it seeks to establish its nationalist state by learning from Western science and institution building.[70] Whereas one may argue that Arab nationalism at the beginning of the twenty-first century in the first sense has been totally weakened, it is not correct to say that in the second, Arab nationalism has passed away. The Arab nation is still alive and healthy, culturally speaking. More and more people realize that the current political elites object to the grand philosophy of Arab nationalism: total liberation from imperialism.

One must examine the decline or weakness of Arab nationalism after 1967 in relation to two broad factors or conditions: first, the change in the international political system after colonialism and the impact it has had on the Arab political system, and, second, the state of Arab economy and society since independence. Arab nationalism, both old and new, has placed its finger on imperialism as the single most antagonistic force against Arab unity. In the old phase, it was both France and Britain that embodied this negative force, and since at least 1967,

America has played this role in concert with Israel. Inarguably, the United States inherited the legacy of British and French imperialism after World War Two and by 1967 had emerged as the major supporter of Israel in its fight with the Arab world. Arab nationalism became weak in proportion to the strength of the American-Israeli alliance in the area and the co-opting of the small Arab states in support of this alliance.[71]

On the domestic front, Arab nationalism has suffered from the absence of real democracy, the narrow social foundation of the political elite, high rates of illiteracy in spite of having nationalized education, huge gaps between rich and poor, and the rise of regionalism in the Arab world.[72] The collapse of the Arab political system after 1967, the withdrawal of Egypt from its leadership position in the Arab world, the initiation of the Open Door policy, and signing of a separate peace agreement with Israel paved the way for the Arab world to be recolonized thus ending the institutional ambitions of state nationalism.[73] In the prophetic words of Naseer Aruri,

> Unless major transformations occur in Arab society during the next twelve years, the twenty-first century will dawn upon the Arab state system with a striking resemblance to the Ottoman Empire of the nineteenth century. The Arab world is in imminent danger of being recolonized during the era of decolonization.[74]

Two years after these prophetic words were written down the Arab world was truly recolonized by the Western powers, especially the United States and Great Britain. The return of colonialism to the Arab world under the pretext of liberating Kuwait from Iraq and defending national American interests in the Gulf is proof, once again, of the importance of the area to the West. Oil is too valuable a resource to be left in the hands of the Arab alone.[75] The period since 1967 has witnessed the death of the most powerful practitioners and ideologues of Arab nationalism, Nasser and Aflaq, although the Arab nation lives.

Can Arab nationalism be revived in the twenty-first century, especially as it has transformed itself into "smaller and smaller units," as Edward Said argues?[76] As it now stands, there are two main paradigms contending for authority in the Arab world. The first is best represented by globalization, better read as Americanization, and the second by Arab and Muslim values. These two paradigms continue to wage battle over the Arab soul and future. We are led to believe that institutionalized globalization in the Arab world has triumphed for the moment over the spiritual domain of the Arab personality.

So far, I have shown the major differences between the Islamic and the liberal Arab trends in their treatment of the "Other." Nationalism is a modern concept emerging first in Europe in the eighteenth century and gaining force in the Arab world in the interwar period.[77] It is possible to speak of two streams of Arab nationalism: one in the Mashreq and the other in the Maghreb. Both streams of Arab nationalist thought have had their distinguished representatives over the decades but are a function of different political, economic, and social forces and conditions.[78]

As we have seen so far, nationalism in the Arab world is not monolithic. There are Arab countries ruled by different political regimes, mainly authoritarian in nature. The 1967 form of Arab nationalism, especially in the case of Iraq, did not benefit much from the debacle of Nasserism and the reasons behind such a disaster. The Iraqi state launched a lengthy and costly war against Iran in the name of Arab nationalism. In retrospect, the conservative Gulf states, which supported Iraq financially in waging this war against Iran, never expected that the Iraqi regime would turn against them. The internal contradictions within Iraq following the war with Iran blinded the regime from correctly assessing the post-Nasserite situation in the Arab world. The Iraqi invasion of Kuwait in August 1990 was a God-sent opportunity for the capitalist world to settle account with Iraq, the last major bastion of Arab nationalism in the Arab world. The main objective of the huge international alliance hastily formed by the United States was not merely to liberate Kuwait or protect the Saudi monarchy; its first and foremost aim was to render the Iraqi economy useless and teach any Third World country that dared to challenge the supremacy of the United States a dear lesson. With the Soviet Union out of the international picture, Iraq had no one upon which to rely except the Arab and Muslim masses.

What is revealing about the Iraqi situation is the fact that the authoritarian regimes in the Arab world have lost their nationalist enemies. Nasserism is dead, Ba'thist Iraq is in the throes of starvation, and Ba'thist Syria betrayed one of its closely-held principles and sided with the international alliance against another Arab nationalist country. International capitalism has bestowed a new sense of legitimacy to the anachronistic states in the Gulf. This, however, has come with a heavy price tag. Arab nationalism is dead at the beginning of the twenty-first century. Can the Arab people resurrect it under the heavy pressures of the international economic and political order? Has the Arab nation given up on the question of Palestine as one of the central questions of modern Arab nationalist ideology?

MARXIST/LEFTIST CURRENT

Marxism has had a rather pained history in the Arab world and the recent collapse of the Soviet system has only aggravated this situation.[79] Although not facing wholesale abandonment by its intellectual elite, like the French Communist Party in the 1970s,[80] the Arab Left was nevertheless greatly weakened by radical problems facing world socialism in the late 1980s. The Arab Left refers to a conglomerate of forces that have offered different readings or interpretations of Marxism. I think that it is important to distinguish between three terms describing the Arab Left: *al-yasār al-'arabī* (the Arab Left); *al-fikr al-ishtirākī* (Arab socialist thought), and *al-fikr al-mārkisī* (Arab Marxist thought). Some important distinctions exist between these categories. For our purposes, however, I mainly deal with Leftist Arab philosophers and thinkers, who have proved to be more analytical than pragmatic in their thought.

Historically speaking, what has distinguished the Left has been the ethos of equality, as the leading Italian Marxist philosopher, Norberto Bobbio, argues.[81] The capitalist system has engendered the most unequal economic and political relations in the West as well as overseas. The globalization of capitalism in the nineteenth century proved to have a lasting influence on the economic and social structures of the Third World, including the Arab world. Furthermore, the dramatic expansion of capitalism into pre-industrial societies forced the native intelligentsia to confront head-on the structural upheavals in their societies and their impact on politics and culture, and issues of poverty and wealth. These intelligentsia raised two complementary questions: (1) why have we declined? and (2) what are the secrets behind European progress?

The leading Arab intelligentsia of the nineteenth century were deeply aware of the immense stagnation present in their societies and they proposed an ambitious program of reform, usually referred to as Nahḍah or renaissance. In the initial encounter with advancing capitalism, two major discourses of reform emerged: the first was Salafī in nature and the second liberal in nature. Afghānī and 'Abduh represented the first model. A number of Syrian émigré intellectuals in Egypt, especially Faraḥ Anṭūn (1874–1922) and Shiblī Shumayl (1850–1917), represented the other.[82] There was quite a major divergence between these two discourses. The latter was not hesitant to adopt the scientific, cultural, and even ethical achievements of the advanced West *en masse* and to ponder ways to lift up the "decadent" East from its slumber and improve the status of women in society.

At this stage, I will attempt no deep analysis of capitalism. The Westernized discourse in Arab thought in the nineteenth century and in the early part of the twentieth century enjoyed the support of a number of major thinkers in the Arab world in the first half of the twentieth century: Salāma Mūsa; Ṭāhā Ḥussain; Nikola Ḥaddād; 'Iṣām al-Dīn Ḥifnī Nāssif.[83] In different ways, these thinkers propagated Western rationalism and liberalism at the expense of the Islamic Sacred and fought for a close cultural and scientific rapprochement between the Arab world and the West. The intellectual legacy of Ṭāhā Ḥussain has been a matter of immense controversy between those who believe that he was totally Westernized and a sell-out to the West and those who believed that his discourse did not deviate from the main tenets of Islam. I think that Ṭāhā Hussain, like many Arab intellectuals in the first half of this century, was extremely aware of the historical contradictions of the Arab people and sought to propagate enlightenment themes at the expense of the return to a sublime past. Neither Ṭāhā Ḥussain nor Salāma Mūsa was a Marxist in any sense of the word, although both sought radical epistemological transformations in the mental worldview of the Arab people. Mūsa, on the other hand, had strong socialist leanings. This is why many say that he was the forerunner of socialist thought in the modern Arab world.[84]

The nineteenth century saw the rise of capitalism on a world scale, to use Samir Amin's favorite term, which betrayed in a sense the economic weaknesses of the Arab world. The Arab thinkers of the nineteenth century were fully aware of the plight of their societies, as mentioned earlier, and they pioneered the first Nahḍah in the modern Arab world.[85] There is reason to believe that the first Nahḍah never materialized in full, in the sense that it did not produce a mass movement in the Arab world, although it encouraged the creation of a significant number of Arab thinkers who were indebted to this Nahḍah in various ways. However, the sense of failure of the first Nahḍah and even the second Nahḍah, begun after independence, is at the heart of the modern Arab Marxist discourse. According to Karīm Muruwwa, a member of the politburo of the Lebanese Communist Party, only internal reasons can explain the failure of the first Nahḍah and the emergence of the Arab Left to deal with this problem. The problem is the result of an historical alliance between several forms of authority: the authority of the dominant religious discourse, which is devoid of real religious values; the authority of the religious institutions, which, according to Muruwwa, are the most backward institutions in Arab society; the authority of the foreign occupier, especially the Ottoman and the British, and, finally, the authority of those national regimes that disdain democracy.[86] Muruwwa argues that it was almost impossible to come up with a creative Arab Marxist discourse because even in the history of the Marxist worldwide movement, creative theoretical production was difficult, except in a few cases: that of Gramsci in Italy and Mao in China. With Arab Marxism early on, theoretical creativity was difficult for the following reasons: (1) the youthful nature of the Marxist movement, and (2) the Arab countries, lying under the Ottoman domination for centuries, fell prey to imperialist Western domination before they were able to achieve independence.[87]

Parallel to the development of socialist Arab thought in the interwar period, a number of Arab communist parties began to emerge, especially under the impact of Stalinism.[88] One must note that in several Arab countries, especially Egypt, Morocco and Algeria, the leaders of the communist parties belonged to the different minority groups and upper classes.[89] In recording the history of the communist movement in Egypt, Rif‘at al-Sa‘īd discovered that most of the leaders were not just of foreign extraction but Jewish, as well. For a number of Jewish intellectuals in Egypt in the interwar period, Marxism was a viable option in their fight against anti-Semitism and Nazism.[90] The establishment of the Arab communist parties was not necessarily a logical outcome of the evolution of Arab socialist or communist thought or the organization of the oppressed members of the working class or peasantry into a radical organization as much as it was the outcome of institutional alliances with the Stalinist Soviet Union. The almost total dependency of the Arab Communist Parties on the Soviet Union forced them to succumb to the policies of the Soviet Union, especially in relation to the nationalist question and the question of Israel. It also forced official Arab Marxist thought to borrow the Stalinist philosophy on a number of questions *in toto*. In other words, Arab Marxism did not develop a unique Arab philosophical or intellectual expression. In a perceptive article, Egyptian Marxist Ghālī Shukrī notes that the Arab Marxists failed to articulate an Arab Marxist vision because of their class background (most if not all belonged to the upper bourgeoisie), police repression, and the widespread illiteracy in the Arab world.[91] Hence it dealt with unreal problematics or with real issues in an idealistic manner.[92] More often than not, dogmatic Arab Marxism did not create the necessary conditions for autonomous and critical Marxism.[93]

What has haunted a number of Arab Marxist thinkers since the death of Stalin has been their inability to develop mature Marxist theorization that is specifically Arab, or that reflects the historical, social, and economic conditions of the Arab world in the twentieth and twenty-first centuries. This notion underlies the work of a number of prominent Arab Marxists, most notably Ḥussain Muruwwa in

Arab-Islamic theology and mysticism, Ṣādiq Jalāl al-'Azm in philosophical and religious criticism, and the Egyptian Aḥmad Sādiq Sa'd in the economic and social history of Egypt.[94]

Because of the Soviet alliance with the West at one stage in World War Two, the Arab communists were asked not to raise questions of nationalist independence and were expected to endorse the creation of Israel in 1948. Neither nationalism nor religion weighed heavily in the thought of Arab communism in this period. Both issues were trivialized. To my mind, this is the real beginning of the crisis of Arab communism. Arab communism failed to express the real concerns of the Arab world in the first half of the twentieth century since it followed outside dictates.[95] In other words, Arab Marxism failed to articulate its own brand of autonomous intellectuals who refuse to be dictated to by an organized and disciplinarian Marxist orthodoxy. Maxime Rodinson highlights this point in much of his writings on the Middle East.[96]

The establishment of Israel in 1948, the death of Stalin in 1952, and the coming to power of Arab nationalist regimes in the 1950s created a totally new environment for the Communist Parties and the Arab Left in general. The Arab Left began to take the nationalist issue more seriously to the extent that in some countries, especially in Egypt and Algeria in the 1960s, the communist parties dissolved themselves and entered into alliance with the ruling bloc.

As with all communist parties in the world, the Arab Left faced a tremendous challenge with the collapse of the Soviet system in 1989 and the official end of the Cold War. One may ironically state that the collapse of the Soviet Union freed Arab Communist Parties and the Left from its dictates and created a favorable atmosphere of self-criticism in the Arab Left. It is important to stress here that the collapse of the Soviet system did not mean the end of the Arab or the international Left. However, the end of the Soviet system abroad and the triumph of the authoritarian forces in the Arab world, especially after the military defeat of Iraq in the second Gulf War, created a difficult situation for the Arab Left and the forces of change in general. Fukuyama's prophecy of the final triumph of capitalism has haunted the imagination of the Arab Left.[97] Alas, his basic arguments of the triumph of neo-liberalism seem to be realized.

In addition to these above factors, internal developments in the Arab world after independence had a marked influence on the Arab Left. The support prominent Marxists gave to Nasserism in 1964 contrasts sharply with the Marxist-nationalist anomaly in the Iraqi state after the communist take-over of the state under General 'Abdul Karīm Qāsim in 1958. Ba'thism and the rule of Qāsim were oxymoronic. On the other hand, the support given by the Egyptian Communist Party to the Nasserite version of Arab nationalism and socialism underlined the importance, from an Arab Leftist perspective, of the Arab Left to collaborate with Arab nationalism in the hopes that Arab nationalism was a stage in the society's transition toward full socialism, as understood by the Arab Left.[98] The fact that the Nasserite experiment in "Arab socialism" received a severe blow in 1967 and was finally dethroned by Sadat and the revived old capitalist classes, who were derailed by the Nasser regime, posed major a dilemma to the Arab Left, at least in Egypt. This dilemma became more acute when it was clear by the mid 1970s that no Arab country was able to take the lead in institutionalizing "Arab socialism" in the same way as Nasserism had done only a decade or two earlier.

In addition to the failure of Arab socialism, which in essence meant the Arab Left, and the *de facto* failure of its alliance with Arab nationalism, the working classes in Arab society, just like the middle classes, failed to develop their consciousness along Marxist/socialist lines and chose instead to dwell on the meaning of their religious identity. The development of the Islamic consciousness of the working and middle classes, although born of societal and political crises, started a brand new movement of Islamic expression at the national Arab level, which was later augmented by two factors: first, conservative Gulf regimes' use of this "consciousness" to support their political and economic *status quo*. Islamic publications and well-known Muslim thinkers were given attention in these states. Second was the Iranian revolution of 1978 and 1979 which gave further new energy, in spite of the Shīʿī character of the revolution, to Muslim activists that the Islamic solution was not just theoretically grounded but had ample practical applications.

However, in the larger Arab context after 1967 it is not just the working and middle classes that took an "Islamic turn," the failure of Arab nationalism also meant the derailment of the Arab decolonization process that was actually at its height in North Africa (Tunisia, Morocco, and Algeria) in the late 1950s and early 1960s and in Southern Arabia (Yemen) in the 1960s. Nasserism was a powerful champion of decolonization, especially in Algeria and Yemen. However, the impasse faced by Nasserism after 1967 damaged the cause of Arab decolonization (Palestine is an example) and, in a fundamental sense, unleashed the power of the conservative Arab regimes in the Gulf to take leading roles in the Arab world in the wake of the collapse of Nasserism.[99]

A combination of important factors enabled the conservative Gulf states to play a role of dominance in the Arab world after the collapse of Nasserism: first was the conservative Islamic ideology that they espoused. They put Islam to use, especially in their attacks on international communism and Arab nationalism. The second major factor was the growing need for oil in the industrial capitalist states in the decades of the 1960s and 1970s to supplement their accelerated process of industrialization. The capitalist West was engaged in a massive process of industrialization that demanded cheap oil. One of the major goals of such a massive industrialization was to drive international socialism, under the leadership of the Soviet Union, bankrupt. The economic policies of the Gulf states, notwithstanding the embargo in 1973 due to the Arab-Israeli war, were in line to support the industrial world with oil, which meant the enlargement of their coffers, and, as a consequence, their ability to modernize their societies, without creating an indigenous class of workers. The import of cheap labor first from the Arab world, and later from South Asia (Pakistan, India, Bangladesh, and Sri Lanka) and from Southeast Asia meant that these Gulf states were saved, for a while at least, from the hassle of dealing with a powerful indigenous working class. The huge influx of money in the 1970s and 1980s enabled the regimes of these states to buy the silence of many classes in society to spread their hegemony worldwide.

As can be seen, the Arab Left was not institutionally strong enough to deal with these huge changes in the Arab world. After the collapse of Nasserism, the Arab

Left was in a severe crisis, which was actually a prelude to the larger crisis affecting world socialism, including the Arab Left, in the wake of the collapse of the Soviet system. The period from the early 1970s to the early 1990s saw the migration of some of the best Arab Leftist minds to Europe and even Japan. This meant that in addition to disorientation, the criticism of the Arab Left was confined to a small exiled Leftist intelligentsia.

The following points summarize the main dimensions of the self-evaluation launched by the Arab Left in the wake of the collapse of the Soviet system:

1. the reasons for the collapse of the socialist system;
2. the role of the party and the intelligentsia in a new era that is dominated by the interests of one superpower, the United States;
3. the prevailing social and economic conditions in the Arab world and widening economic gaps between rich and poor;
4. the failure of the ruling Arab bourgeoisie to advance a viable social and economic project;
5. issues of nationalist liberation, Arab unity, social and economic independence in the age of neo-colonialism;
6. the Arab bourgeoisie, led primarily by the army after independence, has failed to secure nationalist liberation and solve social and economic problems. What can the Arab Left do to solve this continuing dilemma?
7. The gradual recolonization of the Arab world, including the Gulf region, after the defeat of Iraq in the second Gulf War;
8. the decline of oil revenues and the shifting of alliances in the Arab world;
9. the issue of religion. It is important here to transcend the classical Marxist and Leninist formulations of religion, especially when it comes to Islam and to one main brand of Islam, and Islam that fights imperialism and Israel.

The above issues determine, to a large extent, the current preoccupations of the Arab Left and its hard and long search to establish itself as a legitimate intellectual and organizational movement in the contemporary Arab world. For a long time, the Arab Left had been aware of its "foreign roots," so to speak, its dependence on external support, both in the institutional and conceptual senses. There is a need, however, to formulate issues in an Arab Marxist vocabulary. With the rise of the Soviet Union and especially after the creation of Israel in 1948 and the split taking place in the Arab world between the American and Soviet camps, one began to hear of Arab Communist Parties and intellectuals subscribing to one form or another of Marxism.[100] To evaluate Marxist thought in the Arab world, I would like to quote the following from one of its prominent contemporary representatives, the Egyptian Maḥmūd Amīn al-ʿĀlim, who argues that,

> As of yet, no comprehensive Marxist theory, that is specifically Arab, has emerged. In each Arab country, there are some programmatic and activist Marxist ventures that lack deep and meaningful theoretical insights. And that is why Arab Marxist thought remains theoretically aloof and confined to a small circle of elite intellectuals, especially after the collapse and disintegration of the Soviet Union

> and the Socialist camp in general. The socialist experiment in South Yemen, for example, exemplified a tragic dissonance between the elitist theoretical Marxist discourse and the tribal and backward reality of the country.[101]

However damaging this evaluation might be, one must not forget that a good number of Arab thinkers, who subscribed to Marxist ideas and methods of analysis, contributed major theoretical studies about the economic, political, cultural, and religious histories of the Arab world. These thinkers, many of whom were the product of the post-independence phase, were witness to the great historical transformations in their societies and the transition of their countries from the grip of imperialism to the sphere of independence.

Because of the two major factors, that is, the rise of the Soviet Union to world power, especially after the defeat of Nazism in World War Two, and the independence of a great number of Arab countries, the Arab Left, aided by a number of Marxist theories, embraced social change as its major goal. It is possible, therefore, to outline the main characteristics of Arab Marxist discourse as follows: The Arab Left, according to Shawkī Jalāl, is a movement of social criticism that aimed, from the beginning, to introduce drastic changes into the social structure of Arab society as a means of achieving progress and catching up with the advanced West. For this movement to have succeeded, the following conditions must have been present: first, a deep understanding of the system of knowledge and the socio-political conditions that were responsible for stagnation and decline in the Arab world; second, launching a daring enlightenment project that betrays the domination of false-consciousness in Arab society and the absence of harmony between the needs of the modern age and the inherited patterns of thinking, especially of the Salafīyyah movement. It would have been necessary to present a coherent rational, critical and radical theoretical project to deal with the basic underlying issues and problems of Arab society in the twentieth century. Third, to possess a program of political and social change; fourth, to be aware of local and international conditions; fifth, to possess the conceptual and programmatic means to fulfill the above strategies; and sixth, to engage in self-criticism.[102]

However, just like al-ʻĀlim, Jalāl argues that the Arab Left failed to achieve its major goals for the following reasons: instead of producing a comprehensive and radical theoretical project, it produced a partial ideological discourse that lacked real insight into the nature of things in Arab society. Besides failing to generate a mass social movement to reflect its real social concerns, the Arab Left shied away from any self-criticism which left its discourse quite remote from the real conditions of Arab society.

One may argue that the Salafī trend in the Arab world has not met the same failure as the Left. At least certain Salafī movements, such as the Ikhwān, gained a wide popular support and some, as in the Sudan, gained power until recently. This might be ascribed to the fact that the Islamic discourse did not remain in the possession of an isolated elite but, because of the nature of the Islamic congregation, was popularized day by day. Here is the advantage that Salafī discourse has over that of the Leftist in the Arab world: the relatively easy access, in spite of the attempt of some governments to clamp down on the Islamists, to popular religious places. Also, it must be noted that the Salafī discourse, *à la* Ikhwān or Jihad, has a radical political and social agenda. The early social writings of such thinkers as Muḥammad al-Ghazālī, Yūsuf al-Qaraḍāwī, and Sayyid Quṭb bear this out.

The above criticism of the Arab Left must not, in any way, obscure the philosophical, political and intellectual contributions of a good number of Arab Marxist thinkers, philosophers, and political activists to debates about the central issues of the Arab world. Some of these Arab Marxist thinkers have also contributed to the debate about the state of the Third World and Western capitalism. It is important to note the contributions of the following people: Ḥussain Muruwwa, Mahdī 'Āmil, Fawwāz Tarābulsī, and Karīm Muruwwa from Lebanon; Yāssin al-Ḥāfiz, Eliās Murqus, Ṣādiq Jalāl al-'Azm, and Ṭayyib Tizīnī from Syria; Emile Habībī, Nājī 'Allūsh, Māher al-Sharīf, Hishām Sharābī from Palestine; Samir Amin, and the *Ṭalī'ah* editorial board: Lutfī al-Khūlī, Ibrahim Ṣabrī 'Abdallah, Fu'ād Mursī, and Rif'at al-Sa'īd; Aḥmad Ṣādiq Sa'd, Ghālī Shukrī, and Nawal El Saadawi from Egypt; Abdallah Laroui from Morocco; Talal Asad from Saudi Arabia (USA); and Hādī al-'Ulwī from Iraq.

Far from being monolithic in thought, the Leftist trend in the modern Arab world premises its assessment of the "Other" on either a critical evaluation of the "Islamic tradition" or a total dismissal of this tradition as anachronistic religious thought. On the one hand, there are some serious Leftist intellectuals in the Arab world, such as Ṭayyib Tizīnī, Ḥussain Muruwwa, Hādī al-'Ulwī, Ṭawfīq Sallūm, and Maḥmūd Amīn al-'Ālim, who have taken an in-depth look at classical Muslim thought, distilling from it what they consider to be a universal dimension which is, in their view viable in the modern world. In other words, they argue that the classical Islamic tradition possesses a universal epistemology that encourages rationalism, human liberty, openness to the "Other," and appropriation of knowledge. This epistemology belongs to the modern Arabs as much as they belong to the rest of the world. On the other hand, there is another Leftist current of thought, best represented by Salāma Mūsa, Mahdī 'Āmil, Ṣādiq Jalāl al-'Azm, Adonis ('Alī Aḥmad Saī'd), Fawwāz Tarābulsī, Maḥmūd Amīn al-'Ālim, Yāssin al-Ḥāfiz, and Abdallah Laroui, that relentlessly attacks past tradition and considers it as a hindrance toward progress.

According to Yāssin al-Ḥāfiz, for instance, the modern Arab world has been dominated by traditionalist or Salafī ideology (read anti-modernity), which has left a negative impact on a huge number of the Arab intelligentsia, a sign of the internal defeat of the Arab mind and soul. He further maintains that "dogmatic ideologies and conceptions" dominate the modern Arab intellectual environment for the following reasons:

1. schools are unable to teach Arabic in the modern spirit;
2. history is taught in an ideological and partisan way;
3. sciences are taught in a rigid manner;
4. religious education is presented in a traditional and sectarian way;
5. no interest is shown in teaching foreign languages.

He bitterly criticizes the university experience in many an Arab country and concludes that university life has been in decline for the following reasons:

1. liberal thought has been in retreat;
2. free thinking has not emerged as a coherent pattern of thought;
3. a *de facto* separation of university and society exists.

The only solution to this state of affairs is the acceptance of critical Marxism.

Adonis follows in the footsteps of al-Ḥāfiz and argues that there is a predominance of traditional (also read backward, paralyzed, and anti-modern) modes of thinking and cultural and social patterns in modern Arab society. Traditional modes of thinking are maintained by the family, school, university, and mass media, which are to Adonis, to use a favorite Althusserian phrase, the ideological state apparatuses. Adonis argues that the dominant ideological system in the Arab world, far from establishing new conditions and new relationships reproduces the past, exploiting relationships. This dominant ideology is a re-embodiment of the past exploiting ideology, and any superficial political change is no more than a replacement of an old exploitative class by a new one. The modern Arab family is still in the grip of a theocratic-tribal formation, and Arab education is indeed reactionary in both the contents and method of its teaching. Moreover, religion still dominates all of civil life, as well political, legal, and cultural life. Class consciousness is hidden under the impact of religious domination.[103] Adonis maintains that "Arab society still remains in its dominant ideological structure very traditional. Nonetheless, it is led ideologically by a pioneering elite in the direction of modernity." Only a genuine conceptual and systemic revolution that reverses religious and tribal domination would ensure a gradual progression of Arab society toward modernity. In the opinion of many a radical thinker, "revolutionary ideology and religion are essentially contradictory and that religion has not contributed to the Arab struggle against imperialism."[104]

Laroui's thought represents the best example of the Marxist critique of tradition. In his view, the cleric, as the guardian of tradition, cannot rid himself of the ancient polarization and conflict between Islam and Christianity. Laroui claims that he still thinks according to these defunct categories. Thus his religious consciousness does not allow him to grasp the fundamental changes taking place in the West since the Renaissance and their distinctive secular traits. Nonetheless, the religious consciousness of the cleric is marred by a duality, "The conscience of our cleric is religious when he analyzes society, but he becomes liberal when he critiques the West."[105] Also, he dismisses the liberal and nationalist trends as somewhat subscribing to past rules and ideas. Laroui argues that the only means to do away with the traditionalist mode of thinking "consists in strict submission to the discipline of historical thought and acceptance of all its assumptions." Laroui is not quite clear about the real nature of this historical school. Yet his challenge to the functioning categories of the modern Arab mind still awaits an answer.

Leftist thinkers, on the whole, believe in a universal civilization as the progressive "Other." Their analysis of the contemporary Arab world focuses on what they see as widespread mechanisms of social and economic exploitation supported by both "official Islam" and world capitalism. To emancipate the Arab world from its dependency on the outside world, Arab thought must be engaged with critical modernity.

One must note the following about the different trends of Arab thought:

(a) They are not by any means static or mutually exclusive. One may speak of a "Leftist-Islamic" current,[106] or a nationalist-religious current or a liberal-Marxist current;
(b) no classification is monolithic. For example, in the Islamic current, one may discuss such sub-currents as Salafī thought, Wahhabi, Ikhwān, and Sufi thought. Even the Ikhwān thought may be subdivided into Jihad thought, Jamā'ah al-Islāmiyyah, Taḥrīr, and so on;[107]
(c) no classification remains static, that is, one must view each classification in a changing social and economic context.

Each pattern of thought must be examined in light of political and social developments while focusing on the essentials of thought and their adaptation to or understanding of reality; official and counter-official thought. It is important to determine whether a pattern of thought, or a subdivision thereof, represents an official or counter-official thought. For example, whereas the Ikhwān thought of the Islamic movement, represented by Ḥassan al-Turābī and his followers, and its different offshoots, was dominant in the Sudan until quite recently, it is a counter-thought in many Arab countries. It has assumed an oppositional status to the point of a bloody encounter with the state in Syria in the early 1980s and with the military in Algeria in the 1990s.[108] It has also found a legal oppositional role in the semi-democratic political atmosphere of Jordan in the 1990s. One must note that "official thought" is also subject to change. One example is Egypt. In deconstructing the official cultural scene since 1952, one finds that between 1952 and 1970 (Nasserism) there was a strange amalgam of official culture that combined such "Leftist" intellectuals as Maḥmūd Amīn al-'Ālim, Lewis 'Awad, Ṣalāḥ 'Abd al-Ṣabūr, Sa'd al-Dīn Wahbah, 'Abd al-'Azīm Anīs, Ghālī Shukrī, Sherīf Ḥitātah with such "Rightist" intellectuals as 'Azīz Abāza, al-'Aqqād, Sālih Jawdat, Muḥammad Jalāl Kishik, and Yūsuf al-Sibā'ī.[109] This confusion in official culture led one of the most astute observers of modern Egyptian culture to note that the most salient feature of "official thought" in post-1967 Egypt is its lack of a system of thought.[110] However, as one ponders the state of official thought at the turn of the twenty-first century, one may realize that the Arab political elite, most of whom come from a military background, rely on a number of principles in order to preserve their power; these classifications are more ideological than purely academic or "objective." Each current has a worldview or a mental reference and a vision with certain goals to achieve. For example, even after the collapse of the Soviet system in 1989, the Left in the Arab world still speaks about dialectics, class struggle, social justice, neo-imperialism, and the creation of a just and socialist society.

Since these currents are ideological in nature, I prefer to use the above classifications rather than the more academic, such as social, economic, political, philosophical, or religious thought (in the academic sense); the above classifications may not clarify the confusion surrounding some of the most important terms or concepts used in contemporary Arab thought, such as *'ilmāniyyah* (that is, secularism), *uṣūliyyah* (fundamentalism or integrism), and *liberaliyyah* (liberalism). These terms are used by contemporary Arab thinkers, depending upon their ideological bent, to mean different things. The term *uṣūliyyah* is used by the Islamic current to generally denote a return to and reconstruction of the origins of Islam, the period of the Prophet, in the current situation. Other currents use this term in a critical if not pejorative fashion. The term *liberaliyyah* is used to denote a particular phase in modern European history that was distinguished by (a) the rise of the bourgeoisie in its triumph against feudalism with the inauguration of the Industrial Revolution (around the fifteenth century) and (b) the expansion of bourgeois Europe overseas in the guise of imperialism.[111] The essential philosophy of liberalism lies in defending free trade and individual rights, confining religion to the personal sphere and creating a new set of ethics that are not necessarily tied to religious ethics. The political philosophy of liberalism centers around the rule of a class and not that of an individual. The nineteenth century saw the rise of some liberal ideas in the Arab world as a result of colonialism. According to Muḥammad 'Imārah, the nineteenth century Muslim reform movement of Afghānī and 'Abduh was influenced by a number of liberal ideas that reflected, in essence, the genesis of a small bourgeois Egyptian class whose aim it was to liberate itself from the constraints of "individual politics" as practiced in the East.[112] Liberalism was tried in Egypt between 1924 and 1952 and, after de-Nasserization in the early 1970s, came back in the guise of the economic Open Door policy and economic reform. To many Leftist and Islamist thinkers, this type of liberalism is a new form of economic dependence on the West.[113]

CONCLUSIONS

Recolonization is a factual reality in the contemporary Arab world. One need only look at both Iraq and Palestine at the beginning of the twenty-first century. The nationalist movement initiated the process of decolonization, which led to political and cultural independence in the Arab world in the 1950s and the 1960s. A few decades later, recolonization set in and became an entrenched reality by the end of the twentieth century. Contemporary Arab thought faces the formidable dilemma of recolonization. It seems to me that the integrity of every main representative current of Arab thought depends on the creative solutions it might offer to this challenge. Achieving national independence under the current condition must be the criterion against which one can judge the integrity of thought.

I have discussed several representative trends of thought in post-1967 Arab intellectual history. In a sense, there are several planes of thought or perspectives dominating contemporary Arab intellectual discourse. All the above trends, except perhaps the liberal, advocate a radical change in the state of affairs in the contemporary Arab world, ranging from the political elite to economic and social conditions. The Islamic, nationalist, and Marxist trends advocate a number of methods, both peaceful and violent, to secure the envisioned changes. Perhaps the liberal trend is the only one to advocate a democratic method of transition to a better future.

The above trends more or less tackle the same questions and problematics besetting the contemporary Arab world, albeit with methods of analysis that are grounded in different worldviews and philosophies. Since all major contemporary Arab thinkers speak of a pervasive sense of crisis in Arab society, a number of them have launched a wave of self-criticism. This is most apparent in both the Islamist and Marxist trends.

Human thought, however normative it may be, is grounded in historical and social realities. Arab thought is historical in nature; it has delved into various questions with the view to offer solutions to the questions and challenges facing the Arab world. Furthermore, because of the modern conditions, that is, Western superiority over the Arab world in the past several decades, modern and contemporary Arab thought, in its various forms and representations, has fallen under the conceptual influence of outside worldviews. It is almost hard to find a major contemporary Arab thinker who has been able to escape the problematic of modernity. Contemporary Arab thought is, in large measure, the product of modern factors and circumstances, including capitalism, imperialism, science, and progress. What that means in essence is that one must seek the origins of modern Arab thought in the nineteenth century, especially in the historic encounter between two different worldviews: Arab-Islamic and Western. This encounter provided fertile ground for the emergence of the basic intellectual trends in contemporary Arab thought.

The modern crisis in the Arab world, engendered by the imposition of aggressive modernity on, more or less, a traditional worldview and structure in the eighteenth and nineteenth centuries, has challenged to the core the epistemological components of the Islamic worldview and released in the modern Arab mind new forms of expressions that emerged in order to account for new conditions.[114]Although the traditional Muslim intelligentsia, as seen above, resorted to traditional methods in order to come to grips with the shock of modernity, they had to learn the language of the advanced Other in order to uphold the spirit of the Sacred. The most prominent contemporary Muslim thinkers in the Arab world have always associated the dignity of the Sacred with the dignity of the human being. This necessarily entails a radical criticism of prevalent social, economic, and political conditions in the Arab world. In a sense, the Islamic trend vied with the Marxist-Leftist trends in dealing with these issues. Thus, one may speak of an Islamic theory of capitalism or imperialism, as in the writings of Sayyid Quṭb of Egypt, Muḥammad Bāqir al-Ṣadr of Iraq, and Muḥammad Ḥussain Faḍlallah of Lebanon.

A number of prominent Arab thinkers postulate that crisis is at the heart of Arab society and thought and that all attempts at renaissance in the nineteenth century met a deadly failure in the twentieth century. The Islamist Abdul Hamid Abu-Sulayman claims that crisis has been the main characteristic of Arab and Muslim thought since the beginning of the formative phase of Islam. In other words, the roots of the contemporary crisis go back deep in history and that they are political in nature.[115] Abdallah Laroui poses the question of crisis in a different way: it is not just historical in nature but above all is epistemological in nature. Contemporary Arab thought is mostly Salafī; it has not yet freed itself from the

Sacred.[116] Most Arab Marxists would agree with Laroui's hypothesis.[117] Ḥassan Ḥanafī, representing the Islamic Left, argues that all the hopes of nineteenth century Arab thinkers have dissolved into thin air and that all progressive projects produced negative results: rationalism gave way to superstition; liberation from imperialism gave way to neo-imperialism; civil liberties led to imprisonment and oppression and national liberation led to a new occupation, mainly Israeli and American.[118] I think that crisis, *per se*, has been a key factor in regenerating and bringing to new light major debates about various issues. It is quite easy to argue that the Arab world, in spite of some outstanding achievements in the fields of industry and education, still suffers from dependency, social and economic gaps, authoritarian regimes, and the absence of real democratic values.

I think it is important to distinguish Arab thought as a complex theoretical structure belonging to various worldviews from Arab society, as a social and historical reality. No one can deny the challenges posed by modernity since the early part of the nineteenth century. Most Arab thinkers are united on the notion that Arab society has been in the grip of crisis since that time, at least. However, it is hard to pass the same judgment on Arab thought, since, as we have seen, it has been able to regenerate itself either through self-criticism or the necessity of finding theoretical solutions to the many problems of the Arab world.

Since 1967, Arab thought has dealt with a number of political crises both regional and international in nature: the 1973 war between the Arab world and Israel, the 1982 Israeli invasion of Lebanon, the Iran–Iraq war (the first Gulf War), and the 1991 Gulf War in the wake of the Iraqi invasion of Kuwait. These major events forced contemporary Arab thought to reflect on the nature of Arab society and its alliances with the West.

3
Secularism and its Hazards: The Recent Debate in the Arab World

"A significant aspect of the post-colonial structures of knowledge in the Third World is a peculiar form of imperialism of categories. Under such imperialism, a conceptual domain is sometimes hegemonized by a concept produced and honed in the West, hegemonized so effectively that the original domain vanishes from our awareness." Ashis Nandy, "The Politics of Secularism and the Recovery of Religious Tolerance," in Rajeev Bhargava, ed., *Secularism and its Critics* (New Delhi: Oxford University Press, 1998), 321.

"I am now convinced, that no great improvements in the lot of mankind are possible, until a great change takes place in the fundamental constitution of their modes of thought. The old opinions in religion, morals, and politics, are so much discredited in the more intellectual minds as to have lost the greater part of their efficacy for good, while they have still life enough in them to be a powerful obstacle to the growing up of any better opinions on those subjects." John Stuart Mill, quoted in George W. Foote, *Secularism Restated with a Review of Several Expositions* (London: W. J. Ramsey, 1874), 1.

"Defeat goes deeper into the human soul than victory. To be in someone else's power is a conscious experience, which induces doubts about the ordering of the universe, while those who have power can forget it, or can assume that it is part of the natural order of things and invent or adopt ideas, which justify their possession of it." Albert Hourani, *A History of the Arab People* (Cambridge, MA: Harvard University Press, 1991), 300–1.

"We are…confronted with one of the most vexing aspects of advanced industrial civilization: the rational character of its irrationality. Its productivity and efficiency, its capacity to increase comforts, to turn waste into needs, and destruction into construction, the extent to which this civilization transforms the object world into an extension of man's mind and body makes the very notion of alienation questionable. The people recognize themselves in their commodities; they find their soul in their automobile, hi-fi set, split-level home, kitchen equipment. The very mechanism which ties the individual to his society has changed, and social control is anchored in the new needs which it has produced." Herbert Marcuse, *One-Dimensional Man* (Boston: Beacon Press, 1964), 9.

> "The chief danger which always confronts a society is the desire of those who possess power to prohibit ideas and conduct which may disturb them in their possession. They are rarely concerned with the possible virtues of novelty and experiment. They are interested in the preservation of a static society because in such an order their desires are more likely to be fulfilled." Harold J. Laski, *Liberty in the Modern State* (Harmondsworth: Penguin Books, 1938), 207.

In 1988, a major debate took place in Cairo around the viability of religious discourse in the contemporary Arab world. This debate summarizes some of the central problematics underlying contemporary Arab thought.[1] Three distinguished intellectuals were featured: Muḥammad al-Ghazālī, Yūsuf al-Qaraḍāwī, and Fu'ād Zakariyya. It has become a tradition in the modern Arab world, especially in Egypt, to speak of the secularist–Islamist split or debate.[2] Many have joined this debate and some, like Egyptian thinker Faraj Fūda, have fallen victim to its fiery consequences. Others, like Naṣr Ḥāmid Abū Zayd, were forced into exile because they were found wanting, religiously speaking.[3] Even some known for their strong Islamic propensities have been declared apostate, such as Cairo University Islamic Philosophy Professor Ḥassan Ḥanafī, who was charged by the Azhar Scholars' Front, now defunct, of being "responsible for a destructive scheme against which the entire Islamic nation should be mobilized."[4] The secularist–Islamist split is a phenomenon, a dangerous one indeed. We speak here not just of polarization, disagreement or a lack of common intellectual reference, but of what seems to be a restrictive intellectual atmosphere that inhibits freedom of expression. Further, this polarization has obscured the serious issue of secularism and religion with clichés and empty words. Alas, complains contemporary Islamist Egyptian thinker Fahmī Huwaydī, "For a moment, I have realized that the current debates about secularism in our Arab world are very simplistic at best."[5] On the other hand, a leading secularist Arab thinker complains about the continuous rejection of secularism by a large number of Arab and Muslim thinkers, "Is the source of this rejection the fact that secularism hails from the West or is it due to the gulf between the Western and Arab mentalities?"[6] This debate is a continuation, in one way or another, of several earlier debates in modern Arab intellectual history, similar to the one waged by both Ṭāhā Ḥussain and 'Alī 'Abd al-Rāziq in the 1920s and 1930s against the Azhar, and the one waged by Khālid Muḥammad Khālid against religious conservatism in the 1940s and early 1950s.[7]

This debate continues under the close scrutiny of the contemporary Arab state. The Arab political and military elite enjoy such a debate so long as it does not threaten the state's political authority, bureaucratic control, and its definition of social stability. The state feels secure as long as it protects this type of debate. The pioneering generation of such Arab secularists as Farah Anṭūn, Ya'qūb Ṣarrūf, Ṭāhā Ḥussain, Salāma Mūsa, and 'Alī 'Abd al-Rāziq fought hard to establish a modern Arab secularist movement to be guided by the central tenets of the European Enlightenment,[8] which had raised the following mottos: "take the risk of discovery, exercise the right of unfettered criticism, accept the loneliness of autonomy."[9] Taking these to heart, the early Arab secularist movement ushered into the Arab world a novel genre of critical writing that affected almost every aspect of Arab society, thus forcing modern Arab thought to include consideration of some critical questions facing Arab society.[10]

If one were to define secularism, as does the eminent scholar Fazlur Rahman, as "the acceptance of laws and other social and political institutions without reference to Islam, i.e., without their being derived from, or originally linked with, the principles of the Qur'an and the Sunna,"[11] then one would be tempted to speak of two types of secularisms in the modern Arab and Muslim world: one is historically medieval in background and the second is of modern Western creation.[12] There is some historical truth to what has been proposed by the eminent Islamist, Shaykh Muḥammad al-Ghazālī, and popularized in the West by Abdul Hamid Abu-Sulayman, that from the very beginning of Islam, the political elite in medieval Muslim societies placed a wedge between their political authority and the main sources of Islam, that is, the Qur'an and the Sunnah.[13] In other words, Muslim political institutions in the formative phase (seventh to twelfth century CE) did not derive their teachings or inspiration from primary Islamic sources. There is ample room here to meditate on the relationship between politics and religion in early Islamic history; however, it suffices to say that the early Muslim political elite (that is, the Ummayyad and 'Abbaside elite) were primarily concerned about maintaining their political authority, which they did by enhancing the political and legal institutions they inherited from the conquered civilizations of Persia and Byzantium.[14]

The second type of secularism is of recent origin and conforms in the main to the central rational ideas of the European Enlightenment. This secularism emerged after a series of political and religious transformations wrought by European society over a period of several centuries. In other words, it achieved its maturity in the high season of European imperialism in the nineteenth century only after such notions as nationalism, humanism, and rationalism became the cornerstones of the modern European mind. Secularism was the hallmark of the nineteenth century European West.

If the above formulation about the two types of secularism is valid, one may then speak of the historical crisis of the "Arab secularist movement," which has lately been on the increase. Originally, this crisis stemmed from, first, the failure of the classical Arab secularism movement of the nineteenth century, in both its Christian and Muslim components, to establish bridges between "medieval Muslim secularism" and the European type it hoped to emulate and, second, from the fact that the triumphant European colonialism of the nineteenth century spoon-fed its version of secularism to some indigenous intelligentsia in the Arab world, who were the products of the indigenous bourgeoisie and who had gone to the schools of the West.[15] In other words, the Arab secularist movement failed to produce a hybrid secularism or its own version of independent "Arab secularism."

On the whole, the political elite in the Arab world, a small minority compared to the larger society, have jumped on the bandwagon of Western secularism without actually understanding its historical background, intellectual premises, and general objectives.[16] Their intellectual laziness and lack of vision in reorganizing their societies did not much help the cause of Arab secularism. Neither has the fact that a substantial number of the ruling elite in the Arab world hail from military backgrounds helped in enhancing the intellectual independence of the Arab secularist movement. The recent alliance in some Arab countries between the secularist camp and the political elite has merely aggravated the dilemma of Arab secularism and made it look suspicious in the eyes of the masses.

To my mind, the predicament of Arab secularism is not caused by the fanaticism of this or that religious trend, but by the deadly hold the political elite have on Arab society and their intolerance of any critical voice. In an age of advanced technology, the contemporary political elite in the Arab state find themselves armed to the teeth to protect themselves against their own citizens. Convinced that religion is its true enemy, the Arab secularist movement has sided with the state against the possibility of political and public expression of religion. The complicity of the contemporary secular Arab intelligentsia with the political elite is an attempt to drive a wedge between transcendence and moral/social values in Arab society.[17] In an age of global religious resurgence, can the Arab political elite be tolerant of a dissenting religious voice that has a substantial mass following?[18] Why does it seem impossible to construct a new civil society in the Arab world with full Islamist participation? Why has the state in the Arab world resorted to violence and imprisonment to limit the Islamists? It is in the opinion of many astute observers of Islamism in the Arab world such as François Burgat that the Arab state in the 1980s resorted to repression instead of creative political solutions in dealing with Islamism.[19] This fact remains the most obvious in Arab states, such as Syria, Egypt, Algeria, Tunisia, and Morocco. One way to shed some light on this is to discuss the "secularism debate" in contemporary Arab thought.

In answering these questions, I will examine the roots of the secularism debate in both modern Western and Arab thought. The focus will be on the intellectual foundations of this debate in modern Western intellectual history, followed by an examination of the Arab context, especially since 1967.

INTELLECTUAL ORIGINS OF THE "SECULARISM DEBATE"

Scholars of Islam and Middle Eastern studies have questioned the compatibility of Islam and modernity and Islam and democracy for long.[20] Some believe that Islam can be compatible with democracy and secularism only if it is modernized. This statement does not mean much unless one interprets the modernization of Islam as emptying it of its theological principles or submitting its metaphysical foundations to thorough rational criticism. It is clear that Islam is a complex theological and historical phenomenon that is not amenable to simple definitions.[21] One way of approaching these questions is to tackle the issue of Islam and secularism.

The concept of secularization and its derivative "secularism" has elicited the most heated debate in both modern Western and Arab thought. Precisely capturing the history and development of the concept in modern Western intellectual history might be untenable,[22] but it suffices to argue that the term has been obfuscated by much confusion and ambiguity since its circulation in debate. As many scholars have noted, the term "secularism" carries various connotations and is impossible to accurately define.[23] There is much confusion in contemporary Arab writings about the notion of secularism, its intellectual foundations, historical progress, and current manifestations in both Western and Arab societies. For that reason, it is important to restate the position of post-1967 Arab thought, in its different discourses, on the question of secularism. Restating this question may ultimately lead us to understand the many inextricably intertwined questions and challenges facing contemporary Arab thought: the questions of democracy, civil society, rationalism, and the meaning of religion in post-1967 Arab society.

In this effort, I intend to do three things: (1) analyze the philosophical foundations of the term "secularism" in modern Western thought and the historical conditions responsible for its birth and development; (2) analyze the contemporary Arab intellectual response to secularism, which has generated two broad movements of thought: one supportive and the other antagonistic; and (3) discuss in some detail the ideas of Fu'ād Zakariyya, a leading secular Arab philosopher.

At the outset, I propose that the starting point of the contemporary Arab intellectual response to the issue of secularization is not the Muslim theological imperative, that is, state and religion as one, as some scholars have argued,[24] but the historical failure of "Arab modernism," the twin sister of Arab secularism, to articulate a true secularist vision and spearhead a meaningful process of drastic economic and social changes in society since independence from colonialism.[25] "Arab modernism" represents all the intellectual, economic, and political forces present in the Arab world since the early part of the nineteenth century that had aimed to modernize the Arab world while guided by the central tenets of Western modernism as developing historically since the beginning of the sixteenth century.[26] In this sense, the distinction drawn by Hishām Sharābī between "Arab Christian intellectuals" and "Muslim secularists" is untenable, since Arab modernism was an intellectual movement united more by class background than religious affiliation. One must draw a distinction between "Arab modernism" and "Muslim modernism" in the Arab world.[27]

While both responded to the same challenges generated by the Western intrusion in the Arab world in the nineteenth century and shared the vision of total reformation of Arab society, they nevertheless disagreed over both the method and scope of reform. The Muslim reform movement could not envisage reform without resuscitating the Muslim intellectual tradition or parts of it, whereas Arab reform was content to let go of the Muslim intellectual tradition. The Muslim reform movement reinvented a past in order to find its place in the present, whereas the Arab modernist movement focused more on the future than the past. The intellectual pioneers of Arab modernism proposed an ambitious project of modernizing Arab thought without the aid of Revelation or Sacred Text, which forms the central intellectual tradition in Islam. They believed, as in the case of 'Alī 'Abd al-Rāziq, that Islam did not prescribe any particular form of government, and that the future of Arab culture lies in appropriating the modern European tradition.[28] Faraḥ Anṭūn, the pioneer of secularism in modern thought, uses the term in three interchangeable ways: first, secularism does not acknowledge the philosophy of pan-Islamism, especially the wedding of the religious and political realms. Second, secularism means borrowing *en masse* the central ideas of the European Enlightenment, especially in the field of education, and third, secularism is guided by rationalism and is averse to the presuppositions of revelation.[29] Faraḥ Anṭūn's closest disciple, Salāma Mūsa, elaborates on the central tenets of Arab secularism. He argues the following points: first, the East is mentally and socially stagnant. Second, only radical scientific revolution can invigorate mental lethargy to complete freedom. Third, the West represents a model of modernization that the Orient must emulate. Fourth, besides science and technology, the East should discard its past cultural and literary expressions and embrace modern forms of expression. Literature must be connected to social praxis, and both literary criticism and the novel must be introduced to Arab audiences.[30] These arguments are reminiscent of those of Kemal Atatürk in Turkey, who was seen by many Arab secularist and nationalist thinkers as a true revolutionary.[31]

From the start, Arab modernism represented the aspirations of the nascent Arab bourgeoisie, which was too weak vis-à-vis the colonial bourgeoisie to cultivate its own version of secularism. The Arab bourgeoisie adopted the central tenets of Western liberalism, which had been universalized by Western colonialism. In other words, it uncritically accepted European claims of the post-Enlightenment discourse that secularism had universal characteristics that were not necessarily or specifically European. However, one must not assume that there was a simple relationship of correspondence between the Arab bourgeoisie and the post-Enlightenment system of knowledge.[32] Cut off from its indigenous intellectual milieu, it had no better option than to embrace some of the central claims of the European secular movement. From the beginning, however, the Arab modernist movement faced an anomaly: it sought to achieve liberation from colonialism with the aid of a Western worldview that had barely taken root in Arab soil. Secularism's great tragedy in the Arab world has been its complicity with European discourse without having the time or maturity to produce its own indigenous discourse.[33] This failure, to my mind, has unleashed Islamism as the most serious and unabashed contender of secularism in Arab society.

If modernity means the consciousness of being modern,[34] and modernization is the practical translation of this consciousness into institutional frameworks, secularization is the institutional embodiment of secularism. To be sure, modernization has been an inevitable process in the modern Arab world since the early days of colonialism. The history of modernization in the Arab world, written only from the perspective of Western modernization theorists and their Arab students (who carry the banner of modernization in leading Arab universities) has not been written in such a way as to reflect the anguish of the masses whom they claim to be modernizing. In addition, Arab modernism has shown less tolerance vis-à-vis the public expression of religion than its counterpart in the West. If not patronized by the state, that is, the Arab political elite, religion is usually repressed and as a result some religious elements go underground.

To recover modernization from its cultural engineers in the West, we must posit it as the embodiment of the colonial moment in the Arab world and the state or states that inherited this colonial moment. It is true that modernization, as well as urbanization, has been an inescapable political and social phenomenon. A mere vocal rejection of it does not suffice.[35] However, it is important to underline the fact that modernization was introduced into the Arab world under the auspices of triumphant colonialism and was the natural culmination of the philosophy of Western secularism. Many an Arab thinker of the nineteenth century and the early part of the twentieth, who did not question the association of secularism with colonialism, embraced the movement of secularism as a positive, scientific, and rational product of the European Enlightenment.[36] These thinkers argued that since the Arab world needed progress, it had to adopt secularism as its worldview.[37] Therefore, leading secular Arab intellectuals and elite have been in favor of applying such dichotomies as advanced–backward, and religious–secular when speaking of contemporary Arab and Muslim culture. Many have remained silent about the encounter between colonialism and indigenous cultures. As a matter of fact, many considered native cultures to be part of the *ancien régime* that do not warrant serious consideration. This philosophy advocated, at least in silence, the dismantling of the *ancien régime* and its ideological bases.

Modern Arab thought is not unique in its obsession with the impact of modern Western colonialism on its worldview. Modern African thought shares a similar preoccupation. According to one author, "the encounters between Europe and Africa have been anything but free and mutual. Instead of admitting the truth that it saw no purpose and would not really pursue such understanding, Western intellectual culture blessed its political atrocities with lies. One of these lies has been that it could dictate the terms of human convergence and impose them upon the recalcitrant."[38] In the same vein, Western political culture, which is dominant among the secular intellectual elite in the Arab world, has forgotten the errors it committed in its encounter with indigenous Muslim cultures. Fu'ād Zakariyya, one of the most brilliant philosophers in the contemporary Arab world, bypasses this plunder as an unintended historical oddity and advocates secularism as the most positive project of intellectual renaissance and as a civilizational necessity (*ḍarūrah ḥaḍāriyyah*) that Arabs must happily emulate.[39] In the same vein and in spite of his radical intellectual tendencies, Salāma Mūsa, the father of Arab secularism in the twentieth century, advocates borrowing *en masse* the Western intellectual and cultural foundations that made secularism and progress possible. He argues that without these foundations, no Third World society can achieve progress and renaissance.[40]

This chapter attempts to answer the following questions: first, has modernization achieved its stated goals in Arab society? Second, what impact has modernization had on traditional religious discourse in Arab society and, third, why has there been such a severe backlash against it in many Arab countries?

WESTERN SECULARISM

Secularism is a defining conceptual moment in the history of modern Western thought and reflects some important inner developments in modern Western civilization.[41] Since the sixteenth century, it has assumed some essential characteristics that, simply stated, do not tolerate the intervention of the Sacred in life's public domain.[42] This does not mean that secularism, as some Arab thinkers argue, is essentially irreligious or anti-religious. Secularists have in the past sought to limit and perhaps control the role of religion in public life.[43] According to Peter Berger,

> The term "secularization", and even more its derivative "secularism", has been employed as an ideological concept highly charged with evaluative connotations,

> sometimes positive and sometimes negative. In anti-clerical and "progressive" circles it has come to stand for the liberation of modern man from religious tutelage, while in circles connected with the traditional churches it has been attacked as "de-Christianization", "paganization", and the like.[44]

Secularism recognizes only the authority of reason and human conscience.[45]

While its proponents have not been averse to learning from the past, secularism disowns both the past and the sacred scripture as the basis of belief. It creates a new type of authority based entirely on the force of reason. However, one must not forget that the Enlightenment, as a modern philosophical and rational movement, invented classicism.[46] Its main function is to achieve rational truth with the aid of philosophical and scientific investigation. The authority of religious text (the *naṣṣ*, in the Islamic case) has no place in the philosophy of secularism, which leaves the field wide open to the free exercise of reason and all the implications thereof.

Berger, although warning of the impossibility of an accurate definition of secularization, argues that, "By secularization we mean the process by which sectors of society and culture are removed from the domination of religious institutions and symbols."[47] Here, secularization does not refer merely to a social-structural process but to a cultural: it refers to the decline of religious ideas and content in the cultural and intellectual lives of a people. As one Catholic French philosopher puts it, secularization, although of recent connotation, refers to a complex process of social and religious transformation in Christian life in the West that means the following: first, the recession of religious practice; second, the recession of the social influence of the clergy, and third, the recession of the sacred and normative ideas in society.[48]

Secularization has been a major force in Europe since the end of World War Two, mainly as a result of the expansion of urbanization. It has had significant influence on the political, scientific, social, moral, psychological, and cultural realms of life.[49] Although religion constitutes one of the most basic forms of expression and identity in modern Western public life, focus on it has lessened with urbanization.[50] The nineteenth century English thinker George W. Foote offers one potent classical definition of secularism. He defines secularism as naturalism in morality. To him, secularism is based on the following propositions: "Science is the only Providence, Reason the sole guide, Happiness the sole end."[51] Because of its very nature, concern with this world, "Secularism has no message respecting the great problems of theology."[52]

George Jacob Holyoake, one of the original proponents of secularism in nineteenth century English thought, defines secularism as follows:

> Secularism is the study of promoting human welfare by material means; measuring human welfare by the utilitarian rule, and making the service of others a duty of life...The Secular is sacred in its influence on life, for by purity of material conditions the loftiest natures are best sustained, and the lower the most surely elevated. Secularism is a series of principles intended for the guidance of those who find Theology indefinite, or inadequate, or deem it unreliable.

It replaces theology, which mainly regards life as a sinful necessity, as a scene of tribulation through which we pass to a better world."[53]

Moreover, secularism protects the right of the individual to think for oneself, to dissent, and voice one's ideas. No authority exists over that of reason. Secularism unleashes the human mind so that it may fulfill its unlimited potential and, by doing so, engenders fearless and critical thinking, impartial inquiry, and rational curiosity to a high level of respectability. Also, secular education refuses any "admixture of technology with it."[54]

Generally speaking, secularism in Western thought has assumed the following meanings:

1. Faith in reason alone. It is "the conflict of scepticism with faith,"[55] or the philosophical tendency to "do without religion,"[56] or a new trend of thought that "freed history from the parochialism of Christian scholars and from theological presuppositions, secularized the idea of causation and opened vast territories for historical inquiry."[57] Secularism is a revolt against metaphysics, and the inauguration of a new authority based on reason. It is "man's emergence from his self-incurred immaturity. Immaturity is the inability to use one's own understanding without the guidance of another."[58]
2. Secularism means a strict separation between religion and the public sphere. In the second part of the *Leviathan*, Hobbes presents a new ethic motivated by human good and governed by scientific and secular laws. He advocates a clear-cut separation between religion and the public sphere. According to the logic of Hobbes, the state "upholds no religion, pursues no religious goals, religiously-defined goods have no place in the catalogue of ends it promotes."[59] This is the principle that posits that government must pursue a course of complete neutrality toward religion, which is "well established in American constitutional law."[60] Contemporary scholars of liberal thought point to three characteristics of a secular state: liberty, equality, and neutrality. It is the obligation of the state to permit the practice of any religion, ensure no preferential treatment of any religion, and stay neutral on matters of religious faith.[61]
3. Secularism as a form of liberalism seeks to protect the common good and achieve justice in society. It treats all people, regardless of their ethnic and linguistic background, as equal citizens of the same state. One working definition of secularism is the following: "The secular state is a state that guarantees individual and corporate freedom of religion, deals with the individuals as a citizen irrespective of his religion, is not constitutionally connected to a particular religion, nor seeks either to promote or interfere with religion."[62]
4. Secularism often refers to a historical process commonly called modernization. Peter Berger defines modernization as "the process by which sectors of society and culture are removed from the domination of religious institutions and symbols."[63]

As seen above, secularization has more or less been an inevitable intellectual and political process in the West. It was primarily a revolt against Christian metaphysics and ethics in Western societies.[64] In the words of the contemporary Indian thinker T. N. Madan, "secularism has been a gift of Protestant Christianity to mankind."[65] Western paradigms of modernization extol the idea of secularism and believe in the universality of its applications. This universality has been the product of the modern Western worldview which divided the people of the world into two categories: "civilized" and barbarian.[66] In addition, "Models of Westernization, however, prescribe the transfer of secularism to non-Western societies without regard for the character of their religious traditions or for the gifts that these might have to offer."[67] The Third World has witnessed several instances where the state has imposed secularism, such as in Atatürk's Turkey and Mao's China.[68]

Seen against the above, secularization, and its derivative secularism, is a complex concept that posits a modern *Weltanschauung* distinguished at heart by the following characteristics: first, a rational and scientific epistemology that is averse to metaphysics; second, a new ethic derived from the autonomy of civil society from religious authority; third, a new way of management, especially in economic and social spheres and, fourth, a political contract based on the equality of all citizens, regardless of race and religion.

It can be argued that the process of secularization in the West was a natural outcome of scientific, industrial, and philosophical growth combined with the Reformation and the rise of the capitalist spirit. In this sense, it was a natural outgrowth of internal European factors, both intellectual and economic. As such, secularization, as with many other social and political movements after the sixteenth century, was of Western origin and proclivity.[69]

EUROPEAN EXPANSION AND SECULARISM

Armed with immense economic and military power, Europe became a dominant economic and political reality after the sixteenth century.[70] In addition to its overwhelming physical power, Europe imported a special philosophy that exalted secularism in its search for profit in the heart of the Third World. Most European travelers in the eighteenth and nineteenth centuries were placed at the service of the colonial army or companies, such as the British East India Company, whose main purpose was to facilitate their plunder of the Third World.[71] The Renaissance, seeking enlightenment at home, advocated a philosophy of exploitation overseas. This period represented the most advanced historical European phase of breaking away from feudalism and its tributary culture, to use Samir Amin's term.[72] It thus generated enough power to go overseas. Second, the breakdown of the feudal economic structure and its cultural symbols did not necessarily result in the disappearance of religion from public life or Europe's adoption of the Holyoake thesis on secularism, as defined earlier. Europe needed a special form of Christianity, a religious system capable of reflecting the fundamental changes within the European world and give it a helping hand in its adventure overseas. Max Weber, Ernst Troeltsch and Peter Berger often stress this point on the connection between capitalism and Protestantism.[73] In order to survive the profound changes in Europe, "Christianity, confronted with the birth of modern thought, underwent this revolution and separated itself from medieval scholasticism."[74]

As a result, a special form of Christianity emerges, one which does not much resemble the original form in Palestine, the rest of the Middle East, or even in Italy. The transformation of Christianity was a necessary outcome of social and material transformations in Europe. When Europe went overseas, it brought along its newly invented God and its economic structure. As Gauri Viswanathan ably shows in her pioneering work *Masks of Conquest*, both Christianity and colonialism joined hands in erecting a European system of education that made sure that the economic interests of the British ruling elite were not jeopardized and which secured the consolidation of British political power.[75] This important convergence of Protestantism and capitalism, introduced overseas in the guise of colonialism, numbed the inner dynamics of indigenous religious traditions. It neutralized them, at best.[76] Furthermore, as implied above, Europe went overseas with a certain "civilizing mission." The world was divided into "civilized" and "backward," Occident and Orient.[77] The Arab Muslim world, like the rest of the Third World, fell under the expansionist umbrella of Europeanization in the early part of the nineteenth century. Regardless if one accepts the thesis proposed by some scholars[78] that certain Arab countries began to show capitalist ferment before Europe's intrusion, the fact remains that the Arab world failed to thwart Europe's ideological and military intrusion. The pillage of the Third World, as K. M. Panikkar puts it,[79] was also a pillage of its traditional ways of life, its manner of handling coexistence and tolerance among different religions. As such, secularization, as a European process of thought and way of life, was imposed by the triumphant West on the Arab world, creating major societal disequilibrium and crisis of identity from which the Third World has yet to recover.

HISTORICAL ORIGINS OF ARAB SECULARISM

The movement of secularism into the Arab world took place under conditions unfavorable to its internal growth. As Samir Amin notes, although the pre-colonial Arab world was distinguished by a number of coexisting modes of production, both Arabization and Islamization gave the Middle East and North Africa strong and homogenous cultural characteristics that were to a great extent fashioned by a ruling commercial class, "Everywhere it [the ruling class] shares the same language and the same profoundly Islamic culture, which, moreover, is orthodox (Sunni)."[80] That is to say, that if one were to agree with the theory of Peter Gran on the development of indigenous capitalism in Egypt before the advent of the French army in 1798, Egyptian society may have created its own civil society that was free from the tutelage of religious authority, most notably the Azhar institution.

Because the West and its implied process of secularization was on the offensive, a large number of traditional Muslim intelligentsia of the eighteenth and nineteenth centuries were not in positions to comprehend, let alone accept, the main presuppositions of Western secularization. Their response was that uninformed rejection. Before waking from the shock of colonialism, nineteenth century Muslim intelligentsia were unable to comprehend either the implicit or explicit assumptions of the "imperialist epistemological *Weltanschauung*," to use a term from

'Abd al-Wahāb al-Masīrī.[81] These intelligentsia belonged to a pre-modern state, which was not equipped to deal with aggressive colonialism.

A small but influential number of Muslim and Christian Arab intelligentsia, under the pressure of and taken with the allure of secularization, opted to reform those Arab and Muslim practices that did not conform to the spirit of progress and freedom.[82] Perhaps the greatest challenge facing these intelligentsia was their marked devotion to Western ideas of progress that were not yet enshrined in the general culture of the Arab world. The Arab and Muslim world of the nineteenth century was not yet able to form a thorough consciousness of the tremendous scientific, technological, philosophical and religious changes Europe had undergone since the Renaissance. The formation of this consciousness was only possible when Europe became a dominant colonial reality in many Arab states and when a new class of indigenous intelligentsia, mostly the children of the traditional religious classes, who had gone to the schools of the West, began to emerge. Some Arab Muslim reformers of that century looked at Europe through the lenses of their Qur'anic education and saw Europe as nothing more than a deviant form of Christianity. Muslim reformers were not able to fathom the deep religious and economic transformations Europe had gone through by the time it was exposed to the Arab world. Even the most passionate Muslim thinker of the late nineteenth century and early part of the twentieth, Shaykh Muḥammad 'Abduh, drew a distinction between Europe and Christianity. To him, Europe meant materialism, whereas Christianity meant spirituality. He too fails to appreciate Christianity's historical transformation in the nineteenth century and its implicit alliance with Western colonialism.[83]

So far, we have been discussing the indigenous intelligentsia of colonial states who were not privileged enough to stand on par with the colonial ruling elite. The indigenous intelligentsia were quick to grasp the huge power differences. Their embrace of Islam was a reflection of the ongoing battle with colonialist powers, which were desirous of appropriating the Muslim past for its own purposes in addition to the present resources of the colonized society.

Not one of the early reformers, including the most controversial, such as 'Alī 'Abd al-Rāziq (who was steeped in traditional Islamic education), cast doubt on the validity of the theological discourse or preached unbelief at the expense of belief. No Arab Muslim reformer of the modern period posited religion against science/reason, but believed religion to be rational and scientific in nature.[84] In a sense, religion was equated with secular rationalism.

Because of the pervasive presence of colonialism in the Arab world at the turn of the century, new Arab voices of scientific secularism emerged. Their major goal was to follow the methods of progress prescribed by the advanced West in terms of state organization, civil society formation and the separation of the religious and secular.[85] In this study, they did not find anything redeeming in Arab and Muslim culture.

> In most post-colonial societies when religion, politics or religion-and-politics are discussed, there is an invisible reference point. This reference point is the Western Man. Not the Western Man in reality or the Western Man of history, but the Western Man as the defeated civilizations of our times have construed

> him. This Western Man rules the world, it seems to the defeated, because of his superior understanding of the relationship between religion and politics.[86]

The Arab tendency to equate progress with the West was best represented by both Ṭāhā Ḥussain and Salāma Mūsa in the first part of the twentieth century.

Early on, the Arab secular movement parted ways with the Islamic reform movement pioneered by Jamāl al-Dīn al-Afghānī and Muḥammad 'Abduh. Arab secularism aimed at bypassing the arguments of Islamic reform by accepting the European philosophy of progress.[87] In other words, this trend envisioned progress along European lines, where religion would be relegated to the personal realm. In a recent study on the impact of secularism on the modern Arab world, 'Azīz al-'Azmeh argues that the progress of secularism in modern Arab life and thought documents the rise of modern rational, humanistic, administrative and political concepts that have paralleled another process of marginalization of religious institutions and their mental/metaphysical outlook, which had been dominant for many centuries.[88] 'Azmeh's important study on secularism helps define the different modern responses to secularization in the Arab world in systematic, theoretical terms. Theoretically speaking, three broad forms of response have emerged since the nineteenth century: the first is the response of the pre-colonial state, such as the Ottoman Empire[89] or the Muḥammad 'Alī state in Egypt;[90] the second is the response of the colonized state, such as Egypt under Cromer or North African countries under the French,[91] and the third is the response of the post-colonial state, which has been typical of almost every Arab country since independence.

Theoretical production on the origins of the state in the modern Arab world is still meager. It is important to distinguish "old states" in the Arab world, that is, Egypt, from "new states," such as Kuwait, Oman or even Saudi Arabia. Under Europe's increasing pressure, the state began an unavoidable process of modernization beginning with the army and higher echelons of the bureaucracy and moving on to the educational structure and the press.[92] This process is known as Tanzimat in nineteenth century Ottoman history. The Arab territories of the Ottoman Empire were not immune to this process.[93] It was far from complete before the complete disintegration of the Ottoman state, Europe's direct occupation of many Arab countries and inauguration of official colonialism. Broadly speaking, this era witnessed huge changes in Arab political, social, and intellectual life. It produced liberals, nationalists, Islamists, and Marxists, all contesting to create a new definition of Arab society. It was an era of great intellectual and political turmoil and uncertainty; it was pregnant with different possibilities.[94]

The cumulative effects of the modernization programs pioneered by the pre-colonial state and continued in one way or another by the colonial state became apparent on the eve of the establishment of the independent state. We are not talking here about a large percentage of modernizing or secularized classes: the number was still definitely small compared to the size of the population. We are talking about the modernizing institutions that were in place by the advent of the national state, especially the army, bureaucracy, schools, and commercial relations with the West. 'Azmeh speaks at length about the proliferation of secular ideas under the impact of the state and various Western influences. The state promoted a rational and secular form of culture and planted the seeds of major secular societal trends such as liberalism, nationalism, and Marxism. The point of reference became the state rather than religion or religious institutions.[95]

THE POST-COLONIAL ARAB STATE AND RELIGION

Nation-states in the modern Arab world after independence could not free themselves from their intellectual indebtedness to the West; most sought to modernize their societies in the image of the triumphant West. At best, they sought to separate religion from the public domain. When this failed, many encouraged the formation of a new class of ulama who would support the secularization/modernization program of the state. Even the Gulf states, whose leadership looks more traditionally religious than that of other Arab countries, have followed this basic model. In most Arab states, a free exercise of religious ideas is simply not tolerated. But the state does not mind reducing religion to a matter of individual belief. It is possible to argue that the Arab state exhibited the following positions on religion before the 1967 defeat: first, Islam is the religion of the state and the Sharīʻah is the main source or one of the main sources of legislation in society. The official religious elite give their unwavering support to the ruling political elite. Institutional Islam is part of the state. But the main institutions of society are freed from religious tutelage and central religious institutions are "reformed." Second, the state opposes Islam as ideology, or, to be more precise, as a counter-ideology that seeks to topple the *status quo* and establish an Islamic regime. Here the state makes a distinction between Islam as faith and Islam as ideology. It tolerates Islam as faith as long as it does not challenge the state's secular foundations. Third, the modernizing elite in the Arab world, be they intellectual or political, have more or less borrowed and refined the post-Renaissance European view of religion, religion as the domain of the non-rational. The secularized middle classes best represent this. The state trained an elite to see religion as a hurdle to development.

Formally speaking, on the eve of the 1967 war the Arab states proclaimed Islam to be the main religion of the state. Their patronage of religious institutions and major religious personalities was more a reflection of their meddling in politics, that is, exploiting religion for political ends, than of their religiosity. In fact, several Arab states took advanced measures to curb the influence of organized religion on the public sphere before 1967 and place religion under the tutelage of the state.[96]

ARAB RESPONSES TO SECULARISM AFTER 1967

The shock of the 1967 defeat coupled with the failure of the modernization project of the nation-state resulted in several forms of response to the issue of secularization and religion: The first and the most poignant one was the response of the modernizing elite that led the Arab world into defeat. As seen above, the political modernizing elite was heir to a long tradition of modernization that began in the Arab world before the advent of official colonialism. On the whole, it was an elite that did not believe in private but that exploited religious symbols in public.

It placed both Western rationalism and religious symbols in its service in order to keep itself in power. This is true even in the case of the tribal state in the Gulf, which has exploited the tribal fact in order to modernize society. Out of its disarray after defeat, the political elite resorted to camouflaging their defeat with religious symbols and ideas. To this elite, religion is not a matter of piety but a means to achieve political and social ends. Because of its unwillingness to give up power and concede defeat, this modernizing elite betrayed its grandiose modernization symbols by simply resorting to Islamic symbols, however dishonest the attempt has been. The same happened, as is well-known, after the Iraqi defeat in the second Gulf War. The use of religion as an instrument of politics is quite serious in traditional societies that value religious life.

The second major response to defeat was that of the "secular" intellectual elite of all shades and colors. This intellectual elite was of three major orientations:

1. Arab nationalist, Costantine Zurayk is one example;[97]
2. critical Marxist, represented by such thinkers as Adonis,[98] Ghālī Shukrī,[99] Abdallah Laroui,[100] al-'Afīf al-Akhḍar;[101] Ṣādiq Jalāl al-'Azm,[102] Ṭayyib Tizīnī,[103] and Halim Barakat;[104] and
3. liberal or Enlightenment (*tanwīrī*), represented by such people as Zakī Najīb Maḥmūd,[105] Jābir 'Aṣfūr,[106] and Fu'ād Zakariyya.[107]

The critique of this class of intelligentsia centered on the premise that the Arab state lost the 1967 war because both the Arab state and Arab masses were not modernized enough or that their level of modernization was not on a par with that of the Zionists. Lebanese thinker Ḥassan Ṣa'b, best represents this trend when he argues that the Arab-Israeli conflict is civilizational, centered around technological competence. The Arab world faced defeat because of its failure to achieve technological and scientific superiority over "the Israeli settlers."[108] This group was a loosely organized group of public thinkers, many of whom were philosophers in the academic sense and who held teaching positions in the most distinguished Arab universities, especially those in Beirut, Cairo, Damascus, and Rabat.

These thinkers showed bitter disappointment with defeat and its causes. Some blamed the small national bourgeoisie for leading the Arab world into defeat because of its class position or political inexperience. This bourgeoisie considered religion and particularly Islam a major hurdle to the development of Arab society. The extreme of this trend goes as far as to associate everything Islamic with the destruction of civil society. This is clear in the writings of Faraj Fūda[109] and many Algerian and Tunisian thinkers who rushed to congratulate the state for purging Islamic elements from society. The hijacking of the election from the Front Islamique du Salut (FIS) in Algeria in 1992 was seen as the intervention of the army to salvage civil society from the hands of Islamists.[110] In their loose way, they were united on an ambitious program, not just to modernize Arab society but also to rid it of the entire question of religion. This response attacked traditional ways of life and the intellectual/theological structures behind them, and called for a radical transformation of Arab society. The only way for the Arab state to achieve victory is through complete submission to the rule of secularization and modernization;

that is, no authority must exist over human reason and religion and religious symbols must be completely banished from the public sphere.

The philosophical writings of this group of Arab critics, especially the Marxist, are brilliant exercises in comprehensive and piercing social, political, and cultural criticism, a vocalized anguish of many hidden feelings about predicaments and challenges, and a painful expression of the state of affairs in contemporary Arab history.[111]

Out of the last response, an interesting new one emerges: the conversion of a good number of influential Arab intellectuals from critical Marxism and nationalism to Islam. As far as I know, this response has not been analyzed in detail, although it is referred to here and there.[112] This response reflected a collective plea by Arab society to first anchor itself in Islamic authenticity and specificity and then to learn from the universality of ideas. This wave of thinkers completely lost faith in the political elite and looked to the Qur'an as their solace in an unstable world. Some of these thinkers are: 'Ādil Ḥussain, Ṭāriq al-Bishrī,[113] and Muḥammad 'Imārah[114] from Egypt, Rāshid al-Ghannūshī from Tunisia,[115] and Munīr Shafīq[116] from Palestine. This conversion to Islamic themes created an important synthesis and theoretical rapprochement between the critical tradition in which these thinkers were reared and their newly constructed Islamic worldview. Due to their theoretical sophistication, these thinkers converged to create a new rational Islamic discourse that was not tainted with the superstition of petroleum-nurtured Muslim clerics from the Gulf. This discourse was marked by its honest and direct approach.

The above-mentioned discourse shouldered the business of betraying the complicity of the Arab political elite with the colonialist project, both Western and Israeli, and its hidden designs for the Arab world, especially in the so-called "peace era" between Israel and some Arab countries. For example, Rāshid al-Ghannūshī argues that what underlies this complicity is violence on the part of the state and Westernization:

> Violence is at the heart of the relationship between the dependent [Arab] state and its citizens. Inarguably, Westernization is the most poignant and damaging form of violence perpetrated by the state; it is cutting off society from its roots and worldview so that the so-called modernity could be imposed. In fact, this modernity allows the West to exercise its dictatorship on our people with the help of the modernizing elite, so much so that this modernization or Westernization becomes the real antithesis of democracy from all angles.[117]

Besides criticizing the state, this discourse has also brought back to the fore the question of Palestine as the most central question facing the contemporary Arab world. Is this a reactionary approach representing the Arab right or the interests of petroleum-rich countries? It is a new approach born in the throes of defeat and in the hope that only a civilizational Islamic way of thinking can salvage the Arab world and humanity at large from the ills of modernity and from the firing power of NATO.

The Islamic side represents the fourth major response. To my mind, in spite of the plethora of literature on this phenomenon, this is the most underrepresented, misunderstood, and criticized response.[118] So much of what has been written on this phenomenon has been by its critics and enemies. Here I disagree with Fu'ād Zakariyya's main thesis that the Islamist trend has been most dominant in Arab society since 1967 because of its patronage by the state.[119]

At the outset, one must draw a line between the response of the organized Islamic movement or movements and that of the masses. There is a difference between what has been termed "political Islam" and the Islamic religious phenomenon. The latter is a much larger notion and practice than the former. It denotes a living Islamic tradition that has survived against all odds in the modern world. One must agree with Ghālī Shukrī's insightful analysis that the Arab masses practice "Islam" in their daily praxis without theological or legal complications. The collective memory of the masses is based on a simple and pristine Islam, which is based on tolerance and acceptance.[120] In academic and journalistic literature, it has become a cliché to speak of "political Islam" or "fundamentalist Islam" or "radical Islam" in a pejorative sense.[121] These terms do not accurately describe the discourse of organized Islamic movements, a discourse that is not incongruent with the main legal and theological principles of Islam.[122] This response and its various offshoots is the only one that offers a real political alternative to the crisis of the ruling Arab political elite. The immediate response of this trend, a large number of whose proponents have been imprisoned in their own countries, barred from participating in the political process, or in exile either in the Gulf states or the West, was the response of the twice-defeated person or phenomenon: once by Western civilization and its intimate ally Zionism, and the second by the Arab states. The discourse of the doubly-defeated took the position that God destined defeat because of the ungodliness of Arab regimes and their preference of secularism over Islam. With the progress of years, new organized Islamist responses have emerged in different Arab countries, especially in Sudan, Tunisia, Algeria, and Morocco. All argue that religion must furnish the ideological basis of the new state. All call for the formation of a new state.[123]

The second dimension of this response was a product of the masses, including a large number of the middle classes that were adversely affected by the modernization of the state. One must remember that a major social and political cleavage still exists between the "masses" and the "modernized elite." Most of the masses still live either in the countryside or in countryside-like neighborhoods in the cities. It is true that a sizable number of the children of the masses went to the schools of the nation-state, but not many were absorbed by the state and its institutions after graduation. This phenomenon is apparent in most Arab countries, especially Tunisia, Algeria, Morocco, and Egypt. It is doubtful that the recent process of privatization begun in earnest in many Arab countries under the impact of globalization and the IMF will do much to remedy this situation. Al-Jābīrī blames this on the West's successful attempts to suffocate the growth of the national Arab bourgeoisie and its continuing refusal to support democratization and liberalization in the Arab world.[124]

There is a large-scale process of revival not necessarily political, but which revolves around the formation of a new collective identity that follows the broad guidelines of Islamic principles.[125] The bet of the modernizing elite before 1967 was that large doses of state modernization would be enough to reduce if not amputate religious symbols from the public sphere. They are far less preoccupied with "institutional Islam" than with a mass-oriented Islamic movement. The defeat proved the contrary. Large sections of the masses, including the most educated, began to rediscover a new meaning of religiosity and reaffirm the notion that traditional ways of behavior would provide a sense of identity and belonging to a modernization program that had run amok. The bourgeoisie in most Arab countries felt betrayed and a good number began to discover the ways of Islam.[126] The mass response to defeat, which even the state tried to exploit, became manifest not just in the increase in public attendance of prayers or the increased number of pilgrims to Saudi Arabia every year, but also in the increase of interest in Islamic literature.

The mass Islamic response to defeat and predicament was justified by the following factors, which seem to be unchanging in modern Arab political and social life: first, the failure of the modernization program of the nation-state emerging into the scene after the recession of colonialism. The 1967 defeat betrayed the grandiose claims of Arab states, including those that do not share borders with Israel. In several Arab countries, modernization created two countries within one: one urban and advanced and the other rural and backward. In addition, the mass education adopted by a number of Arab nation-states did not deliver the poor from their misery but made them thoroughly aware of the conditions of their misery and the real economic and political causes of these conditions. Second was the accumulation of more power in fewer hands even after defeat and failure of the modernization project and the loss of public freedoms. Harold Laski's observation about the loss of political freedom aptly describes the current situation of the Arab world, "If in any state there is a body of men who possess unlimited power, those over whom they rule can never be free."[127] The history of freedom in the Arab world after 1967 is sad. Besides incurring the wrath of Islamist forces, the expansion in the power of the political elite has led to deep resentment on the part of the masses unseen in the Arab world since the days of colonialism. Third, the recession of democratic freedoms of all sorts and the penetrating crisis of civil society leads to the suffocation of those energies that had been won through education. No new leadership seems to be in sight, except perhaps that of the military. Societal crisis deepens day by day. Fourth, the state, in its attempt to silence dissent and camouflage real problems in society, unleashes the power of technology, that is, the mass media, by encouraging a shallow artistic environment where songs do nothing but promote the trivial side of official Arab culture.

In North Africa, most notably in Morocco, Algeria, and Tunisia, the modernization mind of the state has exhausted its possibilities, as well. The 1967 defeat did not have the same impact on North Africa as it did on the Arab countries in the Middle East. However, similar policies of nation building and modernization had been under way since the time each of these countries achieved independence (Algeria was to achieve independence in 1962). The long history of French colonization in these countries and the bitter struggle for freedom left them in economic shambles. The flight of the poor from the countryside to the cities, the enormous difficulties facing these nascent countries and overpopulation were all major challenges to new regimes. The answer of the modernizing elite, emerging from the shadows of colonialism, was to impose modernization on a poor and backward society.

For example, the Bourguiba regime in Tunisia was perhaps the most radical Arab system to imitate the Kemal Atatürk model of secularization and nation-building.[128] The state imposed secularism on all aspects of society with the double purpose of diminishing the power of religion in social and cultural spheres and creating a new identity congruous with the demands of modernity. The religious institutions, especially the ancient Zaytūna University, were marginalized and a wall of separation between state and religion was erected.[129] However, one major characteristic of the state's imposition of secularization was to ensure its "hegemony over the social imaginaire of people or their collective memory."[130] Here the secularization process in Bourguiba's Tunisia takes on an important function: to create subtle new mechanisms of identity formation through state apparatuses, especially the party, mass media, schools, and the charisma of the leader.[131]

The process of dominating the people's social imaginaire stumbled in the early 1970s with the rise of a new and educated generation of young Tunisians who rebelled against the state's modernization program. The same thing can be said of other countries in North Africa. In the words of 'Abd al-Ḥamīd Ibrāhīmī, the contemporary state in North Africa, after several decades of independence, finds itself dependent on the West, carrying huge foreign debt and its citizens find that the margins of democracy have receded.[132] The modernized state could not absorb its modernization potential and many felt that Islam would provide an answer.[133] In other words, the Islamic response in Tunisia was a translation of deep resistance to the modernization policies of Bourguiba, which were seen and experienced as a policy of full cultural and linguistic subjugation to the West and the loss of the national-religious identity of the nation.[134]

The case of Algeria is also similar to that of Tunisia. Post-independence Algeria went far to modernize society. However, the Algerian intelligentsia, as the most conscious group in society, has experienced a "loss of hegemony" since independence, as Ali El-Kenz puts it, because of excessive control by the army, the Westernization of the Arab collective identity of the country, and the derailment of the economic program of reform in the 1980s. Because of this neglect, the "intellectuals took refuge in the silence of the embassies and factories."[135] In short, the contemporary state in North Africa has imposed its rationalist vision of modernization on a traditional society battered from long years of colonialism. The state's modernization vision is compounded by the fact of the heavy concentration of power in few hands, by overpopulation, inner and foreign emigration, and failed economic development.

CURRENT INTELLECTUAL TRENDS

The complex response to defeat and the failure of the state's modernization program, as shown in its variations above, has basically unmasked three distinct discourses in the contemporary Arab world, each of which has its principal theoreticians and proponents. First, defeat and the failure of modernization have unleashed the power of religious discourse to raise some critical questions about political authority in Arab society, and the viability of the Arab modernizing political elite in a new atmosphere. At the heart of this discourse lies the argument that the *ancien régime* is simply anachronistic. Second, the state, whose interest in preserving authority converged with that of the official ulama and the radical modernizing elite (including in some instances Marxist thinkers), has refused to concede the fundamental question of political authority. Without bothering to camouflage its intentions, it went on the offensive against the counter-state Islamic ideology and any other radical tendency that sought to topple the regime. The state thus does not believe in dialogue except with a neutralized version of Islam, a version that it can manage and is willing to accommodate. Third is the secularization discourse espoused by Arab philosophers and thinkers. As shown above, there are many variations of this discourse. However, one thing is consistent. This discourse has been very much weakened since 1967, and only a handful of Arab thinkers have embraced secularism as a liberating and dynamic philosophy. In secularism's heyday, in the 1950s and 1960s, this movement was on the offensive preaching the emancipation of Arab society from the shackles of tradition only if this society emulated the Western models of secularism and progress. It believed in the possibility of reconstructing the Arab mind along secular Western lines; it was dynamic, positive, highly critical of traditional ideas, and bent on modernizing society. The mood changed after 1967.

Since 1967 and mainly due to the resurgence of Islam, a number of secular thinkers have taken the part of the state. They have advised the state to wage a relentless war on any manifestation of "political Islam." The late Egyptian thinker Faraj Fūda, assassinated in 1996, best represented this argument. He argues that the defense lines of the secular state have been exposed and the only remaining alternative is to repress political Islam by force:

> It is undoubtedly clear that "Political Islam" has succeeded in co-opting and neutralizing the most important defensive as well offensive system of the State – the mass media – not by erecting an antagonistic media system, since this is legally impossible, but by controlling the State's media from within through the use of the most dangerous of weapon, that of money.[136]

Dialogue is therefore impossible with this manifestation of Islam. Moreover, the failure of the state's modernization project, its retreat from building a new civil society, and its severe hold over power, do not help nurture dynamic and responsible leadership. All of these developments, argues Burhān Ghalyūn, forced the marginalized segments of society "to resort to the Islamic reservoir of symbols and to use it as a new medium of expressing its political and conceptual opposition to the status quo."[137] Here the state is a believer in the public domain; it encourages public cultural symbols of Islam, which do not pose a threat to its political authority.[138]

Because of its appeal to a cross-section of the population, especially the poor and marginalized middle classes, the Islamist movement since 1967 has been in the best position to question the political and constitutional legitimacy of the ruling elite in the Arab world.[139] It is not hard to agree with Ayubi that the state, because of the failure of its modernization program, enabled Islamism to appropriate Islam as its powerful weapon:

> the fact that the contemporary State lays claim to secularism has enabled some forces of political protest to appropriate Islam as their own weapon. Because the State does not embrace Islam (except in a "defensive" reactive way), it cannot describe its opponents as the traditional State could as being simply heretic cults. Political Islam now reverses the historical process – it claims "generic" Islam for the protest movements, leaving to the State the more difficult task of qualifying and justifying its own "version" of Islam.[140]

Whatever the advantages or disadvantages of secularization in the Arab world, one must note two major points that often go unmentioned in the discourse on Arab secularism: first that the movement towards secularism in modern Arab history has not garnered sufficient grass-roots support. More often than not, secularism has been imposed by the state from the above. This means the modernizing elite implicitly admit that traditional Muslim culture has inherent mechanisms and procedures that cannot be easily substituted by secularism, especially of the radical nature (that is, secularism as anti-metaphysics). This what justifies an astute observer of the Arab world such as Ṣādiq Jalāl al-'Azm to argue that the secularization movement in most Arab countries has been slow, informal, pragmatic, and full of half measures.[141] Arab secularization has become more and more convinced that a mere carbon copy of Western secularization cannot be transferred to the Arab world, since both the background and current conditions are not the same. The second point concerns the fact that the secularist tendency in the modern Arab world has been the property of a small number of people, people who are either educated in the West or whose economic interests are best served by a strong relationship with Western capitalism. Therefore secularism has been the plea of the minority against the majority, and this plea is enforced because the masses have no say in the major decisions of the state.

4
Contemporary Arab Philosophical Views of Secularism

> "What is renaissance? Is it the [the retrieval of] ancient values? The worst I fear is that we will succeed in expelling the colonialists, and subdue the monopolists, but [meanwhile] fail in defeating the Dark Ages in our lives." Salāma Mūsa, *Mā hiya al-nahḍah?* (Beirut: Dār al-Ma'ārif, 1962), 11.

> "Anyone following the contemporary debates between Islamists and secularists in the Arab world will be surprised to notice the ignorance of both camps of the following fundamental fact: The Sharī'ah has never been implemented, nor a theocratic state has ever existed since the inception of Islam...Muslim jurists and Sunni Imams never thought that the state was indulging in infidelity because it divorced religion from state. The only contemporary salafī jurist, who harbors irrational enmity toward Arabs and Arabism, is Abū al-'Alā al-Mawdūdī, who launched a fierce attack against Muslim jurists and caliphs for their failure to implement the Sharī'ah from the days of Mu'āwiyah up to the rule of Sultan 'Abd al-Ḥamīd." Musṭafa Laṭīfī, "Nihāyat al-dawlah al-dīniyah fī'l islām." *Qaḍāyah Fikriyyah*, special issue on Islamic Fundamentalism in the modern Arab world, October 1993, 303, 305.

> "Egypt resembles an iceberg, one eighth is above sea level. Seven eighths are submerged in the depths. One eighth of our lives take place in the light of the twentieth century, seven eighths in medieval darkness... In the nineteenth century, we went through pangs of birth...but the renaissance was stillborn, and when another embryo was formed in the womb [under Nasser] it was aborted." Lewis 'Awaḍ, quoted by Amos Elon, "Crumbling Cairo." *New York Review of Books*, volume 42(6), April 6, 1995, 32.

> "The Secularist idea is the darling daughter of that major enterprise we have referred to as Westernization and cultural colonialism. By attacking religion and separating it from life, the major intention of this enterprise is to create a doctrinal and conceptual vacuum to be filled thereafter by the philosophies and theories of the West." Muḥammad Yaḥya, *Waraqah thaqāfiyah fī'l radd 'ala al-'ilmāniyyīn* (Cairo: al-Zaharā' li'l I'lām al-'Arabī, 1988), 12.

The preceding discussion leads to one inevitable conclusion: the predicament of the Arab political elite resulting from the 1967 defeat has had a major impact on the intellectual scene in the Arab world. The erosion of Nasserism after 1967, and the disappearance of the Soviet system in 1991 ushered the Arab world into a new era of globalization distinguished by the supremacy of American power. To survive the drastic political changes in the world, especially after 1990, the Arab political elite have begun to show less and less independence vis-à-vis the emerging American power in the area. As such, the debate on secularism must be understood against these deep changes in the world system and its effect on the Arab world.[1]

The last comment begs the question of change in the modern Arab world and the place of religion therein. I do believe that the role of religion in the Arab world (both Islam and Christianity) is as sensitive as ever. However, this view does not diminish the important fact that with the rise of the modern nation-state in the Arab world, most political elite have appealed to religious slogans and ideas in order to preserve the *status quo*, and some regimes have gone as far as to give new life to the official religious intelligentsia for their own political purposes. This means that there has been a major reconstitution of religious values and ideas on the part of the power elite. Therefore, it would be misleading to argue, as Ernest Gellner does for example, that there has not been any change in the strength of Islam:

> It is possible to disagree about the extent, homogeneity, or irreversibility of this trend [secularization]…; but, by and large, it would seem reasonable to say that it is real. But there is one very real, dramatic and conspicuous exception to all of this: Islam. To say that secularization prevails in Islam is not only contentious. It is simply false. Islam is as strong as it was a century ago. In some ways, it is properly stronger.[2]

It is hard to accept Gellner's conclusion in view of the fact that Islam has been tied to, if not dependent on, a very complex socio-economic base that has been subject to enormous changes in the modern era. Further, far from having one collective Islamic presence, a variety of Islamic discourses have mushroomed in the contemporary Arab and Muslim worlds.

In order to shed more light on the secularism debate in contemporary Arab thought, especially in the 1990s, I will focus my analysis on the ideas of the leading Egyptian philosopher Fu'ād Zakariyya.[3] The above begs, once more, the question of the so-called "Arab enlightenment movement" (*al-ḥarakah al-tanwīriyyah*), a dominant trend in contemporary Arab thought and culture.[4] According to Egyptian thinker Galāl Amīn, the contemporary Arab enlightenment trend has lately reached its limits for two reasons: first, it has moved to the orbit of gradual Israeli domination of the Middle East and, second, its propensity to attack any form of religiosity as being terrorist. That the "*tanwīrī* trend" in modern Arab culture has been exhausted indeed is clear from its modern history in the Arab world. The main "*tanwīrī*" representatives in Arab thought, from Ṭāhā Ḥussain to Salāma Mūsa in the first half of the twentieth century, and Jābir 'Aṣfūr and Zakī Najīb Maḥmūd[5] in the second half, are united on an ambitious project of secularization, unfettered criticism, especially of tradition and the sacred, pragmatism and doubt.[6] Most secularist Arab thinkers tenaciously hold to the proposition that the "universalization of modernity" and its acceptance by Arab society and the Arab mind in the nineteenth century was inevitable, and that an appeal to traditionalism in the form of authenticity is just an escape from new conditions created by modernity.[7] Furthermore, this trend has attached its fate to the survival of dictatorial regimes in the Arab world. Its best defense line is that "modernizing elite" have failed to modernize society.

Fu'ād Zakariyya represents the most subtle and serious attempt to salvage the contemporary Arab secularist movement from its current historical impasse, as analyzed in the preceding chapter. He considers the resurgence of Islam and not the failure of "Arab modernism" to be the most serious threat to the integrity and viability of secularism in contemporary Arab society. Zakariyya hopes the Islamic past will jump-start the contemporary Arab secularist movement. He proposes that from Islam's inception, secularism has been pivotal. Contemporary Arab secularist thinkers need not be carbon copies of Western secularists, but must revive the secularist tradition of the Mu'tazilites, Ibn Rushd, al-Fārābī, and others.[8] This is a tempting thesis, although a very difficult one to defend now in view of the indebtedness of the modern Arab secularist movement to Western thought and political hegemony. In principle, Zakariyya does not object to borrowing from Western civilization as long as borrowing meets the criteria of rationalism and progress. Rationalism is universal and it is high time for the Arab intelligentsia to historicize the Islamic past without paying it blind deference.[9] Zakariyya's intellectual project revolves around the following significant issues in contemporary Arab thought: (1) recent attempts at applying the Sharī'ah; (2) the mass orientation of resurgence; (3) "Petro-Islam," and (4) science, reason, and revelation.[10]

To start with, Zakariyya is quite critical of certain political regimes in the Arab world, especially those in the Gulf states. Zakariyya is too subtle to dismiss the "modernization achievements" of Gulf regimes. As a professor of philosophy at Kuwait University in the 1970s and 1980s, he enjoyed some of these benefits. His quarrel is not with the idea of modernizing Gulf States as much as it is with the actors behind modernization, that is, the political elite and their spurious methods. He is right to contend that these elite, and their supporters in larger society, that is, the conservative ulama, are too misguided to appropriate the Enlightenment's intellectual premises *en masse*.

In critiquing the Gulf ruling elite, Zakariyya's point of departure is quite similar to other Islamist thinkers who are critical of the political *status quo*. He argues that social justice must be the hallmark of social and political action in the Arab world. However, contrary to many Islamists, he thinks that the Arab political elite (especially in the Gulf), have lent a hand to both "official Islam" and Islamic resurgence in order to achieve political stability. He says that many current rulers appeal to the Sharī'ah as a last attempt to preserve power. By doing so, they intend to exploit the Islamist movement for its mass appeal. In this regard, he forcefully argues that,

> There is an ocean of difference between the current systems of government [in the Arab world] and the values of freedom, justice, and equality as preached by

> all religions, philosophers, and reformers throughout history. Nevertheless, the proponents of the implementation of the *Sharīʻah* in our land do not heed the astonishing failure of previous experiments. On the contrary, their voices became extremely loud when the implementation of the *Sharīʻah* in the Sudan [under Numeiri] turned into an international scandal.[11]

Zakariyya further argues that the proponents of the Sharīʻah use the Sacred Text, the Qur'an, as a springboard for their thinking while remaining totally oblivious to the social and cultural manifestations of Islam throughout Islamic history. The Qur'an and, for that matter, Islamic tradition, cannot provide adequate solutions to the many dilemmas besetting the modern Arab world. To adopt this view is to become ahistorical, at best.[12] He takes a critical position vis-à-vis the applicability of the Qur'an and the viability of Islamic tradition in the modern era. A critical thinker must subject both the Qur'an and tradition to strict historical criticism if he/she is to learn from them. Zakariyya basically encourages the same critical methodology adopted by both Mohammed Arkoun and Naṣr Hāmid Abū Zayd in the analysis of Islamic religious tradition.[13]

Many a ruler has practiced absolutist rule and made a mockery of the lives, property, and freedom of Muslims. Zakariyya reminds the "Islamist camp" of the distinction they must draw between "textual Islam" and "historical Islam." He argues that implementing the Sharīʻah falls in the domain of "historical Islam," and that as a practical issue, "invoking the power of the texts [that is, the Qur'an and the Sunnah] is insufficient."[14] What is dangerous in Zakariyya's opinion is the mass emotional appeal Islamic movements exert. As a result of this mass appeal, the discussion around the Sharīʻah issue "remains generalized and elastic, although, if it is subjected to rational analysis, it remains ambiguous and messy."[15] Zakariyya, representing the secular Ivy League in contemporary Arab society, contends that the mass appeal of an idea or ideology does not necessarily make it valid. He argues, along Marxist lines, that as a result of deplorable economic and political conditions in the Arab world since 1967, the Arab masses have suffered "loss of consciousness" (*inʻidām wa'y*), and that the recent resurgence of Islam is "a clear reflection of the lack of consciousness among the masses. The spread of these movements becomes inevitable after one third of a century of oppression, the suspension of reason, and the domination of a dictatorial political system."[16]

Zakariyya further criticizes Islamism by accusing its principal leaders of mental poverty and lacking rational values, "In my view, their major problem is that they do not take full advantage of their mental faculty, which they often suspend to the point of complete paralysis."[17] The "monolithic mind" of Islamic resurgence is accustomed to unquestioned premises and to the belief that "doubt is a mistake, criticism is a crime, and questioning is a crime."[18] In other words, these movements are far from embracing the central tenets of modernity as defined above. To my mind, Zakariyya fails to appreciate the central intellectual tenets of Islamism, and the many important historical and religious factors responsible for its birth in the modern period. He relishes the principle that Arab society has only one option for modernization: the uncritical wholesale acceptance of the central premises of secularization and modernity. What this entails is in effect a total disregard of the application of religious values to the governing and daily functioning of Arab society. In addition, he accuses Islamism of being complicit with the ruling political elite in the Arab world. This assumption is problematic.

In the same vein, Zakariyya argues that Islamism has been on the rise in many Gulf states, and that it has principally turned a deaf ear to the misuses of Islam in the public sphere. Zakariyya does not draw clear distinctions between Islamism, as a movement of religious revivalism, and official Islam, as a body of official clergy, which supports the *status quo*. Summarizing Zakariyya's arguments in this regard, he first points out the importance of the Gulf states in the international arena, thanks to their oil resources. However, he notes that from the beginning of Islam, economic factors have been inextricably intertwined with religious factors. Pilgrimage, a central pillar in Islam, has attracted a large number of people every year to a very impoverished region, "One of the main goals of pilgrimage was the alleviation of poverty in this dry desert, and helping its people break out of their isolation so that their territory becomes, for a specific period of time each year, the gathering place of Muslims from all over the world."[19] Undoubtedly, this argument is valid. Zakariyya hits the marks when he says that it is indeed a "civilizational paradox" (*mufāraqah ḥaḍāriyyah*) that this same region, which has attracted people from diverse cultures over the centuries, has been blessed with oil, which has led the political elite of the region into virtual billionaires. Because of the importance of the oil resources to the international economy, the political elites in the Gulf had to modernize the infrastructure of their societies, which in one sense has meant sweeping changes in the educational system for both sexes.[20] Furthermore, Zakariyya argues that oil has not appeared in historically stable agricultural and centralized societies, such as Egypt, but rather in tribal desert societies, which had been under the spell of tribal tradition. Islam itself had been tribalized.[21]

Zakariyya spends little time assessing the impact of the modernization program of the Gulf tribal state on society and the clash existing in many Gulf societies between actual modernization programs and the absence of a modernist consciousness. To camouflage the gap between modernization and modernism, Zakariyya asserts that the political elite are taking full advantage of Islam for their own purposes,

> A specific type of Islam has been gathering momentum of late, and the appropriate name that applies to it is "Petro-Islam." The first and last goal of "Petro-Islam" has been to protect the petroleum wealth, or more correctly, the type of social relations underlying those [tribal] societies that possess the lion's share of this wealth. It is common knowledge that the principle of "the few dominating the largest portion of this wealth" permeates the social structure [of the Gulf region].[22]

This huge wealth is concentrated in the hands of a few families who have refused to share their good fortune with the rest of the Arab world. This is true enough. However, is it true to argue that Islamism supports this behavior? Zakariyya firmly believes that Islamism is indistinguishable from other patterns of Islamic behavior in the Gulf. He maintains that Islam has been held hostage by the Gulf regimes and, therefore, a novel type of Islam has emerged, "the Islam of the veil, beard, and the *Jilbāb*, the kind of Islam that permits the interruption of work during prayers' time, and prohibits women from driving automobiles."[23]

Although he bases his arguments on secular premises, Zakariyya appears to be concerned about the predicament of Islam and Muslims, as have intellectuals of the Islamic movement. He also revives some of their terminology in his secularist discourse. He bemoans the fact that in petroleum-dominated countries,

> It is in the interest of the ruling elite to preempt Islam and reduce it to shallow formalities so that the problems of poverty, the bad distribution of wealth, the predominance of the consumption mentality, and the loss of the final opportunity of a thorough revival of petroleum societies, would escape the attention of the masses.[24]

It is unfortunate, stresses Zakariyya, that the mass consciousness in these countries has been perniciously invaded by and drowned in the ocean of the empty texts and commentaries of ancient jurists and exegetes who have no real understanding of the fundamental challenges facing contemporary Muslims. In the final analysis, Zakariyya reminds us that the current state of affairs is ideal for international and exploitative capitalism:

> Would a country like the United States dream of a better condition than the one dominating the new generations of the petroleum-producing countries who are in perpetual fear of the severe punishment of the grave and its snakes that tear to pieces anyone who dares to question, criticize, or rebel against the prevailing conditions and values? Would the West, including Israel, imagine to dream of a better condition than the one in which the most dynamic and active Islamic movements proclaim that the question of Jerusalem and the problem with Israel must be postponed until the establishment of the Islamic political system?[25]

Zakariyya argues correctly that there is definitely a strong and an unbreakable bond between Petro-Islam and the interests of modern capitalism, "In a nutshell, this Islam is placed at the service of protecting the interests of the ruling elite and its allies of exploiting foreign countries."[26] Zakariyya is certainly critical of the explicit alliance between the political elite of the Gulf region and the United States. He is critical of American political and economic hegemony in the area, which he considers to be one of the main reasons for the absence of true democracy in the Arab world. He warns the Arab world against adopting American ideas simply because they are American.[27] The ruling elite embrace modernity in the name of protecting the type of Islam of which Zakariyya speaks. All of this is fair enough. However, Zakariyya fails to mention the protest Islamic movements in Gulf states against the manifestations of the same. In his brilliant essay on "The Limits of Religious Criticism in the Middle East: Notes on Islamic Public Argument," Talal Asad discusses in detail the Islamic tradition of public criticism in Saudi Arabia and the failure of the state to tolerate it, especially after the stationing of American troops in the Gulf in 1990. This tradition is represented by a group of young Saudi ulama who criticize the prevalent corruption and nepotism made possible by the tremendous oil wealth.[28]

Zakariyya is unwavering in his plea for a rational and progressive Arab secularist movement. He considers the religious solution to have exhausted its limits, at best. He sees no hope in religious ethics or the meaning of tolerance. Zakariyya's ideas are embedded in the secular ideal and owe their inspiration to the historical manifestations of secularism in Arab lands at the end of the nineteenth century. Although not nihilist in a Nietzschean sense, Zakariyya substitutes metaphysics for rationalism.[29] To him, the secularism project, aided by rationalism and ultimately individualism, is a better alternative in contemporary Arab societies than religious ethics. Although he does not declare the "death of God" in his philosophy, he abandons the idea that human ontology should derive its authenticity or essence from Divine Being.[30] Zakariyya is well aware that the modern period in the Arab world, beginning in the early part of the nineteenth century, posed a fundamental challenge to the classical definition of the self in traditional Muslim societies. These societies were challenged by scientifically superior societies and aggressive modernist views. The sum result of this challenge has been the breakdown of the traditional expression of the Muslim self and the creation of multiple centers of self-definition in modern Arab society. Out of the mushrooming of multiple modern Arab historical selves, the secularist-individualist self has commanded the respect of a committed minority of few intellectuals and leaders who see no virtue in the continuation of the classical "Muslim self." Zakariyya considers the "Good" to fall squarely into this modern definition of the "Arab self," which to him cannot be disengaged from the modern world. In other words, the modern "Arab self" cannot be nurtured by historical Islamic tradition, since this tradition has disengaged itself from the "modern self," which had been developing in the West since the Enlightenment. However, it seems to me that Zakariyya fails to consider two additional facts about the multiple expressions of the "self" in the modern period. First, it is true that the nineteenth century was filled with grandiose ideas about progress and human prosperity, which enabled individualism to transcend the boundaries of the classical Western definition of community and self. However, one of the main consequences of the modern definition of the "self" has been the colossal destruction seen in World Wars One and Two.[31] Second, under the pressure of the "Other," that is, the West, the traditional Muslim expression of the "self" had to give way to a new reconstruction of the Muslim Self in the modern period. The idea of revival in modern Muslim thought does not exclusively denote political revival, but social, moral, and philanthropic revival. Zakariyya, like many secularists in the Arab world, does not ponder the many virtues of such a revival in times of severe social crises and change in many Arab countries. The Islamic ethos of generosity, patience, compassion, and kindness have been revived as a result of the encounter with the West.

Against the above, it is possible to argue the following points about secularism in contemporary Arab thought:

1. Far from being a dead issue, religion occupies center stage in the intellectual orientation of Arab secularism. The criticism of religion is still the central

premise of all criticism, even at the beginning of the twenty-first century. Secularist thinkers are perturbed by the fact that the secular state has not taken the issue of religion seriously; they address this "historical error" by examining afresh the complicated relationship between religion and state. This premise is at odds with Binder's observation that "Islam in its various forms, and categories, and applications, is only a part of Middle East culture, and by itself accounts for little."[32]

2. Arab secularists are more determined than ever to produce a discursive secular approach that challenges theological and religious interpretations of social reality and human history. Secularists are convinced that Arab society contains the necessary seeds for secularization and modernization, and that what is needed is a proper implementation of secularist philosophy and worldview. In a sense, it is relevant here to introduce the distinction made by Leo Strauss between political philosophy and political theology. According to Strauss, political theology is made up of those teachings based on divine revelation, whereas political philosophy is limited to what is accessible to the unassisted human mind.[33] Arab secular political philosophy, such as Zakariyya's, rejects any divine intervention in the historical and political process. Political philosophy, as advanced by Arab secularists, is based on the notion that the best context for political action is that of democracy.
3. Arab secularists argue that only secularism and not Islamic resurgence can ensure a smooth transition in the Arab world from "the closed society" to "the open society." One can find similarities between Arab secularist theory and Karl Popper's famous notion of what constitutes an open, progressive, and future-oriented society. For instance, Popper claims that its organic ties, tribal and collectivist mentality, lack of individuality, and religious rigidity are the main characteristics of "closed society." The open (secular) society, on the other hand, is marked by individuality, freedom of expression, rationalism, social mobility, and a critical appraisal of social reality.[34] In other words, secularists assume that Arab society must be able to maintain a degree of tolerance and openness to outside influences, and that a transition from "the closed society" to an open one signals a total breakdown of tribalism and religious rigidity. Then, to the minds of secularists, any reaction against liberalism in the modern Arab world, especially in the form of Islamism or tribalism is in fact a reaction against socio-economic progress, and the scientific culture of modernity.

In addition, contemporary Arab *tanwīrī* thought has intensified its attack on religious thought by ascribing to it fanaticism and extremism because of its doctrinal belief in metaphysics. Amin contends that attacking religious thought as the only source of fanaticism in society is just plain wrong. There are many other sources of fanaticism in Arab society. In addition, this trend has not questioned, not even slightly, American gross violations of the rights of the nations of the Third World to political and economic independence.

The main goal of the first generation of Arab enlightenment was to catch up with the West, whereas the enlightenment in the West represented the economic and political aspirations of the bourgeoisie to make a clean break with feudalism.[35]

Progress and freedom in this sense were synonymous with bourgeois progress and freedom, and this is what Arab thinkers of the Enlightenment missed.[36] They followed the West project blindly, without considering the Arab context. Arab enlightenment took root in the inferiority Arab intellectuals felt vis-à-vis intellectuals of the West. Furthermore, during the Cold War, there were two *tanwīrī* camps in Arab thought, one socialist and the other capitalist. What bound them together were the ideas of progress and rationalism and hatred of religious thought.

According to Amīn, with the eclipse of the socialist camp enters a new phase, which he terms the "Israeli age." In this phase, it is "Islamic fundamentalism" or "fanaticism" or "extremis," which has been defined as the main enemy of Israel, America, progress and enlightenment. With the spread of the NGOs and Western-inspired human rights organizations in the Arab world, the enemy has been well defined: religious fanaticism and Islam.[37]

TRADITIONALISM, MODERNISM, AND SECULARISM

It is perhaps historically fallacious and philosophically contentious to argue that rationalism, the bedrock of modern secularism, has been the creation of European Enlightenment. The identity of traditional worldviews and cultures cannot be understood without rationalism. Rationalism was incorporated as an essential movement of thought, which, in the case of monotheism, functioned as a handyman to revelation. However, one of the main contributions of the European Enlightenment has been a fundamental change in the relationship between revelation and reason. The Enlightenment created a new discourse of rational knowledge that was more in congruence with the demands of an aggressive new civilization than the past. With the advent of colonialism in the Arab world, rationalism was identified with progress and science, which had flourished against the background of early European modernity (roughly from the beginning of the sixteenth century to the end of the eighteenth). In their urgent quest to modernize Arab society, early Arab modernists were anxious to translate Europe's scientific and intellectual achievements without being prepared to undergo the massive industrial and intellectual changes experienced by the West. Some Arab modernists uncritically embraced the main tenets of rationalism. However, these early modernists remained a tiny elite, that was cut off from the masses, or unable to express the concerns of the masses in an adequate manner.

One must agree with the thesis of Syrian thinker Burhān Ghalyūn that Arab rationalism, from the beginning of colonialism, has taken the side of the exploitative classes:

> Western rationalism was a culmination of a long-standing suspicion in all the traditional systems of thought, and was an affirmation of the freedom of man, individual, community, and nation. However, Arab rationalism has affirmed and justified the existing system, the [bipolar] system of modernity and dependency, either in the name of progress or the logic of history, but always against the freedom of the [average] individual.[38]

Theoretically, one might favorably consider Fu'ād Zakariyya's emphatic plea that secularism as an idea, as a movement, and as a worldview is a civilizational necessity (*ḍarūrah ḥaḍāriyyah*).[39] But, is it possible to accept secularism without the political and social package associated with it, that is Western modernity and colonialism? Furthermore, the proponents of international secularism in the West seem to have overlooked the fact that many of their political protégés in the Third World do not practice real democracy and to date nothing has been done to address this problem.

The debate about secularism in contemporary Arab thought is perhaps a reflection of the deformed modernization adopted by the modern nation-state. One may define modernization as the institutional embodiment of modernist ideas. However, in most Arab countries, modernism, as an intellectual consciousness of the necessity of modernization, has not had any real mass support. The educational system in many Arab countries cannot be said to be modernist in outlook. One may even argue that it is not traditional either. The main goal of the educational system has been to create a semi-educated class of people who lack critical skills and vision. It is not in the interest of the Arab political elite to train a mass of critically educated people. Furthermore, the official religious intellectuals (the ulama) have lent their support to this elite, and, consequently, are considered suspect by the masses. This environment has been favorable for the rise of a new kind of religious intellectual who is critical of the *status quo*. Undoubtedly, modernity, with all of its hazards, has been an inevitable movement in the modern Arab world. At the heart of our search for healthy modernity are a number of questions: first, what are the most fundamental lessons the Arab world can learn from the initial growth and evolution of modernity in the West? Second, under what circumstances was modernity transferred to the Arab world? Third, what lessons might one learn from the modernization of Arab societies so far? Fourth, how is it possible to free modernity from the tutelage of the dominant political elite in Arab society? Fifth, is it possible to modernize Islam, or how can it produce a modernity compatible with the main theological tenets of Islam?

Some Arab thinkers who have refused to embrace the modernization paradigms, argue that mainstream Western social sciences have failed to predict the contemporary resurgence of religion. One of the main assumptions that modern political science has taken for granted, for instance, is that all societies, traditional and modern, are gradually disentangling themselves from the grip of religion and that political secularization is inevitable. "How come," asks Ghalyūn, "that history has betrayed itself and produced what had not been expected? And how can one explain this 'historical deviation'?"[40] Ghalyūn notes that one main reason for the rise of Islamism has been the crisis of the modern nation-state. Resurgence presents both doctrinal and political challenges to the secular elite. Islamism has seen the nation-state as an historical extension of colonialism, and believes nationalism and colonialism have one goal in common: crushing the spiritual and religious foundations of modern Arabs. A secular elite that pays only lip service to Islam, especially as represented by the mass media, has controlled the entire cultural space. Ghalyūn discusses three discourses, the first of which is the discourse of Islamism. The second is the discourse of the secular technocratic state that suddenly finds itself facing the formidable challenge of Islamism. The state depends more and more on the official ulama establishment as a means of protection against the challenges of resurgence.[41] The third discourse is loosely called the secularist camp, a fragile alliance of intelligentsia, party and union members, and Leftist thinkers. "This secularist alliance, unlike the Islamic one, is neither based on a strong tradition, nor popular consciousness, which exemplify a strategic depth and a conceptual and political reservoir of the contemporary Islamic movements."[42] "Religious capital" (*ra's māl dīnī*) has become the banner of the dispossessed, the alienated, and a protest movement against the failed mechanisms of the secular state. Arab modernity has failed miserably in alleviating the suffering of the masses and instead, "has created all the necessary conditions for a novel barbarism – a great majority of people who are alienated both mentally and materially and who live a muddy existence."[43] In Ghalyūn's opinion, "New Islamism is a clear expression of the metamorphosis of the shacks' inhabitants from a peripheral social group to a complete society."[44]

CONCLUSIONS

Secularization, which refers to broad cultural, social and political processes in the Arab world, has been inevitable since the advent of colonialism. In the absence of political democracy in the Arab world, the rise of political Islam, and the predicament of the Arab secularist movement, what is the best alternative?

At present, it is important to choose a specifically Arab secular vision in order to guide the different transformations currently under way in the Arab world. The progress of the Arab world in the past century has been inconsistent. However, what has been astonishing about almost every Arab country has been the military hegemony exercised by the ruling elite over the masses. In an important article on the status of secularism in contemporary Indian society, Amartya Sen identifies three challenges to Indian secularism: communal fascism; sectarian nationalism; and militant obscurantism.[45] Sen does not mention a fourth challenge, which is the military suffocation of civil society. With its centralized power, the army in many Arab countries has blocked the formation of healthy civil associations. The Arab secularist movement has been living in crisis due to the general crisis affecting the Arab world. A large part of the secular movement takes the side of the ruling elite against the "religious masses." To gather momentum, the secularist movement must distance itself from the ruling elite and present a critical discourse that reflects the feelings and concerns of the masses. Furthermore, the secularist movement must rethink its position on religion, which should be accommodative rather than confrontational.

It is time to move from political control to democracy and from religious extremism to religious tolerance and pluralism. Religious tolerance should be preached with this secularist vision as one of the major cornerstones of Arab societies. Religious tolerance is not new to the Arab and Muslim world, as Bernard Lewis claims.[46] It must be resurrected in the contemporary era.[47] In addition, there must be a clear-cut separation between Sharīʻah and politics to safeguard both religious tolerance and freedom. To leave the Sharīʻah to the whims of the ruling elite only complicates matters since some rulers in the modern period have tended to exploit religious feeling for their own political ends. Muslims can practice Islam perfectly well without implementing the Sharīʻah from the top down. To argue, as many conservative Muslim thinkers have over the years, that a separation between state and religion is harmful to Islam is contentious at best. This separation has been a fact in Muslim history since the very beginning. I think it is crucial to develop a secularist vision that is protective of religious belief, that is, the theistic dimension of religion. Without such an approach, it is difficult to safeguard Islam and protect it from political manipulation.

It is far from true to argue that an Arab secularist vision should be antithetical to religion. On the contrary, religious identity should be protected as one among many in the Arab world. It is easy to argue, as did Charles Taylor in his magisterial work, *Sources of the Self: The Making of the Modern Identity*,[48] that the modern period of the Arab world has been inundated with new patterns of identity. The religious identity has redefined itself in the midst of the epochal transformations befalling the Arab world in the past two centuries. However, the ruling elite and their intellectual supporters in the Arab world cannot tolerate free expression of the religious identity as an equal among many patterns of identities.[49] In other words, the Arab elite are ready to ascribe the word "terrorism" to any Islamist activity, however innocent, that falls outside of the state's control. Any healthy debate about secularism in the Arab world must start with the premise of "intellectual and religious pluralism." Because most institutions in the Arab world are secular, a public expression of the religious must not diminish this reality. A plurality of religious and secular voices must coexist in order to improve the status of civil society in the contemporary Arab world. Religious people must be allowed to express their identities in public. Increased oppression naturally leads to religious extremism and fanaticism. Undoubtedly, this is a frightening aspect of the current situation in the Arab world. However, one must acknowledge that only a minority of disgruntled religious intellectuals and practioners express religious fanaticism. Most who define themselves as religious are anxious to implement change by peaceful and democratic means. Also, in spite of the oppressive nature of the contemporary state, there has been a marked resurgence in religious life in Arab society. One must admit that the public expression of religion is one of the most central facts in contemporary Arab society.

5
Formation of Contemporary Identities: Nationalism and Islamism in Contemporary Arab Thought

"Although the normative Islamic text is oblivious to the institutionalization of religion and to any priestly intervention (*waṣāṭah kahanūtiyah*) between Man and God, Muslim social history has recognized the caliphate, which was similar, institutionally speaking, to the papacy. It is true that Christ defines the Church as the 'community of believers'; however, Christian social history has defined the Church as an institution wielding tremendous political and economic power which combines this world and the hereafter, and which set up inquisition courts and granted believers the forgiveness of sins for a specified sum of money. The Islamic text promotes freedom of expression, respect of reason, the opening of the door of *ijtihād*, and dialogue between civilizations. However, throughout Muslim social history, many ideas, men, and civilizations were condemned and burned. Also, the text promotes social justice, but Muslim social history has been full with the worst and most oppressive political systems and religious legislations. The Islamic text does not admit of a 'priestly class' since believers are equal. However, throughout Muslim history the men of religion have been abundant." Ghālī Shukrī, *Diktātoriyat al-takhalluf al-'arabī* (Cairo: al-Hay'ah al-Miṣriyyah al-'Āmmah li'l Kitāb, 1994), 118.

"Expansion as a permanent and supreme aim of politics is the central political idea of imperialism. Since it implies neither temporary looting, nor the more lasting assimilation of conquest, it is an entirely new concept in the long history of political thought and action." Hannah Arendt, *The Origins of Totalitarianism* (New York: Meridian Books, 1963), 125.

"Among the many illusions that persisted in modernization theory was one with special pertinence to the Islamic world, namely, that before the advent of the United States, Islam had existed in a kind of timeless childhood, shielded from true development by an archaic set of superstitions, prevented by its strange priests and scribes from moving out from the Middle Ages and into the modern world. The Islamic world seemed indifferent to the blandishments of Western ideas altogether." Edward W. Said, "The Formation of American Public Opinion on the Question of Palestine," in his *The Politics of Dispossession* (New York: Vintage Books, 1995), 59.

"La diversité des cultures fait place à l'unité de l'esprit humain…La culture est universelle; donc les cultures des peuples dits a tort 'primitifs' participent comme celle de l'Europe à l'universalité." ("Diversity of culture gives space to the unity of the human spirit…Culture is universal. Therefore, the cultures erroneously dubbed 'primitive' participate like the culture of Europe in universality." Translation by Abu-Rabi'.) Henri Lefebvre, *Le manifeste différentialiste* (Paris: Gallimard, 1970), 182–3.

There have been many Islamic interpretations of the Sacred Text, but only one Islam. The cultural constructions of Islam throughout Muslim history have taken different shapes while appealing to the most essential theological components of the text. Therefore, one may speak of different "cultural constructions of Islam" reflecting the temperaments and practices of different ideological/religious/intellectual forces in Muslim society throughout history, which were essentially heterogeneous. The history of these different cultural constructions, the different ideological forces they represented, and how they helped to maintain or undermine a certain *status quo* is quite fascinating.[1] Writing such a history might ultimately help clarify the nature of the critical relationship between state and civil society throughout Muslim history, and the role religious authority has played in either reinforcing or weakening this relationship.[2] It is clear that religious authority, in both its sacred and secular senses, has been invoked by almost every major force (tribal, religious, political, or even feminist) within Muslim society for the purpose of guaranteeing and promoting that force's interests. Religion has been deeply intertwined with both culture and politics throughout Islamic history, to say the least. Religious dogma has been inseparable from actual life; it has shaped and been shaped by the synergy of history.

By speaking of the cultural constructions of Islam, I do not mean to imply that Islam as a religion and idea can be comprehended only through its cultural, social, or historical expressions. These are but significant approaches that enable us to come to grips with the manifestations of Islam throughout history and the interesting questions and issues these manifestations have raised. Religion can and has been both a passive and a revolutionary medium. However, it seems to me that religion as doctrine has to be *believed* not so much intellectualized. Most will agree that the main objective of religion is the realization of the ultimate concern, which is God. But since religion as doctrine does not exist in the abstract, the religious quest must also appeal to human reason. Muḥammad 'Abduh notes that, "The Muslims are agreed that if religion can reveal certain things to us that exceed our comprehension, it cannot teach us anything that is in contradiction with our reason."[3]

Perhaps it is impossible to give a precise cognitive definition of Islam, especially when taking belief and human passion into consideration. One may further argue that even the most sophisticated theological formulations cannot accurately describe belief, since belief is not subject to intellectualization and rationalization. However, belief has always interchanged with, and here I do not say defined or shaped, history and human action. On one plane, therefore, it is impossible to draw a clear-cut distinction between belief and history or belief and society. The two are often mixed together and tend to produce certain results with specific intentions. My understanding of Islam goes beyond that of belief or history apart from belief, but is a combination of the interaction of the two. Islam is both normative and historical; in other words, it is both theological and rational. The theological expresses itself as fascination with divine mystery, whereas the rational deals with the fascination of human history.

Although this book discusses in part legal and religious Islamist formulations in the post-colonial era, it deals with the way in which colonial Western modernity has challenged the traditional Islamic worldview, formulated over a long period of time before the modern encounter between the Muslim world and the West, and the different Muslim responses to this challenge. The core of these responses has been a specific theological definition of what the sacred in Islam means and the unanimous, and perhaps implicit, agreement among the major modern Muslim thinkers that the sacred cannot be questioned, whereas the West, Christianity, and the challenges facing the Muslim world can.

COLONIALISM, ARABISM, AND ISLAMISM

In the modern world, cultural constructions of Islam have taken place against the presence of a powerful enemy, colonialism and colonialist culture. Islam, as universality, extended meaning to the anti-colonial struggle in the Muslim world. Thus, modern Muslim identity cannot be grasped apart from modern history. Modern Muslim history, diverse as it is, faced the challenges of Westernization coming from the different corners of Europe. This does not mean that both the West and Islam are essentially at odds. What I mean to say is that the modern historical evolution of the West in the form of an aggressive capitalist modernity put itself on a collision course with the Muslim world. On the eve of colonialism, Muslim societies took a deep introspective look at the nature of their civil societies and states and were forced to contemplate a new pattern of relationships in a new era of colonial and capitalist domination. Different Muslim voices emerged with a heterogeneous set of responses to the one complex political, social, and intellectual challenge: colonialism and its successor, neo-colonialism.

The Muslim response to this complex and multi-layered challenge of colonialism and Westernization has taken different forms: Puritanism, fanaticism, revivalism, reform, secularism, and revolution. Colonialism was not a simple or benevolent transfer of Western modernity to a backward society or culture, but a multifaceted colonial and capitalist encounter of the highest order. It (colonialism) spent many painstaking years trying to set up a highly sophisticated system of colonization to ensure a systematic transfer of wealth from the native populations to the European Center. Against this background, the history of Islamic reform in the modern Muslim world, be it in India or the Arab world, cannot be properly fathomed without understanding the colonial fact in its evolution and structure.[4] Alas, colonialism is at the very foundation of modern Islamic history and thought. To grapple with the meaning of the modern self, that is, the Muslim self, is to grapple by definition with the meaning of the Other, that is, the West. The universality of the triumphant West collided with that of Islam. In other words, the formulation of pre-colonial Islamic identity as faith faced a major challenge with the onset of the modern world.

Nineteenth century Islamic reform grappled with the questions of both colonialism and the construction of a new Muslim society and state, and the answers it has given still represent the launching pad for the responses of many modern Muslim intellectuals to the same questions. One may summarize the classical problematic of the reform movement as follows: How is it possible to catch up with the scientific and intellectual achievements of Western civilization and revive Muslim society and thought without hampering the essential Islamic teachings that relate to doctrine, ethics, law, and worship? By all accounts, Western modernity has posed a crucial challenge to the main legal and historical formulations of Muslim thought in both the nineteenth and twentieth centuries. Therefore, it has been impossible, even for the most conservative of Muslim thinkers, to envisage modern Muslim thought apart from its historical, philosophical, and even religious interaction with or response to Western thought and its complex manifestations in the Muslim and Arab world. Clearly, this interaction, forced or not, between the modern Western and Muslim worlds, has uncovered the enormous socio-political and military gaps between the advanced capitalist and urban West and the less advanced, mainly agrarian, Muslim world. This cornerstone of interaction, unequal at best, has also unraveled two different sets of worldviews or *Weltanschauungs*: the Muslim and the Western. Each has been subject to a complex construction of unique components of enormous epistemological and historical dimensions. At the center of the Muslim worldview is the notion of belief that derives its legitimacy from two sources: the Qur'an and the Sunnah. At the center of the modern Western worldview is the notion of rationalism and its unlimited potential. The post-Enlightenment West went colonial and justified its colonialism with modernity. The Muslim world in the age of colonialism was on the defensive and its religious leadership tried to manage the Western assault with new religious and legal formulations that stressed the compatibility of reason and revelation.

Islamic reform was the first organized Muslim intellectual movement that attempted to give theoretical responses for the reasons behind the decline of the Muslim people, and, inversely, those behind the progress of the West. As a movement with solid foundations in classical Islamic thought and culture (hence the appellation it acquired, Salafīyyah), Islamic reform considered, besides those issues related to the Islamic Sharī'ah and education, new ideas and methods of constructing society and state, while also addressing the issue of forming a modern Muslim identity and creating ways to preserve Islam in the modern age.[5] In this sense, Islamic reform reconsidered Muslim tradition in light of the new conditions engendered by its encounter with capitalist modernity. To the mind of many reformers, the Muslim world was in crisis. Some contemporary observers of Islam believe that Islamic tradition is still in crisis. In Talal Asad's view, for example, "Islam is a major tradition in countries where Muslims live. It is not the only tradition, of course, but one that still constitutes a significant part of the lives of most Muslims. Because Muslim societies are in crisis, Islamic tradition is in crisis too. It has to be defended, argued through and reconstructed if it is to be viable."[6]

Combined with the response of Islamic reform, or parallel to it, has been the nationalist response to the colonial challenge, which focused on cultural constructions, as well. Nationalism did not take "belief" as a starting point; on the contrary, certain trends in nationalist thought in the Arab and Muslim world thought of *belief* as a hindrance to the progress of society.

As a matter of fact, more often than not, Arabism before World War One especially in North Africa and Egypt ensued from the Islamic reform movement, represented in the main by al-Afghānī and 'Abduh. It is important to highlight the idea that Islamism in the first decades of the twentieth century was wedded, more or less, to the same ideals of nationalism: independence from colonialism and development of Arab societies.[7] In Greater Syria, the Arab nationalist movement, which was Ottomanist for a while, reacted against the great decline of the late Ottoman Empire and only after the Committee of Union and Progress (CUP) revolution against Sultan Abdul Hamid, did this movement take a strong Arabist turn. After the institution of both the British and French Mandates, Arabism and Islamism were more or less focused on the same objectives: the unity of the Arab world; the fight against colonialism, and the fight against sectarianism.[8] At the beginning of the twenty-first century, they seem to be the most powerful oppositional forces within Arab societies. However, their journey together has been full of pain and contradiction. What are the common bonds that unite them at the beginning of the twenty-first century?

Nationalism in the Arab and Muslim world has had a rather interesting history and many have written on the introduction of nationalism to the Arab or Muslim collective consciousness.[9] It suffices to say at this juncture that the forces of nationalism in the Arab world fought very hard to lay down a broad emancipatory project that would provide a sense of identity for the Arab masses in the modern era. Two recent books, one by Ralph Coury and the other by Bashir Nafi, document and analyze the rise of nationalism in the Arab world, which in fact was not contradictory to the general philosophy of Islamism.[10] The nationalist Arab consciousness developed hand-in-glove with the social, economic, and political transformations taking place in the Arab world in the first half of the twentieth century, and was faithful to the historical anguish of the Arab people and their desire to achieve political independence. That is to say that the development of Arab nationalism was not predicated on fictitious but very real conditions. That is why Ralph Coury contends, in a path-breaking study on the life of Azzam Pasha, that the shortcomings of many works on Arab nationalism

> stem from a shared idealism and atomism that conceive of Arab nationalism in abstract terms and that do not meaningfully or systematically relate it to a larger social and political environment. Arab nationalism has often been perceived in terms of autonomously decisive essence that has been everywhere the same in its painful deficiencies and inadequacies.[11]

The birth of Arab nationalism was a necessary outcome of the long development of social, political, and economic factors in the Arab world.

Although spearheaded by the bourgeoisie – the notables in Nafi's words and the governing political and educational elite in Coury's – Arab nationalism came to permeate almost every region of the Arab world while developing an inclination towards economic and political unity as a means of transcending division and foreign exploitation. In carefully reading both works, one comes away with the following main conclusions about the history and nature of Arab nationalism: first, one must understand the rise of modern Arabism and Islamism in the Arab world against the backdrop of the following factors:

1. the disintegration of the Ottoman Empire as a multiglot, multiethnic, and multireligious empire;
2. the rise of European imperialism in the Ottoman provinces as a formidable political, economic, and cultural movement;
3. the rise of Zionism with its consistent aim from the start of establishing a Jewish homeland in Palestine;
4. the deep social and economic transformations in the Arab world during that period.

In a sense, nationalism is universal and inseparable from internationalism, to paraphrase some of the words of Benedict Anderson.[12]

Both authors show that the Ottoman Empire faced a long process of disintegration after several centuries of domination both in the Arab world and in Eastern Europe. That this gradual process of disintegration produced fascinating results, one of which was the transition experienced by the Ottoman Empire in its political philosophy from Ottomanism to pan-Turanism (that is, the glorification of the pre-Islamic Turkish past), a process that created a major backlash in the political culture of the ethnic and religious communities making up the Empire. It is this deep adjustment within the Ottoman Empire to the world outside and the pressures of the imperialist demands of the West that had created severe repercussions within the Ottoman Empire. Nafi concludes that Arabism was a natural outgrowth of the decline of Ottomanism and the gradual, although painful, awareness of the Arab and Muslim intelligentsia of the dawn of imperialism.

On the other hand, in his critique of the claims of the Zionist school of historiography[13] that Arab nationalism, specifically in Egypt, was the creation of the Palace in the 1930s and 1940s, Coury proves beyond the shadow of a doubt the real social, political, economic, and cultural conditions that made the rise of Arabism in Egypt and the rest of the Arab world a historical necessity in the interwar period. According to Coury, the following led to the rise of Arab nationalist consciousness in Egypt:

1. Arab unity was perceived as a solution to Egypt's growing unemployment problems;
2. the export of Egyptian goods to the larger Arab market;
3. the central political and cultural role played by Egypt in the Arab world;
4. the impact of the Palestine problem and Zionism on the Egyptian intelligentsia. Both the intelligentsia and ruling elite rejected the Zionist claims to Palestine;

5. the emergence of new political forces that helped to focus Egyptian attention on Arab questions.

To Coury, these factors summarize the inception and growth of the Arab idea in Egypt in the interwar period. In addition, his analysis of the life of Azzam Pasha and the national and economic aspirations he represented reflects Coury's sense of the evolution of Arabism as an historical and cultural movement.

However, it is important to argue that nationalism has presented its own version of "imagined community,"[14] to use Benedict Anderson's most celebrated phrase, over and against the universality of the dominant Western civilization. This was the point of meeting between Arabism and Islamism (read as Salafīyyah) in the nineteenth century. In its secularist manifestation, nationalism is susceptible to becoming Western-oriented; however, in its indigenous manifestation, it was suspicious of the complacent claims of the West to universality, which was translated as creating standardized universal cultural models and traits for the purpose of dominating the indigenous people, including the intellectuals. But indigenous nationalism, in its quest to reconstruct its nationalist personality, hit a snag with Islam, as both a worldview and culture.

It is true that some leading Arab nationalists such as Azzam Pasha were both religious and nationalist. In this sense, both nationalism and the Islamic project of the modern era appealed to the same larger past of the Arab-Islamic heritage and shared the same language, Arabic. Deep cultural and political movement, caused by colonialist challenges, forced the projects of both nationalism and Islam to more or less focus on the same past. In his powerful dismantling of colonialist hegemonic culture, Fanon reminds us that "colonialism is not satisfied merely with holding a people in its grip and emptying the native's brain of all form and content. By a kind of perverted logic, it turns to the past of the oppressed people, and distorts, disfigures, and destroys it."[15] It is precisely colonialism's using the past of the oppressed for the purpose of disfiguring it for its own advantage that unites both Arabism and Islamism in their attempt to salvage a glorious image of the past. Nationalism resurrected Islam as an Arab religion and Muhammad as an Arab Prophet. Both Nationalism and Islamism invented their own versions of the past, and both anchored their ideal in a highly unstable present.

In a curious way, both the nationalist and Islamic projects have dominated the cultural and intellectual scene of the Arab world in the modern age. Both competed over the definition of the cultural personality of the Arab people and their desire to authenticate themselves in a certain construction of the past. After independence, however, Islamism was barred from meaningful participation in the political and economic process in many Arab countries, especially in Egypt. Ṭāriq al-Bishrī considers nationalism in Egypt to have emerged from the sleeves of Islamism. Both were homogeneous and united by common concerns, such as the question of Palestine and the economic and political realities of colonialism.[16] However, in the 1950s and 1960s, Arabism and Islamism stood at opposite poles. Arabism was busy fighting on two fronts: first, forming the institutions of a nationalist state without the aid of the traditional European powers, and second preparing the ground to fight against Israel. In other words, Arabism aimed at achieving two main objectives after independence: first, internal economic development and, second, the liberation of Palestine, all without any real participation from Islamists since, according to Bishrī, Islamists were removed from power in most Arab countries. To a large extent, these two objectives defined the journey of Arab nationalism in the two decades preceding the 1967 war. In achieving these objectives, Arab nationalism created and adapted a secular umbrella and allied itself with the Left, especially in Egypt and Syria. For a while, Nasserism was able to generate mass support in Egypt as well as in the rest of the Arab world.[17] However, Arabism after independence, with its center in Egypt, was not allowed to complete its work of economic and social independence. In the words of Muḥammad H. Haykal, the United States "unleashed" Israel in 1967 to destroy the economic project of Nasserism.[18] It is false to argue that the Arab nationalist movement after independence, including Nasserism, was bankrupt once it was in power. For example, the Sudanese Islamist thinker Ḥassan al-Turābī argues that once the nationalist movement secured power from imperialism, it was not prepared to do anything. The nationalist movement, in his words, was "completely consumed in the business of national struggle and how to achieve national independence."[19]

Although weakened by its resistance to colonialism, nationalism emerged triumphant after the official termination of colonialism in most of the Arab world roughly in the 1950s. Whether or not we agree with Fanon that the national bourgeoisie in the Arab world on the eve of independence was weak, it is a fact that this bourgeoisie resorted to dependence on a charismatic leader who "stands for moral power, [and] in whose shelter the thin and poverty-stricken bourgeoisie of the young nation decides to get rich."[20] Fueled by this find, nationalism in both the Middle East and North Africa sought to embody its success in the erection of institutions and the issuing of constitutional edicts that reflected its vision of a liberal, nationalist, and secularist project. This vision was set against the background of colonialism and also that of the Islamic project, which had failed to articulate its vision back then in institutional and constitutional frameworks. Just as in India, as Ranajit Guha notes, elitism in the form of Arab elite personalities, ideas, and institutions dominated Arab nationalist historiography.[21]

In discussing the interchange or competition between nationalism and Islamism in their different trends and subdivisions over the definition of post-colonial culture in the Arab world, I speak seemingly in the most general terms. In fact, the transition from colonialism to post-colonialism was an extremely complex process. In addition, the transition was not uniformly achieved in all Arab countries. Every country had its specific situation. The levels of colonization in the Arab world varied radically. In response to heterogeneous forms of colonialism, the Arab world began a series of transitions and shifts which enabled it to terminate the political domination of colonialism by creating the modern Arab state. However, one must not confuse political decolonization with cultural decolonization.[22] The latter has been a much slower process and in certain Arab countries it is a still a visible process, especially in relation to the efforts at Arabization in North Africa.

It is important to understand the post-colonial formations of the Arab world against the complex interplay between different factors. The modern Saudi state, for example, which was not officially colonized by Europe, had nonetheless fallen under European/American influence in the early part of the twentieth century. The Saudi state was able to achieve a discernible pattern of political organization only in the 1930s under the leadership of King ‘Abd al-‘Azīz, after a complex series of negotiations, wars, alliances – both internal and external – between the Saudi family and other tribes, and religious forces in the desert.[23] The discovery of oil in the country added a new dimension to political organization. The modern formation of the Saudi state cannot be analyzed apart from king, family, religion, tribe, and petroleum, and the concomitant implications of these categories.[24] All have shaped the alliance formations of the modern Saudi state and uniquely stamped it, which no force (such as Arab nationalism or Islamism) has successfully been able to challenge. The discovery of petroleum in commercial quantities in Saudi Arabia in the 1930s gave the country not just additional sources of income, but immense technological knowledge, which forced it to enter the modern world from its technological door, rather than from an Islamic standpoint. The relationship between the technological and the religious, or between the capitalist forms of economic and cultural penetration and the Wahabi doctrine taking form in the country in the pre-modern era, has been very tense, to say the least. The Wahabi doctrine, which emphasizes a total orientation towards Islam and its forms of cultural expressions of the past, is incompatible with many of the forms of cultural and intellectual expression that have been brought about by the ubiquitous presence of capitalism in the modern Arab world.

In almost every Arab country, the breakdown of the political system of colonization did not mean the disappearance of other forms of engagement, encounter, or relationship between the Arab world and the metropolitan centers. Every Arab country inherited modern forms of knowledge and technology from colonialism. As Moroccan sociologist Abdelkabir al-Khatibi argues, “The [Arab] state became truly dominant only after colonization; that is, its capacity to rule has been strengthened thanks to the instruments and techniques of power bequeathed by imperialism.”[25] However, besides the technological factor, the strength of every Arab political system is predicated on the nature of alliances within the country, which are the result of negotiation between a number of forces: army, party or tribe or family, economic elite, and intellectual and religious elite. The Nasserite project in Egypt, for example, worked hard to change the nature of alliance in pre-1952 Egyptian revolution by summoning the middle and poorer classes to play more active roles in cultural, social, and economic processes. For a while, the pre-1952 Egyptian bourgeoisie seemed phased out of nationalist imagination. In retrospect, however, it seems that one of the failures of the Nasserist project had been not to uproot completely the power of this bourgeoisie. In most present configurations of power in the contemporary Arab world, the Arab political system faces a tremendous image problem at the domestic level. However, this is no way an indication that this configuration is weak or about to give away power.

If revolutionary nationalism or Islamism were to succeed in the contemporary Arab world, it would have to come to grips with the complex alliances in each Arab country before trying to change the political system. Islamism would have to distinguish itself from the current forms of Islamic association with the *status quo* by presenting a comprehensive program of social and economic change.

Since the dawn of the post-colonial Arab state, oppositional Islamism has embraced the cause of the Sharīʿah as a form of protest against the Arab state. Although the Sharīʿah movement, by and large, has failed to dislodge the post-colonial state structure, it has made some headway against the state, especially in many parts of the Arab world where the state itself has made concessions to Islamic forces in society.

THE 1967 DEFEAT AND THE REVIVAL OF THE SHARĪʿAH QUESTION

There are two distinct types of Sharīʿah movements in the contemporary Arab world: one is pacifist in nature and supports the *status quo*; the other, discussed above, is oppositional.[26] Both of these movements pay close attention to the Sacred Text although they derive different conclusions therefrom. The pacifist Sharīʿah movement represents the official side of the governing political elite and is mainly centered in state-sponsored universities and ministries of endowments and religious affairs. The intellectual core of this type of Sharīʿah has been trained in many religious universities in the Gulf states and North Africa. It uses the Sacred Text as an instrument with which to enhance the legitimacy of the ruling elite and the *status quo*. The oppositional Sharīʿah, on the other hand, uses the Sacred Text as an instrument of mobilization and as an avenue by which to express the dissatisfaction of the masses with the ruling elite.

Since 1967, two major events have made it necessary to examine the main arguments of Sharīʿah supporters who take an oppositional stand vis-à-vis the governing elite: first, the 1967 event itself, and second the second Gulf War of 1991. In the first instance, the 1967 Arab defeat with Israel made it possible for the Islamic movement to publicly respond to the predicament of nationalism in the Arab world. Here, the polarization between Arab nationalism and Islamism is most conspicuous. In the second instance, the Islamists did not see the attack on Iraq by Western powers under the auspices of the United Nations as a defeat for the nationalists as much as Western aggression against Muslim people. Initially, the Arab Islamist movement sided with Kuwait against Iraq and criticized the Iraqi attack on Kuwait as illegitimate. However, when it became very clear that the United States and its allies were intent on attacking Iraq, the Islamist movement changed sides and began to criticize the international coalition against Iraq. The Western attack on Iraq created opportunities of rapprochement between Arab nationalism and Islamism. The Islamist movement for a long time had had its disagreements with the Baʿth Party in both Iraq and Syria. This was mainly due to the secularist and nationalist nature of the regimes in both Syria and Iraq and the repression of the Islamist movement in both countries in the 1970s and 1980s.[27]

One may argue that the 1967 defeat put an end to the benevolence of the elite in politics and helped demystify its role in daily life. Arabism faced the most formidable dilemma in its short life. Some radical Islamist groups greeted the defeat of Arabism as a blessing to the Arab world. Intellectualism subsided in Arab society and fanaticism, whether religious or secular, was on the offensive. However, the most direct result of the 1967 war was the collapse of those foundations that promised to support a new Arab civil society after independence.

The Arab world was in a state of disarray, with no sense of how to protect domestic and national security. Regionalism, tribalism, and sectarianism replaced national unity and vision. According to Burhān Ghalyūn, the 1967 defeat ushered the Arab world into an open-ended crisis (*azmah maftūḥah*).[28]

Ṣādiq Jalāl al-'Azm observes that the political defeat was the manifestation of a larger intellectual, cultural, and scientific stagnation in the Arab world.[29] Furthermore, the political elite in the Arab East, most notably in Syria, Jordan, and Egypt, managed to drive itself into political bankruptcy and discredit itself by refusing to give up power. Indeed, the combination of these diverse and strange factors led to the revival of the Islamist project after 1967. The eruption of Islamism was naturally a product of the severe crisis affecting all Arab societies. Islamism promised new hope for the destitute masses.

The aftermath of the defeat led to new resurgence of the Islamic project, one of the most significant political, religious, and cultural events in the Arab and Muslim world at the end of the twentieth century. The Sharī'ah question constitutes the core of this project. Islamists lost no time in presenting its version of new constructions of Islam and the Muslim identity in an age of defeated nationalism and corrupt modernism.[30] These constructions took the form of, although were not limited to, a fresh appraisal of the Sharī'ah question in contemporary Arab society.[31] The Islamist critique of the dominant political, economic, and religious conditions in the Arab world was not confined to particular countries, but it covered almost every Arab country, including those that claimed to apply the Sharī'ah, such as Saudi Arabia and other Gulf countries.[32] Since 1967, the Islamist movement, reemerging as the most viable socio-religious force, has leveled a sustained and popular critique to the Arab political elites, the failure of their modernization program, the loss of political and civil freedoms and the ossification of political leadership. In the Arab East, Ikhwān thinkers throughout the Arab world began to understand the negative implications of their debacle with Nasserism before 1967 and the meaning of the thought of Sayyid Quṭb, executed by the Egyptian state in 1966. A need to transcend the "*jāhiliyyah-takfīr*" dimensions of Quṭb's thought was felt. In North Africa, Malek Bennabi,[33] and 'Allāl al-Fāsī[34] were preaching the necessity of a better expression of Islam in public life, especially after independence.

Therefore, new life was brought to the question of the Sharī'ah, which was seen as a symbol of resuscitating Islamic life after 1967. Here, a number of prominent Arab Islamist thinkers, most notably Yūsuf al-Qaraḍāwī,[35] Rāshid al-Ghannūshī, 'Allāl al-Fāsī, and Aḥmad Kamāl Abū'l Majd,[36] examine the question of the Sharī'ah in the context of the juristic principle of *maṣlaḥah* (welfare) or *maṣāliḥ al-'ibād* (the welfare of people) developed by early Muslim jurists such as al-Ghazālī, Ibn Taymiyya, and most specifically Imām Ibrāhīm Ibn Ishāq al-Shāṭibī (d. 1388). The Sharī'ah question centers around theological, moral, political, and cultural arguments which claim to find a solution to the predicament of nationalism. Although in practical terms, no credible Islamic political system has emerged in the Arab world since 1967 (except until recently the very controversial Sudanese system inspired by Islamist thinker Ḥassan al-Turābī), the Islamic alternative still nourishes the imagination of many in the Arab world.[37]

If the age of colonialism in the Arab world marks the resilience and maturity of nationalism, the 1967 defeat with Israel marks the disintegration of nationalist thinking and political prowess. The graduation of the Arab world from the broad one-nation mentality to the world of tiny, fragmented, and dependent nation-states revived the latent hopes and dreams of the Islamic project for a one united ummah, that very idea which had received terrible blows from triumphant nationalism. The revival of the Islamic project after 1967 was the direct consequence of the failure of Arab nationalism to institutionally implement the notion of the Arab nation as a limited, sovereign, and independent community. The post-1967 Islamic resurgence presented anew its notion of the ummah as an unlimited community, synonymous with "a colossal emancipatory revolution" (*thawrah taḥaruriyah kubrah*) in the words of Sayyid Quṭb, the foremost thinker of Arab Islamism in the 1950s and 1960s.[38] Islamism thus gained a new ground after defeat and emerged as the only reliable mass movement with a possible answer for an exhausted ummah.

As discussed in more details within, Arab nationalism has faced a major debacle since 1967, and the Arab defeat with Israel was a clear manifestation of this. In its ascent to power, nationalism, besides competing with the Islamic project, attempted to put an end to Islamism's political and cultural aspirations by relegating it to a minor position in society. The post-1967 debate around the Sharī'ah is far from a mere religious question. It is, in the first instance, a reflection of the continuing decline of nationalism and its inability to provide plausible alternatives to the complex cultural and political challenges facing the Arab world. The Sharī'ah question, to my mind, is first, an expression of profound societal, political, and intellectual crisis in the contemporary Arab world. Second, it betrays the failure of the Arab state to deal with such issues as Arab political unity, the threat of Israel and neocolonialism, and failure to achieve political and economic independence, generally. Furthermore, raising the issue of the Sharī'ah, which is another way of expressing the Islamic personality at the present, forms a real social, cultural, and even political challenge to the entrenched political elite in the contemporary Arab world and their militaristic, heavy-handed solutions to the problems facing them. However, the optimism of the supporters of the Sharī'ah question was somewhat premature in the late 1960s and 1970s. The foremost living authority in contemporary Islamism, Shaykh Yūsuf al-Qaraḍāwī, best expressed this optimism.

In modern Islamist writings, only a selected number of thinkers have occupied a place of prominence. In spite of his redundant style of writing, Qaraḍāwī has occupied a place of distinction in contemporary Islamist discourse.[39] He has been remarkable in reworking the ideas of Shaykh Ḥassan al-Banna (henceforth referred to as Banna), the founder of the Muslim Brotherhood Movement, in that his thought represents a natural evolution of Banna's in the independence movement in the Arab world. Banna, assassinated in 1949, did not live long enough to further develop his ideas. Qaraḍāwī is also intellectually indebted to the ideas of another leading Islamist thinker, Shaykh Muḥammad al-Ghazālī (d. 1996). Qaraḍāwī's ideas have developed outside the Egyptian context. Since 1962, he has been living and teaching in the state of Qatar in the Gulf. Many agree that his ideas represent a cross-section of the views of the traditional religious intelligentsia in the Arab world, and not in Egypt alone.

Qaraḍāwī's ultimate goal is the creation of a new civil society in the Arab and Muslim world to be ruled completely by the Sharī'ah. The major events of post-colonial Arab history such as the emergence of the nation-state in the Arab world, the 1967 Arab defeat, and the 1970 civil war in Jordan, have made him more convinced than ever of what he calls the "inevitability of the Islamic solution" (*ḥatmiyat al-ḥall al-islāmī*). He does not preach reconciliation between his Islamist philosophy and that of the existing nation-state in the Arab world. Qaraḍāwī believes the nation-state has done its best to replace the Islamic system by a man-made order. To him, Islam has been besieged, cornered, and reduced to bits and pieces by the existing power structure in the modern Arab world.[40] He goes on to say, however, that because of its harmony with pristine human nature and mass appeal, Islam is the only religion and worldview that poses a realistic threat to the systems in place in the Arab and Muslim world.[41]

In order to convince his readers of the viability of the Islamic solution, Qaraḍāwī analyzes at length the failure of the Arab political systems in three major volumes.[42] He believes the political and social projects of most Arab governments, especially those that have carried the banner of socialism and nationalism, have met a disastrous end. The Arab world failed to fulfill the dreams of its masses after independence and the 1967 defeat was a manifestation of this colossal failure. The reason for this lies not in the failure of the Arab economy or technology but rather in the failure of the state to uplift the lot of the Arab masses, preserve and enhance the dignity of the human being, and consistently apply the Sharī'ah.

Qaraḍāwī's attacks on Arabism must be seen against the backgrounds of, first, the conflict between the Egyptian state and the Islamists in the 1950s and 1960s, and second, of the 1967 defeat and the ensuing political and ideological vacuum in the Arab world.[43] Qaraḍāwī's premises are as follows: first, nationalism, socialism, secularism, and liberalism are imported ideologies and philosophies. They do not correspond to the realities of the Arab and Muslim world. Second, neo-imperialists have targeted Islam and specifically Muslim unity by preaching liberalism and the protection of minorities. Third, the modernization of the nation-state has failed. Fourth, Islam has the answer and it is time for the Arab world to apply the Sharī'ah to resolve its numerous problems.

The Sharī'ah question brings back to the front the issues of both identity and authority in the post-colonial and post-nationalist phase of the Arab world. The concept of the sacred is invoked on a collective scale as one of the main sources of authority in the Arab world, but only after the failure of the nationalist modernizing elite to deliver on its promises of modernizing society along Western lines. Regardless if one agrees or not with such scholars as Abdullahi An-Na'im,[44] Ann Elizabeth Mayer[45] or Katerina Dalacoura,[46] who contend that the implementation of the Sharī'ah in its classical form is a violation of the human rights of minorities and women in society and that the Sharī'ah "is not the appropriate vehicle for Islamic self-determination in the present context," it remains to be stated that the calls for the implementation of the Sharī'ah emerged in response to the failure of the modern state in the Arab world and the rigidity of the political elite governing society. Arab modernity has come to a standstill.[47] Self-criticism is the rule. In this sense, the Sharīʻah movement has become the only protest movement with credible mass support and well-developed intellectual and ideological foundations.

At this juncture, it is necessary to distinguish between Arabism as a nationalist movement and the so-called nationalist regimes in such countries as Iraq, Syria, and Libya. The Libyan example is quite interesting. When Muʻammar Qaddāfī came to power in 1969, his thoughts and actions were strongly influenced by Nasser's charismatic personality. Libyan leadership was young, inexperienced and nationalist.[48] But, it is clear that the nationalist regime in Libya has faced a number of debacles since 1969: first, it failed to articulate a true philosophy of secularism in Libyan society. Second, its call for Arab unity has fallen on deaf ears. Recently, the Libyan regime has begun to identify itself more with Africa than with the Arab world and it decided to withdraw from the Arab League in October 2002. Third, Libya faces major problems with the West, especially after the imposition of the air embargo for almost ten years. These factors led to the hemorrhaging of the Libyan Arab nationalist project. Today, few Libyan intellectuals care to speak about Arab nationalism, let alone unity with the Arab world.[49]

Arabism and Islamism face huge obstacles at the beginning of the twenty-first century. Their proponents seem to be promoting disgruntled social and ideological movements that seek a place in the political limelight of the Arab world. Contemporary intellectual leaders of both Arabism and Islamism espouse, more or less, comprehensive ideologies of social and political change. Arabism's major focus is still the unity of the Arab world and issues of citizenship, whereas Islamism's major preoccupation continues to be the implementation of the Sharīʻah.[50] However, a huge difference of opinion exists between the radical element of Islam, as represented by the Egyptian Jihad and Jamāʻah al-Islāmiyyah movements on the one hand, and the mainstream Ikhwān movement on the other. The former believe that the Ikhwān, the largest Islamist movement in the Arab world, has compromised much with the secular "anti-Islamic" regimes and advocated a secular notion of democracy. It is only through a violent means that "true democracy" can be restored and Sharī'ah implemented in the Muslim world, argues Ayman Zawāhirī, main leader of the Egyptian Jihad in a recent book.[51]

Since 1994, Arab nationalists and Islamists opened a series of dialogues to debate ways of tackling the numerous challenges facing the Arab world.[52] In spite of their differences (both political and ideological), they seem to be united on a number of significant points: first, the issue of Palestine and the Arab-Israeli question. Both reject the so-called peace process that began after the Oslo agreement between the PLO and Israel.[53] Second, both seek a measure of unity in the Arab world in order to face the challenges of globalization, the international Zionist movement, and dependency on the West.[54] Arabists and Islamists are well aware that the current Arab state system is fundamentally at odds with the philosophy of Arab and Muslim unity. They note that since 1967, regionalism has incorporated the idea of unity. Third, Arabists and Islamists seek to revive civil society in the Arab world by bypassing the huge and corrupt bureaucracy that exists in several

Arab countries.[55] Fourth, Arabists and Islamists both oppose the increasing tendency of the contemporary Arab state to resort to oppression as a solution to problems.[56]

None of the above can be accomplished until the Islamists review some of the outstanding issues in Islamic thought. Fahmī Huwaydī, a leading Islamist intellectual in the contemporary Arab world, has since the early 1970s called for such a reappraisal. He argues that in the 1990s, Islamist discourse has matured with respect to the following questions: first, democracy and human rights. In spite of the increased calls for violence in different corners of the Arab world, the main Islamist discourse appeals to change via democratic and constitutional means. Second, the question of non-Muslims in the Muslim world. Huwaydī admits that the older category of dhimmis may not be tenable in the modern world. Citizenship has co-opted the concept of *dhimmis* and the law must treat all citizens equally. Third, the question of women. Huwaydī feels this is the most difficult question to address. However, he notes that there has been an increasing tendency in Islamist discourse to consider men and women equally in terms of rights and duties. Fourth, the question of the non-Muslim world, especially the West. Huwaydī argues that the traditional polarity of the "Abode of Islam" and the "Abode of non-Islam" is not viable in the modern era, mainly because the Muslim world has treaties and agreements with the non-Muslim world and there exists a substantial Muslim minority in the West.[57]

It is my contention that these important changes in Islamist discourse can help improve Islamist-nationalist cooperation. In spite of the hopelessness of the Arab political scene, Arabism and Islamism must continue the dialogue. The main challenge lies in the expansion of such a dialogue, especially in relation to the question of the implementation of the Sharī'ah, the question of secularism, and the role of women in society.[58] The two sides must also reach agreement on a common framework of reference, especially in respect to the economic and political independence of the Arab world and the fight against neo-colonialism. However, such an alliance cannot overlook the fundamental changes that have taken place in the Arab world since independence, especially the creation of the regional state in the Arab world and the incessant plan of the ruling elite to create pseudo-mass support, especially through religious support. The Arab world indeed faces a long list of internal and external problems. Therefore, the challenge confronting both Arabism and Islamism, if they are to forge such an alliance, is to first find a common language before any solution can be implemented.

ISLAMIC STUDIES AND THE STATE'S IDEOLOGY IN THE CONTEMPORARY ARAB WORLD

In one of his outstanding chapters on the link between the growth of civilization and the cultivation of scientific research in all fields of knowledge, Ibn Khaldūn,[59] the Arab historian of the fourteenth century, argues that the scientific mind is the product of a sedentary civilization. However, when a civilization experiences an absence of group feeling (*'aṣṣabiyyah*), scientific research tends to deteriorate. This is what happened in Muslim Spain in the twelfth and thirteenth centuries to the extent that the classical Islamic science of jurisprudence became "an empty institution among them [Spaniard Muslims], a mere shadow of its real self."[60] Ibn Khaldūn is primarily concerned about a scientific discourse in philosophy, history, and the traditional sciences as a means of keeping Muslim culture dynamic and vital. He is also concerned with enhancing the role of the intelligentsia in society. For this kind of scientific culture, he says, endowments and years of study are needed. Sedentary life provides the context for such scientific pursuits.

Ibn Khaldūn's proposition of creating a scientific discourse in the Muslim world is on the whole still valid in contemporary Arab or Muslim contexts. It is true that scientific knowledge has greatly proliferated since the fourteenth century and that the Muslim world has for a long time ceased to be the center of civilization for a long time. However, Ibn Khaldūn's remarks help us to understand the position of the "traditional Islamic sciences" in the modern educational systems of Arab and Muslim nation-states in the twentieth century. One may well agree with Ibn Khaldūn that the practitioners of the traditional sciences are "dull or at any rate did not try not to be dull." Various reasons account for this.

The theoretical treatment of Islam in either Western or Islamic literature has been conspicuously meager. At best, Islam is an object of ideological disagreement between different authors and has proven to be the Achilles' heel of modern theoretical reflection. Perhaps a scientific definition of Islam is an impossibility. In a controversial little book on "The Modernization of Modern Islamic Thought," 'Abd al-Majīd al-Charfi of Tunisia advocates the need to distinguish between "Islamic thought" and Islam. Islamic thought refers to all branches of Muslim sciences developing in the formative phases, such as Qur'anic exegesis, Hadīth studies, Kalām, Fiqh, and Sufism. Islam, to his mind, refers to the Sacred.[61] The former meaning is subject to change, while the latter is not.[62] This distinction is very useful, although in the final analysis, unsatisfactory. In speaking of Islam, it is significant to point out the following ideas: first, Islam has become a philosophical, theological, and ideological problematic in modern Arab and Muslim thought. Some speak of elite Islam (that is, official Islam), while others speak of popular Islam (that is, oppositional Islam). However, both agree that Islam can be an either passive or revolutionary force in society. Others go even further in arguing that the concept of Islam as revelation is untenable, and that Islam is what people make of it. It can be used as a movement of progress or as a means to justify social and economic disparities in society.[63] In other words, according to this position, Islam cannot be distinguished by a "sacred core," and practically speaking, Islam is amenable to more than one definition.[64]

Second, on the theological plane, Islam can acquire an open-ended meaning extending from a belief in one God to a theological connection with all revelations preceding it; on the other hand, it can have as simple a definition as the submission to one God. In other words, one can examine the theological nature of Islam from the perspective of the history of religions, especially from Judaism and Christianity, or one can see Islam from an inclusive theological viewpoint, the oneness of God.

Third, the text (*naṣṣ*) has been at the center of Muslim culture.[65] According to the majority opinion of Muslim jurists, both the Qur'an and Hadīth form the textual base of Islam, which furnish the main foundations of Islamic theology.

Therefore, it may be valid to argue that since the inception of Islam, a dialectical relationship has existed between text and (human) history, and text and human thought. In other words, Muslim history and thought have been the products of a complex interchange between the "human" and the "divine"; or between the religious text and socio-economic and political factors.

Fourth, Islam can be presented as a comprehensive anthropological fact, as Rochdy Alili notes in a recent work.[66] It is true that Islam has a normative core. However, in its historical evolution, Islam has given birth to a complex cultural, social, literary, philosophical, and political tradition that still to this day informs the worldview of Muslim people. Islam concerns itself with issues of political and social power and organization. It is important to note that the various intellectual and political movements have interpreted this tradition differently. In this sense, tradition can be either passive or revolutionary.

Both Islamic thought and history, two major dimensions concomitant with the theological essence of Islam, have given rise to a plethora of religious and ideological attitudes and forces that have taken the Qur'an and the Sunnah as their starting point. But, one may ask, what is Islam? There are a multiplicity of meanings inherent in the term *Islam*: Islam as text and theology; Islam as human thought; as history; and as one or several institutions. It is with all these different levels and facets of Islam in mind that I raise the issue of the Islamic problematic.

Why do the political elite in the contemporary Arab and Muslim world, unlike the founding fathers of modern Muslim nation-states, pay so much attention to "Islam" in their official pronouncements? What is the relationship between official culture and the Muslim intelligentsia in the Muslim world? Undoubtedly, Islam took on a revolutionary character in the colonial age, as seen in the careers of 'Abd al-Qādir al-Jazā'irī and Shaykh al-Sanūssī in North Africa. However, the Muslim world in the colonial era lacked the necessary power to arrest the gradual Westernization of Muslim societies. Before Europe intervened in the Muslim world, Muslim society was, more or less, governed by the ideology of Islam, which was interpreted by a traditional class of learned men. But this was not so after European intervention. European influence created dichotomies in all areas of life, including having had a profound impact on Muslim culture and education.

In one important sense, the introduction of European educational and technological systems made the traditional Muslim sciences, especially those that lacked scientific focus, quite obsolete and relegated the traditional Muslim intelligentsia to a secondary status. This drastic change in the system of education was not the result of any inherent superiority of Western over Islamic education, but was mainly due to the complex power structure set up by the colonial West in order to secure its interests in the Arab-Muslim world.[67] The introduction of Western norms of education in India, for example, created a new class of Muslim (as well as Hindu) intelligentsia, which began to use a new language relevant to the problems of Indian society in the nineteenth century. One example of this is the creation of the Anglo Muḥammadan College in India, which became Aligarah Muslim University at the end of the nineteenth century.[68]

With the rise of the nation-state, traditional religious education gained an important edge in society and the traditional religious intelligentsia became, more or less, a prominent class in the new state. Since independnece, the tiny and affluent political elite in the Muslim world very often worked hard since independence to reconstitute the religious class in society as a means of enhancing their *status quo*. One fundamental means of reconstituting this class was through education. The old religious class, belonging as it did to an obsolete social and political system, was dramatically revived with the onset of the nation-state and given a new value by the ruling elite. The new power given to the religious intelligentsia in society created dichotomies, though, between two different educational systems within the new nation-state, one Western-oriented and the other Islamic.

In Pakistan, for example, the religious intelligentsia gained tremendous power under the regime of Zia al-Haq, military ruler of the country from 1977 to 1988. The Dini Madaris, the theological schools of the country that follow an obsolete curriculum of education, became the focus of the state's interest, especially after Zia al-Haq resorted to his dubious program of Islamization. The Dini Madaris survived the colonial era. They have played a significant role in the educational policies of the new nation-state; leading ulama are usually recruited from such schools, and they gave Zia al-Haq his rationale for Islamization in the 1980s.[69] In addition, these Madaris at the height of the Soviet intervention in Afghanistan in the early 1980s, provided many student-fighters to the different Mujahideen in Afghanistan.[70] A detailed discussion of the attempts of the modern Pakistani state to subordinate the traditional educational system to the modern is beyond the scope of this book. It suffices to mention that the control of the different *awqāf* (endowments) by the state and the creation of the Ministry of Religious Affairs augmented the power of official traditional intelligentsia, who, since independence, have given an Islamic voice to the secular elite of Pakistani society.

In considering the previous discussion, it is important to investigate the philosophy of education in the modern Muslim world as closely as possible, especially in relation to traditional Islamic education. One might reach conclusions similar to those of Ibn Khaldūn's on the state of Muslim education in the thirteenth and fourteenth centuries or those of Shaykh 'Abdul Rahmān Jabartī in nineteenth century Egypt: Muslims, by and large, preferred memorization to scientific disputation and study.[71]

Islamic education gained prominence in many Muslim nation-states because of the need of the ruling elite for a group of traditional educated intelligentsia to defend the *status quo*. In the larger Muslim world, official ideology defended a reified notion of Islam as a means of spreading false consciousness. Very often, official ideology dismisses critical or revolutionary articulations of Islam.[72] The official position on Islam is most easily seen in Arab and Muslim academia, where in departments of theology the notion of "production of knowledge" is considered repugnant and "memorization" of classical texts is held in high esteem.[73] Most would agree that knowledge and power are intertwined.

What is blatantly obvious is the absence of a theoretical treatment of Islam in the Muslim world. This is evidenced by the curricular construction of the field of Islamic Studies in leading Muslim universities, such as the Azhar University in Egypt, the Imām ibn 'Abd al-Wahāb University in Saudi Arabia, and Dār al-Ḥadīth al-Ḥassaniyah in Morocco, and the thousands of traditional madrasas in South Asia, most notably in India, Pakistan, and Afghanistan. Because of the centrality and yet sensitivity of the subject of Islam, the state has directly intervened to construct the teaching of Islamic studies so that it does not threaten state interests or weaken its hold on official Muslim clergy. The modern construction by the state of Islamic or Sharī'ah studies has been done in a way to ensure the neutrality of religion in social and political matters. With the blessings of petrodollars, the ulama in leading Gulf universities spend their time debating a dead classical culture that revolves around a closed field, Arabic rhetoric and grammar. The state has reduced these "religious leaders" to mere consumers of its imported products, thanks to the urgent international need for Arab petroleum. A trouble-seeking religious leader faces a grim future. He is stripped of his honorary degrees and thrown in dungeon while denied the advantages of the state's modernization.[74] The Algerian thinker Malek Bennabi comments on the same phenomenon without, however, adducing the necessary conclusions from his remarks. He says that, "In the independent Muslim institutions, the syllabi and methods of instruction also seem to defy time; the principles have remained the same since the Christian Middle Ages."[75] It is clear that these methods of instruction and the knowledge associated with them became obsolete the moment they came up against a superior capitalist civilization in the nineteenth century. The ruling elite of the Muslim world were quick to reconstruct the field of Islamic Studies in the name of authenticity and without critical perspective in order to have the blessings of the religious elite. In one important sense, the secular nation-state in the Arab world has tolerated two official cultures, those of the state and religion, in spite of the epistemological gulf between them.

In this regard, one must agree with the contention of Mohammed Arkoun that "the history of Islam as a school of thought, as a culture, as a system of trans-social and transhistorical beliefs and norms is still written, taught and used as an ideology of legitimization."[76] This is why the work of the Ministries of Education in many Muslim and Arab countries complements that of the Ministries of Religious Affairs in that only a limited and very controlled reading or interpretation of Islam has been permitted.[77] In the minds of the official guardians of Islamic Studies in the Muslim world (that is, the power elite), Islam has ceased to be an intellectual problem and they believe it is high time it ceases to be a question of power, as well.[78] The core of the field revolves around Sharī'ah and Fiqh studies that have often been emptied of critical or political content, or relevance to the present situation. A clear-cut distinction has been made between the "theological" and the "political" or the "theological" and the "social," with the former being understood as rites, symbols, and historical texts only. Furthermore, social science and critical philosophy perspectives are regrettably absent. The field of modern Sharī'ah Studies in the Muslim world remains closed off to the most advanced human contributions in critical philosophy and social science. Those in power do not see the need of employing such concepts as history, class, social structure, criticism, and modernity in their philosophical worldview. Rationalism, which was revealed in classical Islamic thought as the handmaiden of theology and metaphysics, has been reduced to a narrow technical enterprise confined to the fields of Arabic grammar and jurisprudence. Contemporary scholasticism, with the help of foreign currency generated from the production of oil, has waged the most successful "silent revolution" in the Arab world. It has created a fissure between "thought" and reality, between "Islam" and reality.

It is anathema to associate Sharī'ah Studies with a critical appreciation of the science of history. More often than not, the young graduates of Sharī'ah Studies are administered a highly sanitized version of early Islamic history that revolves around morality and the upholding of the *status quo* without any real understanding of the numerous forces at play in early Islamic history. Any different reading of Islamic history is automatically condemned as anti-religious. In other words, the students of Sharī'ah very often lack the scholarly qualifications to examine the rise (or decline) of Islamic ideas in their proper historial and social context. At best, they are made to believe that texts, and not historical conditions, beget texts, and the best way to approach the text is through memorization.

Sometimes, a limited criticism of Western scholariship on Islam (orientalism) is permitted in certain Gulf universities. This criticism seldom goes beyond a number of selected texts or authors, and students are discouraged from conducting a political or historical readings of the texts. It is interesting to note that in spite of the theoretical fact that the notion of social justice is central to Islam, Islam is severely restricted and kept to the realm of the sacred and often is not interpreted in a social or human way.

The secular educational systems in many Muslim countries did not fare better than the traditional. I. H. Qureshi, former Minister of Education in Pakistan, vehemently criticizes the secular educated elite in that country by saying:

> Our secular educated elite is the most spineless, the most unscrupulous and the most mercenary in the world. What has gone during this quarter of a century that has eaten into the vitals of our society and the grit of its leaders except the continuation of a faulty, aimless, and diseased system of education that has bred no social virtues, no depth of feeling, no sense of responsibility – nothing except selfishness, corruption and cowardly lack of initiative and courage?[79]

On the other hand, graduates of the traditional system of education spend the best years of their lives memorizing ancient religious texts without having the understanding or the courage to link or reflect on the themes of these texts in the contexts of modern challenges.[80] Many Sharī'ah graduates, who are lucky indeed to find a job in their field of specialization, are instructed not to tackle the real social and economic problems that face the average Muslim individual on a daily basis. Sharī'ah education in the Arab and Muslim world has been constructed ideologically to maintain, and not question, the *status quo*. It has become a shell without much substance. The end of the Cold War, which may have liberated the field of the humanities and social sciences in the West from narrow dogmatic confines, does not seem to have affected the field of Sharī'ah studies in the Arab world. On the contrary, the end of the Cold War unleashed the power of the authoritarian state to attack any other interpretation of Islam as unacceptable and irrational.[81]

This strange state of affairs has created a backward class of Muslim intelligentsia in Muslim societies; they are well versed in the Islamic text, but who do not necessarily know how to examine the text critically in relation to their surrounding social and political conditions. This state-controlled intelligentsia revels in discussing the most minute theological questions, or raising a battle cry about issues that died hundreds of years ago. This intelligentsia is oblivious to the crises besetting its societies; it simply ignores that such crises exist. It is more interested in authenticity than in real-life problems. In his analysis of the genesis of Pakistan, Hamza Alavi argues that a large number of the ulama in Pakistani society have gone through the Dars-e Nizami,

> a syllabus that was laid down in medieval India and has hardly changed. Generally they [the ulama] have little knowledge of the world they live in, nor even of the world of Islam except for myths and legends. They inhabit little temples of their own uncomprehending and enclosed minds in which they intone slogans, petrified words and dogmas. Affairs of state and society are, generally, beyond their narrowed vision. There are only a few amongst them who have had the benefit of some tolerable education and who, in their own ways, try to follow current affairs.[82]

However, the above analysis cannot be complete if mention is not made of the fact that a small number of traditionally educated intelligentsia have opposed Arab and Muslim regimes and paid for their opposition with either exile or imprisonment.[83] This might explain in part the use of the Sacred Text as an ideological weapon in the hands of the state against those who venture to criticize it and its supporters.[84] Furthermore, the depoliticization and pacification of Islamic Studies may explain one interesting fact in the history of contemporary Muslim revival in the Muslim world: some of the leading activists of Islamic resurgence on campuses do not come from Sharī'ah or arts colleges but from science colleges. Often, the arts colleges are the preserve of Leftist students, whereas science colleges are dominated by Islamists. This explains why, in spite of the millions of dollars spent on "modernizing" this field of study, Islamic Studies in the Arab world has produced only a handful of internationally known scholars.[85]

The multiple sources of education in the Muslim world have created different types of intelligentsia with different worldviews. What underlies these worldviews is the fact that memorization is the rule in all types of education.[86] Egyptian thinker Rif'at al-Sa'īd thinks that memorization is the basis of education in government, private, and Azharite schools in Egypt, which has encouraged the creation of a text-based culture, distinguished at the core by literalism and radicalism.[87]

The absence of social science or critical philosophy perspectives from the field of Sharī'ah Studies is best illustrated by the fact that most students with government scholarships to pursue graduate educations abroad, especially from the Gulf states, study only the hard sciences or business administration, supposedly value-free or criticism-free subjects. In my many years in the United States (almost twenty years now), I have never encountered even one student from the

Gulf pursuing a graduate degree in political science, philosophy, or history. The underpinning of the field of Religious Studies (especially Islamic Studies) is devoid of any type of critical perspective; this has made it quite irrelevant. This fact has also made it quite difficult in many Arab countries to encourage the growth of a scientific tradition, developed mainly in the West, to study the complex interplay between religion and society in the modern Arab world.[88] The discipline of the sociology of religion is looked upon as a *bid'ah*, or innovation, which does not convey the real essence of Islam. Just like the study of the modern Arab state systems, the sociology of religion is a necessity in the Arab world.

This begs the question, once again, of both cultural change and the nature of official culture in the contemporary Muslim world. Undoubtedly, the modernization drive in the Arab world since 1945 created, on the whole, a much more literate culture than that which existed a century ago. In this sense, cultural change has been an inevitable process. There are various methods of assessing the extent of cultural change in a society over a certain defined period of time. One such method is the number of books and/or newspapers published in a country and the contents of such publications. However, the quality and accuracy of what is conveyed by means of the mass media is suspect. One must agree with Raymond Williams' brilliant observation that means of communication are themselves means of production.[89] That is to say, as with any means of production, means of communication are owned by a few individuals in the Muslim world, and a host of skilled and non-skilled laborers are employed to support the viewpoints and mandates of those individuals. The Gulf bourgeoisie has taken advantage of the globalization of the mass media since the mid 1970s. A number of television stations and publications in the Arab world offer programs to their audiences from selected European capitals; the programming selected is never at ideological odds with the official culture of the Arab ruling elite. The globalization of official ideology, supported by the influx of oil money, seems to be a major and unchanging characteristic of contemporary Arab culture. With the help of the most advanced capitalist technologies, official culture presents itself globally as the only credible voice in the contemporary Arab world.

It is crucial to elaborate on the question of the globalization of official Arab ideology in relation to the entire Muslim world, which looks at the Arab world, and especially at a country like Saudi Arabia, as the locus of "authentic Islam." The traditional madrasa system in many Muslim countries, such as in Afghanistan, Pakistan, Malaysia, and Indonesia, or in a non-Muslim country such as India, is a replica of the old madrasa system that dominated the Arab world on the eve of the Western intervention. This system uses Arabic as the main language of instruction, in addition to using the Qur'an, Hadīth, and other classical manuals in Fiqh and Arabic grammar. Global "official Arab ideology," especially the conservative ideology of the Gulf, finds a receptive audience with teachers and graduates of these traditional madrasas, even when no financial donations are made to such institutions. The preservation of such a mentality cripples otherwise healthy cultural change that would enable young Muslim or Arab students to accommodate the enormous changes engendered by recent globalization or even to understand the nature of globalization itself.

The salient features of official Arab ideology, in the making for the past few decades, are finally establishing their presence throughout the Arab world and abroad. The hegemony of the ruling classes in almost every Arab state is being reinforced by a careful manipulation of religion and religious intelligentsia. As Raymond Williams observes, "The educational institutions are usually the main agencies of the transmission of an effective dominant culture, and this is now a major economic as well as cultural activity; indeed, it is both in the same moment."[90] Most of the wealthy classes in the Gulf are *nouveaux riches*. They have accumulated most of their wealth in the past few decades by embracing the ethos of the capitalist system in the dominant world. This has given rise to the use of culture by the emerging new classes in the Arab world. Whenever a new class comes into being, it tries to justify its economic and social gains by relying on certain cultural expressions, one of which is religious. The "Arab Right wing," to use the words of Edward Said, has stifled free expression in society. Because of the tendency to control, most Arab universities languish:

> The Student population increases – which is good – yet the curriculum is antiquated as anything can be. We must face the fact that there are no achievements to speak of in modern Arab science or most intellectual effort, at least none that have come out of our universities…There isn't a single decent library in the entire Arab world. To do research on our own past, our culture, our literature, we still have to come to the West, to study at the feet of the Orientalists, many of whom have openly declared themselves enemies to Islam and the Arabs.[91]

In a nutshell, the academic discourse in the Arab world is in crisis.

As I have argued above, one must understand the absence of critical vision that characterizes most of the educational systems in the Arab world, especially in conservative Arab states, as closely linked to the complex process of modernization launched by the Arab political elite after independence. The influx of oil money in the Gulf states made the technical process of modernization a much easier task than in most Arab states. The lack of direct confrontation with Israel and the alliance with international capitalism made the task that much easier. However, one must underline the fact once more that the modernization program, however creative, did not from the beginning entail any substantial change in the political fortunes of the ruling elite or their families. Putting aside the valid argument that international capitalism, which uses democracy as a cover in its home countries, has never worried about the implementation of democracy in the Arab world (except in those countries that turn against the West) democratic forces in the Arab world have a hard time trying to push their discourse in public. Many an Arab and Muslim regime has hijacked democracy, without apology.[92]

As I have argued previously, the ruling elite of the modern nation-states in the Arab and Muslim world, far from stifling the progress of the ancient religious elite, have reinvigorated them with the help of new material and intellectual foundations. As long as this elite pays homage to the ruling classes, its position in society is protected and prestige enhanced. No wonder then that depoliticized Islamic education is a solid pillar of many regimes, even the most secular regimes of Syria, Tunisia, and Iraq. This kind of education is not supposed to play a critical role in the development of society and broadening the social bases of political authority. The religious elite performs a significant function in the new nation-state akin to that of the Church in the *ancien régime* in Europe before World War One.[93] The religious elite are expected to reproduce and defend the ideas of the ruling elite and not criticize them.

6
Traditional Values, Social Change, and the Contemporary Arab Personality

> "But it has been remarked several times that this passionate search for a national culture which existed before the national era finds its legitimate reason in the anxiety shared by native intellectuals to shrink away from the Western culture in which they all risk being swamped. Because they realize they are in danger of losing their lives and thus becoming lost to their people, these men, hot-headed and with anger in their hearts, relentlessly determine to renew contact once more with the oldest and most pre-colonial springs of life of their people." Franz Fanon, *The Wretched of the Earth*, trans. Constance Farrington (New York: Grove Press, Inc., 1968), 209–10.

> "Nationalism is not what it seems, and above all not what it seems to itself...The cultural shreds and patches used by nationalism are often historical inventions. Any old shred would have served as well. But in no way does it follow that the principle of nationalism...is itself in the least contingent and accidental." Ernest Gellner, *Nation and Nationalism* (Ithaca: Cornell University Press, 1983), 56.

> "Nationalism is an assertion of belonging in and to a place, a people, a heritage. It affirms the home created by a community of language, culture, and customs; and, by so doing, it fends off exile, fights to prevent its ravages." Edward Said, *Reflections on Exile and Other Essays* (Cambridge, MA: Harvard University Press, 2000), 176.

> "Any person who is pleased with the current affairs and who dedicates his life fully to worship while leaving society and politics in the hands of the undeserved, the sinners, the infiltrators, and the colonialists, cannot be considered a true Muslim! Indeed, he is not a true Muslim since the reality of Islam is based on *jihād*, deed, religion, and state." Ḥassan al-Banna, "Bayna al-dīn wa'l siyāsah." *Al-Ikhwān al-Muslimūn* (Weekly), March 4, 1945, 1.

Alienation, immigration, and exile have become cliché concepts that describe not just the post-1948 Palestinian experiment but the situation of many Arab countries, most notably Lebanon, Iraq, Algeria, Morocco, Egypt, and Syria. The emergence of the Palestinian refugee problem after the creation of Israel in 1948 was just the beginning of a long series of major social and political upheavals sustained by the Arab world since independence.

A parallel movement of social change took place in many Arab countries in the 1970s, when the need in the Gulf states for Arab labor of all types was at its highest. Men and women joined large ranks in hard labor, education, and other menial jobs that needed to be filled in order to modernize the Gulf states. Whereas in the 1950s and 1960s, only skilled professionals migrated to the Gulf, a mass of skilled and unskilled people continued the trend in the 1970s and 1980s. This immigration, based as it was on financial need, had a major impact not just on the host countries but also on the home countries of the workers. Emigrants came back with more money and social prestige, but with perhaps less hope about the future of the Arab world as a united whole.[1] Exile in a disunited Arab world has its "ravages," to use Edward Said's term.[2] People understood that two Arab worlds were being born: one more or less educated but poor (Egypt, Syria, Jordan, Lebanon), and the other less educated but richer and more modern. This is a strange type of polarization. It is not a simple modern–traditional polarization. It is a polarization that was, to a large extent, created by the need of the international capitalist market – the need for the commodity of oil and its derivatives. Because of this need, some Arab countries enjoyed some prosperity. But it was the elite classes in the poorest but most educated countries who benefited from the prosperity oil has brought.

As part of the international capitalist market, socio-economic and religious changes in the Arab world in the 1970s and 1980s and the failure of the socialist system in the late 1980s, caused the Arab world to undergo great, and unprecedented changes. Women in the Gulf enjoyed the sudden wealth of their countries, but were prevented because of tradition and long-held values from fully enjoying the benefits of modernization. Modernization did indeed build a new social space in the Gulf states. As a matter of fact, capitalism showed remarkable prowess in making the Arabian desert bloom. But questions arise as to the role and position of women in such an environment, a world shaped anew by the modern forces of capitalism! It seems that women, on the whole, were granted more freedom or at least a type of freedom that seemed commensurate with the levels of modernization in their societies. That is, women too would enjoy the cultural and artistic fruits of modernization.

Although it is impossible to objectively gauge the level of freedom attained by women in these societies, it is possible to argue in general that the conservative ideology imposed on society in the name of Islam has given women a limited freedom at home while curtailing their public freedom. Men may explore public zones as they wish, such as cafes and restaurants; women cannot. The flow of money to the Gulf made it easy for young men to travel, especially to Southeast Asia, to explore a different kind of life dominated by sex and alcohol. For better or worse, women have not had the same leisure. Perhaps the flip side of this deformed sense of modernity is the high consumption of commodities and birth rate among women in the Gulf and other conservative quarters in the Arab world.[3] It is hard to know to what extent women are alienated in these semi-nomadic, semi-modern societies. Modernization cannot be effective without a modernist consciousness and modernist values. Can we naively assume that Gulf societies have accepted modernization with its modernist values? Or that traditional values have not been influenced by the introduction of sweeping modernization programs in many of these countries after the 1970s?

No adequate research has been done about the impact of modernization and modernity on the traditional values of society in these countries. But any creative speculation on the matter would lead us to envision a new movement in society, a movement that questions the grip of antiquated values in a society that looks superbly modernized, ordered, clean, and sure of itself. We know that capitalism in the Gulf has initiated lasting changes in the physical structures of the cities there, as well as in the economic, social, cultural, and educational relationships in society. Clearly, Gulf societies have changed deeply in the past five decades. There is a new generation not accustomed to pre-capitalist demands of life in the desert. It is critical therefore to ask about the effects of these drastic changes on the role of women in the Gulf and the impact that such changes have had on their sexuality.

In addition to the drastic domestic changes wrought on Gulf society by capitalism, a huge new sub-community of migrants from other Arab states has been created. This community is based upon the concept of exile in exchange for economic opportunity.[4] Many would agree that this type of internal exile is extremely difficult to endure, both physically and mentally.[5] Under the pressures of daily life and the increasing tendency toward consumerism that characterized most Arab states in the 1970s and 1980s, the individual (especially the poor) feels disconnected from traditional values of patience and divine reward in the afterlife. A conflict then arises between what tradition preaches and what competitive life demands. Contemporary Arab thought, in the main, has expressed the alienation of the youth, their unfulfilled dreams and dark future, in various sociological, literary, and philosophical ways. Arab social thought, in the words of its best representative Sayyid ‘Uways, begins to document culture and society from the 1950s on. By the 1990s, many brilliant students had followed “Uways” footsteps.[6]

In a nutshell, there is a crisis of values in the Arab and Muslim worlds, and the conflict has taken its toll on traditional religious values. Arab libraries are full of studies on this conflict. Two important studies, indebted to the achievements of Sayyid ‘Uways, come to mind: (1) Nadia Raḍwān’s *al-Shabāb al-miṣrī al-mu‘āṣir wa azmat al-qiyam*[7] and (2) Yāsser Ayūb’s, *Warā’ kull bāb: al-infijār al-jinsī fī miṣr.*[8]

What are the broad outlines of Arab social thought in the 1980s and 1990s? Since the 1952 revolution, Egypt has seen huge projects and dreams of modernization collapse under the encroachment of defeat: pre-war modernization programs, socialist style, attempted to place Arabs back into the cycle of history, making a productive, free, and proud people. The 1967 war undermined these goals. Before, the Egyptian economy’s public sector was able to breathe easy and achieved a certain measure of comfort. With the partial success of Egypt in the 1973 war, however, the Sadat regime hastened to offer new formulations of modernization of Egyptian economy and society. In one sense, the Sadat regime repeated the mistakes of 1952, attempting to build an infrastructure without paying sufficient attention to the individuals themselves.[9] According to Aḥmad Bahā’ al-Dīn, the 1952 revolution did not contain a true revolutionary pedagogy and a new ethic, and the post-1973 Infitāḥ lacked any ethics at all except for capitalist modes of competition and consumerism. In the words of Egyptian economist Galāl Amīn, the Infitāḥ meant three things: "the opening of virtually all doors to the importation of foreign goods and capital, the removal of restrictions on Egyptian local investment, and the gradual withdrawal of the state from an active role in the economy."[10] The new miracle term was *al-infitāḥ al-iqtiṣādī* (the Open Door economic policy), which promised every Egyptian family miraculous financial and economic success by the end of the 1980s. The Infitāḥ was a caesarian operation (*'amaliyyah qayṣariyah*) that aimed to eradicate the socialist foundations of the Egyptian economy. According to Ayūb, the Infitāḥ was the beginning of a major change in the class structure of Egypt, which resulted in the rich becoming richer and the poor poorer:

> [The Infitāḥ] was an earth-shaking experience appearing on the surface as though it were a simple economic change. Soon afterwards, this Infitāḥ transformed itself into a coup against all those who did not belong to the new class of the nouveaux riches...The Infitāḥ was not just an economic system, but the beginning of a radical change in the structure of society, its dominant values, and the nature of the Egyptian personality.[11]

The failure of Infitāḥ modernization, the increasing waves of labor immigration to the Gulf, and the signing of the peace treaty with Israel all had a major impact on traditional Egyptian values. *New forms of social control emerged.* People began to associate themselves with their commodities and the food they consume. The problem that contemporary Egyptian sociologists attack, therefore, is a problem of a disjuncture, the result of huge modernization projects that benefited a small business elite without a comprehensive plan to modernize either the overall structure or the values of Egyptian society. The decline of traditional values, the rise of consumerism (especially among the elite) and the increasing debt burden of the state forced many youth to emigrate or remain alienated at home. Even marriage, friendship, and other benign forms of relationship became no more than financial deals between partners. Corruption and theft became the rule. Muḥammad H. Haykal blames the Sadat regime for unleashing these dangerous tendencies in Egyptian society in the 1970s; tendencies, which in his view created a greedy class of people, he refers to as "the beasts of consumerism" (*wuḥūsh al-istihlāk*).[12]

On the other hand, the Infitāḥ, besides its sweeping economic changes, resulted in the disintegration of the social system erected by Nasserism, a devaluation of national values, and a loss of faith in the Egyptian national interest. In short, the Egyptian social structure emerged badly bruised from Sadat's misguided economic policies.[13] In Sonbol's words,

> The social gap between the rich and the poor became flagrant under Sadat; although it had existed under Nasser, it had not been flaunted, and the inflation that came with Infitāḥ meant that many who had been protected under the protectionism of Nasser were now unable to make a go of it financially. The Sadat khāṣṣa [elite] seemed to live in a fantasy land without true realization of the conditions around them.[14]

What are the broad characteristics of the crisis of values? First, after the 1952 revolution Egypt tried to tread a program of social and economic reform that would free it from dependence on capitalist markets and the restrictions thereof. Since the nineteenth century, debt to the international market had been a problem. The 1967 defeat put an end to internal economic and social modernization and all energies were invested in thwarting defeat. The revolution's goal was to eradicate imperialism, feudalism, and capitalism, and establish social justice, a strong army, and a democratic political system. Many of these hopes were dashed in the wake of the 1967 defeat.

Second, Egyptian students, as the state's new intellectuals, were painfully aware of the consequences of defeat and that their rebellions against the state in 1968 and 1972 were reflections of a deep crisis in values in Egyptian society; it was a conflict between generations, a conflict over the future of Egypt.

Third, the beginning of the Infitāḥ phase after 1973 and the signing of the peace agreement with Israel were sold to the Egyptian public as guarantees of prosperity and growth. Infitāḥ enriched a tiny minority who began to live a conspicuously materialistic life style.[15] Infitāḥ has thus benefited the international market, encouraging it to invest in the Egyptian economy and forcing the state to privatize. "The economic open-door policy, a major phenomenon of economic downfall, has led to the marginalization of human relations."[16] What the Infitāḥ has done has been to drive a permanent wedge between the very rich and very poor. Two distinct classes, each alienated from the other, have emerged.[17]

Fourth, the economic modernization of Egyptian society of the Infitāḥ variety was not accompanied by any plan for cultural or scientific change. Modernization was not followed by modernism, a consciousness to be modern. Society lacked rationality while importing technology at a high cost. Because of this huge gap between modernization and modernism, it was quite easy to implant imported new values in the Arab psyche that did not jive with their true personalities. Those values were the products of a different society with specific historical and social conditions. What resulted from the loss of correspondence between social change and values was marginalization and alienation.

Fifth, because of the abasement of traditional sexual values, sex became a commodity, and a cheap one at that. Arab sociologists are perturbed by the rising levels of rape and sexual assaults in their countries, especially in urban areas. The rise of the petro-dollar (Gulf) states to positions of power and influence inside other Arab states intensified the sexual crisis in Arab countries such as Morocco, Tunisia, Syria, and Egypt. Prostitution began to flourish on a wide scale in these countries throughout the 1970s and 1980s.

Sixth, the increasing emigration of Egyptian youth to the Gulf states exacerbated problems of consumerism, individualism, and conservatism. Many returned with conservative and backward ideas that did not help modernize society.

Seventh, the creative cultural and intellectual space receded before this strange explosion of consumerism and fast wealth. The culture of consumerism brought down the high culture of art and values; these things are now cheaply bought.

Eighth, failed economic modernization coupled with the crisis in values led to great pessimism about the future. People are uncertain about what the future holds for Egypt. This situation has created two severe problems: (1) the most educated Egyptians have decided to emigrate overseas, which indicates a major decline in the personal commitment of the educated classes to modernize and develop their native societies; (2) the state ideology and its institutions lost a great deal of credibility. In a very real sense, society proved that it is not ready to accept democratic values but rather is based on a rigid totalitarian ideology.

Ninth, this social confusion has been a natural breeding ground for anti-state movements, especially the religious. A good number of the leaders of these movements are members of the educated middle class who suffer from the "credibility crisis" along with the state and its institutions.

In a general way, the Islamist response is a symptom of the problems described above. The religious problem in some Arab countries takes on new dimensions: it is inextricable from the social, economic, political, and ethical problems of society. The religious problem, by itself, does not revolve around a controversial new interpretation of the Qur'an, Sunnah, or Islamic history, but is actually a reflection of society's concrete problems. The religious solution takes different shapes, the most conspicuous of which is violence in the name of lost values and lost religion. Violence is often unleashed when there is no religious or intellectual tolerance.[18] The Arab emigration to the Gulf in search of work exacerbated the problem both intellectually and religiously. Gulf societies are more or less one-dimensional, having been ruled by the same family or tribe over a long period of time and which lack the ethnic and religious diversity that other Arab countries, such as Egypt, Sudan, Syria, and Lebanon, possess. Fanaticism is but one response. There is a continuous reaction on all levels of society, attempts to rebuild shattered morality by imposing *ḥijāb* or sending girls to Muslim-only schools or simply leaving the city. A silent response to this societal catastrophe is continuously in the making.

In delineating the "Islamic response" to the engineering of Arab societies and cultures in the 1970s and 1980s, it is important to distinguish between the political and the Sacred – or the changing and the fixed. For example, there are three major Islamist movements in Egypt – the Ikhwān, the Jihad, and the Jamā'ah al-Islāmiyyah. The Jihad movement in Egypt, committing violence in the name of the Sacred, believes that Jihad and not dialogue is the solution. The Jihad organization believes that the engineering of society is steeped in *Jāhiliyyah* and only a violent toppling of the dominant regimes will rid the Arab world of these secular tendencies. It seems to me that this is a classic political response to the decline of values in society. There is another type of Islamic response, however, one more social, religious and fixed in nature; religious discourse functions as a subtle mechanism to restore balance to a wounded society. The example of Syrian society in the 1970s and 1980s, the eradication of the Syrian Ikhwān's military and political power as a result of events in Aleppo and Hama did not, by any means, decrease the domain of the Sacred in society. On the contrary, some strata, the middle and lower classes, became more religious in response to the deep crisis affecting Syrian society in the 1980s. Attendance of mosque prayers increased, especially by youth, as did the number of those wishing to perform pilgrimage. There was also a conspicuous movement on the part of some women of donning the veil.[19] These examples point to the fact that the sacred constantly renews itself in times of political and social crises. It becomes a matter of self-preservation, of striking a new balance between addressing social wounds and cherishing deeply-entrenched values.

Most agree that Egyptian society has experienced a decline in values in the realms of both religion and society. A wide spectrum of society feels the pressure of social change and the inadequacy of state institutions to devise appropriate solutions to social, moral, cultural, and economic problems.[20] The religious response to this situation is multi-faceted and sometimes besides calls to implement the Sharī'ah, takes the form of terrorism against the state and its symbols.[21] But where religion shows a violent side, it also permits a new kind of response: a conservative onslaught on the foundations of a bewildered society, a society that has both failed in its modernization project and lost its modernist consciousness. This conservative onslaught takes several forms, one of which is a subtle process of reasserting values in a context of social and ethical erosion. As such, it has the potential to help arrest decay and attrition within society's social and ethical structures.

TOWARD A NEW CIVIL SOCIETY

In general, three complex phenomena have characterized the Arab world in the modern period: the first is colonialism; second is Islamic resurgence, and the third is nationalism. Furthermore, great demographic and economic changes have predicated these phenomena and determined their nature in the Arab world. Once it was officially over, colonialism left behind a complex cultural and intellectual package that the Arab world is still trying to manage. After the departure of colonialism and the deep shifts in the world political and economic order (from roughly the early 1950s on), the fate of the Arab world has become more intertwined than ever with that of the Western world. Even at the intellectual and religious levels, the Arab world is different than it was during the first days of colonization. Colonialism, aided by universal capitalist expansion, has shaken up the parochialism of the Arab world and made it more universally viable than before.

Islamism has offered the most serious religious and cultural response to the multifaceted challenges of colonialism in the modern era. Islamic resurgence has capitalized on the deep economic, demographic, and cultural transformations taking place in the Arab world from the days of colonialism to the present. The population shift in the past several decades from countryside to cities and the cultural/religious consequences associated with this shift, provided Islamic resurgence with a stronger foothold in society than ever before. Besides being a source of both solace and hope, religion brings a certain measure of stability to people when society is in a period of great transition and tension. Resurgence followed the movement of the rural poor and urban outcasts in the cities and gave them hope in the name of religion.

The relationship between the contemporary Arab state and the Islamic movement is problematic at best. Suffice it to mention here that a central theme in the thought of some of the main leaders of contemporary Islamism in the Arab world has been that the contemporary Arab political elites sold out to Westernization and became totally dependent on the Center.[22] In such a state, prospects for true democracy are almost non-existent; despotism runs inherently deep in its foundation. Furthermore, the embodiment of the state in the dictatorship of one party, one family, one tribe, or one individual has made it quite impossible for a true civil society to emerge, that is, if we define civil society as an autonomous entity distinguished from that of the state.[23] Civil and religious associations that were established and nourished by autonomous endowments in the pre-modern Arab state have been destroyed by the modern state and its hegemonic structure. The marginalization of civil society and the concentration of power in the hands of the few, far from eliciting protest from the "democratic world," have gone unchallenged.

Because of this pathetic state of affairs, the prospect of a bloody conflict between the state and Islamism is a real possibility. Syria in the early 1980s and Algeria in the 1990s both evidence this. What concerns us here are the present (that is, post-independence) formulations of Islamist thought in relation to Sharī'ah, civil society, and politics. Those formulations have reached a major stumbling block, not so much at the theoretical level, but at the level of their application. Contemporary Islamist thought is replete with all sorts of theories and inclinations, but the emergence of a coherent system of thought is long overdue. In spite of official attempts to neutralize Islamism, it remains the only attractive alternative in recent years.

When the state miserably fails to deliver on its promises after independence, such has been the case in Algeria, resurgence escalated to the level of resistance of, and even military confrontation with, the nation-state. The current political elite in most of the Arab states stood against the democratization of their societies for fear that such democratization would lead to the accession of Islamists to power.[24] The Islamists, including the most moderate of them, have been placed under the watchful eyes of the state and its secret services. What we are currently witnessing in the Arab world is the retreat of the current political elite and their inability to establish a clear program of social and economic reform. In some countries, however, a complete ban on Islamist activities has been impossible. In Egypt and Jordan, Islamists still control many of the student and labor unions.

Ghalyūn believes that society's crisis in the contemporary Arab world must be attributed to the first days of the encounter between the advanced capitalist West and the less advanced Muslim world in the nineteenth century. He argues that the nature of capitalist expansion into the Arab world and the major political and economic gaps created between the center and the periphery produced an authoritarian, liberal, and later nationalist, state with power concentrated in the hands of the few.[25] The centralization of power, supported by the huge bureaucracy and army of the state, made it impossible for a truly modernized civil society to emerge. The nationalist state tried to follow a different policy from that of the liberal state in focusing state and nation formation. However, by doing so, "the autonomy of civil society has been sacrificed and its very existence has been negated."[26] At present, the political elite is most concerned with amassing more power and spending more money on security matters for fear of losing its grip on power.

Some scholars reduce the complex phenomenon of Islamic resurgence to "political Islam," a term which fails to convey the ethical, spiritual, and educational dimensions of religious resurgence in the modern Arab world.[27] Most literature on resurgence focuses on the political, while neglecting the larger meaning of Islamic resurgence, especially at cultural and intellectual levels. "Political Islam" is just one important expression of Islamic resurgence. I think that in many ways, resurgence is an overall ethical, educational, social, cultural, and political movement that has given rise to a variety of expressions and concerns about the fate of the Arab world, its present and future relationship with the West, and its ability to lead the Arab world into the future. True, there has been some concern about the place of secularism in Arab society from the standpoint of resurgence and, one might add, some Islamists' treatment of the question of secularism has been shallow and intellectually unproductive. However, I think that the most important concern has been how to assert a new cultural and political identity in an age where the destiny of the entire Muslim world lies in achieving a certain measure of balance between international demands and internal concerns for cultural and economic autonomy. From the perspective of resurgence, the question is not about Muslims refusing the process of modernity. Modernity is already a universal phenomenon that no one dares reject. The question becomes how to accommodate and coexist with modernity, while continuing to lead an authentic Muslim life.

CONTEMPORARY BURDENS AND FUTURE PROSPECTS

By and large, Islamist thinkers and activists in the contemporary Arab world (post-1967) are very critical of current political regimes and their social and economic philosophies. Many have suffered imprisonment or exile because of their opposition to the *status quo*. Algerian Islamists are a case in point. However, a minority have been co-opted by the regime in such countries as Morocco and Jordan, and find it useful to pursue their political and religious demands from within the existing political system.[28] Composing a list of the most influential Islamist thinkers in the contemporary Arab world would be difficult, but the following are worth noting: 'Abd al-Salām Yāssīn, 'Abd al-Karīm Muṭī, and 'Abd al-Ilāh Kirān of Morocco;[29] Malek Bennabi, Mahfūdh Nahnāh, and 'Abbās Madanī of Algeria;[30] Rāshid al-Ghannūshī, 'Abd al-Majīd al-Najjār, Ṣalāh al-Dīn Jourshī and Muhsin al-Maylī from Tunisia;[31] Muḥammad al-Ghazālī, Muḥammad 'Imārah, Ṭāriq al-Bishrī, and many others from Egypt; Muḥammad Bāqir al-Ṣadr, Muṣṭafa al-Ṣawwāf, and 'Abd al-Karīm Zaydān from Iraq.

A lot of research has gone into the thought of the so-called "extremist" Islamic movements in the Arab world. I personally find the discussion of these movements least interesting and representative of serious Islamic thought. The main Islamist thinkers in the Arab world, such as those above, refrain from advocating violence as a means of disseminating their ideas. Some have suffered imprisonment and exile simply by advocating that Islam is a religion of peace and Islamic victory will be assured the moment real democracy is practiced. As the contemporary Egyptian lawyer Ṭāriq al-Bishrī notes, the most serious Islamist thinkers present Islam as a comprehensive religion touching all aspects of life, including the political.[32]

ISLAMISM AND THE CRISIS THEORY

As shown above, Islamism, in its various contemporary manifestations, is an outgrowth of the Islamic reform movement of the nineteenth century. Islamism seems to be the only movement of substance that poses a threat to the *status quo*. However, Arab Islamism has not succeeded, as in the Iranian case, to set up an Islamic political system. In the minds of many Islamists, Islamism has failed on the political front due to the multiple crises affecting the Arab world since its painful encounter with the West in the nineteenth century.

The work of Muḥammad al-Ghazālī and Rāshid al-Ghannūshī, discussed in some detail in the coming chapters, belongs to a modern genre of Islamic writing that has been conditioned, more or less, by a severe political and military encounter between two unequal players in modern history: the advanced West and the less advanced Muslim world. This inequality is the result of complex phenomena that cannot be summarized in a simple sentence. Broadly speaking, though perhaps superficially, the premises of this genre of writing are:

1. The Muslim world has been suffering from a pervasive crisis in thought, politics, economics, and social relations for at least the past 200 years. The most poignant feature of this crisis has been intellectual.[33] Many modern Arab and Muslim thinkers, belonging to a variety of intellectual trends, have used the term "crisis" in analyzing contemporary responses to modernity;
2. twentieth century Islamist thought has invented the notion of the ummah as a "religious response" to the political weakening and division of the Muslim world. Islamist thinkers such as Ḥassan al-Banna, Muḥammad al-Ghazālī, Sayyid Quṭb, Ismā'il al-Fārūqī, and Ṭāhā J. al-'Alwānī, have used the term "ummah" to refer to the entire Muslim world without much discussion of the major historical, political, and cultural differences between the many countries that in fact make up the Muslim world. The Islamist thinkers advance the term "ummah" on the presupposition that there have been common religious and historical bonds in the Muslim world that justify the use of such a term;
3. the Muslim world has been locked in a civilizational, military, and political conflict with the West. This is often referred to as the "East–West conflict." This theory is best-expressed by Ḥassan al-Banna, Sayyid Quṭb, Muḥammad 'Imārah, Yūsuf al-Qaraḍāwī, and Ḥassan al-Turābī.[34]

The literature on crisis in modern Arab and Islamic thought is immense. Most Arab and Muslim thinkers, from a variety of intellectual predispositions, assume that modern Arab thought is the product of crisis, either of the mind, in history or in religion. For example, in the nineteenth century, Muslim Arab thinkers were caught unaware by the Western intrusion into the Muslim world and, as a result, were forced to think about conditions of crisis and decline in their societies and appropriate ways to revive the modern Muslim world.[35]

"Crisis" continues to be the main theme in the writings of Islamic resurgence from the work of Ḥassan al-Banna to Sayyid Quṭb, Yūsuf al-Qaraḍāwī, Muḥammad al-Ghazālī, and Rāshid al-Ghannūshī.[36] All agree with Ghannūshī's contention that "the real truth behind crisis is the absence of education or methods of teaching as much as a crisis caused by the disintegration of our civilizational personality (*inḥilāl shakhṣiyatinnah al-ḥaḍāriyyah*)...It is the loss of our civilizational model."[37] While the primary theoreticians of Islamism consider both imperialism and nationalism to be responsible for this crisis, they postulate that establishing an Islamic political system on the model established by the Prophet and the Rightly Guided caliphs is the best way to bypass this state of affairs. In other words, Islamism has attempted to establish itself as a mass movement possessing a definite program to establish a new civil society in the Arab world by reinforcing the Sharī'ah law in all walks of life. Politics, as a result, has dominated philosophy and theology in contemporary Arab Islamist thought. A rupture between the ulama, the custodians and defenders of the classical Sunni tradition, and Islamists, that is, the Ikhwān in the Arab world, as a mass-based movement, was inevitable. The Ikhwān viewed the ulama with great distrust. In its view, the ulama were upholders of the same *status quo* that the Ikhwān were attempting to abolish. Islamist discourse was born in reaction to relatively modern historical and political crises affecting the modern Arab world, and, as a result, has always attempted to provide solutions on the basis of new and sometimes aggressive understandings of the colossal Islamic tradition.[38]

Some leading Arab Marxist and secular thinkers best express another view of this crisis. Such thinkers as Abdallah Laroui,[39] Ṣādiq Jalāl al-'Azm,[40] Maḥmūd Amīn al-'Ālim, Faraj Fūda,[41] Ghālī Shukrī,[42] and Fu'ād Zakariyya[43] begin with different postulates and premises from those of the Islamic modernist school as represented by 'Abduh, Afghānī and Riḍa, or the Ikhwān school as represented by its main theoreticians. To Arab Marxists, the persistence and invention of tradition have dealt heavy blows to secularism. In other words, the persistence of tradition is the cause of crisis.

In addition to the above, Orientalist thought, especially as it appears in the writings of Hamilton Gibb, Wilfrid C. Smith, von Grunebaum and others, pursues the theme of crisis and furnishes the following theses: crisis is caused by (1) the rigid formulations of Muslim *fuqāhā'* and jurists; (2) the atomistic nature of the "Muslim mind"; (3) the enclosed and self-sufficient religious system of Islam; and (4) the lack of individualism in modern Muslim culture. They propose Westernization as the only viable option for the salvation of the modern Muslim world.[44]

One must note, however, that there are some leading Arab thinkers who reject the thesis of crisis in modern Arab and Muslim thought. I have in mind the works of Anouar Abdel-Malek and Ḥassan Ḥanafī. For instance, Ḥanafī[45] argues that in spite of the civilizational shock produced by the encounter between the Muslim world and Western civilization in the nineteenth century, Muslims awakened to the immense possibilities in their civilization, and that Arabo-Islamic civilization has lately taken the initiative of launching a critique and understanding of the West, whereas Western civilization has begun its decline.

Prominent Arab and Muslim thinkers have preoccupied themselves with the question of colonialism, even when discussing the nature of the civil society they envisage. Most Islamist thinkers argue, more or less, that colonialism created a fissure in the Muslim historical consciousness and introduced a new vision of life that is essentially incompatible with traditional Islamic mores. For example, Iraqi Islamist Ṭāhā Jābir al-'Alwānī[46] maintains that colonialism succeeded in driving a wedge between Islamic thought and Islamic practice, thus confining Islam to the domain of theory only, "Western strategists took advantage of the dual system of education to completely isolate Islam from life, and to confine it to mere theoretical issues which served little practical purpose and had no great effect on everyday life."[47] Another Islamist thinker argues that the Western attack on the Muslim world has played a significant role in

> dismantling the Islamic worldview in the modern era...Consequently, many an Arab author and thinker has come under the influence of the orbit of Western conceptual and cultural dependency and hegemony. As a result of the [Muslim] civilizational defeat, many Arab minds were forced to deal with those problematics generated from the concepts and philosophy of triumphant imperialism.[48]

Contemporary Egyptian Islamist Muḥammad 'Imārah, on the other hand, believes that the conflict between Islam and the West is far from over. The West has become the Center and the Muslim world a simple appendage. The most significant aspect of this battle is that it is being waged at the level of identity. The West is attempting to dissolve, dismantle, and do away with the social, cultural, historical, and religious identities of Muslims and Islam so that Muslims will surrender their identities without much resistance.[49]

To be sure, many Islamists have not reconciled themselves with the reality of the nation-state and the civil society it has created. They cannot absolve the nation-state of its failure after independence to stem the tide of what they call "*ghazw thaqāfī wā fikrī*," or "intellectual and cultural invasion," which they consider the most dangerous manifestation of colonialism after independence. To 'Imārah, for example, the circulation of the ideas of the hegemonic culture or civilization to a dominated periphery is a fact in human history. He argues that in looking at the cultural map of the modern world, one can distinguish a number of civilizations, such as the Chinese, Hindu, Islamic, and Western, each of which possesses certain fundamental characteristics. For example, Islamic civilization is distinguished by the role of revelation, the Qur'an and its impact on Islamic history. It is impossible to conceive of Islamic civilization without its distinguishing traits: Sacred Text, prophecy, a class of ulama who became active in preserving and disseminating the holy text, and the Arabic language. These traits notwithstanding, Islamic civilization appropriated many ideas from other foreign (non-Islamic) cultures and gave them Islamic meaning and space. "The Islamic civilization, although the creation of Muslims, is closely linked with Islam as a religion, whose essence is a revelation divinely ordained. Revelation is not a human social product."[50] Islamic history was shaped by the interaction between revelation and the activities of Muslims under particular socio-historical conditions. The main ideas are the consequences of social and economic conditions. In one sense, 'Imārah argues that it is essential to borrow from other civilizations and this need becomes that more urgent when a civilization is in its nascent stage.[51]

However, when a culture or civilization is under stress or threatened by a different quality of ideas, either through direct military conquest, as had been the case with colonialism, or through the impact of modern ideologies, especially nationalism and socialism, we may be justified in speaking of cultural invasion.

In their treatment of crisis, Islamist thinkers posit a dichotomy between the spheres of materialism and the Sacred. According to this position, ideas are not humanly induced, but divinely inspired. For example, 'Imārah argues, in contradistinction to Marx,[52] that Islamic civilization became conscious of itself only in the process of interaction between divine ideas and human history, and that the divine seeped into the consciousness of men and women who made up that civilization. What is not clear, however, is whether the divine element in Islamic civilization has been threatened as a result of the cultural invasion previously discussed. 'Imārah does not develop his argument further. Are we speaking here of the domination of one civilization by another or of one class by another? What role does the divine, in terms of Sharī'ah and moral Islamic rules, play in the modern consciousness of Muslims?

A great number of contemporary Muslim thinkers are convinced that there is a deep conflict between East and West, South and North or Islam and the West. "Many argue," says 'Imārah, "that Muslims exaggerate why they discuss the attitude of the West toward Islam and Muslims. To my mind, the time is opportune to discuss not our attitude toward the West, but the latter's attitude toward us and Islam."[53] In its latest manifestation as the supreme leader of the New World Order, the West, especially the United States, has taken the position that Islam and Muslims are their principal universal enemies.[54] This position was enunciated well before the tragic attacks on the United States on September 11, 2001. It is true that the Muslim–Western conflict is as old as Islam itself, but it has taken on dangerous proportions in the last few decades. According to the Islamist view, Muslims are under attack. What 'Imārah assumes is that the conflict is political and economic on the surface and ideological, philosophical, and religious in principle. The Muslim world has become an appendage to Western interests and forces, but the most dangerous of battles that contemporary Muslims face is that of their identity,

> If a nation gets defeated in the battlefield while preserving its [religious and national] identity, it will be able to maintain its independent will, and endeavor to possess all the necessary means of power to liberate the land and prevent a military invasion. But if a nation loses its identity, it will be forced to submit to the dominant power, which means a complete loss of vitality. Both occupation and dependency lead to the dissipation of authenticity...In that sense, the essence of the battle revolves around the preservation of identity.[55]

'Imārah further argues that as a result of colonialism, the West left behind factories that produce Westernized ideologies and trends of thought that aim at dissolving the true essence of the Muslim ummah. "Colonialism has departed while leaving behind institutions controlled by the Westernized intelligentsia and leaders."[56] The battle with the West was engendered by the major transformations within the

Western world in recent decades, and Muslims have suffered most from these plans. "We are drowned in our blood."[57] Therefore, the West has been busy devising a multifaceted plan to control the Muslim world, mainly because the West cannot tolerate a responsible Muslim leadership in power.

To 'Imārah and many Islamist thinkers, identity is the key issue. However, no one has attempted a clear delineation of "Muslim identity." Is it the Qur'anic identity or the historically-constructed identity or identities? 'Imārah considers the intellectual scene of the Arab world in the past two centuries to have been dominated by two major and even antagonistic dichotomies: Islamic revivalist and Western secularist. In 'Imārah's view, modern Islamic revival originated in response to the Western onslaught on the modern Muslim world. Real revival means civilizational independence and freedom of identity. The West has posed significant historical and civilizational challenges to the world of Islam. Further, there has been an intention to strip the world of Islam of its religious and historical character. The Muslim response to the Western project came in three forms of revivalism: (1) extremist revivalism,[58] wherein the Western media pays more attention to this trend than to others in the modern Muslim world; (2) mainstream Ikhwān; and (3) the trend of renewal, *ijtihād*, and intellectual creativity.

Contemporary Arab Islamism, therefore, considers the West, in its political and intellectual manifestations, to be the real enemy of the Muslim world. It posits that the aggressive capitalist West seeks to stifle the development of an independent Muslim personality. It prefers the rule of dictatorship to that of democracy. That is to say, contemporary Arab Islamism says that the Arab world is going to remain in the throes of crisis as long as the West has a say in its internal affairs.

7
Globalization: A Contemporary Islamic Response?

"By dissolving nationalities, the liberal economic system had done its best to universalize enmity, to transform mankind into a horde of ravenous beasts who devour one another just because each has identical interests with all the others." Karl Marx, "Outlines of a Critique of Political Economy," in Karl Marx and Frederick Engels, *Collected Works*, volume 3 (New York: International Publishers, 1975), 423.

"Europe's centrality reflects no internal superiority accumulated in the Middle Ages, but is the outcome of its discovery, conquest, colonization, and integration of Amerindia – all of which gave it an advantage over the Arab world, India, and China. Modernity is the result, not the cause, of this occurence." Enrique Dussel, *The Invention of the Americas: Eclipse of the "Other" and the Myth of Modernity* (New York: Continuum, 1995), 11.

"We do not live in a modernizing world but in a capitalist world. What makes this world tick is not the need for achievement but the need for profit. The problem for oppressed strata is not how to communicate within this world but how to overthrow it." Immanuel Wallerstein, *The Capitalist World Economy* (Cambridge: Cambridge University Press, 1979), 133.

"Neoliberalism, as a global system, is a new war in the conquest of territory. The end of the Third World War, or Cold War, certainly does not mean that the world has overcome bipolarity and rediscovered stability under the domination of the victor. Whereas there was a defeated side (the socialist camp. It is difficult to identify the winning side. The United States? The European Union? Japan? Or all three?…) Thanks to computers, the financial markets, from the trading floor and according to the their whims, impose their laws and precepts on the planet. Globalization is nothing more than the totalitarian extension of their logic to every aspect of life. The United States, formerly the ruler of the economy, is now tele-governed – by the very dynamic of financial power: commercial free trade. And this logic has made use of the porosity produced by the development of telecommunications to take over every aspect of activity in the social spectrum. The result is an all-out war." Sous-Commandant Marcos, "La 4e guerre mondiale a commencé." *Le Monde Diplomatique*, August 1997, 1.

"We are told that the world is shrinking, that vast distance has been conquered by computer and fax, and the Earth is now a 'global village' in which all of us are connected as never before. It feels, however, quite the opposite. It feels as if distancing and disconnection are shaping modern life. If anything is shrinking, it is the fullness of being that is experienced by the modern self...Psychologists report [high] levels of depression and anxiety...For most people today, the web of friends, nearby family members, and community relationships is a shrunken fragment of what previous generations experienced." Charlene Spretnak, *The Resurgence of the Real: Body, Nature and Place in a Hypermodern World* (New York: Addison-Wesley, 1997), 11.

"I've used the word 'globalization'. It is a myth in the strong sense of the word, a powerful discourse, an *idée force*, an idea which has social force, which obtains belief. It is the main weapon in the battles against the gains of the welfare state. European workers, we are told, must compete with the least favored workers of the rest of the world." Pierre Bourdieu, *Acts of Resistance* (New York: The New Press, 1998), 34.

"Knowledge that was free, open and for the benefit of society is now proprietary, confidential and for the benefit of business. Educators who once jealously guarded their autonomy now negotiate curriculum planning with corporate sponsors. Professors who once taught are now on company payrolls churning out marketable research in the campus lab, while universities pay the cut-rate fee for replacement teaching assistants. University presidents, once the intellectual leaders of the institutions, are now accomplished bagmen." John Harris, quoted in Maude Barlow and Heather Jane Robertson, "Homogenization of Education," in Jerry Mander and Edward Goldsmith, eds., *The Case Against the Global Economy: And for a Turn Toward the Local* (San Francisco: Sierra Club Books, 1996), 62–3.

"In the post-Cold War period, the South can anticipate a worsening of oppression for the large majority while some sectors may be enriched, notably those linked to the masters of the global economy." Noam Chomsky, *World Orders Old and New* (New York: Columbia University Press, 1994), 82.

"We have the fortune and misfortune to belong to a tormented region of the world, Latin America, and to live in a historical period that is relentlessly oppressive. The contradicitons of class society are sharper here than in rich countries. *Massive misery is the price paid by the poor countries so that 6 percent of the world's population may consume with impunity half the wealth generated by the entire world.* The abyss, the distance between the well-being of some and the misery of others, is greater in Latin America; and the methods necessary to maintain this distance are more savage." Eduardo Galeano, *Days and Nights of Love and*

War, trans. Sandra Cisneros (New York: Monthly Review Press, 2000), 169 italics added.

It is almost impossible to give one simple definition of the term "globalization," for it carries with it a plethora of implications in the economic, social, political, ideological, pedagogical, and intellectual realms.[1] My main concerns in this chapter are to raise a number of critical questions about these implications, especially in relation to the contemporary Arab and Muslim worlds, to offer some critical remarks on the state of contemporary Arab and Islamic thought and to suggest ways to grapple with the subtle and deep epistemological, ethical, scientific, economic, and political shifts globalization has recently engendered in the entire world. Also, at the outset, I would like to say that the Islamic perspective on economy and community has not been taken seriously by proponents of globalization, mainly because there has not been a systematic Islamic appreciation and critique of globalization.[2] It is true that there has been a political backlash against Western modernism in many Muslim countries, most notably in Iran, the Sudan, and Egypt; however, a Muslim intellectual response to the problematics engendered by globalization is long overdue.

Regardless of the complex epistemological undercurrents of contemporary Islamic thought in the Arab world, I believe it has not yet fulfilled its intellectual potential in that it has failed to grapple with some of the most critical issues of our times. Where is the Islamic critique and appreciation of modern nationalism, democracy, nation-state, modernity, and even the often discussed colonialism and neo-colonialism? Except for a few sparse individual studies and reflections, contemporary Islamic thought has not presented a comprehensive, let alone convincing, perspective or perspectives on the many issues and questions that beset the contemporary Muslim world. The lacuna is most apparent in the areas of both modernity and globalization.

To shed some light on the nature of modern Islamic thought, one must differentiate among, for example, Islamic thought and Arab thought or Pakistani thought. Modern Arab thought means the intellectual production of Arab thinkers during the last century, both religious and secular. In other words, one must not equate Arab thought with Islamic thought, since the former includes all those tendencies, trends, and patterns of thought, both religious and secular, that reflect the bewildering number of questions and issues that have preoccupied modern Arab thought.[3] Islamic thought, on the other hand, has a theological center and an intellectual frame of reference defined by the central place which the Sacred Text, the Qur'an, holds in Muslim life and thought.

The above remarks beg the question of the nature of the "Muslim presence" in the West generally. It is fallacious to argue that the Muslim world is out there, and is separate from the West, and that the Muslim presence in the West is of no importance to the Muslim world because it either lacks authenticity or is not governed by an Islamic state. With the onslaught of modernity and the migration of substantial numbers of Muslim intellectuals, engineers, doctors, and professionals to the West since the turn of the twentieth century, it is important to raise questions about the nature and direction of Muslim intellectual contributions in the West.

On the whole, the Muslim community in the West has failed to produce its own intellectuals, those thinkers that can be in a position to aid the Muslim community in its daily encounter with modernism and globalization. The failure of the Muslim community in the West to grasp the central problems surrounding its presence in a non-Islamic, though religiously-tolerant environment, reflects the deep social and psychological anguish Muslims suffer from in a Western milieu. The Muslim community is in an ideal position to reflect from within, so to speak, on the nature of globalization and guide the Muslim world in understanding the multitude of hazards created by neo-liberalism and the new forces of the market. It is quite impossible to escape the conclusion that the Muslim community in the West is hard pressed to apply its ethos to the new realities of the world – realities that do not seem to subscribe to any monotheistic worldview, but to the ideals of consumerism and competition.

Because of these factors, there is an almost total obsession with the issue of tradition and ways to conserve that tradition in a fast-changing and sometimes merciless world. I do not mean to imply that the issue of tradition is irrelevant or unimportant, but it seems to me that it is high time to transcend the conceptual formulations of nineteenth century Muslim thinkers, such as Muḥammad 'Abduh, Jamāl al-Dīn al-Afghānī, Sayyid Aḥmad Khān and others, by inventing a novel Islamic manner of thinking that creatively responds to the rigorous rules of critical philosophical and ethical thinking. No thinking can fathom the problematic of globalization unless the thinker is totally abreast of recent trends in critical theory, economic and social thought, their implications for religious thought in the Muslim world and the West, and the ethical response contemporary Islamic thought must present in order to reassert its vitality and relevance. Islamic thought must incorporate critical tools, besides those of revelation, in order to provide constructive answers to the problems of the contemporary Muslim world.

THREE PREMISES, NUMEROUS ARGUMENTS

The first premise is that in order to reclaim vitality, modern Islamic thought, in the Arab or the larger Muslim world, must reinterpret the main theological and normative precepts of Islam in a manner that challenges the totalitarianism of the ruling political and educational systems in the contemporary Muslim world, and the support and encouragement they have received with the onslaught of globalization on the world markets and the universal human psyche. If one accepts the claim that the crux of the Islamic worldview is egalitarianism, then one must conclude that in order to follow the ideals of Islam, one must be opposed to all forms of political, economic, social or intellectual oppression, which seems to dominate the Muslim world. In other words, one must promote an Islamic worldview that is liberationist in nature and meaningful to the average person.

The second major premise is somewhat historical and mainly related to the colossal social and economic changes taking place in the modern capitalist West and their political, intellectual, and cultural impact on the modern Muslim world and thought in general. It would be absolutely naive to assume that modern Islamic thought follows specific internal dynamics that have nothing to do with the complex mutations in modern Western thought or that modern Islamic thought refuses to "borrow" from external sources. To grasp the nature of economic, political, and philosophical transformations in the modern Western world is to seriously wrestle with the whole history of post-Renaissance Western thought, from Marxism and neo-Marxism to capitalism and its latest manifestation, globalization. One may argue that Western history, especially American and European history, has witnessed major transformations in its worldview, the latest manifestation of which is globalization. Islamic or Arabic thought cannot hold itself aloof from these deep-seated changes in the world economic and political scenes. It is true that it may still need some time to grapple with the whole legacy of its encounter with capitalist modernity in the nineteenth century; it is also equally true that it cannot turn a blind eye to the accelerated process of change the world has seen since the eclipse of the Soviet project, and the series of important transitions the Arab world has undergone since then, the most obvious of which has been the military defeat of Iraq in the second Gulf War and the *de facto* occupation of the Gulf by the American military.[4]

To most thinkers in the Muslim and Arab worlds, from the radical to the most conservative, globalization seems to be an inevitable phenomenon. In one sense, it is true that because of the fundamental historical, political, and economic mutations in the modern West, the fate of the Muslim world is highly intertwined with triumphant Western capitalism. However, a number of questions remain. What does globalization mean in the context of a post-modern, post-Soviet, post-Cold War world, and in the context of aggressive/hegemonic Western, especially American, capitalism?[5] What is the fate of the nation-states that were constructed in the Cold War era under globalization? How has civil society in the Muslim world changed in the past decade? Is the recent breakdown in the Indonesian economy and society a direct result of the encroachment of globalization?[6] What role do Muslim intellectuals play in transition?

How can one preserve the essential features of Muslim identity in this context, especially if those features had been construed in a pre-globalization phase? If one is to translate "preservation" as a defense mechanism, what conceptual tools must one create in order to revitalize modern Islamic thinking regarding globalization? Lastly, since manufacturing consent, to use Noam Chomsky's favorite term, in contemporary society is based on the power of ideas, and the leading (capitalist) ideas are taught in private schools and universities across the Muslim world, with whom does the common interest of the people lie?

My third premise derives from the last. The Muslim world is undergoing a dramatic process of change in its educational premises. The best education is privatized and is the preserve of the children of the elite. The elite have indeed waged a silent and highly subtle intellectual revolution against the masses in recent decades. The mushrooming of private educational institutions and distance learning centers in such countries as Turkey, Egypt, Jordan, Malaysia, Morocco, and Saudi Arabia, drives home the point that education is a highly priced commodity sold to the highest bidder.[7] There is no need to bother with "the revolt of the masses" or a liberal synthesis of education.

Because of the progressive privatization, elitization, Westernization, and Americanization of education in numerous Muslim countries, common people have been stripped of their traditional pride, and a new consciousness based on a class education distinction and social-economic segregation has been promulgated. The following observation about a tribal people in the north eastern part of India is also applicable to the Muslim world,

> No one can deny the value of real education – the widening and enrichment of knowledge. But today in the Third World, education has become something quite different. It isolates children from their culture and from nature, training them instead to become narrow specialists in a Westernized urban environment. This process has been particularly striking in Ladakh, where modern schooling acts as a blindfold, preventing children from seeing the very context in which they live. They leave school unable to use their own resources, unable to function in their own world.[8]

In the Third World, indigenous creativity has been sacrificed for academic and scientific specialization that promises financial gain.[9]

THE POST-COLD-WAR MUSLIM WORLD OR THE NEW WORLD ORDER

Globalization is not a brand new phenomenon; it is the direct result of the triumph of the capitalist mode of production in eighteenth century England after centuries of economic activity distinguished by the tributary and feudal modes of production, and long-distance trade.[10] Recently, the term "globalization" has acquired new and powerful meanings. It has been rightly characterized as, "one of the most hegemonic concepts for understanding the political economy of international capitalism. And its uses extend far beyond the business world to embrace questions of politics, culture, national identity, and the like."[11] For instance, Muslim economic history, as Samir Amin and Eric Wolf document, was characterized by long-distance trade, except perhaps in Egypt. This fact enabled Muslims to develop their high culture.[12] Many economic historians have noted the unrelenting expansion of capitalist mode of production and the concomitant drive toward new market and raw material.[13] This explains the rise of imperialism on the heels of the ever-expanding capitalist mode of production.[14] As Andre Gunder Frank shows, the development of the capitalist mode entailed another parallel development, that of underdevelopment.[15] In other words, "Capitalist development created peripheries within its very core."[16] During the nineteenth century and almost until World War Two, globalization's epicenter was in Europe. After American intervention in the war, it shifted to North America. This fact is important since many thinkers in the Arab and Third Worlds equate globalization with Americanization, and for good reasons. Also, the French intellectual climate became wary of the Americanization of the cultures of the world, and so was not hospitable to American thoughts and ideas.

In its European phase in the nineteenth century, capitalist globalization created profound structural, economic, political, cultural and religious transformations in the so-called Third World and led to permanent unequal interaction between South and North.[17] Imperialist domination was double-edged: on the one hand, it led to the modernization of some leading institutions and segments of the colonized world, such as the army, the police force, and the educational system. This modernization was necessary for the colonial state to ensure the smooth application of the capitalist mode of production in the Periphery. On the other hand, however, it created social and economic disequilibria, opening major gaps between the countryside and the urban centers, which in turn led the poor to migrate to the cities, and engendered a bilingual and anxious indigenous intelligentsia.[18]

The nation-state, emerging in response to the penetration of foreign capitalism, and emphasizing an autonomous national economic and cultural independence, sought to create new structures and foundations that bypassed the traditional dependence created by defunct imperialism. The existence of the Soviet Union and the ensuing Cold War after World War Two gave the new nation-states some room to maneuver.[19] However, two major events shifted the balance in the 1970s and 1980s in favor of the Capitalist West: first, the conquest of the huge Chinese market by American capitalism,[20] the collapse of the Soviet System, and the subsequent end of the Cold War, which signaled the triumph of the Capitalist West over the Socialist East.[21] Apart from leaving the socialist and nationalist movements in the Third World caught between a rock and a hard place, these significant changes created for the first time since the Bolshevik revolution of 1917 a unipolar world with a tremendous potential for economic and political chaos in the Third World, especially in that segment deemed insignificant to the strategic and economic interests of the Center.[22] These events, without parallel in the history of mankind, have naturally left the nation-states easy prey to the challenges and dangers of the new geopolitical and economic realities of the New World Order.[23]

This change once again proves the impact of economic decisions on the direction of world politics and the future. Profit-driven and highly competitive capitalism begins a new drive: the conquest of space after the conquest of the terrain.[24] Enter the multinational companies that see the future of capitalism in conquering new space and non-physical territories.[25] To do this, they aim to create a global climate that allows competition free from the controlling hands of the nation-state. This tendency of "aggressive capitalism" to go amok, so to speak, is all the more dangerous in the absence of a multinational economic and political system. In the mono-system of neo-liberalism, one author notes that,

> En cette ère de libéralisme généralisé, mission est confiée aux firmes privées, en collaboration avec les Etats et les organismes internationaux chargés de les assister, de promouvoir abondance et bien-être. Des entreprises productrices de marchandises et, de plus en plus, de services et ignorant, pour les plus performantes, les frontières. Leur seul moteur, leur unique raison d'être étant le profit, force est de constater qu'un immense fossé sépare le but assigné des capacités d'action.[26]
>
> ("In this era of general liberalism, mission is confined to private corporations in collaboration with states and international organizations tasked to help them and promote abundance and well-being. Manufacturing enterprises, and more and more, of services, these corporations ignore the national frontiers. Their

sole incentive and unique *raison d'être* is securing profit. We are forced to conclude that an immense divide separates the original goal from the range of action." Translation by Abu-Rabi'.)

Creating a globalized climate amenable to a new type of international profit has had negative impacts on indigenous economies. In a sense, it creates new sets of rationales and values inconsistent with the cultures, traditions, and histories of indigenous peoples and nation-states. The *raison d'être* of capitalism is not to maintain or develop healthy social and economic systems, but to gain profit in the shortest period possible.[27] Capitalism pursues its goals under the cover of transmitting democratic ideas to the Third World, and this is partially insidious.[28]

This last thought begs the question of the newly-gained relationship between multinationals and the nation-state, the role of the state in society, the enormous changes in power relations, not just between South and North, but also within the countries of the South as well, the nature of civil society, and the implications for democracy in the Third World.[29]

Globalization challenges the nation-state to open up its space and borders for a novel type of competition free of any control.[30] The political elite of the nation-state is expected to fully cooperate with the endorsed economic enterprises. However, the accumulation of national capital is very often impossible in view of the fact that many nation-states in the Third World suffer from onerous debt to the advanced world or the International Monetary Fund. The rules of the game thus change here: national development and growth in the Third World is hopelessly hampered by the accumulation of capital on an international scale. According to Samir Amin, in the 1950s and 1960s, globalization was somewhat controlled by three international factors: the intervention of the capitalist state in the process of capital accumulation; the Soviet project of socialist economy, and the Bandung project of the non-aligned world formed under the auspices of Sukarno, Nehru, and Nasser.[31] With privatization mushrooming in the countries of these leaders, the nationalist/socialist project of self-sufficiency and empowerment of the poor has come to a deadly halt. In the case of the Arab world, for example, the Gulf region was forcibly cut off from the rest of the Arab world by the Center, which intensified its hegemony, both economic and military, in the wake of the military defeat of Iraq in the second Gulf War. What this simply means, in the words of Samir Amin, is that the states of the Gulf have turned into "protectorates that are devoid of any freedom to maneuver both economically and politically."[32] In the words of Immanuel Wallerstein, the Third World was able to win the political battle in the 1950s and 1960s, whereby decolonization "had been achieved almost everywhere. It was time for the second step, national development…The second step was never to be achieved in most places."[33] In the age of liberalization and integration, globalization does not permit local economies to function on their own.[34]

The failure of nationalist economies in such countries as Indonesia, India, Egypt, and Algeria is proof of the triumph of rational technology in the advanced West. However, as some economists have pointed out, the spread of "financial liberalization" or "technological globalization" cannot be determined by technological factors alone; politics have a great deal to do with the spread of rational technology and globalization. It is the Center's political desire to subjugate the nation-states, with the exception of Israel, to the exigencies of capitalist markets.[35]

Advocates of globalization envision a kind of "global village economy" that facilitates the spread of modernization and technological rationalization to every corner of the world. They propose that globalization has led to the integration of those societies that had been hitherto marginalized and impoverished into the world market. In their view, globalization did not just result in the creation of millions of new jobs and the improvement of social and economic conditions of the poor, but also led to an opening in the cultural and mental space of the poorer nations.[36] Even if one is to accept the above views of the advocates of globalization, which has become an inevitable process in many Third World countries, one must turn a blind eye to other no less significant processes accompanying globalization: the "globalitarian regimes" that are more entrenched than the "totalitarian regimes" of yesteryear.[37] The global oppression of the nation-state has created new forms of oppression of civil society by the already "oppressed" nation-state, broken down social cohesion in the Third World, and whittled away the democratic space in society. Civil society is suffocated as a result of the new shifts in power boundaries in society, and freedom of expression becomes rare.[38] Also, as one astute author observes,

> As the industrialized nations are gradually figuring out, the new world order imposed by the globalized economy means a race to the bottom for everyone, as jobs are eliminated in the name of global competitiveness or exported and the transnational corporations assume a level of power above any government. Even in a country like India, where 10 percent of the 980,000,000 residents comprise a new middle class that has benefited from the globalized presence of transnationals, the other 90 percent are simply not in the plan for the dazzling future. The 10 percent with disposable income constitute a large enough market to cause salivation among the global players: India is called a great success story.[39]

In the new nation-state of the 1980s and 1990s, democratic space has been challenged to the core. One would expect the advanced Center, that which carried the slogan of democracy for a long while, would promote real democracy in the South. This has been far from true. Under globalization, a new relationship is forged between the political elite and economic powers, especially the multinationals.[40] In the case of the Muslim world, the tribal, quasi-constitutional state, controlled by the same family or clan, gains additional repressive power. Civil society also suffers from loss of freedom: the working people and women are disempowered.

The multinationals' gradual penetration of the Third World economies, far from eliminating poverty and alleviating the misery of the urban and rural poor, has led to three intertwined phenomena: an increase in the number of the poor and unemployed; the concentration of wealth in the hands of the political elite, and an increase in the repression of the state.[41] Indonesia is one prime example of this. With the onslaught of modern technologies under the guise of globalization, the old mission of the West, the *mission civilisatrice* is reaffirmed in the new/old god of money, technology, investment, and prosperity.

INTELLIGENTSIA AND KNOWLEDGE

In the Third World, the role of the intelligentsia is radically transformed in the age of globalization. In the colonial era, the indigenous intelligentsia played a leading role in both political and cultural independence. Although these intellectuals were, according to Benedict Anderson, a "lonely, bilingual, and highly anxiety-ridden intelligentsia,"[42] they were nevertheless in a position to reflect and draw attention to the anguish and suffering of their people. The majority acted as organic intellectuals, to use one of Gramsci's favorite terms. They fought for independence from their colonial masters, in whose schools they had been educated. The new intelligentsia of "Third World globalization" do not share the anxieties of the colonial intellectual elite. Scientists, technocrats, engineers, and researchers all have something in common: a preoccupation with business and investment, all expressed in a new mode of English exemplified by the London School of Economics or Harvard Business School. In the words of Pierre Bourdieu, those new technocrats tend to favor economic profit at the expense of social and mental dislocation in Third World societies. Technocrats support what he calls a "structural violence" in these societies, that is, an increase in the number of society's unemployed and marginalized.[43]

English, and to be more specific, American English, plays a critical role in the age of globalization. The power of the command of the English language is commensurate with the power of the English-speaking world. One cannot be a successful technocrat without having mastered the secrets of American business English.[44] As a matter of fact, it is hard to be a successful intellectual in the world today without knowing some measure of English. If the study of English in England was from the outset "all about the legitimacy of [British] national origins,"[45] its study by Third World professionals is about the legitimacy of their professions worldwide. The transmission of English as a language and British and American forms of knowledge to the Third World has been a complex process, which traverses the last two centuries. The transmission of English and British forms of knowledge, as Bernard Cohn shows in his masterly *Colonialism and its Forms of Knowledge: The British in India*,[46] was linked with the formation of the new British state in the eighteenth and nineteenth centuries in the same way that the transmission of American knowledge to the Third World since the end of World War Two has something to do with the origins of the new American state, read as empire, forming in the wake of the collapse of Fascism in Europe and the defeat of the Japanese in World War Two.

According to Mignolo, "Modernity, the period of globalization that today is witnessing a radical transformation, is characterized by and shaped from a particular articulation of languages (English, French, German, Italian)."[47] It is true that American English, in the seventeenth, eighteenth, and nineteenth centuries, developed from the womb of British English. But it is equally true that American English during that period was creatively responding to the social and economic conditions of the new world. In their fight against British domination, Americans developed a new linguistic authority that did not subscribe to the old rules of the Queen's English. Leading American linguist of the nineteenth century, Noah Webster promoted the notion that "it is quite impossible to stop the progress of language – it is like the course of the Mississippi, the motion of which, at times, is scarcely perceptible."[48] In the Cold War (1945–1991), American political elite failed to deploy English against their enemies, mainly because academic English was the preserve of Leftist intellectuals who abdicated "curatorship of the great books, abandoned traditional values, and subverted the social order."[49] However, with the end of the Cold War and the collapse of the Soviet Union, those with an investment in formal business English have taken the offensive. The new technocrats of both North and South adopt a formalized type of English that is more suited to the business and financial worlds than to the world of the humanities.

Although Chinese is the most frequently spoken language on the planet, it does not carry the same hegemonic power as the English language. Perhaps if China were to develop itself into a super industrial power in the current century, Chinese would be taught worldwide, just as English has been since the beginning of the twentieth century. Mignolo observes that in matters of language dominance in the world today, the main question, "is not so much the number of speakers as it is the hegemonic power of colonial languages in the domain of knowledge, intellectual production, and cultures of scholarship."[50] And although "globalization is not homogenizing the cultures of the world,"[51] as Nye argues, the dominant elite in many countries value the role of the English language in the maintenance of their system.

As seen previously, English is the most dominant language in the world today. I think that Chinese will have to go a long way before it becomes the dominant language of power and business in the world mainly because the modern Chinese state was born a weak one after World War Two and did not have imperial designs to dominate the world in the same way as the British and American states did. This leads us to raise a question about the transmission of knowledge under the aegis of American-dominated globalization. It is clear that even with the dominance of American English, all sorts of institutions and not mere scholars are needed to collect, order, and disseminate knowledge in the contemporary global age. What makes this process somewhat easier than before, in addition to the breakthroughs in technology, is the fact that the United States is the main beneficiary of the "brain-drain" process, which allows it to receive thousands of experts in all fields of knowledge who enrich its economic and scientific institutions and make it more competitive with other centers of global powers, most notably those of Japan and Europe.

To be sure, the increase in misery and economic poverty is not the sole preserve of the Third World.[52] This same phenomenon is unfolding in countries of the Center too, such as in France, England, and the United States. Urban decay can be easily found in major cities of the Center, which, in a real sense, is symptomatic of its neglect of projects focused on bettering the educational and social welfare of the poor. The increase in the use of drugs and the proliferation of crime indicate among other things that a significant portion of society in the advanced Center has been and continues to be marginalized. In other words, in its steadfast march towards the accumulation of capital, capitalism succeeds in gaining more and more profit only at the expense of creating havoc in the weaker sectors of society, both domestic and overseas. As one author puts it, "le capitalisme engendre à la fois des prospérités et des pauvretés" ("Capitalism simultaneously engenders prosperity and poverty." Translation by Abu-Rabi‘).[53]

As seen above, the New World Order did not emerge from the blue. With the collapse of the Soviet system in the early 1990s, after many decades of severe struggle, the Third World became easy prey to the hegemony of the only remaining superpower.[54] Regardless whether or not it was Iraq's intention to challenge the West's hegemony in general and the United States in particular by invading Kuwait in 1990, the amassing of Western troops under the banner of the United Nations in the Gulf sent shockwaves throughout the modern Muslim world. Iraq's military defeat by the West did in fact preserve, if not enhance, the West's national interests, which, in clear historical irony, further strengthened the authoritarian political regimes in the Gulf states and obliterated any real chance to achieve democracy for many years to come. In addition to signaling major shifts in world alliances and witnessing the rise of the United States as the only major superpower in the world today, these two events, that is, the collapse of the Soviet system and the defeat of Iraq, have raised once again, and perhaps in a much more acute way than before, the issue of Western, especially American, cultural hegemony and its impact on Third World cultures. It is far from true that the American impact on the Muslim world in the post-Cold War era is limited to the economic and political. It is primarily intellectual and conceptual. The ruling elite in the Muslim world take the functioning ideas in the capitalist West as their ideals.[55]

The West's entanglement with the Muslim world since at least the early nineteenth century has caused confusion in modern Islamic thought; baffled by the West as a phenomenon. Since the dawn of colonialism, Muslim intellectuals have always posed the question: "What is the West?" The West poses a major challenge to the modern Muslim and Arab mind, a challenge which has forced modern Islamic thought to critique the past and attempt to appropriate the scientific spirit of the modern West. In spite of the fact that the "West" has remained undefined in modern Islamic thought (does the West exemplify colonialism, liberalism, Christianity, capitalism or socialism?), the West, as a scientific and socio-cultural entity, has always been on the offensive. Nahḍah thinkers of the nineteenth century in the Arab world and liberal thinkers in Muslim India[56] were intrigued by the different possibilities of the "Western mind" and Western science provided. They were aware of stagnation in their societies and that this stagnation went against one of the main principles of Islam: the common good (*al-maslaḥah al-‘āmah*), which was ill-served by this situation. They sought to ameliorate conditions by reviving the doctrine of "the common interest" and linking it to the need for Western science. In other words, in the thought of the Nahḍah intelligentsia, Western science and the Muslim doctrine of common interest were not mutually exclusive; on the contrary, for the Muslim doctrine to be well-served, the logic of modernity (that is, science) must be adopted.[57] In other words, R. R. Al-Ṭahṭāwī, Muḥammad ‘Abduh, Sayyid Aḥmad Khān, and their colleagues thought that the tension between stagnation and science could be resolved only if the intellectual

Muslim elite of the nineteenth century linked its own doctrinal philosophy to the logic of Western science and philosophy. That is to say, all of them advocated the central concept of nineteenth century European modernity: progress. However, in resolving this first contradiction, a second and perhaps more astounding one was revealed: the contradiction of colonialism and science, two givens in the West. Muslim thinkers of the nineteenth century were well aware that the West did not simply mean science but also meant military and political domination.

The above double tensions – Muslim stagnation and Western science, Western science and Western hegemony – have defined the parameters of the main challenges facing the "Muslim mind" since the nineteenth century. This double bipolarity became more complex in the mid 1950s after the end of official colonialism in most Muslim states. The new nation-states sought to modernize without sacrificing the common interest, be it derived from Muslim or nationalist thought, and sought economic and social independence from the West while still relying on it. As globalization began to lay its economic egg in the early 1970s with the economic conquest of China and came to fruition with the collapse of the Soviet system in the 1990s, the Muslim world became inextricably ensnared to the capitalist West. Further, the power gap between the Muslim world and the West began to widen to the extent that a country like Syria, that had used the Soviet Union during the Cold War era to bolster its status, went all the way to appease the West by sending its military to fight against Iraq. The political regimes of the Muslim world soon realized that it would be suicidal to challenge the authority of the only remaining superpower. This fundamental power differential has had and is having a tremendous impact on the internal functioning of Muslim societies and is leading to wider gaps between rich and poor within the Muslim world. The international shift in power is also working to solidify the military and political elite in the Muslim world.[58]

CULTURAL INDEPENDENCE UNDER GLOBALIZATION

The post-independence state in the Arab and Muslim world has inherited many contradictions. On the one hand, it sought cultural and political decolonization after independence; on the other, neo-colonialism began to manifest itself immediately after the colonial period by forging new economic and political relationships that gave the Center the upper hand in international and economic affairs with its former dependents. In the opinion of many Arab thinkers, globalization is the latest stage of neo-colonialism, "It is the culmination of the success of the Capitalist project worldwide."[59] Neo-colonialism has permitted the Center to preserve its markets and cultural influence and sometimes even its troops at a minimal cost.

While it is possible to measure and quantify economic factors, it is of course difficult to measure culture in the same way. The end of official colonialism left behind a complex cultural package that cannot be easily overcome. The intellectual elite of the *ancien régime*, some of whom fought political but not cultural colonialism, found themselves in commanding positions, caught between their adopted Western and the indigenous cultures. Those who opted for Arabization

(North Africa, for example) do support cultural diversity and independence from the dominant culture of the West.

Post-colonialism ensued from neo-colonialism and is in fact its twin brother. It is the product of the New World Order.[60] As an historical event, colonialism very often entails a military occupation of one country by another (that is, a military occupation by a European country). Colonialism also entails direct control of natural resources, which becomes very important to the strategic interests of the colonizer.

The political elite of the new nation-states have sought to modernize their countries by blindly imitating the West. These elite have benefited from political and military protection by the West, which has permitted them to stay in power. For example, the West has never raised the issue of human rights or the absence of democracy in some of these countries. What mattered to the West was preserving its strategic interests, even if that meant sacrificing its principles. The basis of neo-colonialism is a new form of economic domination that allows other discrete forms of domination – political, cultural, and intellectual.[61]

Third World countries felt somewhat relieved from cultural and political pressure by the West during the Cold War between the Soviet bloc and the Western capitalist world, since the balance of world power permitted them to function somewhat freely. However, the *status quo* changed with the collapse of the Soviet system and the military defeat of Iraq in the second Gulf War. These two events left both the Arab world and Arab culture defenseless in face of American hegemony. With the emergence of the United States as the leading superpower, a number of states such as Cuba, Syria, and Libya were and still are accused by the Center of supporting terrorism.

The Periphery has been dependent on the Center since the colonial era, and the diffusion of ideas through satellites instituted a new relationship between the Muslim world and the West. The Center practices what one may call a hegemonic "imperialist culture."[62] Most of the thinkers of the Muslim world who grew up in the shadow of colonialism draw our attention to the major conclusions of European, and even some American, thinkers about the rise of America in recent years and its cultural impact on the whole world, including Europe: "L'empire américain est le seul au monde, c'est une hégémonie exclusive, et c'est la première fois que ce phénomène étrange survient dans l'histoire de l'humanité" ("The American empire is the only one in the world; it is an exclusive hegemony, and it is the first time that this strange phenomenon occurs in the history of humanity." Translation by Abu-Rabi').[63] The United States is a unique empire. It is a major producer of all sorts of goods; however, it is also an avid consumer. The history of America from the very beginning is marked by an extreme tendency toward expansion, "L'histoire américaine tout entière est marquée par une perpétuelle tendance à l'expansion: soif de terre, soif de puissance, soif de nouveau, soif de grandeur, autant de besoins qui se assouvissent d'eux-mêmes" ("American history is marked entirely by a perpetual tendency to expansion, thirst for land, power, the new, grandeur, as many needs as can be self-satisfied." Translation by Abu-Rabi').[64]

One must understand the rise of American power to world dominance after 1945 in the context of the expansion of Fordism, an economic system, which took shape in the United States at the beginning of the twentieth century and came to maturity after World War Two, when the European industrial world was still reeling from damage sustained in the war.[65] The American model of socio-economic development was fully realized after the war, "Leading thinkers heralded a 'postindustrial' order that eliminated industrial capitalism's fundamental sociopolitical divisions."[66] United States capitalism was able to achieve, in the 1950s and 1960s, a high level of "class compromise," where poorer sections of the population bought into the "American dream."

Both David Harvey and Noam Chomsky have noted that the rise of the United States to economic and political prominence in the world order was a result of the tremendous economic possibilities of the United States, the rise of Fordism or the industrial management of American society, and the destruction of key industrial nations in the aftermath of World War Two.[67] In Chomsky's words,

> In 1945 the structure of world power was unusually clear by historical standards. A half-century before that, the United States had become by far the world's greatest economic power, but it was a relatively small player on the world scene. By 1945 that had radically changed, for obvious reasons: the other industrial societies had been seriously damaged or destroyed, while the US economy had flourished through the war; the US had literally half the world's wealth, incomparable military power and security, and it was in a position to organize much of the world, and did so with the assistance of its "junior partner," as the British Foreign Office ruefully described the new reality of the time.[68]

David Harvey, after an enlightening discussion of the history of modernism and post-modernism in the West and their appropriation by Americanism in the 1940s, turns his attention to the economic system created by Fordism in the early part of the twentieth century, which grew to maturity in the interwar period and was launched on the world scene after the destruction wrought on Europe by World War Two. Harvey agues that,

> The problem of the proper configuration and deployment of state powers was resolved only after 1945. This brought Fordism to maturity as a fully-fledged and distinctive regime of accumulation. As such, it then formed the basis for a long postwar boom that stayed broadly intact until 1973. During that period, capitalism in the advanced capitalist countries achieved strong but relatively stable rates of economic growth. Living standards rose, crisis tendencies were contained, mass democracy was preserved and the threat of inter-capitalist wars kept remote…Postwar Fordism was also very much an international affair. The long postwar boom was crucially dependent upon a massive expansion of world trade and international investment flows…This opening up of foreign investment (chiefly in Europe) and trade permitted surplus productive capacity in the United States to be absorbed elsewhere, while the progress of Fordism internationally meant the formation of global mass markets and the absorption of the mass of the world's population, outside the communist world, into the

> global dynamics of a new kind of capitalism...All of this was secured under the hegemonic umbrella of the United States' financial and economic power backed by military domination.[69]

However, both Chomsky and Harvey are quick to point out that in the process of the internationalization of Fordism, or the larger American capitalist system, American policy makers identified indigenous nationalist movements as a threat and worked hand in glove with a tiny indigenous elite, which chose "to collaborate actively with international capital."[70] The capitalist West decided to export its version of Fordism to the less developed world while seeking to suppress any political movement standing in the way of its capitalist agenda. In the case of the Arab world, Nasserism was identified as a threat to the expansion and consolidation of the capitalist system in the Middle East, especially in the Gulf countries. Nasserism was proclaimed pro-communist and anti-Islam.

Fordism had a decisive influence upon the social structure and relations of capitalist societies.[71] The same is true of the Arab world, especially in the Gulf, since 1945. Most Arab ruling elite adopted Fordist ideas. The United States exported these ideas to the Arab world and agreed to transfer Fordist forms of production while "maintaining crucial command and research functions in the metropolises."[72] The question is what has been the impact of such a project on the social composition of modern Arab societies, the rise of new classes, and the increase in the number of the poor in post-1945 Arab society? The Gulf states have worked tirelessly to realize a new social and economic contract with their own people. This became possible with advanced technology and the application of the Fordist project to implement a new form of social contract, one based on the promise of material prosperity and the premise of excessive consumption. Furthermore, the Fordist project in the Arab world was carried out in collaboration with official Islamic forces that justified material consumption in the name of Islam. This is the more poignant in the Gulf states, which further depended on a huge pool of cheap foreign labor to actualize Fordism's economic objectives. No serious force has arisen in any of the Gulf states to challenge the fundamental premises of Fordism, which attained its apogee in the 1970s and 1980s. On the contrary, many people mourn the passing of these decades. Post-Fordism, which entered a crisis in the industrial world in the 1970s, caught up with the Arab world two decades later.

According to the famous American literary critic, Edmund Wilson, American expansion overseas in the wake of the defeat of Nazi Germany in World War Two was not coincidence,

> We thought we were liberating Europe and fending off the imperialism of feudal Japan, but we turned up after the war [World War Two] occupying or controlling foreign countries all over America, Europe, Asia, and the Middle East, and sometimes as unwelcome as the French in Algeria, the British in Cyprus or the Russians in central Europe. After years of being shocked by the imperialism of others, we are developing a new kind of our own, and we find ourselves scowling at the Soviet Union and spending billions for weapons against it – and weapons even the testing of which is dangerous to our own population – without any real provocation and for the simple sub-rational

> reason that we are challenging the Soviet Russians for domination of large sections of the world.[73]

Post-Fordism, which began in the early 1970s, is an advanced form of Fordism. According to one preeminent critic of this phenomenon, post-Fordism has since 1975 exhibited the following characteristics: first, as opposed to the unification of production under Fordism, production in post-Fordism is decentralized among different owners in different localities. Second, although production has been decentralized in various regions and countries, the financial and information sources of production are firmly held by the First World. Third, because of the geographical spread of production, new forms of communication, mostly owned by the Center, have emerged.[74] Fourth, the state becomes an agent of unrestricted economic development. Fifth, the necessity of paying for full-time work comes under scrutiny. Part-time tend to replace full-time employees, which translates as more profit. Finally, the end product of post-Fordism has been the emergence of global capitalism that knows no boundaries.[75] Most of the proponents of the post-Fordism economic development model belong to the First World, especially the United States. Post-Fordism is a refined version of classical capitalism; its goal is the constant expansion of the world market for the sake of wealth accumulation. Policy makers of post-Fordism have pushed the tiny and affluent elite of the Third World to follow suit in order to increase profit. The following quotation from one of Immanuel Wallerstein's early writings points to the direction of American capitalism after World War Two:

> It was the Second World War that enabled the United States for a brief period (1945–1965) to attain the same level of primacy as Britain had in the first part of the nineteenth century. United States growth in this period was spectacular and created a great need for expanded market outlets. The Cold War closure denied not only the USSR but Eastern Europe to US exports. And the Chinese revolution meant that this region, which had been destined for much exploitative activity, was also cut off. Three alternative areas were available and each was pursued with assiduity. First, western Europe had to be rapidly "reconstructed," and it was the Marshall Plan which thus allowed this area to play a primary role in the expansion of world productivity. *Secondly, Latin America became the reserve of US investment from which now Britain and Germany were completely cut off. Thirdly, southern Asia, the Middle East and Africa had to be decolonized. On the one hand, this was necessary in order to reduce the share of the surplus taken by the western European intermediaries...But also these countries had to be decolonized in order to mobilize productive potential in a way that had never been achieved in the colonial era. Colonial rule after all had been an inferior mode of relationship of core and periphery, one occasioned by the strenuous late-nineteenth-century conflict among industrial states but one no longer desirable from the point of view of the new hegemonic power.*[76]

One major net result of the whole process has been the consolidation of the Third World elites' influence in restructuring their societies and making them more appealing to the demands of global capitalism. This fact has exacerbated class differences in the Arab world in the past three decades. In the case of the Center as well, "Under post-Fordism, class lines have grown sharper, more severe, and more easily visible; the alleged postwar trend toward a 'middle class society' is undergoing a reversal."[77] Recent manifestations of globalization, in the view of many Third World intellectuals, are triumphant Americanization that advocates a new kind of cultural and economic model, "Besides being an economic system, globalization is an ideology that serves this system. Americanization and globalization are highly intertwined."[78]

The Arab world needs Western science and technology to further develop. However, Western science cannot be imported without the cultural and ethical values that underlie it. It is a well-known fact that during the imperialist phase, the West used culture and ideas as a means to colonize the Third World. That is why Orientalism, missionary work, and similar activities flourished. Classical imperialism was sustained by the physical presence of its troops overseas; physical and mental conquest went hand in hand. The situation is somewhat different in the age of neo-imperialism with its rapid advances in technology. The intellectual and cultural integrity of small nations is endangered. The purpose was to create an indigenous cultural elite with Western values and plant Western systems of education and thought in the Third World. The culture of colonialism was ideological in nature. Today, cultural invasion through advanced technology leads to the following conclusion: besides being ideological in nature, Western culture was to subdue the means of criticism and rationalism in the Third World. In our case, it is aimed at Arab and "Muslim reason," attempting to make this "reason" oblivious to its unique and glorious past.

One of the unfortunate facts in today's world is that no one can rival the economic and intellectual hegemony of the United States.[79] The United States has huge economic resources, military prowess, advanced technology, and the will to intellectually conquer the whole world intellectually.[80] Therefore, I rephrase an earlier question: What is to be done in order to achieve an overall rational cultural, political, and social renaissance in the contemporary Arab and Muslim worlds? Islamic thought cannot avoid the full implications of the contemporary cultural challenges of the West, especially of the United States, in the context of the New World Order.

The New World Order, inaugurated in the aftermath of the military defeat of Iraq in the second Gulf War, has become a political phenomenon of universal proportion. In the Arab world, for example, the nationalist response to the West took a grass roots orientation after the end of the Cold War. Most states lost interest in Arab unity. What Muḥammad 'Ābid al-Jābīrī, a leading Moroccan ideologue of Arab nationalism, says has some relevance,

> Arab existence is well and alive. The recent war that the allies have launched against Iraq has undoubtedly pointed to the vitality of Arabism and its enshrined presence in the souls of the Arab masses that rallied to support Iraq, very often against the wishes of their governments. Also, what is of significance in this regard is the Arab nationalist position that the Francophone Maghrebi thinkers

took, many of whom were deprived of learning Arabic in their childhood. In addition to rallying their support behind Iraq, they expressed their dismay at and frustration with the European attitude toward Iraq.[81]

During the age of imperialism, the main purpose of the Arab nationalist project was to ensure the independence of the Arab world. The independence of Algeria helped achieve that goal. However, the 1967 war was a major setback in that it did not allow Arab unity and solidarity to take deep organizational and intellectual root in society. The emergence of the regional state in the Arab world, as an Arab and international political fact and as a social, economic and psychological condition that cannot be overstepped places more hurdles in the way of the Arab nationalist project. The Arab world is more divided now than ever. As Noam Chomsky argues, the United States and the West in general opposed the rise of independent nationalism in the Third World during the Cold War. Nasserism was considered to be a virus that had to be cleansed of the body of the Arab world.[82]

Against the above, one would say that the task of the Third World is the more urgent in seeking economic and political liberation from this new mode of hegemony. One of the crucial factors in this liberation is cultural decolonization since the principal goal of post-colonialism is cultural hegemony and the propagation of Western values in the Third World.[83] The North refuses to embark upon a thorough conversation on cultural values with the South on the premise that Occidental values are the norm – that is, they are universal values – and that adopting them will be the solution to the social and economic problems of the Third World.[84] Not counting its nuclear and military prowess or economic and political influence, "post-colonialism is a weapon that aims at destroying cultural diversity"[85] in today's world and creating one universal homogeneous: Occidentalized culture.[86]

It is not coincidence that the majority of "hot spots" in the world are located in the Muslim world. The main reason for this is the West's refusal to come to terms with a system of values other than its own. However, the problem is not caused purely by external factors. The Muslim world, like most of the Third World, suffers from the absence of democracy, a crisis in basic human rights and a lack of democratic channels that enable people to freely express their ideas. This is all perpetrated without objection on the part of the West. Under globalization, arms production in the West is on the increase and its main consumers are in the South, in Africa, the Middle East, and Afghanistan. Civil wars are on the increase, mainly in the South. The West, including the now defunct Soviet Union, learned a great lesson after World War Two: not to wage war in Europe or the North.

The United States has undertaken a war against its new universal enemies in the wake of the collapse of the Soviet system. This is clearly expressed in Samuel Huntington's thesis.[87] The West has become preoccupied with the menace of "Islam," "Islamic terrorism," and Islamic fundamentalism, and the tragic events of September 11, 2001 gave many in the Western media a rationale. The entire Muslim world, with its multitudinous cultural and ethnic complexities, has been demeaned, reduced and atomized by such all-inclusive, discriminatory terms as "Islamic terrorism" and "Islamic fundamentalism." The simple fact that most in the West refuse to acknowledge is that most Muslims live in countries that have authoritarian regimes that are supported by the West and its democracies.[88] In fact, real cultural decolonization begins when the West and the intellectual elite of the Third World seriously consider the thesis that modernization does not necessarily mean Occidentalization, and that there are non-Western ways of modernization.

A fascinating phenomenon that characterizes modern civilization is the profound mutation taking place in the passage of this civilization from a "culture of production" to a "culture of information and scientific knowledge." The relationship between information and economic production is not new; however, "it is only under the current technological, social, and cultural parameters that they become directly productive forces."[89] This is possible because of radical breakthroughs in science and technology. Because of the West's scientific superiority, the information gap between North and South has become insurmountable, and grows larger every day. The information gap between North and South has been compounded in the contemporary age of globalization by what is termed, "Soft power," that is, the power of cybernetics and the launching of technological warfare from a distance. According to Richard Falk of Princeton University, the current thinking of the elite in the West and the United States predicts that the cybernetic potential is unlimited:

> Certains stratèges, aux Etats-Unis, rêvent de prendre le contrôle des réseaux cybernétiques et des fabuleuses richesses que vont produire, semble-t-il, les industries de l'immatériel, du savoir et de la connaissance. Ils veulent construire le nouvel Empire de l'ère électronique. Au centre de celui-ci: un marché mondial totalement innervé par les technologies du futur.[90]
>
> ("Certain plans in the United States dream of taking control of cyber networks and the fabulous wealth which will be produced, it appears, by the unseen industries of knowledge and learning. They want to build the new empire of the electronic age. At the heart of this age, there is a global market supported by the technologies of the future." Translation by Abu-Rabi')

The United States, powerful and young, is still fascinated by the early immigrants' experience of conquering the prairies in the American heartland. That land conquest initially seemed unlimited. But by the end of the nineteenth century, all came to a halt. The American mind had to fnd a new frontier with which to grapple. The new frontier of the New World Order is the conquest of space, which means having full access to cybernet and other resources. With the "brain-drain" from poor countries inexorably continuing, and the migration of high-tech experts from the former Soviet Union, the United States now possesses enormous technological resources. American globalization has begun in earnest.[91] In fact the advanced Center encourages the migration of skilled professionals from the Third World and has begun to enact laws that make it difficult for non-professionals to immigrate.[92]

As stated, globalization has accelerated the "brain-drain" from the Third World to the advanced Center. The place of preference for many Third World intellectuals and professionals is the United States. This process has been rightly termed "intellectual hemorrhage," since it depletes poor countries of much-needed expertise in all fields of science. Many emigrate, not just in search of better economic and social standards, but because the development process in their native countries lacks the appropriate vision to productively incorporate them. Very often, this lack of vision is compounded by blind imitation of the modernized North, leading to the transfer of technology with no creative contribution from the South. In other words, the South can purchase technology, but it must create its own forms of modernity and modernization. However, these forms cannot be created in the context of the continuous exodus of its skilled professionals. As a consequence of this unfortunate state of affairs, the Muslim world and the rest of the Third World countries suffer from the following interdependent problems: illiteracy; an absence of rigorous scientific research, and a lack of democratic values.

Globalization is constructing a new world that will, in a few decades from now, look much different than the one to which we are accustomed. Transformations are already underway: first, the collapse of socialism and the spread of privatization to such countries as China, India, and Egypt; second, the rise of regional powers, such as the European community, in the wake of the rise of the United States to the position of supreme power; third, the widening of social and economic gaps between rich and poor within and between countries; fourth, the globalization of exploitation, which is a natural consequence of privatization and multinational investment; fifth, the rise of ultra nationalism, ethnic cleansing and the creation of new refugee problems; sixth, the internationalization of crime, especially Mafia-related crime; seventh, the destabilization of the nation-state; and lastly, the creation of new international enemies.[93]

8
Contemporary Arab Thought and Globalization

"A hidden pitfall in historiography is disregard for the fact that conditions within the nations and races change with the change of periods and passing of days…The condition of the world and of nations, their customs and sects, does not persist in the same form or in a constant manner." Ibn Khaldūn, *The Muqaddimah: An Introduction to History*, volume 1, trans. Franz Rosenthal (New York: Pantheon, 1958), 56–7.

"In the 1950s and the 60s, a phase in the history [of the Third World] that the supporters of globalization wish to marginalize and assassinate, culture was in fact made up of two kinds: imperialist/hegemonic culture and liberationist/nationalist culture. Those influenced by the ideology of globalization desire to create a new genre of culture: the culture of opening and renewal and that of withdrawal and stagnation." Muḥammad 'Ābid al-Jābīrī, *Qaḍayah fī al-fikr al-mu'āṣir* (Beirut: Markaz Dirāsāt al-Wiḥdah al-'Arabīyyah, 1997), 144.

"What imperialists actually wanted was expansion of political power without the foundation of a body politic. Imperialist expansion had been touched off by a curious kind of economic crisis, the overproduction of capital and the emergence of 'superfluous' money, the result of oversaving, which could no longer find productive investment within the national borders." Hannah Arendt, *The Origins of Totalitarianism* (New York: Meridian Books, 1963), 135.

"Over its modern history, the West has not permitted any Arab liberal [and democratic] experiment to succeed, since, to start with, it has not allowed an Arab bourgeoisie to grow independent of its control. This is the reason why the West has always sought the explicit alliance of patriarchal and theocratic societies which vehemently oppose secularism." Ghālī Shukrī, *Diktātoriyat al-takhalluf al-'arabī* (Cairo: al-Hay'ah al-Miṣriyyah al-'Āmmah li'l Kitāb, 1994), 159.

"It is hard for any Arab aged between fifty and seventy not to feel that his or her generation has not made an all around mess of things. Ours was the generation that supported and lived through the first decade of post-World War II independence which brought to power the very regimes – surprisingly durable – that run things today: the armies, the undemocratic societies, the intelligence services, the hopelessly backward and unreformed educational systems, the growing gap between a small elite and a vast number of disadvantaged citizens, the dependence on the United States, the almost total absence of a thriving civil society, the sinking rate of nearly all forms of productivity." Edward Said, *The End of the Peace Process: Oslo and After* (New York: Pantheon, 2000), 173.

"From New York to Beijing, via Moscow and Vladivostok, you can eat the same junk food, watch the same junk on television and, increasingly, read the same junk novels. In the newly marketized countries of Eastern and central Europe, a book can be consumed just like a McDonald's Hamburger. Indigestion and an excess of wind are no longer the preserve of the stomach." Tariq Ali, "Literature and Market Realism." *New Left Review*, number 199, May–June 1993, 140.

"Perhaps history will one day remind us that 'capital' is not just a stack of money: Capital is the energy that has, over the last four centuries, altered the face of the world and driven away to reservations, jungles, and the outback those peoples who would not compromise. Capital has joined together the peoples of all nations and races through war, trade, destruction, and financial assistance. It has brought people out of their cocoons to fly as economic butterflies. Don't think me to be anticapitalist. I'm not at all. I'm simply cognizant of the fact that capital has the power to effect change, something that has been almost continually demonstrated ever since the sixteenth century. No, it's not capital I dislike. It's the arbitrary use of capital power that I abhor." Pramoedya Ananta Toer, *The Mute's Soliloquy: A Memoir* (New York: Hyperion East, 1999), 253.

"Capitalism [in France] produced a ruling class whose economic imperative was to buy cheap and sell dear. This class reproduced itself by establishing a set of institutions that would guarantee its preponderance within the state and throughout civil society by denying peasants and workers significant access to the levers of power." Michael Sprinker, *History and Ideology in Proust: A la recherche du temps perdu and the Third French Republic* (London: Verso, 1998), 61.

Contemporary Arab thinkers of all hues and inclinations are beginning to grapple with the issue of globalization with a two-fold purpose: to reflect on the enormous challenges this phenomenon has posed to the Arab world and to evaluate the general progress of the Arab world in the past century or so. Aside from the social and economic ramifications of globalization, the main issue to be addressed by Arab intellectuals is that of the contemporary cultural personality of the entire Arab world, both in the Middle East and North Africa. Arab intellectuals seem to agree on a number of major points: first, since the disappearance of the Soviet Union, the Third World has been thrown into huge political and military imbalance. Second, the rise of the United States to its position of hegemony has had adverse effects on the Arab political order. Authoritarianism reigns when democracy is in full retreat.[1] Third, the poverty margin has widened in the past several decades. The ruling Arab political elite, out of uncertainty, have taken a turn to the right in their alliance with their counterparts in the Center, especially in the United States.[2] Fourth, Israel and the Zionist movement have been the main beneficiaries of globalization in the Middle East.[3] Fifth, Islamism seems to gain new ground with the spread of modernization in the Arab world as the new hope for the dispossessed middle classes and the poor. Sixth, while globalization has been an inevitable phenomenon, the Arab world can be culturally united to thwart the spread of Americanization.

Of all contemporary Arab intellectual trends, the Arab Left is pioneer in offering a sustained critique of the phenomenon of globalization, its economic and social origins, and current implications. Some intellectual leaders of the Arab Left, especially Samir Amin and Ṣādiq Jalāl al-'Azm, have gained international prominence as a result of their analyses of this question. A full consideration of the Arab Left's position on globalization is beyond the scope of this chapter. However, it is important to note two prominent Arab Leftist periodicals that have devoted considerable attention to the issue of globalization, the Lebanese *al-Ṭarīq* and the Egyptian *Qaḍayah Fikriyyah*.[4]

In order to give the reader a general idea of the Arab leftist position on globalization, I will devote a few pages to two important contemporary Arab Marxist thinkers, the Egyptian Maḥmūd Amīn al-'Ālim, and the Syrian Ṣādiq Jalāl al-'Azm.

Al-'Ālim places globalization squarely within the historical context of the development of modern capitalism in Europe since the sixteenth century. He takes as his basis the economic insights of Karl Marx, who spent a great deal of time trying to unlock the dynamics of nineteenth century capitalism. As such, globalization is an objective historical process, and not merely ideological construct, which has deeply affected the world since its inception:

> Globalization is an objective realization of a complete human unity attained for the first time in human history...This capitalist civilization, present internationally, is more than a Western European civilization, as some tend to think, but a universal capitalist civilization, in spite of its European origins and its domination by the West currently.[5]

Since its inception, capitalism has been on the global offensive for the purpose of exploiting new markets. The end result, according to al-'Ālim, has been that global capitalism has built a true competitive universal civilization, in spite of its Eurocentric vision.[6] Despite his severe criticism of aggressive capitalism in the eighteenth and nineteenth centuries, al-'Ālim plays down the advanced world's pillage of the Third World in this period. Two companies were primarily responsible for executing this pillage: the East India Company, which became a virtual state in India in the eighteenth century, and the East Dutch Company in Indonesia. The goal of both of these companies was to make maximum profits in trade. To reach this objective, both found it necessary to either maintain or change the power structure in a way that best suited their stated goals.[7]

To contend that contemporary globalization is a much more complex system than the capitalist system of the sixteenth or seventeenth centuries is to assume that current globalization is more pernicious and capable of more damage to the Third World than ever before. However, al-'Ālim's argument follows a somewhat different direction. He says that we can no longer speak of a simple capitalist mode of production in the way that Samir Amin speaks of it in his various writings, but about a complex capitalist civilization, the only acknowledged global civilization that has cut across cultures, religions and regions, at levels of advancement. To al-'Ālim's mind, the capitalist mode of production has given rise to capitalist civilization and culture, which in turn has given rise to the current capitalist globalization. At present, three major conditions define contemporary globalization:

1. the competitive and exploitative nature of the capitalist system. At the heart of this system is the idea of progress, growth or expansion, which has characterized it since the beginning;
2. the collapse of the socialist system, which in a sense left the universal capitalist system in charge of the world's economy. This state of affairs has had major ramifications for the Third World and the political independence of many states;
3. the enormous scientific advances in information and media technology which have redefined the concept of distance. Capitalism has become truly triumphant in the age of globalization.

Al-'Ālim defines contemporary capitalism as "a universal capitalist civilization" [*ḥaḍārah ra'smāliyyah 'ālamiyyah*], which has outgrown previous human civilizations and cultures.[8] That is to say, al-'Ālim believes that under the impact of recent globalization, the world has been moving towards a homogenized economic system, with different levels of acceptance in the world at large. This homogenized economic system has created a dominant capitalist civilization, which is, to al-'Ālim's mind, the only viable civilization in the contemporary world. In other words, al-'Ālim dismisses Samuel Huntington's contention that the near future will witness "a clash of civilizations."[9] Al-'Ālim advises that this thesis is untenable for the simple reason that the world is not teeming with civilizations but is for all practical reasons dominated by one universal capitalist civilization.[10]

To put it bluntly, the Arab and the Muslim worlds cannot boast an Arab or Muslim civilization at present. The political and economic elite in the Arab or Muslim worlds, regardless of their culture, are true participants in the civilization of capitalism. True, there is an Arab or Muslim culture, but it is currently dominated by the larger capitalist civilization. This is an intriguing statement, and a sharp response from a leading Arab Leftist intellectual to the Islamist claim that there is an Islamic civilization and not just culture or cultures in the modern Muslim world. I think al-'Ālim places his finger on one of the most perplexing problems in contemporary Muslim thought in the Arab world: the juxtaposition of normative civilization (Islamic worldview) with a concrete and historically present civilization; that is, the global capitalist civilization. Al-'Ālim cannot fathom modern global identity outside the rubric of capitalism. In other words, religious identity is, at best, secondary to that defined by the domination of the capitalist system. Capitalists (proponents of a capitalist civilization) can be found all over the world, including the Muslim world, and class conflict still defines social relations. Furthermore, implicit in al-'Ālim's argument is the assumption that the Muslim world, unlike Europe, has failed to develop its capitalist system in the modern period and has thus become dependent on the world capitalist system, which has been pioneered by the West. The Muslim world has *culture* but lacks *civilization*.

To al-'Ālim, the capitalist civilization is dominant worldwide, although it has crystallized in various cultural and social forms depending on the country in which it flourishes. Al-'Ālim contends that the capitalist system is strongest in North America, Europe, and Japan, with North America taking the leading role in world economic and scientific affairs.[11] He draws a distinction between globalization and Americanization or between globalization and hegemony. Globalization is an objective socio-historical and economic process that began in the sixteenth century from the remnants of the feudal system. It has gone through major transformations ever since then. On the other hand, Americanization or American hegemony is the product of the leading scientific and economic role the United States has played in the present world capitalist system.[12] Britain was the dominant capitalist power in the nineteenth century and the first half of the twentieth. Therefore, globalization and American hegemony are not necessarily synonymous. At this point in time, however, the United States is the sole leading power, but it is unlikely that it will play this role forever.[13]

Why is it important to come to grips with contemporary globalization? Since the nineteenth century, the Arab world has been hard pressed to find solutions to its dependency on the capitalist West. Although the Arab world has witnessed several political movements, most notably nationalism (which attempted to put an end to the structural and economic dependency of the Arab world on the West), no viable solution has been found. Al-'Ālim argues that the crisis of the Arab social system is predicated on the international division of labor under capitalism and the current hegemony of the United States. The Arab political elite either benefit from this division of labor or are unable to alter it to their advantage.[14]

Al-'Ālim, as pointed out earlier, dismisses the notion of intra-civilizational conflict. However, he argues that an intercivilizational conflict between various or regional economic powers or blocs is very likely, such as the conflict between the European community and the United States, or Japan and the United States. This conflict will not be over the nature of the capitalist system or civilization but over the distribution or exploitation of resources, which has been critical to the capitalist system. Al-'Ālim does not refer to the Chinese in his analysis. His comments about the Chinese economic experiment would be interesting nonetheless.

Although al-'Ālim acknowledges the 'objective' universal nature of capitalist globalization and the enormous scientific innovations of the system, he points out its tragic and ruinous side, as well. Al-'Ālim makes connections between

European modernity and current globalization. Globalization has been one of the main consequences of modernity.[15] But modernity has tragic origins. From the start, it was driven purely by the conquest of the world for profit. Al-'Ālim posits that globalization is presently driven by the greed and hunger of the few and, as it stands, serves the interests of only 10 percent of the world population at the expense of the majority of its people. He believes that the solution to the problems caused by globalization is to first maintain an open attitude to recent world developments while refusing to subscribe to American political and economic hegemony. He states that the Arab world must take a leading role within the contemporary capitalist civilization and support the values of progress, openness and engagement.[16]

Has globalization been advantageous to the political elite in maintaining their authority? Has globalization weakened the contemporary Arab state? Al-'Ālim believes that globalization has aided the Arab political elite in spreading their version of "false consciousness" by means of the mass media and given them the technological means to exercise full hegemony over society.[17]

Capitalism in the Arab world, although concentrated in few hands, is deeply entrenched. It is part of the global capitalist system. As such, it competes with other capitalist groups or formations in the pursuit of unlimited wealth and power, when possible. Domestically, Arab capitalism assumes a relentless pursuit of power in order to protect its economic interests while constantly pursuing greater wealth. Instead of working for the progress of its society, capitalism in the Arab world seeks only the preservation of its hegemony and the expansion of its control. This expansion takes the form of a meager investment in religious institutions in order to exploit the religious feelings of the masses for its materialist ends.

Syrian Marxist philosopher al-'Azm argues that although globalization coexisted with capitalism from its inception, it is only in the past decade that it has made a qualitative break with the old form.[18] A number of prominent thinkers have probed the nature of the global capitalist economy since the days of Marx, most notably Paul Sweezy, Samir Amin, and Andre Gunter Frank. In the old model of globalization, contends al-'Azm, capitalism accumulated wealth on a world scale by creating unequal conditions of exchange between the Center and the Periphery, while maintaining the means of industrial production at home.[19] What is novel about current capitalism has been its ability to globalize the means of production; that is, achieve industrial globalization, thereby reproducing the relations of production on a world scale. The globalization of industrialization under the auspices of Western capitalism has in fact, says al-'Azm, proved Lenin's theory of "imperialism being the highest stage of capitalism" obsolete.[20] Al-'Azm defines globalization as a deep transformation in the capitalist system which engulfs the entirety of humanity, and which is dominated by the Center and guided by the hegemony of a global system of unequal exchange.[21] This new global system is based on the notion of the commodification of everything. In other words, what al-'Azm suggests is that, far from being parochial, globalization's epicenter has gone global. Capitalism is able to reproduce itself on a magnificent international scale without losing its hold on the world economy. What this means is that current globalization has the tendency to destroy all non-capitalist formations in the Third World after invading local economies and producing huge numbers of consumers. Globalization means the complete worldwide victory of the capitalist mode of production. However, the Third World continues to suffer from increasing unemployment, emigration, and pollution.[22]

Al-'Azm thinks that Karl Kautsky's formulation of Super-imperialism or Ultra-imperialism is a good way to describe the recent triumph of global capitalism.[23] Super-imperialism results from the attempt of advanced industrial nations to appropriate resources from the Third World, either through investment or by creating industrial facilities that are owned by the Center. What this means is that in the age of globalization, the Capitalist Center has restructured its relationship to the Periphery in a way that again serves its own interests. In other words, the modernization or industrialization of the Periphery has been carried out for the sake of the Center.[24]

Al-'Azm revisits the issue of the nation-state under globalization. He argues that the state, especially in the Center has gained new strength under the impact of globalization. The state's budget is then allocated to both the army and international investment.[25]

Al-'Azm shares al-'Ālim's position that globalization is an inevitable process that cannot be stopped. Mere opposition to this important phenomenon accomplishes nothing. However, the Arab world must meet globalization with unified economic projects. That is, Arab countries must form a common Arab market in order to safeguard their economic interests.

Both al-'Ālim and al-'Azm propose that globalization has been a somewhat inevitable phenomenon. Galāl Amīn, son of the famous Egyptian modernist Muslim thinker Aḥmad Amīn and a famous economist, advocates cultural resistance to globalization because of what he considers its huge inherent danger to national cultures in the Third World. He thinks it impossible for the contemporary Arab state to resist globalization. While previous thinkers do not directly refer to the Arab state, they seem to share Amīn's indictment of the Arab political elite as collaborators of globalization. However, neither thinker offers an alternative. Amīn calls for cultural resistance. But who is to carry out this resistance in the age of globalization?

Amīn is unsettled by the explosive technological presence of globalization and its dehumanization of the contemporary human individual. He argues that the utilization of too much technology dehumanizes the individual, both in his/her own society and one culture by another. Modern technological society, socialist or capitalist, has stripped man of his inner freedom, innocence, and vitality. Modern technological society has the potential to achieve mass material gratification in an atmosphere of complete cultural and individual homogenization. As defined by Amīn, modern technological society (not just capitalism) is a negation of individual freedom and human culture.[26]

As a leading economist at the American University in Cairo, Amīn understands the Arab world's need for economic growth and high material standards for each Arab individual. However, in spite of the technological advances and the influx of wealth to certain parts of the Arab world, especially during the oil boom of the 1970s and 1980s, "poverty has been merely modernized."[27] Amīn believes that

Egypt under Nasser had embarked on an adventurous economic program which aimed at lessening the economic gaps between classes in society, and its successes were reversed by the Israeli victory over Egypt in 1967. Sadat's economic policy of Infitāḥ (Open Door policy) in the 1970s increased the pace of privatization and the amount of debt Egypt would shoulder. Amīn says that the term Infitāḥ means three things: "the opening of virtually all doors to the importation of foreign goods and capital, the removal of restrictions on Egyptian local investment, and the gradual withdrawal of the state from an active role in the economy."[28] This economic policy, pursued vigorously in Egypt after 1974, paved the way for globalization to establish a real presence in Egypt, even before the Soviet Union collapsed in 1991.[29] However, one must also look to Amīn's analysis of the post-1970 economic structure of Egypt, which began to change dramatically after Nasser's death. The old landed and capitalist bourgeoisie, whose power was greatly curtailed by the 1952 revolution, reappeared on the scene after Nasser's death with the expressed purpose of realizing its economic potential in the new era. This class welcomed globalization wholeheartedly, for it gave it the ability to be a strong player in international capitalism.

In his economic critique of globalization, Amīn invokes the Marxist axiom that the state (that is, political power) expresses the economic interests of the ruling elite. With the recent advances in technology, the function of the state has become more subtle, and is usually facilitated by the invocation of democratic and liberal ideas.

During the Cold War, the bipolarity of the world acted for the benefit of the Third World. However, the pace of privatization has accelerated since the disappearance of the Soviet Union, and many countries place the destiny of their nations in the hands of the multinationals and the IMF. Amīn uses the term "The Soft State" to refer to the contemporary Arab state, which does not take into account the welfare of society in the long run.[30] As an economist who has studied Egypt and several Arab countries,[31] Amīn analyzes the economic changes the non-Gulf Arab countries have undergone since the 1970s. He contends that the Arab state has reduced its role in managing the economy and allowed privatization to rule without accountability. The end result of this practice has been the selling of the fortunes of the Arab states to multinational companies that aim only to maximize their own profits. However, Amīn argues that Israel seems to be an exception to the rule in the Middle East. Although Israel is as much a "soft state" as many Arab countries, if not more so, it does not seem to have been adversely affected by globalization. The Israeli state regulates its private sector while at the same increasing its defense budget. Israel has its own version of local globalization, Middle Easternism, a theory that has been propagated by former Foreign Minister Shimon Peres.[32] Amīn takes up the issue of Israeli in the course of critiquing Thomas Friedman's *The Lexus and the Olive Tree*.[33] He argues that in addition to arguing on behalf of the American model of globalization, Friedman espouses the Israeli version of globalization in his debates with Arab and Egyptian intellectuals.[34]

Globalization is indeed an old phenomenon. So also is the dissemination of the ideas of the dominant culture. The Center's culture, facilitated by the revolution in technology, has spread its technological and rational standards to the Third World.

Jalāl Amīn refers to the question of Arab culture and globalization only in an accidental manner. Contemporary Moroccan philosopher Muḥammad 'Ābid al-Jābīrī takes the issue of culture and globalization quite seriously. He does not share either al-'Ālim's and al-'Azm's views that globalization is more or less an objective historical and economic phenomenon, but believes it is primarily an ideological phenomenon that aims at subordinating the whole world, including Europe, to the cultural demands of the United States. Jābīrī offers ten "cultural theses" in support of his central argument that globalization is a tool in the hands of the United States to express its cultural and ideological hegemony.

As opposed to al-'Ālim's view that the world is dominated by a cross-cultural and transnational capitalist civilization, Jābīrī focuses on the world's cultural diversity and the role of national culture in preventing and overcoming the negative impact of modernity. In elucidating the link between national culture and globalization, Jābīrī offers ten theses. In the first, he argues that far from being dominated by one universal culture (that is, civilization), the world is teeming with cultures that possess internal dynamism that ensure survival and profusion. The multiplicity of cultures is not likely to disappear in the future.[35] In other words, cultural diversity is much more interesting than monolithic and standardized global capitalism. In the second thesis, Jābīrī defines cultural identity as an amalgamation of three essential components: self, society, and nation. What makes national cultural identity unique is the level of interaction between these three. In a dynamic society or nation, there is heightening of individual, societal, and national consciousness. External pressures or challenges tend to increase the level of cultural identity. In the third thesis, Jābīrī argues that cultural identity takes an active and open role in the world's cultures only if its reference point is derived from three factors: country, nation, and state. Here, Jābīrī directly responds to the claims of many Arab rulers (such as in Morocco, Jordan, and Saudi Arabia) that the viability of the national culture is derived from the authority of the king or the person in power. Fourthly, Jābīrī defines globalization as a world system with two sets of components: financial and technological, on the one hand, and cultural, political, and ideological on the other. To Jābīrī's mind, globalization is not merely an extension of capitalist modernity, but a proliferation of the civilizational model or example of the United States. Current globalization has been dominated by American cultural and ideological interests. The export of American culture has had deleterious effects on the integrity of the social and ethical systems of the Third World. To Jābīrī, American culture is dominated by corrosive individualism and rampant materialism. Globalization is a universal ideology that reflects America's desire for universal hegemony.[36]

In his fifth thesis, Jābīrī draws a distinction between globalization (*'awlamah*) and universalism (*'ālamiyyah*). The former implies American containment of other world cultures, whereas the latter implies openness to and reciprocity between cultures. Globalization has embarked on a sophisticated process of penetrating other cultures for the purpose of domination. In its quest to dominate the world, American ideology is given much support by the media which preach as basic "American values," such as individualism and consumerism.[37] Many an Arab thinker has expressed the opinion that the internationally dominant

American mass media promotes Western ideas of consumerist capitalism in its quest to dominate both the material and intellectual tastes of the people in the Third World.[38] Frederic Jameson echoes Jābīrī's concerns in his critique of American globalization, "This is consumerism as such, the very linchpin of our economic system, and also the mode of life in which all our mass culture and entertainment industries train us ceaselessly day after day, in an image and media barrage quite unparalleled in history."[39] This sixth thesis gives rise to the next, which stipulates that accepting the moral and ideological values of American culture in the world would be a sure way to drive a wedge between world cultures and their sources of legitimacy: country, nation, and state. In Jābīrī's words, "globalization is a system that possesses no country, no nation, and no state."[40] Jābīrī goes on to argue that once nations or individuals internalize such values, a pernicious sort of globalization reigns supreme and all sorts of barriers (economic, political, and cultural) give way to relentless American globalization. Jābīrī's condemnation of American globalization has its roots in modern Arab culture and thought, which informs his next thesis. He points out that since the encounter between the capitalist West and the Arab world two centuries ago, modern Arab culture has suffered from internal polarization and tension. Polarization has defined the cultural identity of the individual, community, and nation. Globalization has recently exacerbated this polarization by making it possible for the local elite in the Arab world to enjoy the benefits of technology, thus fostering the isolation of both the masses and their traditional intellectual representatives.[41] The polarization between the few "globalized" elite and the rest of society begs the question of a total reconstruction of modern Arab culture from within, which is Jābīrī's thesis number nine. In the last thesis, however, Jābīrī claims that the best way to preserve Arab cultural identity (which is the product of the interaction between country, nation, and state) is by appropriating the scientific methods of globalization. In other words, Jābīrī advocates the appropriation of "modernization" without its cultural package, modernism or modernity. Is this possible? Perhaps, it is true that globalization is a universal capitalist culture and that the Arab political and business elite have worked hand-in-glove with this process. Jābīrī preaches tough choices: to preserve the integrity of contemporary Arab culture, one must fight not just American hegemony and cultural values, but also the Arab elite themselves since they have long been globalized. What Jābīrī is saying in effect is that the modern Arab state has failed to develop a solid program of Arab culture and that it uses the mass media to encourage certain cultural expressions that are not concordant with the personality of the Arab nation.

This consideration of "the Arab discussion" of globalization cannot be complete without presenting Islamist arguments on the matter. Arab Islamists, like most Arab thinkers, have come late to this discussion but find the issues urgent.[42] The work of two major Islamist thinkers, Yūsuf al-Qaraḍāwī, Muḥammad Quṭb (brother of Sayyid Quṭb) is important in this context. These thinkers represent the ideas of the old generation of the Muslim Brotherhood. They were close disciples of its founder, Shaykh Ḥassan al-Banna.

Both Qaraḍāwī and Quṭb agree with Jābīrī's main thesis that globalization today means American ideological, cultural, and economic hegemony.

Globalization, a concrete expression of American arrogance, is in fact an aggressive form of cultural invasion.[43] The Muslim world must protect its culture and ethical values from globalization's harmful effects. Qaraḍāwī outright equates globalization with Westernization and Westernization with Americanization. He contends that the United States' foreign policy in the Muslim world is guided by its desire to punish Muslim dissenting voices. He gives as an example such countries as Sudan, Libya, and Iran, which have suffered from the United Nations' embargo imposed under pressure from the United States and Britain. Qaraḍāwī posits that globalization is simply neo-colonialism.[44]

In spite of his harsh indictment of globalization, Qaraḍāwī concludes that it is an inevitable phenomenon, "In reality, we cannot escape from globalization; it seems to be our destiny at present. We are unable to reject it or escape from its clutches."[45] Qaraḍāwī calls upon the Arab and Muslim worlds, as well as the Third World, to unify in the face of globalization. He is vague about the methods of achieving such unity. However, like Jābīrī, he believes that in spite of the negatives of globalization, it also possesses some positives. He advocates the use of advanced media technology to spread the Islamic message. He argues that Muslims carry the right medicine, that is, Islam, to cure the world of its psychological and social problems, and it is time for Muslims to use the internet and other advanced technological methods to spread Islam.

From his part, Muḥammad Quṭb is less sanguine about the positive aspects of globalization. He believes Islam is an alien religion in the contemporary world. He quotes the famous Ḥadīth, "Islam began in exile (*gharīban*) and it will be exiled again as in the beginning. Happy are the expatriates of the community of Muḥammad, for they live in solitude, alone with their religion."[46] Quṭb thinks that true Islam has not been applied in society and is known only to those individuals who have believed in the eternal message of the Qur'an. Unlike Qaraḍāwī, Quṭb does not advocate engagement with globalization, since this phenomenon is based on both gross consumerism and massive exploitation.[47] Quṭb sees no positive side. He sees resistance as the only way out of the impasse with globalization.

On the basis of the preceding discussion of Arab voices on globalization, it is possible to come to the following representative conclusions: first, the Arab Marxist thinkers consider globalization to be a self-sustained process that began in the sixteenth century and developed to become a dominant world civilization. In that sense, this argument more or less agrees with Robertson's definition of globalization, which refers "both to the compression of the world and the intensification of consciousness of the world as a whole."[48] Capitalism has achieved a breakthrough in informational technology, which has made it possible for both individuals and nations to reach heightened consciousness. Second, unlike Marxist Arab thinkers, most Islamists and nationalists ponder the current political, economic, and religious manifestations of globalization without delving into its past economic history and the way it has impacted the world since its inception. Some use the term "*khuṣūṣiyyah*" or "authenticity" to refer to the cultural or religious distinctiveness of the Arab world and juxtapose authenticity with the domination of the capitalist civilization. In other words, some Muslim thinkers envisage the problem to be that between Muslim doctrine and Western capitalist civilization. As shown above, this is not exactly the case.[49] Nationalists and Islamists are worried about the export of American culture to the Arab world. Both argue for a certain measure of protectionism to guard against the harmful effects of exposure to American culture. To the Marxists, globalization is a natural product of modernity and an extension of its modernization project of the 1950s and 1960s. Islamists and Arab nationalists, on the other hand, are quick to point out to the Americanization of globalization, and warn about what they term "ghazw thaqāfī," or "cultural invasion." They equate globalization with Americanization or American hegemony in the world. Marxists are less sure about this association, since they consider capitalist civilization to be more universal than Americanization. They argue that the main question is not that of "cultural invasion," but of inseparable structural and economic bonds between the Muslim or Arab world and the West since the nineteenth century.[50] However, Marxists do believe that the main reference point of current globalization is the Western world. Third, more than anyone else, Arab nationalists seem to be more concerned about the function of the state under globalization.[51] As pointed out earlier, Galāl Amīn sees a shrinking of the role of the state under globalization, which is in the long run disadvantageous to the welfare of Arab society. Arab liberals do not share this perspective. To them, the state has increased its authority under globalization.[52] Fourth, Islamist thinkers draw a distinction between *'awlamah* (globalization) and *'ālamiyyah* (universality). They juxtapose the universality of Islam with the globalization of capitalism. They prefer the former and shun the latter. They make *'ālamiyyah* central to their analytical project, thus refusing to subscribe to any moral acceptance of the complexity of the world that has been created by the dominant capitalist civilization.[53] Is it possible to realistically juxtapose what is essentially an economic and scientific system (capitalism) to a religious system (Islam)? The end result of this type of juxtaposition is a collision between two different forms of narratives, the capitalist and the Islamist, or between values that are based on socio-economic relations and those that are based on the primacy of the divine in human life. Fifth, although few Arab thinkers have suggested thorough solutions to the enormous problems engendered by globalization, many would agree that a strong economic and political cooperation among the Arab states is needed. Ismā'īl Ṣabrī 'Abdallah offers such a solution with the view that Arab states should be conscious about a more equitable distribution of economic resources and the uplifting of the status of women and the poor in society.[54]

FROM MODERNITY TO GLOBALIZATION

If the twentieth century with its two savage world wars reflects the cruel character of modernity, the nineteenth century was perceived by many European thinkers as the apogee of modernity; its crowning event being the discovery, and not exploitation, of the whole world. Perhaps, the early Arab discussion of modernity in the nineteenth century was sanguine about the great possibilities of modernity. Arab thinkers then read modernity as science and progress, which they very much desired for their societies, soon colonized by mighty European powers.[55] In due course, this hope as a whole transformed itself into nationalist and Islamic liberation movements that fought very hard to emancipate the Arab world from the yoke of military and cultural colonialism. However, post-colonial Arab discourse has not completely freed itself from modernity. The Arab discussion of modernity is guided more by confusion than by anything else. This confusion is the product of grave social and political conditions as much as it is the result of the decline of good thinking in the Arab world. It is rare to come across good thinkers with a high sense of intellectual integrity who still live in the Arab world. Freedom of thought has been curtailed and the results are disappointing, to say the least.

It is a cliché to state that no modern culture has escaped the problematic of modernity. Arab literature on the phenomenon is immense and understandably so. However, I find it astonishing that many Arab and Muslim authors have taken modernity for granted without delving into its violent and cruel beginnings. Most Western philosophers and thinkers treat modernity as a particularly European event, phenomenon, and situation that has nothing to do with the non-European Other. As such, modernity represents the most promising aspects of European thought and practice, and is the model of development and progress to which the rest of the world must aspire. Modernity represents the triumph of European Reason over the barbarism of non-Europe. Obviously, this is a blatantly Eurocentric notion. Under this treatment, the indigenous people in Latin America, Africa, and Asia have disappeared, and if they do appear, they do so as a nuisance or menace, enemy of the civilized West. Why have so many Arab authors bought this argument?

One of the most sobering discussions of modernity is provided by Argentine philosopher Enrique Dussel, who argues that modernity's beginnings betray a violent, greedy side, and that the misery of the people of the Third World is proportional to the wealth of the ruling elite in both the West and Third World. He goes on to argue that in fact one must account for two modernities, the Eurocentric and the planetary. The first, according to Dussel, "is a Hispanic, humanist, Renaissance modernity, still linked to the old interregional system of Mediterranean, Muslim, and Christian…Second, there is the modernity of Anglo-Germanic Europe."[56] One can understand these two forms of modernity only within the historical context of Europe's ascendancy in the fifteenth century and the decline of the Muslim world, especially in North Africa. Europe discovered Amerindia (Latin America) because it was surrounded by the Muslim Other; its intention was to discover India by avoiding or bypassing the Muslim menace. Europe was blocked on the east by the Muslim world. Columbus was considered to be the first modern because of his discovery of Latin America. He died in 1506, assured that he had discovered the route to Asia. The second form of modernity, the Anglo-German, has become the norm. Very often,

> Progress and modernity replaced the Christian mission of Spain and Portugal, the civilizing mission of France and England, and became the new goal of the U.S. imperial version of previous colonialisms. However, old ideas and prejudices did not vanish: they survive in the present, recast in a new vocabulary.[57]

Before 1492, Europe was a Periphery and not a Center. The Muslim world and the Indian Ocean constituted the Center. The Mediterranean was not part of that

Center.[58] However, Europe began conceiving itself as a major world power and over the centuries, it was able to rise to the Center. The two most important countries in the early genesis of European modernity were Portugal and Spain. Portugal took the lead in the discovery of the world and the conquest of key port cities in the East. Portugal accumulated so much wealth from these colonies. Nowadays, they are considered part of the European Periphery.

It is clear that Europe came to birth in its confrontation with the European Other, especially in Amerindia. Europe defined itself as discoverer, as bearer of religion and civilization, as conquistador, and colonizer. According to Hegel, Europe is absolutely the end of universal history. Nineteenth century European philosophers mentioned Asia in their discourse, but often missed Africa and Latin America. Africa and Latin America stayed outside the domain of universal history.

The Germanic spirit is the spirit of the New World, whose end is the realization of absolute truth. The destiny of the Germanic people is that of serving as the bearers of that which is Christian. (Compare this to what Bush had to say in 1991 about Iraq.) He argues forcefully that,

> Modernity has shown its double face even to this day by upholding liberty… within Western nations, while at the same time encouraging enslavement outside them. European Common Market politics, closed in upon itself, expresses this double face in new guise. Modernity's other face shows up on the map tinted with negritude in the southern United States, the Caribbean, the Atlantic coast of Central America, the north and east of Colombia, the Pacific coast as far as Ecuador, the three Guyanas, and Brazil, home of sixty million Afro-Brazilians.[59]

Modernity, modernization, and globalization have had their positive as well as negative effects on the Arab world. Arab thinkers on the whole are committed to the progress of their societies. Most do agree that the Arab world has been in the grip of a crisis for a long time. Some propose the construction of a new civil society; others think that the economic path to development is the only way to go. However, many agree that the Arab political elite are behind the festering problems, and that the march of Western and rational globalization has only solidified the structures of authoritarianism in the Arab world. Some intellectuals have nothing new to say because they face a deadlock. They cannot criticize from within since their means of livelihood are so easily jeopardized. Other brilliant minds have been simply bought off by the ruling elite. The tension is high. "What is to be done?" is asked every day. A radical revolution needs to take place. Who is able to bring about this radical revolution, the intellectuals or the military? Once again, we are confronted with the same answer. It is the military who has the logistical power to change things. However, the relationship between the military and the intellectuals has been strange in the Arab world, to say the least. The military possesses the sword though intellectuals wield the pen. So far, the sword has proven mightier than the pen. Migrant Arab intellectuals, even if not giving up their independent ideas, cannot fight a successful battle from the outside. True, there is more freedom outside, in Europe, America, or Latin America. However, this freedom has not yet produced a coherent Arab discourse. Perhaps it is in the nature of things to wrestle with the multiplicity of voices in contemporary Arab intellectual life, especially overseas.

One of the main sources of modernity is rationalism. Rationalism means organization and discipline at the concrete institutional level. The process of the introduction of rational modernity to the Arab world has been very complex and very unsettling, as well. As I have argued earlier, modernization can be bought from abroad whereas modernity (which must be a home-bred consciousness) cannot be imported. Some of the most modernized Arab states, especially in the Gulf, have so far been unable to produce their own version of modernism. The dichotomy between modernization and modernism is severe at times in certain Arab countries. What makes it even worse is the fact that some Arab political elite consider modernism a threat to "Islamic values," or, to put it more accurately, to their entrenched political authority.

FINAL THOUGHTS

The Western mindset, which has shaped the socio-economic and intellectual destinies of the world since the Industrial Revolution, has as its center the notion of progress.[60] To some, the potential for progress was unlimited.[61] The Third World was there to occupy and colonize. According to one author, in the modern worldview, "a salvational sense of progress places economic expansion and technological innovation at the center of importance."[62] The phenomenon of progress has indeed posed a major challenge to traditional cultures, their socio-economic bases, and their ethical worldviews. Globalization continues to pursue the notion of progress, even the most damaging forms of progress, which lead to new forms of colonization. According to Hannah Arendt, the classical notion of progress led to a "process of never-ending accumulation of power necessary for the protection of a never-ending accumulation of capital [which] determined the progressive ideology of the late nineteenth century and foreshadowed the rise of imperialism."[63] Globalization is already leading to a new more subtle and destructive form of colonization than has been seen so far.

Furthermore, globalization, as seen in the latest manifestation of the modern mindset, has obfuscated what is really important in life. Traditional notions of prosperity, connectedness, community-building, and aiding the poor have been displaced by new aggressive notions of what life means vis-à-vis the "bottom line." Before the dawn of the twentieth century, the religious intelligentsia of the Muslim world considered European progress to be devoid of any ethical foundations. Some have argued, however, that the Western mindset has been intent on building on ethical foundations that did not subscribe to those of the monotheistic revelations for many centuries. Under the aegis of globalization, the ethic of the Western mindset encourages fast accumulation of wealth and power. Extravagant consumerism is the rule of the day. In the view of Richard Falk,

> At present, it is mainly the consequence of the globalization of Western cultural influence, including its commitment to modernization, that has

> produced a world order crisis of multiple dimensions: nuclearism, industrialism, materialism, consumerism.[64]

In view of the colossal consequences of globalization, a new popular consciousness has to evolve in order to understand and resist the negatives globalization brings. The Muslim world must work hard to revive the social, financial, and economic ethic of Islam, as a monotheistic phenomenon, in order to combat these dangerous inclinations. It is important to revive a sense of community that can withstand the attacks of individualism that are the rule of the day in advanced industrial societies and their satellite societies in the Third World. With increasing gaps between North and South and, within most countries in the South, between the countryside and the city, and the increasing number of the marginalized and impoverished in the cities, there is no escape from reviving the Islamic communal ethic that "commands the good and prohibits the evil."[65]

It is important to keep in mind that for traditional philosophies and worldviews to remain vital in a highly competitive and individualistic world, solutions must be offered on the basis of the traditional worldview that takes into account the social and psychological ravages created by globalization in the Muslim world.[66] In other words, how can we formulate Islamic answers to the economic and cultural problems and dislocations created by globalization and its allies in the Muslim world? We must not forget the example of Indonesia, a country that launched a seemingly adventurous program of modernization in the late 1960s and whose economy collapsed all of a sudden in early 1998! What went wrong? It is disturbing and startling to realize that the personal wealth of the family of ex-president Suharto, almost equals the amount of the approved loan of the International Monetary Fund to Indonesia. Therefore, the question is: why is it that the political and military elite in the Muslim world financially prosper to such unbelievable degrees under the aegis of globalization?

Part Two

Thinkers

9
Rāshid al-Ghannūshī and the Questions of Sharī'ah and Civil Society

"Secularism came to us on the back of a tank, and it has remained under its protection ever since." Rāshid al-Ghannūshī, *Muqarābāt fī'l 'ilmāniyyah wa'l mujtama' al-madanī* (London: al-Markaz al-Maghāribī li'l Buḥūth wa'l Tarjamah, 1999), 175.

Recently, Western scholarship on the subject of Islamism has been prolific. Some have studied this phenomenon with a specific goal in mind: to redefine Western interests in the Arab world, especially in the wake of the collapse of Soviet communism and the need to find a new international enemy. This trend is on the rise since the tragic attacks on the United States on September 11, 2001.[1] Others have focused on the political dimensions of Islamism at the expense of its theological, philosophical, historical, and legal contexts.[2] Some Arab scholars have even followed suit in defining Islamism in mere political terms.[3] It is possible to argue that Islamism is the natural expression of a dominant trend of thought, and one must take its claim that it has remained true to the basic theological principles and historical vision of Islam seriously.

Islamism adheres to the following Islamic theological premises: the oneness of God, the unity of humanity, the oneness of prophecies, and the universality of the Islamic message. First, Islamists believe the Qur'an, the fountainhead of Islamic metaphysics, expresses the Islamic doctrine of man with superb clarity, which is the expression of universal human characteristics.[4] Second, Islamic history is an indivisible part of human history, and is subject to its laws and fluctuations. The Islamic human endeavor must be distinguished from Divine Revelation, but from a normative point of view, Revelation and human history go hand-in-hand. Third, Muslims have been entrusted with a universal message. Their task in the world of today is, perhaps, more arduous and demanding than that of Muslims in the first century of Islam. Contemporary Muslims face new hurdles such as alienation, economic disparities, social injustice, and new forms of colonial domination and hegemony. Fourth, Islam repeatedly affirms the organic connection between Muslims and life. As an historical religion, Islam has never isolated itself from the socio-economic, political, and military processes of life. In the final analysis, these four premises underlie modern Islamic discourse.

In treating contemporary Islamism, one must carefully examine the relationship between Islam and society in the contemporary Arab world.[5] For the most part, Islamism has been an oppositional religious and political movement in the Arab world since independence. Obviously, Islam or Islamism cannot be reduced to politics, ideology or social movements alone. These may, of course, be facets or manifestations of Islam in the modern world but do not represent its totality. In the same vein, Islamic movements, as socio-political and religious movements, are only one facet of Islam, and their theological discourse or/and ideological contention is one among many others. Furthermore, in most Arab countries since 1967, the Arab political elite have usurped official expressions of Islam and made it impossible for other voices to be heard.

The major thinkers of the Muslim Brotherhood movement in the modern Arab world, such as Ḥasan al-Banna,[6] ʻAbd al-Qādir ʻAwdah,[7] Sayyid Quṭb,[8] Muḥammad al-Ghazālī, ʻAlī Gurayshah, Yūsuf al-Qaraḍāwī, Saʻīd Hawwa,[9] Ḥassan al-Turābī,[10] and Rāshid al-Ghannūshī, have discussed a wide range of issues in light of the original theological and Qur'anic formulations of Islam in the context of Western colonialism and the political divisions (the rise of the nation-state) that arose in the post-colonial era. Such issues as Islamic theory of knowledge, the theory of man in the Qur'an, *Jāhiliyyah* (pre-Islamic conditions) and Islam, social justice in Islam, the intelligentsia (religious and secular) and power, the West, capitalism and socialism, the formative phase of Islam and early Islamic philosophy and thought, and the possibility of an overall reconstruction of Islam in the modern world have formed the intellectual core of Islamic social movements. These questions, no doubt, are very complex, and there is no indication that the intellectual leaders of the Islamic movements have discussed them in a monolithic, ahistorical, or superficial past-oriented fashion. Therefore, in studying the religious and societal dimensions of the modern Arab world, or of any post-colonialist situation of the Third World, one must take into consideration the complexity of the relationship between state and religion and the social or political roles that Muslim institutions and ideas play in the contemporary Arab world. Seen in this light, a critical sociology of religion, that is, Islam, must be formulated using the most advanced philosophical methods and social science concepts.

One may delineate two general positions that underlie the debate about the Sharīʻah in contemporary Arab discourse: the first, represented by a variety of Muslim thinkers, Sharīʻah professors, and Islamic activists, argues that the application of the Sharīʻah at all levels of society is the way to guarantee civil liberty for all citizens, Muslims and non-Muslims alike. On the other hand, a number of thinkers, mainly scholars and other academics, argue that the Sharīʻah's application is nothing less than the legalization of irrationalism in Arab society, and that implementing the Sharīʻah in any form would lead to egregious human rights violations, especially those of women and minorities. It is conspicuously clear that the Arab political system, on the whole, has suppressed Islamism as a political force, which has made it difficult if not impossible to ascertain verity of Islamism's claim that implementing the Sharīʻah is the only solution to the predicament of contemporary Arab societies. However, it is clear that the Sharīʻah does not offer ready-made solutions; on the contrary, one has to rethink its salient premises in view of the dramatic changes affecting Arab societies since the birth of the modern nation-state.

CONTEMPORARY ISLAMISM AND THE CONCEPT OF *MAṢLAḤAH*

As has been pointed out earlier, Islamic resurgence in modern history is a complex socio-religious, ideological, and historical phenomenon that has gone through various transformations since the eighteenth century. In the beginning, before the intrusion of the West in the Muslim world, Islamic resurgence in the form of the Wahabiyyah, Sanūsiyyah, and Mahdiyyah stressed the purification of religious doctrine against all sorts of superstitions and innovations in doctrinal principles.[11] The reformers of this period understood the application of Sharīʻah as simply the repair and purification of religious belief. In the second phase, resurgence in the form of Islamic reform in the nineteenth century was a reaction to the severe decline experienced by Muslim societies under the direct threat of imperialism. Ṭahṭāwī, ʻAbduh, Afghānī, and Kawākibī understood the severity of the situation and searched for some sort of rapprochement between the advanced West and the less advanced Muslim world. ʻAbduh sought a new legal formulation and new form of *ijmāʻ*, or consensus. He argues:

> Why do we stop, in legal matters, with the Ḥanafī writings although there is an urgent need to renew in all matters related to this life? We must change those aspects of Muslim civil life that are incompatible with the modern life on the basis of a new *ijtihād* and a new *ijmāʻ*.[12]

ʻAbduh couched his reformist ideas in the legal language of the great Andulasian jurist of the eighth Muslim century, Imām Abū Isḥāq Ibrāhīm al-Shāṭibī, author of *Muwāfaqāt fī Uṣūl al-Sharīʻah*, one of the greatest legal works in Islamic jurisprudence. Shātibī speaks of the intentions of the Sharīʻah (*maqāṣid al-Sharīʻah*) as being commensurate with the general welfare of the people, in this life and in the hereafter. He drew the attention of many of his students to this important work. In the third instance, the Islamic legal response was formulated against the background of the spread of Westernization in the Muslim world and the abolition of the Ottoman caliphate, the symbol of the Muslim ummah's political unity.

This legal response took two forms: one under the auspices of the Ikhwān and Ḥasan al-Banna. Its goal was to apply the Islamic Sharīʻah by establishing an Islamic political regime. The second was represented by ʻAbd al-Razzāq al-Sanhūrī. Although al-Sanhūrī advocated the implementation of Sharīʻah, he also preached the necessity of understanding Sharīʻah in the context of comparative international law.[13] The third response took place in the context of the nation-state. One of the best representatives of the Egyptian case is Shaykh Maḥmūd Shaltūt and Muḥammad Abū Zahra, who espoused the reform of Sharīʻah rules in order to meet the demands of the modern age.[14] In the final instance, there are current legal formulations that are informed by the diverse Islamic legal tradition and by Shāṭibī's *Muwāfaqāt*. Some of the best advocates in the Arab world today are ʻAbd al-Karīm Zaydān, al-Būṭī, Fahmī Huwaydī, Ṭāhā Jābir al-ʻAlwānī,[15] Salīm al-ʻAwwa, Ḥassan al-Turābī, Aḥmad Kamāl Abū'l Majd, Rāshid al-Ghannūshī, though there are many others. On the other side of the debate, four major thinkers, all of whom were Egyptian, tried to prove that the implementation of Sharī'ah is impossible in the contemporary Arab world due to theological as well as modern reasons. These four are: Muḥammad Sa'īd al-Ashmāwī, Naṣr Ḥāmid Abū Zayd, Fu'ād Zakariyya, and Rashād Salām.[16]

The debate over the Sharī'ah, besides reflecting two irreconcilable positions on the nature of civil society in the Arab world, also reflects deep disagreement in modern Arab intellectual history over the meaning of Islamic revelation, the nature of society as erected by the Prophet and the early companions in Medina and Mecca, the role of jurists throughout Islamic history, the meaning of Islamic history in general, and the main components of the Islamic and Arabic personality. The proponents of the Sharī'ah in the contemporary Arab world draw on a plethora of material in classical Islamic legal and theological thought.[17] However, the content of their main arguments is conditioned by two main sources: the first, somewhat practical, is the failure of the current political elite in the Arab world to modernize society. The second is theoretical and focuses on how to safeguard the rules of the Sharī'ah under the above-stated conditions. For the purpose of safeguarding the rules of the Sharī'ah, many begin by defining its main objectives (*maqāṣid al-Sharī'ah*) and how they might be interpreted at the present time.

Proponents of Sharī'ah in the Arab world are united on a vastly ambitious program, an ideal if not a backward program, in the view of their opponents. Proponents often begin with the theoretical premise of the Sharī'ah's main objective, which is to preserve the interests of the people (*maṣāliḥ al-'ibād*). Many agree with Imām Ghazālī's definition of *maṣlaḥah*: "What we mean by *maṣlaḥa* is the preservation of the *maqṣūd* (objective) of the law (*shar'*) which consists of five things: preservation of religion, of life, of reason, of descendants, and of property. What assures the preservation of these five principles (*usūl*) is *maṣlaḥa*, and whatever fails to preserve them is *mafsada* and its removal is *maṣlaḥa*."[18] Most contemporary Islamist thinkers argue, however, that the Sharī'ah's objectives can only be guaranteed within an Islamic political system. In other words, a state is needed in order to enforce the law. In the opinion of Mahmūd Shaltūt, the term 'Sharī'ah' means all those "systems legislated by God, or whose sources are legislated by God, for the purpose of organizing man's relationship with God, with the Muslim community, with the human community, and life in general."[19] I will argue in this chapter that the call to implement the Sharī'ah in many Arab countries is as elusive as ever, especially with the banishment of intellectual leaders of the Islamic movements, one conspicuous case of which is the career of the Tunisian Islamist Rāshid al-Ghannūshī. Almost all Arab ruling elite are united on the notion of preserving the *status quo* against any alternative, Islamist or otherwise.

THE CONTRIBUTIONS OF RĀSHID AL-GHANNŪSHĪ

Rāshid al-Ghannūshī represents the first generation of active Tunisian Islamists who opposed the post-colonial secular state.[20] It is difficult to assess the impact of Ghannūshī's ideas on the intellectual scene within the Arab world, mainly because he has been in exile in England since 1989, and unable to travel to most, if not all

Arab countries.[21] The founder of the Nahḍah Party in Tunisia in the early 1980s, he sought to play the democratic game in a country that pays only lip service to democracy. The result has been his imprisonment and exile, which, to a large extent, define the career of many Islamist intellectuals in the modern Arab world.[22] In a moving introduction to his masterpiece, *al-Ḥuriyyāt al-'āmmah fī'l dawlah al-islāmiyyah* (*Public Liberties in the Islamic State*),[23] Ghannūshī speaks about his three years of *miḥnah* (plight) in a Tunisian prison as well as the *mihnah* of many years of exile. Imprisonment was, to a certain extent, helpful in reflective praxis; it gave Ghannūshī the time and leisure to ponder, in the manner of veritable Sufi shaykhs, the secrets of this world, the nature of power relations in the contemporary Arab world, the destiny of the Muslim world, the meaning of freedom and democracy in the New World Order, and the plight of the Third World in the neo-colonialist age. Ghannūshī's reflection on these matters also represents the thought of many Arab and Muslim intellectuals, living at home or in exile.

Ghannūshī, like many contemporary advocates of the Sharī'ah in the Arab and Muslim world, offers a consistent theoretical Islamic treatment of the prevailing intellectual and religious conditions in the contemporary Arab world, most notably in Tunisia. Within the confines of Islamic religious text, he criticizes what he considers un-Islamic behavior.[24] Ghannūshī's Islamist endeavor is the latest manifestation of the modern renaissance project begun in the eighteenth century, before Western intrusion into the Muslim world. The main question is, why has this project failed to materialize yet in most Arab countries and what can a minor group of Islamist thinkers in exile do to resurrect this project? In my opinion, it is impossible for Islamism to resurrect the Islamist project under the prevailing world political conditions.

Ghannūshī, thought, shies away from advocating violence to achieve the central objectives of his movement. To the contrary, he affirms without hesitation that the first priority of the Islamic movement should not be to reach power, "The Islamic movement must not have the government as its first priority. Takeover of the government should not be the biggest achievement possible. A bigger achievement would be if the people would love Islam and its leaders."[25] This is a radical departure from the main objectives of classical Islamism in the first half of the twentieth century. Islamism then believed that in order to implement "the correct rules of the Sharī'ah," an Islamist political system must be established. Ghannūshī realizes that this classical proposition of Islamism is untenable in contemporary Tunisia, and perhaps in the rest of the Muslim world. Instead, he posits that the Islamic movement should actively enhance the foundations of civil society and promote democracy. In this regard, Ghannūshī rejects violence as a means of solving intractable problems between the Islamic movement and the ruling secular political elite. Violence has proved, however, to enhance the regime's standing and give it more power with which to repress the Islamic movement.[26]

Although critical of the current Arab political elite, Ghannūshī's essential problem is with the worldwide metamorphosis of classical colonialism to neo-colonialism and globalization. He contends that colonialism has changed its tactics since inception; however, it has not altered its aim of manipulating and exploiting the vulnerable Third World. Within the Muslim world, a major conflict exists over the identity of society between two conglomerate forces: the "Islamic school" on the one hand, and the school of "Westernization and dictatorship" and its secular allies in the contemporary Arab world on the other.[27] Westernization is highly entrenched in the Muslim world, and far from representing an enlightened and cultivated school of thought, represents both "violence and hypocrisy."[28]

MODERNITY AND SECULARISM IN GHANNŪSHĪ'S THOUGHT

In his youth, Ghannūshī was very much influenced by Arab nationalism as espoused by Nasserism.[29] However, he found the nationalist project wanting on a number of grounds, especially at the level of "Arab and Muslim identity."[30] Ghannūshī valued the nationalist project for its attempt to achieve political independence from colonialism; however, he faults nationalism for only going half way. Nationalism failed to construct a true project of intellectual and cultural emancipation since it remained, at heart, indebted to the mental and scientific contributions of Western modernity. Nationalism gained politically but lost intellectually.

Nationalist intellectuals in the Arab world, most specifically in Tunisia, remain captive to the contributions of Western modernity without attempting in a real sense to make their contribution to this modernity. The fascination with the culture of the dominant West is the rule rather than the exception. What Ghannūshī powerfully uncovers is the crisis of the bilingual intelligentsia in the post-colonial state in the Third World. This is not specifically an Arab or Muslim problem. Further, this problem goes beyond the dictatorship of the ruling elite in the Arab world. What kind of worldview should the Arab world adopt after colonialism? Ghannūshī's simple answer is Islam, or Islam interpreted in light of the dramatic changes affecting Muslim societies after the end of colonialism. However, are Arab intelligentsia willing to pay a price as has Ghannūshī?

Ghannūshī advocates a new understanding of Islam capable of coexisting with the challenges of the contemporary world. Neither nationalism nor political oppression is the answer, in his view. He posits that a radical examination of early Islamic philosophy is urgent. He argues, "we defeated and backward Muslims who live in countries permeated by all sorts of cultural trends and while our societies undergo the most dangerous contradictions and crises, what benefit can we derive from studying the Mu'tazilite position on the attributes of God, whether they are self-sufficient or an extension of the self, or studying Ibn Rushd's position on the universe, whether it is uncreated or created, or studying Ibn Sina's opinion about the self and its permanence?"[31] Modern Arab and Muslim intelligentsia must put aside these arguments so as to focus on a rationalist Islamic system that can deal with the issues of the modern world, one of which is modernity.

Ghannūshī draws a distinction between two types of modernity: first is what he sees as the genuine modernity of the West, and the other is the fake, aborted modernity of the Westernized elite in the Arab world.[32] To his mind, Western modernity is the product of specific historical and philosophical factors brewing under the surface for many centuries and which resulted in a great scientific and rational movement leading to progress, science, liberalism, unfettered criticism, democracy, and rebellion against political and religious dictatorship.[33] Ghannūshī sees Western modernity as a natural expression of the political, intellectual, and economic evolution of the Western world after the industrial revolution. He is less critical of the genesis of Western modernity than one might expect. He approaches modernity as an idea, which is why he calls on Muslim intelligentsia to accept the positive and liberating aspects of Western modernity. He states, "We want modernity, contrary to the ridiculous allegations made by those opposed to political Islam, but inasmuch as it means absolute intellectual freedom, scientific and technological progress; and promotion of democratic ideals."[34] On the other hand, only a handful of people educated in the schools of the West welcomed the introduction of modernity into Arab and Muslim societies and tied the destiny of modernity to the political and social interests of their class. Modernity thus ceases to be a movement of rationalism and becomes a tool of class and an elite privilege. In other words, modernity is confiscated and its intellectual and cultural foundations obscured. However, it is not clear to which class Ghannūshī refers. Was the nationalist movement under colonialism a beneficiary of Western modernity?

There was a tiny class of indigenous Westernized intellectuals who benefited from the achievements of modernity and who sent their children to the schools of the West. This trend, far from subsiding after independence, became the landmark of the new nation-state. The ruling elite in the Arab world, receiving their basic education and inspiration from the West, were intent on obscuring the rational foundations of that modernity, which also built a somewhat progressive civil society in the West, according to Ghannūshī. The fake modernizing elite in the Arab world has been busy dislodging the masses from their well-entrenched historical and cultural identities, driving a wedge between the masses and their true religious leadership, and making them subservient to foreign powers. Here, Ghannūshī assumes that on the eve of the nation-state there was a well-entrenched and unified religious leadership in the Arab world, which is far from true. The Arab masses grew tired of fake modernity only after it failed to improve their lot. More often than not, official religious intelligentsia were supportive of the introduction of modernity into Arab societies.

Ghannūshī correctly argues that "an authentic modernist perspective" cannot be merely transferred from one culture to another. It must be indigenous, homegrown, so to speak. That is, it must infuse all aspects and levels of society with real democratic spirit. Second, the political elite have exploited modernity in order to maintain their interests. Ghannūshī gives Tunisia as an example of what he calls "deformed modernity." He says that the power elite in Tunisia today, a minority regime, is made up of three complementary power blocs in society that stand against the formation of a new civil society: the police force, the corrupt business elite, and a good number of bankrupt Leftists. These forces are united on a plan to prevent Islamic forces from gaining ground in society for fear of losing their carefully guarded privileges, through either peaceful or violent means.[35] This fake modernizing bloc in Tunisian society has utilized oppression and the banner of democracy and the emancipation of women to remain in power. Ghannūshī argues,

> Language causes us to fall in drastic errors when we state that there is a conflict in the Muslim world between modernity and fundamentalism, between

> democracy and fundamentalism, or between secularism and Islamism. We must be wary of such confusion. For example, the meaning of both Western secularism and modernity has no precedent in the Muslim world. Modernity, secularism, and democracy in the West have freed the intellect and people by granting them authority, and have separated the institution of the state from the personality of the ruler by making him a true servant of the people. However, the alleged modernity and secularism of Bourgiba, Atatürk, the Shah of Iran, and the rest of the world dictators, and their few disciples, have not followed in the footsteps of the Western conception.[36]

I find it surprising that Ghannūshī is uncritical when it comes to the genesis and evolution of Western modernity. In his view, modernity in the West has created a dynamic society built on institutional and legal principles. Seen from this angle, Islamism need not be in conflict with modernity. The Islamist movement would like to implement this productive side of modernity in the Arab world. Practically speaking, however, in the Arab world, modernity has meant total alienation and the loss of cultural and religious values.[37]

In his sustained critique of the Arab political elite, especially in North Africa, Ghannūshī argues that this group prefers violence, both physical and psychological, to solve their problems and blame Islamist forces for the failure of the economy and modernization, "Claiming to undertake a modernizing mission, the state in the Arab Maghreb justifies the pursuit of an authoritarian policy and the exercise of oppression in order to fulfill its mission. Society is, therefore, not the source of authority but its field of action."[38] Modernization and Westernization projects have been crushingly defeated in most Arab countries, especially in North Africa. What has happened is that the military or security forces of the ruling political elite intrudes on the public space of civil society, "In most Arab countries, the project of modernity, or that of Westernization, has rested captive in the efficient hands of the security forces, those who are quick to use physical violence."[39]

Although praising the intellectual and scientific achievements of Western modernity, Ghannūshī is critical of the New World Order and the hegemonic policies of the West, which collude with those of Zionism in the Middle East. Ghannūshī doubts the integrity of the Western political system when it comes to bringing democracy to the Arab world, "Just like the *mission civilisatrice* was the motto representing the hegemony of the West in the past, today democracy represents the ideology of the hegemonic Western world."[40] However, in spite of the failure of the Western world to impose "democracy" on its allies and protégés in the Arab world, democracy remains the preferred option of Islamic movement at the present time. Ghannūshī contends that for the Islamic movement,

> the second best alternative…would be a secular democratic regime which fulfills the category of the rule of reason…What matters in such a system is that despotism is averted. A democratic secular system of government is less evil than a despotic system of government that claims to be Islamic.[41]

MAQĀSID AL-SHARĪ'AH (THE OBJECTIVES OF SHARĪ'AH)

As seen earlier, Islamism emerged as a response to failed modernity, especially after 1967. Contemporary Islamism, being a religious and social phenomenon, has been inspired by classical Islamic legal thought to develop a critique of current conditions. Ghannūshī's point of contention is to bring the objectives of the Sharī'ah to focus in a sea of political trouble and uncertainty. Like many Salafī and reformist thinkers in the modern Arab world, he relies heavily on classical Islamic Fiqh works dealing with the concept of *maṣlaḥah*, and especially on Imām Abū Ishāq Ibrāhīm al-Shāṭibī's *magnum opus*, *al-Muwāfaqāt fī Uṣūl al-Sharī'ah*, referred to earlier.

Shāṭibī begins with the premise that God instituted laws for the purpose of ensuring the common good of the people (*masālih al-'ibād*), in this life as well as in the hereafter. Shāṭibī divides the main objectives (*maqāṣid*) of the Sharī'ah into three broad categories: (1) *maqāṣid ḍarūriyyah* (necessary objectives); (2) *maqāṣid ḥājiyyah* (needed objectives), and (3) *maqāṣid taḥsīniyyah* (commendable objectives).[42] The first category includes five objectives, which revolve around the preservation (*ḥifdh*) of religion, self, procreation, property, and intellect.[43] These objectives are necessary in the sense that without them, the common interests of the people in this life and in the hereafter cannot be maintained. For example, *'ibādāt* (acts of worship) are needed in order to ensure the preservation of religion in man's life. The second category of *ḥājiyyāt* is based on the notion of making the necessary objectives of the Sharī'ah easily accessible by removing any form of hardship or strict literal interpretations of the main rules of the Sharī'ah. Concession in prayer while traveling is one form of removing this sort of hardship. The third category of *taḥsīniyyāt* (commendable objectives) concerns the adoption of moral behavior and the best social customs related to cleanliness, etiquette, and praiseworthy behavior.[44] To Shāṭibī's mind, the purpose of divine legislation is to establish the common interests of the people in this life and the hereafter. Thus, the five necessary objectives of the Sharī'ah, common to all humanity, are absolute and constitute the basis of the well-being of any ummah, political or religious.

Against the context of the above categories, as elaborated by Shāṭibī, Ghannūshī discusses what he terms "the general framework for human rights in Islam," which are based on the following principles: (1) freedom of doctrine; (2) respect for the human self; (3) freedom of expression and movement; (4) economic sufficiency, and (5) social well-being.[45]

To give some balance to our discussion, it is important to highlight the main theses of opponents of Sharī'ah implementation in contemporary Arab society. As has been mentioned above, herein lies a basic, irreconcilable conflict between two opposing worldviews. The opponents of Sharī'ah implementation advance the following premises that support, in their mind, the incompatibility of the Sharī'ah with the prevailing conditions: first, contemporary religious discourse in the Arab world, whether radical or moderate, oppositional or official, elite or popular, stresses some basic features: the supremacy of the text (*naṣṣ*) and God's deputy-ship (*hākimiyyah*).[46] The call to implement Sharī'ah is but an ideological cover to attack rationalism, secularism, nationalism, and modernity in the name of religion. The dominant religious discourse in the Arab world uses *takfīr* (declaring someone or something to be an infidel) as the most effective weapon to attack and discredit opponents of Sharī'ah. Such people as Sayyid Quṭb and Omar 'Abd al-Raḥmān and other Muslim radicals have used this discourse as the Azhar, as an official institution, has used *takfīr* to discredit the enemies of the Sharī'ah application. In an age dominated by ignorance and the absence of rationalism, religious discourse strips Islam of its historicity and diversity: it reduces it to ahistorical essentials.[47]

Second, law is the product of social factors and not revelation. Law, far from being accidental, is the product of a confluence of social, economic, political, and religious factors.[48] Early Islamic law went through three phases of evolution: the Meccan, Medinan, and post-Medinan, that is, empire-bound, law. In the first place, Fiqh was still tribal-bound, and in the second, it was directed by the demands of the nascent state of Medina. However, in the third phase, Islamic law, that was still characterized by the simplicity of Arabia, stood up to the legal and intellectual challenges of the Persian and Byzantine civilizations and amalgamated some of the central principles of these civilizations into its worldview.

Fiqh, as a human Islamic legal science, developed into law and matured to reflect the needs of the expanding Islamic empire. This empire-bound law was more distinguished by reasoning than it was by the use of original sources, that is, the Qur'an and the Sunnah. In other words, Fiqh superseded the text. The primacy of original sources receded whereas reliance on reasoning expanded. In its process of building a multiglot and multiethnic empire, the new Muslim state built by the Ummayyads and Abbasids could not rely on a text (that is, the Qur'an) that was not constitutional, to begin with. The new sciences of the conquered civilizations formed the basis of the constitution of the new empire.[49]

Third, *ijmā'* as a legal mechanism to ensure the consensus of the ummah over the election of a certain person to preside over the state, ensured the continuous hegemony of the ruling political elite throughout Islamic history with strong religious and legal justification. The dominant Islamic discourse throughout Islamic history has been the product of an alliance between "the *fuqahā'* class and the political elite."[50] According to Ḥassan Ḥanafī, the Muslim state, to a large extent, relied on the authority of the *fuqahā'* "to justify and defend its own authority against the attacks of the opposition, and the *fuqahā'* became an important component of authority in our tradition."[51] Muslim rulers throughout Islamic history have used religion to ward off rebellion and dissent.

Fourth, the strong alliance between the *fuqahā'* and the political elite in classical Muslim society created a certain form of religious identity that was protected by the *fuqahā'* and justified by religious text. Human rights were tied up in this religious identity. In other words, not all people shared the same level of citizenship. Non-Muslims were considered inferior to Muslims.[52] The Muslim notion of the welfare of people applies in principle to Muslim citizens, who are in the majority and not to the non-Muslims.[53]

HUMAN RIGHTS IN GHANNŪSHĪ'S THOUGHT

It is beyond the scope of this chapter to analyze the immense literature on Islam and human rights. Others have attempted this analysis elsewhere.[54] In her controversial although useful book, *Islam and Human Rights: Tradition and Politics*, Ann Elizabeth Mayer argues that in its classical form, the Sharī'ah contains principles that are greatly at odds with the Universal Declaration of Human Rights, especially with respect to the following questions: religious freedom (that is, the freedom to convert from Islam); the rights of women,[55] and the status of minority groups within the Muslim world. Mayer argues that in spite of the fact that those involved in the development of international human rights law have treated "Islamic law and Islamic thought" as irrelevant, it remains an undisputed fact that the Sharī'ah falls short of the promulgated international standards. Furthermore, and on the practical plane, there have been gross violations of human rights in a number of Muslim countries, including the Sudan, Pakistan, and Algeria.[56] An-Na'im reinforces this idea by arguing that a substantial revision of those Sharī'ah principles that discriminate against women and minorities must take place. An-Na'im's view, Muslims, if they desire to "exercise their legitimate collective right to self-determination…[they must] not violate the legitimate right of self-determination of individuals and groups both within and outside the Muslim communities."[57] Theoretically, the above positions, although emanating from different theological and ideological premises, incorporate and promote the idea of human equality, in the secular humanistic sense, as the main yardstick against which the issue of Islam and human rights must be judged. In their different ways, each position intends to rid the Sharī'ah of its supposed parochialism and its allegedly faulty theological presuppositions, and open it to the vast field of critical inquiry. Equality of all human beings, regardless of race, religion, language, and origin is the main premise.

Philosophically, Ghannūshī lends his wholehearted support to the notion of equality, which to his mind is one of the absolute principles of the Sharī'ah.[58] However, his premises are somewhat different from those espoused by the two authors above. We must remember that Ghannūshī is first and foremost an *'ālim*/ideologue, who represents an oppositional religious movement and who has suffered punishment and exile because of his ideological and religious commitments. Ghannūshī does not speak purely as a scholar but also as an activist whose main purpose is to change a government that has violated his and others' human rights with the support of Western powers, tacitly or explicitly.

Furthermore, and in spite of his bitterness toward the West for supporting the current government in Tunisia, Ghannūshī sticks to the concept of an unfettered freedom as the main criterion of both individual and human progress. He does not buy into the arguments of many Western legal scholars, such as Ann Elizabeth Mayer, that "individualism is a fundamental ingredient in the development of Western human rights concepts."[59] He believes that what dictates both the domestic and foreign policies of the West, especially in relation to the Third World, is the national interest of the West. This was amply illustrated in the second Gulf War in which the West intervened on behalf of Kuwait against Iraq. In fact, the Western world has thrived on its exploitation of the Third World.[60]

In his treatment of the concept of equality, Ghannūshī marshals a great deal of Qur'anic evidence to prove that the Sharī'ah protects freedom of doctrine and that in Islam, this freedom is the mother of all public freedoms. The Qur'anic principle "No coercion in religion" means that all citizens in the Islamic state constitute one political ummah, although they may belong to a plurality of religious affiliations. Ghannūshī maintains that the Medina constitution was an embodiment of one political ummah with religious pluralism. In other words, religious pluralism does not negate common political and social responsibility in an Islamic framework. Furthermore, religious pluralism means, besides religious freedom, the expression of one's religious identity as long as it does not impose on the public feelings of Muslims.[61] The Islamic doctrine of freedom and the respect for the human individual regardless of his/her race, religion, and social background constitutes the basis of the Islamic worldview developed by the Prophet. In the final analysis, what Ghannūshī is saying is that the Sharī'ah, because it is divinely inspired and its focus is on the common good of the people, any people, cannot be discriminatory in nature. Ghannūshī believes the Qur'an to be a theological text with the highest degree of integrity and comprehensiveness. That is to say that the Qur'an, as the source of Sharī'ah, cannot contain two levels of meaning, as Abdullahi An-Na'im and his teacher Ustadh Mahmoud Ṭāhā claim. According to An-Na'im, Ustadh Mahmoud Ṭaha argues that

> a close examination of the...Qur'an and *Sunnah* reveals two levels or stages of the message of Islam, one of the earlier Mecca period and the other of the subsequent Medina stage...[T]he earlier message of Mecca is in fact the eternal and fundamental message of Islam, emphasizing the inherent dignity of all human beings, regardless of gender, religious belief, race, and so forth. That message was characterized by equality between men and women and complete freedom of choice in matters of religion and faith.[62]

Ghannūshī's perspective differs from An-Na'im's in that he considers the Qur'an to be a theological unity. He also sees real freedom in Islam as an expression of human servitude to God (*'ubūbdiyyah lilah*). It is this servitude which defines the pristine nature of man.[63]

Regardless, it remains to be seen whether the Arab political elite are interested in the implementation of Sharī'ah. As I have argued in Chapter 3 of this work, the Arab political elite only pay lip service to religion in public. Most of them are not religious in private and interested only in a superficial discussion of the precepts of the Sharī'ah.

STATE, DEMOCRACY, AND CIVIL SOCIETY

Political authority is necessary for the purpose of guaranteeing the objectives of the Sharī'ah, and, consequently, of the *masālih* (interests) of the people. Sovereignty rests ultimately with God alone. These are well-known arguments from classical Fiqh manuals. However, actual sovereignty in the Arab world has rested with a Westernized elite that is only superficially supportive of the objectives of Sharī'ah. This elite is assisted by token official ulama who neglect their legal duties as advisors to people in power. This says a lot about the predicament of the official religious class in the contemporary Arab world and about the relationship between religion and society.

As mentioned above, in spite of his deep dissatisfaction with the state of political affairs in the Arab world in general, and Tunisia in particular, Ghannūshī refrains from advocating violence as a means of attaining Sharī'ah's objectives. Although he is skeptical of the Western philosophy of democracy and its modern historical manifestation in the context of colonialism, Ghannūshī is convinced that political authority can be attained only through democratic means. "After idolatry, despotism is the greatest enemy of Islam,"[64] he declares. Islam thrives only in the context of freedom. Islam is both religion and state, or, in other words, political authority is a major dimension of Islam. Authority though is a means to an end, which is to establish justice in society, which is also the principle objective of Sharī'ah.[65] Ghannūshī reiterates the classical legal Islamic position on the state, which can be summarized as follows: "The purpose of establishing the state (that is, *Imāmah*) in Islam, as stated by medieval Muslim political thinkers, is to maintain law and order, to defend the faith, and to protect the community from schism."[66] He argues along the same lines that establishing an Islamic political system is a religious duty, as well as a national, human, and strategic interest. This is a tall order given the state of the world today. When Ghannūshī speaks about Islam, he means the Islamic movement he represents. The question is: can this Islamic movement mobilize enough mass support, as was the case in Iran in the late 1970s, to secure political power? Ghannūshī uses ummatic terms to refer to the entire Muslim world. He says that in the absence of an Islamic political system, the Muslim ummah suffers from political division, exploitation, and dependence on the West. The Muslim ummah is doomed to failure unless a state is first established. To the minds of Islamists, the state, once controlled by the Islamists, becomes a source of liberation and emancipation for the people since it is the embodiment of supreme justice, that of the Sharī'ah. In other words, the state is a practical construct needed to safeguard the Sharī'ah. One is justified, therefore, in defending the state on practical and functional grounds.

Most Islamists do not share the Marxist formulation of the state that, first, it is a coercive apparatus or "the concentrated and organized violence of society"; second, that it is an instrument of class domination, and, third, that it is subordinate to civil society.[67] Islamists envision the state as the historical or concrete embodiment of divine justice. To put it simply, the state is an instrument of Sharī'ah, the only source of justice in this world, and the only embodiment of God's will in history. In this sense, Islamists share some of the central Hegelian premises about the role of the state in history and its embodiment of a divine will.[68]

By identifying the state with Sharī'ah justice, Islamists raise serious doubts about the viability of contemporary political systems in power in the contemporary Arab world, their use of coercion to remain in power, and the failure of their modernization projects. Islamists remain convinced that the contemporary state in the Arab world depends in the last resort on violence. Therefore, the Islamists' practical predicament is how to effect sufficient political and religious change in society to make it possible for them to control the state without having to use violence. This is a difficult dilemma indeed.

According to Islamists, one way of controlling the state is by a gradual application of Sharī'ah. It is possible to distill a number of basic positions shared by contemporary Islamist thinkers about the application of Sharī'ah, with some minor variations. The following propositions form the basis of Islamists' arguments concerning the viability of the Sharī'ah in the contemporary Arab world:

First, Islamic political theory has dealt at length with the subject of public liberties from the angle that Islam is both religion and state or that state is a central dimension of Islam.[69] Authority falls under the category of the means (*wasā'il*) and not objectives (*maqāṣid*) of the Sharī'ah. The function of authority is to guard both religion and life, and the enforcers of authority, the political elite, are the employees and servants of the ummah.[70] In the words of Imām al-Ghazālī, "religion is the foundation or the base and authority is the guard."[71] The foundation of an Islamic state is a legal Islamic duty and a national and humanitarian interest.

Second, the Sharī'ah is immutable in that it intends to safeguard the interests of the people. It has no other function. Justice and compassion reflect divine will. The above is clearly stipulated by the Qur'an and the clear Sunnah of the Prophet. In other words, the Islamic worldview, as opposed to the modern Western mindset, to use a term from Huston Smith, derives from the notion that God is the source of legislation and human beings are God's vicegerents on earth. Islam is a colossal emancipatory, revolutionary system,[72] which guarantees human freedom as a form of trust between God and man. To the mind of Ḥassan al-Turābī, for example, liberty is embedded in the Islamic doctrine of the oneness of God. In other words, liberty has metaphysical absolutes that cannot be defined by reason alone. The Western concept of individual liberty, which evolved after centuries of conflict between the feudal-religious and the capitalist system, produced a centralized form of authority in the hands of the state, which has become the only measure or criterion of freedom in the contemporary capitalist system. Turābī argues that human beings can attain true freedom only if they submit themselves to God, and this submission becomes the true measure of freedom in society, "Liberty is a means to worship God, and a method that liberates man from submission to both things and other human beings in order to worship God alone… Absolute liberty can be achieved only through worship."[73] This metaphysical conception of liberty can take concrete form only in a state that is ruled by Sharī'ah, as the embodiment of divine will in life.

Third, the Islamic state is based on two main principles: the Qur'anic text and *shūrah*. The text establishes the main theoretical principles of doctrine and conduct of life. The Qur'anic text has established the most precise characteristics of the Islamic worldview, and God's will has become embodied in His Sharī'ah, as Ghannūshī would say.[74] Political legitimacy must be based on the text, both the Qur'an and the Sunnah, "The Islamic text, both the Qur'an and the Sunnah, besides being the highest authority, underlies the major foundation on which Muslim society was erected. The text is the foundational authority that has given a sense of organization to the Muslim community, state, and civilization."[75]

The text is the *raison d'être* of the ummah, and without it, the ummah has no meaning or personality. *Shūrah*, on the other hand, is not a marginal Qur'anic injunction but one of the main principles of Islam.[76] For example, the Egyptian jurist Ahmad Kamāl Abū'l Majd argues that Qur'anic text must be the launching pad of any discussion about the Sharī'ah's application in modern Arab society. However, the text must not devalue the role of reason in explicating the right legal rules in a changing social and historical environment. Therefore, *ijtihād* is the most valued process that explains the rules of the text in a changing situation. In other words, reason must be an aid to revelation in creating an Islamic systematic theology that is both modern and authentic. In this sense, Abū'l Majd, as well as many other Islamist thinkers, has defined several issues: first, it is impossible to separate legislative injunctions from their Qur'anic worldview as well as from their social and historical contexts; second, Sharī'ah and Fiqh are not the same. Sharī'ah rules are contained in the Qur'an, whereas Fiqh is a legal science created by jurists. Put simply, Sharī'ah is divine, and Fiqh is human. Third, the exertion of *ijtihād* in Sharī'ah is almost an open field since original texts have not dealt with many issues that still bewilder the modern Muslim mind.[77]

Fourth, Fiqh must reflect the social and cultural realities of Muslims. In other words, one must investigate social phenomena, any change in social structure and mentality, and social dynamics before any Fiqh judgment is passed. Therefore, according to this view, a sociological judgment is critical. In other words, the *faqīh* must be a hidden sociologist, or must seek the aid of sociologists when passing judgments about the state of men and women in society. In discussing modern conditions and their impact on Muslims, Abū'l Majd says that the ulama, who have been entrusted with the responsibility of providing adequate answers to the dilemma of contemporary Muslims, have done their job poorly. The only answer to the predicament of the ulama is the use of *ijtihād*.[78]

Fifth, the classical theory of *ijmā'* must be revisited in order to determine the proper way to ensure the legal conduct of the Islamic state envisaged by Ghannūshī. He implicitly argues that if *ijmā'* exists at all nowadays, it does not reflect the opinion of the Muslim community. *Ijmā'* emerged in the formative phase of Islam as a legal movement reflecting the desire of the whole Muslim community to act in unison in response to the multitude of challenges and problems facing the nascent Muslim community. As the community grew, *ijmā'* became a binding legal and political force, and its authority was justified by a number of Muslim scholars and jurists. Ghannūshī argues that the doctrine of *ijmā'* is an explicit invitation to recognize public opinion and its role in conducting the affairs of Muslim society. In other words, *ijmā'*, as Gibb notes, is "*vox populi*, the expressed will of the community...demonstrated by the slowly accumulating pressure of opinion over a long period of time."[79] Ghannūshī states that *ijmā'*, as a vehicle of public opinion and a progressive and binding force, must be reinstated in the contemporary Arab world in order to ensure democracy. Ghannūshī takes up the issue of '*ahl al-ḥall wa'l 'aqd*' (the people of loosening and binding), those in position to give advice to political authorities about affairs of state. He agrees with Muḥammad 'Abduh and the modernist school in Islam that the *faqīhs* in the strict sense cannot be the only people of "loosening and binding."[80] To him, these people are the open-minded ulama and the intelligentsia who have something to say about the religious and political situation of their society.

Sixth, justice is at the core of Islamic public liberties. The main goal of the Sharī'ah is to safeguard these liberties as a form of upholding the public interest (*al-maṣlaḥa al-'āmmah*).[81] In Ghannūshī's words, man is duty-bound to protect his life by refusing to submit to any form of emotional or physical assassination, and is also responsible for fighting against any form of slavery and for the sake of a progressive and happy community. This duty falls in the realm of the sacred, which means that it is on par with any other sacred duty in Islam, such as worship or fasting.[82] The goal behind the search for knowledge in Islam is not to attain mental leisure or academic neutrality but to achieve an Islamic revolution that eradicates dependency and human forms of authority and liberates the poor and disadvantaged from every form of oppression and injustice.[83]

Seventh, Islam has guaranteed the freedom of belief, which is defined as the freedom of any individual to have the right to choose the religious doctrine that suits his/her needs. "No coercion in religion" is the most primordial theological position that protects man's religious pluralism. Modern Islamists believe that Muslims and non-Muslims can constitute a common political ummah, within which religious pluralism is protected. Non-Muslims have the right to express their different religious and cultural personalities as long as they do not infringe on the rights of Muslims to express their Islamic personality.[84]

Eighth, the contemporary capitalist system, pioneered by the United States, has proven to be an impediment to the implementation of the Sharī'ah, and hence, true justice, in the contemporary Arab world. Since the disappearance of the Soviet system and the beginning of the New World Order, the capitalist system has found a new international enemy in Islamic resurgence and the Muslim world. The capitalist system does not care in principle about the essential rights of human beings; all it cares about is the national interest of this or that state.

Ninth, democracy and nationalism have been intertwined since the appearance of the modern nation-state in Western Europe. However, the nation represents or reflects the aspirations of a limited political and social community, whereas the ummah reflects the aspirations of the larger or more universal Islamic community. Furthermore, democracy, although guaranteeing free elections and rights of citizenry, has failed to express the spiritual and intellectual quest of man. In the absence of the Islamic political system, argues Ghannūshī, the Western political system that has developed over many centuries is the best man-produced system to which Muslims must aspire in their struggle to establish their Islamic state, "a partial or loose freedom is always better than dictatorship."[85]

Tenth, religion preceded state in Islam, that is, religion was the *raison d'être* of political authority, especially during the reign of the Rightly Guided caliphs, before Islam became a complex multiglot and multi-religious empire. However, with the evolution of the state in the post-Ummayyad phase and the increasing ethnic and social pluralization of society as time progressed, the state became primary. In the minds of some early Ummayyad and Abbaside jurists, state was synonymous with civil society. Other jurists dissented and formed their own associations and *awqāf* that were independent from the authority of the state. Civil society evolved in contradistinction to the state by building its autonomous associations and institutions, especially in the area of religious and educational endowments. The modern state in the Arab world began to spread its hegemony over society at large by dismantling all elements of civil Muslim society, nationalizing the religious property and other endowments and placing educational religious institutions under its control.[86] In Ghannūshī's mind, the modern state is totalitarian in principle, and hence the difficulty facing civil society is to shake off its entrenched political and military foundations.[87] In other words, despotism is identical with the origins of the modern Arab state, especially as it destroyed the religious associations of pre-modern society.[88]

The Islamic movement, aided by the teachings of the Sharīʿah, is the only movement to Ghannūshī's mind that offers a new vision of civil society. This vision is comprehensive, patriotic, international, liberationist, and Salafī in orientation.[89] Ghannūshī speaks more like a theologian or philosopher than a politician. It is extremely difficult to determine the strategy needed to achieve the lofty goals he has set for his movement. If the democratic option in the Arab world is out, what other options remain, except the resort to violence?

THOUGHTS ON *IJMĀʿ* AND EARLY ISLAMIC HISTORY

Receptive to any indication of democratic feeling that may manifest from undemocratic arteries of contemporary political systems in the Arab world, Islamists have turned their intellectual ammunition towards reconstructing the legal and religious foundations of the Islamic system they envisage. As has been mentioned earlier, to the mind of the Islamists, authority is the twin sister of religion; religion cannot be established properly unless some form of political authority stands behind it. Most contemporary Muslim jurists are agreed that both the Qur'anic text and *shūrah* represent the most essential foundations of the Islamic state. The text is the embodiment of justice and the *shūrah* is the mechanism to preserve this justice.

Islamists' quest for a just Islamic order (both religious and political) in the modern world has taken them back to early Islam, and the role of the *shūrah* in the famous Saqifah meeting to elect a leader after the death of the Prophet (632 CE). The *ijmāʿ* (consensus) of the meeting leaders was to elect Abū Bakr as the first caliph after the Prophet, an *ijmāʿ* that gained the wrath of future Shīʿis, who saw that ʿAlī was more suitable for the job. To many Shīʿis, the Sunni *ijmāʿ* and the events following from the election of Abū Bakr represent only one version of Islamic history. In fact, to some, the triumph of the Islamic revolution in Iran in 1979 is proof that the Shīʿī version of Islamic history is the most credible, since it has been the most impressive revolutionary event in the history of modern Islam. Although the doctrine of *ijmāʿ* played a central role in spreading the Prophet's message after his death, as ʿAllāl al-Fāsī argues,[90] most contemporary Islamist jurists speak ill of Islamic history since the death of the fourth caliph, ʿAlī bin Abī Ṭālib. By raising this point, I share one of the main theses of Samir Amin, who argues that most modern Islamists think of Islamic history of the past fourteen hundred years as little more than the history of the betrayal of Islamic principles and ideals.[91]

Ghannūshī addresses why things shifted from the sublime principles of Islam, especially that of the *shūrah*. He notes change even during the reign of the Rightly Guided caliphs, especially Othman and ʻAlī, the last two. The dramatic expansion of the early Islamic state, and the conquest of new civilizational centers in Persia and North Africa ushered the nascent Islamic state into a complex new phase that was too much for its founders to handle. The main victim of this was the *shūrah* strategy that led overnight to a new form of dictatorship and usurpation of power from the ummah and its representatives, the people of *Ḥall and ʻAqd* (consultative assembly).[92] The overseers of the institutional caliphate were swept by dictatorship. Sayyid Quṭb calls this period *al-fiṣām al-nakid* (bitter schizophrenia).[93] The usurpation of power is set in a dichotomous process, between the political elite and the religious class. The Muslim world today still suffers from it. The religious class, for fear of losing Islam, tended to be more conservative and less innovative in matters of religious thought and theology.[94]

TOWARD AN ISLAMIC POLITICAL SYSTEM

A great deal of Muslim intellectual focus has gone to the necessity of reestablishing an Islamic political system after the historical demise of the Ottoman caliphate in the wake of the triumph of Kemal Atatürk's brand of nationalism in Turkey. Muslim parties, such as the Ḥizb al-Taḥrīr established by Taqiy al-Dīn al-Nabahānī, and the Muslim Brotherhood movement fought relentlessly with other distinguished Muslim thinkers to justify reestablishing the caliphate. To all Muslim jurists, from ʻAbd al-Qādir ʻAwda to Ḥasan al-Banna and Muḥammad Abū Zahra, establishing the caliphate as a religio-political institution is a religious duty similar to that of jihad or prayer, and the failure to do so is an "undisputed sin."[95] These attempts have come to naught. Modern Islamic political thinking, radical or conservative, does not contemplate the state becoming some sort of classless society, as Lenin envisioned in some of his writings. Most Muslim thinkers consider the state a precursor to the flourishing of religion on earth.

In the mind of famous Egyptian jurist ʻAbd al-Razzāq al-Sanhūrī,[96] the Imāmate, that is, the political leadership of the Muslim ummah, is a religious obligation and the Imām must be elected by the populace. Ghannūshī sees this has been impossible to realize in modern times because of the strong alliance between the political dictatorship in the Arab world and "the remnants of political and religious feudalism."[97] The Imāmate, although based on divine sources, is a civil form of authority that derives legitimacy from the peoples' freely given acceptance. Ghannūshī is, no doubt, uneasy about the cooperation between a significant sector of the ulama, the official ulama, and the ruling power elite, and the attack both have launched against any other interpretation of Islam in the modern age. At the very least, the ulama must engage in peaceful *jihād* against oppressive rulers in the modern Arab world.

It is true that the Muslim community is legally-bound to disobey that ruler if he does not apply explicitly the rules of the Sharīʻah. But do not most Arab rulers claim they apply the Sharī'ah? Ghannūshī notes that the doctrine of obeying tyrant rulers for fear of anarchy is groundless in Islamic law, since the ruler must act as the servant of the community and fulfill its wishes by applying Sharī'ah. Muslims have the right to rebel against any ruler who has suspended Sharī'ah and placed the destiny of the ummah in the hands of foreigners. Most rulers in the Arab world seem to qualify.

CONCLUSION

The critical writings of contemporary Islamists are more than a mere exercise in intellectual futility. They are bitter, piercing, passionate, and revolutionary. Ghannūshī's bitterness with things un-Islamic is reminiscent of Muḥammad 'Abduh in the nineteenth century. Decline and stagnation have suspended Muslim reason and spread many unwanted mental and psychological diseases. If Islam was a giant advance that transcended the unacceptable in Arabia, the "garbage of our decline" (*mazābil inḥiṭātina*) has accumulated over the past centuries.[98] Against this background, it is impossible for the committed Muslim intelligentsia to do its work in peace. Perhaps suffering both imprisonment and exile will become the only alternative to this debilitating and confusing state of affairs. Ghannūshī's *magnum opus*, *al-Ḥuriyyāt al-'āmmah fī'l dawlah al-islāmiyyah*, is a product of both revolution and exile. It is reminiscent of Antonio Gramsci's classic, *Prison Notebooks*. Of course, there are some unbridgeable differences between Gramsci's thought and Ghannūshī's. However, both are preoccupied with similar problematics: state, hegemony, and the best means of establishing civil society.[99] Gramsci suffered imprisonment and death for his ideas, and Ghannūshī has suffered imprisonment and exile. Ghannūshī summarizes succinctly the imagining of the contemporary Islamist intelligentsia, an intelligentsia that was nurtured and bred in secular schools and philosophies of the West, but which rebelled against the West's preordained categories of thought.

Ghannūshī represents a new type of pious Muslim intellectual who envisions a new political community free from repression and injustice. He also envisions a new political community unsupported by a corrupt and feudal-minded religious class. It is paradoxical to note that the resurgence of Islamic activism after 1967 gave the corrupt religious class of the ulama a new legitimacy and role to play by the waning nationalist state. In the age of the nationalist triumph, the state tried to minimize, control, and bypass the authority of the ecceliastical class. After 1967, this class became the spokespersons of religious and political order and the self-proclaimed enemy of terrorism in society. The alliance between the official religious class and the ruling elite in Ghannūshī's native land is as strong as ever. In a sense, this alliance has postponed the fate of Ghannūshī's movement for a long while.

It is important to point out that contemporary Arab intelligentsia is torn between two different worldviews. The Westernized intellectual elite have lost their real affinity and connection with the masses, erected new barriers by aligning with the ruling class, "it is barely different, in its connection with the masses, from the white minority in Apartheid South Africa."[100] The depth of the crisis in contemporary

Arab society is not philosophical or epistemological, or even intellectual, but rather social and historical. The crisis is compounded by the fact that the traditional ulama class has forsaken its position of mediation between the ruling elite and the masses. One must understand mediation as the sustenance of a certain form of relationship between the masses and the power elite, where the latter is placed in a position to listen to the complaints of the former. The new intellectual elite, educated in the West and who prey on its rationalism, have found themselves totally disconnected from the agonies and complaints of the masses. Their alliance with the ruling elite has further cut it off from its indigenous society. "The disintegration of our civilizational personality"[101] (*inḥilāl shakhṣiyatunah al-ḥadāriyyah*) has been made possible by the confluence of international and local factors, all of which reinforce the need of the Arab world for a true democracy. Violence is what distinguishes the contemporary Arab state in relation to society, argues Ghannūshī. Through the medium of modernization and the philosophy of modernity, the ruling elite is unrelenting in superimposing its vision on the rest of society. Meanwhile, the West nourishes its allies in the Arab world with the philosophy of modernity, just another form of Western dictatorship imposed on the Arab world.[102]

In addition to suffering imprisonment and exile, Ghannūshī has been attacked by a number of Muslim groups, especially in Britain, his country of exile. Some members of the Taḥrirī and Salafī groups have accused him of harboring "Western concepts that are alien to Islam, such as democracy and public liberties, for whose benefit he seeks to alter Islam's concepts claiming they are flexible and capable of modifying whenever we want depending on our interests or according to our own reasoning."[103] Contemporary Islamists are highly suspicious of the ruling political elite and their modernization/Westernization project. In their struggle against the prevalent Western legal language in the Arab world, they propose the establishment of the Sharī'ah and following the ultimate authority of the Qur'an and Sunnah,

> the discourse used Muslim vocabulary and terminology and insisted on the right to be different or at least distinctive. Instead of "natural law" it was "God's deputyship"; instead of "human rights" it was 'the legitimate rights stipulated by the Sharī'ah'; instead of "democracy" it was *shūrah*, or "consultation"; instead of "parliament" it was *ahl al-ḥall wa-l-'aqd* (the body of influential people).[104]

Some contemporary Islamists have learned the hard way that attacking society without providing legal or religious alternatives is far from enough. A serious attempt has been made to deal with the Sharī'ah, Fiqh, Islamic history, Islamic political theory, and modern conditions in order to avoid the mistakes of Islamists in the 1950s and 1960s.[105] Although this discourse has appealed to a good number of educated Muslims, it has not yet done much to change the political situation in the Arab world.

10
Muslim Self-Criticism in Contemporary Arab Thought: The Case of Shaykh Muḥammad al-Ghazālī

> "The civilizational decline of the Muslim people has come as a result of a pervasive mental backwardness, and a series of political, social, educational, and scientific betrayals enveloping the Muslim *ummah* from top to bottom." Muḥammad al-Ghazālī, *al-Ghazw al-thaqāfi yamtaddu fi farāghina* (Amman: Mu'assassat al-Sharq, 1985), 108.

> "Some [Muslims] prefer that I discuss the points of weakness in other societies. To my mind, this is self-deceit, and an attempt at satisfying a lying arrogance. The naive feeling that we are better than others engenders this. And this is a costly loss of consciousness." Muḥammad al-Ghazālī, *al-Sunnah al-nabawiyah bayna ahl al-fiqh wa ahl al-hadīth* (Cairo: Dār al-Shurūq, 1989), 112.

> "Other widely-held beliefs, reflected in both popular and scholarly writings, are that the mullah-dominated priestly class, with its paraphernalia, represents 'true' Islam, while liberal and modernist currents are either secondary or peripheral to the more dominant 'separatist', 'communal' and 'neo-fundamentalist' paradigms." Mushirul Ḥasan, *Legacy of a Divided Nation: India's Muslims Since Independence* (Boulder: Westview Press, 1997), 224.

> "There does not exist 'progressive Islam' or 'revolutionary Islam' or 'political Islam' or the 'sultans' Islam' on the one hand, and 'reactionary Islam' or 'pacifist Islam' or 'social Islam' or 'mass Islam' on the other. There is one Islam only, and one book, which God revealed to His Prophet, and which the Prophet conveyed to the people." Fahmī Huwaydī, *al- Qur'an wa'l sultān* (Cairo: Dār al-Shurūq, 1982), 7.

"The ulama of the sultan are the dogs of Hell-fire." This is not a polite statement with which to begin a chapter on Shaykh Muḥammad al-Ghazālī (1916–1996) (henceforth referred to as Ghazālī). However, this statement captures the foremost preoccupation of one of the most influential contemporary Islamist thinkers in the twentieth century: the relationship between religion and power in the Arab world. Many consider Ghazālī to be the Muḥammad 'Abduh of the contemporary era.[1] His singularity stems from the fact that throughout his intellectual career as a writer and thinker (beginning in 1947), he used the tools of critical Islamic thinking in approaching issues of the day. Whether considering the Qur'an and the

Sunnah, discussing the economic and social conditions of modern Muslims, critiquing inner stagnation and the weakness enveloping modern Muslim societies, proposing a sophisticated philosophy of Muslim self-criticism, critiquing the West and imperialism, or presenting his views on matters from Islamic knowledge to the responsibilities of Muslim intellectuals in the contemporary age, Ghazālī brought an enormous intellectual and rigorous style of analysis to the task. Ghazālī began his life as an ideologue of the Islamic movement in Egypt (al-Ikhwān), and ended it as a freelance Islamist critic.[2]

However, at the end of his life, Ghazālī turned out to be a disgruntled critic of religion and culture in the Arab world in the last decades of the twentieth century. He even went as far as to justify the assassination of Egyptian thinker Faraj Fūda.[3] Ghazālī began his career as a promising young Azharite intellectual and disciple of Shaykh Ḥasan al-Banna (henceforth referred to as Banna) in pre-1952 Egypt.[4] In the 1950s and 1960s, however, he took up the state's position against organized Islamic activism and believed it to answer the enormous problems facing religious institutions. In a sense, Ghazālī was more or less faithful to the general line of Azharite support of the Nasserite state, in which he held a very high position.[5] However, the dismantling of Nasserism in the early 1970s and the resurgence of Islamism as a formidable socio-political and religious movement in the Arab world enabled Ghazālī to shift positions and reclaim once again his association with the Muslim Brotherhood. The Ikhwān, arguably out of fashion in the Middle East, were gaining wide support among young Muslim intelligentsia, most notably in Tunisia and Algeria. Ghazālī's work in Algeria in the 1980s gave him a new perspective of the broader problems of post-colonial Arab societies in North Africa.[6] He was invited by the government of Algeria to moderate the radical voices of its youth, a radicalism engendered by a number of complex social and political factors in that country after independence.[7]

Ghazālī's passion for criticism and things Islamic did not brand him an eccentric thinker. On the contrary, he has been considered by many as one of the most distinguished religious thinkers in modern Islam, a man who had a feel for the problems of the entire Muslim ummah. As a distinguished intellectual holding important posts in Egypt and throughout the Arab world, Ghazālī was concerned with the decline of Muslim culture in the present, ways of reconstructing this culture, and ways of solving other predicaments of modern Islam. Ghazālī was a prolific author. It is impossible to discuss the multitude of his ideas in one chapter. My intention in this chapter and the next is to document and analyze his main theses as they evolved over the years, and shed some light on the origins of these ideas, their implications for the contemporary Arab and Muslim world and their impact on Muslim thinkers. Until his death in 1996, Ghazālī had been totally immersed in the same problematics of Muslim renaissance of the nineteenth century.

ISLAM BETWEEN THEOLOGY AND CLERGY

The Qur'an is inexhaustible. It is the ultimate revelatory text that has given Muslim culture its dazzling radiance and immense power. If not read with the rigor of a true believer, it ceases to guide man's spiritual and ethical life.

The Qur'an never ceased to puzzle Ghazālī or millions of other Muslims for that matter. As a child, he memorized the Qur'an in the village of Kuttāb and, as an adult, he unlocked its basic meaning at the Azhar University.

Revelation has made human reason the most substantial symbol of its reality: revelation has enchanted reason. Furthermore, it unleashed in the believer the power of rational bewilderment, and gave Muslim culture a unique outlook on life. God occupies center stage, and He never falls silent even after the cessation of Revelation or the sealing of Prophecy. His presence predicates every living being. Whether or not this is the manifestation of the Hegelian *Geist*, Ghazālī strongly believes the Qur'an to be the most important of the different sources of Islamic culture. Although the Qur'an contains the eternal epistemological foundations of the Islamic worldview, Muslims have differed in their interpretations of it, because, according to one important ḥadith, "difference within my community is surely a sign of mercy" (*ikhtilāf ummatī raḥmah*). Nowadays the issue is much more than a healthy difference of opinion. The Muslim world has been subjugated by Western modernity, imperialism, and its arrogant missionary activity. Alas, the Qur'an has ceased to bewilder the believer or give contemporary Muslim culture its radiance and zeal. People no longer read the Qur'an in the way they did before and, if they do, it is to avail themselves of a hope of an afterlife. Sterility is the norm in contemporary Muslim societies; dynamism belongs to the culture of the triumphant "Other," including the "infidel" Other. The modern historical enemy has been quick to grasp the secrets behind the grandeur of Islam, at least in its classical historical phase. Contemporary Muslims, emptied of their substance, suffer from dependency and meaninglessness.

The most substantial manifestation of sterility and stagnation in modern Muslim life is the loss of those principles, means, and objectives that made the early Islamic community a dynamic and historically conscious. Stagnation has become rampant in the contemporary Muslim world mainly because Muslims have failed to revitalize the Qur'anic *Weltanschauung* and link it to the secular realm of their lives.

Qur'anic principles enabled the early Muslim community to commit itself to the principle of *shūrah*, social justice, and to stand against racism and arrogance.[8] The Qur'an contains a practical worldview, that is on the one hand speculative in nature and, on the other, relevant to the social and cultural needs of the people. In other words, the Qur'an has been revealed for people.

To speak of sterility and stagnation is to imply the loss of creativity in a world that does not tolerate blind imitation. Innovation or *bida'h*, condemned by some Muslim jurists of the past as an assault on the submission to the authentic pattern of the ancestors, is the essence of the modern spirit of life. The main schools of Islamic thought and culture of the past have disappeared since the loss of *ijtihād*, or, simply stated, since the assassination of Muslim reason.[9] The exile of reason from the Muslim world enabled one obsolete school of jurisprudence to survive with pomp and authority, the Ahl al-Sunnah (the people of the Sunnah). This group is currently prominent in the Gulf and in certain parts of India, Pakistan, and Afghanistan. It confines itself to the science of Sunnah and rejects a comprehensive outlook of Islam or larger civilizational message. Its flirtation with reason goes only as far as to concern itself with a small number of juristic issues that revolve around the jurisprudence of worship (*fiqh al-'ibādāt*), while neglecting the jurisprudence of social engagement (*fiqh al-mu'āmālāt*) and other more substantial challenges that face the contemporary Muslim world.[10]

The Qur'an contains an all-encompassing view of life, man, and the Divine. This comprehensiveness is at the heart of the Islamic notion of universalism. Ghazālī, like any Muslim thinker, opposes any separation between social and religious life,[11] and draws Muslim attention to the fact that the Qur'an is the primary source. However, as mentioned above, modern Muslims have largely deserted the Qur'an. There exists a need to rediscover it against the context of new conditions. Furthermore, the Sunnah is the science of interpreting the Qur'an, and not vice versa. As a secondary source, the Sunnah can only aid the believer in comprehending the primary text; the Sunnah documents the major deeds and sayings of the Prophet, the role model of all Muslims, in great detail.[12]

In deserting the Qur'an and its teachings, modern day Muslims pose the most formidable threat to the survival of the Qur'an and its application to actual life. Muslims have allowed the external challenges presented by the missionaries, whose aim has been to eradicate the influence of the Qur'an, to influence the way they apply the Qur'an to their lives. The missionaries have adopted the following methods: (1) influence the Muslim political elites by trying to prevent them from applying Islamic law; (2) spread Christianity through medical, social, educational, and humanitarian services, and (3) create governments that are dependent on Western imperialism. Mission, in fact, is inseparable from colonialism.[13]

In addition to being a comprehensive religion that encourages people to be socially cognizant, Islam contains rich psychological and emotional aspects, which people have termed mysticism. This is the subject of *The Emotional Side of Islam*.[14] Modern Muslim education must be restructured to include study of the psychological factors affecting the modern Muslim personality, so that doctrine is supported both rationally and emotionally. Belief is a matter of rational and scientific discourse, which investigates the mysteries of the universe as well as providing psychological reflection into the mysteries of the heart.[15] One of the first important steps of belief is total submission to God. How can this be accomplished in the present time? Belief, to be effective, must be both a dynamic rational presence and a creative emotional movement. "As a spiritual condition, belief cannot spring up from a stagnant intellectual activity, or it cannot result from the influence of myths and superstitions on the human mind."[16] Clearly, Muslims must invest in religious education in order to achieve the above. The search for knowledge is a religious duty, one that if pursued, will lead to knowledgeable and highly ethical Muslims.

In view of the above, there is an urgent need to reformulate modern Islamic thinking on the basis of the two main sources of Islamic knowledge: the Qur'an and the Sunnah, while not neglecting the conditions of the modern world in general and the Muslim world in particular. What Ghazālī calls for is Islamic systematic theology, which must be capable of producing new tools of thinking in order to come to grips with both theory and practice.[17] The basic *élan* of this implicit systematic theology, according to Ghazālī, is to emancipate Muslim reason from blind imitation, reductionism and atomism, expose it to the recent scientific contributions of mankind, and facilitate its access to a well-rounded critical theory aided by the most advanced tools of social and humanistic criticism. This Islamic systematic theology must reaffirm the need for a new work ethic in the Muslim world in order to replace the philosophy of predestination (*falsafat al-jabr*). This philosophy, the product of the dark ages and the absence of real enlightenment, has permeated classical and modern Muslim culture and led to one noticeable result: the abdication of human responsibility, thereby negating the necessity of human action.

A WEDGE BETWEEN ISLAM AND POLITICS?

The concept of predestination has confined Muslim reason to the spurious, the unverified, and the indeterminate. Worse yet, predestination is the twin son of conceptual impairment (*khalal fikrī*), which conspicuously underpins the cultural reality of the modern Muslim world. Where does one situate the Muslim intelligentsia (both lay and religious) relative to this cultural fact? Ghazālī maintains that one of the saddest historical facts in early Muslim history is the creation of a wedge between the Muslim intelligentsia and the power elite, beginning with the Ummayyad caliphate (662–750 CE). In spite of their deep awareness of transience, the lovers of this world were relentless in their refusal to allow the Muslim mind to exhaust its possibilities and delve in the complex historical and social realities. The leaders of Muslim thought, the authentic ulama who were burdened with the Islamic message, were given no chance to produce a true Muslim philosophy of governance or to advise the people of their political duties in an Islamic state. Submission to the power elite took precedence over the unfettered exercise of Muslim reason. Authoritarianism has impeded the true progress of Muslim thought from the very beginning. The result has been abysmal. Muslim political thought, as we know it today, does not deal with real issues of power, neither does it reflect the progress of Muslim history, "Those who possessed great scientific abilities, mature conscience, and a deep experience in life as well as the politics of the masses were removed from power and, consequently, Islam and Muslims were deprived of their intelligence, courage, and piety."[18] The wedge between the power elite and the true ulama has had dire consequences. When the caliphate was transformed into a kingdom during the Ummayyad rule, Muslim thought in the areas of constitutional freedoms, political philosophy, international relations, and finance began to stagnate. Those who did not accept the bribe of the comfort of the sultan withdrew to silence and mysticism. The bloody conflict between the Kharijites and the Shī'īs, on the one hand, and the state on the other was too painful to contemplate. However, this double-edged process of withdrawal and conflict led to a clear defeat of the system of the *shūrah*.[19] In other words, Islam did not succeed in influencing the philosophy of power in early Islamic history. The political elite loathed *shūrah* and valued allegiance instead. The triumph of the political over the sacred was not without severe consequences. It was first a division over political authority, and it evolved into a division about doctrine. The natural outcome was the basic violation of human rights in classical Islam.[20]

What kind of historical philosophy does Ghazālī preach? Ghazālī is convinced that as a result of the separation between religion and politics since early Islam, Islamic governments of the past fourteen centuries have not been truly Islamic. Corruption has been the rule.[21] The modern political arena in the Muslim world has not seen any fundamental progress in its political philosophy or political structure. It is true that the state bureaucracies have expanded over the years; however, in almost every Muslim country, major political decisions are still made by a handful of individuals. In contrast to this sorry state of political affairs, Islamic knowledge and culture was revived throughout Muslim history by a number of prominent and erudite figures. In the area of Fiqh, such major Muslim thinkers as Abū Ḥanīfa, Imām Mālik, Imām al-Shāfi'ī and Ibn Hanbal, Ibn Ḥazm, Ibn al-Qayyim, and Ibn Taymiyya became well-known. In matters of reform and renewal, Muḥammad ibn 'Abd al-Wahāb, al-Sanūssī, al-Afghānī, 'Abduh, al-Kawākibī, Riḍa, and Banna were pioneers.[22]

Historically speaking, therefore, it was not in the interest of the political elite to develop a true Muslim theory of governance. The wedge placed between Muslim thinking and politics (or Muslim intellectuals and power) was followed by the division of Muslim sciences between jurists and mystics, each group having its own method of fathoming the Qur'an. Jurists became exclusively interested in domains such as legislation, society, and the externals. Mystics focused on education, ethics, and internal matters. This separation of Islamic sciences into two distinct unrelated domains has been the landmark of weak Muslim culture.

Ghazālī distinguishes between two presences of Islam in the wake of the termination of the Rightly Guided caliphate: (1) official Islam, and (2) popular Islam. Official Islam, which lent itself intellectually and religiously to preserving the *status quo*, was a contradictory and self-evading discourse that failed to come to grips with the universal essence of Islam and, as a result, failed to spread it. But "popular Islam was able to bridge the gaps created by official Islam, and to continue marching without any hindrance."[23] Ghazālī maintains that the masses embraced Islam in the wake of Islamic conquest and made it a viable social and religious force. In a sense, Islam has survived due to the efforts of the masses and not the elite in Muslim societies.

It is interesting to compare Ghazālī's ideas on governance and those of the famous Muslim historian Ibn Khaldūn. Ibn Khaldūn, who was in many ways responding to the political and social conditions of the Muslim world in the thirteenth and fourteenth centuries, was aware that royal authority was needed as a form of organization and an incentive for commerce and scientific activity. However, in his view, political organization cannot supersede the religious law since the goal of the latter is to lead people to happiness in the other world, "The religious laws guide it [humanity] along the path of religion, so that everything will be under the supervision of the religious law."[24] The caliphate, to Ibn Khaldūn's mind, was a necessary institution in Islam because it functioned to preserve divine commands, "[The caliphate] substitutes for the Lawgiver (Muḥammad) in as much as it serves, like him, to preserve the religion and to exercise political leadership of the world."[25] Although, according to Ibn Khaldūn, there were substantial disagreements among early Muslims about the necessity of the caliphate, he took the side of those who said it was necessary to administer Muslim justice. However, Ibn Khaldūn did not concern himself with the implied schism between political and religious authorities in early Islam. What he worried about was the Arab, and more specifically, Qurashite sense of *'aṣṣabiyyah* (group feeling) and its role in the solidification of the early Muslim (Arab) community in Arabia, which was necessary for the expansion of Islam and its emergence as a world civilization under the banner of Arabism and Islam. The Quraysh tribe was the only group, historically speaking, that was capable of leading the Arabs into a world civilization at the time, and that is why the Prophet, in Ibn Khaldūn's view, warned against dissension in the ranks, "The Quraysh were able to assume the responsibility of doing away with division and of preventing people from splitting up."[26] Because of their strong group unity, the Arabs were united and "Muslim armies entered the most remote countries. It remained this way in the Ummayyad and 'Abbaside dynasties until the power of the caliphate dissolved and the Arab group feeling vanished."[27]

It is clear from the above that Ibn Khaldūn's main point of contention was Arab group feeling, which was translated into the unity of Quraysh, the Arabs of Arabia, and then the Muslims under Arab rule until the end of the Abbaside caliphate. This feeling of Arab *'aṣṣabiyyah* was a necessary precondition for the spread of Islam. As long as the political authority of the Arab dynasties was able to enhance the position of the Muslim world vis-à-vis other powers, Islam was in a good position. Ibn Khaldūn did not consider the theory of the split between political and religious authority to be of much importance.

Ghazālī's point of departure, on the other hand, is more on the fate of the religious intelligentsia in the classical and modern Muslim worlds and less on the preservation of the Arab group feeling within Islam.[28] Ghazālī argues that although the modern world is much more complex than the ancient, the condition of the contemporary Muslim intelligentsia is not that different. Those not in the service of the sultan are either dying of starvation, finding comfort in silence, or prospering in exile. The "sultans are twins of devils" *(al-salāṭīn Ikhwān al-shayāṭīn)* is an apt description of this state of affairs. Those intellectuals who have dared to raise their voices, even in the form of *naṣīḥah* (advice) to the sultan, have fallen prey to the sultan's bullets, and the more opponents these bullets can kill, in more comfort does the sultan sleep, "The thinkers of this ummah are persecuted one after another and they are forced to live in exile."[29] Genuine Muslim thinkers are either assassinated, as in the case of Ḥasan al-Banna and Sayyid Quṭb, exiled, or prevented from having real contact with the masses. Therefore, to Ghazālī's mind, the question is not the absence of sources. Although Muslims possess the right sources, a crisis exists in thinking, comprehension, and jurisprudence, "The saddest things of all is that those who possess proper thinking are controlled by the sword wielders."[30]

The ulama of the sultan, the brothers of Satan (*Ikhwān al-shayāṭīn*) condemned so fiercely by Imām Abū Ḥāmid al-Ghazālī of the twelfth century,[31] are condemned with the same ferocity by Ghazālī in the twentieth century, "The ulama of the power elite (*sulṭah*) possess no religion…They are the dogs of Hell-fire (*hum kilāb jahanam*)."[32] The power elite have suffocated true intellectual thinking.

As a result, there is a real intellectual starvation in the contemporary Muslim world. The ruling classes in the Muslim world understand very well the power of ideas and words. Ghazālī adopts a revolutionary path reminiscent of that of Banna in the first half of the twentieth century. To be faithful to the message of Islam and the highest level of religiosity, the ulama must launch an intellectual and religious revolution in the contemporary Muslim consciousness. As in the revolutionary era in France, great ideas precede great revolutions. The seed of these great ideas is contained within the Qur'an. Courage, with a dose of Qur'anic philosophy, is needed to really change things in the Muslim world.[33]

Yet, in spite of his impatience with the political elite and their attempts to suffocate the educated Muslim voice, Ghazālī finds immense hope in the masses. The most interesting observation about the current Muslim world is that mass religiosity is still alive and kicking. This is the Achilles' heel of the political elite. The masses give the true ulama the balance they need vis-à-vis the elite. The umma, in spite of the many internal and external enemies devouring its divided body, is able to resist.[34] A new consciousness is needed. Ghazālī says, "Political corruption in our midst has had the most damaging effect. Muslims must realize that political corruption will impede their renaissance as long as dictatorial politicians remain in power."[35] Furthermore,

> Number wise, the Muslim umma is one fifth of the world population. It is absent from the fields of [human] knowledge and production…[It is ruled by] feudal and pharoanic governments. Its people are in constant search for sustenance, and its art revolves around pure pleasure and ways to attain it. Its religious-minded people are preoccupied solely with mental garbage (*qumāmāt fikriyah*)…As for the developed world, it worships itself and it spares no effort to enslave the backward nations, the Muslims included.[36]

This severe condemnation of the Muslim world sounds like a cry in the wilderness, the sigh of the oppressed in a vulnerable time, and a plea for rationality in an age of chaos and uncertainty.

Ghazālī greatly values Western technology and progress. He ascribes Western success in these fields to diligence and an openness to others. Where quality is the foundation of modern Western scientific life, corruption and mediocrity are the hallmarks of contemporary Muslim life. The current Muslim state of affairs, according to Ghazālī, is due to the fundamental fact that Muslims "have deserted the Qur'an," which translates as another form of deserting the methods of research and inquiry into the secrets of the universe.[37] In addition to being absent from all fields of human enquiry and from international conferences, Muslims are preoccupied with trivial juristic and theological differences and revel in their dependence on the economic and technological aid of the West. People in positions of authority in the Western world make major decisions only after consulting a group of learned and reliable people, called by Ghazālī *ahl al-ḥall wa'l 'iqd*.[38] On the Muslim side, however, the people in the position of power tolerate no opinion and seek no advice. These people are "half-learned, arrogant dwarfs [*aqzām*]."[39]

ISLAM AND SOCIAL JUSTICE

The 1940s was a crucial decade in the history of modern Egypt. These years saw the gestation of major movements of thought representing Marxism, liberalism, and voices of resurgent Islam. All competed to represent the poor and members of the working classes in the last days of an opulent and stagnant monarchy. As President Sadat did before his assassination in 1981, King Fārūq placed the major dissidents from different parties in detention camps before his final eclipse in 1952. Even this did not silence the intellectuals. It was an important era for social and political criticism.

The growth of criticism in a society is a true measure of its mental progress; it is also a reflection of its deep anguish and prolonged pain. Very often, criticism flourishes in reaction to a severe *status quo*. There has been a sustained effort on the part of a small number of Muslim intelligentsia to glorify the Muslim critical spirit. Sayyid Quṭb, ʻAbd al-Qādir ʻAwda,[40] Muḥammad Bāqir al-Ṣadr, and Muḥammad Ḥussain Faḍlallah are some of its major representatives in this century. They revived a genre of critical Islamic literature tackling such issues as "Islam and Our Economic Conditions," or "Islam and Our Legal Tradition," and "Islam and the Challenges of the Modern World."

As a comrade-in-arms to this school, Ghazālī does not deviate from this genre. His first book is about Islamic economics. In it, he shows a passion for criticism and makes an anguished cry for the poor. In his first book of 1947, *Islam and the Economic Conditions*,[41] Ghazālī tackles the problematic connection between religion, the economic systems of both capitalism and socialism, the prevailing economic conditions in Egyptian society, and the role Islam might take in alleviating the suffering of the poor. Although he is not as bitter in his condemnation of "feudalism and capitalism" as Sayyid Quṭb is in his *Social Justice* or *The Battle Between Islam and Capitalism*,[42] Ghazālī nevertheless argues that the spirit of Islam stands against economic exploitation and class differences.[43] Stagnant economic conditions produce their own Rasputins and charlatans. Ghazālī, the village boy who struggled to make ends meet while a student at the Azhar, discovers upon graduation a class of "*nouveaux riches*," a "leisured class," as he calls it, which is hard at work asserting its political and economic hegemony. Its way of preserving class differences in society is to preach "mental gaps" (*tafāwut ʻaqlī*) between the different classes.[44] What this means is that social and economic differences cannot be explained by purely social factors; they are God-ordained. The poor do not have much intelligence or wit, although they have many children. The unfortunate rich have just a few.

Ghazālī argues that the supposed intelligence of the wealthy always gets translated into educational and political hegemony.[45] In the case of Egypt in the interwar period, only the rich had private schools; the poor were nurtured on ignorance in the countryside. Because of its privileged educational training, the "leisure class" adopts elitist (Ghazālī calls it "Latin" or "Western") manners of cultural and social expressions that are fundamentally divergent from those of the poor. There is an ocean of difference between poor and rich. The "leisure elite" thus pose a great social danger to other people. Ghazālī invokes the authority of the sacred text.

The Qur'an, he argues, levels heavy critique of the "leisured class" in many of its verses. Consider the following argument proposed by the Qur'an: first, the "leisure class" stands against any kind of reform in the *status quo*, since reform places their prestige, hegemony, and arrogance at a great peril; second, the Qur'an stipulates that the "leisure class" is "the source of enormous corruption and the cause behind the eruption of infighting and discord (*fitnah*) in society."[46] *Fitnah* is surely a great plight, and sometimes it is more difficult to fathom than killing (*wa'l fitantu ashad mina al-qatl*). The structure of corruption it creates is the first to crumble under outside pressure and threat. Ghazālī argues that colonialism in Muslim lands has always thrived on such people, who maintain their prestige and influence only by becoming completely dependent on outside powers. The colonialists, cognizant of the oppressive social and economic conditions in the Muslim world on the eve of their occupation, "Paved the way for their prolonged stay in the countries they conquered by causing the class system (*nizām al-tabāqāt*) to flourish, and securing for the 'leisure class' what it desires of material goods."[47] Furthermore, the "leisure class," a product of oppression and corruption, proves to be the true enemy of the masses, of the *naṣṣ* in the Qur'anic text.[48] It seeks no equality with the masses and above all it considers the masses to be inferior, both mentally and socially.[49]

Ghazālī encourages us to be mindful of the Muslim present before we can plan for a healthy future. One of the major ills in the modern Muslim world is the preponderance of an unholy alliance between "poverty, ignorance, and disease."[50] The poor and the masses, the true stewards of Qur'anic revelation, cannot correctly practice the essential teachings of Islam as long as they are deprived of the basics in life. As a woodcutter by night, ignorance makes sure that the energy of the community is wasted, and helps to keep the masses from practicing their religion. Social conditions, as a consequence, reach a boiling point, or a very "dangerous social upheaval" (*iḍṭirāb ijtimā'ī khaṭīr*). Ghazālī contends that the oppressive economic and social conditions at home are hand in glove with outside colonialism. Internal colonialism precedes the external one.[51] Class differentiation and social injustice are incompatible with the demands of true freedom. Freedom of the press, as is practiced in Egyptian society, protects only the interests of the elite.

Ghazālī repeats the classical phrase that religion can be a double-edged sword. Although a great number of righteous ulama have stood against social and economic oppression and voiced their criticism against the prevailing conditions without fear, others have always resorted to the Qur'an to justify oppressive social and economic conditions. Whatever the case, the Islamic philosophy of life is in actuality more socialist than capitalist. It is in the best interest of Islam to eradicate differences between classes. These differences cannot be completely overcome; after all, some people are just more industrious than others.

Just like Sayyid Quṭb, his comrade-in-arms of the early 1950s, Ghazālī resorts to Marxist terminology in order to analyze the prevailing economic and social conditions. Human knowledge is after all universal. Ghazālī marshals a great number of Qur'anic verses against exploitation, class system, and the leisure class. Colonialism is not a transient phenomenon precisely because it parasitically thrives on these corrupt economic conditions. From this angle, Ghazālī does not see a swift or radical end to colonialism in the Muslim world. Oppressive internal conditions engender external colonization. Imperialism as a historical system and political fact may change colors, but will not easily disappear.[52] Imperialism will evolve and use more subtle methods of exploiting the rest of the world. It has discovered that the Middle East is a strategic area for its economic and military interests. Ghazālī makes a grim analysis of the future of the Muslim world, saying that the only way to fix the situation is to improve the lot of the masses who have preserved religiosity since the beginning of Islamic history, "Before they can comprehend Islam and promote its cause, the masses of the Muslim East are in need of gigantic efforts to improve their ethical and material levels. That is to say that the human value [of those Muslim masses] must be restored first...Without taking this step, the efforts of the reformers would become like waves of water pouring on desert sand, waiting in vain to bear fruit."[53]

IN DEBATE WITH ARAB LIBERALS

Early in his intellectual and religious career, Ghazālī waged a major battle against a number of liberal Egyptian thinkers, especially Khālid Muḥammad Khālid and 'Alī 'Abd al-Rāziq.[54] The essence of this battle centered around the various definitions of identity (both national and religious) in the modern Arab world and the role of religion in shaping these definitions. As mentioned above, Ghazālī considers Ḥasan al-Banna to be his spiritual and intellectual mentor.[55] Ghazālī's ideas of the 1940s and 1950s were the product of his indebtedness to al-Banna's thought as well as to Ghazālī's own creative response to the liberal theses about the national identity of Egypt.

What is interesting about Egypt's intellectual milieu in the first half of the twentieth century is the preponderance of aggressive liberal voices calling for a redefinition of the social and political roles of Islam in the modern world. What is more surprising, however, is that the most effective of these calls came from an unexpected corner: the Azhar University and one of its teachers, 'Alī 'Abd al-Rāziq. In *Islam and the Principles of Government*,[56] 'Abd al-Rāziq raises a number of crucial although controversial questions about the nature of government in Islam and whether or not the Qur'an stipulated a government at all. A summary of his ideas is in order since it will elucidate the evolution of Arab political discourse since 1925, the year when the book came out.[57]

'Abd al-Rāziq argues the following points: first, as a political concept, Imamate[58] (that is, for Muslims to be ruled by an Imam) is not mentioned by either the Qur'an or the Sunnah. In other words, the Qur'an and the Sunnah, the two primary sources of Islam, do not promote an explicit political philosophy, neither do they command Muslims to establish a religious or theological state.[59] Second, although Arabs and Muslims were fascinated by Greek philosophy, especially the works of Plato and Aristotle, they neglected the discipline of political science, "whose place in their scientific activity was indeed modest."[60] Third, as an institution, the caliphate was established and maintained through military power, "The caliphate, in Islam, was founded upon repressive power, and this power, except in rare cases, was an armed physical force."[61] Fourth, Islam is inherently egalitarian promoting justice and freedom. That is to say, Qur'anic philosophy abhors repressive power. In addition, it is not necessary to have such an institution as a caliphate for Muslims to fulfill their religious duties and rites and manage their spiritual lives, "The caliphate has brought calamities upon Muslims and has been a great source of evil and corruption."[62] Fifth, Muslims have always believed that the Prophet was both a messenger and a political leader and that he established an Islamic political regime of which he was the head. Muḥammad was a messenger of God who communicated the divine message to all people. Muḥammad never desired to establish a government or preach the virtues of this transient life. He was in essence like the prophets who preceded him.[63] The Prophet exercised a spiritual power over his followers.[64] The human heart is the center of this spiritual power, whereas the caliphate is the center of physical power. Sixth, on the eve of Prophet's death, it was religious faith that united the Arabs, not political power. The Arab submission to the Prophet was of a spiritual and doctrinal nature and one of outright allegiance to political authority.[65] Seventh, the Prophet's religious (and spiritual) authority ended the moment he passed away. The choice of Abū Bakr to rule after the Prophet's death was a response to the political conditions in Arabia that had been gathering momentum since the early days of the Prophet's message. But Abū Bakr established an Arab state for Arabs, which was supported solely by the Arabs. Islam, on the other hand, was not addressed solely to Arabs; it was universal. The new state "supported the Arabs, served their interests and enabled them to control different realms which they colonized fully and exploited greatly. They did just what other nations do when they have the means to achieve conquest and colonization."[66] Eighth, from the first days of the caliphate onward, educated and lay Muslims have assumed that the caliphate is a religious title. Some *fuqahā'* even made it a religious requirement. The rulers propagated these notions and prohibited Muslims from reflecting on the discipline of political science. "All of this ended with the death of research faculty and intellectual activity amongst Muslims, who were afflicted by paralysis in political reflection and research into every aspect that may have a connection to the caliphate and caliphs."[67]

This debate illustrates a theme that has preoccupied the intellectual leadership of the Ikhwān since its founding, namely, the relationship between the ulama establishment and the Ikhwān. Egyptian Leftist thinker Rifa't al-Sa'īd argues that although Ḥassan al-Banna was antagonistic to the ulama and the interests they represented, he never severed his relationship with them. Moreover, he was careful about developing a relationship, albeit a cautious one, with the official religious establishment, and never went so far as to condemn the ulama.[68] To my mind, this assessment is inaccurate and obscures the bitter debate which arose shortly after Banna's death between several of his supporters, most notably Shaykh Ghazālī and the secular intelligentsia represented by the famous Khālid M. Khālid, about the nature and function of the ulama class in Egyptian society.

The debate that sparked the controversy revolved around two issues: the Ikhwān's call for "a return to religion," and the ulama's seizure of the new opportunity created by the Ikhwān's activism to promote a state-oriented religion.

The liberal attack on the ulama as a priestly and parasitical class was spearheaded by Khālid M. Khālid.[69] This debate, to be sure, was reminiscent of two previous cases in Egyptian intellectual life also represented by Azharites-turned-liberals Ṭāhā Ḥussain and ʻAlī ʻAbd al-Rāziq.[70]

In his still-relevant but controversial work, *From Here We Start*,[71] Khālid bitterly argues that there is a strong priesthood in contemporary Muslim societies, which is "pregnant with pernicious doctrines and deadly principles."[72] The sole aim of this class has been to exploit spirituality and the devotion to religion. It also

> commingled its interests with religious doctrine itself, thereby completing the desecration of religion...Later on, the priesthood, with consistency and with perseverance, went about envenoming everything with its deadly poison, consecrating economic and social reactionism and preaching eloquently the virtues and excellence of poverty, ignorance and disease.[73]

In Khālid's view, then, the type of truth represented by the priestly class is "a form of mental and religious terrorism."[74]

Nourished by critical liberal ideas, Khālid goes on to criticize, implicitly at least, the Ikhwān's doctrine of religion-society and religion-state compatibility by advocating the notion of liberating society from the bonds of religion. This is necessary in his view because any "priestly class," ancient or modern, ulama- or Ikhwān-oriented, serves as the embodiment of social injustice and exploitation of the poor. This class, "the fastest runner after booty, wealth, and pride,"[75] promotes superstition instead of rationalism and poverty instead of wealth. Khālid draws the conclusion that any meddling of religion in the affairs of society is apt to "annihilate the personality of the nation, to drag the whole people down into an abyss of servility and subjection, and to breed an instinct of following."[76] Religion, therefore, is far from being a liberating force in society; it subjugates humankind to the whims and desires of an egotistical, stagnant, and wealth-driven mentality.

Ghazālī also said that some of the ulama he knew acted like parasites sucking the blood of the poor.[77] In a scathing critique of Khālid M. Khālid's book, *From Here We Start*, Ghazālī writes, just a year after Banna's assassination, that there has indeed been a number of influential ulama who cared more about their personal welfare than the general happiness of Muslims:

> The men who now lead the defense of Islam are, without exception, bringing shame to themselves and their cause...The service of God and Mammon cannot be combined; nor can the duty of jihad be compatible with the pursuit of pleasure and comfort. It requires a really deranged mind to bring these opposites together in any system of human life. Such must be the minds of those Azharites who grow fat while Islam grows thin, and repose in comfort while [Muslims] suffer in anguish. These deceivers have devised devilish means for escaping the genuine duties of Islam. They are more crafty and sly than those hashish smugglers who escape justice and the police. On one hand, we have a group of men satisfied merely with the performance of personal worship. When they are asked to take care of the public, or observe the social duties of Islam,

> they answer despondently, "politics is not our business"...On the other hand, we have a group that fights sectarianism and worship of the dead, yet its members profess to belong to Muḥammad bin 'Abd al-Wahāb. They silently worship the living and sheepishly submit to the tyrants and despots of their "Wahābī" [Saudia Arabia] land...We have seen many leaders of al-Azhar who did not leave their office chairs until their pockets bulged with riches, though they claimed to be the "spiritual continuation" of the legacy of Muḥammad 'Abduh and Jamāl al-Dīn.[78]

One must keep in mind that these "internal Islamic debates" contain a large degree of self-criticism that may have affected the intellectual environment in which the early Ikhwān leadership grew. In one sense, what one witnesses here is a harsh critique directed by one Muslim group or camp against another. The view held by some that the Ikhwān avoided intellectual and theological disputations with other Muslim groups for the sake of unifying the diverse views in Islam does not hold water. The Ikhwān launched their movement in protest to what they perceived as "the declining state of Islam" and in response to the ineffectiveness of the guardians of Islam in defending and promoting it. The thesis that "the Brethren belong to no one special sect but are devoted to the bare essence of religion"[79] cannot be tested against the historical background of the Ikhwān. Secondly, Ikhwān thought on many matters, although shaped by the intellectual veracity of Banna, did not end with his death; new developments were necessary in the post-Banna stage.

A great deal of contemporary Arab thinkers assume that the past three decades in the Arab world, besides witnessing the resurgence of social movements using Islamic discourse to express political and social concerns, have witnessed the rise of intellectual liberalism, which can offer the only viable alternative to resurgent Islam.[80] One of the greatest intellectual engineers in the modern Arab world carrying the legacy of 'Alī 'Abd al-Rāziq is Khālid Muḥammad Khālid.[81] He begins where 'Alī 'Abd al-Rāziq leaves off in *al-Islām wa uṣūl al-Ḥukm* in 1925. As shown above, 'Abd al-Rāziq's main thesis revolves around the incompatibility of Islam and politics. The caliphate was an Arab invention. Both 'Abd al-Rāziq and Khālid acknowledge, however, that the relationship between religion and society in the modern Arab world is far from clear or over.

In *From Here We Start*, *Citizens and Not Slaves*,[82] *Democracy Forever*,[83] and *The Crisis of Liberty in Our World*,[84] Khālid argues a number of points: first, religion is a social phenomenon that satisfies indispensable social and psychological needs. A class of "religious men," or a "priesthood" always exploits religion for economic purposes, and its alliance with the most reactionary class in society, the feudalists, has always justified its existence.[85] As a reactionary force in Egyptian society today, the religious hierarchy "works for the impediment of evolution and progress, seeks to keep all social, economic and cultural principles at a standstill and prevents the inflow of new blood – that reactionary is a useful simpleton in the hands of imperialism and ignorance."[86] Second, democracy and the priesthood are incompatible. Priesthood, by virtue of its economic and political position, impedes progress and human rights.[87] Freedom is a divine right that is obliterated by unjust social and economic conditions. Third, priesthood opposes the evolution and progress of reason. In its true nature, religion is democratic and rational. It encourages free speculation and it respects all humans as the creation of one God. Fourth, Islam does not stipulate the establishment of a religious state throughout history; theocracy has proved to be anathema to humanity throughout history.[88]

What is the nature of Islam? Why are its basic principles unknown to Muslims and non-Muslims alike? Ghazālī takes up these questions in many of his writings, especially in *How Can We Comprehend Islam?*[89] The reason the world's people know about "Arab petroleum" more than they do "the Arab Qur'an" is because Muslims have failed to understand and disseminate the Qur'an, its principles and values. Ghazālī bitterly criticizes the contemporary Muslim generation for "insulting their religion" by abandoning it, and for "committing treason" as a result of neglecting its teachings. He angrily declares, "I am not aware of any treason that is worse than the one committed by the Muslims against their religion. They have neglected its call and busied themselves instead with their whims and personal desires."[90]

In his 1950s critique of the "Muslim priesthood," a response to Khālid M. Khālid's call for establishing a liberal, secular society where religion is relegated to the individual and religious liberty is safeguarded, Ghazālī ponders the meaning of the "religious class" in Islam specifically, its role in transmitting Islamic knowledge. He maintains that contrary to some socio-religious facts, Islam, in theory, does not sanction any religious hierarchy, especially the one that allies itself with the power elite and that gets rich at the expense of others. Religious education must not be the privilege of a special class of people, but should be available to every Muslim man and woman. Nevertheless, as a result of the accumulation of knowledge and the division of educational labor in most contemporary societies, a need arose in Muslim societies to train certain emotionally, mentally and religiously equipped people in the field of Islamic studies. This field, according to Ghazālī, needs to delve into the Islamic branches of knowledge – Qur'an, Hadīth, Arabic, history – and interpret these sciences in light of modern conditions. In other words, one must find a Fiqh for each branch that provides answers for the contemporary situation of Muslims. When examining existing Muslim institutions of learning and the way Islamic scholars are formed, Ghazālī finds both wanting. He bemoans the plight of traditional Islamic learning and intelligentsia "in a world that does not shed tears on the backward." He argues that in actuality, the Muslim hierarchy as it exists in modern society is so backward and weak that it cannot fulfill its mission, Islamically speaking. There is a scarcity of specialists in Islam who are equipped to lead Muslims both intellectually and religiously, "To my mind, the calamities befalling Islam lately are attributable to the lack of knowledgeable experts [in religion] and to the scarcity of deeply-learned ulama."[91] Religious education is in decline. The most capable students prefer a secular education to a religious for two fundamental reasons: (1) the state gives priority in filling its offices to secular graduates, and (2) secular education is more assertive in teaching students all sorts of interesting disciplines and languages.[92]

In a highly volatile age, Muslim religious education has failed to meet the necessary conditions of success for the following reasons:

1. a great number of the students in religious institutions lack the necessary skills, and mental and emotional preparedness to become ulama and preachers. As a result, many of the preachers who work in mosques do so because they have no other option in life;
2. religious institutions pay only lip service to the "secular sciences," such as the humanities and social sciences. Graduates of such schools usually abhor the non-religious sciences and fail to take advantage of this learning for the benefit of Islam;
3. even Islamic learning is transmitted in a debilitating manner. Most religious education is confined to the *fiqh al-'ibādāt* (Fiqh that deals with doctrinal matters). The Azhar as well as the Wahabi universities in Saudi Arabia are guilty of the same thing;
4. a gap exists between the idealistic preaching of religious institution graduates and their actual behavior in society. Many are alienated from society either because they are poor or are not equipped to deal with social and cultural change.[93]

In summary, the future of Islamic education is bleak. What are the ways of modernizing this educational system? This disintegration reflects negatively on the state of contemporary Muslim culture.

IN DEBATE WITH THE INNER ENEMIES OF ISLAM

For an Islamic movement in any part of the Muslim world to survive, it must engage in the difficult task of rational and critical enquiry, have theological depth, and fathom the intellectual and rational contributions of other nations. Blind submission to any doctrine thwarts the possibility of gaining healthy knowledge. There are many forces brewing under the surface in the contemporary Muslim world which have neglected the call of rational duty, and which operate under either false or ignorant doctrinal pretenses. Blind submission is the natural outcome of the marginalization of reason and the reduced space of rationality in the Muslim world. Ghazālī courageously takes up the question of contemporary Wahabiyyah, especially in Saudi Arabia, and criticizes its leading theologians of failing to equip Islamic thought and Fiqh with appropriate rational criteria. In daring to attack Wahabiyyah, Ghazālī incurred the wrath of its proponents; some have gone as far as to accuse him of being infidel to the mainstream teachings of Islam.

Ghazālī's *al-Sunnah al-nabawiyah bayna ahl al-fiqh wa ahl al-hadīth* represents the most daring critique of the modern historical formulations of Wahabi Fiqh. Ghazālī was not afraid to become embroiled in controversy as he was in his younger years, when he waged his attack against liberalism. Ghazālī was convinced that the most dangerous enemy comes from within, especially if this enemy is supported by petroleum wealth.

Ghazālī does not hide his appreciation of Islamic revivalism (*al-Ṣaḥwah al-islāmiyyah*). In this book, he warns both the leadership and youth of the Islamic movement lest they fall prey to the ideas of Ahl al-Hadīth, who control the religious scene in the Gulf states. He also encourages Muslim men to revisit the question of women in Muslim society, and examine that question in light of a fresh appraisal of Qur'anic text and the numerous traditions that discuss Islamic women.[94]

In a previous book, Ghazālī points out that Ahl al-Hadīth are so much preoccupied with the Sunnah that they purposely neglect the basic Qur'anic teachings.[95] For the Islamic movement to succeed, it has to digest the basic facts of Islam, be aware of the extent of colonialism in Muslim lands, and cognizant of the fact that the current governments[96] in the Muslim world desire that the intellectual leadership of the Islamic movement waste its time on trivial, petty, and irrelevant issues. An example of one such issue is whether or not shaking hands with a woman abrogates ablution.

Ghazālī bemoans the fact that the Azhar University, the oldest in the Muslim world and the pioneer institution in the spread of Islamic teachings, has lost its central position in the last three decades and has denied the Muslim world of valuable Islamic legal knowledge. Against this background, an aggressive new movement by the name of Ahl al-Hadīth has begun to fill the vacuum. Ghazālī was undoubtedly aware that this movement would not have arisen if it was not for the newly-gained status of the Gulf states, especially Saudi Arabia after the discovery of petroleum. With the decline of the Azhar and the rise in the economic fortunes of the Gulf states, a shallow "nomadic Fiqh" has taken root, and an immature conception of doctrine and legislation has taken hold.[97] Ghazālī documents some examples that prove the influence of the nomadic Fiqh on contemporary Muslim culture:

1. in a Gulf state, a nomad intentionally killed an American engineer and the Ahl al-Hadīth school opposed the killing of the Muslim on the basis that the blood of a non-Muslim is unequal to that of a Muslim;
2. Ahl al-Hadīth claim that the blood ransom for a killed woman is half that of a man's;[98]
3. some Ahl al-Hadīth claim that merchants are absolved of paying *zakāt* money.

The question of women's rights is still subject to much controversy in contemporary Muslim discourse. Ghazālī takes the side of women without claiming to be the Qāsim Amīn of his time. In *Dustūr al-wiḥdah al-thaqāfiyyah*, he emphasizes without any sort of hesitation that women are the sisters of men. This is a sacred principle. Both must search for knowledge equally since this is a religious duty. Women, within the ethical limits of religion, bear the responsibility of building the social and political foundations of Muslim society.[99]

Appalled by the abysmal condition of women in the contemporary Muslim world, Ghazālī unleashes his anger on Ahl al-Hadīth, whom he calls those "stagnant Muslims" who have darkened the image of Islam. They are the last stronghold impeding the progress of women in society. Ahl al-Hadīth and other backward Muslims devalue and dehumanize women.

Such a lamentable attitude in some corners of the Muslim world has given the enemies of Islam the opportunity to defame it in the name of human rights and freedom of expression. Alas, Muslims have miserably failed in presenting the real position of Islam, that of emancipation, toward this central issue. However, the battle over women's rights is far from over, and it is not confined simply to their dress. Ahl al-Hadīth stipulate that not only the head but also the face must be veiled, justifying this judgment by the Islamic principle that Islam stands against idolatry and showing a woman's face leads to idolatry. Others have taken the extreme view that on the basis of certain Hadīths, women leave their homes only twice throughout their lifetimes: one to go to their husband's house and the second to the grave.[100]

One must make no mistake about the widespread influence of Ahl al-Hadīth beyond the boundaries of Saudi Arabia. This movement has been very influential in the subcontinent of India since the early part of the nineteenth century.[101] Of late, it has established an important presence in several African countries, most notably Nigeria, and in the United States and Canada, as well. Its missionary zeal and undisputed presence in the holy sites of Islam has enabled it to spread its ideas far afield. Ghazālī speaks for another kind of Islam, an enlightened Islam that carries the burden of both sexes, since it is the sanity and viability of Islam in the contemporary world that matters. If Ahl al-Hadīth succeed in pushing their message, "it is inevitable that Islam will become a wide prison for women," Ghazālī concedes. Ahl al-Hadīth espouse an obsolete system of knowledge; it fails miserably on the issue of human liberties. The only solution is to stress the perfect emotional and mental equality of men and women, although there are some false Hadīths that stipulate that "women lack both religion and reason." Modern-day Muslims have inherited these defunct normative principles and the practices associated with them from the ages of decline. The net result has been the emotional, mental, and physical imprisonment of women. Ghazālī argues that the Qur'an does not prohibit women from seeking work, although it is the preference of many Muslim jurists that women take care of their household, which includes a proper education for the children. Women must participate in the social reconstruction of Muslim society. There is no stipulation that prevents them from being teachers, nurses, physicians and even soldiers. "I have noticed," says Ghazālī, "that the Jewish woman was responsible for our defeat [in 1967] and did participate in the creation of the state of Israel. She has done her religion and country great military and social services."[102] Many Christian women too have dedicated their lives to the service of the Muslims as part of their missionary philosophy.

Some Western voices have taken advantage of the negative Muslim treatment of women. Muslims must be blamed for this. To change things for the better, women must reclaim their autonomous personality, decide for themselves whom to marry, and be as active in congregational prayers as men. Ghazālī argues that Islam is not a regional and narrow-minded religion. It does not belong to one particular nation and must not be confined to some narrow juristic interpretations.[103] In the final analysis, the absence of democracy and the abundance of authoritarianism, parochialism, and extremism are the most powerful reasons for the decline of the Muslim ummah in the modern world.

ISLAM IN THE GULF

Throughout his intellectual career, Ghazālī was preoccupied with the Gulf region for two main reasons: one religious and the second economic and political. The Gulf area, especially the Arabian Peninsula, does not play the same Islamic role as it did in the past because of religious stagnation and scientific backwardness. The religious hierarchy in the Gulf is preoccupied with superstition and trivial religious and cultural issues. Europeans, on the other hand, have discovered oil and have invested a great deal of their scientific energy in extracting and processing this resource. Ghazālī laments the lack of aggressive and dynamic Muslim thinking. He feels that Muslim thought must parallel the modern situation. To enter the future encumbered with the failure of the age of decline would certainly lead to more failure and intellectual confusion.[104] In this age of military and scientific production, what have Muslims done? Ghazālī bitterly notes that Muslims are preoccupied with metaphysical issues and juristic questions with no relevance to the modern world. They lag behind the developed world because of the wrong views they have adopted, focusing on a materialistic mode of living, depending on corrupt political system, and lacking a future philosophy.

11
Islam and Muslims in Crisis

> "Today, Islam is a wounded religion. The majority of the nations that belong to it are the poorest of the Third World." Muḥammad al-Ghazālī, *Turāthuna al-fikrī fī mīzān al-shar' wa al-'aql* (Herndon: International Institute of Islamic Thought, 1991), 75.

> "No religious principle prevents Muslims from competing with other nations in the social and political fields of knowledge. Nothing prevents them from destroying that ancient system [of government] to which they have succumbed, and to build the edifice of their state and the system of their government on the basis of the most recent creation of the human mind and the strongest foundation of rule that was experienced by other nations." 'Alī 'Abd al-Rāziq, *al-Islām wa uṣūl al-ḥukm* (Beirut: Dār Maktabat al-Ḥayāh, 1978), 201.

> "[Our] pulpits carry out a negative, destructive program. Nine-tenths of our mosque preachers are still ignorant of the message that they should bring to people. Accordingly, they attempt to cure poverty with poverty and evil with evil. They urge the people to give up their society, and they incite them against it, teaching them to see in it such great evil that it appears unworthy of any respect or love." Khālid M. Khālid, *From Here We Start*, trans. Ismā'īl R. el-Faruqi (Washington, D.C.: American Council of Learned Societies, 1953), 55.

Ghazālī's unwavering support for a critical interpretation of Islam in the modern age has placed him at the forefront of the most advanced movement of modern Islamic criticism, which was pioneered by the reformers of the nineteenth century. In an age of competing philosophies and worldviews, no one can speak about passive and antiquated Islam. Criticism must be the *raison d'être* of the Islamic method. From the vantage point of critical Muslim scholarship in the modern Arab world, the Muslim *Weltanschauung* must first be revived if alleviation of "intellectual impairment" is to be achieved. Ghazālī poses the question, "What has gone wrong with modern Muslim culture?" to his Muslim audience with a bitter acknowledgment that the Muslim world is far from sound and that the road to recovery is long indeed. There is so much anger in Ghazālī's tone, so much disappointment with the state of affairs. Ghazālī's anger with the current Muslim conditions is the symbol of his passionate appeal to revive the critical soul of the modern Muslim world.

Although reason and criticism have their own limitations, they have not been exercised to their fullest. Fiqh, the heart of Islamic reason, was developed by early Muslim thinkers in their quest to produce a critical Muslim *Weltanschauung*. Fiqh, which derives its legitimacy from a thorough reading of Qur'anic principles and the Sunnah's elucidation of these principles, cannot be confined to pure theological science. On the contrary, Fiqh is the most serious Islamic religious discipline, which studies the interplay between the normative and the social, or the theological and the real. One can verify the sociology of Islam with the aid of Fiqh alone.

Ghazālī examines what he calls the "constitution of cultural unity amongst Muslims" (*dustūr al-wiḥdah al-thaqāfiyyah bayna al-muslimīn*) in an effort to determine the religious and ethical foundations of contemporary Muslim culture and the place of the concept of the "ummah" in this foundation. To this, Ghazālī utilizes his vast and complex knowledge of Islamic religious sciences while heeding the conditions and demands of the twentieth century. Against this background, he appeals to the life and teachings of Ḥasan al-Banna (henceforth referred to as Banna), the founder of the Ikhwān, and finds in Banna's tragic life the religious and cultural examples toward which Muslims must strive. He also emphasizes the important role of a movement, such as the Ikhwān, in the life of modern-day Muslims.

Although he was terminated from the Ikhwān movement in 1953, Ghazālī considered it as the most vital movement in modern Islam to achieve cultural unity in the Muslim world. In other words, cultural unity is the vehicle by which real transformation can take place and the legitimacy of this unity lies in a movement and not in the work of one or few individuals.

The foundation of a strong religious movement is not only necessary, but must be the first priority on the agenda of Islamic revivalism. Conceptually speaking, Fiqh must be at the heart of this movement if it is to survive. As Banna applied critical Fiqh in his quest to revive the Muslim world in the first half of this century, a reexamination at the end of the twentieth century has become quite necessary. The current state of the Muslim world has not improved much since independence: (1) colonialism is still a fact and continues to dominate the Muslim world both in terms of its modernity and modernization, and (2) corruption is still rampant in the Muslim world in politics, the economy, and social, moral, and individual conditions.[1] These two basic facts, according to Ghazālī, have had major consequences: colonialism has used political and economic pressure to maintain its interests in the Muslim world and it has developed its version of "cultural imperialism" (*al-isti'mār al-thaqāfī*) that "constantly appropriates hearts and values, and invades both doctrine and legislation."[2] Fiqh is the means out of this conceptual chaos.

The most unfortunate consequence of Muslim cultural decline, however, has been the inability of Muslim Fiqh, as a real Muslim discipline, to promote adequate concepts and methods with which to study the complex evolving social and historical conditions of Muslims. Fiqh philosophy has been confined to a narrow arena of Muslim life, to some areas of worship. What this means is that Fiqh was separated early on from the political engineering of the state. Also, two types of educational systems concurrently exist: the secular and religious. The ulama are mainly to blame for this condition since they were not able to comprehend the spirit of the modern world. Many even kept quiet when confronted with the polarization of the educational system.

As a matter of fact, Muslims have retreated from reason to unreason, from universalism to parochialism. This complex situation, however, has led to some major ruptures in the modern Muslim soul and mind. Muslims in general, and the Muslim intelligentsia in particular, have not been able to learn from the sciences and histories of other nations and religions. In others words, few have accepted the challenges of globalization. Second, Muslims have not appropriated the fruits of the technological and scientific progress for their own benefit. The advanced Western world has benefited from the "brain-drain." Third, the enemies of Islam have awakened to their enormous possibilities; they have made their desire to "assassinate Islam" very clear.[3]

This retreat from the "open-society mentality," that Ghazālī preaches is analogous to inner stagnation. It is naive to blame current Muslim problems solely on external enemies, that is to say, imperialism. Muslims were poised for colonization because of their inner division and weaknesses. This retreat, moreover, has led to what Ghazālī calls "scientific shortsightedness" (*al-quṣūr al-'ilmī*), by which he refers to two basic things: (1) Muslim misunderstanding of the objectives and principles of the Qur'an and how to apply them in their secular life, and (2) misuse of the Sunnah as the second basic source of Islamic knowledge.[4]

The revival of Fiqh stands at the heart of contemporary Muslim renaissance and cultural unity. The ascendancy of Fiqh in early Islam was made possible by the devotion of a great number of Muslim ulama who rejected the patronage of the political elite. Fiqh, luckily, escaped the clutches of political corruption. Jurisprudence was nurtured in more or less a free speculative environment. As a result, the four major schools of Sunni Islam have had many things in common, especially the belief in the general principles of Islamic revelation. But a number of factors – a combination of political corruption and mental leisure – has led to some unbridgeable gaps between the different schools. In the modern period, both Muḥammad 'Abduh and Rashīd Riḍa were exemplary in attempting to revive Fiqh as a source of unity among Muslims. They formed the most distinguished "School of Opinion" (*madrasat al-ra'y*) in modern Islam to which Ghazālī himself subscribed.[5]

This school proposed rigorous prescriptions for the revival of Islamic sciences. First, although it respects the opinions of its predecessors, it is not bound by their judgments; second, it prefers the Qur'an to the Sunnah as a source of knowledge, especially if the Ḥadīths are weak; third, it places reason at the source of judgment and, fourth, it does not believe that "abrogation" is an Islamic principle.[6] This school is flexible, open-minded, and rational. The Ikhwān have been the natural heirs to this school of thought.

The retreat from contemporary challenges is best exemplified by the Ahl al-Ḥadīth or Wahabi school of jurisprudence, as mentioned above. Although this school is very tiny, it has had a major impact on the modern Muslim world for two major reasons: first, the Wahabiyyah ensues from Arabia where the sacred Muslim places are and, second, with the discovery of oil, this school has been able to use money in order to influence people in other Muslim countries. Ghazālī claims that the Wahabiyyah attempt to impose a simple-minded Fiqh on a highly developed situation. He says, their "brains need a new overhaul."[7] These people are not cognizant of the civilizational gaps between the Muslim world and the rest of the world. They choose to face this world with the thought of the age of decline. As a result, there exist in modern Islam manufactured bridges between the different schools of Fiqh, Kalām, and mysticism. Every science has become an autonomous entity.[8]

The real decline of Fiqh as an independent Muslim discipline began when some *fuqahā'* (jurists) became subservient to the power elite. The rulers in the Muslim world, as in any religious society, had taken advantage of Fiqh to maintain their control, "A great number of Arab and Muslim rulers have become wealthy at the expense of the wretched [Muslim] people. They triumphed in the wake of spreading amongst the masses moral and mental damage (*damār 'aqlī wa khuluqī*)."[9] Some *fuqahā'*, unfortunately, supported these rulers and argue that the masses must be ruled by a strong individual.

In light of this bleak religious and cultural situation, what remedies does Ghazālī offer, philosophically speaking? The "frozen Fiqh" of yesteryear must give way to a new and dynamic Fiqh that can transform modern Muslim culture. Although Muslims must not borrow doctrines and ethics from other nations, they can borrow certain ways of thinking that serve the common interests of Muslims. Why can't Muslims borrow those rules that regulate finance? It is true that Ghazālī opposes "cultural imperialism," but he feels strongly that there are Western principles that must be adopted by the Muslim world. One such principle is democracy, which has the benefit of controlling political corruption and mitigating the effects of dictatorship. In this sense, Ghazālī differs from Muḥammad Quṭb and Sayyid Quṭb in their characterizations of the modern world as living in a state of *Jāhiliyyah*.[10] Democracy is a political system whose main aim is to ensure a proper relationship between ruler and ruled.[11] Ghazālī argues that the philosophy of democracy is not antithetical to Islam, but in fact is a requirement of correct Islamic thinking because "dictatorship has been the ghoul that has eaten up both our religion and our life."[12] Ghazālī states that Muslims should borrow those rules and ways of thinking that can meet their common interests. In other words, true Muslim intellectuals have to learn from the intellectual experience of other nations. One of the main principles of modern democracy is that opposition is healthy in a political system and is acceptable by both ruled and ruler.[13] Muslims have borrowed only the externals of the triumphant Western democracy during their period of decline and stagnation.

THE MISSION OF THE *DĀ'IYAH* (PREACHER)

In an age of competing philosophies and worldviews, Muslim preachers (*du'āh*) cannot afford to be ignorant or self-complacent. The field of *da'wah*, contends Ghazālī, is not a place for the shortsighted and non-educated. The *du'āh*, as a special category of the ulama, emerged with the gradual historical evolution and sophistication of Islam, which needed people to preserve and spread its essential message.[14] In the present time, the Islamic movement paid a close attention to the training of *du'āhs*, who must assume their role as the backbone of modern Islam. However, in many Arab and Muslim countries, the Ministry of Religious Endowments or Awqāf has shouldered this responsibility, competing with popular Islamic activism. Ghazālī, first and foremost, was an Islamic preacher, a person well versed in the Qur'an and Muslim tradition, who sought to spread the Islamic message.

It is unfortunate, maintains Ghazālī, that Muslims have not done much in the twentieth century to disseminate their message. Even in petroleum-dominated countries, the Islamic *da'wah* is sluggish and has been curtailed. Several reasons explain the servility of the *da'wah* mission: first, the Muslim world is not as organized as the Christian missionaries have been in spreading their message to remote corners of the world. Only a group of loosely connected people have shouldered this immense responsibility.[15] Second, the Arabic language has been neglected in many Muslim countries. Third, the sectarian (*madhabī*) differences among Muslims have impeded the process of *da'wah* and, fourth, the Muslim ummah, in its state of weakness, has forgotten to communicate its essential social and political messages to people of other nations.[16]

However bleak this picture is, Muslims have created popular means to spread their message in the absence of assistance from the state. Once again, Ghazālī refers to the popular engagement with and preservation of the Islamic ethos. To communicate effectively, the *du'āh* must be equipped with the following: first, closeness to the Sacred. The *du'āh* must take the Qur'an as their main criterion of truth and must be in constant communication with God. Second, they must improve their ethical and spiritual standards. Third, they must fully understand both the main principles of religion and the actual world situation. No *dā'iyah* can succeed if he fails to take these facts into consideration. No one operates in a vacuum. To be effective, preaching must reflect people's problems and concerns.[17]

Ghazālī connects *da'wah* with education and even enlightenment. It is tragic that modern Muslims have neglected the ethic of serious reading. The *du'āh* must rediscover this ethic and be abreast of recent theories in the natural and social sciences and humanities. A new brand of *du'āh* must be organized to combat several centuries of religious stagnation and disengagement.

By identifying *da'wah* with education and enlightenment, Ghazālī encourages the *du'āh* to discover the paths of analysis and criticism. The first thing they must do is take an analytical look at the definition of Islam itself, "Islamic thought is not the same as Islam, but is the mental creation of the Muslim thinkers who ponder the principles of Islam."[18] Both are serious endeavors. Islam is the creation of the divine, whereas Islamic thought is the creation of humans, "Islamic thought is contingent [*mustaḥdath*], and it is subject to the law of evolution and the factors of decline...Islamic thought is not immune to weakness and errors, whereas Islam is infallible."[19] There is nothing in the duality between the normative and the historical that prevents the Muslim *du'āh* from producing a critical religious discourse that promotes the Islamic message.

To be totally equipped with both analytical and critical tools, the modern *du'āh* must learn from history. In its formative phase, Muslim thought did not hesitate to learn from foreign sources, incorporating ideas from cultures that were more advanced than were the Arabs of the time. Doing so enables Muslims to better comprehend the Qur'an and see it from different perspectives. Muslim thought divided the Islamic sciences into main branches, "*ulūm naqliyyah*," that is, those sciences that deal with matters of doctrine and belief and which are not accessible to human reason and "*ulum 'aqliyyah*," such as philosophy and logic. The evolution of Islamic thought was a function of the movement and dynamism adopted by the early Muslims.

Muslim thought espoused a progressive and rational perspective, and Muslims were thus able to develop a unique brand of modernity that was rational, dynamic, creative, and risk-taking. However, the cancellation of *ijtihād* as a primary principle of Islamic jurisprudence had drastically negative effects on Muslim thought. Ghazālī more or less adheres to the Orientalist thesis that from the thirteenth century on, the Muslim world ushered in a state of rigidity and was awakened in the nineteenth century under the trampling feet of Western imperialism.[20]

Ghazālī's critical analysis of the state of Islamic thought and the needs of modern *du'āh* points to the urgent need to recognize and then overcome the reasons behind decline, which seems to have been self-perpetuating since the thirteenth century. Ghazālī contends that decline was predicated more on philosophical-epistemological than on socio-economic factors. He enumerates the following reasons: first, Islamic thought in the age of decline failed to express the essential *raison d'être* of the Qur'an and the objectives of the Prophetic message. Second, the science of Kalām, as a symbol of the expansion of Muslim reason, lost its original purpose. Third, some sects deviated from mainstream Islam. Fourth, mysticism took the place of Fiqh in the Muslim rational discourse; and fifth, Muslim theologians became more concerned with rhetoric and sophistry than with the revival of true Muslim thinking.[21]

In addition to re-establishing a critical and rational Muslim discourse within the limits set by the Qur'an, Ghazālī argues that the modern-day *du'āh* must profoundly consider the main purpose of the Islamic doctrine or *'aqīdah*. Reminiscent of Sayyid Quṭb's discussion of the role of *'aqīdah* in modern Muslim life, Ghazālī espouses the revival of the *'aqīdah* against a backdrop of increasing spiritual and intellectual chaos in modern Muslim culture. A revived science of Kalām that is in tune with spirituality is urgently needed. In the classical age, Kalām defended Muslim doctrine rationally. However, it failed to promote itself for a number of reasons: first, it became a highly abstract and logical science to the point of only paying lip service to the emotional and spiritual dimensions of Islam. In other words, the science of Kalām, akin to a "dryness in the rational thinking of Muslims,"[22] ceased to inspire Islamic thought, especially during the age of decline. Second, this science became an easy target for those who promoted dissension; it was used for political ends. Third, the science of Kalām, which developed in Islam's Golden Age, stayed an empty shell after this period ended. It dealt only with dead issues that had no relevance to the revival of Islamic sciences and the Islamic way of life. As a result, many books dealing with the science of Kalām and transmitted to the modern Muslim world do not adequately explain the objectives of the *'aqīdah*, nor do they reflect the real interplay between the normative and historical in the Islamic consciousness.[23]

In an age of metaphysics, decline and confusion in speculative thinking in the Muslim world, rationality and spirituality must complement one another. No modern *dā'iyah* or religious person can afford to survive without both. Furthermore, rationality and spirituality reflect the *'aqīdah*'s dual nature. On the one hand, there is the Creator, the infallible, the first and the last;[24] and, on the other, there is the created world, where man is given a leading position as vicegerent of God on earth. God has endowed man with strong rational faculties with which to understand the main purposes of revelation and perform his role as God's vicegerent.[25] Ghazālī argues that,

> In the Islamic Sharī'ah, God gives reason the most privileged position in comprehending the principles of the revealed text and in formulating rules where no revelatory text is present...This reason...permeates every meaning in the universe, from the most trivial, such as clearing the road from dirt, to the most sublime, such as the meaning of divinity and unity.[26]

The reason–spirit duality reflects another long-standing duality in man's life: freedom of choice versus predestination. A human cannot choose the facts of his birth, although he may be free to choose his destiny. Predestination and freedom of choice go hand in hand. To live a meaningful life, man must possess a certain measure of autonomy, "Our feeling points out to both the autonomy of our will and our ability to carry out those functions that fall under their jurisdiction."[27] The theological philosophy of Islam revolves around the notion of *taklīf*; that is, giving man a good measure of responsibility in order to fulfill the will of the divine. However, it is impossible to carry out *taklīf* if human will is abolished.[28] In one sense, what Ghazālī argues is that predestination is not absolute. Man has goals in life and possesses the abilities to reach those goals.

Responsibility is at the heart of the Islamic message. No *du'āh* can succeed in spreading the Islamic message unless the dust of lazy ages is removed. Islam has no place for stagnant and uneducated *du'āh*. The individual or ummah that carries no message is doomed to eternal failure and disease.[29]

VIEWS OF THE WEST AND NATIONALISM

The West has been an object of fascination, fear, and envy in the contemporary Muslim world. A good number of Muslim thinkers have tried to grab hold of the West, so to speak, and they stumbled on a huge presence, to say the least.[30] Following in the footsteps of Ḥasan al-Banna[31] and other modern Muslim thinkers, Ghazālī distinguishes between three entities in the West: Christianity, Western civilization, and Western imperialism.

In the nineteenth century, Muḥammad 'Abduh distinguished between Western civilization and Christianity. He felt sorry for the latter and bitterly attacked the former.[32] Ghazālī's point of departure is not the materialism of the West as much as the weakness of Islam. He states that the main difference between the modern

Muslim world and Western civilization is that where the former has been constrained by blind imitation and its negligence of reason, the latter has been characterized by creativity and the supreme utilization of reason in discovering the rules of nature and science in general. As a Muslim thinker,

> I do view the Western brand of life with an eye of justice. The Western civilization has paid its utmost respect to the universe – and this is a main principle in Islam – , it has studied it, and as a result, it has come closer to the pristine nature of man (*fiṭrah*), much more than we have. Blind traditions have eaten up our ummah and put constraints on its ways of progress.[33]

In the age of imperialism, the Muslim ummah found itself prey to inner stagnation and insurmountable external challenges. The most difficult of these was how to revive Muslim thought after many centuries of decline and in the absence of freedom of thought. It is likely that the onslaught of colonialism awakened in Muslims a deep desire to shoulder their responsibility as an ummah endowed with a divine mission. The Muslims' economic, military, and political defeats betrayed this urgent need. The current leadership of the Muslim ummah faces a formidable task. How is it possible to come to grips with the perplexing state of affairs in the Muslim world when intellectual confusion reigns supreme, worldviews have collapsed, and Muslims display their failure to envision the tremendous challenges posed by imperialism?[34]

Ghazālī does not scapegoat imperialism as much as he criticizes the ineptitude of Muslim leadership. In the absence of cultural and intellectual creativity, the Muslim world has fallen prey to what Ghazālī and many other Arab scholars term "cultural invasion," which is the most dangerous form of Western imperialism initiated to date against Muslim and Third World people. The imperialist, according to this analysis, is not satisfied with pure conquest of territory, but is hard at work plotting to destroy Muslim doctrine (*'aqīdah*) by creating a "novel colonialist religion" in the name of Muslim lethargy and stagnation. However, the main goal behind creating this "colonialist religion" is to distract the attention of the most intelligent Muslims from the real social and political challenges and place them in a defensive position. Qadianism in India and Bahaism in Iran are such "colonialist religions."[35] In short, the West, responsible for the birth of new religious movements in the Muslim world, uses these movements to then attack the central premises of Islamic monotheism.

Progress, to be sure, is not an inherently Western quality. The human race has known progress in a multitude of different forms and expressions. However, the modern Muslim world stands behind other nations in civilizational achievement. Its people do not fathom the depth of science and embrace progress. One may forward a number of reasons for the absence of progress in the contemporary Muslim world. However, the main reason lies in the failure of Muslims themselves to appropriate and assimilate the different sciences and to live productively in the world.[36]

To speak of decline is to target many ills, one of which is that Muslims, according to Ghazālī, are infested by "false religiosity" (*tadayyun maghshūsh*).[37]

The root of this phenomenon lies deep in the past, long before Western intrusion. Muslims were in the habit of self-flagellation, accumulating gloomy pictures of their collective personalities and ways of life. In the struggle against colonialism, it was not Islam, which was defeated, since it was not part of this battle, but those onerous notions and stagnant traditions.[38] The historical Muslim self, therefore, was betrayed, and a new sense of historical self has taken shape in the Muslim consciousness.

However, the West benefits from giving creativity a free hand in enhancing man's mental and cultural propensities. Because of this immense creativity, modern Western civilization has succeeded where pre-modern cultures have not. Man, instead of being subservient to nature, becomes its master. Europeans, driven by the new spirit of progress, made great advances in both the physical and the mental worlds. On the other hand, the Muslims acquiesced to a suspended state of lethargy and dependency. The abysmal decline of Muslim reason in the modern period is one major reason for today's Muslim backwardness.

In the same vein, the West created its own form of democracy. No one can sanely deny Western achievements in this field. "As Muslims," says Ghazālī,

> we cannot deny Western progress at both the social and political levels. But, alas, the virtues of democracy are not for export. I do congratulate the Western countries for the disappearance of dictatorship from their midst, the stability of their legislative councils, the freedom attained by every individual, and the competition of the intelligent minds to serve the common good.[39]

It is with such argument that Ghazālī revisits the question of "cultural invasion" (*al-ghazw al-thaqāfī*), which was not an issue in the Muslim culture in the formative phase. Ghazālī and other contemporary Islamist thinkers use the term to define three distinct but interrelated items: first, a historical process begun by the Western occupation of many Muslim countries in the nineteenth century; second, the transfer of Western ideas to Muslim culture, or the infusion of the ideas of the expanding Center into a retreating Periphery and, third, the resulting battle over ideas in contemporary Muslim culture.

The historical Muslim self, due to its antiquated nature, offered no significant resistance to "cultural invasion," which went hand in hand with the military invasion of the Muslim world. While the West was preoccupied with the achievement of both progress and democracy at home, it exercised a double-edged policy in the Muslim world: first, it aimed to control the resources of the Muslim world while, second, unleashing its "historical anger" against Islam and Muslims.[40] The modern West has revived the religious spirit of its past. Ghazālī claims that a number of facts substantiate "the cultural invasion" of the Muslim world by the West: first, communism fed into the ancient Christian and Jewish rivalry with the world of Islam. Second, imperialism principally aims at "assassinating" the Islamic religious sciences by creating a counter-culture, a culture infused with the materialist values of the West. This has already been accomplished through the creation of a dual system of education in the Muslim world and creating a new Westernized intelligentsia that looks at the Arabo-Islamic tradition with suspicion and fear.

Third, because they were backward, Muslims did not participate in the creation of the modern scientific culture, for which "We certainly deserve defeat."[41] Fourth, "cultural invasion" was facilitated by the misuse of political power and the maintenance of dictatorship by a "gang of politicians." This dictatorship has always "usurped private as well as public money and has constantly driven people to the wall."[42] Fifth was the spread of superstitions and mystical ideas.

These daunting factors have created much confusion in contemporary Muslim society; the direct result has been deviation from the main path of Islam. In other words, the Muslim world has not digested well the central lessons of modernity; neither has it taken to heart the main teaching of Islam. The net result of all of this is that Muslims have suffered both psychologically and mentally. Corruption in religious feeling; the consistent declining value of the Muslim individual; suspension of reason, and the refusal to follow the true teachings of Islam characterize the state of culture in the modern Muslim world.[43] Because of all of this,

> Undoubtedly, imperialism has succeeded in creating a generation of Muslims who cooperate with the enemies of Islam to destroy their own religion. Unfortunately, a good number of educated men believe that Islam is a religion only and not a state. More unfortunately, a number of ulama have been converted to this trend of thought, perhaps without realizing its full import.[44]

Clearly, the Western world has advanced ahead of the Muslim world. Muslims establish research foundations in order to bridge these scientific gaps. Ghazālī asserts that one of the historical mistakes Muslims have committed in recent times is to not understand the advanced "Other" and the real scientific and cultural reasons behind the progress of the "Other," "Our research about the 'Other' is zero."[45] In order to be faithful to the commands of revelation, Muslim intellectuals must pursue the following:

1. examine and fathom the cultural creativity demonstrated by advanced cultures;
2. comprehend ways and means that lead to urban, technological, and civilization modernization;
3. research military power, political and social trends in the advanced world;
4. fight corruption and intellectual deviation in modern Muslim culture so that Muslims reconsider their sources of knowledge, the Qur'an and the Sunnah;
5. rebuild the foundations of the Muslim ummah on the eternal principles of Islamic revelation;
6. come to grips with Islam as a practical and gradual religion;
7. ascertain the *turāth* (Muslim tradition) with a critical eye and examine it against the Qur'an and Sunnah.[46]

As stated before, religious circles in the Muslim world are characterized by "stagnation and narrowness of mind [*quṣūr wā jumūd*]."[47] This results in "psychological and scientific defeats [*hazāi'm nafsiyyah wā 'ilmiyyah*]."[48] The Islamic movement has been besieged by an inexperienced staff of callers who carry "forged knowledge and double ignorance [*'ilm maghshūsh wā jahl murakkab*]."[49]

For contemporary Muslim culture to revive, it must adopt the following principles:

1. women and men must be seen as equal in terms of their human, emotional, and mental capacities, as well as in their religious duties and rights;
2. the family must be seen as the core unit of society and both men and women should collaborate in building strong families;
3. human rights should be recognized as a prerogative of every man and woman and people must be defined by their ethical and intellectual values;
4. rulers must be seen as the servants of their people;
5. *shūrah* or democracy must be the basis of government;
6. private property must be protected on the basis of certain conditions;
7. communicating the Islamic message should be the responsibility of Muslim political and social institutions;
8. religious differences in the world should not lead to dispute;
9. Muslim international relations must be based on the brother- and sisterhood of men and women;
10. Muslims must contribute, along with other nations, toward the progress of man.[50]

Ghazālī devotes a good part of his writing to attacking the secular and Westernized indigenous intelligentsia who, in his view, are:

1. the product of Western and missionary education;
2. consider Islam as backward and anti-rational;
3. conspire with foreign enemies to destroy the remaining foundation of Muslim culture;
4. are pawns in the hand of the Cold War that aims at destroying the political unity of Egypt.

> There are Egyptian Orientalists who were born in this land of ours, but whose hearts and minds were reared in the West...Although they are of our book and speak our language, they pose a mortal danger to our existence. As proponents, out of conviction or interest, of the Cold War that imperialism launched against us, following the war of destruction that tore our human *ummah* apart in the past century, they disbelieve in both Arabism and Islam.[51]

He poses the question: how can we salvage this "exhausted ummah" from imperialism and internal decline? This is the question facing the ulama.

As a religion, Islam strongly values reason. The values of Western civilization have placed a wedge between reason and religion, and this explains the pervasiveness of materialism in the West. The ethic of materialism is antithetical to religious principles. Ghazālī reminds us that we must respect Western civilization for its scientific spirit. Many Muslim thinkers and people of letters, schooled in the West, adopted Western materialistic ideas *en masse*. Consequently, "they pay only little attention to the religion of their defeated ummah. Meanwhile, their hearts have been greatly saturated with great admiration of the conquering civilization, and its customs, even if they were the most trivial of all."[52]

Some Arab thinkers have fallen prey to Western attitudes toward modern Islamic thought and history. They attack the school of 'Abduh and Riḍa, and claim that Islam is a backward religion. Ghazālī argues that some of us mistakenly assume that "achieving political independence from the West means automatically civilizational and intellectual independence...This is but an illusion."[53] He rebuts the ideas of Jubrān Shāmiyah of the American University in Beirut who holds that secularism is the natural child of freedom of thought. Religion must not be imposed by the state or clergy. It should be left to the individual to decide. Europeans and Israelis took advantage of reason and developed scientific and intellectual capacities, whereas Arabs presented a medieval religious mentality. Atatürk built a modern and secular state. If they are to achieve progress, Arabs must follow suit.[54] "European culture [education] assumes the lead position in our national cultural and mental life as well as in our systems of thinking. We do not expect these [missionary] schools to create committed citizens who are endowed by a strong nationalist feeling."[55] To Ghazālī, secularism means treason to Muslim language and heritage.[56]

Ṭāhā Ḥussain is one of the major symbols of Western culture in the Arab world. Ghazālī, in his criticism of Ḥussain, points to the following: (1) Ḥussain considers Islam and Muslim history to be subservient to national education; (2) liberals and Westernized intellectuals in Egypt prefer Ḥussain to al-'Aqqād, although the latter is considered to be more knowledgeable than Ḥussain. Ḥussain is a challenge to the reconstruction of modern Muslim culture.[57]

At one time in his life, Ghazālī believed in the power of Arab nationalism to find a solution to the Arab predicaments. We must remember that before 1967, Ghazālī was serving in the Ministry of Religious Affairs in the Egyptian government. It is interesting to see how his ideas evolved after 1967; that is, after the political defeat of Nasserism in the 1967 war. Ghazālī gives credit to Arab nationalism in the form of the Egyptian nation-state for the great service it provided the masses: freeing them from colonialism, granting them political and social freedoms, and improving their economic conditions. But these governments will not realize their major goals of economic prosperity and social freedom as long as they insist on separating Islam from the public realm. As a state functionary under Nasser, Ghazālī was dissatisfied with the state of Islam, especially when the nation-state permitted all sorts of foreign ideas to flourish.

> The Arab *ummah* is the heart and brains of Islam. The aim of crusaderism [*al-ṣalībiyyah*] behind its intervention in the Muslim world is to achieve both *fitnah* and deviation. However, it is cognizant of the fact that its efforts will meet in failure if Arabism becomes part of a new renaissance that unifies it and makes its mission flourish...We do realize, however, that crusaderism is gathering enormous political, economic, and cultural forces in order to create a wedge between the Arabs and Islam and belittle its principles in their eyes.[58]

To Ghazālī, any Arab renaissance without Islam at the center is a missionary endeavor. He opposes the brand of Arab nationalism that argues that the Arab reality is the source and Islam has only been a stage in Arabism. The Prophet was an Arab hero and the Arab mind was completed by the resurgence of Arab nationalism.[59]

Revolution often paves the way for change. Ghazālī believes that Arab nationalism, wedded to the spirit of Islam, is the solution to the predicament of colonialism. Arab nationalism is the correct response to colonialism and the backward social, economic, and political conditions in which Muslims live. As a result of the success of nationalism and the Syrian-Egyptian unity of 1959, colonialism resorted to (1) reviving regional and tribal feelings, and (2) reviving sectarian differences after it had realized that the nationalist response was going to liberate the Eastern church from the influence of the West and Western missionary activities.[60]

MODERN MUSLIM RATIONALISM?

Islamist movements in the contemporary Arab world are haunted by a dilemma or they are stuck with the impossible. The dilemma exists simply in the ideal of Islamist movements to establish an Islamic political system. In addition to being incapable of establishing an Islamic political regime, the contemporary Arab elite have successfully competed to win the allegiance of the religious masses. How did Ghazālī deal with such a fact? Didn't he lend a helpful hand to the Egyptian state in thwarting the attempts of the Ikhwān to establish an Islamic political system? Here we have a traditional Muslim thinker identified from the start with the class of the ulama and becoming a member of the Muslim Brotherhood movement in the 1940s. Ghazālī's career proved to be different from that of the founder of the Ikhwān, who was murdered by the Egyptian secret police in 1949, and was also different from that of Sayyid Quṭb, who was hanged by the nationalist Egyptian regime in 1965. Both of these important figures were slated to become martyrs in the modern Islamist consciousness. Ghazālī, just like other major thinkers of the Ikhwān who supported the Nasser regime, such as Shaykh Ḥassan al-Baqūrī and Ahmad Kamāl Abū'l Majd, was able to ride the storm of the tumultuous events in Egypt before and after the eclipse of the monarchy in 1952. He was even given an important post by the Nasser regime. Ghazālī rose to prominence after the death of Nasser in 1970 and became known as the most significant preacher (*dā'iyah*) in the Muslim world. He was sought after not only by the young Islamists in the Arab world, Asia, Europe and North America, but also by a number of Arab regimes, which saw him as a voice of moderation in the midst of the roaring Islamic revival in Algeria and the Gulf states.

As stated above, although terminated from the Muslim Brotherhood movement in 1953 for accepting to work with the Nasser government, Ghazālī remained committed to the broad outlines of Banna's thought.[61] Ghazālī also stressed once and again his indebtedness to Afghānī's and 'Abduh's Islamic reform movement. The Ikhwān literature is replete with references to these two major figures in modern Muslim thought and practice. However, one must draw certain distinctions between the thought of Islamic reform and that of the Ikhwān. The principal aim of the Ikhwān has been to achieve political authority as a means of building its ideal society and state. The reform movement, on the other hand, preached reform without placing political authority at the top of its agenda. Ghazālī was surely influenced by the philosophical arguments of the reform movement, especially in relation to restoring the role of the reason in modern Islamic thought. To his mind, both Afghānī and ʻAbduh made great effort in salvaging Muslim reason and redefining the role of the ulama in the modern Muslim world. They fought very hard to rid the modern Arab world of its stagnation and backwardness,

> Afghānī was cognizant of the fact that superstitions permeated the social space of the defeated Muslims [*muslimīn munhazimīn*], and was cognizant of the evil, desire, and exploitation accompanying the European renaissance. He then began to interpret and present Islam in a way that attacks the arrogant [Europeans] and awaken the defeated [Muslims].[62]

Afghānī fiercely rejected any separation whatsoever between Islam and reason, *shūrah* and governing, man and freedom. He was strict in his connection between matters of worship and the purity of the soul, between dependence on God and showing piety vis-à-vis life and the friendship of the elite.[63]

However, Ghazālī remained convinced during his collaboration with the Nasser regime and after Nasser's death in 1970 that Islam cannot be fully realized in the modern age without an Islamic state; a state that rules in the name of the Sharīʻah. Hence, his disdain of what has been termed the "secularist camp" in the modern Arab world and those ulama who did not make politics as their priority. The Islamic state remained a priority in Ghazālī's discourse until the end of his life.

Although leading to some forms of revival of Islam, the post-1967 Arab world has not, on the whole, embraced the political or legal philosophy of the Ikhwān. Before his death, Ghazālī found some solace in new youth of the Gulf and North Africa, especially in Algeria, who were searching for the meaning of Islam in their lives. He was invited to teach in Qatar by one of his students, Yūsuf al-Qaraḍāwī, perhaps the most famous preacher in the contemporary Muslim world. However, he decided to leave Qatar for Algeria after being enticed by the regime there. Ghazālī received a great welcome from the Algerian regime in the 1980s, just a few years before the Islamist storm flooded the poor neighborhoods of that country. Although he became the most famous preacher in contemporary Algeria since the days of Bin Badīs, his preaching failed to calm down the storm there. Algeria became embroiled in violence a few years after he left the country.[64]

Ghazālī's death in 1996 closed a major chapter in contemporary Islamist thought. Regardless of the criticism one may level at Ghazālī or the "fundamentalist" attitudes that he may have espoused, he was and still is an inspiration to many Islamist thinkers and activists in the contemporary Arab and Muslim worlds. Many of these thinkers have heeded his passionate plea for the restoration of Muslim society and law.[65] Will his vision be fulfilled in the twenty-first century? Will there be more angry preachers like him? Only the future will tell that. On the whole, however, Ghazālī, like Banna and Quṭb before him, did not see the "Islamic state" materialize during his lifetime. The Arab and Muslim world remains as divided as ever, if not more so. Contemporary conditions in the Arab world are still very ripe for Islamism to reinvent itself and once again become a major player in the religious and political life of the Arab world.

12
Towards a Critical Arab Reason: The Contributions of Muḥammad ʿĀbid al-Jābirī

"At the very moment when the native intellectual is anxiously trying to create a cultural work he fails to realize that he is utilizing techniques and language which are borrowed from the stranger in his country. He contents himself with stamping these instruments with a hallmark, which he wishes to be national, but which is strangely reminiscent of exoticism." Franz Fanon, *The Wretched of the Earth* (New York: Grove Press, 1968), 223.

"[Philosophy] is the first cause of man's intellectual activity and his emergence from the sphere of animals, and it is the greatest reason for the transfer of tribes and peoples from a state of nomadism and savagery to culture and civilization. It is the foremost cause of the production of knowledge, the creation of sciences, the invention of industries, and the initiation of the crafts." Jamāl al-Dīn al-Afghānī, "The Benefits of Philosophy," in Nikki R. Keddie, *An Islamic Response to Imperialism: Political and Religious Writings of Sayyid Jamāl al-Dīn al-Afghānī* (Berkeley: University of California Press, 1983), 110.

"[F]urthermore, can a national culture be achieved completely in countries where the material bases of power are not indigenous but are dependent on foreign metropoli?" Eduardo Galeano, *Days and Nights of Love and War*, trans. Sandra Cisneros (New York: Monthly Review Press, 2000), 175.

Does the process of decolonization come to a close by the time the "natives" achieve their independence, as Franz Fanon seems to imply in his classic, *The Wretched of the Earth*?[1] Or does decolonization encompass the cultural aspects of a nation, besides its political freedom? One has to agree with Fanon that decolonization is first and foremost a violent process. Often, a strong coalition of heterogeneous forces embarks upon a violent program of decolonization, taking its cue from other liberation forces around the world. In the case of Morocco under French colonization, the nationalist coalition put its faith in the king as the symbol of opposition against French colonial presence.[2] However, once the king is installed after political independence is achieved, his status escalates and those around him begin to spread the false assumption that besides being the "father" of the nation, the nation's prosperity and stability also lie in his hands.[3]

Although the process of political decolonization is successfully completed, it is unlikely that the country has achieved economic independence, even decades after the termination of political colonialism. In the same vein, it is unlikely that the country has broken away from the cultural influence of the colonial center, which will have left behind its indelible cultural imprint. All of these realities challenge the "native intellectual" in his capacity as theoretician of culture once the colonizer has departed. The task of the post-colonial nationalist intellectual is indeed formidable.[4] The intellectual, philosopher, or writer does not possess the material means, the physical force, to single-handedly construct the new nation-state. This important task is left to the bureaucracy, police force, and new people who surround the king. These people often mediate between the palace and the people, as in the colonies of yesteryear. The philosopher possesses the power of his argument, his logical charm, and perhaps a series of long forays into the cultural and religious history of his nation's past. The revolutionary philosopher takes a leading role in providing the masses with a quality education. Typically, the masses have had long been dehumanized and deprived of this valuable commodity and made backward by the colonizer. In the new nation-state, the philosopher finds him or herself in competition with the Ministry of Education, which is set up by the government to regulate, order, and dominate the "thinking habits" of the people.[5] The post-colonial nationalist intellectual and philosopher, although steeped in the cultural ways of the West, turns his/her attention to the cultural legacy of the people, looking for ways to salvage the cultural values of a broken nation.

It is unrealistic to expect such an intellectual to accomplish much alone. He or she usually represents a whole nationalist movement, a political, economic, and cultural attitude or way of life. The nationalist movement in Morocco, as in Algeria, was a coalition of heterogeneous forces that represented both Berber and Arab, rural and urban, and rich and poor.[6] Post-colonial North Africa, especially Morocco, Algeria, and Tunisia, emerged from colonialism carrying a heavy economic, political, and cultural burden. In the long struggle against French colonialism, the nationalist movement articulated three major positions on independence: pan-Arabism, pan-Maghrebism, and local nationalism. In each of the three countries, local nationalism was to triumph and pave the way towards its country's independent industrialization without significant economic or political coordination with other Maghrebi or Arab countries.

In Muḥammad 'Ābid al-Jābīrī's view (hereinafter referred to as Jābīrī), the idea of the Maghreb evolved from the local to regional to Arab levels in response to the complex structure of colonialism imposed on each of the three Arab countries. Internally, the reaction against colonialism was spearheaded by a mixture of Salafī and nationalist forces, who were aware of the importance of Arab-Islamic culture in the fight against cultural colonialism.[7] However, this alliance, which fought a winning battle against colonialism, for all sorts of reasons, did not succeed in achieving regional or Pan-Arab unity after independence.[8] To a large extent, Jābīrī's thought has matured against the absence of regional or Pan-Arab unity in North Africa. The intention of this chapter is to examine Jābīrī's philosophical project as an expression of contemporary Arab nationalist thought, which seeks to make profound changes, not just in the political and social map of post-independent North Africa, but also in the epistemological structure of twentieth century Arab Reason. One must read Jābīrī's identification with Arab Reason and Arab-Islamic history as the first ambitious attempt to create an independent nationalist cultural project in the post-colonial era. This cultural construction reflects the aspirations of a good number of people who participated in the nationalist struggle against colonialism.

Jābīrī has emerged as one of the most distinguished thinkers in the contemporary Arab world. His work is read differently by different people.[9] His intellectual formation in both Syria and Morocco and his refusal to write in French have made him the favorite of a new generation of Arab intellectuals and students. Jābīrī's *oeuvre* is widespread; he has written on subjects ranging from the academic to the political. Some of Jābīrī's writings can be sometimes quite difficult to follow. Jābīrī discusses the following themes: first, the problem of knowledge in Islam and the meaning of "Arab Reason"; second, the historical evolution of Muslim society and the role of the intelligentsia; third, the Arab world and the West; fourth, contemporary Arab thought and universal ideas and, fifth, the implementation of the Sharī'ah and future directions of Arab societies.[10] The purpose of this chapter is to critically discuss these major themes by linking them to the ongoing discussion in contemporary Arab thought.

Jābīrī received his primary education in the philosophy of science and epistemology. The evolution of his thought put him in the driver's seat of the contemporary Maghrebian school of Arab and national renaissance. The salient features of his intellectual system resonate with those of 'Allāl al-Fāsī,[11] Mohammed Arkoun,[12] Abdallah Laroui, Muḥammad al-Kettānī,[13] 'Abdel Ḥamīd bin Badīs,[14] Muḥammad Talbi,[15] Ali Merad,[16] and many others from North Africa.[17] These thinkers have proposed that only a critical process of transformation can lead to real renaissance in the Arab world. Criticism is the common denominator in their thought.[18] Like Ibn Khaldūn of the fourteenth century, who attempted a renaissance of Arab-Muslim civilization by way of a powerful *'aṣṣabiyyah*,[19] Jābīrī stands at the crossroads of both national and intellectual independence. He envisions a plan of modern Arab renaissance, which can be achieved with the power of reason. Philosophical renaissance is a precondition for the renaissance of the entire Arab culture and civilization in the modern period. Does such a project of "intellectual emancipation" have a chance of succeeding under the current political conditions of the Arab world?

THE APPEAL TO CLASSICAL ARAB REASON

Jābīrī's preoccupation with the problem of knowledge in Arabic and Islamic philosophy underlies his philosophical quest. The problem of knowledge is a deeply complex issue and a truly in-depth discussion of this topic is unfortunately beyond the scope of this chapter. However, it suffices to say that Jābīrī's fresh, if not controversial, examination of this problem in the context of Islamic philosophy is pertinent to the question of the meaning of knowledge and rationalism in the contemporary Arab world. In his major philosophical work, Jābīrī's main objective is to create bridges between the huge Arab/Muslim intellectual tradition and the modern Western intellectual tradition, on the one hand, and the post-colonial Arab world, on the other. In one sense, Jābīrī's is an advanced formulation of the Nahḍah thinking on intellectual revival. In another, however, his thought is part of the cultural decolonization project that began after independence in North Africa, and which seeks to anchor modern Arab thought in certain rational patterns of classical intellectual tradition. Jābīrī thus follows a double process: a deconstruction of the past and a reexamination of the most pressing issues facing post-colonial Arab thought. Unlike Laroui, Jābīrī does not dismiss Islamic philosophical and religious tradition, neither does he espouse a wholesale acceptance of any form of European school of thought or philosophy.[20] Jābīrī's intellectual quest is primarily anchored in the field of philosophy. He argues that there is a strong link between the professions of philosophy and political criticism, a link which is indispensable to the task of cultural decolonization. He maintains that the contemporary Arab political elite cannot "put up with the rudeness (waqāḥah) of philosophy and the philosophers"[21] mainly because they represent the most serious hurdle in the quest for full liberation of the Arab world. Since political methods have proven barren in the Arab world, it is philosophy and not politics that offers real solutions.

Jābīrī's point of departure is philosophy, not metaphysics or theology. The problems of Islamic theology developing in the Classical Age concern him only to the extent that they impinge on reason and culture. Although he does not directly condemn theology, his identification of Arab renaissance with philosophy, especially critical philosophy, casts doubt on the usefulness of theology as an intellectual medium in contemporary Arab culture. Jābīrī believes philosophy can free contemporary Arab culture from the parochialism of the theological mind (that is, Salafī mind) and distance it from those theological presuppositions that belong to a bygone era. To his mind, it is possible to utilize philosophy as a method of reviving the grand Arab nationalist project, in both the Maghreb and the Mashreq, to be anchored in the grand environment of Arab rationalism that existed before Islam. Therefore, Jābīrī preaches the birth of a new Arab age of Tadwīn, that is, writing down the main principles of modern Arab thought and culture.[22]

In Jābīrī's thought, turāth (tradition) encompasses a wide array of intellectual and cultural activities, and must not be equated only with theology or religion. Since the encounter with the West in the nineteenth century, Arab thinkers have turned to turāth to derive the necessary lessons to help them out of their predicament. The process of examining turāth accelerated after the 1967 Arab defeat with the view of understanding the reasons behind such a defeat. "What are the reasons behind defeat and how can we achieve progress?" is a question often asked by a number of Arab intelligentsia. Contemporary Arab discourse on turāth is very complex and revealing by virtue of the tremendous intellectual energy devoted to it by the world's most important Arab thinkers, representing different perspectives.[23] In Jābīrī's, turāth is understood in a specific way: it is the contemporary articulation or re-articulation of Arab Rationalism, which has shaped the Arab world since the time of Jāhiliyyah, and which was active in the formative phase of Islam in producing Arab-Islamic philosophy and scholasticism. Unlike Abdallah Laroui, Jābīrī is convinced that no one can adequately meet the challenges facing the contemporary Arab world without taking into account the colossal Arab and Muslim philosophical heritage of the past. Simply put, to ignore the past is to commit intellectual suicide.

Jābīrī's thought is anchored in the urgent concerns of the modern Arab world. His definition of rationalism as the organized habit of critical reconstruction allows him to examine the rationalist undercurrents of the Arab and Muslim past for the purpose of reconstructing the rational foundations of modern and contemporary Arab culture. The past poses many problems indeed, and its legacy has entangled the modern Arab world in parochialism, superstition, and anti-rationalism. A past reconstructed in an enlightened and rational manner paves the way for the contemporary Arab world to appropriate the fruits of Arab and universal reason and turn modernity into a creative process. One must understand Jābīrī's thought, then, as an engagement with those rational trends of the past that can furnish a direction for contemporary Arab thought.

Because part of his quest is to bring *turāth* into contemporary Arab intellectual discourse, Jābīrī focuses his efforts on the deconstruction and critique of Arab Reason (*al-'aql al-'arabī*). More or less following the logic of Edward Said in his appraisal of Orientalism, Jābīrī elicits what he considers to be the underlying and essential religious, linguistic, philosophical, and political components and epistemological underpinnings of Arab and Islamic thought. For this, he consecrates a trilogy that centers on criticism: (1) *Takwīn al-'aql al-'arabī* (*Genesis of Arab Reason*), appearing in 1984; (2) *Bunyat al-'aql al-'arabī* (*Structure of Arab Reason*) appearing in 1986, and (3) *al-'Aql al-siyāsī al-'arabī* (*Arab Political Reason*), appearing in 1991.

Jābīrī does express appreciation for the efforts of nineteenth century Arab Nahḍah thinkers in reviving Islamic heritage and attempting to meet the challenges of the West.[24] However, he believes that the nineteenth century reform movement failed because it was not committed to an overall critical appreciation of Arab Reason. The Nahḍah thinkers bitterly criticized the stagnation and backwardness of their societies; however, their criticism was bereft of deep philosophical content. In their rush to condemn what they considered the concrete social and political manifestations of stagnation, they employed inadequate theological methods, in the case of religious thinkers, or borrowed European rational concepts, in the case of liberal thinkers, without stirring the rational passion of the people.

Reason and only reason can lead to the end of cultural chaos in the modern Arab world. With this as his thesis, Jābīrī presents rationalism as Arab society's only defense against the shackles of the past and to negotiate the hurdles of the present. A systematic investigation into the foundations of "Arab Reason" becomes fundamental. Jābīrī does this with the aid of universal reason, that is, the thought of French deconstructionist philosophers such as M. Foucault, Godelier,[25] Lacan, Barthes, DeLeuze and others. To be sure, Jābīrī is not the only Arab philosopher to enlist the aid of universal deconstructionist reason. Other Moroccan philosophers have done this in the past as well.[26] But Jābīrī is the only Moroccan philosopher to have gained a reputation across the Arab world for his ambitious work of deconstruction.

The main goal behind Jābīrī's archeological project is to investigate the historical growth and movement of Arab Reason for the purpose of uncovering its most fundamental components, its underlying and hegemonic concepts, methodological tools, and main political and ethical objectives. This is a daunting task, indeed. Although fully aware of the ideological consequences of ideas, especially religious ideas, Jābīrī proposes that it is important to reveal and understand the basic epistemological components of Arab Reason before investigating its ideological formation and the hegemonic culture it created in the medieval period. Epistemology, he maintains, has never been free from ideology, which in turn describes the nature of hegemony in Muslim and Arab culture and the different elite or communities who have been active in either supporting or opposing this hegemony. Jābīrī does not directly refer to the Antonio Gramsci writings on hegemony, although he seems to have learned quite a bit from Gramsci's insights into this important concept.

By identifying epistemology with hegemony, Jābīrī tries to explain what is most puzzling about the interplay between reason, ideology, and society throughout Arab history. To deconstruct the role of hegemony in classical and modern Arab society, Jābīrī proposes to uncover the deep epistemological foundations of Arab Reason and the mechanisms that give rise to concepts and ideas. To his mind, Arab epistemology is distinguished by a certain way or logic of producing ideas. In other words, both the thematic and problematic of Arab Reason are products of the tools of this reason and its surrounding social, economic, religious, and political conditions. Before any useful critique is made of Arab Reason it is necessary to reexamine its different components within the framework of modern philosophical methods and approaches. This task is indeed immense and one person, however astute and learned, cannot shoulder it alone. Yet, Jābīrī embarks on an ambitious, although still partial, deconstruction of the epistemological components and ideological consequences of Arab Reason.

Jābīrī's philosophical passion and breadth of analysis allow him to write down the main outlines of the historical development and epistemological mutations of Arab Reason. In this, he follows in the footsteps of a small number of modern Arab philosophers, such as Aḥmad Amīn, Muṣṭafa 'Abd al-Rāziq, 'Alī Sāmī al-Nashār, Ibrāhīm Madkūr, Ṭayyib Tizīnī, Ḥussain Muruwwa, and 'Abd al-Raḥmān Badawī, all of whom have had a major impact on the intellectual environment of the twentieth century Arab world. However, Jābīrī seems to stand alone in tracing contemporary Arab Reason to pre-Islamic or *jāhilī* origins. Although Jābīrī considers Islam to be the greatest mutation in Arab Reason, it is wrong to consider it the beginning of this Reason.[27] Jābīrī, therefore, undertakes defining the most stable features of Arab Reason over 1,500 years of history. He considers Arab Reason to be endowed with epistemological unity, the product of deep ruptures experienced by Arab Reason over a long period of time. One of these major ruptures is the rise of Islam in Arabia in the seventh century. Although this comprehensive approach may not present an accurate assessment of the major contributions of Arab thought over that period of time, it nevertheless is the only method available that can shed some light on the structure of Arab thought and its progress over the centuries.

In almost all of his writings, Jābīrī struggles to uncover what he terms the "epistemological nucleus" (noyeau épistémologique) of the subject at hand. Jābīrī is highly indebted to the contributions of the modern French school of structuralism, especially in the writings of Gaston Bachelard,[28] Georges Canguilhem,[29] and Michel Foucault.[30] The notion of "epistemological break," borrowed from Bachelard, presupposes that "scientific progress always reveals a break, or better perpetual breaks, between ordinary knowledge and scientific knowledge."[31] The matrix of his scientific thought is to develop an epistemology capable of meeting the scientific demands of the new age, and which challenges our common-sense acceptance of traditional epistemologies. Canguilhem developed Bachelard's notion of "scientific break," especially in post-Renaissance European thought. Foucault credits both Bachelard and Canguilhem in the introduction to his The Archeology of Knowledge and the Discourse on Language. He says that:

There are the epistemological acts and thresholds described by Bachelard: they suspend the continuous accumulation of knowledge, interrupt its slow development, and force it to enter a new time, cut it off from its empirical origin and its original motivations, cleanse it of its imaginary complicities: they direct historical analysis away from the search for silent beginnings, and the neverending tracing-back to the original precursors, towards the search for a new type of rationality and its various effects. There are the displacements and transformations of concepts: the analyses of G. Canguilhem may serve as models; they show that the history of a concept is not wholly and entirely that of its progressive refinement, its continuously increasing rationality...but that of its various fields of constitution and validity, that of its successive rules of use, that of the many theoretical contexts in which it developed and matured.[32]

One of the key points here is that what defines the history of human thought is not just links and connections but also breaks and discontinuities, which mostly arise in periods of transition and change. However, what is important to note is that under the pressure of transformation, human reason is able to develop new categories and classifications of thought, relationships to both past and future, and either acceptance or rejection of certain attitudes. In spite of Foucault's highly mechanical approach in dealing with epistemology, he never forgets, under the influence of Bachelard and Canguilhem, to give space to both history and human activity.

Jābīrī's indebtedness to the French school of epistemology enables him to focus on epistemology, history, and transformation in the classical Arab and Muslim age and on epistemology, society, and liberation in the modern era. Jābīrī embarks on an ambitious project of epistemological and historical analysis. In addition to linking epistemology with history (both scientific and socio-economic history), he identifies ideology as a salient feature of human thought. Examined through the lenses of history, the marriage between epistemology and ideology reflects the progress of social and cultural realities and the different players in each situation or epoch. In his faithfulness to French structuralism, Jābīrī's critical rationalism does not give much credence to the claims of metaphysics or abstract theology.[33]

THE ROLE OF PHILOSOPHY

In an illuminating piece on the differences between theology and philosophy, Paul Tillich argues that "epistemology, the 'knowledge' of knowing, is a part of ontology, the knowledge of being, for knowing is an event within the totality of events. Every epistemological assertion is implicitly ontological. Therefore, it is more adequate to begin an analysis of existence with the question of being rather than with the problem of knowledge."[34] Although Jābīrī begins his analysis with the problem of knowledge in the Arab world, his major focus is post-colonial Arab existence. Ontology and epistemology are absolutely linked in his approach.

Jābīrī locates the beginning and progress of Arab epistemology and rationalism in the field of philosophy. He identifies two primary schools in the formative phase of Islam: first, the Mashreqi school of philosophy, which was Hermetic[35] in orientation, and second is the Maghrebi Zaherite school, which was rational in nature. Ibn Sīna and al-Ghazālī belong to the former and Ibn Rushd, Ibn Ḥazm, Ibn Bājjā, and Ibn Khaldūn belong to the latter.[36] Jābīrī ascribes every evil in Muslim philosophical thinking to Hermeticism, which he wrongly considers a pre-Islamic Persian school of philosophy that influenced a number of early Muslim philosophers.[37] Jābīrī considers Hermeticism to have had a pernicious impact on early Arab thought because of its preoccupation with esotericism, astrology, and magic. In this sense, he differs from Nasr's assessment that,

> The Muslims identified Hermes, whose personality they elaborated into the "three Hermes," also well-known to the West from Islamic sources, with Idrīs or Enoch, the ancient prophet who belongs to the chain of prophecy confirmed by the Qur'an and the Ḥadīth. And they considered Idrīs as the origin of philosophy, bestowing on him the title of Abū'l-Ḥukamā', the father of philosophers.[38]

Ibn Rushd, of the Maghrebi school of philosophy, is Jābīrī's ideal philosopher.[39] Ibn Rushd represents the victory of Arab Reason over the Hermetic and irrational mind of Ibn Sīna, patron of the eastern school of philosophy. Many philosophers would find this premise highly debatable. Jābīrī seems to say that occidental Arab Reason has preserved its rational purity, unlike oriental reason, which was very much influenced by Persian ideas. "L'histoire de la pensée arabe et musulmane est, chez al-Jābīrī, une histoire dialectique qu'anime l'opposition entre irrationalisme et rationalisme, entre l'obscurantisme et les Lumières." ("The history of Arab and Muslim thought, according to Jābīrī, is a dialectic history which breathes life into the conflict between irrationalism and rationalism and between obscurantism and the enlightened ones." Translation by Abu-Rabi'.)[40]

One has reason to agree with Majid Fakhry's assessment that "Islamic philosophy is the product of a complex intellectual process in which Syrians, Arabs, Persians, Turks, Berbers, and others took an active part."[41] Undoubtedly, the dramatic expansion of Islam in the first century, the amalgamation of a heterogeneous number of people into the matrix of Arab/Islamic culture and thought, and the appropriation of medical, astronomical, philosophical, and literary traditions of the conquered people created a very dynamic Islamic civilization, which was intent on bringing universalism to its intellectual achievements. The preceding statement proves to be shallow if not examined against the different social, political, religious, and intellectual forces that exploded on the scene after expansion. The point to be underscored here is that Jābīrī's distinction between "Oriental Arab Reason" and "Occidental Arab Reason" misses the point of the Muslim/Arab mind's dynamic appropriation of all sorts of sciences; this process was as true in the western part of the Muslim world as in the eastern.

Jābīrī, however, hastens to emphasize that a complete assessment of the Arab/ Muslim philosophical tradition must begin with the Age of Tadwīn, launched in the eastern part of the Muslim world around a century or so after the birth of Islam.[42] Unlike theoreticians of contemporary Islamic resurgence in the Arab world, Jābīrī's point of departure in treating the Islamic foundations of Arab Reason is not the age of the Prophet or the Rightly Guided caliphs, but a much later phase. In this later age, philosophy was integral to the formation of the rational spirit of Arab culture, thus stretching the rational imagination of Arab Reason and philosophers. Jābīrī underlines the function of philosophy in that age as "a struggling ideological discourse that committed itself to serving science and progress in Arab society."[43]

Jābīrī avoids confining philosophy to the field of epistemology; in the formative phase of Islam, it was engaged with all sorts of ideological and philosophical discourses. In the process of building the rational edifice of classical Arab Reason, philosophy was destined to incur the wrath of Manichean philosophers who, under the cover of Islam, began to spread their old Persian ideas in subtle and destructive ways. Although Jābīrī does not belittle the importance of the assimilation of ideas in the age of Tadwīn, he nevertheless believes that the old Persian aristocracy defeated by the Arab forces of Islam was bent on wreaking havoc on the Arab mind of the classical era. In order to compensate for its humiliating defeat in the battle field, this aristocracy used its arsenal of ideas or intellectual ammunition to conquer Islam and the Arab world from within. During the Ummayyad and early 'Abbaside ages, "The tense Persian aristocracy launched an extensive ideological attack using its rich Mazdakian, Manichean, and Zoroastrian heritage in order to cast doubt on the nature of the Arab religion and lead to its destruction so that Arab authority and state will crumble."[44] Jābīrī argues that the Persian aristocracy used the cover of Shī'īsm and its esoteric symbols to attain its objectives. He further argues that the Arab backlash to this movement took the form of rational philosophy, which was supported by the caliph al-Ma'mūn in the east.[45]

Jābīrī reaches the logical conclusion that Arab philosophy was ideologically motivated from the very beginning and not just a fruitless exercise in rationalism. This motivation was justified by the attacks of esoteric and mystical philosophers who took the side of ambiguous metaphysics against rational philosophy. Jābīrī gives as an example the Arab philosopher, al-Kindī who to his mind struggled against two types of thinkers: the gnostics and the *fuqahā'*. To Jābīrī, al-Kindī advocated unity between religion and philosophy, a method, which could ultimately lead to the knowledge of God. The next important philosopher in Jābīrī's view is al-Farābī, who committed himself to establishing the unity of the Arab ummah by proposing the universality of reason against the insidious plots of the Persian aristocracy and Shī'īs. Jābīrī says that Ibn Sīnā, because of his Persian background, spread Gnostic ideas that were anti-rational in nature.[46]

Jābīrī's strong condemnation of pre-Islamic Manichean philosophy, Shī'īsm, and Persian influence on classical Islamic and Arabic thought diverges from the acceptable theoretical position that whatever classical Arab or Muslim Reason accepted from outside sources "was all transformed and assimilated into a matrix that was characteristically Islamic."[47] He downplays the notion of Islamic universalism and underscores instead the importance of Arabism in thought and culture in that age.

Jābīrī highlights the importance of four thinkers whom he considers all Arab in building the edifice of Arab rationalism. These four are al-Kindī, al-Fārābī, Ibn Rushd, and Ibn Khaldūn. Jābīrī's favorite philosopher is Ibn Rushd (Averroes).[48] He argues that Ibn Rushd's thought must be considered primary in modern Arab thought, as Descartes' ideas are in modern French thought. Jābīrī maintains that Ibn Rushd's philosophy deals with the following central questions: (1) how to correctly read and interpret the Qur'an; (2) how to interpret the philosophy of Aristotle, and (3) how to define the relationship between religion and philosophy in a manner that protects the autonomy of each. Jābīrī argues that according to Ibn Rushd, philosophy utilizes a different system from that of religion. The two subjects begin with different premises that lead to different conclusions. The philosopher must not dispute the principles on which the Sharī'ah is based and by the same token, the *fuqahā'* must not dispute the foundations of philosophy. In the final analysis, however, religious truth does not contradict rational truth.[49]

Against the above, Jābīrī raises the following question that summarizes his intellectual preoccupation: "How can contemporary Arab thought retrieve and absorb the most rational and critical dimensions of its tradition and employ them in the same rationalist direction as before – the direction of fighting against feudalism, gnosticism, and dependency?" The Arab world of today badly needs such a reason, whose sole objective must be to create justice, socialism, and democracy.[50] To achieve true renaissance, the point of departure for modern Arabs must be "philosophical rationalism," as construed by Arab philosophers of the medieval and early modern period. It is only by reconstructing the foundations of the Arab heritage that Arabs can preserve their uniqueness and secure a place in the world of nations.

HISTORICAL OUTLINES OF ARAB REASON

The broad outlines of Arab Reason, as discussed by Jābīrī, emerge fully after an exhausting process of deconstruction. On the whole, Jābīrī thinks that although Arab Reason has from the beginning exhibited a number of essential characteristics, its primary epistemological formation has responded only to three major shifts or discontinuities in its long history, all of which took place during the Jāhiliyyah, early Islam, and the nineteenth century. These three epochs exhibited many coexisting epistemological modes and reflected a number of ideological forces competing to shape the Arab world, each according to its own image.[51]

The coexistence of different modes of epistemology and the great ideological and cultural competition between the different modes has created a unique phenomenon in the modern Arab world, that of the "migrating intelligentsia" – those intellectuals who migrate from one plane of thought to an antithetical; from the rational to the irrational, from the scientific to the metaphysical, and from the mystical to the philosophical. Many traditionalist intellectuals try to interpret and apply ancient knowledge without the predicate of proper philosophical scrutiny. This phenomenon carries with it cultural and intellectual alienation, an inability to form a coherent image of the "cultural self," and a failure to adequately assume a progressive vision of the present.[52]

Jābīrī claims that the true intellectual history of the Arab world has not yet been written for the simple reason that Arab history as we study it today is a history of schisms and not of epistemological breaks, opinion formation, or scientific refinement. A new Age of Tadwīn is past due. We are still far from appreciating the epistemological components of Arab Reason and the tools used to lay down the foundations of Arab culture and thought. Modern Arabs are apt to confuse the ideological and the epistemological, and thus fail to appreciate those components that gave their system of thought its coherence and viability. This fact "made our historical consciousness the product of the accumulation of and confusion in facts and not succession or systemization of historical facts."[53]

Jābīrī does not attribute much weight to the Islamic intervention in Arabian history in the formation of Arab Reason. Neither the Qur'an nor Ḥadīth played a significant role in Arab epistemological formation. The Age of Tadwīn takes precedence over the first few years of Islam. This is an odd position to take in light of the importance of Islamic revelation in shaping Islamic history. One must agree with Ḥassan Ḥanafī that *waḥy*, or revelation, had a significant impact on the Muslim mind, both past and present.[54] The classification of the Islamic sciences and the formation of the Islamic *oeuvres* all took place during the Tadwīn Age and not the early Islamic. Therefore, the Age of Tadwīn inaugurates a new epistemological and intellectual authority in the world of Islam; it constitutes the primary system of reference (*al-sulṭah al-marja'iyyah*).[55] However, Jābīrī hastens to add that, as a matter of fact, two primary systems of Islamic reference arose in this age: the Sunni and Shī'ī systems. Although the epistemological components of both systems were more or less the same, they exhibited different social, political, and ideological formations. Dissension over political authority in early Islam led to the rise of these two different systems of reference.[56]

What is important to underline here is the Jabirean notion that the epistemological foundations of Arab Reason primarily took shape during the Tadwīn Age. Hence, the Arab appeal to the Tadwīn Age in the nineteenth century, during colonial expansion into the Arab world. The broad outlines of the Arab system of knowledge were shaped in the Tadwīn Age, and this historical fact must guide our thinking about the historical progress of Arab thought.[57] The first task performed by Tadwīn thinkers was to lay out the principles and bases of the Arab language – to write down its grammar and to shape its universal traits. Language is both a tool that leads to the production of ideas as well as a coherent form, shape or system of these ideas. For example, *Lisān al-'Arab* was the dictionary that gave coherence to Arabic grammar. In other words, the Tadwīn Age enabled the Arabic language to evolve from non-scientific to scientific. It has solid rules which enable it to evolve and be flexible enough to include novel elements.

The canonization of language and grammar was followed by that of jurisprudence. Jurisprudence lies at the heart of the Arab-Muslim heritage. Jābirī argues that Arab-Muslim civilization was based on Fiqh. The Fiqh of early Islam was pragmatic, whereas in the Age of Tadwīn, it was theoretical and epistemological in nature. The function of Fiqh was to produce laws to regulate society's social, economic, and political affairs, whereas the main goal of Fiqh (*'ilm al-uṣūl*) was to produce rules for the mind, or to enable the mind to legislate rules. Shāfi'ī, the Descartes of Islamic jurisprudence, gave coherence to the principles of Fiqh that helped Muslim jurists deduce rational rules. Shāfi'ī understood the need to establish rules and systems that give a sense of organization and discipline to meanings and legislations. Shāfi'ī established rules for every opinion. Although the problem of authority or caliphate was the first challenge facing Muslims in the wake of the death of the Prophet, it was the last question that jurists examined in a systematic manner. This examination established the political foundation and outlook of such groups as the Shī'īs, Sunnis, Mu'tazilites, and so on. Shī'ī thinkers began to formulate the theoretical bases of this question during the Tadwīn Age as a means of protecting their claims to authority. They based their theoretical justification on a text – they claimed the Prophet left a text promising the caliphate to 'Alī and his family. The Sunnis, on the other hand, followed the precedent of Abū Bakr being appointed by the Prophet to lead people in prayer. The importance of al-Asha'rī, similar to the job of Shāfi'ī, was to lay down the foundations and principles of Sunni doctrine. Therefore, in matters of language, doctrine, Fiqh, and Kalām, Muslim thinkers in the Tadwīn Age introduced the epistemological foundations of these sciences and established the reference system of Bayān (*al-niẓām al-ma'rifī al-bayānī*).[58] Canonization establishes internal coherence and gives authority to certain texts, "The hidden and discursive purpose behind the canonization of both language and Fiqh was to achieve social and political unity,"[59] which was badly needed for the expansion of the Islamic state. However, the epistemological formation of the Tadwīn Age and the classification of its various sciences took place against the influence of Greek philosophy. Jābirī does not seem to object to Greek influence in the same way that he does to pre-Islamic Persian philosophy.

Jābirī introduces the concept of the "Arab religious thinkable" (*al-ma'qūl al-dīnī al-'arabī*), which is based on the belief in the absolute oneness of God and the idea of prophecy. Unlike the ancient Greek thought, God plays a central role in Muslim thought. In other words, the concept of "God" is placed at the center of the relationship between man and nature. Man cannot conceive of causal or natural laws without first conceiving of God. Comprehending nature and its laws leads to comprehending God. Thus, the knowledge of nature leads to that of God in Islamic thought, and the comprehension of God leads to that of nature in Greek and European thought. What is important about this thinkable in Islam is the Nature/God/Man relationship established in the Tadwīn Age, which has been translated as the most important part of the Sacred Text, especially the Qur'an and Ḥadīth. The fact is that the Islamic thinkable cannot be examined solely in reference to the sacred text or texts. The sacred thus becomes the basis of Islamic rationalism.

Jābīrī maintains that the concept of "the religious thinkable" in Islam took shape in negation to Persian Manichean philosophy, which had an important presence in the formative phase of Islam. Islamic ideas flourished in the second century of Hegira and their interaction or confrontation with the philosophical and intellectual heritage of other civilizations. This opening or mushrooming of ideas was not possible during the time of the Prophet for the simple reason that Arab culture at the time was not mature enough to be cognizant of the philosophical achievements of other civilizations or even evolved enough to grasp its own theoretical and epistemological foundations and principles. This was only possible during the time of the Tadwīn.[60] At the apogee of conquest, Muslims were able to politically and militarily dominate and began to take notice of the intellectual achievements of these cultures through various means, such as translation, assimilation, and thus were able to distill the intellectual integrity of these cultures, assimilate their central ideas, and spread a new form of Islamic hegemony over them. Arab Muslim space was totally dominant in Arabia, but faced new enemies in the periphery, especially in Persia in the form of the battle of the books launched by Zoroastrian and Manichean philosophers and ideologues who did not disguise their distrust of the ascending Islamic culture.

Jābīrī highlights three major systems of conceptual reference that emerged during the Tadwīn Age: the Bayān, 'Irfān, and Burhān systems. He calls the first *al-Niẓām al-ma'rifī al-Bayānī*, developed by Muslim jurists, which grants the Sacred Text primacy over reason or philosophy. The sciences of Fiqh, Qur'anic exegesis, and philology are products of this system. The 'Irfān system, discussed above, emerged hand-in-glove with the Persian philosophical and mystical influences upon early Arab and Muslim thought. Hermeticism is the core of such a system, which Jābīrī calls *Allā ma 'qūl 'aqlī* (uncomprehended reason). The third system of Burhān is the product of Arab philosophical activity in North Africa and Spain and is best represented by al-Kindī, al-Fārābī, and Ibn Rushd.[61]

Jābīrī critically discusses the writings of Imām Ghazālī, held in high esteem in the Muslim world for his work in theology and Sufism. Jābīrī accuses him of falling victim to the 'Irfān school and Hermetic ideas.[62] It is because of this system of thought that Ghazālī, according to Jābīrī, turned a blind eye to the danger the Crusaders presented to the Muslim world in the last ten years of his life. Jābīrī accuses Ghazālī of masterminding a pernicious plot to unseat Arab Reason. Ghazālī's Hermetic thought, he claims, "has left a deep wound in Arab Reason that still bleeds profusely."[63] Jābīrī does not provide much evidence to back up such a harsh accusation, neither does he discuss in any detail the ideological or social forces that might have been in play at that particular juncture in Islamic history. Jābīrī points to Hermetic influences without analyzing in any depth Ghazālī's religious or philosophical views and their positive reception in the Muslim world. However, Jābīrī points out that during Ghazālī's time (the eleventh and twelfth centuries), the Muslim world was at a crossroads, beset by political and social turmoil and in search of stability in the midst of chaos. As a result, the three epistemological systems, which developed during the Tadwīn Age, were in a state of friction and competition. To appease the conservative jurists in Islam and to satisfy his Hermetic bent of mind, Ghazālī spent many years working on a synthesis between jurisprudence and mysticism. However, one of the main consequences of such a synthesis was the blocking of philosophical and rational progress in Arab and Muslim minds, which ultimately reduced the influence of rational philosophy in many parts of the Muslim world.[64]

As seen above, Jābīrī examines what he calls "Arab Rationalism" over a period of 15 centuries. Arab Rationalism predates Islam. Its constituent elements have been shaped by three major mutations, discontinuities, breakthroughs and cataclysmic events. Arab rationalism is uniquely Arab, which means that Jābīrī implicitly dismisses the notion of "universal reason." There exists a multiplicity of reasons in the world. Jābīrī looks at Arab Rationalism as a living reality that transcends the limits of tradition. The concept of tradition refers only to the past, or a certain ordered and well-defined past. Jābīrī looks at Arab Rationalism as a sort of progressive system, which renews itself with every moment of dramatic change.

Jābīrī does not explain how "Arab Rationalism" emerged. He only mentions in passing that it first emerged in pre-Islamic Arabia. What are the conditions which led to the rise of Arab Rationalism? Also, as mentioned above, Jābīrī does not accord any significant epistemological or doctrinal importance to Islam in the development of Arab Rationalism. The historical eruption of Islam on world history is brushed aside. He focuses instead on the Age of Tadwīn, which began at least a century after the appearance of Islam. In the Age of Tadwīn, all the basic Arab sciences were written down, commented upon, argued, critiqued, elaborated, and classified.

In one sense, Jābīrī follows in the footsteps of Egyptian thinker Ṭāhā Ḥussain, who traced "Egyptian rationalism" to the philosophical formations of pre-Islamic Egypt. However, the conclusions of each are entirely different. In *The Future of Culture in Egypt*, released in 1936, Ḥussain aimed at establishing a transhistorical link between modern European Reason and ancient Egyptian Reason.[65] Jābīrī, on the other hand, was busy tracing the roots of modern Arab Reason to the Jāhiliyyah Age of pre-Islamic Arabia. Although he ended up discussing the Tadwīn Age and its intellectual ramifications, he was able to establish some major links between the formative phase of Islam and modern Arab thought.

On the basis of the above arguments, Jābīrī argues that the triumph of the Hermetic philosophy and its propagation by such major thinkers as Ibn Sīna and Ghazālī led to the decline of Arab Reason. It is only by freeing Arab Reason from such a capitulation that sound rational progress can be achieved. "The Europeans," he says, "achieved progress the moment European Reason began to wake up and raise questions. Capitalism is the daughter of Reason."[66] Jābīrī, therefore, gives a purely epistemological answer to a vexing social and economic problem. Although his epistemological approach is essentially rational, it lacks a socio-economic dynamic or reference to social forces inside the Arab world as well as outside, that have no vested interest in the advancement of capitalism within their societies.

POLITICS AND RENAISSANCE

After treating the epistemological formations of Arab and Muslim history, Jābīrī turns his attention to the question of politics while highlighting certain notable examples in Islamic history. "Islam and politics are one" is a cliché often recounted, especially by Islamist thinkers. It is impossible to understand what is meant by this statement unless a thorough examination of the classical environment of Islam is undertaken. Therefore, a good number of modern Arab thinkers have studied the perplexing relationship between Islam and politics in early history and come up with different conclusions. We all remember the famous arguments of Shaykh 'Alī 'Abd al-Rāziq back in 1926. He postulated that the Prophet was not concerned about politics or even this world but was totally immersed in worship in order to attain the best station in the other world.[67] A great number of contemporary Arab thinkers try to understand the complex relationship between politics and Islam in the present Muslim world through the lenses of the past relationship between Islam and politics. The work of Hichem Djaït on this matter is qualitatively different from that of Sayyid Quṭb. Djaït speaks about tension in early Islam;[68] Quṭb prefers to speak of early Muslim pioneers, the builders of a God-ordained civilization. Jābīrī ventures into the much-trodden territory of early Islam in order to ascertain the complex relationship between religion and society/state in the modern Arab world.

What Jābīrī has in mind, I suspect, when writing about the relationship between politics and religion is the argument proposed by many Islamists: that Islam constituted a total revolution against *Jāhiliyyah*, tribalism, and disunity, and that from the beginning, the Islamic state was religious in nature, that is, was not based on secular foundations. Jābīrī does not think so. He proposes that it is impossible to come to grips with the formation of the early Islamic state under the Prophet and the Rightly Guided caliphate without investigating the importance of three major concepts or factors: tribe, doctrine, and booty. These concepts do not elicit any epistemological or hidden arguments, but provide an explicit appraisal of socioeconomic and political forces throughout Islamic history. Whereas Jābīrī does not accord any importance to Islamic revelation and the role of the Prophet in his earlier argument, he seems to think that in any political or economic treatment of early Islamic society, these factors are central. Jābīrī contends that the Prophet made full use of all of these factors in the formation of the early Islamic state in Medina, while giving preference to the tribal factor in order to protect his mission in its infancy. After his death, the early caliphs used a combination of the tribe/booty/doctrine to build a multiglot, multiethnic Islamic empire. The political was not divorced from the religious in early Islam, and this could be taken as the genesis of secularism in early Islamic thought.[69]

In *Naqd al-'aql al-siyāsī* [*Critique of Political Reason*], Jābīrī raises the following main questions: first regarding the relationship between the religious and political in early Islam; second, the basic constituent elements underlying the formation of the early Islamic state; third, the absence of a coherent Qur'anic political theory and the constitutional vacuum left after the death of the Prophet; fourth, the political mechanism in place to elect the caliph and questions of political despotism in Islamic history and, fifth, the state in the modern Arab world and the meaning of both democracy and civil society.

Jābīrī's launching pad in the treatment of religion and politics in early Islam is the primacy of the political over the theological during that period. The Islamic message was political in nature, "From the beginning, the Muḥammadan message was carrying a conspicuous political project with the aim of bringing to an end the political foundations of both the Persian and Byzantine states and controlling their treasures and riches."[70] In other words, Jābīrī argues that even in the Meccan phase, the Islamic message was political in nature and it is false to argue, as did 'Alī 'Abd al-Rāziq, that the Prophet and his early followers were not interested in this world or that they did not understand the political threat the Islamic message posed to the authority of Quraysh in Mecca or even the dominant tribal system in Arabia as a whole. Quraysh itself was alerted to the political implications of the Islamic message, and therefore chose to fight it politically to kill it in its infancy. Jābīrī also argues that the Prophet was aware of the importance of ideology, which was the same as *'aqīdah*, in reinforcing his political ideas in the hearts and minds of early believers. In this, Jābīrī does not differ much from the main claim of Arab Islamists that Islamic doctrine played a critical role in the diffusion of Islam.

Jābīrī shows that the Prophet offered his life as a political model by fighting against the Meccans with the aid of revelation. He attacked the Meccan idols, the supreme religious symbols of pagan Arabia, criticized the wealthy as a means of attracting the poor and giving them a political space in his message of radical change, and aimed at attracting the young and oppressed (*musṭaḍa'fīn*).[71] That is to say, the Prophet was well aware of the religious importance of Quraysh before Islam. His critique of the religious practices of the Meccan aristocracy was a necessary prelude to the dissemination of new ideas. The Prophet accomplished his critique with the aid of *'aṣṣabiyyah*, a new form of solidarity, that of the poor and the marginalized in Arabian society.

Jābīrī poses the following questions: Why weren't the enemies of the Islamic message capable of putting an end to the Prophet's preaching at an early stage in Mecca? The answer lies in the tribal system and the role of the tribe in protecting the Prophet and many of his early followers. In a sense, argues Jābīrī, the Prophet derived his legitimacy not so much from the Qur'an as from tribal solidarity, or tribal *'aṣṣabiyyah*, if we are to use Ibn Khaldūn's term. This mechanism was essential to the survival of his message; this becomes even more conspicuous in the second important phase of the *da'wah* in Medina, when the Prophet secured the help of several tribes in Medina against his enemies in his native town of Mecca. Thus, Jābīrī correctly argues that, "These complex tribal connections did not permit the tribe of Quraysh to kill the followers of the Muḥammadan message for the simple reason that any physical attack or shedding of blood would have led to a dramatic explosion and an overall civil war."[72] The tribal "imaginaire," in a sense, protected the Islamic message and ensured its progressive spread throughout Arabia.

In Medina, the Islamic message begins to operate on a higher political and economic plane. It lays down the seeds of a state, or a mini-state, of political and social organizations led by the Prophet and made successful by the novel sense of solidarity discovered by the Medinian tribes supporting Muḥammad. Those tribes begin to envision a larger political and military battle with Quryash in which they will play significant roles. In Medina, the Prophet follows a number of strategies: internal consolidations of his ranks; fighting enemy tribes in Medina, especially the Jewish, and preparing to consummate his final battle against Mecca.

The conquest of Mecca in 630 inaugurates a new progressive phase in the life of the message. Muslims are ready to fight a larger battle for the future of Arabia and later on the Near East as a whole. Jābīrī maintains that the booty that accrued to Muslims from the attacks on the commercial caravans of Mecca played a major role in the spread of Islam, since the followers of Muḥammad were motivated by material gains, in addition to the Islamic doctrine. Booty was taken not just to prepare armies against Quraysh but also to excite the imagination of the Muslim individual.[73] That is, when Muslims with the aid of the Qur'an were able to see that the notion of the ummah was far from parochial, they were challenged to think of it in universal terms.

The death of the Prophet created a number of important challenges to the nascent Muslim state: first, the question of political authority. The Qur'an as a text does not stipulate exactly how a caliph is selected after the death of the Prophet. Therefore, to find a solution to this dilemma, the early followers of the Prophet sought a purely political solution based on their tribal background and their Islamic experience until then. They met and chose Abū Bakr. The followers applied a tribal mentality to the selection of the shaykh, leader or head, taking into account the expanding territory of the state and common interest of the members of this emerging state. This was a purely political process, unaided by Qur'anic text, which later proves to be an important precedent in Islam and a basis for the development of Islamic political theory, especially for Sunnis. It was neither *'aqīdah*'s logic nor booty that decided this sensitive political matter, but the logic of the tribe.[74]

A second important problem facing the new Muslim state was the Ridda wars. On hearing of the death of the Prophet, many tribes (especially outside of the Ḥijāz) withdrew their pledges of allegiance to the young Muslim state and opted for their centuries-old freedom. Abū Bakr, with the help of that political nucleus built in Ḥijāz, was able to crush the Ridda with his followers, especially those from Medina. In summation, Abū Bakr used a number of strategies: booty, *'aqīdah*, and politics to reconstruct the Muslim state and continue conquest beyond Arabia. Both he and Omar used the tribes that had tried to recede from the body politic of the ummah in a new series of campaigns of expansion. As a result of the political possibilities emerging after the conquest of Mecca and the re-conversion of the tribes, both could envision the possibility of further expansion, even to the point of laying down the foundations of a new Islamic empire. The center becomes more powerful with the return of the tribes. They become extremely busy in their efforts to reap booty and in focusing on the expansion of Islam.[75] The Islamic state under the leadership of Abū Bakr and later on Omar succeeds in embodying a new political discourse, that of pragmatism and commitment to the vision of the Prophet of creating a large state.

Abū Bakr's death led again to the intervention of the logic of the tribe again in the selection of Omar as the second caliph. Here, the caliphs were careful to differentiate between the religious/theological and political functions of the Prophet and their political functions. They did not inherit the Prophetic mission of the Prophet but his political mission and message. Abū Bakr and Omar were the caliphs of the Messenger of God and not the caliphs of God. Being close to the Prophet in this sense gave them a strong sense of legitimacy in addition, of course, to recognizing the eternal values of Islam, such as forbidding evil and commanding good.

The dramatic expansion of Islam during the Rightly Guided caliphate and the booty Muslims gained from their conquests led to mass conversions to Islam for the sake of material and other gains and created a new class of *nouveax riches* in the Muslim ummah. This was an indication of the creation of a class society in which a minority, especially of some sahabah, become rich, and the majority consist of commoners.

So far, religion underlies the universal values of the Muslim ummah; conquest and booty were the dynamos behind expansion, which was also motivated by doctrinal issues. Religion is important in a metaphysical sense as a new bond of unity, although it could not completely annihilate the tribal mentality and sense of allegiance that is revived during the Ummayyad caliphate. But one must note that even the Ummayyads, who were known for their Arab ethnocentrism, immense wealth, and love of this life could not abolish religion as a bond among believers. But the egalitarian quality inherent in Islam moves some people to protest the amassing of wealth. This was clear in the career of Abū Dhar al-Ghifārī and 'Ammār bin Yāssir who strongly believed in the absolute concepts of Islamic egalitarianism and support for the poor and downtrodden. Abū Dhar and 'Ammār took the *'aqīdah* to heart, especially as they themselves underwent harsh treatment from the Meccan aristocracy. In this new phase, they begin to apply their early efforts towards a doctrinal rather than worldly Islam. The state, on the other hand, especially the Ummayyad state, although it could not escape the umbrella of Islam, began to use both latent and manifest coercion as a means of asserting its authority. Here, we are confronted with two imaginaires: one is statist and supported by a tribal mentality with Islamic legitimacy and the other is anti-statist and reclaims the early experience of Islam, especially Meccan Islam and frowns upon the excessive materialism of the Muslim consciousness, the worldliness of the Ummayyad state, and the co-opting of large numbers of the Prophet's followers by the Ummayyad state.

Jābirī correctly notes that the explosion of Islam on the world scene then took place under the auspices of the Rightly Guided caliphate. This "was an age of transition – a transition from Paganism to Tawhid; from revelation to explanation and from the state of message to the state of conquest. Before this transformation, the caliphs followed an open-door policy that was antithetical in nature to both sectarianism and orthodoxy. The essence of the behavior of the Prophet's followers was based on the Ḥadīth: 'you are indeed cognizant of the affairs of your world'."[76]

Mu'āwiyah and the Ummayyads generally begin a new phase of state formation after they win the early civil war against 'Alī and the Shī'īs. This was an era of deep political and some doctrinal divisions with the Muslim ummah. According to Jābīrī, many Sunni *fuqahā'* lent Mu'āwiyah their support because he infused the Muslim state with new energy by expanding its physical and mental territories and actually beginning to lay down its foundations as an empire.[77] Mu'āwiyah was indeed able to create a new political model in Islam in which the three factors mentioned above – tribe, booty, and *'aqīdah* – began to interact in a new way, thus giving the nascent Ummayyad state its social, economic, and religious legitimacy and integrity. Here, the political game takes on its strong shape, the purpose of which is to retain the power of Ummayyad family, build new institutions that parallel the whole plethora of complex changes affecting state and society, and rule from Damascus, which becomes a new intellectual and political center competing with the old centers of the Rāshidūn caliphate in Ḥijāz.

One other major difference between the Ummayyad and the Rightly Guided caliphs is the fact that the latter were totally immersed in the religious problematic; they were religious and political leaders who used their influence to build the foundations of Islam. With Mu'āwiyah, the central game becomes political. In the time of Mu'āwiyah, a split takes place between religion or doctrine and politics, or between the ulama and the sultan (between power and religion).[78] Politics becomes the profession of the elite to the exclusion of the masses. Mu'āwiyah begins his rule with the strength of his tribal background and the support of a large army. He embodies a novel phase in the world of Islam where the political takes precedence over the religious.

Because of the domination of the political ethos over the doctrinal one, a new ideological warfare erupts between the Ummayyad state and its opponents. Although a number of the Prophet's followers abstained from politics because of its divisive nature, others were co-opted by the state and went on the attack against its enemies, particularly the Shī'īs, Kharijites, and others who stood against the Ummayyads. Kalām begins to take shape, especially with the conversion of large numbers of non-Arabs to Islam. A new intelligentsia begins to emerge, an intelligentsia that quickly puts to use its past intellectual and cultural heritage in the service of this party or that, and the result is a great enriching of the ideological and cultural space of the Ummayyad state. The Shī'īs used their ideology of the Imāmate (that, in fact, there was a text in which the Prophet promised authority to 'Alī and his family) in order to wage their warfare against the Ummayyads and later the 'Abbasides. This state used the ideology of predestination to justify its existence and a great number of Ḥadīths were invented to justify this ideology.[79]

As long as the Ummayyad state was able to maintain a balance between the three factors that went into its construction – tribal power, distribution of booty, and predestination ideology – it was able to thwart the attempts of various enemies. The great expansion of the state and the success of its opponents to forge a new alliance, which was based on Mawali allegiance, Hashemite lineage, and a seemingly new egalitarian ideology, allowed the 'Abbasides to win their battle against the Ummayyads. Here a new relationship takes place between the three factors enumerated above. To use Gramscian terminology, the world of Islam witnesses the emergence of a new "historical bloc" that mobilizes its force against the *ancien régime*. Jābīrī discusses the influence of Persian political writings on this new historical bloc, and the caliph begins to rule in the name of God.

During the Rightly Guided caliphate, the caliph ruled in the name of the Prophet of God; where the Ummayyads relied mainly on their army, the ‘Abbasides begin to rule in the name of God.[80]

Islam was primarily a political community developing in Arabia, however, it lacked a coherent political theory. Politics evolved from a delicate balance struck by successive rulers in early Islam between tribe, booty, and ideology. As the Islamic political community became more complex, the relationship between these three factors became more complex, although they remained constant. In his writings, Jābīrī does not treat the Prophet as a saint or religious figure but primarily as a charismatic politician with a tremendous vision for the unification of Arabia. It was therefore for the first caliphs to translate this political ambition to a higher plane, which was achieved with the explosion of Islam on the world scene a few years after the death of the Prophet.

What is interesting about Jābīrī's argument is his emphasis on the development and consolidation of the religious elite in the early Islamic state.[81] The disciples of the Prophet and the Sādah (descendents of the Prophet) climbed on the bandwagon of Islamic expansion. Social mobility was made possible by the tremendous political expansion of the early Islamic state. However, the disciples of the Prophet were shortchanged when it came to control of the Islamic polity. Most could not develop into an oppositional group, since many were co-opted by the state. The dramatic expansion of Islam gave them a chance to migrate and settle in different regions of the state and enjoy the material benefits of such an expansion. Some fought with Muslim armies and died on the battlefields. Others, of course, stayed behind in Arabia, without showing any interest in the riches of this world.

The Ummayyad state in particular used the ulama in its expanding administrative structures. Did the Ummayyad state take an active role in the institutional training of the ulama in order to meet the increasing religious needs of society and place it under tighter political control? Jābīrī does not answer this question directly. However, what he proposes is interesting. He argues that the formation of the religious elite in early Muslim society was totally contingent upon their acquiescence to political authority. Jābīrī does not believe, as Gellner argues, that Muslim society had a weak state but a strong culture, which kept "a relatively open, non-hereditary and thus non-exclusive class, but without a central secretariat, general organization, formal hierarchy or any machinery for convening periodic councils."[82] It was in the interest of the state from the very beginning to organize the religious hierarchy in order to defend its expanded interests. In addition, Jābīrī's argument about the centrality of the state in the formative phase of Islam and the general dependence of the literati class or religious elite on the state made Islam a weak component of both the social and political fabric of society. Once again, Gellner argues that what is distinctive about Muslim society is that "Islam is the blueprint of a social order."[83]

Because of the support they lent the state and the great advantages they derived, the ulama were uninterested in applying the Sharī‘ah; in their view, this was not necessary.[84] The ulama did not dare raise the banner of the Sharī‘ah because in theory, at least, it contained a higher metaphysical authority than the worldly authority of the rulers. The function of the ulama did not change much with the advent of the ʻAbbaside caliphate. On the contrary, in its affluent days the ʻAbbaside caliphate built more schools and mosques, mainly to support its religious authority over both the religious elite and the masses. Therefore, any modern call to implement the Sharīʻah has no historical precedent in Islamic history. The call to apply the Sharīʻah was a direct result of Western intervention in the Muslim world. Undoubtedly, Jābīrī's thesis is intriguing and is damaging to the religious claims of modern Islamic fundamentalism. What makes his claim stronger is the fact that the Sharīʻah movement in the main has been spearheaded in the modern Muslim world by people with no formal Islamic education, but by lay Muslim intellectuals and activists impatient with the delicate balance of forces in modern Muslim societies, in which the official ulama play a conspicuous role.

In analyzing the evolution of Islamic political discourse, Jābīrī attempts to determine the ideological and discursive bases of political hegemony and dictatorship. He argues that his commitment to democracy as a concept and a process in the modern Muslim world led him to investigate these bases.[85] This is all the more justifiable in view of the fact that Islamic political theory did not stipulate a specific kind of Islamic government. Many believe that modern Muslims must choose democracy if they are to revive their political consciousness. In a sense, Jābīrī is not at all satisfied with the political unfolding of events, especially in early Islam, which is commonly used as an ideal by contemporary Muslims and Islamists. Jābīrī argues that early political Muslim thinking failed in the following areas: (1) it did not establish clear mechanisms for the appointment of the caliph, nor did it canonize the appointment of the successor; (2) it did not specify the duration of the rule of the caliph, and (3) it did not specify the functions of the caliph; in a sense, these functions were open-ended. The lack of legislation in early Islam left a major political vacuum that the Ummayyads utilized in their own way. The political language of the Qur'an is very thin in that it does not help us understand the normative discourse. The Qur'an functions as an ideal or model, point of view, and reference that lends support to such universal concepts as justice, equality, distribution of wealth, and brotherhood. Jābīrī envisions these qualities as forming the basis of the democratic society he aspires to attain.

Against this background, Jābīrī shows that the political game, as practiced in the classical phase, centered on the control of power by one sultan or family. This fact proved to be a hurdle to the growth of political modernity in the medieval Muslim world and an obstacle to real authority for the masses through the process of democracy. Therefore, Jābīrī's basic contention is that the logic of the contemporary Arab state does not much differ from that of the medieval Muslim state; the political elite still rely on a combination of different factors: the tribe, army, ideology, and religion.

The modern Islamic movement has spearheaded a campaign for the application of the Sharīʻah in the Muslim world. What is the historical and religious context of such a call? Jābīrī discusses this important issue from the point of view of the relationship between religion and politics and its evolution throughout Islamic history. He maintains that this relationship must be examined against the context of the work of the Rāshidūn caliphs; their historical and social experience must work as the model. This relationship has evolved according to the following factors:

1. On the eve of Islam, Arabs lacked any organized political structure;
2. the Prophet was aware of the theological integrity of his religious message. He was not a statesman but a messenger;
3. the Islamic message evolved into social and political projects, not merely the religious, even during the time of the Prophet, and it was natural that his death caused "institutional vacuum," since which neither the Prophet nor the Qur'an left any clear rules about how to govern or type of government should emerge. The Qur'an states only general rules;
4. the meeting taking place in Medina between the *ṣaḥābah* after the Prophet's death and their decision to elect Abū Bakr as the first caliph was purely political. Tribal mentality dominated; it was not a religious decision *per se*. What that means is the issue of the relationship between state and religion was not subject to discussion during the Prophet's life or during the time of the Rāshidūn caliphs.

Further, early Muslims were aware of the evolution of the Muslim community to an ummah, but to their mind, this was a social and spiritual ummah that shouldered the responsibility of the last religion, the perfect religion, in the view of the Qur'an. This ummah did not look at itself as establishing a new state, but as bearing the heavy responsibility of the final call. "From the point of view of the Muslims, the Muslim ummah emerged from the Islamic message and its own identity was formed before it evolved into that political system that we call today a state. The term 'state' emerged only on the eve of the victory of the 'Abbaside revolution when the 'Abbasides and their followers used the term 'this is our state' to denote the transition of authority from the Ummayyads to them."[86]

Against the above context and in the wake of the expansion of Islam and the growth of contending ideologies and political theories, Islamic political thinking developed three positions vis-à-vis the relationship between politics and religion:

1. The Shī'ī position stipulated that the question of Imāmah (political authority) was the heart of the Islamic message and that its centrality derives from the importance of spreading the Islamic message; further, the Prophet left a clear text promising the transition of political authority to 'Alī and his family.
2. The second position is best illustrated by the Kharijites, who argued that the Imāmah was not necessary as long as the common good was protected and every Muslim family applied the Sharī'ah to its own life. But if Muslims should establish such an Imāmate without bloodshed or chaos.
3. The third position is held by the majority of the Sunni ulama, who believe that the Imāmah is a must to ensure the common good and protect Muslim life and property.[87]

Jābirī therefore shows that Muslims were not unanimous on the question of politics and religion and that, historically speaking, this relationship was subject to the socio-political and military conditions of the Muslim state. However, the Sharī'ah itself did not mean politics all the time. The Sharī'ah revolved around the common social and economic good of the Muslim community. The common good of modern-day Muslims is an important question and is subject to much dispute. Some propose reviving the example of the Rāshidūn caliphs, their example to be correct, having evolved apart from political and doctrinal conflicts taking place later.[88] Many insist Muslims must rely on *ijtihād* in order to decide the best rule for them, but agree that rule must recognize that the Muslim world is in a totally unique phase and to competently address the challenges of Western modernity.

13
Towards Modern Arab Reason

"It [is] the role, indeed the obligation, of the intellectual to challenge established wisdom, to practice the fine art of negativism, and to remain aloof from corrupting power." Michael Wreszin, *A Rebel in Defense of Tradition: The Life and Politics of Dwight Macdonald* (New York: Basic Books, 1994), 381.

"Par définition, [les intellectuels] ne se contentent pas de vivre, ils veulent penser leur existence." ("By definition, [the intellectuals] are not content to just live; they want to think their existence." Translation by Abu-Rabi'.) Raymond Aron, *L'opium des intellectuels* (Paris: Gallimard, 1968), 289.

I have shown so far that Jābīrī's analysis of the problem of knowledge in Arab and Muslim history is a prelude to his own examination of the impact of colonialist intervention in the nineteenth century Arab world on modern Arab thought and philosophy. His final goal, however, is to make a link between Arab rationalism and the possibility of scientific/capitalist revolution in the Arab world. This is a difficult task indeed in view of the fact that Jābīrī, who embraces the theoretical presuppositions of modernity, has argued against the violent imposition of imperialist European modernity on the Arab world.[1] A good number of colonial and post-colonial Arab thinkers have pondered the same goal, for example, such authors as Mohammed Arkoun, Zakī Najīb Maḥmūd, Abdallah Laroui, Hichem Djaït, Malek Bennabi, as well as many others.[2]

Although the nineteenth century imperialist intrusion in many Arab countries was an earth-shaking experience, it created perfect conditions in which to create an epistemological break with all the stagnant ways of thinking. One would have hoped that Arab Reason had no choice but to incorporate some of the achievements of Western Reason. However, Jābīrī seems to think that the possibility of "epistemological impregnation" did not materialize for a number of reasons. The nineteenth century provided a ripe atmosphere for the assimilation of two incompatible systems of epistemology: the Salafī system of reference and the European.[3] Each had a different image of the world and of course had been subject to its own historical growth and evolution. Jābīrī's ideal model is not the Salafīyyah movement *per se* but Arab Rationalism as it developed in Spain and North Africa with the efforts of Ibn Rushd, Ibn Hazm, Imām *Shāṭibī* and many others. The dominant form of Salafīyyah in the Arab world on the eve of Western intervention was a far cry from this type of Arab Rationalism. The problem with this type of analysis is that Jābīrī's form of Rationalism was absent in the midst of the huge political, economic, and mental transformations of the Arab world in the nineteenth century.

How is it possible to achieve modernity (any type of modernity) with the absence of this ideal? Furthermore, the European imperialist project, which was a post-Enlightenment project focusing on rationalism, individualism, and secularism, did itself appeal to reason, while aiming to create appropriate conditions for a Western exploitation of the Arab world. European rationalism of the nineteenth century, although propagating certain humanistic values, also possessed an ugly face of exploitation and Eurocentrism.

If High Rationalism, as discussed above, was absent, it was normal for the second best alternative, the Salafīyyah of the late nineteenth century, to take a leading role in achieving modernity. In its enlightened form, the Salafīyyah was an urban social and religious movement that expressed its anger at deteriorating social and economic conditions in the Muslim world and fought very hard to achieve political and intellectual independence. The intellectual leadership of the Salafīyyah was treading water in many different worlds; it was caught between several antagonistic currents, and sometimes found itself in the embarrassing position of expressing contradictory concepts and worldviews. It realized early on, that the way out was not at all simple. To achieve its objectives, this Salafīyyah spoke the language of High Islam and not folk or popular Islam. It was intent on purifying Islam of negative influences, but without losing sight of the necessity of modernizing Muslim societies. However, Jābīrī seems to think that in spite of its failures, the Salafīyyah movement did create some enlightened individuals, such as Jamāl al-Dīn al-Afghānī and Muḥammad 'Abduh, who were passionate about the renaissance of their societies. That is why Arab thinkers of the nineteenth century envisioned renaissance while planting their feet deep into the soil of Arab thought and tradition.[4] However, the Nahḍah discourse of most Arab thinkers in the nineteenth century was ambivalent, at best. It was subject to many epistemological tensions. On the one hand, the liberal discourse of the Nahḍah invoked a liberal Europe minus colonialism and, on the other; the Muslim discourse invoked the Golden Age of Islam while turning a blind eye to several centuries of stagnation and decline.[5]

Various Arab authors – liberal, religious, nationalist, and Marxist – have been preoccupied with renaissance and, as a result, various interpretations of the conditions of renaissance have emerged. The 1967 defeat ignited the debate in the Arab world about the failure of the Nahḍah, the post-colonial nation-state, and the reasons for this failure. It is clear that Jābīrī's vision is at odds with the one proposed by Arab thinkers of the twentieth century, such as Ṭāhā Ḥussain, Salāma Mūsa, and Zakī Najīb Maḥmūd. In their various writings, these thinkers proposed that Arabs couldn't achieve renaissance unless they first adopt, without hesitation, the liberal ideas of Europe such as liberty, equality, and constitutionalism.[6] Jābīrī claims that the Eurocentric views of some Arab intellectuals impose European systems of reference on a completely different culture.

The 1967 defeat dealt a deadly blow to Arab attempts at renaissance that had begun in the previous century. On the one hand, defeat shook the foundations of historical Arab Reason to the core, and challenged modern Arab thought to produce an efficient scientific knowledge capable of competing with the triumphant Israeli and imperialist mind, which is rational in nature. Jābīrī argues that pre-1967 Arab Reason did not live up to the challenges of reality, mostly because of its flight into romanticism and idealism. Defeat, like a piercing sword, reawakened Arabs to their difficult reality.[7] That is to say that the same colonialist process encountered by the Arabs in the nineteenth century is again replayed in 1967. On the other hand, defeat has not so far led to radical change in the social, economic, and political structure of Arab societies, especially those adjacent to Israel. This is not to diminish the radical social changes taking place within the matrix of Arab societies after 1967. Undoubtedly, many new classes were created after 1967, thanks mainly to the demographic explosion in the Arab world as well as the increasing need of the industrial world for oil. However, this massive social change did not adequately translate into political changes or breakthroughs. Instead of progressing after 1967, the Arab political system retained its basic pre-defeat characteristics.

Jābīrī believes both Arab liberalism and Salafīyyah offer the most rewarding prospects for the exercise of Arab rational criticism. Neither can achieve the expected renaissance in the Arab world because of their inherent shortcomings. On the one hand, the liberal Arab mind invokes Western categories of progress that are incongruent with Arab thought and reality. On the other, the Salafī mind invokes the Golden Age of Islam without offering much historical or critical insight. In other words, the Salafī mind invokes the career of pristine Islam, that of "innocent and simple Islam" before it emerged on the world scene as a complex and synthetic religion. Islam became a mature religion, historically speaking, after the onset of the Tadwīn Age, and the Salafī mind, in Jābīrī's view, does not pay sufficient attention to this major progress in classical Islamic thought. The Salafī mind is therefore ahistorical; it lacks the proper bent of mind needed to aid modern Arab thought in its quest for growth.[8] It is ironic, notes Jābīrī, that the Arab liberal invokes Europe before it went colonial in the same way the Salafī invoke Islam before it went colonial. Both offer complex epistemological models that have developed over centuries and reacted against all sorts of forces and currents of thought. Although both worldviews were very much fashioned by historical conditions, they are invoked in an idealistic, ahistorical manner. Consequently, the "invoked" Arab and Islamic past runs parallel to the invoked European present, and this creates disharmony. In one sense, the modern Arab mind is divided against itself, is alienated from its real essence, and ambivalent about its present prospects. We must pay sufficient attention, says Jābīrī, to the extensive presence of the "Other" in our intellectual and political life:

This "other", that is to say the West, has realized its own renaissance without an intellectual, social, or economic adversary. However, an internal struggle took place between different classes and trends and past and future visions. As for us, our struggle has been double-edged: on the one hand, we were engaged in a conceptual, political, economic, and social struggle with the West as an oppressive power. As much as the West put an end to the military, intellectual, and economic renaissance of Muḥammad ʿAlī [in nineteenth century Egypt], it put an end also to the intellectual project of Tahtawi and his disciples. One normal result of this Western oppression has been a relapse to the past,

> and clutching to the past heritage as a form of identity, and a means of self defense. This explains the persistence of reactionary traditional trends and even their growth in contemporary Arab society since this is but a normal mechanism of self-defense. On the other hand, the West projects another image: that of enlightenment, liberalism, Marxism, and rationalism. If we are to weigh the two faces of the West – that of imperialism and enlightenment – separately, we will be astonished to discover that the former will outweigh the latter. The West of enlightenment and liberalism has given us dreams and hopes, while the West of imperialism has hindered our political and economic progress. This hindrance is double-edged: on the one hand, it has stopped our progress, and, on the other, it has led to a relapse to the past in Arab behavior and thought.[9]

The following conclusions are in order: first, Jābīrī forcefully contends that the Arab Nahḍah discourse, be it religious, liberal, nationalist, or Marxist, has absorbed ready-made patterns of thinking and methodological approaches. This has prevented the modern Arab mind from producing its own coherent worldview. Jābīrī calls this "the discourse of hijacked consciousness."[10] Second, because several renaissance discourses have simultaneously existed since the nineteenth century, there has been a great deal of tension between proponents of these various discourses. Third, Jābīrī argues that as long as the various Arab discourses do not liberate themselves from the oppressive and hegemonic rule of past models, Nahḍah will not be possible. Nahḍah can only take place if these models are invoked in assistance to the current process.[11]

After surveying the different models for renaissance in the modern Arab world, Jābīrī reaches a grim conclusion:

> Arab Reason has, then, failed to construct a coherent discourse around any of the basic issues forming the intellectual space of the Arab world for the past century. It has failed to erect the foundations of a renaissance ideology with which to dream, and it has not been able to lay down the foundations of a revolutionary theory that may serve as a guide for both action and change.[12]

The main problem has been the failure of the Arab intelligentsia to reconstruct "Arab Reason" in the modern period. A unified Arab discourse is needed because, Jābīrī argues, the concepts constituting the modern and contemporary Arab discourse do not reflect or convey the true meaning of Arab actuality,

> For the most part, these concepts are borrowed from either European thought – where they express an actuality that has either been realized or in the process of becoming – or medieval Arabo-Islamic thought, where they expressed a particular reality and content. In either case, these concepts are used to envision a sought-after and vague "reality"...The logical result has been a clear rupture between thought and content in the modern Arab discourse.[13]

Since thought and ideology are often intertwined, the two thought structures discussed above – the Arabo-Islamic and European – have produced two broad ideological currents in the modern Arab discourse with various sub-currents. Jābirī argues that:

> Ideological conflict in the contemporary intellectual Arab environment reflects essentially the difference between two contending systems of reference (*sulṭah marji'yyah*), two epistemological and cultural spaces, and indeed, two ideological spaces that share no common bondage: the Salafī uses the lenses of the old Arabo-Islamic ideological-epistemological field of knowledge in order to reflect on his modern problems, and the liberal (and also the Marxist) thinks according to the problematics produced by the European ideological-epistemological field of knowledge.[14]

This lack of common epistemological foundation has turned into an ideological conflict between two epistemological views and discursive views.

> What must be ascertained in the most specific way is the absence of linkage between thought and reality in contemporary Arab ideology. The theoretical and ideological differences of the Arab discourse are far from over interpreting and assessing reality as much as they are over the differences in the epistemological authorities used.[15]

Thus, the most fundamental challenge facing contemporary Arab thought is how to link the two contending systems of reference, while at the same time using adequate concepts to express the modern Arab reality.

Jābirī advocates the emancipation of contemporary Arab Reason and, on the whole, contemporary Arab thought and culture from the shackles of both the Western and Islamic traditions. What does emancipation mean? Arabs cannot easily dismiss the West because their history of the past two centuries has been highly intertwined with that of the West. However, the Arab world can only be emancipated through critical engagement with the "Other." To critically engage the West means

> to approach its culture, which is becoming universal day after day, with the spirit of critical dialogue by reading and assessing its historical depth and grasping its concepts and problematics at they relate to its evolution. In addition, we must understand the foundations of Western progress and must work to plant these foundations in our culture and thought…What we need the most is rationalism and most specifically critical rationalism (*'aqlāniyyah naqdiyyah*).[16]

On the other hand, emancipation from tradition does not mean bypassing or discarding it but rather grasping its components and facts of historical growth and allowing growth from it, without being bound by its limitations. There is a need nowadays to construct a new intellectual foundation for Arab culture, which must by necessity begin with reason. Therefore, Jābirī seeks a total epistemological rupture with the Arab Reason that was formed during the age of the stagnation and decline (*inḥiṭāṭ*), since this reason has had a negative impact on modern Arab thought. He does not delineate the nature of stagnation or its historical context. He tends to agree with the broad formulations of some Nahḍah thinkers on decline, especially those of ʻAbduh and Afghānī.[17]

Jābīrī considers the question of decline to be one of the main problematics of modern Arab thought and philosophy. He declares that no intellectual trend has been immune. He argues that Muslim thinkers, especially "revivalist" Muslim thinkers, have failed to present a viable alternative to the problem of decline.[18] He further argues that both "the Islamic tendency" and "the liberal Westernized tendency" have not succeeded in diagnosing the intellectual malaise of the Arab world: the former tendency locates the solution in the Islamic past, the Golden Age, whereas the latter locates it in the European Renaissance, the antecedent of European colonialism. In other words, the liberal tendency, according to Jābīrī, cannot seek Western philosophical answers to questions and issues arising in the context of the modern Arab world. Finally, Jābīrī concludes that the Nahḍah discourse in modern Arab thought – be it Islamic, liberal, nationalist, or Marxist – is compromising and self-contradictory, mainly because it offers ready-made solutions and theses.

ARAB INTELLECTUALS

As seen above, Jābīrī, as a post-colonial nationalist intellectual, participates in the revival of national culture, which had extended over 14 centuries of cultural, religious, philosophical, and literary achievements. Jābīrī's predilection to classical Arab-Muslim culture encourages him to examine afresh the role of the intelligentsia in medieval Arab-Muslim society. In this regard, he raises many questions about the social origins of the intelligentsia, their educational and pedagogical formation, their political and educational roles in society, their transfer or preservation of ideas, their resistance, exile, or prestige and elevation. Although the term "intelligentsia" is not an Arab product, the Arabo-Islamic culture has produced its own intellectuals who have thought within the mental framework of the Islamic heritage and whose thought cannot be understood today except in relation to their epistemological-cultural worldview and their position in society.

As seen above, Jābīrī advocates a fresh reexamination of the whole Arab "epistemological tradition" as a means of reviving modern Arab Reason. In this reexamination he raises the question of the role of Arab science and its relation to wider Arab society and culture. He asks, "How come that the tools of knowledge (concepts, methods, and vision) in medieval Arab culture did not develop enough to lead to a progressive scientific and conceptual renaissance similar to that achieved by Europe in the fifteenth century?"[19] Jābīrī answers the question by arguing that from the beginning, "Arab science" remained aloof; it did not become part of the ideological debate between the different intellectuals of Islamic culture.[20] The question now is how to place science and rationalism at the center of debate in the modern Arab world.

In the nineteenth century, when the Arab world was facing a dim future and at a crossroad facing a dangerous situation, the intellectual leadership revived its interest in Arab intellectuals of the past, their religious and intellectual preoccupations, educational backgrounds, and personal crises. The expansion of capitalism into Arab society of the nineteenth century under the aegis of imperialism blocked the independent development of this society and the free evolution of classes of intellectuals within this society. One may argue that one of the salient features of post-colonial Arab society is the persistence of the "blockage mentality," which has not allowed intellectuals a free say in political and social affairs of their nation. Therefore, any examination of the role of intellectual in classical and modern Arab society is apt to shed light on the relationship between the intelligentsia and the state.

Jābīrī agrees with Gramsci that intellectuals do not form a coherent class since they belong to diverse social and economic formations. This idea allows us to reexamine the social and economic backgrounds of the great many intellectuals the Muslim civilization produced in its heyday.

One of Jābīrī's main concerns is the relationship between intellectual authority and political power in Muslim society. Undoubtedly, the question of political authority (that is, who is to rule after the death of the Prophet?) throughout Islamic political history has been one of the most irksome questions facing the Muslim intelligentsia.[21] This question gains prominence in the post-colonial Arab world and becomes even more urgent in view of the resurgence of Islam in recent decades, the triumph of the Islamist revolution in Iran and the appearance of many movements in the Arab and Muslim world competing for political authority in the name of Islam. Lay Muslim intellectuals, who lack the traditional religious formation of the ulama class in Muslim society, have led some of these movements. Very often, the nationalist intellectual does not subscribe to the ideological rationale of either the traditional religious class in the Arab world or the Islamists. The traditional religious class, far from disappearing in the modern nation-state, has become a powerful voice in support of the *status quo*. The question of power is still at the center of debate in contemporary Arab intellectual discourse.

Jābīrī argues that the dramatic expansion of Islam in the early period created many new opportunities for the intellectuals to spread Islam and universalize Arab culture. This is true to the extent that the explosion of Islam on the world scene led to dramatic social and political change, which enabled intellectuals to play a prominent role. Jābīrī says that the intellectual in classical Muslim society is very often a member of the masses, that is, of the lower classes, and often performed manual labor in addition to fulfilling their intellectual duties. However, those intellectuals who aspired to fame or money may have lent their intellectual services to the Sultan, but rarely did they become members of the elite. In the 'Abbaside period, for example, the elite were made up of the caliph, his inner circle (that is, family members and confidants), his Arab and sometimes Persian friends, and the top officers of the state.[22] Very often, the intellectual who opted to work for the state received his salary from the state and, being urban, he depended less and less on money earned from manual labor.[23] His ideological discourse was couched in a religious language.

The above position needs some qualification. Early Muslim society began to show signs of complexity and social diversification with the Ummayyad caliphate in Damascus and its dependence on a large number of Christians and Persians in the running of its bureaucratic affairs. The moving of the caliphate seat from Arabia to Damascus and the incorporation of a large number of intelligentsia of the old regimes in the Ummayyad state created a fissure in the traditional Muslim intelligentsia of Arabia. On the whole, some of the disciples of the Prophet supported the nascent Ummayyad state in the name of the unity of the ummah, while others remained neutral, especially in relation to the bloody struggle between 'Alī and Mu'āwiyah over political authority. That neutrality, of course, helped solidify the Ummayyad state, since many of the Prophet's prominent disciples did not take an active interest in the political or social affairs. Some turned to mysticism, while others were more interested in their personal affairs.[24] Although worldly in their overall orientation, the Ummayyads used a religious philosophy (the doctrine of predestination or *jabr*) in order to legitimize their rule. Yet, a third but tiny class emerged which attacked the political and social practices of the Ummayyad elite on the premise that they were not consistent with true Islamic practices.[25]

As Muslim society moves from Ummayyad to 'Abbaside rule and with the additional expansion of the frontiers of the Muslim state, society becomes more complex. Many new elements are incorporated in the expanding arenas of the 'Abbaside state. The early 'Abbaside society reaches the age of maturity with the beginning of the Tadwīn Age. Here, society becomes more aware of the need to institutionalize different sciences in order to preserve its continuation. According to Jābirī, the 'Abbasides used the intellectual project of the Kalām philosophers, who spoke about political authority, God and His traits, to topple the Ummayyads. What this means in essence is that the intellectual horizons of the 'Abbasides was wider than that of the Ummayyads, who principally ruled in the name of the Arabs of Quraysh. All sorts of intellectual currents mushroomed in 'Abbaside society: (1) collectors of Islamic tradition; (2) grammarians of Arabic language; (3) Kalām philosophers (primarily the Mu'tazilites and the Asha'rites) and (4) state intellectuals and bureaucrats.[26]

Of the many intellectual classes in classical Muslim society, Jābirī takes the side of the Mu'tazilah. He argues that they formed the higher echelons of Muslim intelligentsia and took a pioneering role in "applying rational criteria to the religious texts, including the Ḥadīth collections."[27] However, some of these intellectuals were hired by the state to more or less improve its ideological apparatus, whose function was to spread state ideology. When not in the employ of the state, these intellectuals used the environment of freedom to ponder of issues ranging from divine justice to the meaning of life. Jābirī says that the jurists or *fuqahā'* did not occupy the same leading role in 'Abbaside society as did the Mu'tazilites. However, during the decline of the 'Abbaside caliphate, the *fuqahā'* began to play such a role. This is clear in the life of al-Mawārdī (d. 450 H.). Therefore, what defined the position of the intelligentsia to a large extent throughout Islamic history was their relationship or lack of the same to the state and their position vis-à-vis authority. The state needed them and they needed the state. There has been fluctuation in the relationship between authority and state, as was the case with the *miḥnah* of Ibn Hanbal.

On the whole, Jābīrī dismisses the notion that Arab rulers of the past, in acquiring the services of the intelligentsia, were bound by the ethic of *shūrah* or democracy. It is interesting to follow this argument against its historical, political, and religious background. Undoubtedly, the Arab state of the Ummayyads and later the 'Abbasides evolved against all sorts of factors; however, the leading political authority remained the same, a kind of scenario one still sees in the contemporary Arab world. Furthermore, the rules of Islamic Sharī'ah evolved not so much from the implementation of its rules in the medieval period as of the desire of the jurists to extrapolate on the legal theories of Islam. Therefore, the contention made by Esposito and Voll in their comments on the rule of law in medieval Islam has no historical basis:

> In the long-standing concept of "oriental despotism," there is no sense of a separation of powers or structures limiting the power of the ruler. However, such unlimited power was not available to leaders in classical Muslim societies and this situation is visible both in Islamic law of political structures and in actual historical experience…It was the consensus of those scholars, and not the commands and rules of the Caliphs, that provided the basis of formal Islamic law. No ruler was recognized as being above the law, and all rulers would be judged by that law.[28]

This assessment, Orientalist at best, does not reflect the major political transitions undergone by early Muslim society and the subjugation of the official ulama to the rules of the political elite. In addition, this statement presumes an ideal Islam that was not practiced in reality.

Jābīrī does not discuss the role of Shī'ī intelligentsia in classical Muslim society. Undoubtedly, disagreement over political authority after the death of the Prophet led to the rise of Shī'īsm, which had been the quintessential oppositional movement throughout Muslim society.[29] In the same vein, Jābīrī does not discuss the rise of the Sufī shaykhs, their social origins, educational backgrounds, differences with the traditional established ulama class, and their position towards political authority.

It is clear that modern Muslim society, diverse as it is, has religious classes of diverse religious, political, and social inclinations. In the nineteenth century, children of the religious classes were at first the main beneficiaries of colonial education. The educational base of many Arab countries began expanding after the nineteenth century until the age of the nation-state and the nationalization of education in such countries as Egypt, Morocco, Algeria, and Syria. With the dramatic expansion of educational opportunities after independence, many graduates suffer from unemployment and some choose to join the long train of the "brain-drain." The migrant Arab intellectual is a modern phenomenon of major implication for the future of the Arab world.

There are Sufīs, Ulama, Islamists, and Muslim writers and thinkers in both Sunnism and Shī'īsm who in their writings and speeches articulate different positions on political authority and what ought to be done in the post-colonial state in the Muslim world. Perhaps Jābīrī's reflections on the intelligentsia in medieval

Muslim and Arab society opens the door for a more fruitful discussion of the function and nature of the intelligentsia in contemporary Arab societies.

MODERN PREOCCUPATIONS

Recently, Jābīrī has started paying close attention to issues, which are relevant to the contemporary Arab world. These include: Arab national culture after independence; democracy and human rights in the Arab world; the question of Sharī'ah and the question of Arab identity. In Jābīrī's view, the pressures of globalization have made extensive discussion of such issues quite necessary.

In his discussion of national Arab culture after independence, Jābīrī takes his cue from Fanon's discussion of the matter. To a large extent, he expands Fanon's argument with a view to shedding light on Arab culture in the 1970s and 1980s. Jābīrī argues that despite the fact that the regional state has become a virtual reality in the contemporary Arab world, different educational and cultural policies are pursued by each state and the complex ethnic and religious structure of the Arab world. Further, he states that this world is still defined by a national Arab culture, which possesses various components such as language, religion, a common past and common future challenges.[30] Jābīrī strikes an optimistic note about the profound service culture performs in contemporary Arab society: "Arab culture has indeed functioned as the basic constituent of the identity of the Arab world, and, as a consequence, of the Arab personality and unity."[31] Culture, and not politics or economics or even education functions as a common denominator in the Arab world. Jābīrī posits Arab national culture as an autonomous variable, which does not have much to do with the economic and social conditions of the Arab world. That is to say, Arab national culture took its definite shape during the Tadwīn Age in the medieval Arab period, and in spite of the political differences in the Arab and Muslim world since then, this culture has retained its integrity or historical mission and acted as a unifying culture factor. With this system of reference in mind, Jābīrī argues that it is impossible to deal with modern Arab culture without delving into the past. As a matter of fact, Jābīrī calls upon Arab national culture to fulfill its historical mission of imparting moral, spiritual, and mental unity on the diverse Arab nations. The historical mission of national culture resides in guiding the Arab nation from a mere geographical area to a unified culture capable of facing the challenges of the future.

The most important challenge facing contemporary Arab culture is aggressive capitalist globalization and its attempts to undermine national cultures in the Third World. Jābīrī says that modernization has been inevitable. Here, he more or less airs some of the ideas of exiled Saudi novelist 'Abdul Raḥmān Munīf on the state of contemporary Arab culture. Munīf argues that culture too is an independent component in the Arab world and that lately there has been an attempt to abolish culture in order to water down Arab resistance to globalization and dependency. Munīf accuses both Israel and the United States of waging a "cultural war" against the Arab world in order to pave the way for the Arab world's full capitulation to the Zionist political and cultural project. One sign of this manipulation has been the persistent attempts of American foundations to "buy off" Arab intellectuals and makers of opinion.[32]

Is it possible to speak of one independent Arab culture at present? Also, is it possible to proceed with modernization, at an even faster pace, while safeguarding the specificity of national Arab culture? True, the technical and scientific civilization of the West fundamentally differs from all preceding civilizations in its aggressive expansion. Modern globalization tends to destroy the material foundations that give Third World societies their historical and cultural specificities.[33] That modernization and rationalization is something contemporary Arab society needs is beyond dispute. What is also needed, however, is to protect national culture from a hegemonic and aggressive "cultural invasion." Jābīrī goes on to argue that even many European countries, especially France, are weary of American cultural hegemony. The Arab world must protect itself against a double cultural invasion originating in both the United States and Europe. One of the intriguing things about the Cold War era is the fact that national Third World cultures were somewhat protected from breach by either superpower. However, the creation of a unicultural world led by the United States has opened the door wide for the penetration of American cultural ideas and practices, an ethos that preaches individualism and consumerism at the expense of traditional cultural practices.

Although influenced by Fanon's ideas, Jābīrī does not provide concrete solutions to the predicament of national culture in the contemporary Arab world. To Fanon, the solution was quite easy: create an indigenous intelligentsia capable of leading the nation out of its cultural colonization. Jābīrī finds solace in the historical mission of national Arab culture, born during the Tadwīn Age. However, in the age of the nation-state, which globalization has not yet weakened, what to do with national culture and the national intelligentsia? Jābīrī does not propose any clear options. He does not tell us, for example, whether the nationalist intelligentsia must work with the state in order to improve education and culture. In the colonial era, the native intelligentsia risked exile and imprisonment; this was a source of personal as well as social pride. Few intellectuals in the nationalist era are willing to undergo exile or imprisonment. Jābīrī's diagnosis of contemporary Arab national culture is nevertheless true. He refuses to take political or even educational divisions at face value. Jābīrī feels Arab culture can overcome these divisions and create and project a unified vision for a future Arab nation.

As seen in Chapter 3 of this work, the question of secularism has been persistent in modern Arab thought since the nineteenth century. Jābīrī argues that the call to separate religion from politics, especially in the Arab East, was important in the nineteenth century for the following reasons: first were the challenges presented by Western ideas. Second was widespread Ottoman oppression of the time, a subjugation that spared neither Muslims nor non-Muslims. Because of Ottoman abuses, many Arab thinkers (especially Christian Arabs) called for the separation of state from religion. Third was emergence of Arab nationalist movements, which identified nationalism with secularism (or state–religion separation). Jābīrī proposes that the question of separation of religion and state in the Arab world has been a regional issue, and must therefore be treated separately by each Arab state. However, any viable solution to this problem must not prevent the modern Arab world's comprehensive renaissance by taking into account the common good of the Arab and Muslim people. Jābīrī notes that the common good can be achieved only if a way is found to stop the power elite's manipulation of religion. He posits democracy as the only means of achieving the common good and, in its essence, democracy does not contradict the Islamic spirit of *shūrah* or consultation.

Jābīrī warns the Arab thinkers not to use the term *'ilmāniyyah* (secularism) if it means distancing religion from its focus on the public good. Notions of the public good are not inconsistent with the principles of cultural independence, philosophical rationalism, democracy, and religious contribution. Jābīrī feels democracy's primary function must be judging what is or is not useful for the public good. But religion must be an integral component of the system, because the very nature of the religious quest establishes clear guidelines for relationships between God and man, and man and man.

Jābīrī claims that the Islamist movements emerged in the wake of the failure of the modern Arab political elite to both apply the principles of democracy and ensuing social justice. The oppressed classes in society have long carried the banner of Islamic activism because of their marginalization by the political elite. This can be quite decisive in countries where Christians and Muslims live together, as in Lebanon, Sudan, and Egypt. What this means is the sectarian issue is not religious in nature; it is both political and economic. Jābīrī supports the right of the Islamic movement to practice politics as long as that does not, first, lead to further divisions and, second, lead to the imposition of veiling and applying the *ḥudūd* principles of the Sharī'ah. The movement must deal with the larger political and economic issues that the masses face.[34] Jābīrī supports an enlightened Salafīyyah that values both democratic and nationalist values. This is feasible; for instance the Salafīyyah, especially in the Maghreb, supported the nationalist project against French colonizers.

Major Arab intellectuals agree that democracy is the framework most Arab countries must adopt in order to meet present challenges.[35] Jābīrī agrees with this basic contention. Although he had difficulty accepting Western modernity because of inherent imperialism, Jābīrī contends that democracy in its European orientation is the solution to political authoritarianism in the Arab world. One would expect Jābīrī to couch his arguments about democracy in traditional Islamic or Arab terms, terms that derive from the political traditions of Islam. However, Jābīrī surprises his reader by arguing that democracy has not been practiced throughout Arab or Muslim history and that the tribal mentality has been dominant in Arab and Muslim political management.[36] "The Arab and Muslim civilization, which has conditioned our present reality, has been characterized by an authoritarian rule." Democracy is a uniquely European and Western phenomenon, to Jābīrī's mind.[37] The Islamic political tradition, in contrast, was premised on complete obedience to the ruler, ideas inherited from Persian civilization.[38] Jābīrī preaches a total revolution in political philosophy. He stresses the importance of democracy in the Arab world and the need to substitute individual authority with institutions and rules. Jābīrī's invocation of Western democratic tradition as a solution to the predicament of contemporary Arab political culture has been hailed by one Arab author as "the idea of a deep convergence between Islamic principles and the ethical foundations of democracy and human rights."[39] However, another Arab author accuses Jābīrī of following the footsteps of Orientalists who gave credence to Western forms of democracy at the expense of native political traditions.[40]

It seems that democracy is indeed the way out of the deteriorating Arab and Muslim predicament in view of massive social and demographic changes taking place in the Arab world in the modern era. New social forces have coalesced and aspiring new social classes flocking to cities from the countryside have challenged the old Arab aristocracy. Jābīrī presents a new social map for Arabs and posits four main categories: the first is the traditional aristocracy, both bourgeois and landed, which emerged during the colonial era. The second is the nationalist bourgeoisie, derived from the latter category, which led most of the Arab world to independence. The third social class emerged in the wake of independence and took shape in the 1950s and 1960s, forming a new middle class and competing with the old classes for power and social prestige. The formation of this class was possible after the nationalization of industry in several Arab states, such as Egypt, Syria, and Algeria. The fourth category represents the majority of the population, especially the urban and rural poor, which like the third category, expressed itself using Islamic symbols and ideas.

Undoubtedly, the massive social change taking place in almost every Arab country since independence has created new dimensions of social and political friction that had hitherto been absent. The basic authoritarian state structure has not changed in response to the massive social changes in society. As mentioned in Chapter 9 of this work, the state in the Arab world gained its strong political structure in the age of colonialism and independence, which people hoped would broaden mass participation in the political process but came to naught in most Arab states. The modern Arab state has remained all along strongly military and bureaucratic without a comparably strong political culture. To manage massive social change, authoritarianism in the post-independent Arab state, as John Waterbury argues, "was founded on broad-based corporatist coalitions that were party to 'social contracts', according to which regimes pledged welfare benefits in exchange for political discipline and quiescence."[41] The breakdown of civil society in a country like Algeria happened exactly because the Algerian state was not able to pledge "welfare benefits," especially to the emerging middle and poor classes in society. These classes then naturally turned to Islamic protest and ideas by which to express their anger at the state.

Undoubtedly, democracy would lead to far-reaching political change in the Arab world. Jābīrī does provide guidelines for the best way to make the transition from authoritarianism to democracy and whether or not this is possible despite vested military interests in modern Arab states. The new social classes in Arab society, including those who identify themselves with Islamist politics, believe that democracy is the best solution to the current Arab political system. Jābīrī, however, is correct in noting that the modernized elite/traditional class dichotomy is not a true reflection of the massive social change taking place after independence. He points out that there are four social groupings in the Arab world, each contending for political power. The weakening of the state's economic base complicated matters. The "modernized elite," which is actually made up of the top echelons of the army and the bourgeoisie, have used a European liberal discourse to distinguish themselves from the poor masses, who use Islam as an expression of protest.[42] It is therefore normal in Jābīrī's view that "the Arab 'modernized elite' suffer from the absence of an organic connection with the masses at the political, social, cultural, and even spiritual and religious levels."[43] Further, what makes democracy a difficult objective to achieve is the fact that it has not been in the interest of the so-called liberal West to support the few liberal experiments in the Arab world, most notably those in Egypt and Morocco, and help Arab countries build strong economic foundations that allow for the burgeoning of modernized countries. On the contrary, in the 1940s, the imperialist West suffocated the growth of the nationalist Arab bourgeoisie and prevented it from modernizing its society.[44]

Jābīrī advocates a deep convergence between the universal conditions of Western modernity and the needs of modern Arab societies. Democracy, as both a condition and a concept, is an expression of such a convergence. The Arab world needs to implement democracy in order to modernize.[45] This conviction, however, does not blind Jābīrī from realizing that democracy as both a modern concept and process (a) has been the product of deep changes in the intellectual, social, and economic foundations of modern Europe, or the product of a constellation of factors, and (b) the Arab and Muslim world has not known democracy in the Western sense; instead it has fallen prey to authoritarian regimes that have based their justification in religion and military power, "Arab history has never witnessed, not even once, a struggle to limit the authority of the ruler or to impose restrictions or supervision on him."[46] Jābīrī argues that authoritarianism in Arab and Muslim thought has not grown from the Sacred Text, but was the reaction of the early Muslim community to the political vacuum created after the death of the Prophet.

In its evolution, the Islamic political system has known the system of consultation, without jeopardizing in principle the authoritarian rule of the sultan or caliph. Jābīrī contends that the state in Muslim history has known no association to the person in power, while democracy is nothing but association.[47] The principle of *shūrah* was used by the Islamic political system, but this does not simply translate into the Western notion of democracy, which has different roots than the Islamic concept of *shūrah*. Therefore, democracy in a Western sense has been alien from the body politic of the Muslim world and accepting its message and meaning in the contemporary Arab world necessitates radical transformation in the mental and political space of the modern Arab world.[48] In another sense, collective political loyalties to parties and other civil organizations must replace loyalties to individuals, tribes, or sects in Arab society. A mental change must take place to limit if not totally change authoritarian rule and put an end to social and economic cleavage and division. The challenges facing the "democratic bloc" in Arab society are:

1. achieving social cohesion;
2. the transition of authority to the modern elite in Arab society;
3. building new foundations for a comprehensive Arab unity.[49]

This new historical bloc must be aware of its historical function and, above all, must take into account the post-independence changes in the Arab world, the role of imperialism and Israel in impeding the democratic process in Arab society, and the fact that internal factors in the Arab world have come up, especially since 1967, with two major elite: one is modern and revolutionary in nature and the other traditional in nature. Both are, of course, very diverse in their composition and loyalty. "The democratic bloc" in Arab society must be cognizant of this fact.

The transition to democracy in Arab society must take into account the existence of two conflicting trends or sets of elite and create political pluralism in society. Pluralism is achieved when the following pillars are established:

1. human rights and equality in citizenship and the right to compete for jobs, and so on;
2. civil institutions that make up the social, economic, and political fabric of the state;
3. authority is held by the majority without jeopardizing the rights of political or religious minorities.[50]

Jābīrī comments on the New World Order by saying that with the collapse of the Soviet system and the emergence of many democratic voices in Eastern Europe, the prospects for democracy are good for the following reasons: first, the collapse of the Soviet Union, which acted as a model for revolutionary and socialist forces in the Arab society. That model in actuality hindered the emergence of true democracy; second, the Western world, which "always acted against the popular feelings of the masses" during the Cold War will feel less enthusiastic than before about dictatorial Arab regimes. So far, this has proven to be illusory.

From there, Jābīrī moves on to discuss civil society in the Arab world. He contends that the state in the modern sense was created in the age of imperialism and that civil institutions were inherited from Europe to ensure the civil rights and privileges of the colonizer and a tiny indigenous elite. As for the rest of indigenous society, the democratic process was used to ensure the hegemony of colonizer over colonized. The new nation-state in many Arab countries, especially that nation-state that rebelled against the domination of imperialism and its political philosophy, created a highly centralized state with new civil institutions that were supported by the army. This nation-state has failed for two reasons, one internal and the other external. Internally, the nation-state was able to create genuine institutions, but largely depended on the army, tribe, centralization, and religion. Externally, neo-colonialism moved to destabilize the foundations of the nascent nation-state; this collapse was utterly clear in 1967.

THE NEW WORLD ORDER AND THE ARAB WORLD

The Cold War and the Soviet Union provided the Third World a cover, an opportunity to practice relative freedom away from the hegemony of a major superpower. The collapse of the Soviet and the military defeat of Iraq left the Arab world and as a consequence Arab culture vulnerable to American hegemony. A number of states, Cuba, Syria, and Libya, for example, stand accused of supporting terrorism. The Periphery is dependent on the Center, and the diffusion of ideas via satellites enshrined a new relationship between the Arab world and the West. The Center practices what Jābīrī calls a hegemonic "imperialist culture."[51]

How is it possible to reconstruct Arab Reason in the new age of globalization? Jābīrī notes that Europe and the United States have competed with each over the control of the Third World, which is making it that much more difficult for Arab countries to achieve cultural independence.[52] During imperialism, the main purpose of the Arab nationalist project was to ensure the independence of the Arab world, which was achieved with the independence of Algeria. 1967 was a major setback in that it did not allow Arab unity and solidarity to take deep organizational and intellectual root in society.[53] The emergence of the regional state in the Arab world, as an Arab and international political fact and as a social, economic, and psychological condition that cannot be overstepped, creates hurdles for the Arab nationalist project. The Arab world is more divided than ever. In addition to the cultural challenge and political division, the Arab world must contend with the Zionist project and its metamorphosis in the context of the New World Order and the spread of American globalization.[54]

Jābīrī supports Arabization but it is doubtful that he supports Islamization. He is for an Arabized Islam but not an Islamized Arabism. His project of Arabization is at odds with the historical and religious vision of contemporary Islamism in the Arab world. They perhaps use the same terms, but with different references in mind. The Arabization project Jābīrī envisions is closely linked to national independence and the emancipation of the contemporary Arab mind from all of its shackles or impediments, internal and external; an Arab Reason that is not disjointed by conditions of the past and demands of the present, but one true to both, one that is simultaneously authentic and contemporary. Neither projects – Islamism nor Arabism – seem to support cultural or intellectual pluralism. They search instead to build solid and unified foundations for the contemporary world.

CONCLUSIONS

Jābīrī admits, implicitly at least, to a profound crisis not just in Arab Reason, but also in Arab culture, economy, politics, and course of modernization. He communicates a deep sense of anguish, of the dream of renaissance from the ashes of defeat and the profound hope that the Muslim world can correct the crises of the past. To Jābīrī's mind, the question is not confined to the mediocre; the problems are enormous and include the level of Arab and Muslim knowledge, cultural appreciation, and meeting the challenges of modernity by reinventing a system of rationalism that is faithful to the rationalism of the most prescient of Muslim ancestors and does not demean the achievements of the "other," especially the West.

Rationalism in itself lacks meaning and profundity if it is not applied in a socio-historical domain and if it is not accompanied by an ethos of difference. Jābīrī proposes the ethos of difference as long as the current political elite in the Arab world are interested in enforcing democracy in their land. As two individual thinkers, who represent two different types of intelligentsia in the Arab world, Jābīrī and Laroui stand apart on a number of questions: (1) *turāth* and (2) state.

Jābīrī maintains his distance from the state with his criticism of its shortcomings. Laroui in contrast has drawn near the state, the very same that had banned his *L'idéologie arabe contemporaine* from distribution for 20 years. Why is this? Jābīrī frames his criticism of the state in Arab nationalist terms. He also begs the support of the masses, not just in Morocco but in the Arab world at large. Laroui does not exhibit the same urgency. He maintains his elitism vis-à-vis the masses who may not understand his message. He opts for a modernized state as long as the ruler is enlightened and who, at the same time, welcomes such elitist philosophers as Laroui.

Jābīrī concludes the following:

1. Arab thought, with the expansion of Islam, grew wildly in all sorts of directions, a fact that was the prelude to the rise of different contending intelligentsia in medieval Muslim society;
2. the intelligentsia were connected to power, and in fact their rise in Islam was a result of the early political disagreement about the caliphate;
3. with the decline of Muslim society, the position of the intellectual declined also;
4. the intellectual faced Western challenges in the nineteenth century.

14
Costantine Zurayk and the Search for Arab Nationalism

> "Costantine Zurayk [is a] consulting don to a whole generation of [Arab] nationalists." Albert Hourani, *Arabic Thought in the Liberal Age* (New York: Oxford University Press, 1970), 309.

> "Intellectual and moral excellence....like all values, personal and collective, is not inherited or given by an outside agency; it has to be won by every individual and every generation and must be constantly guarded against dispersion or contamination. It is the fruit of diligent exertion. It can only come as a result of sweat, of continued and often painful labor." Costantine Zurayk, "Abiding Truths." In *al-A'māl al-fikriyyah al-'āmmah li'l dokṭor Costantine Zurayk*, volume 4 (Beirut: Markaz Dirāsāt al-Wiḥdah al-'Arbīyyah, 1994), 49.

> "Living, as are all people today, in an age of accelerating change, and facing tremendous external and internal challenges, the Arabs will not be able to participate positively in contemporary life and to respond creatively to the mounting challenges of the times without undergoing a total transformation in which the cultural element plays an important, if not a primary, part." *Ibid.*, 101.

> "Modern Colonialism won its great victories not so much through its military and technological prowess as through its ability to create secular hierarchies incompatible with the traditional order. These hierarchies opened up new vistas for many, particularly for those exploited or concerned within the traditional order. To them the new order looked like – and here lay its psychological pull – the first step towards a more just and equal world. That was why some of the finest critical minds in Europe – and in the East – were to feel that colonialism, by introducing modern structures into the barbaric world, would open up the non-West to the modern critical-analytic spirit." Ashis Nandy, *The Intimate Enemy: Loss and Recovery of Self Under Colonialism* (New Delhi: Oxford University Press, 1998), v.

Costantine Zurayk was one of the most distinguished Arab nationalist thinkers and historians in the twentieth century Arab world in spite of the fact that he was marginalized by his native country, Syria.[1] Zurayk had been trained at the American University of Beirut, the University of Chicago, and Princeton University. Before his death in 2000, he had been active in academic, intellectual, and political work in the Arab world, beginning in 1936. A remarkably creative intellectual, he was able to construct and present a coherent theoretical project that involved a detailed discussion of four major intertwined issues in the modern Arab world: (1) the question of nationalism; (2) the question of Palestine; (3) the question of Arab renaissance, and (4) the question of futurology in the Arab world.

Although referring to himself as an "ivory tower" intellectual,[2] recent research shows that Zurayk was deeply involved along with his colleagues at the American University in Beirut, among them Amin Nabih al-Faris, in formulating the theoretical guidelines of the Arab Nationalists' Movement (Ḥarakat al-Qawmiyyīn al-'Arab) of George Ḥabash and his comrades.[3] Zurayk, however, remained committed to the ideals of Arab unity until his death and did not become a Leftist ideologue as did, for example, George Ḥabash. Arab nationalism was Zurayk's passion, in spite of the tremendous obstacles it faced in practice in the modern Arab world. A careful analysis of his reaction to the Arab defeats in both 1948 and 1967 reveals the genesis of Arab bourgeois nationalism, its current historical impasse, and the small space into which Western imperialism has pushed it for the sake of the Zionist movement and the state of Israel.

Zurayk devoted over sixty years of his intellectual life to elucidating and teaching these concepts. His intense intellectual seclusion allowed him to be fully engaged with those values and factors that make modern life both rational and meaningful. In his thought, one finds not only a lucidity of ideas, superb scientific organization, and a depth of analysis, but also a passionate telos that transcends particular emotional and mental predicaments. One must take Zurayk seriously. Indeed, he has been taken seriously by a whole generation of Arab intellectuals in both the Arab world and in exile in the West, who still refer to his ideas for guidance, wisdom, and inspiration.

To a certain extent, ideas have a force of their own, and Zurayk's ideas are no exception. One reason for their power is his implicit and explicit stinging criticism of the state of the Arab world in the twentieth century. Throughout his life, Zurayk showed rare courage in directly confronting the most formidable problems in modern Arab life and thought. In his quest toward constructing a theoretical project of Arab renaissance, he was not afraid to address the major points of weakness in contemporary Arab life, citing where leadership had gone wrong, and what Arab society must do to deal with its many and diverse problems.

Neither was Zurayk hesitant to criticize individual Arab leaders, as he did Jamāl 'Abd al-Nasser and Ṣaddām Ḥussain for their failure to implement meaningful projects of national renaissance in their countries.[4] Nor was he hesitant to critique those traditional religious tendencies, both Christian and Muslim, in the Arab world that had lost their dynamism and passion. The Arab culture of the past, a product of many peoples and civilizations, was "animated by an open mind and a tolerant spirit,"[5] he argues. However, with the progress of time and the rise of European civilization to power, Arab-Islamic civilization disintegrated. Zurayk looked to why this was the case and how best to revitalize it. To begin with, Zurayk was in favor of a secularized and totally modernized Arab world. He believes that though religion had formed the greater part of Arab consciousness in the past, especially after the birth of Islam, it should only be a small part of the private sphere of man's existence. This theme runs throughout his work.

GENEALOGY OF WRITING

Zurayk's writings belong to an influential critical, liberal, and nationalist Arab genre of writings best represented in the twentieth century by 'Alī 'Abd al-Rāziq in *Islam and the Principles of Government*, Ṭāhā Ḥussain in *The Future of Culture in Egypt*,[6] Khālid Muḥammad Khālid in *From Here We Start*,[7] and Fu'ād Zakariyya in *Reality and Myth in the Contemporary Islamic Movement*.[8] These writings elicited vehement responses from a certain class of Arab-Muslim intelligentsia who accused the authors of espousing Western philosophies of life. However, we must recognize that we can in fact trace this genre of writing to the nineteenth century Arab Nahḍah movement, which was a result of the encounter of modern European and Arab thought.[9] Many Arab thinkers have at different times raised the issue of Arab decadence and suggested various ways to enact renaissance and achieve unity.

All of these intellectuals were somewhat vulnerable because of their traditional Islamic upbringings. 'Alī 'Abd al-Rāziq fell silent after the publication of his book in 1926 and remained so until his death in 1953; Ṭāhā Ḥussain tried to appeal to the Islamic worldview by writing on Islamic themes, and Khālid Muḥammad Khālid radically changed his ideas about the secularization of the Arab world toward the end of his life. Zurayk was not as vulnerable for three main reasons: his Christian upbringing; his American education in both Lebanon and the United States, and the fact that he lived in Lebanon for most of his life.

Zurayk sought to redefine how the West was understood. He saw the West as representing both rationalism and progress. He strongly advocated the Arab world learn from the many scientific, political, cultural, and economic achievements of the West. In order to undergo renaissance, he believes the Arab world must create a new identity, that of the Western "Other." This West is not the Orientalist "Other" portrayed by Edward Said as calculating, controlling, and aggressive.[10] To Zurayk, the West is the most progressive human culture ever to exist. Even the West's negative Orientalist aspects have resulted in the renaissance of modern Arabic literature and thought.[11] In Zurayk's thought, modern civilization cannot be separated from the Western. Of course, the Westernization of the Arab people does not necessarily translate to the Arabization of the West. We know it has not. Along with the huge number of people who constitute what has commonly been called the "Third World," Arabs have yet to be considered equals by the West. Arabs occupy a unique position: though they are not the most backward people making up that entity known as the West, neither are they the most advanced people of the Third World.

Zurayk's infatuation with the West did not carry over to one main product of nineteenth century Western civilization: Zionism. Like a true Arab nationalist, Zurayk considers Zionism to be the most highly articulated form of Western aggression against the Arab world. He agues that the secrets behind the success of Zionism are its alliance with the Western power elite and its adoption of the West's scientific outlook. To Zurayk, Zionism is both the subject of anger and envy, anger because of its usurpation of Palestine and envy because of its relative sophistication. To him, the Arab world suffers from "brain-drain" (*hijrat al-admighah*), while Israel in contrast enjoys the "marshalling of brains" (*Ḥashd al-admighah*).[12] This will be discussed further within.

Zurayk's absolute belief in the rationality and correctness of the Western project of modernity is sometimes vexing. He seems to consider colonialism an accident of history rather than as a constituent of modernity. The Arab people were colonized because of their "colonializability," to use Malek Bennabi's favorite term.[13] Zurayk is unmoved by the writings of Third World Leftist intellectuals and liberation theologians on this issue.[14] He strongly believes that colonialism is and has been a function of Arab weakness.

In Zurayk's view, the Arab people's marginalization and decline was caused by a combination of ignorance, poverty, and disease, and are in fact the problems the Arab intelligentsia must shoulder. Like many others, Zurayk believes the intelligentsia is the last hope of stagnant nations and that hard times create tough-minded people. This is a somewhat hopeful viewpoint. Hard times, mixed with proper exposure to the secrets of Western progress would ensure the smooth transition of Arab society from a closed-minded state to an open one. Even with this seemingly healthy diagnosis, however, contemporary Arab society hits a snag, and the very serious problem of the "brain-drain" from which it suffers, as do most Third World countries.

THE MEANING OF NATIONALISM

In his development of a nationalist project, Zurayk sharply differs from many Islamist, Leftist, and even liberal formulations in modern Arab thought. His Christian background, Western education, and leading role as an educator in both the American University in Beirut and the University of Damascus, as well as tireless efforts to promote nationalist philosophy have put him in the forefront of modern Arab theoretical production on this question.

In his early formulation of a comprehensive philosophy of Arab nationalism, Zurayk relies heavily on key classical Islamic terms such as the *ummah*, *jihād*, *rūḥ*, *'aqīdah*, *azmah rūḥiyyah*, and so on. Zurayk's point of departure in the foundation of his philosophy is the same as that of modern and contemporary Islamists: that the Arab world lacks conceptual clarity. He maintains that there has been rampant intellectual confusion in the modern Arab world caused by the absence of a "nationalist consciousness" (*wa'y qawmī*).[15] To him, "nationalist consciousness" is a whole *Weltanschauung* that, if properly understood, could "unite our efforts, organize our spiritual powers, and envelope our souls with purity, contentment, and satisfaction."[16] Zurayk contends that for the Arab world, the "nationalist consciousness" possesses the following criteria: (1) the Arab past, its complex history and the role of both language and religion in the making of this history; and (2) the modern world. Western civilization and the Arab past together define the modern historical moment of nationalism.[17]

In bitterly criticizing the points of weakness in the soul of the Arab world, Zurayk says:

> Our true nationalist consciousness forces us to both feel and deeply ponder the factors behind the weakness of the present Arab personality and its concomitant problems. We must confront these problems in practical and honest terms.

> The Arab world suffers from pervasive ignorance, deep poverty, and a moral and mental lack of discipline whose full only God appreciates. In addition, there are nearly unsolvable spiritual, social, and economic problems. It is both unproductive and unwise, therefore, to escape these diseases and problems by resorting to empty rhetoric.[18]

In addition to being one of the direct products of the interaction between the modern Arab world and the West, Arab nationalism is also a powerfully expressed manifestation of religion, particularly Islam. In this, Zurayk differs from Arab Islamists, who deny any link between Islam and nationalism and who argue that nationalism is a European creation. Zurayk sees no contradiction between Islam and nationalism:

> True nationalism cannot in any way contradict true religion, for it is nothing in its essence but a spiritual movement which aims at resurrecting the inner forces of the nation and at realizing its intellectual and spiritual potentialities in order that the nation shall contribute its share to the culture and civilization of the world.[19]

Both Islam and nationalism are powerful spiritual movements that define the character and future direction of the Arab nation.

Being a spiritual, nationalism is the only modern movement that can unify the Arab world and place it on a par with Western civilization. Zurayk of course considers nationalism to be the most important manifestation of the modernity project after the industrial revolution, and that the true spirit of Islam and the teachings of the Qur'an, progressive as they are, do not conflict with the underlying principles of modernity. Zurayk maintains that, "In its true meaning, nationalism has been the creation of the modern age and its emerging social, economic, and political forces."[20] In the same sense, Orientalism, or the Western academic of Islam and the Muslim people, must be credited with the preservation and publication of important Arab and Muslim literature, which constitutes an essential part of modern Arab culture.[21]

As a modern philosophy, nationalism cannot take root in society without first establishing a scientific outlook. Zurayk bemoans the lack of scientific spirit in modern Arab society. He argues the Arab world suffers from "scientific poverty" (*faqr 'ilmī*) that manifests itself in poor scientific writing and the lack of a role for science in modern Arab culture. In summary, Zurayk believes the only way to modernize Arab society is through science, and scientists must stop being a silent majority.[22]

In his reflection on the Arab world on the eve of World War Two, Zurayk argues that the Arab intelligentsia suffered from "conceptual confusion" (*fawḍah fikriyyah*) for several reasons: first, conceptual confusion was a pervasive worldwide phenomenon by the end of the war; second, Arab society was making a transition from the old to the modern, which reflected its desire to move from backwardness (lacking a scientific spirit) to modernity (distinguished by science and progress); third, the lack of uniformity in Arab educational systems contributes to conceptual confusion. With this lack of uniformity, there are no consistent goals or strategies.[23] Zurayk believes the modern Arab needs to wage Jihad in order to achieve systematic thinking and intellectual freedom.[24]

In delineating the concept of "world-wide conceptual confusion," Zurayk states that he does not believe that modernity has a destructive edge. To the contrary, all the destruction that the world saw during World War One and World War Two was the result of human selfishness and innate destructiveness and was not the fault of modernity *per se*. Zurayk posits that Arabs experienced conceptual confusion because of the absence of a truly modernized intelligentsia capable of assimilating the modern tools of knowledge and giving them an indigenous meaning.

Zurayk establishes his method by first clarifying some key concepts, one of which is "culture." As a concept, culture is based on two primary foundations: first, inner proclivity to acquire knowledge, and second, a person's constant struggle to cultivate himself/herself in life.[25] Zurayk blames the Arab intelligentsia for not doing their part in acquiring culture and leading a renaissance of the Arab world. He considers the general failure of the Arab intelligentsia reflects the stagnation of the masses in the Arab world. Therefore, he argues that the modern Arab individual needs a new doctrine (*'aqīdah*) in order to be able to envision the range of issues facing his society and the prospects for its survival. That is to say, the Arab world's crisis of rationalism and new ethics does not stem from the lack of innate scientific logic but the failure of intellectual leaders to translate this logic into daily practice.[26] As can be seen so far, Zurayk uses a combination of Islamic terminology and Western solutions to reflect upon Arab society and it could progress.

Arab movements of unity in the twentieth century failed precisely because their leaders lacked a full-fledged doctrinal or philosophical vision of nationalism. In spite of waging successful battles against imperialism in the Arab world in the first half of the twentieth century, Arab leaders had no well-defined philosophy of Arab nationalism. In the age of the nation-state, few Arab leaders opted for Arab unity: most were moved either by tribal or regional concerns and paid little attention to calls for Arab unity.

THE WEST AND MODERNITY

As I have stated, to Zurayk's mind, the West is the most advanced civilization in the modern world. The entity known as the West includes all the European countries, the United States, Canada, and Japan. It is distinguished by three major factors: (1) a superb economic organization; (2) a pioneering scientific spirit, and (3) a progressive philosophical worldview. Zurayk notes that the industrial revolution, represented by the modern machine, was responsible for the creation of a sophisticated economic system that from the start aimed to exploit both natural resources and human skill in order to increase and organize productivity. The scientific spirit, combined with an analytical and philosophical mind, was the impetus for the industrialization of the West and the creation of an international economic system. It is impossible for the modern Arab world, argues Zurayk, to "catch up" with Western progress unless it adopts the Western philosophical and scientific spirit *en masse* and recognizes the principles elucidated by such Western philosophers as Plato, Aristotle, Aquinas, Descartes, Kant, Hegel, and Nietzsche.[27]

Zurayk advocates that modern Arab thought assimilates the philosophical and scientific discourse of modernity. The reason is obvious, "After four hundred years of dormancy, the Arab East began in the last century [nineteenth century] to awaken under the impact of this terrifying dynamic civilization, and to look for security, dignity, and progress in the troubled modern world."[28] Imperialism, at this stage, does not play a permanent role. Zurayk seems to advocate capitalism as the way toward development. However, he argues that a totally modernized Arab consciousness or personality is not possible without the confluence of three factors: (1) an appropriate appreciation of the Arab past; (2) a balanced consideration of the present, and (3) a strong belief in the future.

To make further sense of Zurayk's commitment to modernity, I would like to discuss the parameters of this project from the viewpoint of a number of contemporary Western scholars. What is modernity? American political philosopher Marshal Berman defines modernity as a "mode of vital existence and experience." He states:

> There is a mode of vital experience – experience of space and time, of the self and others, of life's possibilities and perils – that is shared by men and women all over the world today. I will call this body of experience "modernity." To be modern is to find ourselves in an environment that promises us adventure, power, joy, growth, transformation of ourselves and the world – and, at the same time, that threatens to destroy everything we have, everything we know, everything we are. Modern environments and experiences cut across all boundaries of geography and ethnicity, of class and nationality, of religion and ideology: in this sense, modernity can be said to unite all mankind. But it is paradoxical unity, a unity of disunity: it pours us all into a maelstrom of perpetual disintegration and renewal, of struggle and contradiction, of ambiguity and anguish.[29]

There are two "streams" of modernity, so to speak, and Zurayk does not identify the second destructive stream of modernity until his work in the 1970s. In his pre-1967 work, he still believed in the unlimited possibilities of Western modernity and advocated the adoption of Western civilization. In contrast, in his post-1967 writings, he demonstrates more awareness of the dangers of modernity and of the West's and Israel's use of its weapons of modernity to kill the project of Arab renaissance.

However, the point made above did not weaken Zurayk's conviction that for the contemporary Arab world to succeed, it must acquire a new theory of knowledge that is based on reason and not revelation. Knowledge is and must be undertaken secularly. In the words of American philosopher Richard Rorty the secularization of knowledge is at the basis of the triumph of the Western project of modernity and the pushing away of the religious epistemological problematic:

> The secularization of moral thought, which was the dominating concern of European intellectuals in the seventeenth and eighteenth centuries, was not

> then viewed as a search for a new metaphysical foundation to take the place of theistic metaphysics. Kant, however, managed to transform the old notion of philosophy of metaphysics as the "queen of sciences" because of its concern with what was most universal and least material into the notion of "most basic" discipline – a foundational discipline. Philosophy became "primary," no longer in the sense of "highest" but in the sense of "underlying."[30]

Zurayk advocated a new Arab philosophical perspective, a new *Weltanschauung* that rejects traditional epistemologies and worldviews.

In his work, Zurayk presents an overall picture of the development of modern Western civilization; he is deeply aware of the historical and cultural changes it has engendered. Following in the footsteps of historians of modernity, he identifies five underlying moments or phases in its history:

1. Renaissance;
2. Reformation;
3. industrialization or scientific culture;
4. Enlightenment;
5. post-Enlightenment.

In his pre-1967 writings, he seems to identify only the positive features or products of modernity, such as scientific philosophy, secularization, rationalization, individualism, humanism, and progress. As stated within, he focuses more on the destructive stream or edge of modernity, its consumerism, excessive waste, and nihilism in post-1967 writings.

Although he becomes critical of Western neo-colonialism, particularly as it appears in the case of Israel and the Western attack against Iraq, he still proposed to translate the concept of modernity into the theory of modernization. This view, in simple terms, seeks to transform the Third World into the image of the technologically triumphant West. According to Habermas, for example,

> "Modernization" was introduced as a technical term only in the 1950s. It is the mark of the theoretical approach that takes up Weber's problem but elaborates it with the tools of social-scientific functionalism. The concept of modernization refers to a bundle of processes that are cumulative and mutually reinforcing: to the formation of capital and the mobilization of resources; to the development of forces of production and the increase in the productivity of labor; to the establishment of centralized political power and the formation of national identities; to the proliferation of rights of political participation, of urban forms of life, and of formal schooling; to the secularization of values and norms; and so on.[31]

These forms of modernity have not proliferated in the post-1967 Arab world. Is it because the Arab world has failed to adopt the Western scientific spirit or is it because the nationalist interests of the West preclude the development of real democratic structures in Arab society?

PALESTINE IN ZURAYK'S THOUGHT

Besides the project of modernity, the Palestine question has a central place in Zurayk's nationalist philosophy. Zurayk's analysis of the West takes a critical turn: he no longer sees the West as only modernity, but also as an imperialist system with designs for the Arab world, and in particular, Palestine. This revelation constitutes the bases of two of his major books on the Palestinian problem: *The Meaning of Disaster* and *Revisiting the Meaning of Disaster*, respectively.[32]

Zurayk uses the term "*nakbah*" (disaster) when he references the Arab defeat with the nascent Israeli state in 1948. Zurayk argues that the main reason for the 1948 Arab defeat was: the inability of the Arab world and Arab culture to absorb the main principles of modernity. Zionist nationalism, a byproduct of the West, has in contrast subscribed to its basic principles of economic organization, political influence, and future planning and has flourished.[33]

This disaster has had radical implications for the nature of Arab society and its future in world affairs. The most important implication of this disaster is not the physical flight of Palestinian refugees to various Arab countries, but the confusion in the minds and souls of the intellectual leaders in Arab society. Zurayk contends a new brand of Arab intellectual thinking is needed to express the depth of the crisis and find appropriate solutions. He thus advocates the creation of a new kind of Arab intelligentsia, one guided by the critical spirit of scientific philosophy.

Zurayk also believes that it is only tragedy that can create serious intellectuals guided by a critical philosophic scientific spirit and a passion for engagement with real problems.[34] It is impossible, he argues, to become an intellectual without first being revolutionary at heart. Conscious intellectuals must identify the real causes behind disasters and predicaments, and then pave the way for solutions. However, Arab culture seems to have few genuine intellectuals who are open-minded, engaged, and dynamic enough to contribute to the real progress of their societies.

For engaged thought to take root in society, it must come as the result of the concerted effort of the state and its citizens to promote real intellectual activity. The Arab world lacks this. Engaged thought, to be successful, must fulfill the following tasks: first, it must alert people to impending danger. The Arab masses and a large number of Arab intellectuals have been unable to fathom the depth of Zionism, comprehend the challenges it poses to Arab society, and fully understand its nature and international connections; thus, they have been unsuccessful in this first task. Second, engaged thought must bring about Arab military preparedness to face the Zionist challenge. Third, engaged thought should work toward achieving unity among Arab states. Fourth, engaged thought should permit the masses to contribute toward the struggle. Fifth, engaged thought should encourage Arabs to be pragmatic. Pragmatism might mean compromise in order to safeguard Arab interests.[35]

What is needed is an overall spiritual and scientific revolution, a revolution in the Arab personality and mind, so that it can deal with the dangers of Zionism and world imperialism. Here, Zurayk agrees with the main theses of a good number of Arab intellectuals who wrote on the meaning of disaster, most notably Ṣādiq Jalāl al-'Azm, Amīn al-Ḥāfiẓ, and Ṣalāḥ al-Dīn al-Munajjid.[36] Zurayk maintains that

> the main reason behind the Zionists' victory, a victory denied only by the blind and self-conceited, does not lie in the superiority of one nation over another, but in the distinction of one system over another. This victory is mainly due to the fact that the roots of Zionism are highly entrenched in modern Western life, whereas we are still alien to and rejecting of this way of life. Moreover, they live in the present and plan for the future, while Arabs still cherish the dreams of the past and intoxicate ourselves with its bygone glory.[37]

Zionists, although not constituting a nation in the modern sense, have been united by "both religion and suffering,"[38] which, combined with their superior sense of organization and indefatigable will, has enabled them to establish their state to the detriment of Palestinians. For the Arab world to overcome the challenges of Israel and Zionism, a true "Arab science of *nakbah*" or disaster must take root.[39]

To be truly nationalist, the Arab world must adopt a radical revolutionary strategy to achieve the following:

1. industrialization of the Arab world in order to diminish, if not destroy, the power of both tribalism and feudalism and increase material productivity;
2. observe a strict and absolute separation between state and religion or religious organization. In its true sense, nationalism opposes theocratic rule;
3. give primacy to reason by focusing on the study of positive sciences;
4. appropriate the best spiritual and mental values of world civilizations.[40]

In *Revisiting the Meaning of Disaster*, first published in 1967, Zurayk elaborates on his earlier theses on the predicament of the Arab world, the absence of scientific spirit, and the Israeli victory in 1967. He reiterates the same position that the real salvation of the Arab world lies in adopting, without question or hesitation, the scientific and philosophical spirit of modernity, and that the real Zionist victory in both 1948 and 1968 lies in the concept of civilization, "Our Arab society and Israeli society belong to two different civilizations or to two different stages of civilization's development."[41] Zurayk believes this is the truth of the matter, in spite of the historical fact that the Western world militarily, morally, and financially supported the state of Israel, and that Zionism has fully adopted the West's civilizational mission.[42] That is to say that before any military victory against Israel is possible, the Arab world must assimilate the cultural achievements of the West and learn to think in scientific ways. Modernity cannot be imposed from outside, it must come from the Arab people themselves.

In evaluating the nature and progress of Arab nationalism between 1948 and 1967, Zurayk argues that only scientific, social, and economic reasons explain the failure of Arab nationalism to accomplish its goals of political and national independence. The nation-state, after independence, has not generated enough social and economic change to warrant the creation of a strong national bourgeoisie capable of carrying the banner of secularism and progress in backward societies. Nationalism, far from being born in primitive societies or in the old and medieval age, was born in Europe in the wake of the following colossal revolutions that transformed the *ancien régime* radically and opened up vistas for the new order. These colossal revolutions were European renaissance, religious reform, geographical discoveries, commercial expansion, scientific renaissance, and rationalism preached by the Enlightenment age. Out of these revolutions, the middle class was born. This class was able to effect a major transition in the economic, social, and cultural relations in society. Furthermore, it carried the burden of nationalism, political democracy, and capitalist productivity and other components of modern life before the appearance of communism, whose explicit aim was to unseat this class from power. Zurayk believes that it was the European middle class that was primarily responsible for national unity and emancipation from the yoke of feudalism.

For the Arab world to achieve a similar renaissance, the middle class must shoulder the responsibility of effecting a major transition to modernity. "What I would like to stress is that the main reason for the failure of [Arab] nationalism is that…society was not cognizant of its conditions and premises – premises that are closely linked to rationalism, science, and technology."[43] Concomitant with nationalism is unity in the Arab world. In an article published in 1990, Zurayk argues that the main condition for the success of Arab unity is the democratization of the Arab world. Arab political systems, for a number of external and internal reasons, have failed to unify, spread democracy, promote social justice, and put an end to the forces of irrationalism.[44]

Out of its concerns for reform of social and economic conditions, the nationalist leadership in several Arab states, especially in Egypt, Syria, and Iraq, adopted the socialist (read Marxist) philosophy of class conflict and class alliances without much thinking. Class conflict and the division of society into "progressives" and "reactionaries" superceded the nationalist spirit in Arab society.[45] Thus, Arab nationalists failed to engineer a true nationalist alliance including all segments of society.

Once again, Zurayk comes back to the question of modernity. The main reason for the failure of the Arab nationalist project and the success of Zionism lies in the degree to which both projects have taken up modernity, technology, and Westernization. Zurayk considers all other factors, including Western support for Israel and Zionism as secondary. In this he echoes some of the major premises of Lebanese thinker Ḥassan Ṣa'b, who also argues that the reason behind the defeat of the Arab world with Israel has been the Arab failure to appropriate Western technology and science.[46]

Zurayk proposes a dual strategy of development to be adopted by both the political elite and the masses in Arab society to overcome the failure of the Arab world to assimilate and subscribe to the main principles of modernity. The state can ensure productivity only if proper scientific planning is followed. The Arab world is fighting a multifaceted battle, against Zionism and also against backwardness and underdevelopment.[47] The Arab state must establish centers for research and guarantee freedom for this critical and scientific research. Zurayk believes it is only by following these strategies that the Arab "brain-drain" can be contained and Arab reason used to its full potential. As for the Arab people, Zurayk says that rationalism must take the place of ignorance, work must take the place of laziness, organization must replace disorganization, and belt-tightening must take the place of irresponsible spending.[48]

Zurayk considers Zionism a fundamental threat, not just to the Palestinian people, but also to the larger Arab world. According to Steppat, Zurayk regards Zionism "as an expansionist, imperialist movement which does not only want to destroy the Arab people of Palestine, but threatens also the resources and the existence of the other Arab countries."[49] It is incumbent, then, on the Arab world to study Zionism and the state of Israel, which to date remains undone. Zurayk says:

> The matter is not solely confined to the scarcity of research and studies [on Israel] but also to the scarcity of [Arab] students and researchers in this field. It would be hard to find trustworthy Arab researchers on the subject of Palestine. They are too widely dispersed all over the place and are hard-pressed to devote their energy to this question. It is common knowledge that any field of specialization or serious [intellectual] product requires complete commitment…We are hard-pressed to find Arab scholars fluent in Hebrew and who can convey to us what is being published and produced in Israel.[50]

Zurayk also discusses the nature of imperialism and the dangers it has posed to the Arab world in the modern period. His solution is for the Arab world to attain political independence and begin to reunite. Zurayk, however, does not consider imperialism as posing an intellectual, cultural, or scientific danger to the modern Arab world, as Islamists do. To him, imperialism is a military and political fact only. We Arabs can appropriate its scientific, technological, and rational aspects. In other words, the spirit of the "Other" must be ours. Here, Zurayk's views as representative of the nationalist trend, do not much differ from Ṭāhā Ḥussain's or that of an other liberal in the Arab world.

NATIONALISM AND HUMANISM

What are the ways to reconstruct the modern Arab nation? Zurayk provides these answers in *What Future?*[51] Here, Zurayk takes up the whole question of culture and the role of the Arab intelligentsia in creating a responsible and scientific-minded culture. Although written in 1957, that is, at the height of the success of Nasserism as a nationalist project, the author rejects the notion that the Arab nation was in good stead. He believed appropriating the main principles of modernity remains the only viable road to the renaissance and development of the Arab world. This is a big responsibility for the Arab intelligentsia, but as we have seen in other chapters, Zurayk is not the first to assign responsibility for change to the intellectuals.

With Arab society in the throes of a major crisis, the intelligentsia must have clear cognizance of its function and role. The first function of the intellectual is to have a solid understanding of the reasons for the crisis in the first place, to recognize Arab society's pain and be ready to identify and meet the challenges. The second important job, and this is related to the first, is to define key issues and problems facing society and individuals. This comprehensive vision is only one step in understanding the nature of the crisis in contemporary Arab society.

Zurayk posits the following to explain this crisis:

1. The universality of the crisis. Arab minds cannot ponder their problems in isolation from the world at large. The world has in many ways become a small village.
2. The roots of this crisis lie in man's failure to keep his human destructiveness in check. In other words, although modernity provided new ways in which man could control nature, man did not take full advantage of these opportunities to develop his personality.
3. The Arab nation, in addition to the above problems, experiences a unique dilemma, which is the underdevelopment and suspension of its reason.

Zurayk argues that it is far from possible to ward off the modern Western attack on the Arab world with a primitive economic system, a sectarian and feudal social system, or mentality that belongs to the medieval period. It is not at all possible to erect a nation-state on these foundations.

As a matter of fact, the modern state created in the modern period was established on opposite foundations.

> To solve our crisis and protect our entities from both external control and internal collapse, our first duty must be to engage in the world in which we live. We must be receptive to the methods and ways developed by Western reason in exploiting nature, organizing its economic relationships, and developing its scientific resources...We must speak the language of the West.[52]

Therefore, the modern Arab intellectual must tackle the issues of organization, rationalism, and colonialism.

At this stage, Zurayk tries to distinguish between two Wests or two streams of the West: one positive and emancipatory in nature and the other exploitative and destructive. Arabs must emulate Western scientific spirit and discipline. But in doing so, they must be wary of the Western propensity toward exploiting other nations. He calls these inclinations "desires" (*gharā'iz*) that lead to economic and social exploitation of the working classes.[53] The West is full of progressive and humanitarian forces that work for the interests of the world at large, and Zurayk believes it is these the Arab world should use.

Zurayk contends that modernity is the only means of salvation for the modern Arab world. In order to be part of modernity, the Arab world must adopt a new philosophy, one that gives man new meaning. The culture of modernity represents a qualitative leap from that of the medieval period, both Islamic and Christian.[54] Modernity is this world-oriented, whereas the medieval cultures of both Islam and Christianity are other world-oriented. Modernity posits a progressive human and technological project that relegates religion to a secondary status.[55] The modern view credits man's reason and ability to do good and achieve happiness. In both Christianity and Islam, however, reason is a means of aiding revelation, which promises happiness in the afterlife. The Renaissance in the West freed man of such a view.

Zurayk advocates historical consciousness of modernity and not reliance on antiquated modes of thought. He delineates four major historical patterns or positions in the modern Arab world: (1) traditionalist, (2) nationalist, (3) Marxist, and (4) scientific.

The traditionalist Islamic pattern of history draws its legitimacy and strength from the past centuries. Zurayk argues that this pattern is incompatible with the true spirit of modern history for several reasons. First, proponents of this trend advocate an ummatic version of history whose goal is to revive the Muslim ummah, Arab and non-Arab, rather than an Arab nation. Second, this philosophy explains human history through the prism of the divine, and it consequently obliterates any connection between human historical events and their surrounding social and economic factors and circumstances. Third, the historical method of this philosophy is based more on imitation and acceptance than on criticism and reason. Besides being medieval in nature, the rationalism of this discourse has lost its dynamism and vision in the modern world. In other words, it has failed to ally itself with modernity.

The nationalist philosophy of history distinguishes the modern world. It seeks to revive a nationalist consciousness and history amenable to the demands of the modern age. Further, in the case of Arab nationalism, the nationalist consciousness seeks to create a secular Arab society that nurtures conceptual positions and practical policies that are congruent with or viable in a modern world. Zurayk argues that,

> nationalism possesses a specific meaning and particular characteristics without which it loses its essence. The most essential characteristic is the secular underpinnings of the nationalist movement and the state to be established. Secularism in this sense does not mean the denial of spirituality or God's existence. On the contrary, nationalism allies itself with whatever deepens belief in the human soul and drives away evil...Nationalism purports to create society on secular foundations while it fights against sectarian fanaticism and any distinction whatsoever between citizens on the basis of religion and doctrine.[56]

The Marxist philosophy of history, utopian as it may be, has attracted a good number of Third World intellectuals because of its critique of imperialism. However, this philosophy is not compatible with the spirit of nationalism either, since it considers nationalism to be a byproduct of the bourgeois state. The state will disappear with the disappearance of the bourgeoisie and the triumph of socialism.[57] The fourth philosophy of history is based on a scientific appraisal of various things. It is the way to the future.

Zurayk argues that new social and political forces are emerging in Arab society. These forces have expressed their anger at the United States and its unabashed support for Israel. In this context, a true secular nationalist force must emerge:

> The movement of Arab nationalism has carried the banner of political independence [from imperialism] and unity [amongst the Arab states]. However

> history teaches us that it is not possible for any nationalist movement to succeed in a society unless that society attained a certain stage of development and harmony. In brief, one may say that nationalism in the West did not emerge in a society dominated by the medieval age...Nationalism and theocracy are incompatible. The first requirement of a healthy nationalism is a secularized state. Secularism is the true foundation of any viable nationalism, including Arab nationalism. Moreover nationalism is at odds with feudalism, a system that confines the resources of a society in a few hands that exercise political, social, and economic control. Finally, to be viable, nationalism requires the following: economic growth, to be based on the machine and the efforts of the middle class; social progress to ensue from the spread of knowledge and science, liberating the people from disease and want, and from regional, sectarian, and tribal tendencies.[58]

In his posthumously published *In the Battle of Civilization*,[59] Zurayk, invoking the authority of leading post-Renaissance Western intellectuals, considers the extent of the modern Western debate on the meaning and growth of civilization or civilizations. His main objective is to draw essential lessons from Western discussion on the subject and inject them into contemporary Arab thought. Reading between the lines, Zurayk expresses frustration with the dearth of Arab intelligentsia in this major field and urges them, once and again, to look to modernity for answers.

Zurayk returns his focus to the role that the Arab intelligentsia must play in these critical times, especially when the Arab masses are anxious and waiting for fundamental change in their societies. The role of the intellectual, the "ivory tower" intellectual, becomes more critical than ever. The intellectual, argues Zurayk, must seclude himself from society to theoretically reflect on its underlying radical changes, needs and future expectations. The task of the intellectual must be to grasp the underlying essential concepts, summarize the historical, political, and social factors that give rise to current events, to deeply reflect on these concepts and weigh them in light of benefit to the larger society. A creative intellectual is born in the battle for the civilizational uplifting of his society and nation.[60]

How can contemporary Arabs emancipate themselves from the shackles of backwardness unless they absorb the essential elements of modern Western civilization? It is true, says Zurayk, that before the triumph of monotheism, there emerged several disparate human civilizations that progressed slowly for lack of interaction and communication with other civilizations. The monotheistic traditions produced a far more unified vision of the objective of civilization than preceding religions. Regardless of the theological and historical differences between Judaism, Christianity, and Islam, they also came up with a mature *Weltanschauung* that organized the relationship between man and God and man and man. Monotheism proposed "divine unity" (*tawḥīd* in Islamic theology) as the main criterion distinguishing the religious civilization from others.

Zurayk says that the concept of "the unicity of civilization" as advanced by monotheism was adopted by post-Renaissance Western civilization in its development of a more mature meaning of human civilization. Instead of being based on theological unity, modern civilization is based on human unity. The Enlightenment advocated collective human reason as a substitute for "theological" or "primitive reason."[61]

Arguing on behalf of the concept of progress as envisaged and actually applied by modern Western civilization, Zurayk says that progress was only possible when Western civilization, the most advanced human civilization to date, envisioned an underlying human unity and emancipated collective reason. Reason and only reason is the criterion of human unity and progress. Any other factor that does not fall under this cognitive umbrella is a mental charade. In other words, revelation as divinely inspired cannot stand the test of critical and scientific reason that Zurayk and the European Enlightenment philosophers advocate.

The unification of collective reason does not deny the multiplicity of human cultures and civilizations. Each is distinguished by a primary symbol or *Weltanschauung*. However, multiplicity does undermine one of the most important discoveries of the human mind in the past several centuries: the underlying unity of human civilization and the primary role of human reason in achieving this unity.

Modern Western civilization has elevated human reason to the highest degree possible, unleashed its power to discover nature's secrets, and develop means and methods to secure as many material benefits as possible for the happiness of mankind. By so elevating human reason, Western civilization has logically elevated man and emphasized this concrete world over the imaginary afterworld. It is a humanistic civilization, by definition. The maturity and seriousness of any civilization depends on the human factor in society.[62]

It is a simple truism that a reason-based human civilization is universal in nature; it cannot exclude any human being on the basis of ethnicity, gender, or religious background. What this means in effect is that human civilization as developed by the West argues for a much more tolerant and open identity than religious models in their many historical forms. Historical religious identity, of any religion, has not emancipated itself from the constraints of both theological worldview and historical conditions. To the contrary, the principal values of modern civilization "express the most authentic human needs and proclivities and address the human side of man."[63]

In his quest for a viable human and Arab culture, Zurayk proposes that the *raison d'être* of any mature civilization is the byproduct of the interaction of the following factors: societal-human, technological-nature, and individual-human.[64] Modern Western civilization progressed only after it encouraged the human mind to interact with nature and society so that it resulted in full control over the forces of nature and full productivity of the social and economic forces in society. In this sense, Western civilization, says Zurayk, differs sharply from preceding civilizations, namely Hinduism, Christianity, and Islam, in that these civilizations focused solely on individual reform while ignoring the multiplicity of factors that give rise to a dynamic civilization.

In the course of its development over the past several centuries, Western civilization amassed and assimilated the scientific and cultural achievements of other civilizations. This civilization has two springs or two sides: the Western and democratic world, and the communist-socialist world.[65] Zurayk argues that in spite of economic and political divides between these two springs of Western civilization,

> they are, civilizationally speaking, two streams of the same fountain and two sides of the same civilization expressing some real contradictions within this civilization. In addition, there is the Third World that had been, until a short while ago, secluded from this civilization, in spite of the fact that some of its people had produced civilizations that played a major role in history.[66]

What lessons can the Arab world draw from the preceding discussion? The Arab world quite understandably faces severe challenges to its existence and collective identity as an Arab society. The first of these challenges is how to come to grips with the essential reasons for its backwardness and lack of scientific and social progress. The following conditions define the "problem of backwardness" (*mushkilat al-takhalluf*) in the contemporary Arab world: (1) mental stagnation and apathy, and (2) the absence of scientific and technological development. As stated before, the Arab world has failed to digest the essential lessons of modernism. Zurayk says:

> Inarguably, this fundamental disease, the disease of backwardness, is the source from which other diseases and plights have ensued. If we had not been suffering from this disease, we wouldn't have succumbed, in the first place, to imperialism, nor poverty and ignorance would have infiltrated our midst, nor we would have suffered a plight in Palestine or other places, nor our plans for unity and cooperation would have faltered.[67]

The second major challenge facing the Arab people is self-honesty and self-criticism. Here, one must agree with Zurayk that to curtail self-criticism in an age of crisis is akin to sacrificing the intellectual and emotional energies of a whole nation. Self-criticism is complemented by a third factor, which is a passionate popular commitment to the proliferation of civilizational goals and methods. This can be done only if a deep belief in reason and a passionate attachment to truth are manifested in society at large. Nothing will place Arabs on equal footing with advanced nations except a mental attitude characterized by curiosity and an orientation toward the future. Arab reason must engage itself in the sacred task of transforming Arab society from a closed system to an open one: "One major reason for the retreat and ultimate decline of civilizations and people is self-enclosure; nascent nations and prospering civilizations possess enough inner strength and self-confidence to open their doors and windows to both light and air."[68]

By facing these challenges, the Arab nation can resurrect itself in the modern world, develop its natural and human resources, and promote social justice. Zurayk argues that it is appaling that the Arab world has not taken advantage of its natural and human resources. Too much land goes uncultivated: rampant consumerism is the norm among the elite in society, who pay no attention to productivity. What exacerbates this state of affairs is the fact that the "brain-drain" has taken its toll on Arab society:

> It is indeed unfortunate that not a small part of the human skills we train and nurture find their way to other countries, in spite of the heavy price we have paid

> and our urgent need to them. A number of our youth, spending, as it were, a good portion of their lives preparing and training for specialization in foreign countries, either prefer not to return or, if they return, they find no fulfillment, appreciation, and encouragement. Ultimately, some find their way overseas and, in either case, their countries become deprived of their hard-won abilities.[69]

What is needed to improve the *status quo* is a real revolution, an authentic mental transformation and commitment from every citizen.

It is only by understanding and applying the main principles of civilization that the Arab people can survive the challenges of the modern world. Indeed, Arabs face two major battles: the battle for survival and that of construction. The goal of the first is to protect Arabs from foreign colonialism and the goal of the second is to construct a unified Arab nation.[70]

POST-1967 CONCERNS

As discussed within, the 1967 Arab defeat with Israel had a major impact on Zurayk's thought. In addition, two more significant events in Arab political life after 1967 shape his writings in this period: the 1982 Israeli invasion of Lebanon that ended in the expulsion of the Palestine Liberation Organization from Lebanon and its dispersal throughout the Arab world, and the defeat of Iraq in the second Gulf War after its occupation of Kuwait and the intervention of the United States and the West against the Iraqi army. These events were, in a sense, proportionate to the 1967 Arab defeat in Zurayk's mind. They highlight continuing deficiencies in Arab cultural and intellectual life, especially as they relate to establishing specialized research centers in all aspects of science, both physical and social, and in the study of futurology. Zurayk advocates the establishment of a specialized Arab center in American studies whose goal would be to prepare detailed studies and give advice regarding American influence on two major Arab issues: Palestine and petroleum.[71]

What has distinguished the West since the Industrial Revolution is its scientific and futurist spirits. Its classical theological philosophy failed to produce a critical futuristic spirit because it rejected the secular, did not understand the human role in history, and blindly believed in revelation at the expense of reason.[72]

Zurayk is a firm believer in human reason and its unlimited potential. However, he is aware of the enormous difficulties associated with the project of modernity worldwide, especially with respect to the limits of growth.[73] He argues that five major challenges face the whole world and in particular, the Third World:

1. population explosion;
2. scarcity of natural resources;
3. environmental pollution;
4. increased urbanization and the decline of the countryside;
5. an increased crime rate, especially in urban areas.[74]

In addition to the above factors, the Third World, including the Arab world, has in recent decades suffered the loss of democratic space because of the centralization of power in few hands. This offers multiple challenges to the Arab world, especially the challenge of backwardness:

> Besides our Arab identity, our social reality is characterized by another factor, that is, we are a backward world. As a matter of fact, this is the most dominant feature of our contemporary life and the principal source from which other problems have emerged: our sluggishness in achieving Arab unity and establishing efficient social, economic, and political systems that meet the demands of both the present and the future; our failure to overcome Zionism and secure our rights; and our retardation in raising the level of our people and in shouldering the cultural and social burdens inherited from the periods of stagnation and disintegration.[75]

Zurayk does not understand backwardness only as economic underdevelopment, but as an absence of a collective policy in society to marshal human forces toward the achievements of societal progress at all levels. One of the least understood sides of underdevelopment is the marginalization of the talents of the young and the educated, some of whom cannot get a job because they lack the necessary connections to the centers of power in society. Hence, the most fundamental problem of the Third and Arab worlds: the "brain-drain" and the emigration of its professionals.

To ensure the proper development of society and achieve change, the following conditions must be fulfilled:

1. national policy must be geared toward research and distinguished by dedication and determination. It must also have at its disposal the financial resources to underwrite this;
2. human resources must develop;
3. research institutions and committees must be established;
4. there must be cooperation and coordination in matters of scientific research within the Arab world.[76]

All of these conditions will lead to success if the Arab world produces a new identity, one that is truly Arab, or that is not determined by narrow familial, tribal, and regional factors. Also, the Arab world must reject the negatives associated with growth in the West, especially consumerism and waste. Zurayk aptly says,

> Living…in an age of accelerating change and facing tremendous external and internal challenges, the Arabs will not be able to participate positively in contemporary life or to respond creatively to the mounting challenges of the times without undergoing a total transformation in which the cultural element plays an important, if not primary, part. This need became evident to a number of Arab analysts who attempted to examine the failures of the Arabs in their resistance, military or otherwise, to Zionism and Israel. The deep-lying factors that have so far determined the course of this struggle and produced unfortunate

> results have not been political, military, or economic, local or international, but basically cultural in the widest sense of the term. To overcome these factors, nothing less than a cultural transformation is necessary.[77]

One must not underestimate the impact of the international arena on the Arab world and the position the Arab world holds in both economic and international affairs. Zurayk once again raises two points in this regard. First is the Zionist threat as a neo-colonial entity, which differs from classical colonialism in that it seeks to transplant a whole nation and build an aggressive modern state that aims to dominate the larger part of the Arab world. The second point is that the West has developed enough technological capacity to think of practicing neo-colonialism itself. In order to maintain high standards of living for its people, the West finds itself in the role of neo-colonialism, especially as it relates to sources of oil in the Gulf.[78]

Zurayk is convinced that in spite of the tremendous scientific and cultural achievements made by the Arab world after 1967, three huge impediments still exist: (1) population explosion; (2) scarcity of water resources; and (3) the autocratic nature of Arab political elite. The latter factor is perhaps one of the most perplexing of the three, mainly because the Arab world, it seems, was not affected by the spirit of democratization that swept Eastern Europe after the collapse of the Soviet Union. Arab political culture is still very often dominated by a one-man rule and this, in principle, explains Iraq's political plunder a result of its occupation of Kuwait in the summer of 1990.

In Zurayk's view, Ṣaddām Ḥussain, lacking a democratic political system and a group of specialized advisors in American and world affairs, underestimated the huge political and economic transformations in the world in the wake of the decline of socialism, and turned a blind eye to the political consequences of the Iraqi invasion within the Arab world. The West, supporting Iraq in its war against Iran, was in fact unhappy with Iraq's interest in developing nuclear weapons. This has resulted into a fierce United States media campaign against Iraq after the end of the Iran–Iraq war.[79]

CONCLUSIONS

Zurayk's thought is centered in the critical question raised by Nahḍah pioneers in the nineteenth century Arab world, "What are the roots of Arab decadence and what is to be done to achieve renaissance?" Zurayk's unequivocal answer throughout his life was that for the Arab world to achieve true renaissance and compete with other modern nations, the fruits of Western science and civilization must be appropriated *en masse* by intellectuals and masses alike. Zurayk did not see any innate Arab resistance to progress; he ascribed the lack of progress to historical, social, and scientific factors. Both regimes and intellectuals were responsible for this state of affairs.

Zurayk remained committed to a liberal, Arab nationalist project with the aim of establishing an Arab democratic system to enable the modern Arab world to open to the intellectual and scientific achievements of the West. Although not dismissing the religious spirit in shaping the modern life of the Arab nation, he firmly believed that individual freedoms and human rights were at the heart of the modern Arab renaissance.

In spite of his criticism of the West and its continued support to the state of Israel, Zurayk did not share Islamists' perspective that Westernization was the true culprit of division in the modern Arab world. Whereas Islamists advocated an almost total disengagement with Westernization and called for the appropriation of "authentic" sources of knowledge and practice, Zurayk advocated a total break with the past. Although in his initial writings, he used key Islamic terms to describe his Arab project of nationalist renaissance and did not see any real contradiction between Islam and Arabism, Zurayk advocated a future-oriented scientific method; Westernized, and progressive.

Arab unification cannot be achieved by a simple military coup or class warfare. Modern Arabs must be convinced to radically change their perception of the world and ultimately themselves in order to survive the tumultuous changes of the present. Zurayk believes secularism lies at the center of modern Arab renaissance. He does not buy Islamists' arguments that secularism is a Western design to drive a wedge between the Arab world and its heritage. On the contrary, he sees secular nationalism as the only road to salvation for the modern Arab world.[80]

Although not opposed to Islam in principle, Zurayk does not believe that it should function as a source of political authority in the Arab world. Islam is based on fixed revelation, whereas nationalism is based on science and historical change. Religion should not take the place of state and vice versa.[81] Islam possesses a unique ethical spirit that should move the Arab world toward national renaissance and not theocracy. A theocratic state is not the answer, since it cannot guarantee legal equality among all citizens. A national secular state supported by a strong constitution and representing the aspirations of various strata in society should be at the heart of the Arab quest for renaissance.

Unlike Marxists, Zurayk did not think that regenerating the Arab nation was contingent upon class conflict. Arabism was more about the inculcation of scientific modern ideas and less about class conflict. Therefore, Zurayk spoke less about military coups and more about internal scientific or intellectual change in the Arab mind. However, what Zurayk shared with Arab Marxists was his desire to establish a secular Arab system that limited religion to the domain of individual practice and minimized its institutionalization in society.

Zurayk maintains that Zionism's victory over the Arab world was mainly due to the lack of scientific spirit in the Arab world and less to alliances with Western powers. In order to succeed, he says, the Arab world must embrace Western scientific outlook. Zurayk died before a true project of nationalism could materialize. It is hard to tell whether he had any personal contact with nationalist Arab leaders such as Nasser, Qaddāfī, and Asad. However, it is clear that Zurayk's primary concern was intellectual and not political life, especially after the 1950s. In the final analysis, Zurayk thought that the absence of a true nationalist system in the Arab world was due to the fact that no fundamental differences existed between "progressive" and "reactionary" regimes. Both lacked a true vision of unity, failed to build institutions to achieve unity, overlooked economic or cultural integration, and were in one or another tied in their destiny to internal disunity and external dependence.[82] However, what Zurayk considered most paralyzing to the Arab quest for unity was the fact that the Arab world was wracked with tribal, sectarian, religious, and ethnic solidarities that prevented *de facto* the rise of a comprehensive nationalist solidarity.[83]

15
Mahdī ʻĀmil and the Unfinished Project of Arab Marxist Philosophy

"If two intellectuals got into an argument in Paris, their dispute could turn into an armed encounter here. Because Beirut had to be in solidarity and up-to-date with everything new, with every old thing that renewed itself, and with each new movement or theory." Mahmoud Darwish, *Memory for Forgetfulness: August, Beirut, 1982*, trans. Ibrahim Muhawi (Berkeley: University of California Press, 1995), 53.

"Political economy came into being as a natural result of the expansion of trade, and with its appearance elementary, unscientific huckstering was replaced by *a developed system of licensed fraud*, an entire science of enrichment." Karl Marx, "Outlines of a Critique of Political Economy," in Karl Marx and Frederick Engels, *Collected Works*, volume 3 (New York: International Publishers, 1975), 418.

"The modern world economic system, which came into existence in the sixteenth century, is seen instead as reproducing the duality inherent in the traditional structure of an empire with a *core* and *peripheral* regions which subsidize the core by means of their tribute." Gershon Shafir, *Land, Labor and the Origins of the Israeli-Palestinian Conflict, 1882–1914* (Berkeley: University of California Press, 1996), 25.

"Bourgeois thought judges social phenomena consciously or unconsciously, naively or subtly, consistently from the standpoint of the individual. No path leads from the individual to totality; there is at best a road leading to aspects of particular area, mere fragments for the most part, 'facts' bare of any context, or to abstract, special laws." Georg Lukacs, *History and Class Consciousness: Studies in Marxist Dialectics*, trans. Rodney Livingstone (Cambridge: MIT Press, 1971), 28.

"Philosophy is, in the last instance, class struggle in the field of theory." Louis Althusser, *Essays on Ideology* (London: Verso, 1984), 67.

Contemporary Lebanese Marxist thought offers some illuminating insights into the attempts of various distinguished Arab thinkers to achieve rapprochement between the grand Islamic philosophical and intellectual tradition and some aspects of Western Marxist theory. It is from this corner of the Arab world that the most serious reinterpretation of Islamic philosophical tradition from a Marxist perspective has been accomplished. I think that the world of scholarship is indebted to the historical, philosophical, and critical reconstruction of classical Islamic thought by Ḥussain Muruwwa in his masterpiece, *Materialist Tendencies in Arabo-Islamic Philosophy*,[1] accomplished several years before his tragic assassination in Beirut in 1986.[2] Muruwwa was the first Arab Marxist thinker to attempt, on a grandiose scale, to apply the complex corpus of Marxist-Leninist philosophy and criticism to the study of the growth and progress of classical Islamic religious thought, especially in its philosophical and mystical dimensions. In spite of the questions that one may raise about Muruwwa's Marxist-Leninist approach, his discussion of the material is both coherent and refreshing. Mahdī 'Āmil, less well-known than Muruwwa but perhaps as theoretically rigorous in his study of Marxism and the Arab world, was also assassinated, three months after Muruwwa was assassinated in Beirut in 1987. These two thinkers, more than any other Arab Marxist philosopher in the modern period, attempted to forge a synthesis between their Marxist philosophical orientations and their field of study: Arabic literature and Islamic philosophy, in the case of Muruwwa, and socio-economic history and the Lebanese civil war in the case of 'Āmil. A delineation of the central ideas of such an approach in contemporary Arab thought is long overdue.

It is a cliché now to speak of the historical impasse of world communism and fashionable to attack Marxist thought as having failed, or as a system of thought that has outlived its utility. The vulnerability of Marxism worldwide has been made possible, to a certain extent, by the economic and political collapse of the Soviet system and the much-applauded historical triumph of Western capitalism over socialism. The collapse of the Soviet system has had profound repercussions on the Arab world since the early 1990s, only some of which are visible. 'Āmil did not live long enough to witness these dramatic changes in the world system and how they have impacted Arab Marxism. However, he planted the seeds of an advanced methodological approach guided by Marxist philosophy that has the potential of shedding much light on the economic and political nature of imperialism, the post-1967 evolution of the Arab bourgeoisie, and its current condition. What are the main outlines of 'Āmil's theory?

'Āmil's central preoccupation in his philosophical *oeuvre* is devising a workable method with which to interpret the modern economic and social history of the Arab world and its underlying ideological and religious structures, with a special focus on Lebanon. As a Marxist, he is heavily indebted to the works of Karl Marx, of course, but via the interpretations of French philosopher Louis Althusser.[3] While a student in France in the 1960s, 'Āmil came under the influence of French Marxist thought in its Althusserian articulation. In addition to Althusser, 'Āmil is indebted to the theoretical formulations of Nicos Poulantzas[4] and Yves Lacoste. Althusser is known only to a small segment of Arab Leftist intellectuals. As far as I know, only a few of his books have been translated into Arabic.[5] 'Āmil was of the opinion that Althusser's Marxist structural philosophy could provide Arab researchers with an arsenal of concepts with which to analyze the structure and social relations of the contemporary Arab world.[6] Although 'Āmil's work suffers from theoretical loopholes, he succeeded in uncovering the reasons behind economic and social domination in the Arab world. Thus he escapes one of the harshest criticisms leveled to Althusser's work, namely that, "His thought is the child of economic determinism ravished by theoreticist idealism."[7] Nevertheless, Althusser has had a major impact on thinkers in other countries, most notably in England.[8] 'Āmil's Arab Marxist project is not without its faults. However, to my mind, it is the most brilliant Arab synthesis of Marxist thought to date, especially in its Althusserian version.

Here we are confronted with critical Marxist Arab thought that is committed to the conceptual formulations of the Lebanese Communist Party, especially after the 1967 Arab defeat, the military expansion of Israel, the move made by the PLO to Beirut after the civil war in Jordan in 1970, the death of Nasser in that same year, and the collapse of the state system in Lebanon in the mid 1970s. Our analysis of Mahdī 'Āmil's main ideas, therefore, is apt to shed some significant light on the development of the ideology of Lebanese communism, especially after 1967, and on the above interrelated questions. It is important to note that the whole area has experienced much change since 1967. Communism in particular entered its historical impasse with the dismantling of the Soviet Union at the end of the 1980s.[9]

'Āmil was born in South Lebanon in 1936 of Shī'ī background. In 1968, he obtained a Ph.D. in philosophy from France, where he came under the influence of the French students' movement and Althusserian Marxism. In 1960, he joined the Lebanese Communist Party and in 1987 was elected a member of the Central Committee of the party.[10]

THEORETICAL UNDERPINNINGS

'Āmil's Arab Marxism was prompted by the limitations of official and traditional Arab scholarship in critically dealing with the social and economic history of the modern Arab world. 'Āmil's is a project of historical materialism that seeks to interpret Arab history and culture afresh in light of Althusserian Marxism and pave the way to transcending bourgeois thought and structure in Arab societies. Although deeply steeped in Marxist thought in general and Althusserian philosophy in particular, 'Āmil is weary of superimposing ready-made patterns of thought on the Arab world. In order to transcend dominant patterns of thought, he espouses a radical method of analysis that gives credence only to the historical mission of the Arab proletariat to liberate itself and the rest of the Arab world from those patterns of social and economic dependence created by the Arab bourgeoisie in the early part of the nineteenth century.

'Āmil argues that the Arab bourgeoisie worked hard to achieve hegemony over society. In this, he agrees with the Marxist dictum that, "Morality, religion, metaphysics, and all the rest of ideology as well as the forms of consciousness corresponding to these,...no longer retain the semblance of independence."[11] 'Āmil discusses the cultural and intellectual aspects of the Arab world in relation to the dominant mode of production and class in power, namely the bourgeoisie. His starting point is the Marxist dictum that, "The production relations [the relations of production] of every society form a whole."[12] Social relations, ensuing from the relations of production, make visible the historical forces at play in a society. Because of its privileged position in society, the bourgeoisie articulates its mission in progressive terms in order to reproduce its class domination. It seeks the services of an intelligentsia who articulates its worldview in return for financial benefits. Instead of using the Gramscian term "organic intellectual," 'Āmil uses "the mercenary intellectuals," who perform service to the dominant class in power. The only true radical class, to 'Āmil's mind, is the proletariat that faces the challenging task of understanding and opposing the designs of the bourgeoisie.

'Āmil's theoretical *oeuvre* wrestles with the following questions: first, a correct theory to interpret the reasons behind underdevelopment in the Arab world; second, an appreciation of modern Arab social and economic history; third, an examination of the structure of domination in the modern Arab world and the ideological apparatus needed to maintain this structure; and, fourth, a study of the particular sectarian case of Lebanon as an exercise in failed politics and engineered social and economic structure.[13] According to Egyptian philosopher Maḥmūd Amīn al-'Ālim, 'Āmil surprisingly discovered that the absence of Arab Marxist theory of underdevelopment is itself a sign of underdevelopment *par excellence*.[14] 'Āmil diligently applied himself hard to postulate a Marxist explanation of backwardness in the Arab world.

Although not an historian in the strict sense, 'Āmil discusses the economic and social history of the modern Arab world at great length, or the post-capitalist Arab world, to be more precise. He analyzes the history of the Arab economic structure with the view toward highlighting the changes within it since the introduction of capitalism in the Arab world in the nineteenth century. In this regard, 'Āmil employs such terms as "means of production," "historical materialism," "class," "ideology," and "domination" in order to understand the above historical process. 'Āmil is more interested in examining the post-capitalist history of the Arab world than the pre-capitalist, with the specific aim of coming to grips with the class structure of contemporary Arab societies. Against the above, the concept of the state takes major precedence in his "historical-materialist" analysis. He concludes that, besides the strong link in Lebanon between the state and the bourgeoisie, there is a parallel link between the state and sectarianism that does not exist in Arab society. Therefore, one must understand the evolution of these two links in the general relationship between the Lebanese and the world capitalist economies, which had been evolving since the nineteenth century. The Arab world, he argues, has fallen under the domination of imperialism by being part of "the network of the international capitalist system."[15] This materialist base or reality has in turn determined many other political, social, ideological, and educational relationships in the modern Arab world.

The general starting point of his philosophical project is the impact of modern Western capitalism on Third World societies and the resulting "structural differentiations" between Western capitalism and Third World economies. Since the advent of capitalism in the Third World, roughly around the end of the eighteenth century,[16] two different economic structures were created: one capitalist and the other dependent. Although they seem to be mutually exclusive, on the surface, they are in fact horizontally related. To his mind, the bistructural reality of the Third World since the triumph of capitalism is the most crucial factor in helping us understand the deep socio-economic, political, and cultural alterations in the Arab world since the early part of the nineteenth century. 'Āmil highlights the economic at the expense of the political. Although in the final analysis, he considers them to be inseparable from each other, he seems to think that the political aspect of society is totally determined by the economic one.

Like many contemporary Arab thinkers, 'Āmil takes the Napoleonic invasion of Egypt (1798–1801) as his starting date in dealing with what he calls the intrusion of capitalist imperialism on the Arab East. However, unlike a good number of Arab thinkers, he does not look at "thought" as an accumulation of ideas over years but as a response to their changing material base throughout history.

Unlike Arab Islamists and nationalists, 'Āmil's initial conceptual launching pad, so to speak, is deeply rooted in modern social and economic history and not in metaphysics or doctrine. He theorizes that to be properly understood, one must examine both religious and nationalist identities against the dominant mode of production in society and its ideological cover. However, it strikes one that 'Āmil, just like many classical Marxist thinkers, does not pay sufficient attention to the question of nationalism in the Middle East. This seems to be one of the weakest points in his theoretical edifice. One might well be with total agreement with Tom Nairn's intelligent observation that "The theory of nationalism represents Marxism's great historical failure."[17] 'Āmil seems to have downplayed the issue of nationalism. It is rarely mentioned as a central component in his theoretical formulation. This is surprising in view of the fact that after 1967 the Lebanese communist party began to look seriously at the nationalist question.[18]

'Āmil argues that both individual and collective identities develop primarily from their position vis-à-vis the dominant mode of production in society. Religious identity does not exist as such except in relation to the economic factor. In the modern Arab world, one must examine identities, religious or otherwise, against the background of the "structural differentiations" created by capitalism since the nineteenth century. Thought reflects the actual economic and social connections in reality.

What are the parameters of Mahdī 'Āmil's theory?[19] In an article published in 1968,[20] 'Āmil argues that it is both historically and philosophically necessary to produce an Arab Marxist version of underdevelopment.[21] To do so does not necessarily translate to a mechanical imposition of the universal Marxist theory of capitalism or the Leninist theory of "imperialism as the final stage of capitalism" on specific modern Arab social and economic conditions. 'Āmil argues that the Arab Left finds itself impaired in its political struggle against imperialism and its corollaries in the Arab world because it has thus far failed to produce an Arab Marxist theory of underdevelopment. Theoretical struggle is the twin brother of political struggle. Marxist thought contains an elaborate and critical social theory that can offer a comprehensive theory of underdevelopment. What that means in effect is that it is important to analyze the modern historical factors behind underdevelopment using Marxist tools of analysis.[22]

In his seminal work *Muqadimmāt nadhariyya*, 'Āmil studies the social and economic changes in the Arab world in general and in Lebanon in particular in order to come to grips with the roots of Arab crisis. With this goal in mind, he presents the following main theses: first, the pre-colonial Arab world was not feudal in nature. Different modes of production coexisted in the same region. Internal capitalist formations were beginning to take shape in the region before the imperialist intrusion in the nineteenth century. Here ʻĀmil agrees with a well-known thesis developed in English by Peter Gran in *Islamic Roots of Capitalism*[23] and in Arabic by Aḥmad Ṣādiq Saʻd.[24] Second, the imperialist intrusion into the Arab world created a structural dependency between the advanced imperialism and the economy of the Arab world. These two structures engendered by the intrusion of European capitalism signified an advanced imperialist capitalist structure and a colonized and dependent indigenous economic structure.[25] It is within the relationship of these two structures that one must examine the creation of classes in the post-imperialist Arab world. If one agrees with Wallerstein's definition that "Capitalism is first and foremost a historical social system,"[26] which aims at the commodification of the "social processes in all spheres of economic life,"[27] then it is easy to argue that the *most advanced* form of capitalism deploys more efficient methods than the *less advanced* in maximizing profit. One of these methods is the creation of a servant capitalist class in the Periphery. Third, in comparison to the development of the bourgeoisie in the capitalist Center from the womb of the middle classes in Europe, the main Arab bourgeoisie came from the feudal classes and secured its position by allying itself with imperialism.[28] Fourth, the petty bourgeoisie, and not the colonial bourgeoisie, finds itself in a leading position of political struggle against imperialism, especially after independence. This political struggle does not necessarily translate as economic struggle against dependency on world capitalism. Samir Amin, for example, calls this a "state of dependent state capitalism."[29] Fifth, the nationalist struggle in the Arab world to achieve unity and fight both imperialism and Zionism can best be represented by the Communist Party and its allies. The Communist Party (that is, the Lebanese Communist Party) is the true representative of the working class. No party can become truly revolutionary unless guided by a revolutionary theory. Here ʻĀmil dismisses the role of the petty Arab bourgeoisie in achieving true unity. He does not distinguish between "progressive" and "reactionary" Arab petty bourgeoisie.[30]

ʻĀmil says that the starting point of understanding underdevelopment is to analyze the "colonial relationship," that is, the relationship between the advanced capitalist West and the less advanced Arab East, as a relationship between two different modes of production or two different infrastructures: one advanced and powerful and the other less advanced and weak. This "structural differentiation" is the most important cause of the emergence and growth of underdevelopment in the Arab world since the nineteenth century.

ʻĀmil argues that Marxism can provide only some signposts in understanding the nature of imperialism and underdevelopment in the Third World, since Marx does not treat the "colonial question" as an independent problem, but as a secondary one:

> Marx's principal theoretical burden has been to determine the scientific laws behind the historical development of capitalism. Therefore, he does not treat colonialism except in relation to his clarification of some aspects of the development of capitalism. In other words, Marx treats colonialism in relation to capitalism. We must, therefore, treat this issue from a different perspective, that of colonialism and not of capitalism.[31]

In other words, 'Āmil perceives the need for a radical Marxist Arab theory that may determine the "scientific laws behind the development of the socio-economic infrastructure of the colonized world" and not that of the capitalist world, which Marx and Lenin thoroughly analyzed in their various writings. 'Āmil begins where Marx and Lenin end.

Marx and Lenin believed the specter of capitalism had touched every corner in the world and modernized many hitherto underdeveloped countries. To 'Āmil's mind, the worldwide expansion of capitalism was a logical outcome of its huge potential, productive possibilities, and historical movement. Capitalism has been the only modern universal force to produce the material foundation of a unified human history.[32] In other words, capitalism was able to unleash the process of globalization in the wake of its expansion overseas. The contemporary Arab world came under the influence of world capitalism since the first phase of its historical expansion. In other words, the expansion of capitalism was not so much a result of the transformation of capitalism as much as a realization of its colonial potential. Capitalist expansion, resulting as it did from its structural differentiation, was initially the reflection of a successful modernization project at home.

TOWARD AN ARAB THEORY OF UNDERDEVELOPMENT

It is doubtful that 'Āmil was familiar with the works of the systems' theorists such as Immanuel Wallerstein,[33] Giovanni Arrighi,[34] and Andre Gunder Frank.[35] However, he follows similar lines of arguments in his discussion of the nature of underdevelopment in the Arab world. He argues that,

> The deep changes produced by capitalism in the structural foundation of the colonized countries cannot, in any way, be considered as the realization of the potential and movement of these countries. Far from it, this change has grossly impeded the movement of indigenous development in these countries, leading to a fundamental alteration of their historical line of development and the skewing of their horizon of becoming. History thus emerges anew in these countries, in a newly created spatial-time structure.[36]

The dominant mode of production in the pre-capitalist world is innately fragile; it cannot contribute in any meaningful way to the development of the colonized society. Capitalist imperialism is the new historical mover and shaker. In this analysis, 'Āmil agrees with the main thesis of Charles Bettelheim about India that the underdeveloped economy is characterized by disequilibrium.[37]

We thus face two different modes of production: one capitalist and the other pre-capitalist and colonized, which belong to the historical horizon of capitalism. The relationship between the imperialist-capitalist mode of production and the colonial, defined by the supremacy of the former, does necessarily produce a specific social structure in the colonial moment, that is the subjugation of the ruling economic elite to the needs of the capitalist market. In other words, the indigenous bourgeoisie developed in the Third World under the impact of Western capitalism. That is, the development of capitalism within the colonized world has produced a new indigenous class, the bourgeoisie, which is an integral part of the capitalist-colonized situation. Colonized countries cannot develop their different means of production and political systems without these historically-defined relationships between Western capitalism and the indigenous countries. That is to say that the national bourgeoisie develops within this colonial condition imposed by Western capitalism.

What we have seen so far is a creative reproduction of Althusser's concept of "structural causality" in the Arab and Lebanese contexts.[38] 'Āmil argues along the same lines as Marx that the productive forces of capitalism are constantly expanding, since conservatism is a mark of the pre-capitalist modes of production.[39] Constant expansion is the secret behind capitalism's stable instability and worldwide expansion, which can sometimes mean resort to military force. Structural causality produces some drastic changes in colonized countries to the extent that their economic structures and social relations are radically transformed. Capitalism has been an extremely significant phenomenon in the modern Third World.

'Āmil argues that in the process of colonizing the economic structures of the Third World, Western capitalism, which is industrial in nature, barred the colonized bourgeoisie from developing industrially. The indigenous bourgeoisie was only allowed to deal with commerce, which is why the Lebanese bourgeoisies, for example, have been commerce-oriented since the beginning.[40] The colonial bourgeoisie is made up of two sub-classes: merchants and landlords who benefit from selling their agricultural products to capitalist markets. Because of this state of affairs, 'Āmil argues that the bourgeoisie, although a leading political movement of independence from the West in the middle part of the twentieth century, has never been, historically speaking, in a position to rebel against the "structural relationship" imposed by the West on the colonized world in the nineteenth century. Even after independence, this bourgeoisie fails to emancipate itself from this "economic subjugation" to the capitalist market. The relationship between the two structures has been that of differentiation and not identification.

Capitalism engendered far-reaching economic and social changes in the countries it colonized. To keep its grip on the colonies, argues 'Āmil, it promoted a two-tier economic structure: one highly modernized and assimilated by the Metropole and the other backward and isolated from the Metropole.[41] The sectors of Arab petroleum, Algerian wine, and Cuban sugar industries all fall in the former category. 'Āmil is indebted to the theoretical formulations of French Marxist geographer Yves Lacoste, who wrote extensively on underdevelopment in North Africa:

> Les guerres coloniales furent donc des conflits entre sociétés différemment structurées. Celle dont les forces étaint les mieux articulées, donc les plus cumulatives, l'emporta. Cependant, et ceci est essentiel, l'action des Européens fut d'autant plus facile qu'ils trouverent dans les sociétés indigènes des appuis décisifs chez tous ceux qui allaient profiter de la déstruction des structures traditionelles pour renforcer leurs pouvoirs.[42]
>
> ("The colonial wars were therefore conflicts between differently structured societies. That society whose forces were the best deployed, therefore, was the

most cumulative one. However, and this is essential, the action of the Europeans was that much more easy that they found in the indigenous societies decisive support from all those who would profit from the destruction of traditional structures to reinforce their power." Translation by Abu-Rabi')

'Āmil disagrees with Lacoste's thesis on the subject of colonialism, that the Arab world was colonized because of its proclivity toward colonization or colonialiability.[43] Lacoste argues that internal reasons led to the colonization of the Third World by the West. Many Third World countries witnessed some brilliant civilizations, such as those in India, China, and the Muslim world, but most of these countries that belong to these civilizations suffer from underdevelopment. Why? Lacoste ascribes underdevelopment to purely internal historical reasons,

> Une première cause historique de l'absence d'implantations des "semences" du développment dans les pays qui sont aujourd'hui sous-développés paraît donc bien être l'absence préable de structures sociales propices à cette implantation: absence d'une classe d'entrepreneurs, d'une bourgeoisie, persistance de structures sociales paralysantes (sujétion des masses paysannes, absence de mobilité sociale, monopolisation des profits commerciaux par des artistocraties compradors, etc). Ces formes d'organisation sociale étaient d'origine plus ou moins ancienne: vieilles de plusieurs siècles en Asie, elles étaient relativement récentes en Amerique latine, par example, ou s'était implanté un mélange complèxe de structures féodales, ésclavagistes et de mercantilisme colonial.[44]
>
> ("A primary historic cause of the absence of the planting of the seeds of development in those countries which remain underdeveloped today appears to be the absence of social structures conducive to this implantation: absence of a class of entrepreneurs, of a bourgeoisie, persistence of paralyzing social structures (subjection of the peasant masses and absence of social mobility, monopolization of commerical profit by comprador aristocracies, and so on). These forms of social organization were, more or less, of ancient origin: of several centuries in Asia, these social organizations were relatively recent in Latin America, for example, where there was implanted a complex mixture of feudal and slave-oriented structures and of colonial mercantilism." Translation by Abu-Rabi')

'Āmil argues that colonization, a historical necessity in the logic of capitalism, took place under complex historical circumstances when the structure of capitalist development came into contact with a less developed economic structure that was in the process of evolving to a higher economic level. Imperialist capitalism stifled the growth and development of the economic structure of the Third World. Therefore, underdevelopment is the direct product of imperialism.

'Āmil pushes his discussion further in the domain of political conflict in the colonized world. He argues that one distinguishing factor was the coexistence of several modes of production in the colonized world under the political and economic influence of the West. Imperialism was able to ward off movement of political independence for a while because the different classes in the colonized world waged disparate political struggles that were not connected to a unified meaning of nationhood: "It is possible to argue that each class of exploited classes such as the workers, the peasants and segments of the small bourgeoisie, waged an independent political struggle with no real coordination as though each belonged to an independent social structure."[45] As history progressed and the colonized social structure became more complex, the exploited classes began to be aware of the structural subjugation of their societies and classes to imperialism. The emergence of a unified political vision, or what 'Āmil calls "the unity of class struggle" was responsible for the emergence of united political activity against the West.

'Āmil has admirably succeeded, with the guidance of Althusser's theoretical insights, in presenting a convincing picture of the social and economic transformations in the Third World following capitalist-imperialist intrusions, especially in the nineteenth century. As previously discussed, 'Āmil's sole preoccupation is the socio-economic transformation of the Arab world (both the Middle East and North Africa) and not that of South Asia or Southeast Asia. Therefore, 'Āmil only indirectly refers to India or China or only to the extent that either Marx or Lenin refers to each of these countries. One does not find him drawing on Third World Marxist sources or analyses.

'Āmil argues that a great number of Arab historians ascribe to the Napoleonic invasion of Egypt and Syria in 1798 some "genie impact" without understanding the impact of the socio-economic conditions of the post-Napoleon Middle East on the production of intellectual and political movements. To 'Āmil's mind, the most important consequence of this invasion was the imposition of the more advanced Western capitalist structure on the less advanced indigenous structure, throughout the entire area. The nineteenth century witnessed this historical marriage, this forced marriage, between Western capitalism and the Arab world. One major consequence of this marriage was the birth of what he calls the colonial or national bourgeoisie. However, there are fundamental economic and ideological differences between the European bourgeoisie, such as the French bourgeoisie, and the colonial bourgeoisie. The former made its distinct mark on French history by (1) obliterating the material bases of feudalism, and (2) developing the structural bases of capitalism and aspiring to an international role. It is only against this background that one can understand the revolutionary character of the Western bourgeoisie, as an anti-feudal class. Against this context, one may understand the real nature of the French bourgeois revolution and its slogans of liberty, fraternity and equality. The Arab colonial bourgeoisie, an extension of the feudal system in the pre-capitalist Arab world, was the product of the advanced economic structure of world capitalism. As a result, it cannot assume as revolutionary a form as the French Revolution.[46]

On the whole, 'Āmil is unimpressed by the economic career of the Arab bourgeoisie since the nineteenth century. He refers to it as an "undifferentiated monolith" and essentially assumes that it has not achieved any form of independence since its creation by imperialism.[47] 'Āmil assumes that the bourgeoisie became an ally of colonialism and its interests did not collide much with those of the European powers. This position does not accurately reflect the struggle of the national bourgeoisie to keep its autonomy vis-à-vis European powers in such countries as Iraq and Egypt in the first half of the twentieth century.[48]

Here, ʻĀmil stands in opposition to the whole project of modernity preached by Costantine Zurayk. Zurayk believes that for the Arab world to progress, it must give birth to an Arab bourgeoisie that will lead to the roads of modernity and progress. To ʻĀmil's mind, this is both historically and structurally impossible because the colonial bourgeoisie, emerging in the wake of the expansion of capitalism, is dependent by nature. It is only the communist part, that can wage such a revolution of renaissance in the Arab world.

ʻĀmil's theorization on the question of imperialism and underdevelopment leaves out the whole question of ideas and ideologies and the impact they might have on the movement of history. He returns to this complex question in his leading theoretical work, *Muqaddimāt nadhariyya*, initially written in 1971. Here, ʻĀmil's starting point is the "conceptual structure" (*al-bunyah al-fikriyyah*) of thought. Such terms as "intellectual history," "individual ideas," and ideas in general cannot be fathomed except in relation to the "conceptual structure" of thought. ʻĀmil maintains that the "conceptual structure" of a philosophy or worldview has always been conditioned by the "economic structure" of society. This conditioning or interaction, which has been a product of historical necessity, has given birth to numerous ideologies corresponding to the complex relationship between the conceptual and economic.[49] In his own way, ʻĀmil tries to elaborate on the famous premise of Marx that:

> The production of ideas, of conceptions, of consciousness, is at first directly interwoven with the material activity and the material intercourse of men – the language of real life. Conceiving, thinking, the mental intercourse of men at this stage still appear[s] as the direct efflux of their material behavior. The same applies to mental production as expressed in the language of the politics, laws, morality, religion, metaphysics, etc., of a people. Men are the producers of their conceptions, ideas, etc., that is, real, active, active men, as they are conditioned by a definite development of their productive forces.[50]

EDUCATION AS CLASS IDEOLOGY

In discussing the role of ideology in securing control for the political leadership in society, ʻĀmil reproduces Althusser's famous article on "Les appareils idéologiques d'état."[51] A brief recap of what Althusser says is in order to shed light on ʻĀmil's treatment of the subject.

Althusser points out the following: first, the basic function of the state is to preserve the material interests of the ruling classes and help the bourgeoisie in the modern world conduct its class struggle against the proletariat. Second, in its struggle to maintain state power, the bourgeoisie develops a comprehensive state apparatus based on ideological domination. Althusser calls this "the ideological state apparatus," which must be distinguished from repressive systems used by the state, such as the army, police, and so on. Third, Althusser identifies several ideological state apparatuses such as religious, educational, political, and legal. Althusser maintains that, "no class can hold state power over a long period without at the same time exercising its hegemony over and in the State Ideological

Apparatuses."[52] Fourth, in the past, the Church in Europe fulfilled important educational and religious functions that were congruent with the maintenance of the power elite, especially in pre-capitalist societies. As the hold of the Church under capitalism waned, new institutions were created to replace the Church, namely schools and the mass media. Althusser says that, "In fact, the Church has been replaced today in its role as the dominant Ideological State Apparatus by the School."[53] The main function of the ideological state apparatus is the reproduction of the relations of productions; that is, to reproduce capitalist relations of exploitation.[54]

Here 'Āmil distinguishes between *class control* and *class hegemony*. Class control is defined as the political and economic control of one class over the rest of classes in society, which does not necessarily translate to hegemony. Hegemony means a more subtle form of control exercised by the educational and religious institutions in society. Again, 'Āmil does not benefit from the important discussion of Antonio Gramsci on the topic, although Gramsci's ideas were well-known in France in the 1960s, 'Āmil's student years.

Although education has been the colonial bourgeoisie's most subtle weapon to ensure its hegemony, it also, "betrays the undemocratic class foundations on which the system of education is based in its colonial or capitalist structure."[55] Education leads to a certain form of class consciousness. In its capitalist expansion in the Third World, capitalism and its heir, the colonial bourgeoisie, preaches a certain form of mass education in order to meet its expanding structural and economic needs. This is apt to create educated people who belong to the poorest classes in society.

In his analysis of the modern history of education in Lebanon, 'Āmil argues that the Lebanese bourgeoisie makes full use of the educational system in order to realize its ideological domination in society, "which is necessary to reproduce the same social relations of production."[56] The dominant educational system embodies the material foundation of the bourgeois ideology in Lebanese society. The educational system reflects various trends of pedagogical philosophy, which represent both foreign and sectarian interests. 'Āmil says that the American system of education is dominant at the college/university level, whereas the French is dominant at the high school level.[57] In spite of the curricular differences in the official education system, "one ideological unity contains all of these trends in one structural system, which is the system of the dominant bourgeois ideology."[58] 'Āmil places his fingers on a major issue that has been perplexing since Arab states gained independence, the issue of national versus colonial cultures. Arab bourgeois culture is dependent on the West. However, in Lebanon at least, national culture has not found real expression in the educational system. What that means in effect is that most of the Arab intelligentsia who go to Lebanese universities are guided by a sort colonial education and vision. A true liberation of the Arab intelligentsia and of national culture begins with dismantling the foundations of the dominant educational system, and creating an independent one free from colonial hegemony.

In achieving radical change in the educational system, 'Āmil discounts the state since it has itself fallen to the ideological hegemony of the bourgeoisie. 'Āmil does not tell us how to change this state of affairs except through a radical change of the class structure of Lebanese society.[59]

CLASS AND CHANGE

'Āmil turns his attention, in the course of analyzing the meaning of ideology in society, to discussing the political and ideological situation in the post-independence Arab world. As stated previously, he argues that the colonial, that is, national, bourgeoisie leads the nation into political independence not so much because of its structural economic independence from world capitalism but because of its political struggle. In other words, political independence in the newly-emerging countries does not translate to economic independence from the Center. The petty bourgeoisie, through the support of the military and not mass revolution, achieves power in the post-independence Arab countries.[60] He argues that after independence in such countries as Syria, Egypt, and Algeria, the "colonial social structure" came under the political control of the petty bourgeoisie and its party. These countries, in spite of the so-called progressive side of their regimes, have not experienced real rupture with capitalism; their structural foundation is still nourished and maintained by world capitalism.[61] However, the petty bourgeoisie uses both its party and state machinery to promote itself, "In essence the petty bourgeoisie, which is part of the colonial social structure, lacks hegemony since it cannot produce a distinctive social and class system that is different from the colonial system of production. Its acquisition of power is political in nature only. In other words, its formation as a dominating class has not ensued from a position of 'class hegemony' as in the case of the capitalist bourgeoisie."[62] Because of its lack of hegemony, the Arab petty bourgeoisie appropriates for itself such terms as Arab and Islamic socialism in order to obtain ideological hegemony. 'Āmil remains silent about the alliance forged between the progressive wing of the Arab petty bourgeoisie and the Soviet Union in the 1960s. He reiterates that the proletariat is the only revolutionary class in society, which is capable in the long run of introducing drastic changes through its alliance with the Communist Party.

Furthermore, 'Āmil does not provide any insight into the Arab economy in the 1970s, and the increasing incorporation of the Arab world into the capitalist market, especially after the collapse of Nasserism in Egypt. The Infitāḥ policies of the Egyptian state after Nasser's death paved the way for the old landed bourgeoisie to return to the social and political scene of Egypt without disguise. After the 1952 Egyptian revolution, this class lost most of its material base in Egypt, either because of the nationalization of industry or the confiscation of the assets of this class. The return of this class to power, usually from its exile in Europe and North America, accelerated the process of incorporating Egypt into the capitalist market, which had the primary effect of driving a major wedge between Egypt and the socialist bloc. The small and middle classes benefited a great deal from the economic policies of the Nasserite regime. However, with the debacle of Nasserism after the 1967 war, Egypt lost its creative vision of a nationalist economy and appealed to conservative Arab states for help. The weakening of the Nasserite project after 1967 paved the way for the old Egyptian bourgeoisie to dominate the scene once again. This was possible during Sadat's regime.[63]

'Āmil postulates that the Communist Party possesses the vision to replace the petty bourgeoisie that is in power in the Arab world.[64] It is the only party that can effect real transition to socialism. In other words, 'Āmil criticizes the claim made by the liberals or the representatives of the small bourgeoisie in Arab society that only a charismatic figure can salvage Arab society and lead it to the road of development. This belief is similar to Orientalists' argument that Arab societies, because of their patriarchal natures, need patriarchal figures. Here 'Āmil is critical, not just of the petty bourgeoisie in Syria, Egypt, and Algeria, but also of Arab leadership in the Gulf states and Jordan. To him, their rule, which is supported by the army and world capitalism, lacks a real hegemony in society.[65]

'Āmil's critique of the Arab petty bourgeoisie as a non-revolutionary class has elicited a major controversy within the ranks of the Arab Left.[66] He insists that the small bourgeoisie cannot be considered, from a theoretical standpoint, a progressive class since it fears real structural evolution in society. In his response to the critique of some Leftist thinkers that it is important to forge alliances with the "progressive classes" in society in order to counteract imperialism and Israel, 'Āmil argues that real Marxists must not blind themselves to the fact that these "progressive classes" use every means at their disposal to impede the transition of society to socialism. Furthermore, the class position of these classes obscure from them the necessity of class conflict.[67] The real struggle against imperialism and Zionism begins in principle at the structural plane: a real structural revolution must take place in order to emancipate the country and its different classes from the economic hegemony of world imperialism. 'Āmil argues that this is the only true meaning of national liberation that the small bourgeoisie cannot shoulder precisely because of its class position.

MARXIST THEORY AND SECTARIAN POLITICS IN LEBANON

'Āmil's long excursion into Marxist thought is intended to shed some light on the sectarian question, the most sensitive issue in modern Lebanon. Besides being a religious structure, sectarianism is a political system, as well. After 1967, the sectarian question became the most complex political and religious question facing the country, which triggered the intervention of Syria, Israel, the United States, and France.

Sectarianism was at the heart of the Lebanese civil war of the 1970s.[68] To 'Āmil, the fundamental reason for the Lebanese civil war lies in the nature of the Lebanese colonial bourgeoisie, as a dependent bourgeoisie, and its ideological use of sectarianism as a weapon to preserve its political power. Although the tension in Lebanon seemed political on the surface, it was caused by economic factors that go back to the first half of the nineteenth century. In this regard, 'Āmil assumes that no modernization of the Lebanese state is possible unless the sectarian nature of the state is eradicated. In other words, Lebanon will continue to be prey to inner explosion and foreign intervention until the sectarian foundations of the state are abolished.[69]

In one of his major books on the subject, *A Treatise On Negating Sectarian Thought: The Palestine Question in the Ideology of the Lebanese Bourgeoisie*,[70] 'Āmil treats in great detail the main ideas of Lebanese bourgeois thinker Michel Shīḥa and the current ideology of the Lebanese bourgeoisie.[71] 'Āmil argues that Shīḥa is the spiritual father of the Lebanese bourgeoisie and the main ideologue of the Phalange Party. 'Āmil claims that the Lebanese bourgeoisie has more or less remained faithful to its nineteenth century ideological vision as sectarian ideology. The Lebanese bourgeoisie emerged in the latter part of the nineteenth century in the wake of European and particularly French expansion of capitalism in Lebanon and the Middle East. It was given its economic shape as a dependent class, structurally speaking, by the nature of the capitalist expansion and its needs for certain commodities from Lebanon. ʻĀmil says that this bourgeoisie grew in the context of this structural dependency and became preoccupied with commerce as the main expression of its economic activity. It was not permitted, because of its dependent nature, to establish significantly income-producing industry in the country so that it would not compete with European capitalism.[72]

ʻĀmil argues that the Lebanese civil war ushered the Lebanese bourgeoisie into one of the worst political crises in its long history. This crisis betrayed its economic condition and used sectarianism as a weapon to maintain its political authority. The political system upheld by this bourgeoisie has become a matter of negotiation between the different parties that make up the complex political map of contemporary Lebanon.[73]

ʻĀmil draws a distinction between two main groups in conflict in Lebanon: (1) the Lebanese bourgeoisie; and (2) progressive forces, at the heart of which is the Palestinian national movement. He argues that one major accomplishment of the progressive forces in the 1960s was their gradual consciousness of being one large oppressed class by the bourgeoisie and not merely a congregation of sects or classes. He further maintains that it is in the interest of the Lebanese ruling class to maintain sectarianism as the basis of its political and ideological systems. Above all, this class controls the state; it exercises power through the constitution it had drawn.

What does Lebanon mean to Michel Shīḥa? First, Shīḥa believes that since time immemorial Lebanon has been distinguished by several characteristics: the centrality of mountain life; its international commercial role; peaceful Christian-Muslim coexistence; openness to the Middle East and the world at large; and its connection with the Lebanese Diaspora. Lebanon is a unique country. Second, Lebanon is a country of immense economic freedom. Shīḥa prefers commerce to industry. Third, Lebanon needs outside investments so that it can prosper economically. In describing Lebanon, Shīḥa says: "Le Liban est par essence, il est de naissance et par necessité, une nation maritîme; et chez nous la montagne est exactement la citadelle qui couvre la mer, qui défend la mer,"[74] and "La présence du Liban, on la découvre d'abord dans son coeur." ("By essence, birth and necessity, Lebanon is a maritime nation. And at home, the mountain is precisely the citadel which covers and defends the ocean." And "We find the existence of Lebanon first in one's heart." Translation by Abu-Rabiʻ.)[75]

In his critique of Shīḥa's bourgeois ideology, ʻĀmil argues the following points: first, Shīḥa reflects the political vision of the ruling Lebanese bourgeoisie by presenting the idea that Lebanon is simply made up of a mosaic of cooperating and coexisting sects, and that the common denominator in their lives is the political balance that has been forged and controlled by the bourgeoisie.[76] Second, Shīḥa's proposition about the "mosaic" of Lebanese society is oblivious to nationhood. Democracy in a sectarian sense means the elevation of the sect at the expense of the nation.[77] Third, Shīḥa pays no attention whatsoever to the concept of social class in his portrayal of Lebanon. In this sense, he refuses to ascribe social reasons to any imbalance that may occur in the sectarian structure of Lebanon. Imbalance would occur because of people and not because of the social or political system. Fourth, the mountain and the bourgeoisie forming around it have given shape and stability to the Lebanese political and social systems. ‘Āmil argues that the Lebanese bourgeoisie, because of this essential definition by Shīḥa, has been isolationist from the beginning. Its belief in the uniqueness of Lebanon and its sectarian nature has, by definition, made it different from the rest of the Arab world, which believes in nationhood as the basis of identity. ‘Āmil says that the Lebanese bourgeoisie has used isolationism in order to preserve its economic and political prestige and interests. Also, the isolationism of this class, dominant in both the political and commercial spheres, is predicated on its structural dependency on world capitalism and the political inspiration it receives from Western imperialism.[78] Fifth, Shīḥa, according to ‘Āmil, sees a political function in religion which is to preserve the social harmony of the dominant sectarian system. Shīḥa argues that the worldwide confusion in this century did not result from the historical division between Islam and Christianity *per se*, but from the negation of the existence of God. Thus, atheism is responsible for the chaos.[79]

Charles Malik, another representative of the Lebanese bourgeoisie, elaborates on Shīḥa's view of the uniqueness of Lebanon. Malik points to seven major principles that define the Lebanese personality or heritage:

1. the Lebanese village that represents freedom and hard work;
2. the art of negotiation or mediation. Lebanon is a distinguished commercial country and the art of negotiation learned from the ancient Phoenicians defines its basic social and behavioral ethic;
3. language. The Lebanese have adopted Arabic after Syriac and Greek and excelled in its uses;
4. a tolerant sectarian environment;
5. the state as the symbol of Lebanese democracy;
6. educational systems and freedom;
7. the Church as a symbol of continuity in the Lebanese personality.[80]

To both Malik and Shīḥa, Lebanon in essence is Phoenician Lebanon:

> Pour ce qui est de notre ettitoire, le Liban d'aujoud'hui s'idenifie à peu pres avec le Liban-Phencis des origins; mais, pour retrouver entirement le Phenicie métropolotaine du passé, nous devrions longeant du sud au nor le litteroal mediterraneen, aller du Mont-Carmel et d'Acre à l'antique Aradus.
>
> ("For its territory, Lebanon today identified more or less with its Phoenician past. But in order to rediscover the Phoenician world of the past, we would have to cross the country along the Mediterranean coast going from Mount Carmel and Acre to the ancient Aradus." Translation by Abu-Rabi‘)[81]

‘Āmil's treatment of the Lebanese bourgeoisie and the Palestinian question is interesting for the questions it raises about the relationship between the Lebanese bourgeoisie, on the one hand, and both Israel and Europe, on the other.[82] 'Āmil condemns the Lebanese bourgeoisie. In his mind, it has committed treason from the first days of independence until the civil war in 1975–76:

> The determined march of the Lebanese right in the Zionization (*ṣahyanat*) of Lebanon [turning Lebanon into another Israel] is but a culmination of a long history of forging conspiracy with imperialism, Zionism, and the Arab reactionaries against the struggle of the Palestinian nation to liberate its land, the struggle of the Arab peoples to free themselves from imperialism, and the struggle of the Lebanese people to achieve democracy and national independence.[83]

Shīḥa has always claimed that Lebanon, unique and easily distinguished from the rest of the Middle East, is an integral part of Europe, especially Mediterannean Europe. To Shīḥa, the enemy is not the West or imperialism, but any force that tries to destabilize the relationship between Lebanon and the West.[84] To 'Āmil's mind, Shīḥa has called for an alliance with the West against what he calls "communism," or atheism or Marxism.

Historically, the sectarian system was the brain-child of the West and was absorbed into the Lebanese political system on the eve of independence.[85] The Lebanese constitution embodied this philosophy. However, 'Āmil raises another important point, which is that it is possible to argue that imperialism might have from the beginning envisaged the creation of a "national homeland for the Christian people" in Lebanon following the Zionist model in Palestine.[86]

Next, 'Āmil analyzes the historical position of the Lebanese bourgeoisie on the Palestinian question. He says that, logically speaking, the Lebanese bourgeoisie's position toward the "Arab liberation movement" *(ḥarakat al-taḥarrur al-'arabiyyah)* is not different from their position on the Palestine question. History proves to us, he argues, that the Lebanese bourgeoisie has been explicitly anti-nationalist and pro-Zionist, and that its political and commercial interests were in full tune with the interests of the Arab reactionary movement, Zionism, and Western imperialism.[87] Shīḥa believes that Lebanon's connection to the Arab world derives from its historical connection to Mediterranean Europe. Lebanon falls under the Mediterranean umbrella and not that of the Arab.[88] Shīḥa believes that Israel is an expansionist state, but is there because of historical destiny.

'Āmil takes up the controversial work of some of the thinkers from the University of the Keslik, who represent the views of the Phalange party in Lebanon. According to 'Āmil, this group argues the following points:

1. the main reason for the current conflict in Lebanon is the doctrinal difference between Islam and Christianity;
2. the history of the Arabs in the Middle East is the history of Islam and the sliding of Christians into *dhimma* status;
3. Islam represents the backward and decadent Orient, while Christianity represents the dynamic and advanced Occident.

'Āmil responds to these formulations by saying that these doctrines or principles betray a clear ideological function. The first maintains that, far from being socio-economic and political, the current conflict in Lebanon is religious and doctrinal in nature. Second, the ideological function of the second principle maintains that Lebanese Christians face two major dangers: either Islamization, that is conversion to Islam, or living as second-class citizens (*dhimma*) in the world of Islam. Third, Lebanese Rightists claim that all the Arab world is Muslim and that Islam is essentially one dimension of Arabism. Identifying Islam and Arabism in this way negates the nationalist component of Lebanon's conflict, it is then reduced to a religious struggle between Islam and Christianity.[89]

LANGUAGE AND CREATIVITY

I am not aware of 'Āmil's *ouevre* being criticized as the product of a snobbish or ivory-tower intellectual. Many intellectuals, especially in the Third World, have been accused of this. In his own philosophical way, 'Āmil holds close the everyday concerns of the masses, especially the Lebanese working class. Although his thought is mostly abstract, his primary concern is the liberation of the masses, the poor and downtrodden from the domination of the bourgeoisie, which to his mind controls the state and its various ideological apparatuses.[90] 'Āmil dedicates two books for the purpose of unveiling the ideological control of the Arab bourgeoisie on everyday thought: *Crisis of Arab Civilization or the Arab Bourgeoisie?*,[91] and *Criticism of Everyday Thought*.

In the first book, 'Āmil investigates the key concepts and methodologies of the Arab bourgeoisie's worldview, as discussed in a major conference held in Kuwait in 1974 on the "Crisis of Civilizational Progress in the Arab world" (*Azmat al-taṭṭawwur al-ḥaḍārī fi'l waṭan al-'arabī*). He defines two contesting worldviews or philosophies in contemporary Arab intellectual discourse: the bourgeois worldview and the "scientific Marxist-Leninist" worldview of the Arab working class. Under the first, he places such intellectuals as Costantine Zurayk, Zakī Najīb Maḥmūd, and Fu'ād Zakariyya, and in the second, people like Maḥmūd Amīn al-'Ālim and Ṣādiq Jalāl al-'Azm.

In his treatment of the Arab reflection on the problematic of underdevelopment, he departs from two interdependent premises: first, Arab social relations are closely bound up with productive forces, and second, in order to maintain its privileged social and economic position, the Arab bourgeoisie has exercised intellectual and ideological domination since the intrusion of European capitalism into the Arab world in the nineteenth century. No doubt, 'Āmil elaborates one of the main postulates of Marxist philosophy that, "Economic categories are only the theoretical expressions, the abstractions of the social relations of production."[92] In their social intercourse, humans produce ideas that reflect their economic positions. As a dominant class in Arab society since the nineteenth century, the bourgeoisie has sought the services of the intelligentsia in order to produce ideas and categories of thought that maintain its economic, social, and political dominance in society.[93]

'Āmil presents a simple argument in his refutation of the main ideas discussed at the Kuwait conference: the capitalist mode of production, introduced into the Arab world at the beginning of the nineteenth century under the aegis of European imperialism, has been the determining factor in political and social relations in the modern Arab world. In other words, he espouses the premise explained earlier that

"Arab backwardness" owes its existence to the structural dependence of the Arab economic system, led by the bourgeoisie, on world capitalism. Any other explanation of backwardness tends to obscure the real modern crisis of the Arab bourgeoisie.

In its quest to secure ideological hegemony, the bourgeoisie espouses the Enlightenment discourse of progress and individualism. It places itself on a par with the Western bourgeoisie by creating parallels between itself and the Western bourgeoisie. By doing so, the structural dependence of the Arab bourgeoisie on the West becomes mystified and, as a result, the main problem, which is the liberation of the Arab world from imperialist economic and political domination, is marginalized.[94] The Arab bourgeoisie refuses to admit any contradictions between the Arab world and the capitalist. Its intellectuals argue that the real problem is a "civilizational gap" between the Arab world and the West. The Arab world needs to catch up with and follow the "advanced" West if it is to modernize. What this means is that bourgeois intellectuals have unduly dwelt on the problematic of tradition versus modernity, which is, by definition, a false problematic. On the surface, the bourgeois thesis that the Arab world is traditional and in need of modernity is a logical one. However, this position does not reflect the real structural reasons behind backwardness. 'Āmil correctly argues that Arab or Muslim tradition cannot be seen as a reason for backwardness, but is rather a consequence of the structural dependence on world capitalism.[95]

Against the above background, 'Āmil rejects the position espoused by some bourgeois thinkers that the religious worldview is at the heart of contemporary Arab discourse. He agrees with one of Samir Amin's main formulations that capitalism introduced a decisive break in modern Arab history. Capitalist culture has been dominant in the Arab world since its wholesale purchase. He implicitly argues that the capitalist mode of production has ruptured the seemingly old social and religious unity of the Arab world. Harking back to utopian discourse of unity means the failure to come to grips with the fundamental changes in the Arab world since the nineteenth century. 'Āmil does not see much difference between those who are faithful to a *Salafī* vision and those who espouse a bourgeois: both wage class conflict at the level of theory. The real problem is not the crisis of "Arab or Muslim reason" but the real social and economic conditions of dependency. The bourgeoisie, through its intellectual representatives, claims that the real problem is just intellectual or ideational. It refuses to shoulder any responsibility for the backwardness of Arab society. By creating a semblance between itself and the "advanced" Western bourgeoisie, it glosses over real issues. Once these conditions disappear, Arab intellectuals will be emancipated. National liberation entails a revolutionary transformation of the dominant relations of production in the Arab world.[96]

'Āmil scores a bull's eye in his analysis of the historical role of the Arab bourgeoisie. He highlights the role of ideology in reinforcing hegemony; however, he paints a grim picture of the role of the Arab proletariat in achieving its historical mission. To put it differently, 'Āmil's analysis of the nature and role of the Arab proletariat bypasses the peasantry and feudal/tribal social relations in Arab society. 'Āmil posits a mature industrial working class that does not exist in many Arab countries, especially in the Gulf. The ruling classes in the Gulf have been able to bypass the historical impasse of Western capitalism by bringing *en masse* transient immigrant laborers, people who can be easily deposed of by the dominant classes. Those classes have succeeded in postponing the historical emergence of the domestic working class. What does Marxist theory do about that? At best, 'Āmil is silent about this historical alteration, especially by regimes in the Gulf. Furthermore, in his preoccupation with dismantling the ideological foundations of hegemony in Arab society, 'Āmil neglects to discuss the use of physical coercion by the power elite to maintain their hegemony and engineer consent in society. It seems to me that the ruthless use of force has gone hand in hand with ideological hegemony.

'Āmil's last work, *Naqd al-fikr al-yawmī*, is dedicated to his preoccupation with issues of everyday life. It is an argument with and an elaboration of the ideas of some leading Arab intellectuals about such issues as the Lebanese civil war, the role of religion in public life, the relevance of Marxist theory to contemporary Arab culture, and the conceptual expressions of the Arab bourgeoisie. 'Āmil's main concern, besides critically approaching the main trends of contemporary Arab ideology, especially in Syria and Lebanon, is to drive the point home that Marxism can play a prominent role in contemporary Arab thought if used correctly by the revolutionary intelligentsia. His main ambition was much like Althusser's, who desired "to give back to Marxist theory something of its status as a revolutionary theory and thereby to make it effective in producing results in the real world."[97] The first major challenge facing 'Āmil is to make Marxism an acceptable and relevant philosophical discourse in contemporary Arab thought. To embrace Marxism as the most viable critical theory human thought has produced, the Arab intelligentsia must distance themselves from old methods of analysis and embrace *in toto* the Marxist approach. The second major challenge is to devise a Marxist theory that is specifically Arab, and which is able to raise serious questions about the complex Arab reality.[98] To my mind, 'Āmil goes a long way in addressing these challenges; yet, his mission remains incomplete.

One has to agree with 'Āmil that Marxism, if interpreted in a specifically Arab manner, could become one of the most effective theoretical tools in studying and deconstructing the Arab world. There are few Arab Marxist thinkers who are steeped in Marxist theory. One has to ask: is there a true Arab Marxist movement? 'Āmil's implicit answer is that the Arab Marxist movement is in the process of being born. Has this movement digested the central ideas of Marxism and applied them to the leading questions facing the modern Arab world? Or would one agree with the Egyptian Marxist 'Abd al-'Aẓīm Anīs that, besides dogmatism, Arab intelligentsia have not yet had the chance to digest the central theses of Marxist theory?[99]

In attempting to achieve his goals, 'Āmil follows a polemical approach. He launches a vitriolic attack on a good number of prominent Arab intellectuals, such as Hishām Sharābī, Edward Said, Burhān Ghalyūn, Adonis, and Wajīh Kawtharānī, accusing them of spreading false consciousness in the Arab world. He claims that most Arab thinkers have embraced the mental worldview of the Arab bourgeoisie, whose main objective is to demystify dominant social and economic relations in society. He also claims that although these thinkers represent different trends within bourgeois Arab thought, there is a strong sense of unity in bourgeois thought, which refuses to loosen its grip over everyday thought. ʻĀmil is quite harsh in his criticisms of the Arab intelligentsia, many of whom are considered to be on the Left, such as Hishām Sharābī and Edward Said. There seem to be few intellectuals who meet the criteria he has in mind. In this approach, ʻĀmil seems to be faithful to one of Althusser's main philosophical axioms that "philosophy represents class struggle in theory."[100]

As a philosopher, ʻĀmil is precise in the choice of language. He believes language must adequately reflect a society's socio-economic structure. However, he also thinks that writers must be endowed with enough creativity to distinguish "wheat from chaff." In his last uncompleted book, ʻĀmil turns his attention to a genre in contemporary Arab writings that, to his mind, seeks to stifle progressive thinking by rationalizing certain activities on the ground. In *Naqd al-fikr al-yawmī*, ʻĀmil preaches the birth of a new Arab world from the painful pregnancy of the *ancien régime*.[101] An author's creative writing is born in negation to the cultural practices of the old, and true modernity triumphs only after the old forms of sanctity, priesthood, and sovereignty are exhausted. These forms only perish when a new political order, to be run by the oppressed and downtrodden, is born.

ʻĀmil examines the impact of the 1982 Israeli invasion of Lebanon and the crisis of the Lebanese state in the context of various Arab writings on this question. He isolates four central trends of thought that have shaped contemporary Arab ideology: (1) dominant [bourgeois] thought *(al-fikr al-muṣayṭir*); (2) nihilistic thought (*al-fikr al-ʻadamī*); (3) thought of the Dark Ages (*al-fikr al-dhalāmī*); and (4) the Muslim bourgeois trend (*al-tayyār al-islāmī al-mutabarwij*). ʻĀmil ponders the question of political authority in relation to these trends of thought by pointing out that whomever controls political power is able to determine the economic nature of society. Politics is a movement that unites society. The dominant bourgeois thought marshals all sorts of powers, be they nihilistic, backward, or even scientific, in order to maintain its subtle and explicit hold over the masses by defining what is and is not acceptable. Thus ʻĀmil follows to the letter one of Karl Marx's most famous conclusions:

> The ideas of the ruling class are in every epoch the ruling ideas: i.e., the class which is the ruling material force of society is at the same time its ruling intellectual force. The class which has the means of material production at its disposal, consequently controls the means of mental production, so that the ideas of those who lack the means of mental production are on the whole subject to it.[102]

Undoubtedly, this is a fascinating argument not easily rebutted. Its gist seems to hold true if the political and economic history of the modern Arab world is interpreted in its light. ʻĀmil fully utilizes Marx's position in his scathing criticism of the dominant intellectual environment in modern Lebanon.

According to ʻĀmil, the juxtaposition between the dominant trend and the revolutionary trends summarizes the movement of contemporary Arab thought. Both dominant bourgeois thought and nihilistic thought join hands by creating a type of expression that lessens the importance of politics in daily life. Bourgeois thought trivializes common consciousness by preaching the neutrality of politics.

This action forms the cornerstone of the ideological counterattack mounted by the bourgeoisie against the working class.[103] As a prelude to its political attack, the bourgeoisie uses its rational arsenal in attacking all forms of scientific (read Marxist-Leninist) thinking in history, economics, and politics. It seeks the services of mercenary intellectuals who deny any association between politics and the concerns of daily life. Bourgeois thought uses the weapon of logic to convince people of order and dissuade them from chaos. From the womb of chaos, a new order is born.

However, 'Āmil believes that the 1982 war afforded a great opportunity for revolutionary Arab thought to create a new society in Lebanon. The civil war in Lebanon, which started in the early 1970s and continued in one way or another until the 1980s, is a class conflict between two classes, visions, and historical movements: the bourgeoisie and the working class. The bourgeoisie represents the entrenched social and political order and class conflict takes place at all levels, including the cultural.

'Āmil does not believe that the Arab bourgeoisie can play a radical or nationalist role in the Arab world. He argues that this bourgeoisie distanced itself from the nationalist question after its historical defeat in 1967. In the case of Egypt, the bourgeoisie was united behind Sadat's economic Open Door policy, launched only a few years after Nasser's death. In Lebanon, successive civil wars did not prevent the bourgeoisie from renewing its pact with the international imperialist bourgeoisie.

Against the above background, 'Āmil discusses the relevance of Marxist thought to the central problems of the Arab world. One must examine 'Āmil's preoccupations with the relevance of Marxist theory to the Arab world against the background of the Lebanese civil war and the role of the Lebanese Communist Party in the war. Officially, the party saw the war as an intense manifestation of class conflict. However, the predicament of Lebanese communism is a result of the failure of the party and other Leftist forces to effect a socialist revolution.

The political impasse of Lebanese or Arab communism does not often translate as a theoretical limitation of Marxism. On the contrary, Marxist theory experienced an ostensible resurgence in the Arab world after 1967. The writings of Ṣādiq Jalāl al-'Azm,[104] Ṭayyib Tizīnī and others attest to that. An impressive number of dedicated Arab intellectuals who joined its ranks sought to apply its basic formulations to the social and political problems of the Arab world. Since 1967, Arab Marxism, as a theoretical discourse, has fought very hard to establish an authentic intellectual presence in Arab thought. 'Āmil is a pioneer in this effort. Other Arab thinkers of this age, such as al-'Azm, Sharābī, Tizīnī, al-'Ālim, saw an altered historical space in the post-1967 Arab world. Like many Arab Leftist intellectuals, 'Āmil believed that Marxism was the only viable theory to explain the structural reasons for what went wrong in the Arab world. He did not see Marxism as just another theory of the European Enlightenment focusing on issues of democracy and human rights, as much as he pondered it as a revolutionary theory of radical change. 'Āmil was critical of some Arab intellectuals who accepted Marxism just as a method of analysis without really taking the side of the working class in its struggle to liberate itself from the hegemony of the dominant classes.[105] However, it is important to emphasize that the resurgence of Marxist theory, perhaps just like the resurgence of Islamism after 1967, originated from the historical impasse of the contemporary Arab world. The 1967 defeat was merely a nuance of this impasse.

'Āmil notes that socialism as a system and Marxism as a structure of thought have been greatly attacked in the Arab world by a number of thinkers who speak the language of cultural specificity (that is, Arab nationalists) or the language of religious authenticity (that is, the Islamists) or those who have a vested interest in maintaining the *status quo*. However, he believes Marxism is the only philosophy that uncovers the class and exploitative nature of capitalism and the persistence of all forms of domination in the modern Arab world. As we have seen so far, 'Āmil spent a considerable amount of time trying to work out Marxist theory in light of the economic and social history of the modern Arab world and the sectarian situation in modern Lebanon.

'Āmil is weary of criticisms leveled against Marxism because of its European origin. He considers such to be a mark of cultural provincialism on the part of the Arab or Islamist critics. Responding to such critics, he convincingly argues that Marxism was born in opposition to bourgeois universal thought, and is thus the only theory that can in a sustained fashion explain the universal expansion of capitalism and its effect on the modern Arab world. He therefore dismisses the claim made by some authors that capitalism did not succeed in penetrating the traditional structure of Muslim or Arab society and that many traditional forms, if not remaining intact, have been revitalized under the threat of capitalist expansion. According to this view, capitalism has not substantially altered the Islamic identity and/or doctrine of modern Arab society. It is correct to assume that a pure doctrinal or conceptual reading of modern Arab history falls short of providing adequate answers to the socio-economic realities of the Arab world. "There is no such thing as an innocent reading," as Althusser would say. However, a theoretically nuanced materialistic reading of modern Arab history is preferable to a doctrinal reading that distorts or mystifies the economic reality being considered.

'Āmil argues that modern Islamist thought shares some common features with Marxist thought, especially in connection with the notion of dependency. However, there are important differences between the two streams of thought. Islamist thought, which speaks of specificity and authenticity, presents the West as a reified concept and not as a set of evolving social and economic relationships that affected the Arab world at least since the beginning of the nineteenth century. This thought cannot explain the historical and materialist reasons behind the expansion and domination of the West.

As mentioned above, 'Āmil undoubtedly wrestles with a very complicated question in contemporary Arab culture: the relevance of Marxism to the modern Arab world and the need to develop an Arab Marxist theory that can take on the religious problematic. Many an Arab author has attacked Marxism as a foreign philosophy or an abstract system of thought that cannot be easily appropriated by the masses, and found in Islam, especially after the Iranian revolution of 1979, an appropriate vehicle with which to express the masses' sentiments. Adonis, one of the most creative of Arab authors, believes that since the inception of Islam, Arab society has been distinguished by a primary religious structure, and that "Arab culture has been essentially a reflection of this structure which makes it impossible to understand apart from its religious dimension."[106] Adonis goes on to argue that Marxist philosophy has functioned as a weighty tool of conceptual machinery masking reality instead of explaining it more clearly. Marxism cannot come to grips with the religious structure of Arab societies and with the Arab-Muslim tradition in general, argues Adonis.[107]

Adonis and other Arab authors were theoretically responding to the Iranian revolution and the role of Muslim ideas and leadership in fomenting this revolution. To them, the main reason behind the revolution was not class conflict but religio-ideological conflict. 'Āmil does not concede that Islamic ideas or Muslim tradition, as interpreted by the religious leadership of Iran, may have played any role in this revolution. It is mainly the revolution of the dispossessed using Islamic slogans to attack the power structure of the Shah. 'Āmil contends that such an ideological interpretation of reality is at loggerheads with the materialist interpretation of history that considers history to be a movement between two opposing social/economic poles: socialism and capitalism and not between the meaningless concepts of the "self" and the "Other."

Both nihilistic and Dark Ages trends of thought in contemporary Arab culture are at odds with the thinking of the working class. In one way or another, they lend major intellectual services to the dominant bourgeois thought, especially as the bourgeoisie, in its daily behavior, "has cleansed its hands of the nationalist question."[108]

'Āmil thinks that the main reason for the Arab defeat of 1967 lies in the class nature of Arab society and the alliance between the military elite and capitalists in the Arab world.[109] This defeat uncovered the structural weaknesses of the Arab bourgeoisie and its deeply entrenched submission to the exigencies of world capitalism. He does not buy into the contention of some Arab authors, including Islamists, that the reasons behind defeat can be ascribed to civilizational gaps between the Arab world and the West. He points to the attempt of some Arab authors to ascribe essentalist and reified reasons for defeat; reasons that go back to the early phase of Islamic history and the Arabs' intellectual defeat before the Persians. 'Āmil dismisses any argument of religious and cultural specificity, as well as the contention that with the rise of capitalism in the Arab world in the nineteenth century, Arab culture lost its specificity and was submerged in the universality of capitalism.

Cultural specifists in modern Arab thought forget that they borrow their central concepts and essential arguments from the dominant bourgeois thought of the European Enlightenment of the eighteenth and nineteenth centuries. To juxtapose the Arab or Muslim "self" against the European "Other" is to consider imperialist expansion an attack on cultural specificity and an alienation of Arab and Muslim spirit.[110] This metaphysical formula masks the complex social and economic transformations engendered by European capitalism in the modern Arab world and the creation of two social structures: an imperialist structure and a subservient colonial structure. 'Āmil argues that the discourse of the "self" and the "Other" and all of its central concepts is primarily a bourgeois discourse that has underlined most trends of contemporary Arab thought, except the revolutionary one.

'Āmil's Marxist interpretation of the religious question in Islamic history as well as in contemporary Arab culture is refreshing for the many questions it raises about the social nature of religion and its connection to political authority. 'Āmil argues that a great many interpretations of Islam have been made possible because of the social and economic backgrounds of their interpreters. A huge gulf exists between the Islam of the rulers or the rich and that of the weak or dispossessed. Various social and political forces used Islam as a launching pad from which the *status quo* was either justified or attacked. 'Āmil argues that the Muslim state in the past and present has used the Sharī'ah to enhance its political authority. No wonder, then, that the ruling class in Muslim society, like the bourgeoisie, has justified authority in the name of the people at large, that is, in the name of the Muslim ummah. The state has used the concept of a permanent, reified, and Sacred Sharī'ah: anyone who dares to attack the state is implicitly attacking the Sharī'ah, which is often translated as attacking Islam itself. Institutionalized Islam has been by necessity a state Islam. According to Althusser, institutionalized religion becomes an apparatus of the state. 'Āmil also argues that Sufism has been the only movement in Islam that has dared to criticize the state in the name of an esoteric interpretation of Islam. He also sees a common denominator between the revolutionary thinking in the Muslim world and the Sufī. Both sought to attack the state by embodying concepts of freedom using different language than that of the state.[111] 'Āmil does not elaborate much on the revolutionary potential of Islam. Can Islam be a tool in the hands of Arab revolutionaries fighting internal oppression and external domination?

'Āmil subjects all major trends of Arab thought to a ruthless criticism. He is not even appreciative of the creative thinking of such people as Adonis or al-Ḥāfiz, precisely because they do not pay sufficient attention to economic factors. He thus concludes that all major trends of Arab thought suffer from social and economic paralysis; they are utopian at best, and their utopianism can fall into intellectual and ideological service of the bourgeoisie. This harsh criticism has escaped Sufī trends in the modern Arab world. 'Āmil seems oblivious to the fact that many a Sufī shaykh has sided with the ruling elite against the masses and the poor. However, 'Āmil measures Arab writings with the rod of historical and social realism.

In his reflections on the predicament of contemporary Arab culture and the economic realities of the Arab world, 'Āmil remains an objective thinker more or less committed to a scientific theory explaining the modern history of the Arab world. He is convinced that Marxism-Leninism, if interpreted correctly, remains the only scientific and revolutionary theory available to the masses in the Arab world. Subjectivity does not play a prominent role in his thinking, which leads one to conclude that he does not see a role for human passion and sentiment in the historical process. 'Āmil, like Althusser, returns to Marx, but not the young and Hegelian Marx. He embraces the legacy of the mature or scientific Marx, which began, according to Althusser's periodization, with the publication of the 1846 Marxian masterpiece, *The German Ideology*.[112] 'Āmil does not refer to Marx's *Economic and Philosophical Manuscripts of 1844*,[113] where Marx seems to be heavily indebted to Hegel, especially in his treatment of such concepts as alienation and creativity.[114] One may infer from 'Āmil's methodological approach that he thinks that historical materialism and theoretical humanism are conceptually incompatible. 'Āmil seems to prefer an economist reading of Marxist theory to a humanist. Again, like Althusser, he belongs to a generation of intellectuals who was trying "to escape Hegel."[115]

In this way, 'Āmil reduces the religious to the ideological. Although this position is appealing, since religion has indeed functioned as an ideological tool in the hands of the powerful and dispossessed alike, it negates the subjective role religion may play in the human psyche. 'Āmil argues that the religious-ideological dimension cannot replace the social and economic in human history. That is why one can apply materialist interpretations to Arab history, which is a summation of the contradiction between rich and poor, between the forces of production and the relations of production that have been maintained by the bourgeoisie.[116]

Finally, 'Āmil's project is mainly philosophical in orientation. 'Āmil was a high-profile member of the Lebanese Communist Party. However, this party, along with other Communist Parties in the Arab world, failed to achieve any sort of unity in their home country or in other parts of the Arab world. A number of reasons account for this, especially military repression in the Arab world. A number of anti-Leftist Arab intellectuals have criticized the Arab Left for its intellectual snobbishness and for "borrowing ideas and concepts that are alien to Arab and Muslim heritage." One can agree with the charge that the Arab Left has been in the main confined to a minority of intellectuals and activists, and aside from the short-lived experience of Arab Marxism in Yemen, Communist Parties did not make much headway in the Arab political scene. This is all true. However, the approach used by 'Āmil and other intellectuals has shed significant light on the historical and economic conditions of the modern Arab world. Arab Leftist intellectuals have been on the whole more realistic in their approach than Islamists, especially in relation to the political economy of the Arab world. This is what makes 'Āmil's thinking very vital and relevant to the concerns of the present Arab world. 'Āmil's ideas have much to say about the present predicament of the Arab world. He always argued that contradictions within the Lebanese political system were exploited by all sorts of foreign powers, especially Israel. An appreciation of both the economic history of modern Lebanon and the role of sectarianism in public life shed important light on the troubled history of modern Lebanon, but also on the anguish of the Leftist Arab intelligentsia as they tend to establish a socialist system in an Arab world dominated by dictatorship.

16
Abdallah Laroui: From Objective Marxism to Liberal Etatism

> "The central inner-European event of the imperialist period was the political emancipation of the bourgeoisie, which up to then had been the first class in history to achieve economic pre-eminence without aspiring to political rule. The bourgeoisie had developed within, and together with, the nation-state, which almost by definition ruled over and beyond a class-divided society." Hannah Arendt, *The Origins of Totalitarianism* (New York: Meridian Books, 1958), 123.

Cultural decolonization, to use a favorite term of contemporary Moroccan thinker Mahdi Elmandjra,[1] analyzes a process undertaken but not yet finished in the intellectual and political evolution of the contemporary Arab world. We are indeed indebted to Franz Fanon for raising the issue of cultural independence from colonialism as the most coherent expression of the struggle of the oppressed against their oppressors in the twentieth century.[2] In the same vein, it is quite impossible to grasp the cultural struggle waged by the indigenous intelligentsia after independence without full recourse to the mental worldview and cultural policies of imperialism in the colonies. After independence, the most distinguished North African intellectuals thoroughly immersed themselves in the imperialist cultural problematic. Some attempted to find creative solutions to the onerous legacy of imperialism by advocating a sort of synthesis between their culture and that of the West. Only a few advocated a sharp separation between the "indigenous" and "foreign." In other words, even the most committed nationalist intelligentsia dared not advocate cultural or intellectual disengagement with the Center. All these of this class were born during the reign of colonialism and most of them studied in schools espousing its philosophy either at home or abroad.[3]

In spite of this "forced engagement" with the culture of imperialism, the North African intelligentsia have suggested new approaches to constructing a cultural space for their newly-independent countries. These approaches have inherently dealt with questions of freedom from imperialism, and the vision needed to create a new civil society. How far intellectuals have gone in envisioning this new society is a matter of debate in contemporary Arab thought. The question is, "What type of intelligentsia are we discussing?"

As a leading North African intellectual, Abdallah Laroui offers a critical reading of the state of indigenous culture immediately after independence. As I shall later argue, although painfully aware of the great burden of colonialism on the modern Arab world, Laroui in part at least rejects Arab-Islamic culture by advocating Arab total immersion in the culture of the West. Furthermore, he has recently assumed the role of disgruntled intellectual, for, in the end, he takes the part of the state against both the intelligentsia and the masses. In spite of this major lapse, Laroui offers some of the most original insights on the state of contemporary Arab thought and culture, and must be taken seriously for this reason. One may vehemently disagree with his analysis; however, even his detractors must acknowledge his daring in the formulation of his cultural and historical analysis. He challenges the Arab intelligentsia to seriously reflect on its role in instituting change relative to its inherited cultural environment.

Because of his extensive travel in the Arab world, especially in Egypt, and his French education, Laroui is comfortable dealing with the most problematic questions besetting contemporary Arab societies.[4] His intellectual breadth and the significant transformations in his thought reflect the anguish and concern of many Leftist and nationalist intellectuals in North Africa. Laroui's generation was deeply affected, although not humiliated, by French colonialism.[5] It was a generation that hoped to lay the intellectual foundations of a young, independent, and nationalist state. However, this generation was still intellectually indebted to European thought in its different manifestations, especially Marxism, Liberalism, and Hegelianism. It is a generation that could not escape the problematic of the "Other."

Although born of an historical reflection on the Moroccan cultural and social situation, Laroui deeply reflects on the epistemological content and historical movement of modern and contemporary Arab thought. His intellectual enterprise and the attention it gained among a small but influential segment of Arab intelligentsia summarizes the cultural movement of Arab society since the official end of colonialism. Laroui's theoretical reflections on social, economic, political, and cultural conditions in the Arab world have influenced the work of such intellectuals as Eliās Murquṣ,[6] Maḥmūd Amīn al-'Ālim, Mahdī 'Āmil, Yāssīn al-Ḥāfiz, Burhān Ghalyūn, Hishām Sharābī, Hichem Djaït, Muḥammad 'Ābid al-Jābīrī, as well as many other Moroccan and non-Moroccan thinkers. Also, Leftist students in Moroccan universities in the 1970s and 1980s embraced Laroui's work as a means of deconstructing society.

A careful reading of Laroui's work presents a number of questions about his writing style, which has been described by a leading Moroccan intellectual as "an essay within an essay."[7] Although he poses more questions than he can answer, Laroui is fully able to focus on the pulse of the cultural and intellectual movement underway in the contemporary Arab world. He does this not merely as an objective and analytical academician and critic. Laroui evokes the dialectical ideologue, he who is anxious to investigate radical transformations and forever dismantle the intellectual paradigms that have dominated the Arab world for so long. He engages the reader, sometimes in a provocative and bitter way. Laroui forces one to take a position on the issues at hand right away. The force of his argumentation is clear in his major work, especially in *L'idéologie arabe contemporaine* and in *La crise des intellectuels arabes*, which were written in the same critical spirit. Laroui's real strength is in cultural and philosophical analysis rather than political. His unstated goal seems to be political transformation of the Arab world, whereas his articulated goal is simply to subject the Arab world to rigorous criticism.

Laroui's method in his early works is informed by both critical Marxist philosophy, and political economy. He is obsessed with the machinations of intellectual, cultural, and economic domination in Arab society. He sees a strong link between the structures of power and the reproduction of ideology. He believes the intelligentsia can, at least in theory, play a very radical role in transforming their societies. However, in his later writings, his obsession with the intelligentsia turns to a scathing critique. In spite of this accusation of conceptual lethargy, Laroui seems to think, at one point, that the intelligentsia can play a major role in the intellectual and political transformation of Arab society. To be effective agents of change, however, the intelligentsia must subject their inherited "mental structure," epistemological worldview or intellectual framework to a radical and thorough deconstruction. They must completely break from the intellectual practices and premises of their predecessors. That is to say, Laroui argues that the roots of backwardness in the modern Arab world are to be found in the epistemological and cultural environment, and not so much in the realms of economics or politics. This is an interesting and highly controversial thesis. Laroui insists that the intelligentsia must first emancipate themselves from "the slavery of inherited epistemology" if they are to effect radical change in their societies. The logical question that follows is this: "Can the Arab intelligentsia conform to Laroui's theoretical ideal?" The answer is no. No intelligentsia, however homogeneous and concordant, can totally free themselves from deeply ingrained patterns of intellectual practice.

Judging from the ideal Laroui posits, one must conclude that his predicate is the assumption of internal mental backwardness in the post-colonial Arab world. In addition, the proletariat, envisaged by Marx as the historical enemy of exploitative capitalism, may not be capable of fulfilling its historical mission in a backward society that lacks industrialization, among other things. This is a valid point. However, Laroui seems to be optimistic when he places full confidence in the intelligentsia. If Laroui's main point of departure is valid, can one assume that the real task of liberation falls on the shoulders of the intelligentsia? What role does the state play in this type of liberation? From this simple point, Laroui launches an in-depth analysis of the composition of the intelligentsia in modern Arab society and their responsibilities to the new nation-state created after colonialism.

Perhaps, Laroui's *oeuvre* is illuminating not for the answers it provides but for the insightful questions and issues it beings to the fore. Throughout his work, Laroui raises the following fundamental questions:

1. What is colonialism? Is it just economic and political hegemony or can it also be mental exploitation?
2. What is revolution and what role does the intelligentsia play in such revolution?
3. What are the reasons behind decline and stagnation in Arab society?
4. What position does the religious question with its ever-present weapon, *turāth*, occupy in the modern context?[8]

In the work he wrote immediately after the 1967 war, Laroui considers political defeat as symptomatic of a larger problematic condition in modern Arab life: the dominance of old mental and epistemological structures. Laroui offers a critical reading of the "epistemological map" of the entire Arab world, not just North Africa, in his first work, *L'idéologie arabe contemporaine*. This book, he admits, was written in response to the central formulations of Sayyid Quṭb, the ideologue of Islamic resurgence in the 1950s and 1960s, as stated in his major work, *Social Justice in Islam*.[9] Laroui does not attempt to disguise his dislike of Islamism, which he considers reactionary. He thinks that in spite of its popular following, Islamism has failed miserably to effect a radical change in its worldview. Its philosophy is under girded and dominated by an anachronistic text, he argues. In pursuing this line of thought, it is important to be cognizant of the explicit differences between Laroui's thought and Sayyid Quṭb's.

In this book, Laroui speaks on behalf of the Arab nation. He posits what he terms "*La Problematic Arabe*," as opposed to the "Islamic problematic." In other words, in his early writings, Laroui is more inspired by the concept of nationalism than by religious universalism, that is, Islamic universalism. At this point, he shares Arab nationalist concerns expressed by some leading Moroccan intelligentsia, especially by 'Allāl al-Fāsī, leader of the Istiqlāl Nationalist party who was exiled by the French to Egypt in the 1950s.[10] The "Arab problematic" is the product of the radical and abrupt transitions the Arab world experienced at the beginning of the twentieth century.

According to Laroui, four criteria define the "Arab problematic": authenticity, continuity, universality, and artistic expression. Authenticity refers to the definition of the self, the collective self. This, by nature, implies a negation, specifically the West as negation. One must understand the history of the modern Arab self against the background of the modern West, its intervention in the Arab world, and Arab reactions to the challenge the West presented. The situation of the Arab world, though impermanent, has produced a unique genre of literary and cultural expression that reflects its deep anguish.[11]

At one point, Laroui seems to be more Hegelian than Marxist in his analysis. He postulates an undifferentiated "Arab Self" that has been uniformly affected by the exposure to the West. One gets the feeling that Laroui sees the West as an undifferentiated monolith. In later sections of the book, however, Laroui clarifies his conception of the West: the capitalist Western bourgeois that developed against modern history. Further, authenticity implies a certain continuity with the past, a complex Arabo-Islamic heritage, which Laroui condemns because of its "anti-reason."

Because of the failure of the "past" to accommodate or prepare society for the demands of modernity, Laroui offers universality as a substitute. He defines universality as a *Weltanschauung* that permits modern Arabs to act and think in a rational way. However, Laroui's notion of universality is vague, he calls it *raison universelle*. Furthermore, his argument that the past must be opposed to reason is not entirely convincing. Laroui seems to consider Western reason to be the ultimate expression of "universal reason." He definitely situates this reason within the Western philosophical discussion of "Reason" and its development in modern times. Furthermore, Laroui argues that no region in the modern world has escaped the problematic of modernity, which has been primarily engineered by the West. The Arab world must dare to change and to change means to accept the conditions imposed on the world by modern Western history and forces.[12] Does Laroui fall victim to the grandiose schemes of Eurocentrism, a philosophy described by Samir Amin as belittling the intellectual achievements of other nations and cultures?[13]

Laroui's reflections on the modern Arab world is born of his particular situation as a Moroccan thinker.

> Il est né d'une réflexion sure une situation particulière: celle du Maroc d'aujord'hui. Personne ne peut empecher de s'etonner de l'impuissance politique et de la stérilité culturelle, que l'élite marocaine montre depuis dix ans. Pour rendre compte de cet état de choses, on peut certes s'orienter vers une analyse politique ou sociale; mais on peut egalement commencer par l'investigation culturelle, et c'est cette voie qui à été suivi dans ces pages.[14]
>
> ("It is born of a reflection on a particular situation, that of Morocco today. Nobody can help being surprised by the political powerlessness and the cultural stagnation which the Moroccan elite have shown for ten years. To understand this state of affairs, we can certainly look toward a political or social analysis, but we can also begin by a cultural investigation, and this is the path which has been followed in these pages." Translation by Abu-Rabi‘)

He posits that Moroccan society must modernize in order to "catch up" with the West. But who constitutes the elite in post-independence Moroccan society? Laroui focuses on both the intellectual and political elite in Moroccan society. He takes for granted the notion that the intellectual elite betrayed its historical mission of offering a critical analysis of society on the eve of nationalist independence. What are the reasons behind this assumption?

Although the starting point of his discussion is the particular situation of Morocco and the Arab world, Laroui calls for a critical examination of the inherited Arab "mental tools," "Our world is indeed subject to various influences: in order to think, we use concepts, images, and models that are derived from a different reality than ours. If we do not embark on a rigorous analysis of our mental tools (*outillage mental*), we can never be confident of our discussion of ourselves."[15] It is only by performing such an analysis that the weak points of Arab reason can be discovered and a new intellectual map can be suggested in order to remedy the dilemmas of modern Arab culture. These various notions enable us to understand the central cultural problems of the contemporary Arab world but only if they are understood in larger contexts, those of religion and history, religion and society, Islam and the West, the Arab world and the West, imperialism and the nation-state, the intelligentsia and the modern Arab state, etc.

How does one study the mental structure of the modern Arab world? Is it necessary to follow the precedent of Michel Foucault, as does Muḥammad ‘Ābid al-Jābīrī, for instance, and perform an "archeological" deconstruction of Arab reason? Laroui does not consider this necessary. His approach is straightforward: there is no need to delve into archival material or even into the construction of Arab Reason in the formative period of Islam. Contemporary cultural and mental material is abundant and pervasive. The main point to be underlined concerns the correct method of studying recent development in the Arab world.

Laroui's approach in dividing the modern political and intellectual histories of the Arab world into colonial, liberal, and nationalist reminds one of Albert Hourani's famous statement that, "It is commonplace that we cut up history into periods at our peril: the artificial frontiers made for convenience may seem to be real."[16] Laroui is aware that this division is more figurative than practical. However, in order to grasp the social, political, and cultural transformations in the twentieth century Arab world, Laroui supplements this division with another one. He argues that three main trends of thought have dominated the Arab world's intellectual scene since the onset of imperialism: religious, liberal, and technical.

In the first instance, the colonial state is the logical outcome of imperialism. The liberal state, heir to the colonial state, accepts imperialist exploitation as a matter of destiny, whereas the nationalist state struggles against this exploitation without being able to uproot it. Laroui argues that the international capitalist market will not facilitate the economic plans of the nascent nationalist state, which tried to stop the economic pillage of its resources instituted by imperialism.[17] Laroui has Nasser's Egypt in mind when he discusses the impasse of the nationalist state in the Arab world. In spite of this impasse with world capitalism, the nationalist state imposes an ambitious program of secularization that extols the virtues of bourgeois culture and universal Western reason, "The nationalist state imposes a bourgeois, rationalist, and universal culture on a society that has not developed such a culture internally."[18] In other words, Laroui implies that the nationalist state faces a terrible dilemma after independence: it aims to catch up with thc "advanced" West while facing two gruesome hurdles. The first is the globalization of the international market under capitalism and the receding window of economic competition for the nationalist state. The second hurdle centers on the state's awareness of a huge gap between its bourgeois or petty bourgeois culture and that of the people it is determined to modernize. In both cases, the danger is real. The capitalist world does not favor an independent nationalist state, and for nationalist culture to take root in society, the infrastructure needs to be modernized and a new set of mental criteria need to be in place.

By taking Egypt as the primary example, Laroui cites two primary reasons for backwardness in the contemporary Arab world; one is political/economic and the other is cultural/intellectual. In the first instance, after independence the Arab world failed to achieve political unity and economic independence and, in the second, failed to emancipate itself from its inherited cultural worldview. One must note at this juncture that Laroui underlines the theme of the state as a modernizing agent in the Arab world, a theme he later revisits.

Laroui's political and economic typology is complemented by another that reflects the three mental structures, spaces, phenomena, and conditions that define the modern Arab cultural scene. As mentioned above, Laroui delineates three basic intellectual trends, each represented by a major figure, that summarize the progress of modern Arab thought:

1. the religious trend, represented by the religious intellectual;
2. the political trend, represented by the liberal intellectual;
3. the scientific rational trend represented by technocrats and men of science.

The first trend is situated in religious faith, the second in political modernization, and the third in scientific and technical activity and product. Each trend is made up of several strata, of a complex structure, and many voices and dimensions.

These three trends coexist in various degrees of interrelatedness in modern Arab society. However, it is important to realize that no trend is monolithic by nature. The religious, which is Salafī at best, disavows Western progress on the premise that religion in the West has been marginalized. It posits that materialism is the rule of the day in the West. Many agree with Laroui that the Salafī trend is the most dominant in contemporary Arab thought. To a certain extent, though, this trend is bereft of historical vision. For example, it deals with Western Christianity, but not from the perspective of the historical struggle of a new brand of Christianity, namely Protestantism, to define a new mode of religious and economic behavior for the nascent European bourgeoisie after the sixteenth century. On the contrary, it deals with Christianity from the perspective of the Qur'an, or, at best, the perspective of modern Islamic history. What Laroui addresses here is a valid point. Arab intellectuals have failed to produce specialists on the modern West and the cultural changes therein. That is to say, the Arab world has failed to produce its Occidentalists, a point taken up by leading and contemporary Arab thinker Ḥassan Ḥanafī in his book, *al-istighrāb*.[19] The problematic can be put in the following way: Why is it that the nationalist or even Islamist Arab culture after independence failed to produce specialists in European, American or even Israeli studies?

In Laroui's view, the cleric, as the guardian of tradition, cannot distance himself of the effects of the ancient polarization and conflict between Islam and Christianity. He still thinks according to these defunct categories. Thus, his religious consciousness does not allow him to grasp the fundamental changes taking place in the West since the Renaissance and their distinctive secular traits. What this means is that the Salafī thinker, more or less, is guided more by text than history, belief than analysis, and dogma than reflection. This particular criticism has long supplied intellectual ammunition to the critics of "Islamic dogmatism," such as Ṣādiq Jalāl al-'Azm and Ḥāmid Naṣr Abū Zayd.[20] Nonetheless, the cleric's religious consciousness is beset by a duality, "The conscience of our cleric is religious when he analyzes society, but liberal when he critiques the West."[21]

The liberal politician, although not dismissing Islam in public, has borrowed all of his basic concepts about consultation and democracy from the West, though he sometimes gives them an Islamic umbrella, as in his use of the terms *shūrah* and *ijmā'*. He still appeals to Islamic tradition as both a symbol of legitimation and an indicator of cultural authenticity.

The technocrat, on the other hand, pays lip service to both religion and politics. He sees the differences between the Arab world and the West not in terms of religion or political organization, but in the way each has acquired applied science.[22] Laroui notes because of the limitations imposed on the nationalist state, the Arab technocrat is emotionally depressed, but is a mental terrorist. He is weary of arguments unrelated to his preoccupation, which is the technical modernization of society. In his quest to achieve modernization, especially in the new nationalist state, the technocrat often reminds others of the following maxim: "Today's civilization is entirely based on industry and its culture is science and nothing but science, whereas the culture of agrarian societies is that of literature, religion, and philosophy."[23] In addition, the technocrat, according to Laroui, has totally neglected the religious question and tradition: "The technocrat does not feel any need of interpreting the dogma or even changing its traditional meaning; he simply ignores doctrine totally."[24] Laroui is perhaps justified in drawing our attention to this latter idea, mainly because the modern Arab technocrat grew up in the shadow of either colonialism or secular nationalism, both of which attempted to relegate religion to the periphery. However, it seems that technocrats as a class have lent their total support to politicians in modernizing the state without the aid of the religious intelligentsia. In most Arab countries, this intelligentsia, whether oppositional or quietist, is unhappy with its status after independence.

The three individual types mentioned above reflect the dominant intellectual phenomena in the Arab world after independence. Laroui seems to be saying that these three trends must be overcome with an enlightened and critical nationalist philosophy. This is a most daunting task. Is it possible to move beyond the confines of these trends without a ground of common agreement between the State and the intelligentsia? The intelligentsia must spearhead intellectual change and the state must provide assistance. A great gulf exists and methods are needed to bridge that gulf. Laroui attempts this in *The Crisis of the Arab Intelligentsia*, which is a sequel to *L'idéologie arabe contemporaine*.

To a large extent, the nationalist state emerging after independence inherited the cultural environment of colonialism, as mentioned earlier in this chapter. Franz Fanon is one of the few Third World authors who sharply criticized the state of culture under colonialism in view of constructing the foundations of a free national culture after independence. Many Arab authors are indebted to Fanon's contributions.[25] Laroui, however, mentions Fanon only in passing and rarely elaborates on his ideas on culture. However, he correctly notes that the new state is led by the triumphant petty-bourgeoisie, a class intent on thoroughly modernizing society.[26] In its rush towards modernization, the state abandons intellectuals of the *ancien régime* and gives power to technocrats instead, most of whom are graduates of modern European universities. In spite of the rich heritage of the new leading class and the experience it gained in its struggle against imperialism, it continues to function against many odds, most notably against the absence of stable criteria and in an international climate that is not amenable to economic or political stability. In order to establish its foothold in society, the nationalist state raises the banner of nationalist socialism and cultural authenticity. Laroui contends that at best this is a "synthèse de la force et de la fidelité aux ancêtres" ("Synthesis of power and loyalty to ancestors." Translation by Abu-Rabi').[27] In other words, the nationalist state places itself between a rock and a hard place, or between the technical reason of the modern West and the totalistic vision of its cultural past. Is it possible to simultaneously choose both modernity and authenticity? Laroui's answer is clearly no.[28]

I think the above analysis hits the mark, especially in relation to what seems to be the stable nature of many unstable regimes in the Arab world. Laroui does not discuss the military state in the Arab world; however, his discussion of the new state after independence allows us to examine the background of the contemporary military state that has more or less inherited the failed nationalist state.

Is Laroui accurate in his analysis of dominant cultural trends after independence, especially those related to classical Arab and Muslim culture? He seems to suggest that with the advent of the nationalist state, classical Arab and Muslim heritage lost its relevance, has been made redundant. To him, modern Arab culture is antithetical to society's real needs, since it is the product of a closed mental and theological system. Arab culture reflects the inner alienation of the modern Arab individual from modern civilization. This is a serious charge, indeed. Like other Arab intellectuals before him, most notably Ṭāhā Ḥussain, Laroui advocates a clear disengagement with the Arabo-Islamic heritage. Simply stated, he believes this heritage represents dead weight from the past. If this thesis is to be accepted, the Arab world must diligently search for new alternatives. However, I believe it is impossible as well as irresponsible to accept this position as it dismisses out of hand all historical continuities and cultural specificities.

What are the main characteristics of Laroui's alternative structure of thought? Laroui uses the notion of ideology – a complex notion indeed – in three different ways: first, as a system of epistemological analysis that inadequately reflects reality because of the poor conceptual tools used. Second, as a system that obscures reality, for it is difficult to analyze and critique that reality, and finally, as a theoretical construction taken from another society, used as a model for development and a plan for action. It is in this last sense that Laroui uses the term "ideology" throughout his work.[29]

Laroui has in mind the Salafī thinker, who uses the old tools of Fiqh and jurisprudence in reading new situations, " 'Abduh's traditional conceptual tools, which derive from Islamic dialectical theology (Kalām) and Fiqh, permitted him by necessity to look at his society, after it was radically transformed by Western capitalism, in the context of a collapsing traditional society."[30] What this means is that the resurgence of traditional thought in the process of reacting to imperialism and retrieving the notion of authenticity is not helpful in dealing with radical economic and social changes in the Arab world engendered by capitalism since the beginning of the nineteenth century. Laroui analyzes an inevitable process of transformation that brings the Arab world head-on with both liberalism and socialism and their constituent meanings.[31]

Needless to say, Laroui is very much influenced by Western Marxist thinking in his early writings. He is a Marxist in the sense that he uses Marxist philosophical insights to gain some understanding of the Arab world after independence. He suggests adopting Marx, not so much as a political leader, but as a teacher or guide who can direct Arab intelligentsia toward unlimited sources of wisdom and knowledge. That is to say, Laroui thinks that what distinguishes Marxism most is its universal, and not merely European, character and reach. Marx's homeland was the world at large. As stated above, Laroui delineates the major characteristics of post-colonial Arab culture with the guidance of Marxist philosophy. His method is not a simple adaptation of Marxist theory to the exigencies of the modern Arab world but a reworking of some central issues in Marxism in light of the evolution of the modern Arab world from colonialism to nation-state.

In *L'idéologie arabe contemporaine*, Laroui uses the term "Objective Marxism" in describing his method of analysis. He is convinced that Marxism is the most advanced system of social and economic analysis and represents a significant moment in modern European history. It is the methodological summation of modern Western thought.[32] Because of its analytical uses, Marxism can play an ideological role in unmasking systems of exploitation in twentieth century Arab thought. Marxism is born of the capitalist problematic and is the simplest and most rational method of understanding capitalist development:

> Le marxisme…est, de toutes les théories du développement capitaliste, la plus claire et il n'est rien autre. Le marxisme met à jour une rationalité étonnante de simplicité; il fixe l'ordre des priorités et concentre toute sa critique contre le système féodal dans toutes ses manifestations: économiques, humaines et culturelles.[33]
>
> ("Marxism is, of all the theories of capitalist development, the clearest and it is nothing else. Marxism brings to light a rationalism astounding in its simplicity; it fixes the order of priorities and focuses all its critique against the feudal system in all its manifestations: economic, humanistic, and cultural." Translation by Abu-Rabi')

As method, Marxism can interpret the following three planes of Arab society: economy, society, and ideology. In other words, to go deep into the roots of the modern Arab economy, one must have some familiarity with the development of capitalism on a world scale, especially as it evolves under the auspices of imperialism. To understand the class nature of modern Arab societies, it is first necessary to perform an historical analysis of the class composition of this society and the roles of both capitalism and the national bourgeoisie in either maintaining or dismantling class structure. Marxism, in Laroui's view, is the most advanced ideological system in existence.

Therefore, *to Laroui, Marxism offers the most reliable philosophical and theoretical* system. As a scholar, Laroui weds philosophical analysis to historical research. In this he departs sharply from the Althusserian legacy, which has influenced a number of Arab thinkers, such as the Lebanese Mahdī 'Āmil. It is Althusser's opinion that, "Marxism, as a theoretical and a political practice, gains nothing from its association with historical writing and historical research. The study of history is not only scientifically but also politically valueless."[34] Laroui calls himself a historian with a philosophical bent of mind. His use of concepts such as state, class, bourgeoisie, capitalism, political elite, and the masses is necessary in order to analyze some of the dynamics of the modern Arab state. Modern Arab thought cannot escape the problematic of capitalism and the Arab world's engagement with the West. Only Marxism as a philosophical framework is capable of unlocking the mysteries of capitalism and its worldwide expansion. Further, the state, in its quest to establish cohesive structures for Arab society, imposes its notions of unity and community from the top down. In fact, Laroui is highly indebted to Franz Fanon's insights on the colonial question and his views on how to achieve intellectual and political independence.[35]

THE RELIGIOUS PROBLEMATIC

The "religious problematic" has proven to be at the center of modern Arab intellectual debate. Is this problematic a reflection of deformed ideological development in Arab society? What impact did the expansion of capitalism into modern Arab societies have on religion, especially Islam? Although on the whole, secular Arab thinkers pursue different premises and methodologies from those of religious-oriented thinkers, they nevertheless cannot escape dealing with the religious issue and its ideological manifestations. Laroui's thinking on the matter represents certain forms of Marxist critique of Arab society, culture, and its religious underpinnings. "Criticism of religion is the premise of all criticism," declares Marx in one of the most perceptive pieces on the use of religion as ideology in the West. Abdallah Laroui passionately buys into this thought and applies it to the intellectual history of the modern Arab world, which, in his estimation, has not yet transcended the "problem of religion." Laroui proposes the coexistence of a variety of modes of consciousness in the contemporary Arab culture. He also concedes that imperialist intrusion has reinvented the religious question in the form of Islamist activism. As many scholars have noted, Islamism in the Arab and Muslim worlds was born in the age of colonialism as a direct response to it. However, is that not also true about nationalism and other forms of indigenous resistance against foreign intrusion?

How is it possible to methodologically deal with the religious question? Philosophical analysis is one of such means. "Philosophy," Laroui tells us, "is born, develops, and lives again in polemic. It is not by reexamining old problems with the old terminology that it can save itself from ever-threatening anachronism; it renews itself only by occupying itself with the questions that are the stuff of everyday social practice, and these first appear in the form of critical polemic."[36] Laroui seems unsure about the final purpose of religion in Arab society. Will the ruling classes always use religion as an ideological weapon? Laroui seems to think that religious effectiveness in terms of shaping Arab consciousness will recede with the progress of time. His own philosophy is guided by a secular, "democratic," progressive, and even atheist vision that aims to transform Arab society from a state of "backward tradition and religion" to one that seeks radical transformation, the liberation of the Arab individual and the creation of a socialist society. To achieve this end, religion must be abolished. But his obsession with the problem of religion, which permeates Laroui's entire work, is a reminder of the centrality of religion in modern Arab discourse, as pointed out earlier.

THE WEST AS A PROBLEM

Modern Arab consciousness in its different expressions and dimensions is highly intertwined with the West as colonial event, religious expression, political thought and technical creativity. Laroui proposes the following two premises: (1) the Arab world, more or less, forms cohesive cultural unity; and (2) colonial occupation represents a point of rupture between medieval and modern Arab history and thought.[37] Colonialism, like the defeat in 1967, awakened modern Arabs to high levels of consciousness, regarding both their weaknesses and the progress of the West. The nineteenth century problematic of stagnation versus progress reemerges in a new light in the twentieth century. Progress is most lacking in those Arab countries that were able to avoid experiencing direct colonialism.

The complicated engagement between the Arab world and the West profoundly influenced the thought of the religious intelligentsia; it is a modern religious consciousness that cannot be measured in purely religious or traditional terms. The three intellectual trends go through a metamorphosis in the context of colonialism. Although the religious trend loses its dominance in the liberal but colonized state, it reinvents itself in the form of a religious movement speaking the language of universal Islam. The universal language of utopian and ideal Islam – that of colonialism-bred resurgence – masks the great anxiety of post-colonial religious consciousness, the enormous challenges it faces, and the uncertain path it treads. This post-colonial universal Islam does not appeal to Sufi literature or supplications, as in the case of pre-colonial Islam of Egypt, as mentioned by al-Jabartī. Alarmed by the noisy approach of the infidel's troops, the ulama cannot do better than to read *Ṣaḥīḥ al-Bukhārī* in order to be saved from the West. However, universal Islam in the twentieth century is more aggressive and pragmatic in its approach than it proved to be in the nineteenth. It seeks to present new formulations of Islam, even in the name of a utopian "return to the past." This compels Laroui to postulate that "although it loses its dominant role, religious thought (or consciousness) does not totally disappear in the liberal independent state."[38] Neither Laroui nor many Leftist intellectuals can account for the reticence of the Islamic consciousness in the modern era. Liberalism was supposed to control religious consciousness by empting it of social meaning; that is, acknowledging only its private meaning.

According to Laroui, these three trends do not disappear with the advent of the post-colonial nation-state. Instead, they adopt new forms and relationships. The new nation-state represses universal Islam but permits official Islam – a type of submissive Islam – to fill the vacuum and establish bridges between the political elite and the masses. The liberal trend is weakened but not totally annihilated. And the technocrat who cares neither about Islam nor politics forms the backbone of the emerging new state. All these three trends, no doubt, go through another major transformation after 1967. Universal activist Islam celebrates the defeat of the Arab nation-state, especially the Egyptian, the liberal trend assumes its role of defending democracy and human rights, and the technocrats are asked to focus their energies anew in order to rebuild the state.

The three intellectual trends mentioned above are reminiscent of three different moments in European history and thought. They address the question "What is the West?" in three different ways.[39] In other words, one may conclude from Laroui's analysis that the most important common denominator in the various trends of Arab thought is the West. The cleric, although unhappy about the stagnation of the modern Muslim spirit, bemoans the loss of moral and ethical values in the West. Religious consciousness in the modern Arab world determines that the West has lost on moral ground and that Islam still has the upper hand. In other words, the cleric follows a double attitude: he attempts to understand his society from a religious viewpoint, and the West from a critical liberal perspective.[40]

The West is the catalyst, or in Laroui's expressive words: "In attempting to comprehend itself, the Orient [the Arab world] acts as an archeologist in that it digs up the [intellectual and cultural] roles of the Western consciousness. It is always the West that furnishes the elements of discussion."[41] In other words, contemporary Arab thought is greatly indebted to the West. The profound transformations of the West since World War Two, the establishment of the state of Israel, and the end of the Cold War have all affected the Arab world and Arab thought in various ways. All trends postulate that there is a deep crisis affecting the Arab world. The religious intellectual, of various levels, seeks a solution to this crisis in religious faith, and the politician in liberal thought and political modernization, and the technocrat in scientific progress and learning.

Laroui deals with the issue of national culture after independence in Morocco and the rest of the Arab world as the central issue dominating the cultural agenda of the new state, the various Arab intelligentsia and even the popular masses. What direction does national culture take after independence? Laroui mocks the doctrinal attitude of the clerics, criticizes the liberal consciousness of the liberal, and finds fault in the scientific attitude of the technocrat.[42] Laroui's desire is to overcome the major faults of the three trends and even bypass some of their basic formulations. National culture in the new Arab nation-state cannot succeed unless it meets two conditions: first, employing the discoveries of science in the service of the masses without establishing whether these discoveries are concordant with Islam. Second, because national culture is more future than past oriented, Arabs must "catch up" with modern civilization and progress and a spirit that emancipates man from myth and constructs society on solid scientific foundations.

STATE AND MODERNIZATION

The classical Islamic debate on the state centers around its legitimation from the perspective of the Sharī'ah. Laroui correctly argues that the modern Arab state cannot be the product of the classical Islamic state, as envisioned by jurists and traditional Muslim thinkers, mainly because of colonial intervention in the Arab world, which produced new political forms.[43] Laroui argues that the contemporary Arab state does not fit the classical paradigm of Islamic political authority (that is, the caliphate is a political institution that rules in the name of the Sharī'ah), neither is it developed enough to imitate the bureaucratic achievements of colonialism. Arab intellectuals have not concerned themselves with the theory of the state, and some have been used as easy prey by the military. In classical Islamic theory, the state is perceived as both dominating and coercive; the gap between the governor and governed is huge. The Islamic literature on political theory and the state is immense, and as a political philosopher, Laroui does not belittle its importance. However, his interest in political philosophy is dictated by the role of the modern Arab state as an agent of modernization. Today in the Arab world, the state justifies its existence by appealing to notions of public good; this is the rational way to achieve economic prosperity.[44] But the modern Arab state lacks real legitimacy because the individual is suspicious and the unionist consciousness has lost its appeal.[45]

Laroui defines the national state (*état national*) as a state of technology and industrialization led by the triumphant petty bourgeoisie in Arab society.[46] The engineering of the new Arab national state takes place in the context of aggressive neo-colonialism and capitalism that seeks to destroy its economic and cultural foundations. Imperialism that expresses the scientific and political wishes of the Center, especially that of the United States, refrains for a while from using an explicitly brutal means to widen the gap between the Center and the Periphery. The inequality generated by this gap represents a major challenge to the economic and political aspirations of the nascent nationalist state. Laroui argues that, "L'Etat national ne hait pas tant l'Occident que son retard et sa faiblesse"[47] ("It is not the West that the nationalist state hates as much as its weakness and retardation." Translation by Abu-Rabi'). In order to meet these new challenges, the nationalist state begins to form a new national culture and discovers that the old paradigms do not suffice or are backward in this new context. The old culture is both arid and inefficient. In producing a new culture capable of competing with conditions created by modernity, the nationalist state bypasses the old and attempts to present new formulations. In its attempt to engineer a new culture, three types of enemies coalesce: the defeated liberal, the dethroned cleric, and the unfulfilled youth. All are impatient with the state, since it does not fulfill their dreams. So far, Laroui has Nasserite Egypt in mind. However, he fails to articulate the reasons behind the resurgence of religion in the new nationalist state.

Besides adopting rationalization and modernization as supreme goals, the nationalist state begins to speak on behalf of the masses. It aspires to represent the masses in the name of technology and productivity. In order to engineer a new social order, the nationalist state employs the thesis of authenticity to the past. It claims that it is the true heir of the past, a revolutionary and socialist past, "the nationalist state imposes through force the main premises of technical reason although it fiercely criticizes those mutilations that this Reason has caused the Western self and man."[48] According to Laroui, neo-imperialism forever aims to dismantle this new system, which combines both technology and authenticity. Neo-imperialism does not tolerate real competition in the Periphery, especially one masked by authenticity and love of heritage. This analysis is sound in that if we read history retrospectively, as does Muḥammad Haykal, imperialism unleashed Israel against the nationalist state in 1967 and the result was a shaking of its foundations and dreams.[49]

Undoubtedly, the 1967 defeat provided a golden opportunity for critics of the nationalist state to be more courageous and even vengeful in their criticism of the failed experiment of the nationalist state. I am not speaking merely of those Muslim activists imprisoned by the state, but also of liberals and Westernizers in Arab society who saw defeat as a blessing in disguise. Therefore, new forms of national culture emerge after 1967 – a synthesis of liberal and Islamist factors that competes with a state trying to reassert its authority in the spheres of politics and culture.

In addition, Laroui establishes the idea that the major dynamic in the study of modern Arab thought is the East–West dynamic and not the East–tradition dynamic. This axis (Arab world–West) has generated not just capitalism and colonialism, that is, concrete economic and political conditions, but also the complex and multi-layered ideology of Orientalism as a means of studying and relating to the Arab world in the modern era. The ideology of the West has penetrated modern Arab thought in two ways: the three representative Arab intellectuals have related to three different types of Western consciousness: faith, democracy, and science. Second, Orientalism as philology, social science, and structural analysis, has affected many Arab intelligentsia who apply these methods in their work and teaching.[50] Modern Arab ideology is formed against a constant interaction with the movement of Orientalism.

THE CRISIS OF THE ARAB INTELLECTUAL

In a recent interview, Laroui explicitly states that the state is the only agent of modernization in the Arab world and that the intelligentsia has failed to carry its banner.[51] Laroui's dissatisfaction with the Arab intelligentsia is the subject matter of his second major book, *La crise des intellectuels arabes*. He devotes his energies to a major critique of the Arab intelligentsia, their intellectual product, their understanding of the past and the West, and their role in transforming modern Arab thought. He states that any real transformation of modern Arab culture and society must begin with the critique of the dominant intelligentsia and their various ideologies and expressions. In addition to studying and critiquing the Arab intelligentsia, Laroui tries to deconstruct the discursive thought structure of Arab society (the hidden mentalities) as a way of emancipating Arab society from bondage to the past.

Since the nineteenth century, the West has posed a major challenge to the Arab world to the extent that the history of the modern Arab world can be summarized as a history of struggle against imperialist domination externally, and a conflict between two types of forces internally. Throughout his work, Laroui grapples with the notion of the West. The West is a double-edged sword: it is a symbol of universal progress; however, it has functioned as a universal oppressive force, as well. One may therefore define the West as "economic exploitation, political domination, conceptual system, and ethical practice."[52] Modern Western thought, historically speaking, is bourgeois thought produced against the background of a severe conflict between the European mercantile class and the feudal system. In the same vein, Marxism is an extension of bourgeois thought in that it favors the most liberal and socialist ideas of the bourgeoisie. It is with the latter type of thought that Laroui identifies for a while.

The intellectual elite in the contemporary Arab world have reflected, from various angles, the desire of the Arab masses for emancipation from imperialism and to achieve economic independence and social progress. There has been a decline in the cultural situation in the Arab world since 1967. The "progressive camp" composed of Nasserites, Ba'athist and Leftist Arab intellectuals in general, carried the banner of progress and revolution and were determined to form a progressive national culture in response to the conservatives. Laroui speaks of two camps: progressive and conservative. The progressive camp has been in a state of decline since 1967 and the conservative has been on the rise since 1967. Laroui refers here to the rise of the Gulf states to national and international prominence after the decline of Nasserism following the 1967 war. However, he is not explicit about this; he hesitates to mention any country by name. He argues that in most cases contemporary Arab institutions are controlled by conservative camps. The Arab progressive camp has failed to realize its aims of liberation, socialism, and unity mainly because it has been guided by a traditional method, which, in turn, allowed the conservative camp to control the political movement of the post-1967 Arab world. Once again, Laroui is not explicit about the nature and meaning of "traditional method," except perhaps to denote the absence of rationality in politics and administration and the prevalence of personal, tribal, or family factors.

Laroui offers the following observations. First, although Arab intelligentsia are capable of offering a radical methodology of change, it does not necessarily follow that the masses will embrace this methodology. Laroui does not believe the masses can be an agent of change and resigns himself to the notion that the intellectual elite can offer such a change. Second, in its varied ideological and political expressions, modern Arab thought is the product of imperialist pressure as well as class relations within Arab society.[53] The different classes in Arab society express their interests through their respective intellectuals. The conflict among classes of intellectuals is a reflection of the conflict among classes. This is a well-known thesis that Laroui borrows from Italian thinker Antonio Gramsci. Third, the conservative intellectual camp is dominant and is the one that has remained faithful to the traditional vision. There is a real need to achieve a breakthrough in method in order to achieve progress and unity.

Fourth, in spite of their campaign against intellectual imperialism and carrying the banner of authenticity, the conservative intelligentsia, in Laroui's mind, are paving the way for reconciliation with the West.[54] The traditionalist intelligentsia, in its different expressions, was born as a result of the failure of bourgeois liberal thought, the precursor to Marxist thought, to rule in the 1930s. The failure of liberalism in the 1930s and consequent failure of the Arab bourgeoisie to achieve its capitalist goals enabled the Ikhwān to represent the working class and speak in the name of social justice and equality. To Laroui, modern Arab thought has conspicuously failed to appropriate the gains of modern reason, such as rationalism, objectivity, and dynamism. Laroui seems to think of the "traditionalist" trend in monolithic terms; he does not differentiate between the Ikhwān, as a Salafī oppositional trend, and between the ruling religious elite in a country like Saudi Arabia.

Fifth, according to Laroui, one must draw a line between the content of modern Western thought and the ideology of contemporary imperialism. That is, a distinction must be made between classical liberalism – the fruit of the struggle of the middle class against feudalism – and contemporary liberal and capitalist ideology that basically aims at maintaining capitalist hegemony.[55] Europe has gradually distanced itself from the spirit of classical liberal thought that emerged in the seventeenth and eighteenth centuries, especially in connection to the Third World. In a sense, the West betrayed its original ideals, especially in the process of imperialist expansion. Europe speaks a language that it does not practice overseas – the language of human rights and democracy.

Sixth, one must draw a line between authenticity and specificity. Authenticity means different things: religion, culture, or past history. Authenticity tends to preserve anachronistic ways of thinking and behavior. On the other hand, specificity denotes the uniqueness of a society resulting from its objective social and historical conditions. Laroui argues that the dominant social classes in Arab society, which represent the aspirations of the conservative camp, defend authenticity in various forms as a means of affirming its control not just over the past but the present, as well. Although modernity has invaded every social, educational, political, and economic aspect of Arab society, many traditionalist intellectuals still carry the banner of authenticity versus modernism or inner spirit versus historical change.[56] The progressive camp must present new ideas for a liberal and progressive Arab culture.

Seventh, Arab society betrays a major gap between modernity and modernization. One may argue that such Gulf countries as Saudi Arabia and Kuwait have taken important strides toward modernization, but the dominant consciousness in society is traditional and even conservative. "Is it possible to imagine a modern society without a modern ideology?"[57] Traditional thought is dominant. To revolutionize Arab society, modern methodologies must be used and a new thought structure (*mentalité*) must be built.

Eighth, the Arab intellectual elite lacks a developed historical consciousness, "the concept of history – a concept playing a capital role in 'modern' thought – is in fact peripheral to all ideologies that have dominated the Arab world till now."[58] In a sense, Laroui condemns the Arab intelligentsia for their "historical retardation" vis-à-vis the liberal age – their inability to understand this important historical phase and currents of thought, especially Marxism. This is a severe criticism that does not take into account the fact that catastrophes have forced modern Arab thought to look into all sorts of directions in order to come up with a clear and coherent meaning of disaster in contemporary Arab consciousness. Contemporary Arab thought recognizes the importance of the "Other," its different possibilities and the danger it poses to much of the Third World.

All the above observations revolve around some salient features of contemporary Arab culture. In criticizing the traditional intelligentsia, Laroui downplays the major role a good segment of this intelligentsia played in the national struggle against imperialism. All the national movements in the Arab world contained many traditional classes that fought for independence. The case of 'Allāl al-Fāsī and the Istiqlāl Party in Morocco illustrates this point. Second, Laroui seems weary of the final product of the intellectual elite; neither does he trust the masses enough to produce positive movements of change in the Arab world.

ARAB SOCIETY, LIBERALISM AND MARXISM

Laroui follows the movement of modern European history, especially from its feudal to bourgeois phases and the efflorescence of liberal ideas in the nineteenth century. Since he believes that neither the Arab intelligentsia nor the masses can change their histories, Laroui resorts to a well-established historical model. He poses the question, "Can Arab society appropriate the gains of liberalism without experiencing a liberal phase?"[59] In other words, Arab society is basically agricultural and its bourgeois class is small. Above all, its educated intelligentsia is small. In Europe, a certain logic of liberalism dominates – a logic that organizes the relationship between state and individual on the basis of rationalism and effective management. Liberalism has not known any real success in the Arab world except in some few cases, especially at the educational level. This creates a real dilemma, if one were to accept Laroui's basic thesis, toward the development of contemporary Arab society. Liberalism has been a failed experiment since the 1930s, especially in Egypt. Furthermore, Arab nationalism, the only real hope of the masses, received its first deathblow with the 1967 war and its second in the second Gulf War in 1991. One may push Laroui's conclusions further by noting that in the context of the expansion of multinational companies, globalization, and the economic dependency of the Arab world on the West, the objective conditions are far from ripe in the contemporary Arab world for classical liberalism – the liberalism of real democracy and human rights – to assert itself. The Arab bourgeoisie lacks the strength to effect such a change.

It has been already established that Laroui is convinced that philosophical Marxism is the only effective method of scientific analysis. One reason for his condemnation of the modern Arab intelligentsia lies in the fact that they have not appropriated philosophical Marxism as their method of analysis. Laroui goes a bit further by attacking even the revolutionary Arab intelligentsia that failed, in his opinion, to absorb modern Western thought, especially Marxism. Because this intelligentsia possessed only fragmentary knowledge of Western thought, its analysis of the historical, political, social, and economic conditions of the Arab world in the 1950s and 1960s was strewn with shortcomings. Laroui calls this "ideological paralysis" (*al-'ajz al-aydiūlūjī*).[60]

There are two intellectual tendencies in contemporary Arab society: one is traditional and seeks to reestablish the permanence of tradition over new outlooks of life and the other is modern in the sense that it appeals to modern and scientific methods in studying society, and the economy and in its educational vision, generally speaking. Traditionalism is a form of "ideological prostitution." Marxism has absorbed the intellectual gains of liberalism and it is the only intellectual system that can provide us with the logic of the modern world. "Marxism is the best approach that is able to absorb the logic of modern science that befits our mentality and condition."[61] Only an "unhappy" revolutionary class can lead the Arab world away from conservatism and open up hidden vistas of progress in thought and action.

After outlining the main currents of "contemporary collective Arab ideology," Laroui discovers that the tenacious presence of tradition and the traditional mentality, far from being anachronistic and obsolete, still dominate contemporary Arab thinking. Laroui's relevance to our present endeavor is derived from his scathing critique of what he terms "Islamic traditionalism," and its pervasive presence in contemporary Islamic societies. Laroui specifically struggles with the notion of the Islamic tradition *per se*. Although he ends up dismissing the entire theological and philosophical heritage of Islam as obsolete, he maintains that traditional categories of thought still dominate the mental product of a large number of Arab intelligentsia. "Arab intellectuals think according to two rationales: Most of them profess the traditionalist rationale (*salafi*); the rest profess eclecticism. Together, these tendencies succeed in abolishing the historical dimension."[62] According to Laroui, the real crisis of the traditionalist Arab intelligentsia is to be sought in the "foundations" that give birth to their thought. This mental dependency on and refuge in the past makes the chances of historical consciousness and progress quite remote. What therefore, is the alternative? Laroui argues that the only means to do away with traditionalist modes of thinking, "consists in strict submission to the discipline of historical thought and acceptance of all its assumptions."[63] Laroui is not quite clear about the real nature of this historical school. Yet his challenge to the functioning categories of the modern Arab mind still awaits an answer. In the words of Hourani, Laroui calls for the adoption of historicism: "that is to say, a willingness to transcend the past, to take what was needed from it by a 'radical criticism of culture, language and tradition', and use it to create a new future."[64]

It is true that Laroui utilizes a number of important terms that illustrate his position on a number of crucial issues. Such terms as hegemony, tradition, historicism, and revolution cannot be valued in an historical sense unless they are understood in the context of the power dynamics in modern Arab society, and the way this society produces knowledge and culture. One could argue on the basis of Laroui's thinking that the real problem facing the modern Arab world is not Westernization, cultural alienation, or historical alienation, but the preservation of rigid and traditional categories of thought which are incapable of combating and solving current problems.

Laroui's central theses and the solutions he proposes revolve around one vision of history: European history as universal history. As Abdallah Saaf notes, in Laroui's eyes, "Europe…has become the center of universal history, the focus of historical progress, and the principal axis of modern civilization."[65] Laroui seems to toss authenticity and even specificity out the window: historicism is the answer, "The European historical role – extending from the Renaissance to the Industrial Revolution – furnishes the only model for those revolutionary policies that aim to rid non-European countries of medieval conditions and lead them to modern ones. This premise, far from being a priori, is the result of reflecting on historical reality."[66] It is the re-creation of eighteenth and nineteenth century European liberalism in the heart of the Arab world. The intellectual enemies are clear: once the eclectic and traditional Arab intelligentsia are defeated, it will be possible to effect a major cultural revolution that will pave the way for major political change in the Arab world.

FREEDOM AND ARAB SOCIETY

It can be argued that the central problems besetting modern Arab thought originated in the nineteenth century under the pressures presented by Europe. One such problem is that of freedom in Arab society. Under pressure, Arab thought borrowed the idea of freedom from bourgeois Europe. This significant matter has stood at the heart of modern Arab thought, reflecting the needs of Arab societies and the levels of their economic and social maturity.

Overwhelmed by the dogma associated with European onslaught in the nineteenth century, some traditionalist and non-modernist Muslim thinkers equated liberty with atheism. For example, Aḥmad al-Nāṣīrī, a traditional Moroccan scholar of the nineteenth century, says: "Know that this liberty that the Europeans speak of is the invention of the atheists for sure. Such liberty does not subscribe to the rights of God, family, and man. As for legal (*shari'yah*) liberty, you are apt to find it defined in the Book of God, explained by His Prophet, and formulated by the Jurists in a legal manner."[67] Traditional Muslim thought fundamentally differs from European thought on the matter of freedom. The Islamic concept is guided by a unique tradition, a different worldview, and perhaps different objectives. Laroui contends that from an Islamic perspective, liberty is treated in a moral and metaphysical sense, whereas in European thought it revolves around political and social meanings and begins with the question of the relationship between state and individual and the meaning of freedom.[68]

Laroui contends that it is erroneous to assume that the only meaning of liberty in classical Islamic society is the psycho-metaphysical.[69] It is true that, on the one hand, we must understand liberty in juristic Islamic terms that reflect the level of the Islamic state's development and the interaction between the state and the intellectual elite, namely the ulama. On the other hand, however, it is important to understand the notion of liberty as a counter-state concept and movement that flourished in medieval Muslim society under the following guises: (1) nomadism; (2) clanism; (3) piety, and (4) mysticism.[70] Each of these important concepts reflected a social and mental structure that was at odds with the urban structure of the state. Nomadism represented authenticity and originality, clanism provided social meaning for the individual, and both piety and mysticism gave the individual the means to be connected to a higher metaphysical and spiritual realism than that preached by the urban ulama. All of these genres of discourse existed in almost every traditional Islamic society, and they still exist in various forms. That is to say, the domain of freedom in traditional Arab society is much larger than in that of the state. The real challenge facing the contemporary state in the Arab world is how to build strong relationships between the state and the individual or community, and how to reduce the domain of anti-state freedom. In other words, the concept of citizenry must be the guiding philosophy of the contemporary Arab state. If this is accomplished, individual freedoms would then ensue from the state and not from other sources.[71]

These counter-statist notions affirmed the idea that "state and individual freedom are at odds in traditional Arab society."[72] These notions and anti-statist structures survived the Western assault on the Arab world in the nineteenth century, and, in fact, some of them were strengthened by such a Western presence.

Against this background, how can one evaluate the rise of Islamic revivalism in the modern Arab world? It is a known fact that Islamism rose as a socio-political and religious response to the problem of colonialism and the colonialist state in the Arab world. Islamism, from the beginning, disavowed the Western liberal notion of liberty, since liberty in this sense was equated with servitude. Islamism's philosophy of liberty is based on the notion of divine sovereignty (*ḥākimiyya*), which opposes the liberal notion of freedom. Sayyid Quṭb, for example, the theoretician *par excellence* of Arab Islamism, defines *ḥākimiyya* as man's freedom from the slavery of man and the affirmation of a higher authority, God's, which is above any temporal secular authority. What this means in effect is that for the modern nation-state in the Arab world to survive the challenge of Islamism, it must expand its legal structures and affirm the freedom of the individual in a bourgeois sense so it can then counter ideas of Islamic solidarity proposed by the Islamic movement.[73]

There is no doubt that in its confrontation with the capitalist and imperialist West, the nineteenth century Arab world assimilated some Western ideas of freedom. The Arab nationalist movement in the Middle East used the liberal notion of liberty to challenge Turkish hegemony which was based on the rule of one family as justified by a Sacred Text. As a result of European pressure, both physical and philosophical, the Ottoman legal and political structure began to erode. Journalists, essayists, and writers of the new secular intelligentsia were the best propagandists for such a new movement of thought. However, these intellectuals were doubly frustrated: they wanted to get rid of Ottoman domination with the help of Western hegemonic ideas. They opted for nationalism at a later stage in order to affirm their newly discovered notions of solidarity and unity.

Laroui maintains that modern Arab thought incorporated liberalism in different disguised manifestations. For example, there is the liberalism of Ṭāhā Ḥussain, who without hesitation opted to imitate the West in *The Future of Culture in Egypt*. Another sort of liberalism practiced through the lenses of Islam is that of Aḥmad Amīn and Khālid Muḥammad Khālid. The goal is to create a balance between Islamic and Western values. However, liberalism and the notion of liberty cannot find true acceptance in the Arab world unless the socio-economic and political environments are ripe to absorb them and reprocess them in a uniquely Arab way. This challenge is posed to not only the Arab intelligentsia, but also to Arab society as a whole.

Laroui argues that, on the whole, the modern Arab state is a weak formation because so many incompatible factors, Islamic, Western, and nationalist, have gone into its making. A strong state cannot take control unless there is with it a strong bureaucracy based on rationalism. The state as an oppressive structure exists in most Arab countries and there has not been enough discussion in modern Arab thought of the nature of the modern state.[74] The Arab consciousness of the state is therefore weak, and is even more so in relation to the process of Arab unity. One main reason for the failure of Arab unity is the fact that the collective Arab consciousness of Arab unity, politically speaking, has been fragile or non-existent, and that regionalism has had the upper hand in the political discourse of the Arab world.

MUḤAMMAD 'ABDUH REVISITED

Thirty years after publishing *L'idéologie arabe contemporaine*, Laroui returns to one of his favorite subjects, Muḥammad 'Abduh and the experience of the Nahḍah movement.[75] Laroui discusses 'Abduh sympathetically. Undoubtedly, 'Abduh is the most influential figure in the Nahḍah movement. He fought relentlessly for an enlightened, modern, and viable interpretation of Islam and the Islamic tradition in the context of modernity. His intellectual project exemplifies the maturity of Arabo-Islamic thought in the late nineteenth and early twentieth centuries. His genius stems from the fact that he considered both the "religious problematic" and the question of stagnation to be at the center of modern Arab intellectual debate. This has been the case even in the most advanced nationalist or Marxist literature in the contemporary Arab world. As an enlightened religious intellectual and a critic of those conditions that he saw as stagnant, rigid, and un-Islamic, especially in the Arab world, 'Abduh's point of departure in his appreciation of the "Other" is the "Muslim self," which he understands as both normative and historical. To retrieve the "normative self" from many centuries of socio-economic, political, and religious decline and marginalization (that is to say, from its stagnant "historical self"), he focuses on the following factors:

1. The stagnation of the traditional Islamic educational institutions, such as the ancient Azhar university. In a fiery discussion with Shaykh Muḥammad al-Buḥairī, a member of the Administrative Council of the Azhar University (c. 1903), 'Abduh urges the Council to introduce new courses that permit the teaching of Ibn Khaldūn's *Prolegomena*, Mathematics, and other sciences. Buḥairī objects to this suggestion and asks 'Abduh: "Haven't you studied at the Azhar and attained the highest level of Islamic learning?" 'Abduh counters bitterly, saying: "If I ever attained the sublime learning that you are referring to, it is because I spent ten years cleansing my brain of the garbage of the Azhar [*wasākhat al-Azhar*], and, to this date, it has not attained the cleanliness I meant for it."
2. In addition, 'Abduh devotes considerable time to the issue of stagnation in Muslim religious thought, and the spread of the philosophy of predestination among the masses. According to 'Abduh, it was in the interest of Muslim rulers in the age of decline – roughly from the tenth to the fifteenth centuries CE – to spread this philosophy as a means of easily attaining control over the masses. The main components of the philosophy of predestination are inaction, laziness, and apathy.
3. The rigidity of the Arabic language.
4. The superstition of the mystics and the "deceitful dervishes."
5. The corruption of the political and religious elites, and the backwardness of general social and economic conditions.

'Abduh was a Salafī in a revolutionary sense. Laroui forcefully argues that 'Abduh, like Muslim and Arab societies in the nineteenth century, was challenged to the core by the Western problematic, by an advanced capitalist, imperialist, and liberal civilization that took science and progress as its criteria of excellence and quality. In its encounter with the Muslim world, the expansionist West claimed that Islam was an inherently backward religion; in other words, that Islam and stagnation are two sides of the same coin. 'Abduh was attracted to the Western problematic and began to see the question in its proper Western context: Is there a connection between Islamic doctrine and stagnation? 'Abduh, according to Laroui, was in no position to represent the class of the stagnant ulama [the turbaned shaykhs] in the nineteenth century and refused to dialogue with them because he held them responsible for any existing backwardness. 'Abduh expected no less than utter purification of nineteenth century Muslim reason. Laroui argues that 'Abduh expected the ulama to subject themselves to "mental assassination" (*intiḥār fikrī*) if they were serious about the progress of their societies. Undoubtedly, the real enemy is *taqlīd*, which is simply translated as the absence of rationalism in both institutional and intellectual practices. Laroui notes that the question of *taqlīd* remains pivotal in contemporary Arab thought, "What transpired in the past (in terms of the quarrels between the ancients and the moderns) in the style of the Azhar repeats itself today in the style of Oxford and the Sorbonne."[76]

In addition to stagnation, 'Abduh seriously contemplated the questions of both liberty and dictatorship in his society. If he was successful in defending Islam in high moral and metaphysical terms, he was unreserved in his staunch criticism of the backward social conditions and in placing the responsibility for this squarely on the shoulders of corrupt rulers and shaykhs. However, the problem that 'Abduh faced was how to implement his modernist vision in a society that was basically illiterate. His answer was overall reform: of the religious and intellectual elite, the basic institutions of society, and the underlying mentality. 'Abduh's answer to this state of affairs was reform and not faith.[77]

What is surprising about Laroui's portrayal of 'Abduh and the whole modernist legacy in his recent writings is the sympathy with which he approaches his subject. In a sense, Laroui dismantles the ideal he erects in his two first books. He no longer invites us to overcome the mental structures that dominate the thinking or achievements of the reform movement in the Arab world. Further, he notices the revolutionary potential of the Islamic idiom used by 'Abduh and his comrades. In attacking stagnation, backwardness, dictatorship, and inequality in Arab and Muslim societies, they do not use traditional language. Laroui does not say who represents 'Abduh's position in contemporary Moroccan society, but he is apt to find somebody who represents the tradition of Islamic reform. My guess is that Laroui would prefer a contemporary Muḥammad 'Abduh to a contemporary Ḥasan al-Banna or Sayyid Quṭb.

CONCLUSIONS

A cursory review of Laroui's work reminds us yet again of the colonial origin of the modern Arab cultural problematic. The modern nation-state in the Arab world more or less expanded the colonial cultural enterprise after independence. Building national universities along Western models, sending students to Western universities and importing foreign professors in different faculties enhanced the nation-state's cultural indebtedness to the West. The colonial project indoctrinated indigenous intelligentsia and put in place structures that still impinge on contemporary Arab society.

Laroui's intellectual project appears to be based on radical notions of change in the spheres of society, politics, thought, and culture. It contains the following premises:

1. emancipating the individual from the control of the ulama and the traditional intelligentsia;
2. liberalizing the state;
3. abolishing the pedagogical function of religion in society;
4. creating secular schools;
5. liberating the poor masses and workers from the hegemony of religion and traditional ideas.[78]

As such, this project is ideological in nature. The language of ideology under girds a complex philosophical and epistemological understanding of the questions at hand. Further, Laroui equips his ideological-philosophical project or vision with a deep historical outlook and uses a certain historical model in his writings.

Laroui's project, it seems to me, is much like that of Ṭāhā Ḥussain, as articulated in his leading work, *The Future of Culture in Egypt*. The progressive Arab intelligentsia must adopt the central problematics of Westernization, in the words of Ḥussain, or liberalization, in the words of Abdallah Laroui, in order to create a rational and future-oriented society.

One would have hoped that Laroui, who has solid understanding of both Western and Arab social, economic, and intellectual history would dwell more on colonialism and post-colonialism and their impact on the Arab world. As a reader, I feel Laroui could have but chosen not to continue the critical cultural and political project begun by Franz Fanon, especially in *The Wretched of the Earth*. Although he touches upon some of Fanon's ideas, Laroui instead advocates a totally Westernized national culture or one completely immersed in the liberal problematic.

Laroui's analysis has a mysterious force. It is a critique produced by a highly intelligent mind. He deeply engages in critical thought, which he employs in grasping the less obvious aspect of Arab culture. However, he asks too much of the intelligentsia; he asks them to disavow centuries of thought, tradition, and behavior. Every intelligentsia is nourished by certain traditions, legacies, and worldviews. Is it possible to productively address problems in the modern world without implicitly relying on assumptions given to us by such traditions, legacies, and worldviews? Is it possible to totally dismantle the past? Laroui is contemptuous of the Arab intelligentsia. He charges them of failing to diagnose and provide solutions to the central problems facing Arab society.[79] In fact, this is a preposterous charge. He also maintains that the Arab intelligentsia do not merely live in a crisis-ridden society, but are themselves in crisis.[80] As stated before, the relationship between the intelligentsia and the ruling elite in the Arab world has been problematic at best. Intellectuals who dared offer solutions or plans of action have been silenced, imprisoned, or banished, though Laroui fails to see their dilemma.

Furthermore, Laroui's project of "epistemological liberation" hits a major snag in the 1990s. His ideas are the flawed product of an irreconcilable strain between his role as philosopher-theoretician idealist and the official head of the Royal Moroccan Academy of Arts and Sciences. These factors combined result in Laroui's blindness to many of the requirements of a healthy national culture, in both Morocco and the Arab world half a century or so after independence. He expresses frustration with every dominant intellectual current in Arab society; he proves himself to be elitist at best.

In his earlier works, he invites the Arab intelligentsia to fully embrace critical Marxism, or what he calls "Objective Marxism." Half way through his intellectual career, however, he disavows Marxism.[81] He no longer shows interest in the reproduction of ideology in the contemporary Arab world and the role that the intelligentsia plays in supporting to political authority. Although he continues to use "crisis discourse" while discussing the contemporary Arab issues, he turns away from the former focus on the role of the state and turns the heat up on the intelligentsia. He changes his mind about the contemporary Arab political system, especially the Moroccan monarchy. In his earlier works, Laroui pays only scant attention to the state in the Arab world. He seems to be more interested in the intellectual freedom of the intelligentsia than he is in the legalities of state. In his later writings, however, he changes course. He concludes that the Arab state must adopt liberal notions of citizenry. The individual must be bound to the state alone, not to his clan, tribe, or shaykh. He also advocates that the state is the only guarantee against the breakdown of civil society. Laroui contends the contemporary Moroccan state is the most modernized, saying, "No historian can deny that King Ḥassan II was more successful than the past Moroccan kings in constructing a highly modern state."[82] Laroui admits that most of the intelligentsia have not lent their support to such a state, and for this he blames the intelligentsia. He sincerely believes that the state has been the most powerful agent of modernization in contemporary Moroccan history and should be supported. Although he admits that there are pockets of "traditional resistance" here and there, he is certain that the state modernization program will soon embrace every dimension of society. Laroui ignores the process of globalization and the negative impact it may have had on the contemporary Moroccan state. In this, one is led to assume that contemporary globalization is the natural heir of yesterday's modernization. Furthermore, Laroui completely ignores increasing social and economic gaps in contemporary Moroccan society, the entrenchment of the old guard, and increasing corruption among the ruling elite. The result is that his analysis is highly flawed.

Still, Laroui appears not to trust the intelligentsia that he initially intended to push along a revolutionary path of mental change. He places so much of his hope in the state not because he believes that the contemporary Moroccan state, like its neighbor Algeria, is on the verge of anarchy, but because he thinks it is impossible for the intelligentsia to revolutionize itself. Does this mean that Laroui has aborted his intellectual project? Perhaps so, and especially if examined against the context of the recent collapse of the Soviet system. His thought is the child of theoretical idealism nourished by a well-paid government position: As the head of the Royal Moroccan Academy of Arts and Sciences, he cannot escape this mindset.

As I finish reading most of what Laroui has written, I find I am disappointed. I expected Laroui to expand Franz Fanon's work, one of the greatest Third World intellectuals in the twentieth century, and write the history of national Arab culture after independence. Instead, he takes a rigid, unduly critical position without offering sound alternatives. He alienates himself not just from the intelligentsia but also from the masses. He ends up condemning Arab culture without offering practical solutions. It is a pity that such a great mind, one who has done much to enlighten us about the dynamics of modern Arab thought, seems to go nowhere in his critique of Arab society.

17
Conclusions

I have set my discussion of post-1967 Arab intellectual history in the context of the enormous social and economic transformations taking place in the Arab world since the eclipse of colonialism and dawn of the nation-state. In the good old days, modernization theorists considered these transformations as a victory of the Western liberal model over that of socialism. It has been my contention throughout that although most if not all regimes in the Arab world have been repressive, they have initiated massive transformations in their societies and used them, among other things, as a source of legitimization. It is certainly true that the scope and pace of these transformations differ from one country to another. What accounts for these differences is the size of the country, its wealth, and the education, or lack thereof, of its rulers. Because of oil revenues and the need to "modernize," the Gulf countries initiated drastic changes in their societies without enlarging their power base. Power is still concentrated in the hands of a few members of the ruling family in every Gulf country and in the hands of one party in the case of Iraq or Syria.

What is troubling about most studies on the Arab world is the absence of a clear and conclusive analysis of the concepts of the Arab state and elite. The state formation in the Arab world, just like in many Third World countries, was a colonial phenomenon inherited by the nation-state. In its progress in the past 50 years or so, the Arab state system has faced tremendous internal and external challenges. There are various configurations of the contemporary Arab elite, ranging from the military, to the political, and the tribal. The concentration of power in a few hands and the stunning stability of many Arab regimes are an indication of the expansion of the role of the military in civilian lives, and the increasing dependency of the Arab state on world capitalism.

Militarism seems to be the core factor or code that gives the contemporary Arab state its durability. Overall militarism in the Arab world, unlike that in Israel,[1] lacks a unified ideology. One could say that in the 1950s and 1960s, Arab nationalism gave some coherence and justification to militarism. However, after the decline of Arab nationalism in the 1970s, new factors have emerged to support the *status quo*. Exploiting Islam ideologically has been one of these factors.

To maintain domination[2] over society, the ruling elite in the Arab world have worked hard to ensure the compliance of the largest number of people through either concrete mechanisms or intellectual hegemony. Religion as interpreted by the state is a major source of hegemony, although not the only one. Therefore, in understanding the nature of domination in the Arab world, one must take note of the three grounds on which legitimate domination is based: (1) rational grounds;

(2) traditional grounds; and (3) charismatic grounds. According to Max Weber, the first one is based on legal authority; the second on religious and traditional authority; and the third on exceptional qualities.[3] Of these three, the most prominent in the Arab world is the second. One must add another category, which is militarism as mentioned previously.

The ruling elite in most Arab countries hail from the military or have a strong military support. To preserve their hegemony over society, this elite have participated in forging all sorts of alliances, especially with the religious elite in society. To say that the political elite in the Arab world is anti-religious is far from true.

In my study of contemporary Arab intellectual history, I made sure to account for some significant international factors affecting the Arab world in the past century. One of these major influences on almost every Arab country has been the United States and its economic, political, and military policies vis-à-vis each Arab country since the end of World War Two. It is in this context that one must understand the rise of the Israeli state after 1948 and its immense impact on the Arab world and the Palestinians. I think it is quite naïve to study the Israeli factor apart from the European and American factors. Before the establishment of Israel, Zionism's alliance with the main European powers, especially Britain after World War One, enabled it to achieve its political objectives. After the defeat of the Ottoman Empire in World War One, Britain assumed the mantle of hegemony in the Middle East and established a colonial regime in Palestine, which ultimately proved to be highly beneficial to the Zionist enterprise. Zionism's main success was the establishment of Israel in 1948. Israel became strong militarily due to the enormous channeling of arms and money from the West, and Israel could not have afforded to continue its occupation of the West Bank and Gaza and enlarge its settlement activities there without the active financial and military support of the United States.

As we examine the Arab world at the beginning of a new century, we are haunted by its social, political, and economic divisions. Arab nationalism came to a standstill with the 1967 debacle and more so with the withdrawal of Egypt from the Arab camp after signing a separate peace agreement with Israel in 1979. Some external and internal factors have been responsible for the regression of nationalism, such as foreign intervention, absence of legal foundations of the state that treat all citizens equally irrespective of religion or economic background, and the failure of modernization.

The Arab world of the twenty-first century is disunited. This disunity is further complicated by the rise of a new form of aggressive globalization that is more interested in profit for multinational companies than it is with a healthy process of social and economic changes in the Arab world. Globalization has posed a fundamental challenge to the global claims of both Arabism and Islamism in the contemporary Arab world.[4] Both have failed so far to construct a global Arab or Islamist order that can withstand the huge challenges of the contemporary era. Privatization is already weakening social solidarity in many Arab countries and is creating a wealthy class of compradors who already play a major role in transferring the wealth of their countries to the multinational companies.

In this work, I do not use the term "modernity" at face value. A good number of scholars in Arabic and Islamic studies think that modernity is simply good and is beyond criticism. I have relied more on the concept of capitalism since it accurately describes the transformations in the world in the past three centuries and the Arab world in the past two centuries. Capitalism has had enormous energy to change the world in many positive ways; however, it has wreaked havoc in many countries as well. I am not sure that I agree with Marx that "capitalism contains the seeds of its destruction"; however, the deep transformations wrought by capitalism in the world have produced many problematic results, one of which is the fact that financial power is concentrated in the hands of a small privileged elite.

I have focused in this work on the leading ideas of the Arab Left and Arab Islamism, two major, and on the whole, oppositional movements in the Arab world. The Arab Left has not succeeded in establishing a mass support in different Arab countries for the following reasons:

1. the official ban on the Leftist movements in most Arab countries;
2. the ideology of the Left has not been rethought in an Arab social context;
3. the use of Islam as a weapon by some Arab regimes to attack Leftist ideas.

Religion occupies a central place in the various discourses of modern Arab intellectual history. Although it can be defined adequately, "religious space" as a term includes, amongst other things, the following dimensions or manifestations:

1. religious institutions, such as mosques, madrassas, Islamic colleges and universities, charitable associations, endowments, clinics, parties, and religious organizations of various kinds;
2. religious intelligentsia. I have roughly accounted for "official religious intelligentsia" and "oppositional intelligentsia";
3. religious masses, who form the bulk of the Arab Muslim people;
4. religious consciousness, which is the most difficult dimension of "religious space" to define.

Islamism was initially established by charismatic religious intellectuals who, more or less, had a well-defined mission: the establishment of an Islamic state or society. Since this well-defined objective seemed to be elusive with the progress of time, the charisma of the founding leaders of the Islamic movements either lacked institutionalization or lost energy in the second generation of the leadership. Furthermore, the Arab world in the 1970s and 1980s witnessed the rise of a number of extremist Islamist groups that lacked the patience and wisdom of the older generation of Islamism, the generation of the 1930s and 1940s. The increasing repression of the state coupled with the impatience of the young leadership of the new Islamist movement led to an inevitable head-on collision between the state and these movements. In addition, what accounts for the various dilemmas of Islamism in the contemporary Arab world is the fact that most of the Arab regimes have been unwelcoming of Islamism and some have treated it as enemy number one. This unhappy state of affairs was enhanced after the tragic attacks on the United States on September 11, 2001.

The term "Islamic fundamentalism" or revivalism might not be adequate to describe the social and political phenomenon that we call the Islamic movement. There have been a plethora of Islamic movements in the Arab and Muslim world in the modern period interacting under a unique set of historical circumstances and responding to a multitude of religious, social, economic, educational and political issues. The Islamic movement is basically a social/political movement, which adopts a religious ideology with the primary aim of bringing the whole of society under the rule of the Sharī'ah. That is to say that the Islamic movement, besides being interested in individual salvation, purports to achieve salvation for the whole community under the rules of the Sharī'ah. In that sense, the Islamic movement is primarily a social movement. And it has been subject to different historical circumstances in the modern Muslim world. Take for example the Wahabi movement. Its fortunes have risen and declined with those of the modern Saudi state. Its strong alliance with the state has defined its character in the twentieth century and has therefore curtailed its major objectives. Can the Wahabi movement claim that it has succeeded in implementing the Sharī'ah under the auspices of the modern Saudi state and that the communal welfare of the Muslim ummah has been safeguarded?

It is impossible for any social or political movement to survive without two conditions: (1) ideology and (2) community. It is interesting to examine how the different religious movements in the Arab world have interpreted or used Islam in their struggle to achieve their essential goals. For example, who can claim that the modern Sufī brotherhoods in the Arab world are not social religious organizations that have sought to implement the Sharī'ah in their own way, without necessarily aspiring to oppose the political *status quo* or control the state? These brotherhoods are movements that have a set of ideologies and strong communities that use Islamic spiritualism as a defining criterion to measure their own work.

We are often told that the Islamic movements, in their attempt to achieve their political or religious goals in the present, have a strong tendency to create their own past. What kind of a past have the Islamic movements created? We hear often about the early Islamic period in Mecca and Medina and little about the following periods in Islamic history that stretched over 1,400 years in different continents. In spite of this historical failure on the part of different Islamic movements to consider Muslim history creatively, the main concern of these movements is with the present. How is it possible to create the new Islamic order? The leaders of the Islamic movements who have been forced into exile, such as Rāshid al-Ghannūshī, realize fully that whereas exile has been liberating intellectually for the leaders, it has curtailed the activities of the movement in its home country and has virtually shelved its plan to establish an Islamic political or social order. The ruling elite in many Arab countries are not interested in democracy. As a matter of fact, democracy is the quintessential enemy of many Arab regimes since democracy would open the way for the Islamic movement to achieve its major objective, of pushing its social and religious claim on a grandiose scale.

On a wider plane of action, if most regimes in the Arab world are not interested in democracy, how is it possible to release the multiple sources of tension in the contemporary Arab world without the presence of responsible oppositional groups, be they on the Left or the Right? It is logical to conclude that each and every Arab country will be subject to dramatic social and religious explosions, small or big in the coming years, and that the social religious movements, because of their mass appeal, are going to spearhead these explosions.

The central problem in the Arab world remains the unequal distribution of wealth and concentration of power in a few hands. These two facts have hindered the healthy progress of the Arab peoples and forced the youngest and more educated to seek their fortunes outside the Arab world. The "brain-drain" is a deep problem affecting the Arab world.

The Arab world lacks economic integration, as well. The migration of workers and professionals to the Gulf in the 1970s stemmed less from economic coordination and more from the need of the host countries for skilled labor in the age of petroleum. Ideally, Arab professionals prefer to leave the Arab world to either Europe or North America, and not to the Gulf.

Finally, the absence of economic and political integration in the Arab world has more or less accentuated the polarization between Maghreb and Mashreq. On the whole, the Arabs of the Mashreq are not very familiar with the Maghreb, its modern history and present problems. The division among the various political regimes in the Maghreb has not translated well in economic integration or unified political or social outlook.

Notes

INTRODUCTION

1. "Neoliberalism is the defining political economic paradigm of our time – it refers to the policies and processes whereby a relative handful of private interests are permitted to control as much as possible of social life in order to maximize their personal profit." Robert W. McChesney, "Introduction," in Noam Chomsky, *Profit Over People: Neoliberalism and Global Order* (New York: Seven Stories Press, 1999), 7.
2. See Francis Fukuyuma, "The End of History?" *The National Interest*, volume 16, Summer 1989: 3–18. Fukuyama expands his arguments in *The End of History and the Last Man* (New York: Free Press, 1992). For an analysis of Fukuyama's ideas, see Fred Halliday, "An Encounter with Fukuyama." *New Left Review*, number 193, May–June 1992, 89–95.
3. Samuel Huntington, *The Clash of Civilizations and the Remaking of World Order* (New York: Simon & Schuster, 1996). For Arab responses to the "clash of civilizations thesis," see Fakhry Labib and Nehad Salem, eds., *Clash of Civilizations or Dialogue of Cultures* (Cairo: Afro-Asian Peoples' Solidarity Organization, 1997).
4. Anthony Giddens, *The Third Way: The Renewal of Social Democracy* (Cambridge: Polity Press, 1998).
5. Pierre Bourdieu, *Acts of Resistance: Against the Tyranny of the Market* (New York: The New Press, 1998), 35.
6. See David Reynolds, *One World Divisible: A Global History since 1945* (Boston: Norton, 1999), and J. M. Roberts, *Twentieth Century: The History of the World, 1901 to 2000* (London: Viking, 2000).
7. For more elaboration, see Aijaz Ahmad, *In Theory: Classes, Nations, and Literatures* (New Delhi: Oxford University Press, 1994), especially 1–42.
8. The late Albert Hourani argues that what is interesting about the modern Arab world is its popular discourse, which reveals more about the essential characteristics of the Arab world than discourse of the elite. See Albert Hourani, "How Should We Write the History of the Middle East?" *International Journal of Middle East Studies*, volume 23(2), May 1991, 133.
9. Eric Wolf, *Europe and the People Without History*, 2nd edition (Berkeley: University of California Press, 1997), 5.
10. On the Cold War, see John Lewis Gaddis, *The United States and the Origins of the Cold War* (New York: Columbia University Press, 2000) and *We Now Know: Rethinking Cold War History* (New York: Oxford University Press, 1998).
11. Aijaz Ahmad, *In Theory: Classes, Nations, Literatures* (New Delhi: Oxford University Press, 1994), 25.
12. *Ibid.*, 21.
13. Noam Chomsky, *World Orders Old and New* (New York: Columbia University Press, 1994), 83.
14. See David Henrickson, *The Future of American Strategy* (New York: Holmes & Meier, 1988), and Annelise Anderson and Dennis Bark, eds., *Thinking about America: The United States in the 1990s* (Washington, D.C.: Hoover Institution Press, 1988). In his economic vision of the 1940s, President Truman promised a new economic age with the "old imperialism": "We must embark on a bold new program for making benefits of our scientific advances and industrial progress available for the improvement and growth of underdeveloped areas. The old imperialism – exploitation for foreign profit – has no place in our plans. What we envisage is a program of development based on the concepts of democratic fair dealing. Greater production is the key to prosperity and peace." Quoted by Arturo Escobar, *Encountering Development: The Making and Unmaking of the Third World* (Princeton: Princeton University Press, 1995), 3.
15. For an elaboration on some of these points, see John L. Mearsheimer, *The Tragedy of Great Power Politics* (New York: W. W. Norton, 2002).

16. "As the citizens of the *fin de siècle* tapped their way through the global fog that surrounded them into the third millennium, all they knew for certain was that an era of history had ended. They knew very little else." Eric Hobsbawm, *The Age of Extremes: A History of the World, 1914–1991* (New York: Vintage, 1994), 558–9.
17. Ahmad, *In Theory*, 32.
18. See Martin Wolf, "The Need for a New Imperialism." *Financial Times*, October 9, 2001, and Sebastian Mallaby, "The Reluctant Imperialist." *Foreign Affairs*, March–April 2002.
19. Amy Kaplan, *The Anarchy of Empire in the Making of U.S. Culture* (Cambridge, MA: Harvard University Press, 2002). See also Joseph S. Nye, Jr., *Bound to Lead: The Changing Nature of American Power* (New York: Basic Books, 1990).
20. See Burhān Ghalyūn, *Le malaise arabe: L'Etat contre la nation* (Paris: La Découverte, 1991), and "La fin de la stratégie nationale: Stratégie et nouvel ordre mondial." *Jusoor: The Arab American Journal of Cultural Exchange and Thought for the Future*. Spring–Summer 1993.
21. According to one liberal interpretation, "*Pax Americana* was the product of deliberate policy-making. American elites reflecting on the lessons of the century, concluded that a peaceful and liberal global system was impossible without American leadership, since Europe had grown incapable of managing the world or itself. The time has come for the 'American Century'." David P. Calleo, *Rethinking Europe's Future* (Princeton: Princeton University Press, 2001), 89. *Pax Americana* was enhanced after the attacks on the United States on September 11, 2001. See Tariq Ali, "The Color Khaki." *New Left Review*, number 19, January–February 2003: 5–28. According to one author, "In the months before September 11 [2001] the Bush Administration matched its surprisingly ideological programs with what Democrats politely described as a 'go-it-alone foreign policy'. Bush officials called a halt to negotiations with North Korea amd withdrew from attempts to negotiate peace in the Middle East. They refused to sign the Kyoto Protocol on global warming and blocked a series of international arms control treaties. Then, while promising to make cuts in US Strategic nuclear weapons, they declined to make an agreement with Russia on mutual reductions...In a speech on June 1 [2002] Bush announced a new doctrine of preemptive warfare...Apparently he had decided to let Sharon deal with the Palestinians while he went ahead with an attempt to bring down Ṣaddām Ḥussain." Frances FitzGerald, "George Bush and the World." *New York Review of Books*, volume 49, September 26, 2002, 80. On the roots of American power, see Fareed Zakariyya, *From Wealth to Power: The Unusual Origins of America's World Role* (Princeton: Princeton University Press, 1998), and Warren Zimmermann, *First Great Triumph: How Five Americans Made Their Country a World Power* (New York: Farrar, Straus and Giroux, 2001). It should be noted that some leading American thinkers opposed the idea of *Pax Americana* after World War Two. See the moving biography of American expert on China Owen Lattimore, Robert P. Newman, *Owen Lattimore and the Loss of China* (Berkeley: University of California Press, 1992). In his comment on Asia after World War Two, Lattimore says, "All of these countries [India, Pakistan and Afghanistan] can be made allies, and very reliable allies, but they cannot be made puppets. In all of them, the passion that runs through men's veins is a passion for freedom from foreign rule. All of them are repelled by any policy that looks like restoration of colonial rule." *Ibid.*, 299.
22. In achieving its goals in Iraq during the 1991 Gulf War, the United States, according to British political scientist Peter Gowan, "campaigned to criminalize the Ṣaddām Ḥussain regime. (Just as the US first decided to support the regimes of Israel and Indonesia and *then* ensured the decriminalization of these countries' actions in occupying and annexing.) This process involved anthropomorphizing the Iraqi state and its political-administrative organization into a single person – Ṣaddām Ḥussain, criminal. And the more his human features were enlarged, the more other men and women in the 'criminal' state were dehumanized. The army of conscripts became the murder weapon, the lives of millions of Iraqis the various limbs and resources of their leader. Hence they were fair game; or else they became collateral, in the sense of standing alongside the criminal – by-standers in the police shoot-out." Peter Gowan, "The Gulf War, Iraq, and Western Liberalism." *New Left Review*, number 187, May–June 1991, 31.
23. Edward W. Said, "The Formation of American Public Opinion on the Question of Palestine," in his *The Politics of Dispossession* (New York: Vintage Books, 1995), 57.
24. Mark Lilla, "The New Age of Tyranny." *New York Review of Books*, October 24, 2002, 28–9.

25. Arno J. Mayer, *The Persistence of the Old Regime: Europe to the Great War* (New York: Pantheon, 1981).
26. High birth rates in the Arab world have perplexed many demographers. Egypt is a case in point, "The sheer dimensions of Egypt's problems are best measured by a population growing by one million every nine months and expected to reach seventy million in the early decades of the twenty-first century...Besides, of Egypt's sixty-three million people in 1999, 40 percent are under the age of fifteen." Amira El-Azhry Sonbol, *The New Mamluks: Egyptian Society and Modern Feudalism* (Syracuse: Syracuse University Press, 2000), 194.
27. See Muḥammad ʻImārah, ed., *al-Aʻmāl al-kāmilah li'l Imām Muḥammad ʻAbduh*, 5 volumes (Cairo: Dār al-Shurūq, 1995).
28. Wallerstein says that, "The first step we must make if we wish to understand our world is radically to reject any and all distinction between history and social science, and to recognize that we are part of a single discipline of study: the study of human societies as they have historically evolved." Emmanuel Wallerstein, *The Capitalist World Economy* (Cambridge: Cambridge University Press, 1970), 133–4.
29. "In my view, it is irresponsible to invite readers to regard Islamicist politics as an outgrowth of tendencies essential to an *original* politico-religious Islam. The idea that Islam was originally – *and therefore essentially* – a theocratic state is, I argue, a nineteenth-century European one, developed under the influence of evolutionary theories of religion. Of course its European origin does not in itself render it invalid. My reason for mentioning that nineteenth-century origin is simply that if today's Islamic militants have accepted this perspective as their own, this does not make it *essential to Islam.* (It is necessary to add, however, that my argument is not intended to undermine the validity of any kind of 'politicized Islam'; I claim only that a 'religious state' is not essential to the tradition of Islam.)" Talal Asad, "Europe Against Islam: Islam in Europe." *The Muslim World*, volume 97(2), April 1997, 191.
30. See Chapter 5 of this work, and also Ṣalāh ʻĪsa, *Muthaqafūn wa ʻaskar* (Cairo: Madbūlī, 1986).
31. Tharwat ʻUkāshah, *Mudhakurātī fī'l thaqāfah wa'l siyāsah* (Cairo: Dār al-Shurūq, 2001).
32. On the 1967 war, see Michael B. Oren, *Six Days of War: June 1967 and the Making of the Modern Middle East* (New York: Oxford University Press, 2002).
33. See for example the writings of Muḥammad ʻAbduh. See also Ibrahim Abu-Rabiʻ, "The Concept of the 'Other' in Modern Arab Thought: From Muḥammad ʻAbduh to Abdallah Laroui." *Islam and Christian-Muslim Relations*, volume 8(1), 1997, 85–97.
34. Faraḥ Anṭūn, *Ibn Rushd wa falsafatuhu* (Beirut: Dār al-Ṭalīʻah, 1981).
35. Shiblī Shumayl, *Falsafat al-nushū' wa'l irtiqā'* (Cairo: Dār Salāma Mūsa, 1910).
36. Luṭfī al-Sayyid, *Mabādi' fī al-siyāsah wa'l adab wa'l ijtimā'* (Cairo: Dār al-Kutub al-Miṣriyyah, 1963).
37. Salāma Mūsa, *The Education of Salāma Mūsa* (Leiden: Brill, 1962).
38. Ṭāhā Ḥussain, *Fī al-shiʻr al-jāhilī* (Cairo: Angelo, 1926).
39. See Kamāl ʻAbd al-Laṭīf, *Qirā'āt fī'l falsafah al-ʻarabiyyah al-muʻāṣirah* (Beirut: Dār al-Ṭaliʻāh, 1994), 18.
40. This view is held by Nassif Nassar, "Remarques sur la renaissance de la philosophie dans la culture arabe contemporaine." *Renaissance du monde arabe* (Paris, 1972).
41. Muḥammad Lahbabi, *Le monde de demin: Le Tiers-monde accuse* (Casablanca: Sherbrooke, 1980).
42. Mahdi Elmandjra, *La décolonization culturelle: Défi majeur du 21ème siècle* (Marrakech [Morocco]: Editions Walili, and Paris: Futurbiles, 1996).
43. Galāl Amīn, *The Modernization of Poverty* (Leiden: Brill, 1972); *al-Tanwīr al-zā'if* (Cairo: Dār al-Maʻārif, 1999).
44. Muḥammad Ibrāhīm Mabruk, *Amerika wa'l islām al-nafīʻ* (Cairo: al-Maḥrūsa, 1989), 125.
45. On the Arab intellectual response to the attacks on the United States, see Markaz Dirāsāt al-Wiḥdah al-ʻArabiyyah, *al-ʻArab wa'l ʻalam baʻda 11 Aylūl* (Beirut: Markaz Dirāsāt al-Wiḥdah al-ʻArabiyyah, 2002).
46. See, for example, the formulations of Karīm Muruwwa, from the Lebanese Communist Party, on the issue of religion in Arab society: Dār al-Fārābī, *Ḥiwārāt: mufakirrūn ʻarab yunaqishūn Karīm Muruwwa fī'l qawmiyya, wa'l ishtirākiyyah, wa'l dimūqrātiyyah, wa'l dīn wa'l dawlah* (Beirut: Dār al-Fārābī, 1990).

47. *Ibid.*, 32.
48. L. Carl Brown, *Religion and State: The Muslim Approach to Politics*. (New York: Columbia University Press, 2000), 27.
49. *Ibid.*, 33.
50. Burhān Ghalyūn, "al-Islām wa azmat ʻalāqat al-sulṭah al-ijtimāʻiyyah," in ʻAbd al-Bāqī al-Hirmasī *et al.*, *al-Dīn fī'l mujtamaʻ al-ʻarabī* (Beirut: Markaz Dirāsāt al-Wiḥdah al-ʻArabīyyah, 1990), 305. See also Ghalyūn, *Le malaise arabe*.
51. Aḥmad Kamāl Abū'l Majd, "Sūrat al-ḥalah al-islāmiyyah ʻalā mashārif alfiyyah jadīdah." *Wijhāt Nadhar*, volume 1(11), December 1999, 6.
52. On this point, see Muḥammad Mahdī Shams al-Dīn, *Fiqh al-ʻunf al-musallaḥ fī'l Islām* (Beirut: al-Mu'assassah al-Dawliyyah li'l Dirāsāt wa'l Nashr, 2001).
53. In explaining the September 11, 2001 attacks on the United States, Anderson argues that, "The Republican administration is as well aware as anyone on the Left that September 11 was not simply an act of unmotivated evil, but a response to the widely disliked role of the United States in the Middle East. This is a region in which – unlike Europe, Russia, China, Japan or Latin America – there are virtually no regimes with a credible base to offer effective transmission points for American cultural or economic hegemony. The assorted Arab states are docile enough, but they lack any kind of popular support, resting on family networks and secret police which typically compensate for their factual servility to the US with a good deal of media hostility, not to speak of closure, towards America. Uniquely, indeed, Washington's oldest dependency and most valuable client in the region, Saudi Arabia, is more barricaded against US cultural penetration than any country in the world after North Korea." Perry Anderson, "Force and Consent." *New Left Review*, number 17, September/October 2002, 16.
54. See for example, Aftab A. Malik, ed., *Shattered Illusions: Analyzing the War on Terrorism* (Bristol [England]: Amal Press, 2002).
55. One must agree with the intelligent observation that what threatens the United States nowadays is not "fanatical Islam" but other forces, "In the face of darkening global conditions and its own transigent post-bubble recession, the real threat to the US today comes not from a handful of Wahabi fanatics but from Japan's deflating economy. The process of decay, now gathering momentum, risks triggering an implosion that could suck in the entire region, if not the globe." Gavan McCormack, "Breaking the Iron Triangle." *New Left Review*, number 13, January/ February 2002, 5.
56. For a disappointing analysis of Islamism, see John L. Esposito, *Unholy War: Terror in the Name of Islam* (New York: Oxford University Press, 2002).
57. For an elaboration on Islamism and violence in Egypt, see the following: Abū al-ʻAla Māḍī, *Jamāʻat al-ʻunf al-miṣriyyah al-murṭabitah bi'l islām: al-judhūr al-tārikhiyyah wa'l usus al-fikriyyah wa'l mustaqbal* (Cairo: al-Markaz al-Duwalī li'l Dirāsāt, 1997); Muḥammad Ṣalāḥ, "Kharīṭat ḥarakat al-ʻunf fī miṣr." *Wijhāt Nadhar*, volume 1(4), May 1999: 20–5; Nabīl ʻAbd al-Fattāḥ, *Taqrīr al-ḥālah al-dīniyyah: al-taqrīr al-awwal* (Cairo: Markaz al-Dirāsāt al-Siyāsiyyah wa'l Istrātījiyyah fī'l Ahrām, 1997); Nabīl ʻAbd al-Fattāḥ, *Taqrīr al-ḥālah al-dīniyyah: al-taqrīr al-thānī* (Cairo: Markaz al-Dirāsāt al-Siyāsiyyah wa'l Istrātījiyyah fī'l Ahrām, 1998); and John Cooley, *Unholy Wars: Afghanistan, America and International Terrorism* (London: Pluto Press, 2000). Cooley offers an exhaustive map of the different Islamist movements that fought in Afghanistan in the 1980s and 1990s. He argues that many of the movements were supported by Saudi Arabia, Pakistan, and the United States. He thinks that the United States had made a big mistake by supporting Islamic Jihad in Afghanistan, "When you decide to go to war against your main enemy, take a good, long look at the people behind you whom you chose as your friends, allies and mercenary fighters. Look well to see whether these allies already have unsheathed their knives – and are pointing them at your own back." *Ibid.*, 247.
58. Majdī ʻAbd al-Ḥāfiẓ Ṣālih, "al-Uṣūliyyah: hal hiyah taʻbīr ʻan ikhfāq an-taḥdīth?" *Qaḍāyah Fikriyyah*, numbers 13 and 14, October 1993, 307. See also Ḥāzim Munīr, "ru'yat al-yasār li mawqiʻ al-uṣūliyyīn al-islamiyyīn ʻalā al-kharīṭah al ṭabaqiyyah wa'l siyāsiyyah." *Al-Yasār*, number 8, October 1990, 43–58.
59. al-Fattāḥ, *ʻAql al-azmah*, 149–50.
60. On this phenomenon, see Yūsuf al-Qaraḍāwī, *Islamic Awakening Between Rejection and Extremism* (Herndon: IIIT, 1991), and Zaki Ahmad, "Developmental Changes in Islamic-Arab

Movements." *Middle East Affairs Journal*, volume 3(1–2), Winter–Spring 1997, 3–11. In response to fanaticism and other challenges facing the Islamic movement in the Arab world, Islamist Zaki Ahmad argues that, "Over the past two decades, contemporary Islamic movements have increasingly re-evaluated their priorities, including reviews of methodology, strategy, and principles. Islamic movements are, in essence, seeking out fresh perspectives designed to restructure the way they operate to overcome the problems plaguing them." *Ibid.*, 3.

61. Munīr F. 'Abd al-Nūr, "Nāqus al-khaṭar yadduq." *Wijhāt Nadhar*, volume 2(13), February 2000, 30–1.
62. An important feature of "colonial politics was the attention paid to sectarian, ethnic and tribal divisions, generally for the purpose of some strategy of 'divide and rule'." Roger Owen, *State, Power, and Politics in the Making of the Modern Middle East* (London: Routledge, 1992), 17.
63. On the Marshall Plan, see Michael Hogan, *The Marshall Plan* (Cambridge: Cambridge University Press, 1987).
64. Europe could not compete with the military and economic powers of the United States after World War Two. On this matter, see David P. Calleo, *Rethinking Europe's Future* (Princeton: Princeton University Press, 2001). For a different opinion, see Joseph S. Nye, Jr., *The Paradox of American Power: Why the World's Only Superpower Can't Go it Alone* (New York: Oxford University Press, 2002), 29. Nye argues that "The closest thing to an equal that the United States faces at the beginning of the twenty first century is the European Union. Although the American economy is four times larger than that of Germany, the largest European country, the economy of the European Union is roughly equal to that of the United States; its population is considerably larger, as is its share of world exports." *Ibid.*, 29–30.
65. On modernization in the Arab world, see Hishām Sharābī, "Islam and Modernization in the Arab World," in Jack Thompson and Robert Reischauer, eds., *Modernization of the Arab World* (New York: Van Nostrand, 1966), 26–36 and Charles Issawi, "The Arab World's Heavy Legacy," in *ibid.*, 13–25.
66. Benedict Anderson, "The New World Disorder." *New Left Review*, number 193, May–June 1992, 10.
67. "The Middle East is characterized by what is peculiar to oil, the anomalous economic and social consequences of its production. Less than half of the Middle East states are oil producers, and the majority of those have small populations. The majority of [Arab] states with large populations do not have oil. This asymmetry of population and oil resources has provoked substantial migration from oil-less to oil-producing states, while at the same time enabling the oil producers to use their wealth for individual political purposes in the region." Fred Halliday, *Islam and the Myth of Confrontation: Religion and Politics in the Middle East* (London: I. B. Tauris, 1995), 39.
68. Massive modernization in the Gulf has been made possible by the discovery of oil. In commenting on the origin of some states in the Middle East, Halliday says that Jordan, for example, "is a praetorian monarchy, created ex nihilo or at least ex deserto, by Britain after World War I. Saudi Arabia is a product of tribal conquest, while the smaller Gulf states are towns that became states because of colonialism and oil." Fred Halliday, *Nation and Religion in the Middle East* (Boulder: Lynne Rienner, 2000), 99.
69. Anderson notes that, "On the one hand, as a result of the oil crisis of 1973, the world saw for the first time immensely rich *weak*, agrarian states, such as Saudi Arabia, Iran, and Iraq, which had the purchasing power to acquire 'firstclass' arms from the industrial core." Benedict Anderson, "The New World Disorder." *New Left Review*, number 193, May/June 1992, 10. In commenting on the Saudi political elite, Roger Owen argues that unlike Jordan and Morocco, the Saudi family "was large enough to keep members of the new educated elites resolutely out of policymaking, with the exception of certain rare individuals like Zaki Yamani, the minister of oil for most of the 1970s and 1980s. There was also no serious attempt to create representative institutions of any kind, while incorporation as a subsidiary member of the ruling elite was based almost exclusively on loyalty to the family and a shared perception of the values of Saudi culture and a pride in its social achievements." Owen, *State, Power, and Politics*, 69.
70. *Ibid.*, 40.
71. See Tariq Ramadan's analysis of the Saudi state: Tariq Ramadan, *Islam, the West and the Challenges of Modernity* (Leicester: The Islamic Foundation, 2001), 178–82.

72. Usually, there is a small circle of notables surrounding a president or king in the Arab world. In his comment on King Ḥassan II of Morocco, a small elite surrounded him which numbered no more than one thousand people. "As in Jordan, Ḥassan II was personally acquainted with most of them and very much aware of their personal idiosyncracies and rivalries. Like Hussein [of Jordan] he was adept at keeping them all in play. It was they who provided his advisers, the executors of his policy and his eyes and ears throughout the rest of Moroccan society." Owen, *State, Power, and Politics*, 67.
73. Chomsky, *World Orders Old and New*, 193. In the words of Edward Said, "Democracy in any real sense of the word is nowhere to be found in the Middle East; there are either privileged oligarchies or privileged ethnic groups." Edward W. Said, "The Arab-American War: The Politics of Information," in his *The Politics of Dispossession* (New York: Vintage Books, 1995), 296.
74. Ghālī Shukrī, *Diktātoriyat al-takhalluf al-'arabī* (Cairo: al-Hay'ah al-Miṣriyyah al-'Āmmah li'l Kitāb, 1994), 50.
75. Edward W. Said, "The Arab Right Wing," in his *The Politics of Dispossession*, 224.
76. *Ibid.*, 227.
77. On the formation of such a class in Europe and North America, see Robert Cox, *Production, Power, and World Order: Social Forces in the Making of History* (New York: Columbia University Press, 1987); Stephen Gill, *American Hegemony and the Trilateral Commission* (New York: Cambridge University Press, 1990); and William Robinson, *Promoting Polyarchy: Globalization, U.S. Intervention, and Hegemony* (New York: Cambridge University Press, 1996).
78. Nabīl 'Abd al-Fattāḥ, *Khiṭāb al-zaman al-ramādī: ru'ah fī azmatī al-thaqāfah al-miṣriyyah* (Cairo: Yāfa li'l Nashr, 1990).
79. Eric Wolf, *Europe and the People Without History*, 2nd edition (Berkeley: University of California Press, 1997), 78. Wolf argues that, "The capitalist mode thus shows three intertwined characteristics. First, capitalists retain control of the means of production. Second, laborers are denied independent access to means of production and must sell their labor power to the capitalists. Third, the maximization of surplus produced by the laborers with the means of the production owned by the capitalists entails 'ceaseless accumulation accompanied by changes in methods of production'." *Ibid.*
80. On the development of Samir Amin's ideas, see his intellectual autobiography, *Re-Reading the Postwar Period: An Intellectual Itinerary* (New York: Monthly Review Press, 1994).
81. I have in mind the following theoreticians: Andre Gunder Frank, Paul Sweezy, Eric Wolf, Immanuel Wallerstein, Giovanni Arrighi, and others whose writings will be treated in the course of this work.
82. "It took two or three centuries before the new dominant [capitalist] ideology crystallized, the period of transition from mercantilism to fully developed capitalism." Samir Amin, *Eurocentrism* (New York: Monthly Review Press, 1989), 87.
83. Samir Amin, "Présentation," in Fahima Charaffeddine, *Culture et idéologie dans le monde arabe* (Paris: L'Harmattan, 1994), 10.
84. Amin, *Eurocentrism*, 1.
85. *Ibid.*, 23.
86. *Ibid.*, 31.
87. According to Samir Amin, "The new world is freed from the domination of metaphysics at the same time as the material foundations for capitalist society are laid." *Ibid.*, 71.
88. Amin, "Présentation," 15–16.
89. Amin contends that "The Renaissance breaks with medieval thought. Modern thought distinguishes itself from that of the medieval period by renouncing the dominant metaphysical preoccupation. The importance of partial truths is systematically valorized, while the pursuit of absolute knowledge is left to amateurs." Amin, *Eurocentrism*, 79.
90. See V. Y. Mudimbe, *The Invention of Africa: Gnosis, Philosophy, and the Order of Knowledge* (Bloomington: Indiana University Press, 1988).
91. "Dans ce sens, on peut dire que la culture islamiste n'est déjù plus la culture véritablement dominante dans la région, malgré les apparences. Elle est déjà une forme creuse qui n'élimine pas la véritable dominance, celle de la culture capitaliste." ("In this sense, one can say that Islamic culture is no longer the truly dominant one in the region, in spite of appearances. It is already a

hollow form that does not eliminate the virtual dominance of capitalist culture." Translation by Abu-Rabi'.) Amin, "Présentation," 16.

92. See Amin's extensive discussion in *Unequal Development: An Essay on the Social Formations of Peripheral Capitalism* (New York: Monthly Review Press, 1976), 36–51.
93. Samir Amin contends that the reason for the impasse of Islamic revivalism is that "modernity requires an abandonment of metaphysics." Amin, *Eurocentrism*, 133.
94. Samir Amin and Burhān Ghalyūn, *Ḥiwār al-dīn wa'l dawlah* (Casablanca: al-Markaz al-Thaqāfī al-'Arabī, 1996), 26.
95. Samir Amin, *Fī muwājahati azmatī 'aṣrina* (Cairo: Dār Sīna, 1997), 133.
96. Amin, *The Arab Nation: Nationalism and Class Struggles* (London: Zed Books, 1983), 24.
97. Samir Amin, *Unequal Development*, 302.
98. Samir Amin, *Capitalism in the Age of Globalization* (London: Zed Books, 1998), 2.
99. See Kāmil Dāgher, "al-Ummah wa'l ummah al-'arabiyyah fī fikr Samīr Amīn." *Al-Ṭarīq*, volume 55(2), April 1996, 193–7.
100. Shams al-Dīn al-Kīlānī, *Maṣīr al-jamā'ah al-'arabiyyah: naqd fikr Samīr Amīn* (Damascus: Dār 'Ashtarūt li'l Nashr, 1997), 195.
101. In discussing future scenarios of the relationship between North and South, Amin contends that, "There is another possible scenario – for lack of an alternative – a kind of second edition, American hegemony. There are many variations of this. The most likely one is 'a sharing of the burden' associated with neoimperialist regionalization: hitching Latin America to the US wagon and Africa to the German-European one (with some crumbs for France) and with the Gulf oil region and a 'common market of the Middle East' remaining the domain of the United States. The American presence is already felt by its military occupation of the Gulf and less directly by its alliance with Israel." Amin, *Capitalism in the Age of Globalization*, 9.
102. Samir Amin, *Empire of Chaos* (New York: Monthly Review Press, 1992), 16.
103. Moroccan intellectual Muḥammad 'Ābid al-Jābirī thinks otherwise. In Morocco, he says, the state has not interfered much with culture (intellectual production) and this has been to the advantage of the intelligentsia.
104. See Anne Showstack Sassoon, *Gramsci's Politics* (London: Hutchinson, 1987), 256.
105. Antonio Gramsci, *The Modern Prince and Other Writings* (New York: International Publishers, 1987), 63.
106. See Pedro Cavalcanti and Paul Piccone, eds., *History, Philosophy and Culture in the Young Gramsci* (Saint Louis: Telos Press, 1975), especially part one on culture.
107. Gramsci, *The Modern Prince*, 118.
108. Laclau, *Politics and Ideology in Marxist Theory*, 162.
109. Gramsci, *The Modern Prince*, 119.
110. Alastair Davidson, *Antonio Gramsci: The Man, His Ideas* (Sydney: Australian Left Review Publications, 1968), 46.
111. "In keeping with the usual view, the goal of sociology is to uncover the most deeply buried structures of the different social worlds that make up the social universe, as well as the 'mechanisms' that tend to ensure their reproduction and transformation." Pierre Bourdieu, *The State Nobility: Elite Schools in the Field of Power* (Stanford: Stanford University Press, 1996), 1.
112. On Bourdieu's ideas, see the path-breaking book by David Swartz, *Culture and Power: The Sociology of Pierre Bourdieu* (Chicago: University of Chicago Press, 1998), and Alex Callinicos, "Social Theory Put to the Test of Politics: Pierre Bourdieu and Anthony Giddens." *New Left Review*, number 236, July–August 1999, 77–102.
113. On the intersection between education and power in American society, see Christopher Lasch, *The Revolt of the Elites* (New York and London: W. W. Norton, 1995); Ira Katznelson and Margaret Weir, *Schooling for All: Race, Class, and the Decline of the Democratic Ideal* (New York: Basic Books, 1987); Peter Cookson, Jr. and Caroline Persell, *Preparing for Power: America's Elite Boarding Schools* (New York: Basic Books, 1985); William Powell and Lionel Lewis, eds., *High Status Track: Studies of Elite Schools and Stratification* (Albany: State University of New York Press, 1990); G. William Domhoff, *The Power Elite and the State* (New York: Aldine, 1989).
114. See Michael W. Apple, *Education and Power* (New York: Routledge, 1995).

115. Bourdieu, *The State Nobility*, 102.
116. Pierre Bourdieu, *Distinction: A Social Critique of the Judgement of Taste* (Cambridge, MA: Harvard University Press, 1984), 466.
117. David Swartz, "Bridging the Study of Culture and Religion: Pierre Bourdieu's Political Economy of Symbolic Power." *Sociology of Religion*, volume 57(1), Spring 1996, 71.
118. Bourdieu, *The State Nobility*, 266.
119. *Ibid.*, 279.
120. Alexi Vassiliev, *The History of Saudi Arabia* (New York: New York University Press, 2000).
121. "Orthodoxy is not easy to secure in conditions of radical change. This is not because orthodoxy discourse is necessarily against any change but because it aspires to be authoritative." Talal Asad, "The Limits of Religious Criticism in the Middle East: Notes on Islamic Public Argument." In Talal Asad, *Genealogies of Religion: Discipline and Reasons of Power in Christianity and Islam* (Baltimore: Johns Hopkins University Press, 1993), 211.
122. "I dream of journeys repeatedly: of flying like a bat into a narrowing tunnel, of driving alone, without luggage, out a long peninsula. The road lined with snow-laden second growth, a fine dry snow ticking the windshield..." Theodore Roethke, "The Far Field," in *The Collected Poems of Theodore Roethke* (New York: Doubleday, 1975), 193.
123. "There is a mode of vital experience – experience of space and time, of the self and others, of life's possibilities and perils – that is shared by men and women all over the world today...To be modern is to find ourselves in an environment that promises adventure, power, joy, growth, transformation of ourselves and the world – and, at the same time, that threatens to destroy everything we have, everything we know, everything we are. Modern environments and experiences cut across all boundaries of geography and ethnicity, of class and nationality, of religion and ideology; in this sense, modernity can be said to unite all mankind. But it is a paradoxical unity, a unity of disunity; it pours us all into a maelstrom of perpetual disintegration and renewal, of struggle and contradiction, of ambiguity and anguish. To be modern is to be part of a universe in which, as Marx said, all that is solid melts into air." Marshall Berman, *All That Is Solid Melts Into Air: The Experience of Modernity* (London: Penguin, 1982), 15.
124. Alvin Toffler, *Future Shock* (New York: Bantam, 1991).
125. See H. Gibb, *The Travels of Ibn Battuta*, 3 volumes (New Delhi: Munshiram, 1993).
126. Massignon thinks this is a *Hadīth qudsī*. See Louis Massignon, *Essay on the Technical Language of Islamic Mysticism*, trans. Benjamin Clark (Notre Dame: University of Notre Dame Press, 1997), 165.
127. According to T. E. Lawrence, Mecca forms "an alien belt, continually reinforced by strangers from India and Java and Bokhara and Africa, very strong in vitality, violently hostile to the Semitic consiousness, and maintained despite economics and geography and climate by the artificial factor of a world-religion." T. E. Lawrence, *Seven Pillars of Wisdom* (New York: Garden City, 1938), 35.
128. See Clinton Bailey, *Bedouin Poetry* (Oxford: Clarendon Press, 1991).
129. In his impressive study of the condition of postmodernity, David Harvey discusses the change in space engendered by modernity in the world. He says that one of the most distinguishing facts of the time-space compression achieved by modernity has been "to accentuate volatility and ephemerality of fashions, production techniques, labor processes, ideas and ideologies, values and established practices." David Harvey, *The Condition of Postmodernity* (Oxford: Blackwell, 1989), 285.
130. According to exiled Saudi novelist Abdelraḥmān Munīf, "The tragedy is not in our having the oil, but in the way we use the wealth it has created and in the future awaiting us after it has run out...In underdeveloped countries...oil becomes a damnation, a ceiling that screens the future from view. In twenty or thirty years' time we shall discover that oil has been a real tragedy for the Arabs, and these giant cities built in the desert will find no one to live in them and their hundreds of thousands of inhabitants will have to begin again their quest after the unknown. Oil could have been a road to the future; it could have made possible a natural and continuous progress from nomadic life to civilization...but what actually happens is nothing like that. As a result we shall again have to face a sense of loss and estrangement, this time in complete poverty." Quoted by David Gilmour, "Desert Ruritania." *New York Review of Books*, March 26, 1992, 20.

On Munīf's thought, consult 'Abdul Raḥmān Munīf, *Cities of Salt* (New York: Vintage, 1991) and *The Trench* (New York: Pantheon, 1990).

131. According to Lawrence, the Bedouins "were a people of spasm, of upheavals, of ideas, the race of the individual genius. Their movements were the more shocking by contrast with the quietude of every day, their great men greater by contrast with the humanity of their mob. Their convictions were by instinct, their activities intuitional. Their largest manufacture was of creeds: almost they were monopolists of revealed religions." Lawrence, *Seven Pillars of Wisdom*, 39.

132. Ibn Khaldūn says that "the Arabs are by nature remote from royal leadership...This is illustrated by the Arab dynasty in Islam. Religion cemented their leadership with the religious law and its ordinances, which, explicitly and implicitly, are concerned with what is good for civilization. The caliphs followed one after another. As a result, the royal authority and government of the Arabs became great and strong. When Rustum [the Persian ruler] saw the Muslims assemble for prayer, he said: 'Umar eats my liver. He teaches the dogs how to behave'." Ibn Khaldūn, *The Muqaddimah: An Introduction to History*, volume 1, trans. Franz Rosenthal (New York: Pantheon, 1958), 307.

133. Ibn Khaldūn says that "Bedouins are more disposed to courage than sedentary people. The reason for this is that sedentary people have become used to laziness and ease. They are sunk in well-being and luxury. They have entrusted defense of their property and their lives to the governor and ruler who rules them, and to the militia which has the task of guarding them." *Ibid.*, 257.

134. According to Friedrich Engels, "The Bedouin, poor and hence austere in their manner, contemplate the wealth and enjoyment with envy and lust. They unite under the direction of a prophet, a Mahdi, to punish the faithless, to reestablish the ceremonial law and true faith, and by way of recompence to appropriate the treasure of the faithless." Quoted by Ernest Gellner in *Muslim Society* (Cambridge: Cambridge University Press, 1981), 46. Ibn Khaldūn theorizes that "urbanization is found to be the goal of the Bedouin. He aspires to that goal. Through his own efforts, he achieves what he proposes to achieve in this respect. When he has obtained enough to be ready for the conditions and customs of luxury, he enters upon a life of ease and submits himself to the yoke of the city...Sedentary people, on the other hand, have no desire for desert conditions..." Khaldūn, *The Muqaddimah*, volume 1, 253.

135. On the present state of Bedouin life, see Jibrail S. Jabbur, *The Bedouins and the Desert: Aspects of Nomadic Life in the Arab East* (Albany: State University of New York Press, 1995).

136. Muslim theologians and mystics have discussed the meaning of *gurbah* extensively. According to Abū Ḥayyān al-Tawḥīdī, "The stranger (*gharīb*) is the one whose beautiful sun has set (*gharabat*), who is far from (*istaghraba*) his beloved and those who blame (lovers in love), who acts strangely (*aghraba*) in word and action, who enters strange ground (*gharraba*) in both progress and retrogression, who presents a strange picture (*istaghraba*) in his tattered clothes. The stranger is the one whose appearance speaks of one tribulation after the other, who bears the mark of disturbance after disturbance, and whose reality becomes clear to him in the continuity of time. He is the one who is absent when he is present and who is present when he is absent. He is the one whom you do not know when you see him and whom you do not wish to know when you do not know him." Quoted by Franz Rosenthal, "The Stranger in Medieval Islam." *Arabica: Journal of Arabic and Islamic Studies*, volume 44(1), January 1997, 57.

137. See the moving memoirs of Elias Chachour in *Blood Brothers* (Tarrytown: Chosen Books, 1984) and *We Belong to the Land* (Notre Dame: University of Notre Dame Press, 2001), and Emile Habiby, *The Secret Life of Saeed, the Ill-Fated Pessoptimist: A Palestinian Who Became a Citizen of Israel*, trans. Salma K. Jayyusi and Trevor LeGassick (London: Zed Books, 1985). The following is a list of serious academic studies that have appeared on the Palestinians in Israel: 'Azmi Bishāra, *al-'Arab fī Isrā'īl: r'uyah mina'l dākhil* (Beirut: Markaz Dirāsāt al-Wiḥdah al-'Arabīyyah, 2003); Baruch Kimmerling, *The Invention and Decline of Israeliness: State, Society, and the Military* (Berkeley: University of California Press, 2001); E. Zureik, *The Palestinians in Israel: A Study in Internal Colonialism* (London: Routledge & Kegan Paul, 1979); Alisa Rubin Peled, *Debating Islam in the Jewish State: The Development of Policy Toward Islamic Institutions in Israel* (Albany: State University of New York Press, 2001); Rhoda

Ann Kanaaneh, *Birthing the Nation: Strategies of Palestinian Women in Israel* (Berkeley: University of California Press, 2002); and I. Lustick, *Arabs in a Jewish State: Israel's Control of a National Minority* (Austin: University of Texas Press, 1980).

138. "Soft power rests on the ability to set the political agenda in a way that shapes the preferences of others...Soft power arises in large part from our values. These values are expressed in our culture, in the policies we follow inside our country, and in the ways we handle ourselves internationally." Joseph S. Nye, Jr., *The Paradox of American Power: Why the World's Only Superpower Can't Go it Alone* (New York: Oxford University Press, 2002), 9. The United States has the soft power to influence decision making in other countries, "The success of US primacy will depend not just on our military or economic might but also on the soft power of our culture and values and on policies that make others feel they have been consulted and their interests have been taken into account." Joseph S. Nye, Jr., "Lessons in Imperialism." *Financial Times*, June 17, 2002. On the same subject, see Anthony Lewis, "Bush and Iraq." *New York Review of Books*, November 7, 2002, 4–6, and "Bush at War." *New York Review of Books*, February 13, 2003, 4–8.

1 CONTEMPORARY ARAB THOUGHT AND GLOBALIZATION

1. Samir Amin, *Eurocentrism* (New York: Monthly Review Press, 1989) 53, and I. Wallerstein, "Eurocentrism and its Avatars: The Dilemmas of Social Science." *New Left Review*, number 226, November–December 1997, 93–107.
2. In this work, I use the term "Arab world" instead of the "Middle East." In the words of Keddi, the concept of the Middle East was used by European strategic circles in the nineteenth century and it is no more than an "artificial nineteenth-century abstraction." Nikki R. Keddi, "Is There a Middle East?" *International Journal of the Middle East*, volume 4(3), July 1973, 257. See also Rashid Khalidi, "The Middle East as an Area in an Era of Globalization," in Ali Mirsepassi, Amrita Basu, and Frederick Weaver, eds., *Localizing Knowledge in a Globalizing World* (Syracuse: Syracuse University Press, 2003), 171–90.
3. See Galāl Amīn, "Ḥawla mafhūm al-tanwīr: nadhrah naqdiyyah li tayyār assāssī min tayārāt al-thaqāfah al-'arabiyyah al-mu'āṣirah." *Al-Mustaqbal al-'Arabī*, volume 20(7), July 1997, 35–51.
4. Albert Hourani, *Arabic Thought in the Liberal Age, 1798–1939* (Cambridge: Cambridge University Press, 1970), and Hishām Sharābī, *Arab Intellectuals and the West: The Formative Years, 1875–1914* (Baltimore: Johns Hopkins University Press, 1970). See also the following: Hamilton Gibb, *Modern Trends in Islam* (Chicago: University of Chicago Press, 1947); Issa Boullata, *Trends and Issues in Contemporary Arab Thought* (Albany: State University of New York Press, 1990); Adel Daher, *Current Trends in Arab Intellectual Thought* (Washington, D.C.: Rand, 1969); R. Khuri, *Modern Arab Thought: Channels of the French Revolution to the Arab East*, trans. Ihsān 'Abbās (Princeton: Princeton University Press, 1983); P. Khoury, *Traditions et modernité: thèmes et tendances de la pensée arabe actuelle* (Beirut: n.p., 1983). I have been greatly indebted to the work of Albert Hourani on modern Arab intellectual history. On the importance of his *Arab Thought*, see Donald M. Reid, "*Arabic Thought in the Liberal Age* Twenty Five Years After." *International Journal of Middle East Studies*, volume 14(4), November 1982, 541–57.
5. In London, for example, writings on all aspects of Iraqi society and literature have flourished since the migration of not a small number of Iraqi scholars and thinkers to England after the Gulf War. It is important to point out in this regard the important books that Dar Riyād al-Rayyis and Dār al-Sāqī have put out in London.
6. On the economic and historical background of the Maghreb–Mashreq dichotomy, consult Samir Amin, *The Arab Nation: Nationalism and Class Struggle* (London: Zed Books, 1983), especially chapter 2.
7. By the Maghreb I mean the following countries: Libya, Tunisia, Algeria, Morocco, and Mauritania. France occupied Morocco in 1912.

8. "But, under the Arabization programs, much Francophone writing, especially in the late 1960s and early 1970s, was rejected by the religious authorities and Arab publishing houses because of its inherently, and sometimes offensive, Western nature. In these circumstances, Francophone writers became disaffected and were forced to realize their limitations within the new system, choosing self-censorship if they stayed, or opting for exile if they wished to continue writing freely and being published in French." Anne Armitage, "The Debate Over Literary Writing in a Foreign Language: An Overview of Francophone in the Maghreb." *Alif: Journal of Comparative Poetics*, number 20, 2000, 41.
9. See M. Lahbabi, *De l'être à la personne: Essai de personnalisme réaliste* (Paris: PUF, 1954); *Le personnalisme musulman* (Paris: PUF, 1964), and *Le monde de demian: Le Tiers-monde accuse* (Casablanca: Sherbrooke, 1980).
10. Mohammed Arkoun, *Essais dur la pensée islamique* (Paris: Editions Maisonneuve, 1977), and *Pour une critique de la raison islamique* (Paris: Editions Maisonneuve, 1984).
11. H. Djaït, *La personnalité et le devenir arabo-islamique* (Paris: Seuil, 1974), and *al-Kufa: Naissance de la ville islamique* (Paris: Editions Maisonneuve, 1991).
12. See A. Laroui, *The Crisis of the Arab Intelligentsia: Traditionalism or Historicism?* (Berkeley: University of California Press, 1976).
13. This is also true in the case of Samir Amin's writings.
14. See Ibrahim Abu-Rabi', *Intellectual Origins of Islamic Resurgence in the Modern Arab World* (Albany: State University of New York Press, 1996); Anouar Abdel-Malek, *La pensée politique arabe contemporain* (Paris: Seuil, 1970); Boullata, *Trends and Issues in Contemporary Arab Thought*; Daher, *Current Trends in Arab Intellectual Thought*; Khoury, *Traditions et modernité*; Sharābī, *Arab Intellectuals and the West: The Formative Years.*
15. In this work, I am using the terms "intellectual history" and "cultural history" interchangeably.
16. According to D. R. Woolf, intellectual history in the past 50 years has adopted "the vocabulary, techniques and even agendas of other historical subdisciplines, of related humanities subjects such as philosophy and literary theory, and even of some more far-flung disciplines within the social sciences." D. R. Woolf, "The Writing of Early Modern European Intellectual History, 1945–1995," in Michael Bentley, ed., *Companion to Historiography* (London: Routledge, 1997), 307.
17. See Francis Fukuyama, *The End of History and the Last Man* (New York: The Free Press, 1992).
18. On these themes see Halim Barakat, *The Arab World: Society, Culture, and State* (Berkeley: University of California Press, 1993).
19. According to Cohn, "America's emergence as a world power immediately after World War II had an immediate effect on the organization of academic activities, which was designed to increase and disseminate knowledge of those parts of the world in which the United States had continuing strategic, economic, and political interests. Anthropologists quickly found themselves taking leading roles in the organization of 'area programs' in which collectivities of various academic specialists were organized on the basis of knowledge about a particular part of the world." Bernard S. Cohn, *An Anthropologist Among the Historians and Other Essays* (New Delhi: Oxford University Press, 1987), 27. In the field of Arabic and Islamic, Orientalists of all sorts of orientations took the lead.
20. See Henry Kissinger, *Diplomacy* (New York: Touchstone Books, 1995).
21. See Yvonne Haddad and Jane Smith, eds., *Muslim Communities in North America* (Albany: State University of New York Press, 1995).
22. Perry Anderson, "Renewals." *New Left Review*, number 1, January–February 2000, 18.
23. See Arthur O. Lovejoy, *Essays in the History of Ideas* (New York: George Braziller, 1955) and George Boas, "Some Problems in Intellectual History," in A. O. Lovejoy, ed., *Studies in Intellectual History* (Baltimore: Johns Hopkins University Press, 1953), 3–21.
24. "Intellectual history really began to come into its own as a kind of 'elite' branch of the historical discipline as a whole after the First World War, as repugnance towards political history followed the collapse of the nineteenth-century empires, amid a general cynicism towards European leaders who had so recently led Europe into catastrophe." D. R. Woolf, "The Writing of Early Modern European Intellectual History, 1945–1995," 309.
25. Lovejoy, *Essays in the History of Ideas*, 1–2.

26. Leonard Krieger, "The Autonomy of Intellectual History," in Donald Kelley, ed., *The History of Ideas: Canon and Variations* (Rochester: University of Rochester Press, 1990), 108.
27. On the significance of political economy in the study of the modern Arab world, see Peter Gran, "Political Economy as a Paradigm for the Study of Islamic History." *International Journal of Middle East Studies*, volume 11(4), July 1980, 511–26.
28. F. Gilbert, "Intellectual History: Its Aims and Methods." *Daedalus*, volume 100(1), Winter 1971, p. 94. Leonard Krieger defines five distinct Western schools of intellectual history: "The five schools are: first, the German-Italian historicist school featuring a mix of historical philosophers and philosophic historians running from Dilthy and Croce to Cassirer, Meinecke, and Carlo Antoni; second, the group of social-intellectual historians centering on Marc Bloc, Lucien Febvre, and the periodical *Annales*; third and fourth, the two schools that can be regarded as American counterparts of these two Europeans tendencies, the History of Ideas group of Arthur O. Lovejoy and George Boas, and the New History of Robinson, Becker, and Beard; and fifth, the historians of assorted philosophical, literary, artistic, and politico-scientific theories and theorists." L. Krieger, "The Autonomy of Intellectual History," in Kelley, *The History of Ideas*, 113–14.
29. R. Darnton, "Intellectual and Cultural History," in M. Kammen, ed., *The Past Before Us: Contemporary Historical Writing in the United States* (Ithaca: Cornell University Press, 1980), 337.
30. See Antonio Gramsci, *Selections from the Prison Notebooks* (New York: International Publishers, 1978).
31. See Antonio Gramsci, *The Modern Prince and Other Writings* (New York: International Publishers, 1957). On the influence of Gramsci on modern Arab thought, see Ṭāher Labīb, "Gramsci nel mondo arabo." *GI Informatziori*, number 4, Instituto Gramsci, Roma, 1989, and Ṭāher Labīb, "Gramsci al-'arab." *Al-Ṭarīq*, volume 57(3), 1998, 10–30. Labīb argues that Arab Marxist orthodoxy has dismissed Gramsci's thought as irrelevant to Arab society. By this he refers to such Arab Marxist thinkers as Ṣādiq Jalāl al-'Azm, Ṭayyib Tizīnī, Maḥmūd Amīn al-'Ālim and Ḥussain Muruwwa. *Ibid.*, 17.
32. Paulo Freire, *Pedagogy of the Oppressed* (New York: Continuum, 1988).
33. Ali Shari'āti, *On the Sociology of Islam* (Berkeley: Mizan Press, 1979).
34. Pierre Bourdieu, *Acts of Resistance: Against the Tyranny of the Market* (New York: New Press, 1999).
35. "Apart from the immediate fall-out from the 1967 war, the Arab environment changed in a number of important ways during the 1960s and early 1970s. One factor was the decline of Egyptian power and prestige as a result of military defeat, economic exhaustion and the death of President Nasser. A second was the growing influence of Saudi Arabia, and a third the new political importance of Syria following the consolidation of President Asad's regime in the early 1970s." Roger Owen, *State, Power and Politics in the Making of the Modern Middle East* (London: Routledge, 1992), 90.
36. On the role of the military in politics in the Arab world, see Anouar Abdel-Malek, *Egypt: A Military Society* (New York: Random House, 1968).
37. Compare this to what Ranajit Guha says about India: "Thus there were the metropolitan bourgeoisie who professed and practised democracy at home, but were quite happy to conduct government of their Indian empire as an autocracy. Champions of the right of the European nations to self-determination, they denied the same right to their Indian subjects until the last days of the Indian raj and granted it without grace only when forced to do so under the impact of the anti-imperialist struggles of the subject population." Ranajit Guha, *Dominance without Hegemenoy: History and Power in Colonial India* (New Delhi: Oxford University Press, 1998), 4.
38. I. Wallerstein, *After Liberalism* (New York: The New Press, 1995).
39. According to Peter Gowan, the United States, which had lent the regime of Ṣaddām Ḥussain enormous support during the Iran–Iraq War in the 1980s decided to criminalize Ṣaddām Ḥussain after his troops invaded Kuwait in 1990. The process of criminalization involved "anthropomorphizing the Iraqi state and its political-administrative organization into a single person – Ṣaddām Ḥussain, criminal. And the more his human features were enlarged, the more other men and women in the 'criminal' state were dehumanized. The army of conscripts became the murder weapon, the lives

of millions of Iraqis the various limbs and resources of their leader. Hence they were fair game; or else they became collateral, in the sense of standing alongside the criminal – by-standers in the police shoot-out." Peter Gowan, "The Gulf War, Iraq and Western Liberalism." *New Left Review*, number 187, May/June 1991, 31. On the history of modern Iraq, see the following: Samira Haj, *The Making of Iraq, 1900–1963* (Albany: State University of New York Press, 1997); Hanna Batatu, *The Old Social Classes and the Revolutionary Movements in Iraq* (Princeton: Princeton University Press, 1978); J. F. Devlin, *The Ba'th Party: A History from its Origins to 1966* (Stanford: Stanford University Press, 1976); Charles Tripp, *A History of Iraq*, 2nd edition (Cambridge: Cambridge University Press, 2000).

40. In the view of 'Abdul Raḥmān Munīf, one of the most distinguished contemporary Arab novelists, since 1967 the Arab world has been going through the most difficult phase in its modern history. In addition to the absence of real democracy and civil society, economic dependency, and increase in consumerism, the margin of poverty has increased and the conflict between states has been on the rise. See 'Abdul Raḥmān Munīf, "al-Thaqāfah wa'l muthaqqaf fi'l mujtama' al – 'arabī," in Sayyid Yāssin, ed., *al-'Arab wa tahadiyyāt al-qarn al-hādī wa'l 'ishrīn* (Amman: Mu'assassat 'Abdul Hamīd Shūmān, 2000), 132.
41. This seems to be the same problem in modern American thought. See Alexander Bloom, *Prodigal Sons: The New York Intellectuals and Their World* (New York: Oxford University Press, 1986), and Alan M. Wald, *The New York Intellectuals: The Rise and Decline of Anti-Stalinist Left from the 1930s to the 1980s* (Chapel Hill: University of North Carolina Press, 1987).
42. On the issue of the intellectual and migration, see Salman Rushdie, *Imagined Homelands* (New York: Granta, 1990).
43. John Waterbury, "From Social Contracts to Extraction Contracts: The Political Economy of Authoritarianism and Democracy," in John P. Entelis, ed., *Islam, Democracy, and the State in North Africa* (Bloomington: Indiana University Press, 1997), 142.
44. This picture has changed a bit recently. See the important work done by the Ahram Strategic Center.
45. 'Abd al-Wahāb al-Masīrī, *al-Insāklūbidyyah al-ṣuhyūniyyah*, 7 volumes (Cairo: Dār al-Shurūq, 1999).
46. Of the several books on this issue, see Edward Said's latest, *The End of the Peace Process: Oslo and After* (New York: Pantheon, 2000). See also Edward Said, "America's Last Taboo." *New Left Review*, volume 6, November/December 2000, 45–54.
47. See Rif'at al-Sa'īd, *Ḥasan al-Banna, kayfa wa limādha* (Cairo: Dār al-Thaqāfah al-Jadīdah, 1984).
48. See Haydar Ibrahim 'Alī, "al-Usus al-ijtimā'iyyah li'l dhāhirah al-dīniyyah: mulahādhāt fī 'ilm al-ijtimā' al-dīnī," in Markaz Dirāsāt al-Wiḥdah al-'Arabiyyah, *al-Dīn fi'l mujtama' al-'arabī* (Beirut: Markaz Dirāsāt al-Wiḥdah al-'Arabīyyah, 1990), p. 33, and Muḥammad Ḥijāzī, ed., *Naḥwa 'ilm ijtimā' 'arabī: 'ilm al-ijtimā' wa'l mushkilāt al-'arabiyya al-rāhina* (Beirut: Markaz Dirāsāt al-Wiḥdah al-'Arabīyyah, 1986).
49. One of the best representatives of this view is the Egyptian philosopher Zakī Najīb Maḥmūd. See his *Tajdīd al-fikr al-'arabī* (Cairo: Dār al-Shurūq, 1980).
50. Ṭāhā Ḥussain, *The Future of Culture in Egypt*, trans. S. Glazer (New York: Octagon Books, 1975).
51. Maḥmūd, *Tajdīd al-fikr al-'arabī*. See Ṣalāḥ Qunṣuwwa, "Ḥawla al-'aql wa'l thaqāfah al-'arabiyyah: ḥiwār ma' Zakī Najīb Maḥmūd." *Al-Mustaqbal al-'Arabī*, volume 11(8), August 1988, 121–33, and al-Bukhārī Hammānīi, "Makānat Zakī Najīb Maḥmūd fi'l ḥarakah al-falsafiyyah al-'arabiyyah al-mu'āṣirah." *Al-Mustaqbal al-'Arabī*, volume 20(8), August 1997, 48–55.
52. Lewis 'Awad, his memoirs. I do not agree with the contention of Jalāl Kishik that 'Awad is missionary at heart. See Kishik, *Suqūt al-'ilmāniyyah* (Cairo: Dār al-I'tiṣām, 1994).
53. Maḥmūd Shākir, *Risālah fi'l ṭarīq ila thaqāfatinah* (Cairo: Dār al-Hilāl, 1991).
54. Samir Amin's writings represent this trend.
55. See Kamal Abu-Deeb, "Cultural Creation in a Fragmented Society," in Hisham Rabi, ed., *The Next Arab Decade: Alternative Futures* (Boulder: Westview Press, 1988), 160–81.
56. See *ibid.*

57. Ghassān al-Rifā'ī, "Mulāḥadhāt ḥawla al-manhajiyyah fī ba'd turūhāt al-tajdīd al-fikrī." *Al-Ṭarīq*, volume 52(3), April–September 1993, 30–8.
58. Samāḥ Idrīs, *al-Muthaqaf al-'arabī wa'l sulṭah: baḥth fī riwāyat al-tajribah al-nāssiriyyah* (Beirut: Dār al-Ādāb, 1993), and Richard Jacquemond, "Retour à Nasser des intellectuels égyptiens." *Le Monde Diplomatique*, July 1997, 15.
59. Mohamed Heykal, *L'Autonome de la colère: L'assassinat de Sadate* (Paris: Editions Ramsay, 1983).
60. Nawal El Saadawi, *Mudhakārtī fī sijni al-nisā'* (Cairo: Dār al-Mustaqbal al-'Arabi, 1986) and *A Daughter of Isis: The Autobiography of Nawal El Saadawi* (London: Zed Books, 1999).
61. Ghālī Shukrī, *Egypt: Portrait of a President* (London: Zed Books, 1981).
62. Farīda al-Naqqāsh, *Yawmiyyāt al-mudun al-maftūḥah* (Cairo: Dār al-Thaqāfah al-Jadīdah, 1987).
63. See S. Amin, *Unequal Development: An Essay on the Social Formations of Peripheral Capitalism* (New York: Monthly Review Press, 1976), and *The Arab Nation: Nationalism and Class Struggle* (London: Zed Books, 1983).
64. The Lebanese novelist Eliās Khury says that the 1967 defeat represented a threefold absence in Arab thought: (1) absence of consciousness; (2) absence of planning, and (3) absence of the self. See Eliās Khury, "al-Nakbah wa'l ṣirā' 'ala al-kalimāt." *Al-Ṭarīq*, volume 57(3), May–June 1998, 4–9.
65. Ghassān Kanafānī, "Thoughts on Change and the 'Blind Language'," in Ferial J. Ghazoul and Barbara Harlow, eds., *The View from Within: Writers and Critics on Contemporary Arabic Literature* (Cairo: American University of Cairo Press, 1994), 43.
66. Tharwat 'Ukāshah, *Mudhakarāt fī'l thaqāfah wa'l siyāssah*, volume 2 (Cairo: Dār al-Hilāl, 1990), 375.
67. Yāssīn al-Ḥāfiz, *al-Hazīmah wa'l idiūlujiyyah al-mahzūmah* (Beirut: Dār al-Ṭalī'ah, 1979).
68. Ṣādiq Jalāl al-'Azm, *al-Naqd al-dhātī ba'dah al-hazīmah* (Beirut: Dār al-Ṭalī'ah, 1969). 'Azm contends that defeat had something to do with the nature of the Arab personality, which is fahlawi in nature, or in the words of Fouad Moughrabi, "This syndrome is related to what others have called the 'lack of reality testing' among the Arabs." Fouad Moughrabi, "The Arabic Basic Personality: A Critical Survey of the Literature." *International Journal of Middle East Studies*, volume 9(1), February 1978, 104.
69. Ṣādiq Jalāl al-'Azm, *Naqd al-fikr al-dīnī* (Beirut: Dār al-Ṭalī'ah, 1969).
70. Abdallah Laroui, *L'idéologie arabe contemporaine* (Paris: Maspero, 1970).
71. Yūsuf al-Qaraḍāwī, *al-Hall al-islāmī, farīdah wa ḍarūra*h (Beirut: Mu'assassat al-Risālah, 1989).
72. Costantine Zurayk, "Ma'nah al-nakbah mujaddadan," in *al-A'māl al-fikriyyah al-'āmmah li Costantine Zurayk*, volume 2 (Beirut: Markaz Dirāsāt al-Wiḥdah al-'Arabiyyah, 1994).
73. See Sayyid Yāssin, *al-Shakhṣiyyah al-'arabiyyah bayna sūrat al-dhāt wa mafhūm al-ākhar* (Cairo: Maktabat Madbūlī, 1993).
74. See Abu al-Ḥasan al-Nadwi, *Islam and the World* (Kuwait: IIFSO, 1977).
75. Edward Said, *The End of the Peace Process: Oslo and After* (New York: Pantheon, 2000), 161.
76. Rajā' al-Naqqāsh, *al-In'izaliyyūn fī misr: radd 'ala Tawfīq al-Ḥakīm wa Luwīs 'Awad* (Cairo: al-Hay'ah al-Miṣriyyah al-'Āmmah li'l Kitāb, 1996).

2 CONTEMPORARY ARAB INTELLECTUAL TRENDS

1. Ḥassan Ḥanafī, "al-Fikr al-'arabī al-mu'āṣir: al-judhūr wa'l thimār." *Qaḍāyah Fikriyyah*, volumes 15–16, June–July 1995, 201. For a different classification, consult Abdulwahab Bebaeir, "Intellectual Currents in Contemporary Islam." *The Muslim World*, volume 81. July–October 1991, 231–44.
2. On this issue see Neil Jumonville, *Critical Crossings: The New York Intellectuals in Postwar America* (Berkeley: University of California Press, 1991), especially chapter 2.
3. Hishām Sharābī, *Neopatriarchy: A Theory of Distorted Change in Arab Society* (New York: Oxford University Press, 1988).

4. Mohammed Arkoun, *Pour une critique de la raison islamique* (Paris: Editions Maisonneuve et Larose, 1984). Some of Arkoun's work is also available in English. See Mohammed Arkoun, *The Unthought in Contemporary Islamic Thought* (London: Saqi Books, 2002).
5. Maḥmūd Amīn al-'Ālim, *al-Fikr al-'arabī bayna al-khuṣūṣiyyah wa'l kawniyyah* (Cairo: Dār al-Mustaqbal al-'Arabī, 1996), and Fahima Charaffeddine, *Culture et idéologie dans le monde arabe* (Paris: L'Harmattan, 1994).
6. See Aḥmad Ṣudqī al-Dajānī, " 'An al-'urūbbah wa'l islām wa qaḍāya al-mustaqbal," in Markaz Dirāsāt al-Wiḥdah al-'Arabīyyah, *al-Ḥiwār al-qawmī al-dīnī* (Beirut: Markaz Dirāsāt al-Wiḥdah al-'Arabīyyah, 1989), 62.
7. Abdallah Laroui, *The Crisis of the Arab Intelligentsia: Traditionalism or Historicism*? (Berkeley: University of California Press, 1976), 153–4.
8. Fahmi Jad'ān, "al-Salafīyyah: ḥudūduhah wa taḥawulātuhah." *'Ālam al-Fikr*, volume 26, January–April 1998, 62.
9. *Ibid.*, 73.
10. See Ahmad Dallal, "Islamic Revivalist Thought, 1750–1850." *Journal of the American Oriental Society*, volume 113(3), July–September 1993.
11. See Ḥaydar Ibrahim 'Alī, "al-Itijāh al-salafī." *'Ālam al-Fikr*, volume 26, January–April 1998, 31.
12. Al-'Ālim argues that the Salafīyyah is "a national reformist movement, which opposes and rejects corruption, stagnation, social chaos, and dependency on the West. It is a call to adopt the religious foundations and the past heritage as a criterion to get rid of these conditions." Mahmūd Amīn al-'Ālim, *al-W 'y wa'l wa'y al-zā'if fi'l fikr al-'arabī al-mu'āṣir* (Cairo: Dār al-Thaqāfah al-Jadīdah, 1986), 238.
13. On the problem of stagnation in modern Muslim thought in general see G. E. Von Grunebaum and R. Brunschvig, eds., *Classicisme et déclin culturel dans l'histoire de l'islam* (Paris: Maisonneuve, 1957).
14. Samir Amin, "al-Thaqāfah wa'l aydiyūlojiyyah fi'l 'ālam al-'arabī al-mu'āṣir." *Al-Ṭarīq*, volume 52(1), May 1993, 74.
15. On the attempt to resurrect Mu'tazila Kalam, see R. Caspar, "Un aspect de la pensée musulmane moderne: Le renouveau du Mo'tazilisme." *Mélanges*, volume 4, 1957.
16. Amin, "al-Thaqāfah," 77.
17. See Albert Hourani, *Arabic Thought in the Liberal Age: 1798–1939* (Cambridge: Cambridge University Press, 1970).
18. See Louis Althusser, *Essays on Ideology* (London: Verso, 1976).
19. On Moroccan Salafīyyah, see Abdallah Laroui, *Les origines du nationalisme marocain, 1830–1912* (Paris: Maspero, 1977).
20. Mohamed El Mansour, "Salafis and Modernists in the Moroccan Nationalist Movement," in John Ruedy, ed., *Islamism and Secularism in North Africa* (New York: St. Martin's Press, 1996), 60.
21. Ghālī Shukrī, *Diktātoriyat al-takhalluf al-'arabī* (Cairo: al-Hay'ah al-Miṣriyyah al-'Āmmah li'l Kitāb, 1994), 210–17.
22. On the position of Christianity in the West, see W. Nicholls, ed., *Modernity and Religion* (Waterloo: Wilfrid Laurier University Press, 1987).
23. Ghālī Shukrī, *'Aqni'at al-irhāb: al-baḥth 'an 'ilmāniyyah jadīdah* (Cairo: al-Hay'ah al-Misriyyah al-'Āmmah li'l Kitāb, 1992), 19.
24. See Yūsuf al-Qaraḍāwī, *al-Ḥall al-islāmī: farīḍah wa darūrah* (Beirut: Mu'assassat al-Risālah, 1989). A critical examination of this book is by Khalīl 'Abd al-Karīm, "Min āfāt al-fikr al-'arabī al-mu'āsirah: dirāsah naqdiyyah mujmalah li kitāb al-hall al-islāmī farīdah wa *darūrah* li fadhīlat al-Shaykh Yūsuf al-Qaraḍāwī," in Maḥmūd Amīn al-'Ālim, ed., *al-Fikr al-'Arabī 'ala mashārif al-qarn al-ḥādī wa'l 'ishrīn* (Cairo: Qaḍāya Fikriyya, 1995), 259–68.
25. On the history of the Salafīyyah in Syria, see Bruce Commins, " 'Abd al-Qādir al-Jazāi'ri and Islamic Reform." *The Muslim World*, volume 78, April 1988, 121–31.
26. See 'Abdul Raḥmān Munīf, "al-Thaqāfah wa'l muthaqqaf fī'l mujtama' al-'arabī," in Sayyid Yāssin, ed., *al-'Arab wa taḥadiyyāt al-qarn al-ḥādī wa'l 'ishrīn* (Amman: Mu'assassat 'Abdul Ḥamīd Shūmān, 2000), 139.
27. See Mamoun Fandy, *Saudi Arabia and the Politics of Dissent* (New York: Palgrave, 1999).

28. See Maxime Rodinson, *Marxism and the Muslim World* (New York: Monthly Review Press, 1981) and Michael Gilsenan, *Recognizing Islam: Religion and Society in the Modern Arab World* (New York: Pantheon, 1982).
29. Aḥmad Kamāl Abū'l Majd, one of the most enlightened Islamist thinkers, argues that the Muslim world has known three harmful trends of late: first, the trend of the literalists [*tayyār al-ḥarfiyyīn*], who consider nothing but the Sacred Text; second, the trend of "folk culture," and third, the trend of Arab and Muslim anger [*tayyār al-ghadab al-'arabī wa'l islāmī*]. He says that these trends have coalesced to produce a very harmful front against the voices of reason and progress in the mainstream Muslim community. See Aḥmad Kamāl Abū'l Majd, "Min ajl wihdah thaqāfiyyah 'arabiyyah," in Yāssin, *al-'Arab wa taḥadiyyāt al-qarn al-ḥādī wa'l 'ishrīn*, 404–7.
30. See Yvonne Haddad, "Muslim Revivalist Thought in the Arab World: An Overview." *The Muslim World*, volume 76, July–October 1986, 143–67.
31. 'Alī, "al-Itijāh al-salafī."
32. Immanuel Wallerstein, "The Bourgeoisie as Concept and Reality." *New Left Review*, number 167, January/February 1988, p. 92. Wallerstein goes on to add that, "But admirers and critics have generally combined to agree that the bourgeois, this bourgeois the capitalist, has been the central dynamic force of modern economic life, for all since the nineteenth century, for many since the sixteenth, for a few even longer than that." *Ibid.*, 92–3.
33. Harold Laski, *Liberty in the Modern State* (London: Faber & Faber, 1930), 254–5.
34. Anthony Arblaster, *Democracy* (London: Open University press, 1994), 96.
35. According to Maḥmūd Amīn al-'Ālim, the liberal concept of democracy in the West (Europe and the United States) constitutes an integral part of the dominant capitalist system. Democracy was the result of negotiation between different segments of the nascent bourgeoisie in the nineteenth century and it expressed the desire of the capitalist system to spread overseas. Maḥmūd Amīn al-'Ālim, *al-Wa'y wa'l wa 'y al-zā'if fi'l fikr al-'arabī al-mu'āṣir* (Cairo: Dār al-Thaqāfah al-Jadīdah, 1986), 43.
36. "The philosophic thought of the seventeenth century makes it plain that the human mind had largely freed itself from dependence upon theological authority. Its predominant notes are secular and rational." Harold Laski, *The Rise of European Liberalism: An Essay in Interpretation* (London: George Allen & Unwin Ltd., 1936), 125.
37. *Ibid.*, 19. See also C. B. Macpherson, *The Life and Times of Liberal Democracy* (Oxford: Oxford University Press, 1977).
38. Laski, *The Rise of European Liberalism*, 60.
39. Irene Collins, *Liberalism in Nineteenth-Century Europe* (London: The Historical Association, 1957), 4. See also Richard Bellamy, *Liberalism and Modern Society* (Cambridge: Polity Press, 1992); Allen Brinkly, *Liberalism and its Discontents* (Cambridge, MA: Harvard University Press, 1997); John Dewey, *Liberalism and Social Action: The Later Works, 1925–1953* (Carbondale: Edwardsville, 1987); Charles Forcey, *The Crossroads of Liberalism* (Oxford: Oxford University Press, 1961), and C. P. Macpherson, *The Political Theory of Possessive Individualism: Hobbes to Locke* (New York: Oxford University Press, 1962).
40. "The European states achieved national unity at a moment when the national middle classes had concentrated most of the wealth in their hands. Shopkeepers and artisans, clerks and bankers monopolized finance, trade, and science in the national framework. The middle class was the most dynamic and prosperous of all classes." Franz Fanon, *The Wretched of the Earth* (New York: Grove Press, 1968), 95–6.
41. Ibrahim Ibrahim, "Ṭāhā Husayn: The Critical Spirit," in John Spagnolo, ed., *Problems of the Modern Middle East in Historical Perspective* (London: Ithaca Press, 1992).
42. 'Alī al-Dīn Hilāl, "Azmat al-fikr al-liberālī fi'l waṭan al-'arabī." *'Ālam al-Fikr*, volume 26(3–4), January–June 1998, 109–29.
43. Fanon, *The Wretched of the Earth*, 149. Fanon goes on to say that, "The national bourgeoisie of underdeveloped countries is not engaged in production, nor in invention, nor in building, nor labor...Because it is bereft of ideas, because it lives to itself and cuts itself off from the people...the national middle class will have nothing better to do than to take on the role of manager for Western enterprises." *Ibid.*, 149–50.

44. Muḥammad Kāmil al-Khaṭīb, " 'An al-liberaliyyah wa'l 'ālamiyyah: muḥāwalah fi'l tafkīr." *Al-Ṭarīq*, volume 52(2), July 1993, 102.
45. Wallerstein argues that the middle classes began to develop in the Third World only after independence, "As one country after another became independent after the Second World War, analysts began to take note of the rise of a very significant stratum-educated cadres employed by the government, whose income levels made them quite well-to-do in comparison with most of their compatriots. In Africa, where those cadres stood out most sharply in the virtual absence of other varieties of 'well-to-do' people, a new concept was created to designate them, the 'administrative bourgeoisie'. The administrative bourgeoisie was quite traditionally 'bourgeois' in style of life and social values. It represented the social underpinning of most regimes." Immanuel Wallerstein, "The Bourgeoisie as Concept and Reality." *New Left Review*, number 167, January/February 1988, 97.
46. Al-'Ālim, *al-Wa'y wa'l wa'y al-zā'if*, 121.
47. 'Alī al-Dīn Hilāl, "Azmat al-fikr al-liberālī fi'l waṭan al-'arabī", 123.
48. *Ibid.*, 124.
49. Aḥmad Bahā' al-Dīn, "Mādha yurād bi misr?," in Markaz Dirāsāt al-Wiḥdah al-'Arabīyyah, *Min ḥamalat mashā'il al-taqaddum al-'arabī: Aḥmad Bahā' al-Dīn* (Beirut: Markaz Dirāsāt al-Wiḥdah al-'Arabīyyah, 1994), 141–5.
50. Shukrī, *Diktātoriyat al-takhalluf al-'arabī*, 159.
51. Robert Springborg, "The Arab Bourgeoisie: A Revisionist Interpretation." *Arab Studies Quarterly*, volume 15(1), Winter 1993, 14.
52. "The immediate post-independence period was fraught with peril for ruling elites in the Third World. The process of independence itself engendered revolutions of rising expectations. Even prior to total independence many governments in the Middle East had vastly expanded public education, and by so doing facilitated the emergence of a new, more stridently radical, middle class (or petit bourgeoisie) with superior organizational and intellectual skills." *Ibid.*, 23.
53. Salāh al-Dīn Mansī, "al-Fikr al-liberalī fi'l sab'ināt," in Tāher Labīb, ed., *al-intellijentsia al-'arabiyyah* (Tunis: al-Jam'iyyah al-'Arabīyyah, 1995), 442.
54. *Ibid.*, 446.
55. See Raymond A. Hinnebusch, *Authoritarian Power and State Formation in Ba'thist Syria: Army, Party, and Peasant* (Boulder: Westview Press, 1989) and Hanna Batatu, *Syria's Peasantry, the Descendants of its Lesser Rural Notables and their Politics* (Princeton: Princeton University Press, 199).
56. *Ibid.*, 449.
57. "Pan-Arabism is not dead. On the contrary, it is a living and vital force." R. Stephen Humphreys, *Between Memory and Desire: The Middle East in a Troubled Age* (Berkeley: University of California Press, 1999), 81. In Edward Said's words, "Arab nationalism has not died, but has all too often resolved itself into smaller and smaller units." Edward Said, *Culture and Imperialism* (New York: Alfred Knopf, 1993), 298.
58. See Avi Shlaim, *The Politics of Partition: King Abdullah, the Zionists and Palestine, 1921–1951* (New York: Columbia University Press, 1990).
59. See Sayyid Yāssin, *Tahlīl madmūn al-fikr al-qawmī al-'arabī* [*Towards an Analysis of the Contents of Arab Nationalist Thought*] (Beirut: Markaz Dirāsāt al-Wiḥdah al-'Arabīyyah, 1980).
60. See Albert Hourani, "The Arab Awakening Forty Years After," in Derek Hopwood, ed., *Studies in Arab History: The Antonious Lectures, 1978–87* (London: Macmillan, 1990), and Aziz al-Azmeh, "Nationalism and the Arabs." *Arab Studies Quarterly*, volume 17(1 and 2), Winter and Spring 1995, 6.
61. Al-Azmeh argues that the 1917 Arab revolt against the Ottomans was not motivated by nationalist feelings: "It was an Islamist rebellion, undertaken in the name of, not the Arabs, but a Meccan Caliphate under the Sharif Husayn Bin Ali, who was later to be declared Caliph by a conclave of 16 Hijazis, 3 Indians, 3 Sudanese, 2 Bukharans, and 2 Javanese, in addition to one Moroccan, one Syrian, one Turk, one Afghan, and one Daghestani." Al-Azmeh, "Nationalism and the Arabs", 7.
62. See M. 'Imārah, *al-A'māl al-kāmilah li 'Abd al-Raḥmān al-Kawākibī* (Cairo: al-Hay'ah al-Miṣriyyah al-'Āmmah li'l Ta'līf wa'l Nashr, 1970).

63. M. Darwaza, *al-Wihdah al-'Arabiyyah: Mabāhith fī ma'ālim al-watan al-'arabī al-kabīr wa muqawimmāt wihdatihi wa'l 'aqabāt allatī taqif fī tarīqiha wa mu'ālajatiha wa'l marāḥil allatī yajib an yusarfiha ila tahqīqiha* (Cairo: n.p.; n.d.)
64. M. 'Aflaq, *Fī sabīl al-ba'th* (Beirut: Dār al-Ṭalī'ah, 1959).
65. Marlene Abou Nasr, "L'idéologie nationale arabe dans le discours de Gamal Abd-El Nasser, 1952–1970." Thesis. Paris: Université de Paris, 1979.
66. See Walid W. Kazziha, *Revolutionary Transformation in the Arab World: Habash and His Comrades from Nationalism to Marxism* (London: Charles Knight & Co., 1975).
67. On the dramatic changes in the Egyptian cultural scene from Nasser's rule to that of Sadat, see J. Crabbs, Jr., "Politics, History, and Culture in Nasser's Egypt." *International Journal of Middle East Studies*, volume 6(4), 1975, and Ghālī Shukrī, " 'Abdul Nasser wa'l muthaqaffūn," in his *Mudhakarāt thaqāfah tahtadir* (Cairo: al-Hay'ah al-Miṣriyyah al-'Āmmah li'l Kitāb, 1995), 369–422.
68. Anouar Abdel-Malek, "The Occultation of Egypt." *Arab Studies Quarterly*, volume 1(3), Summer 1979, 177.
69. Aḥmad Bahā' al-Dīn, "Mādha yurād bi miṣr?," in Markaz Dirāsāt al-Wiḥdah al-'Arabīyyah, *Min hamalat mashā'il al-taqaddum al-'arabī: Aḥmad Bahā' al-Dīn* (Beirut: Markaz Dirāsāt al-Wiḥdah al-'Arabīyyah, 1994).
70. Chatterjee argues that "anticolonial nationalism creates its own domain of sovereignty within the colonial society well before it begins its political battle with the imperial power. It does this by dividing the world of social institutions and practices into two domains – the material and the spiritual. The material is the domain of the 'outside', of the economy and state-craft, of science and technology, a world where the West had proved its superiority and the East had succumbed. In this domain, then, Western superiority had to be acknowledged and its accomplishments carefully studied and replicated. The spiritual, on the other hand, is an 'inner' domain bearing the 'essential' marks of cultural identity. The greater one's success in imitating Western skills in the material domain, therefore, the greater the need to preserve the distinctness of one's spiritual culture. This formula is, I think, a fundamental feature of anticolonial nationalisms in Asia and Africa." Partha Chatterjee, *The Nation and its Fragments: Colonial and Postcolonial Histories,* in *the Partha Chatterjee Omnibus* (New Delhi: Oxford University Press, 1999), 6.
71. See Adeed Dawisha, *Arab Nationalism in the Twentieth Century: From Triumph to Despair* (Princeton: Princeton University Press, 2003).
72. Aḥmad Bahā' al-Dīn, "Sanat al-tamazzuq al-'arabī," in Markaz Dirāsāt al-Wiḥdah al-'Arabīyyah, *Min ḥamalat mashā'il al-taqaddum*, 154–61.
73. "With the signing of a separate peace treaty between Egypt and Israel in 1978, the death knell was dealt to the idea of an Arab nationalist order, particularly one centered around Egypt." Saleh Omar, "Arab Nationalism: A Retrospective Evaluation." *Arab Studies Quarterly*, volume 14(4), Fall 1992, 23.
74. Naseer H. Aruri, "The Recolonization of the Arab World." *Arab Studies Quarterly*, volume 11(2 and 3), Spring/Summer 1989, p. 278. Aruri goes on to argue that, "The Arab political order, which had undergone a process of reconstruction between the early 1950s and the June 1967 defeat, collapsed again in the aftermath of that defeat. The end of the Nasserist thrust and the ascendency of Anwar Sadat's open door policies constituted a juncture in the history of Arab polity. The concept of a common Arab good became less tangible, less binding and less rewarding. Henceforward, the Arab world would be atomized and pacified; its dissidents would be contained and its wealth would be used to uphold orthodoxy. The Arab national interest would be replaced by state interests, claimed by no less than twenty two different regimes." *Ibid.*, 280. See also James Petras, "The U.S. and the Middle East: Recolonization or Decolonization?" *Arab Studies Quarterly*, volume 2(2), Spring 1980, 150–61. According to Petras, "U.S. imperialism has several strategic interests in the Arab world: oil trade and investment, preventing social revolution, and creating a sphere of influence opposed to the U.S.S.R." *Ibid.*, 155.
75. A number of Arab nationalist thinkers and journalists predicted the recolonization of the Arab world. See for example, Riyād Najīb al-Rayyis, "al-Khalīj al-'arabī: 'awdat al-isti'mār," in Riyāḍ al-Rayyis, ed., *'Awdat al-isti'mār: min al-ghazw al-thaqāfī ila harb al-khalīj* (London: Riad El-Rayyes Books, 1991), 13–18. Al-Rayyis argues that a number of Western strategists in the 1970s,

especially British and American, were advocating the idea of occupying the Gulf for economic reasons. *Ibid.*, 23.

76. Edward Said, "Ignorant Armies Clash by Night," in Edward Said, *The Politics of Dispossession: The Struggle for Palestinian Self-Determination* (New York: Vintage Books, 1995), 290.
77. See Benedict Anderson, *Imagined Communities: Reflections on the Origins and Spread of Nationalism* (London: Verso, 1991); Partha Chatterjee, *Nationalist Thought and the Colonial World* (London: Zed Books, 1986), and Eric Hobsbawm, *Nations and Nationalism Since 1780* (Cambridge: Cambridge University Press, 1994).
78. On the Arab nationalist movement in the East, see Sylvia Haim, ed., *Arab Nationalism: An Anthology* (Berkeley: University of California press, 1974). On Arab nationalism in North Africa, that is, Morocco, Algeria, and Tunisia, see Nabīh al-Asfahānī, "Tatawwur al-harakah al-siyāsiyyah fi'l maghrib al-'arabī" [Evolution of the Arab Political Movement in North Africa] in Markaz Dirāsāt al-Wiḥdah al-'Arabīyyah, *al-Qawmiyyah al-'arabiyyah fi'l fikr wa'l mumārasah* [Arab Nationalism: Thought and Practice] (Beirut: Markaz Dirāsāt al-Wiḥdah al-'Arabīyyah, 1980), 30–51.
79. On the assessment of the British Left of the Soviet fall, see Robin Blackburn, *After the Fall: The Failure of Communism and the Future of Socialism* (London: Verso, 1991).
80. Sunil Khilnani, *Arguing Revolution: The Intellectual Left in Postwar France* (New Haven: Yale University Press, 1993), 121; Marc Lazar, *Maisons rouges: Les Partis communistes français et italien, de la Libération à nos jours* (Paris: Aubier, 1992).
81. See Norberto Bobbio, *Left and Right: The Significance of a Political Distinction* (Chicago: University of Chicago Press, 1997). See also Perry Anderson, "The Affinities of Norberto Bobbio." *New Left Review*, number 170, July–August 1988.
82. Faraḥ Anṭūn, *Ibn Rushd wa falsafatuhuh* (Beirut: Dār al-Ṭalī'ah, 1981) and Shiblī Shumayl, *Falsafat al-nushū' wa'l irtiqā'* (Cairo: Dār al-Muqṭatif, 1910).
83. On the thought of these Leftist pioneers in the Arab world, see Rif'at al-Sa'īd, *Tārīkh al-fikr al-ishtirākī bī miṣr* (Cairo: Dār al-Thaqāfah al-Jadīdah, 1969) and Rif'at al-Sa'īd, *Thalathut lubnaniyīn fi'l qāhirah* (Beirut: Dār al-Ṭalī'ah, 1973).
84. Kamāl 'Abd al-Laṭīf, *Salāma Mūsa wa ishkaliyāt al-nahdah* (Beirut: Dār al-Ṭalī'ah, 1982).
85. On early socialist thought in the Arab world, see Mourad Wahba, "The Meaning of Ishtirakiyyah: Arab Perceptions of Socialism in the Nineteenth Century." *Alif: Journal of Comparative Poetics*, number 10, 1990, 42–55.
86. Karīm Muruwwa, "Ishkāliyat al-nahḍah wal fikr al-mārkisī al-'arabī." *Al-Ṭarīq*, volume 75(6), 1998, 29.
87. *Ibid.*, 31–2.
88. Criticism of Stalinism is still a trend in Arab Leftist circles. According to a prominent Iraqi Leftist, "Although Marxism began as a revolutionary idea hoping to change the *ancien régime*, Stalin was able to relegate it to a barbaric ideological system in the mid 1920s. Ideology became a totemic rite, and death awaited any violation of the Stalinist taboos." Fadil al-'Azzawi, "Min wahm al-diktatoriyyah ila mamlakat al-huriyyah," in al-Rayyis, *'Awdat al-isti'mār*, 82.
89. See Selma Botman, *The Rise of Egyptian Communism, 1939–1970* (New York: Syracuse University Press, 1993), 21–2.
90. Rif'at al-Sa'īd, "al-Ḥarakah al-shuyū'iyyah al-miṣriyyah 'abra sabī'n 'āman." *Qaḍāyah Fikriyyah*, volumes 11 and 12, 1992, 25. In this volume, *Qaḍāyah Fikriyyah*, a distinguished Leftist periodical edited by Maḥmūd Amīn al-'Ālim, devotes a special issue on "Seventy Years in the History of the Egyptian Communist Movement."
91. Ghālī Shukrī, *Mira'āt al-manfa: asi'lat fī thaqāfat al-naft wa'l ḥarb* (Cairo: al-Hay'ah al-Miṣriyyah al-'Āmmah li'l Kitāb, 1994), 224.
92. According to Ṭayyib Tizīnī, Marxist thought was introduced to the Arab world in the 1920s with its Stalinist coloration. Arab thought, just like Stalinist thought in the interwar period, was sterile. Ṭ. Tizīnī, *Ṭarīq al-wuḍūh al-manhajī* (Beirut: Dār al-Fārābī, 1989), 261.
93. See Maxime Rodinson, *Marxisme et monde musulman* (Paris: Editions du Seuil, 1972), especially chapter 1.
94. Aḥmad Ṣādiq Sa'd states that in the 1940s, a number of Egyptian Leftists began to memorize the major works of Marx, Engels and Lenin and view the Egyptian situation through the prism of

these works. However, these thinkers were not able to unravel the Egyptian specificity and the major role the peasantry has played in Egyptian society since the beginning. See A. S. Sa'd, *Ṣafaḥāt mina al-yasār al-miṣrī: 1945–1946* (Cairo: Madbūlī, 1976), 36.

95. Haytham Jābir, "Min ajl i'ādat wasl ma inqaṭa' aw niqāsh fī afkār Karīm Murruwwa." *Al-Ṭarīq*, volume 49(4), July–August 1990, 36.
96. Rodinson defines himself as an independent Marxist. He says: "On peut l'appeler indépendant s'il refuse de se laisser enfermer, sur le plan des idées, dans une des syntheses idéologiques totalitaires qui prétendent chacune être le 'vrai marxisme' et si, sur le plan de l'action, il refuse d'être intégré dans un groupe marxiste organisé." ("One can say that an independent person is the one who refuses to allow himself to be confined, in the realm of ideas, in one of those totalitarian ideological formations which pretend to be the 'real Marxism' and if, on the level of action, he refuses to be absorbed into a Marxist organization." Translation by Abu-Rabi'.) Rodinson, *Marxisme et monde musulman,* 44.
97. Francis Fukuyama, *The End of History and the Last Man* (New York: Free Press, 1992).
98. Ghālī Shukrī elaborates on this point in many of his writings and especially in *Min al-arshīf al-sirrī li'l thaqāfah al-miṣriyyah* (Beirut: Dār al-Ṭali'ah, 1975).
99. See Ghālī Shukrī, *Bidāyāt al-tārikh: min zilzāl al-khalīj ila zawāl al-soviet* (Cairo: Dār Su'ād al-Ṣabāḥ, 1993).
100. See R. Khuri, *Modern Arab Thought: Channels of the French Revolution to the Arab East,* trans. Ihsān 'Abbās (Princeton: Kingston Press, 1983).
101. Maḥmūd Amīn al-'Ālim, "al-Fikr al-'arabī bayna al-nadhariyyah wa'l taṭbīq." *'Ālam al-Fikr*, volume 26, January–April 1998, 31. See also Rifa't al-Sa'īd, "Salafiyat al-fikr al-mārkisī: mata wa kayfa?," in Maḥmūd Amīn al-'Ālim, ed., *al-Fikr al-'Arabī 'ala mashārif al-qarn al-hādī wa'l 'ishrīn* (Cairo: Dār Qaḍāyah Fikriyyah, 1995), 379–86.
102. Shawqī Jalāl, "al-Yasār al-'arabī wa sosiolojiyat al-fashal." *'Ālam al-Fikr*, volume 26, January–April 1998, 191–2.
103. Adonis, *al-Thābit wa'l mutahawwil: Sadmat al-hadātha*, volume 3 (Beirut: Dār al-'Awdah, 1979), 239–40.
104. Hādī al-'Ulwī, *Fī'l dīn wa'l turāth* (Jerusalem: Salāh al-Dīn, 1975), 14.
105. Abdallah Laroui, *L'idéologie arabe contemporaine* (Paris: Maspero, 1970), 35.
106. This is best represented by Ḥassan Ḥanafī and 'Ādil Ḥussain. See Ḥanafī, "al-Yasār al-islāmī: turāth al-sultah wa turāth al-mu'āradah." *Al-Qāhirah*, number 164, July 1996, 10–15.
107. See Nabīl 'Abd al-Fattāh, ed., *The State of Religion in Egypt Report* (Cairo: Al-Ahram Center for Political and Strategic Studies, 1996).
108. On Algeria, see Hugh Roberts, *The Battlefield: Algeria 1988–2002* (London: Verso, 2003).
109. See Jamāl al-Sharqāwī, "al-Ishkāliyāt al-thalāth allatī hakamat al-'alāqah bayna al-shuyū'iyyīn wa thawrat yūlio." *Qaḍāyah Fikriyyah*, volumes 11 and 12, 1992, 297–302, and Fouad Mursi, "Ḥawla ḥall al-ḥizb al-shuyū'ī al-miṣrī." *Qaḍāyah Fikriyyah*, volumes 11 and 12, 1992, 309–22.
110. Ghālī Shukrī, *Mudhakarāt thaqāfah tahtadir* (Cairo: al-Hay'ah al-Miṣriyyah al-'Āmmal lil Kitāb, 1995), 374.
111. Abu Sayf Yussef, "al-Liberaliyyah fi nadhar al-mārkisiyyah." *Al-Ṭalī'ah*, volume 8(8), August 1972, 12.
112. Muḥammad 'Imārah, "Mawqi' al-fikr al-Islāmi al-hadīth min al-itijāh al-liberalī." *Al-Ṭalī'ah*, volume 8(8), August 1972, 25–35.
113. See Salāh 'Īsa, *Muthaqaffūn wa 'askar* (Cairo: Madbūlī, 1986).
114. See Kamāl 'Abdel Latīf, *Qira'āt fi'l falsafah al-'arabiyyah al-mu'āsirah* (Beirut: Dār al-Talī'ah, 1994).
115. A. H. Abu-Sulayman, *Crisis in the Muslim Mind* (Herndon: International Institute of Islamic Thought, 1995).
116. A. Laroui, *The Crisis of the Arab Intelligentsia: Traditionalism or Historicism?* (Berkeley: University of California Press, 1967).
117. Maḥmūd Amīn al-'Ālim, "al-Hashāshah al-nadhariyyah fi'l fikr al-'arabī al-mu'āasir," in Maḥmūd Amīn al-'Ālim, ed., *al-Fikr al-'arabī 'ala mashārif al-qarn al-hādī wa'l 'ishrīn* (Cairo: Qadāyah Fikriyyah, 1995), 9–18.
118. Ḥassan Ḥanafī, "al-Fikr al-'arabī al-mu'āsir," in al-'Ālim, *al-Fikr al-'arabī 'ala mashārif*, 202.

3 SECULARISM AND ITS HAZARDS: THE RECENT DEBATE IN THE ARAB WORLD

1. N. Gallagher, "Islam v. Secularism in Cairo: An Account of the Dar Hikma Debate." *Middle East Studies*, volume 25(2), April 1989. See also the summary given by Yūsuf al-Qaraḍāwī, *al-Islām wa'l 'ilmāniyyah wajhan li wajh: rad 'ilmī 'ala Fu'ād Zakariyya wa jama'āt al-'ilmaniyyīn* (Cairo: Dār al-Ṣaḥwah, 1978).
2. A recent controversy arose in Egypt and the Arab world over an old novel written by the Syrian Haydar Haydar. See Sabry Hafez, "The Novel, Politics and Islam: Haydar Haydar's Banquest for Seaweed." *New Left Review*, number 5, September–October 2000, 117–41.
3. See Naṣr Ḥāmid Abū Zayd, *al-Tafkīr fī zaman al-takfīr* (Cairo: Dār Sīna, 1995). For a comprehensive overview of the Abū Zayd question refer to 'Abdul Ṣabūr Shāhīn, *Qissat Abū Zayd wa inḥisār al-'ilmaniyyah fī jāmi'at al-qāhirah* (Cairo: Dār al-I'tisām, n.d.), and Fauzi M. Najjar, "Islamic Fundamentalism and the Intellectuals: The Case of Nasr Hamid Abu Zayd." *British Journal of Middle Eastern Studies*, volume 27(2), 2000, 177–200.
4. Shaden Shehab, "Philosopher Faces Apostasy Charge." *Al-Ahram Weekly*, May 8–14, 1997, 7.
5. Fahmī Huwaydī, '"An al-'ilmāniyyah wa tajaliyatihah," in his *al-Maqālāt al-maḥdhūrah* (Cairo: Dār al-Shurūq, 1998), 239.
6. Murād Wahbah, "al-'Aql al-'arabī wa'l 'ilmāniyyah," in Maḥmūd Amīn al-'Ālim, ed., *al-Fikr al-'Arabī 'ala mashārif al-qarn al-ḥādī wa'l 'ishrīn* (Cairo: Qaḍāyah Fikriyyah, 1995), 216.
7. See Midḥat Basyūnī, *al-Ḥaqīqha al-ghāi'bah bayna Khālid Muḥammad Khālid wa Muḥammad al-Ghazālī* (Cairo: n.p., 1997). For a general treatment of secularism in early twentieth century Arab thought, see Kamāl 'Abd al-Laṭīf, *Salāma Mūsa wa ishkāliyat al-nahḍah* (Casablanca: al-Markaz al-Thaqāfī al-'Arabī, 1982).
8. See Ghālī Shukrī, *al-Nahḍah wa'l ṣuqūt fī'l fikr al-miṣrī al-ḥadīth* (Beirut: Dār al-Ṭalī'ah, 1982). For a general discussion of Arab secularism in the first half of the twentieth century, consult Albert Hourani's classic, *Arabic Thought in the Liberal Age, 1798–1939* (Cambridge: Cambridge University Press, 1970) and Hishām Sharābī, *Arab Intellectuals and the West: The Formative Years, 1875–1914* (Baltimore: Johns Hopkins University Press, 1970), especially 70–6. Sharābī discusses what he terms "Christian Arab intellectuals" and "Muslim secularists" who exhibited an open attitude towards modernism which he defines as "a positive attitude toward innovation and change and toward Western civilization generally." *Ibid.*, 6.
9. In his path-breaking study on the Enlightenment, Peter Gay maintains that secularism means taking the risk of discovery, exercising the right of unfettered criticism, and accepting the loneliness of autonomy, "The men of the Enlightenment united on a vastly ambitious program, a program of secularism, humanity, cosmopolitanism, and freedom, above all, freedom in its many forms – freedom from arbitrary power, freedom of speech, freedom of trade, freedom to realize one's talents, freedom of aesthetic response, freedom, in a word, of moral man to make his own way in the world." Peter Gay, *The Enlightenment: An Interpretation* (London: Weidenfeld & Nicolson, 1966), 3. At the end of the book he argues that, "Secularization is a word easy to use and therefore easy to misuse. To speak of the secularization of life in the eighteenth century is not to speak of the collapse of clerical establishments or the decay of religious concerns. The age of Enlightenment…was still a religious age." *Ibid.*, 338.
10. Jacques Berque, "Laïcité ou islamisme: Refuser la tentation de l'insularité." *Le Monde Diplomatique*, March 1991, 13. Sharābī assumes wrongly that the Enlightenment influenced "Arab Christian intellectuals only." See Sharābī, *Arab Intellectuals and the West*, 66.
11. Fazlur Rahman, "Islamic Modernism: Its Scope, Method and Alternatives." *International Journal of Middle East Studies*, volume 1, 1970, 331.
12. British philosopher Ernest Gellner does not buy the argument of the "secularization of Islam," "To say that secularization prevails in Islam is contentious. It is simply false. Islam is as strong now as it was a century ago. In some ways, it is probably stronger." Ernest Gellner, *Postmodernism, Reason and Religion* (London: Routledge, 1992), 5.
13. Abdul Hamid Abu-Sulayman, *Crisis in the Muslim Mind* (Herndon: International Institute of Islamic Thought, 1993).

14. For more elaboration on this, see Ira Lapidus, "The Separation of State and Religion in the Development of Early Islamic Society." *International Journal of Middle Eastern Studies*, volume 6(4), 1975, 363–85.
15. In deconstructing Israeli society, Baruch Kimmerling argues that, "Secularism as a loosely defined ideology and way of life, however, is still regarded as the prerogative of elite groups and is a class phenomenon. It is linked with the highly educated, affluent Ashkenazi middle and upper middle classes." Baruch Kimmerling, *The Invention and Decline of Israeliness: State, Society, and the Military* (Berkeley: University of California Press, 2001), 11. Along similar lines, one can argue that secularism in the Arab world is a class phenomenon as well.
16. See Mohammed Arkoun, *Pour une critique de la raison islamique* (Paris: Editions Maisonneuve et Larose, 1984).
17. Muḥammad Iqbal argues that, "In Islam the spiritual and the temporal are not two distinct domains." Muḥammad Iqbal, *The Reconstruction of Religious Thought in Islam* (Lahore: Sh. Muḥammad Ashraf, 1988), 154. Also, Fazlur Rahman argues that "secularism destroys the sanctity and universality (transcendence) of all moral values – a phenomenon whose effects have just begun to make themselves felt, most palpably in Western societies. Secularism is necessarily atheistic." Fazlur Rahman, *Islam and Modernity: Transformation of an Intellectual Tradition* (Chicago: University of Chicago Press, 1982), 15. For a similar argument, see Syed Muḥammad N. Al-Attas, *Islam and Secularism* (Kuala Lumpur: International Institute of Islamic Thought and Civilization, 1993).
18. See Paul Valadier, "Intolérance et laïcité: la religion dans le débat démocratique." *Le Monde Diplomatique*, June 1989, 3.
19. François Burgat, *L'islamisme en face* (Paris: La Découverte, 1995).
20. See Khurshid Ahmad, "Islam and Democracy: Some Conceptual and Contemporary Dimensions." *The Muslim World*, volume 90(1 and 2), Spring 2000, 1–21.
21. See Sādiq Jalāl al-'Azm, "Sur l'islam, la laïcité et l'Occident." *Le Monde Diplomatique*, September 1999, 16–17.
22. One of the most concise discussions of the intellectual history of secularism in modern Western thought is carried out by the Indian thinker T. N. Madan. See T. N. Madan, *Secularism and Fundamentalism in India: Modern Myths, Locked Minds* (New Delhi: Oxford University Press, 1998), especially chapter 1.
23. See Charles Taylor, "Modes of Secularism," in Rajeev Bhargava, ed., *Secularism and its Critics* (New Delhi: Oxford University Press, 1998), 31, and Kamāl 'Abd al-Laṭīf, *Mafāhīm multabasah fi'l fikr al-'arabī al-mu'āṣir* (Beirut: Dār al-Ṭalī'ah, 1992), 38.
24. Such thinkers as Charfi, Ben Achour, and Filali-Ansari think that the theological imperative is the measure. See Abdou Filali-Ansari, "Islam and Secularism," in Gema Martin Munoz, ed., *Islam, Modernism, and the West* (London: I. B. Tauris, 1999), 125–35; Yadh Ben Achour, "Islam et laïcité: propos sur la recomposition d'un système de normativité." *Pouvoir*, 62, 1992: 15–31, and Abdelmajid Charfi, "La sécularisation dans les sociétés arabo-musulmanes modernes." *Islamochristiana*, volume 8 (1982). See also Bernard Lewis, *The Political Language of Islam* (Chicago: University of Chicago Press, 1988).
25. See Munīr Shafīq, *Fī al-hadāthah wa'l khiṭāb al-ḥadāthī* (Casablanca: al-Markaz al-Thaqāfī al-'Arabī, 1999).
26. Dussel states that the beginning of modernity coincides with the discovery of the New World and that Columbus was the first modern man. See Enrique Dussel, *The Invention of the Americas: Eclipse of the "Other" and the Myth of Modernity* (New York: Continuum, 1995).
27. On the meaning of "Islamic modernism" in the Muslim world in general, consult Rahman, "Islamic Modernism," 317–33. Also see W. C. Smith, *Islam in Modern History* (New York: New American Library, 1957).
28. This is the gist of Ṭāhā Ḥussain's book, *The Future of Culture in Egypt*, trans. S. Glazer (New York: Octagon Books, 1975).
29. Kamāl 'Abd al-Laṭīf, *Mafāhīm multabasah fi'l fikr al-'arabī al-mu'āṣir* (Beirut: Dār al-Ṭalī'ah, 1992), 41.
30. Salāma Mūsa, *The Education of Salāma Mūsa*, trans. L. O. Schuman (Leiden: Brill, 1961), 38–40 and 126–7. In his autobiography, Mūsa discusses a trip he took to Morocco when he was young.

He says, "Then I went to Tanger, the town of Ibn Battuta. I spent some twenty days there, during which I strengthened in my conviction that the East was corrupt, and that the pattern of culture by which it lived and which it had sought to make the basis of its society must be changed. The Moroccan government was selling hashish to its subjects; having a monopoly of this trade, it made a nice profit indeed at the expense of the people's health." *Ibid.*, 62.

31. 'Abd al-Karīm al-Khaṭṭābī, the hero of the Rif war against the French (1921–26) says, "I admired the political course followed by Turkey...The Islamic countries cannot achieve independence unless they free themselves from religious fanaticism and follow the path of the European peoples." Quoted by Mohamed El Mansour, "Salafis and Modernists in the Moroccan Nationalist Movement," in John Ruedy, ed., *Islamism and Secularism in North Africa* (New York: St. Martin's Press, 1996), 59. For a similar argument, see the memoirs of the Syrian nationalist leader Akram al-Ḥawrānī in *Mudhakarrāt Akram al-Ḥawrānī*, 4 volumes (Cairo: Madbūlī, 1999).
32. The same can be said about the transfer of nationalism in the nineteenth century to the Third World. According to Partha Chatterjee, the relationship between nationalist discourse in India and the forms of modern Western thought was not simply a relationship of correspondence, even of derivation. Nationalist thought had to be selective in its borrowing from the Western forms of knowledge. See Partha Chatterjee, *Nationalist Thought and the Colonial World: A Derivative Discourse?* in *The Partha Chatterjee Omnibus* (New Delhi: Oxford University Press, 1999), 41.
33. Berman defines modernity as a way of life that started in the West at the beginning of the sixteenth century and whose aim has been to transcend the intellectual and material roots of "traditional modes of life and thought'." Marshal Berman, *All That Is Solid Melts Into Air: The Experience of Modernity* (New York: Penguin Books, 1982).
34. See Jean-François Lyotard, *The Post-Modern Condition: A Report on Knowledge* (Minneapolis: University of Minnesota Press, 1991).
35. For example, the influential Islamic scholar Yūsuf al-Qaraḍāwī argues in simplistic terms that secularism is anti-Islamic. He argues, "For this reason, the call for secularism among Muslims is atheism and a rejection of Islam. Its acceptance as a basis for rule in place of Sharī'ah is downright *riddah*. The silence of the masses in the Muslim world about this deviation has been a major transgression and a clear-cut instance of disobedience which have produced a sense of guilt, remorse, and inward resentment, all of which have generated discontent, insecurity, and hatred among committed Muslims because such deviation lacks legality. Secularism is compatible with the Western concept of God which maintains that after God had created the world, He left it to look after itself. In this sense, God's relationship with the world is like that of a watchmaker with a watch: he makes it then leaves it to function without any need for him. This concept is inherited from Greek philosophy, especially that of Aristotle who argued that God neither controls nor knows anything about this world." See <www.islaam.com/challenges/secular_moral_values.htm>. See also Yūsuf al-Qaraḍāwī, *al-Islām wa'l 'ilmāniyyah wajhan li wajh* (Cairo: Dār al-Ṣaḥwah, 1987).
36. This is still the view of a small number of secular intellectuals in the Muslim world. For example, contemporary Iranian intellectual Abdul Karim Soroush argues that, "Secularism is nothing more than behaving, looking and thinking in a scientific way...It has nothing to do with hostility to religion." Robin Wright, *The Last Great Revolution: Turmoil and Transformation in Iran* (New York: Alfred A. Knopf, 2000), 55.
37. John Gray, a leading British thinker, argues that few people in the West have questioned the association between the Enlightenment project and imperialism. In addition, this project contains the seeds of rational individualism that has characterized the recent process of neoliberal globalization. He says that "The Enlightenment project...is not only, or even mainly, a project of philosophers, but also, and chiefly, the project of modern liberal individualistic society." John Gray, *Enlightenment's Wake: Politics and Culture at the End of the Modern Age* (London: Routledge, 1995), 150.
38. Peter Amato, "African Philosophy and Modernity," in Emmanuel C. Eze, ed., *Postcolonial African Philosophy: A Critical Reader* (Oxford: Blackwell, 1997), 75.
39. Fu'ād Zakariyya, "al-'Ilmāniyyah darūrah hadāriyyah." *Qaḍāyah Fikriyyah* (1989), 274. See also his book, *Khiṭāb ila al-'aql al-'arabī* (Kuwait: Kitāb al-'Arabī, 1987). See also Fu'ād Zakariyya, *Laïcité ou islamisme. Les Arabes à l'heure du choix* (Paris: La Découverte, 1991).

40. Salāma Mūsa (1888–1958) says that "I cannot imagine the renaissance of a contemporary oriental nation without being based on the European standards of freedom, equality, and order, combined with a scientific outlook towards the universe." Mūsa, *Mā hiya al-nahḍah?* (Cairo: Mu'assassat Salāma Mūsa n.d.), 116. He also says, "Both education and experience have convinced me that in order to secure progress, we must leave Asia and join Europe. The more I know the East, the more I become averse to it, and the more I know Europe, the more I become enchanted with it." Mūsa, *al-Yawm al-ghad* (Cairo: Dār al-Mustaqbal, 1928), 67. Some major studies have appeared in Arabic on Mūsa. The main one remains, Kamāl 'Abd al-Laṭīf, *Salāma Mūsa wa ishkāliyat al-nahḍah* (Beirut: Dār al-Farābī, 1982). See also Ghālī Shukrī, *Salāma Mūsa wa azmat al-ḍamīr al-'arabī* (Beirut: Dār al-Āfāq al-Jadīdah, 1983); Maḥmūd al-Sharqāwī, *Salāma Mūsa: al-mufakir wa'l insān* (Cairo: Dār al-Hilāl, 1968); Anwar 'Abd al-Malik, *Dirāsāt fī'l thaqāfah al-waṭaniyyah* (Beirut: Dār al-Ṭalī'ah, 1967), and Aḥmad Māḍī, "Salāma Mūsa wa'l falsafah," in Markaz Dirāsāt al-Wiḥdah al-'Arabīyyah, *al-Falsafah al-'arabīyyah al-mu'āsirah* (Beirut: Markaz Dirāsāt al-Wiḥdah al-'Arabīyyah, 1988), 333–66. See also *The Education of Salāma Mūsa* (Leiden: Brill, 1961).
41. Iranian philosopher Abdolkarim Soroush traces secularism to ancient Greek thought, "The gateways leading to secularism and separating God and his designs from the world and its explanation were thrown open once the philosophers (primarily the Greek ones) embarked on the project of philosophizing the world order and subsuming it under nonreligious metaphysical categories." Abdolkarim Soroush, "The Sense and Essence of Secularism," in Mahmoud Sadri and Ahmad Sadri, eds., *Reason, Freedom, and Democracy in Islam: Essential Writings of Abdolkarim Soroush* (New York: Oxford University Press, 2000), 65.
42. "The secularization thesis implies the privatization of religion, its continuing operation in the public domain becomes confined to a lingering rhetorical invocation in support of conventional morality and human decency and dignity – as a cry of despair in the face of moral panic." Bryan Wilson, "Secularization: The Inherited Model," in Philip E. Hammond, ed., *The Sacred in a Secular Age* (Berkeley: University of California Press, 1985), 19.
43. Harvey Cox rightly observes that, "The forces of secularization have no serious interest in persecuting religion. Secularization simply bypasses and undercuts religion and goes on to other things." Harvey Cox, *The Secular City: Secularization and Urbanization in Theological Perspective* (New York: Macmillan Co., 1966), 2. Madan argues that, "No serious scholar anywhere believes any longer that Enlightenment philosophers, particularly the English and the Germans, rejected religion completely. They rather sought to bind it with the limits of reason alone." Madan, *Secularism and Fundamentalism in India*, 11.
44. Peter Berger, *The Social Reality of Religion* (London: Faber & Faber, 1973), 106.
45. See Huston Smith, *Beyond the Post-Modern Mind* (Wheaton: Theosophical Publication House, 1989).
46. See Gay, *The Enlightenment*, chapter 4.
47. Berger, *The Social Reality of Religion*, 107.
48. Christian Duquoc, *Ambiguïté des théologies de la sécularisation* (Paris: Duculot, 1972), 14.
49. "The rise of urban civilization and the collapse of traditional religion are the two main hallmarks of our era and are closely related movements. Urbanization constitutes a massive change in the way men live together, and became possible in its contemporary form only with the scientific and technological advances which sprang from the wreckage of traditional world views. Secularization, an equally epochal movement, marks a change in the way men grasp and understand their life together, and it occured only when the cosmopolitan confrontations of city living exposed the relativity of the myths men once thought were unquestionable." Cox, *The Secular City*, 1.
50. *Ibid.*, 17.
51. George W. Foote, *Secularism Restated with a Review of the Several Expositions* (London: W. J. Ramsey, 1874), 6.
52. *Ibid.*, 9. Foote proceeds to say that, "With the doctrine of a future life Secularism has no concern, except so far as that doctrine, or, rather, certain forms of it, interfere with the utilitarian character of its ethics. The mere naked belief in immortality may be entertained by a Secularist without any detraction from essential Secularism; but the very moment that belief interferes with the principles of Secularism, the very moment other-worldly considerations are permitted to influence conduct, that very moment the doctrine of a future life becomes pernicious." *Ibid.*

53. George J. Holyoake, *The Principles of Secularism* (London: Austin & Co., 1870), 11.
54. *Ibid.*, p. 27. For more details, see David Spadafora, "Secularization in British Thought, 1730–89: Some Landmarks," in W. Warren Wagar, ed., *The Secular Mind: Transformations of Faith in Modern Europe* (New York: Holmes & Meier, 1982), 35–56.
55. Franklin Baumer, *Religion and the Rise of Scepticism* (New York: Harcourt, Brace, 1960), 3.
56. Owen Chadwick, *The Secularization of the European Mind in the Nineteenth Century* (Cambridge: Cambridge University Press, 1975), 156.
57. Gay, *The Enlightenment*, 37.
58. Immanuel Kant, "What is Enlightenment?," in *Kant: Political Writings*, ed. Hans Reiss (Cambridge: Cambridge University Press, 1991), 54. Secularization is the deliverance of man "first from religious and then from metaphysical control over his reason and his language." C. A. Van Peursen, a Dutch theologian, quoted by Cox in *The Secular City*, 1.
59. Taylor, "Modes of Secularism," 35.
60. Michal J. Sandal, "Religious Liberty: Freedom of Choice or Freedom of Conscience," in Bhargava, *Secularism and its Critics*, 74.
61. Partha Chatterjee, "Secularism and Tolerance," in Bhargava, *Secularism and its Critics*, 358.
62. D. E. Smith, "India as a Secular State," in Bhargava, *Secularism and its Critics*, 178.
63. Peter Berger, *The Social Reality of Religion* (London: Allen Lane, 1973), 113. See also, H. H. Gerth and C. W. Mills, eds., *From Max Weber: Essays in Sociology* (Routledge & Kegan Paul, 1948), 155.
64. Secularism describes an undeniable process in Western societies, "the regression of belief in God, and even more, the decline in the practice of religion, to the point where from being central to the whole life of Western societies, public and private, this has become sub-cultural, one of many private forms of involvement which some people indulge in." Charles Taylor, *Sources of the Self: The Making of the Modern Identity* (Cambridge, MA: Harvard University Press, 1989), 309.
65. T. N. Madan, "Secularism in its Place," in Bhargava, *Secularism and its Critics*, 307.
66. Samir Amin, *Eurocentrism* (New York: Monthly Review Press, 1989).
67. Madan, "Secularism and its Place."
68. On secularism in Turkey, see Niyazi Berkes, *The Development of Secularism in Turkey*, second edition (London: Hurst & Co., 1998) and in China see Immanuel Hsu, *The Rise of Modern China* (London: Oxford University Press, 2000).
69. Eric Wolf, *Europe and the People Without History* (Berkeley: University of California Press, 1982); K. M. Panikkar, *Asia and Western Dominance* (New Delhi: Somaiya Publications, 1999); and Karl Polyani, *The Great Transformation: Political and Economic Origins of Our Time* (Boston: Beacon Press, 1957).
70. Anderson summarizes Western expansion into the Third World in the following manner, "The Portuguese and Spaniards arrived in the late feudal sixteenth century, the Dutch in the mercantilist seventeenth, the British in the Enlightened eighteenth, the French in the industrial nineteenth, and the Americans in the motorized twentieth." Benedict Anderson, *The Spectre of Comparisons: Nationalism, South East Asia and the World* (London: Verso, 1998), 5.
71. Any cursory reading of the life of eminent British traveler Richard Burton in the nineteenth century will reveal his insatiable search for new resources and riches for the British Empire. See the following: Mary S. Lovell, *A Rage to Live: A Biography of Richard and Isabelle Burton* (London: Abacus, 1998), and Edward Rice, *Captain Sir Richard Francis Burton* (New York: Harper Perennial, 1990).
72. "The Renaissance is not only the moment of the break with tributary ideology. It is also the point of departure for the conquest of the world by capitalist Europe." Amin, *Eurocentrism*, 72.
73. Berger, *The Reality of Religion*, and H. Gerth and C. W. Mills, eds., *From Max Weber: Essays in Sociology* (London: Routledge & Kegan Paul, 1948).
74. Amin, *Eurocentrism*, 85.
75. In an interesting analysis on the state of education in British India, Viswanathan argues that the British exhibited two different attitudes toward the education of the natives in India, secular and missionary. Both fought to control the Indian soul. She says that in their struggle to spread the Bible in India, "The missionaries got...support from an unexpected quarter. The military offices who testified in the parlimentary sessions on Indian education joined hands with them in arguing that a secular education in English would increase the Indians' capacity for evil because it would

elevate their intellects without providing the moral principles to keep them in check." Gauri Viswanathan, *Masks of Conquest: Literary Study and British Rule in India* (New York: Columbia University Press, 1989), 75. For similar arguments, see Benita Parry, *Delusions and Discoveries: India in British Imagination, 1880–1930* (London: Verso, 1998).

76. Madan, "Secularism in its Place," 308.
77. Edward Said, *Orientalism* (New York: Vintage Books, 1978).
78. Peter Gran, *Islamic Roots of Capitalism* (Austin: University of Texas Press, 1979).
79. Panikkar, *Asia and Western Dominance*. Pannikar makes a distinction between two broad phases of European hegemony in Asia. In the early phase, the main objective of Europeans had been to "get round the overwhelming land power of Islam in the Middle East, supplemented by an urge to break through the 'prison of the Mediterranean' to which European energies were confined. By the nineteenth century, Europe, with its social, economic and political structure, reorganized by the tremendous industrial and revolutionary upheavals of the end of the eighteenth century, represented indeed a civilization on the march. It challenged the basis of Asian societies; it imposed its will on them and brought about social and political changes in Asia which are of fundamental importance." *Ibid.*, 17.
80. Samir Amin, *Unequal Development: An Essay on the Social Formations of Peripheral Capitalism* (New York: Monthly Review Press, 1976), 47.
81. 'Abd al-Wahāb al-Masīrī, "al-Ru'yah al-ma'rifiyyah al-imberialiyyah." *Qira'āt Siyāsiyyah*, volume 2(4), 1992, 137–59, and "The Imperialist Epistemological Vision." *American Journal of the Islamic Social Sciences*, volume 11(3), Fall 1994, 403–15.
82. For a thorough analysis of this, consult Ghālī Shukrī, *al-Nahḥah wa'l suqūt fi'l fikr al-miṣrī al-ḥadīth* (Beirut: Dār al-Ṭalī'ah, 1982). See also Tamara Sonn, "Secularism and National Stability in Islam." *Arab Studies Quarterly*, volume 9(3), Summer 1987, 284–305. Sonn persuasively argues that the early Muslim modernizers of the nineteenth century utilized central legal Islamic concepts, such as "*maṣlaḥah*," in order to achieve reform. *Ibid*., 287.
83. See Ibrahim Abu-Rabi', "The Concept of the 'Other' in Modern Arab Thought: From Muḥammad 'Abduh to Abdallah Laroui." *Islam and Christian-Muslim Relations*, volume 8(1), 1977, 85–97.
84. See the discussion of 'Abd al-Rāziq's ideas in Chapter 8 of this work.
85. See Muḥammad J. al-Anṣārī, *Taḥawwulāt al-fikr wa'l siyāsah fi'l sharq al-'arabī: 1930–1970* (Kuwait: 'Ālam al-Ma'rifah, 1980), 81–107.
86. Nandy, *ibid.*, 334.
87. Rahman defines secularism as follows: "Secularism in Islam, properly speaking, is the acceptance of laws and other social and political institutions without reference to Islam, i.e., without their being derived from, or originally linked with, the principles of the Qur'ān and the Sunna." Rahman, "Islamic Modernism," 331.
88. 'Azīz al-'Azmeh, *al-'Ilmāniyyah min mandhūr mukhtalif* (Beirut: Markaz Dirāsāt al-Wiḥdah al-'Arabīyyah, 1992), 10.
89. See Şerif Mardin, *The Genesis of Young Ottoman Thought: A Study in the Modernization of Turkish Political Ideas* (Princeton: Princeton University Press, 1962), and Niyazi Berkes, *The Development of Secularism in Turkey* (Montreal: McGill University Press, 1964).
90. Ahmad 'Izzat 'Abd al-Karīm, *Ṭārīkh al-ta'līm fī miṣr min nihāyat ḥukm Muḥammad 'Alī ila awā'il ḥukm Tawfiq*, 1848–82 (Cairo: Wazārat al-Ma'ārif al-Ḥukūmiyyah, 1945).
91. Ali Merad, *Le réformisme musulman en Algérie de 1925 à 1940: essai d'histoire religieuse et sociale* (Paris: Mouton, 1967); Arnold Green, *The Tunisian Ulama, 1873–1915: Social Structure and Response to Ideological Currents* (Leiden: Brill, 1978).
92. The same happened in India in the nineteenth century. Partha Chatterjee argues that, "As the institutions of the modern state were elaborated in the colony, especially in the second half of the nineteenth century, the ruling European groups found it necessary to lay down – in law-making, in the bureaucracy, in the administration of justice, and in the recognition by the state of a legitimate domain of public opinion – the precise difference between the ruler and the ruled." Partha Chatterjee, *The Nation and its Fragments: Colonial and Postcolonial Histories*, in *The Partha Chatterjee Omnibus*, 10.
93. See Albert Hourani, "Ottoman Reform and the Politics of Notables," in Albert Hourani, Philip S. Khoury, and Mary C. Wilson, eds., *The Modern Middle East: A Reader* (Berkeley: University of California Press, 1993), 83–110.

94. 'Azmeh, "al-'Ilmāniyyah min mandhūr mukhtalif," 194.
95. *Ibid.*, 268.
96. See Mohammed Arkoun, "The Adequacy of Contemporary Islam to the Political, Social, and Economic Development of Northern Africa." *Arab Studies Quarterly*, volume 5(1 and 2), Spring 1982, 34–53.
97. See Costantine Zurayk, *al-Mu'lafāt al-kāmilah li'l doktor Costantine Zurayk*, 4 volumes (Beirut: Markaz Dirāsāt al-Wiḥdah al-'Arabīyyah, 1995).
98. See Adonis, "Reflections on the Manifestations of Intellectual Backwardness in Arab Society." In *CEMAM Reports* (Beirut: St. Joseph's University Press, 1974), and *al-Thābit wa'l mutaḥawwil*, 3 volumes (Beirut: Dār al-'Awdah, 1983).
99. See mainly Ghālī Shukrī, *al-Nahḍah wa'l suqūt fī'l fikr al-miṣrī al-ḥadīth* (Beirut: Dār al-Ṭalī'ah, 1982), and *Mudhakarāt thaqāfah taḥtaḍir* (Cairo: al-Hay'ah al-Miṣriyyah al-'Āmmah, 1995).
100. Abdallah Laroui, *L'idéologie arabe contemporaine* (Paris: Maspero, 1970), and *The Crisis of the Arab Intelligentsia: Traditionalism or Historicism?* (Berkeley: University of California Press, 1976).
101. Al-'Afīf al-Akhḍar, "Min naqd al-samā' ila naqd al-arḍ," in F. Lenin, *Nuṣūṣ ḥawla al-mawqif mina al-dīn*, trans Muḥammad al-Kabbe (Beirut: Dār al-Ṭalī'ah, 1972).
102. Ṣādiq Jalāl al-'Azm, *Naqd al-fikr al-dīnī* (Beirut: Dār al-Ṭalī'ah, 1969); *al-Naqd al-dhātī ba'da al-hazīmah* (Beirut: Dār al-Ṭalī'ah, 1969), and "Sur l'islam, la laïcité et l'Occident," 16–17.
103. Ṭayyib Tizīnī, "Naḥwa 'ilmāniyyah takūn madkhalan li mashrū' 'arabī nahḍawī jadīd." *Al-Ṭarīq*, volume 55(6), 1996, 4–6.
104. Halim Barakat, *The Arab World: Society, Culture, and Change* (Berkeley: University of California Press, 1993).
105. Zakī Najīb Maḥmūd, *Tajdīd al-fikr al-'arabī* (Cairo: Dār al-Shurūq, 1978).
106. Jābir 'Aṣfūr, *Hawāmish 'ala daftar al-tanwīr* (Cairo: Dār Su'ād al-Ṣabāḥ, 1994). 'Asfūr argues, along the famous lines of Hishām Sharābī, that patriarchal thought and structure permeate contemporary Arab societies. Neo-patriarchy in Arab society has marshalled both physical and mental powers to safeguard its interests. The result has been a new type of irrationalism, which is supported by unlimited amounts of funds and the official mass media. See *ibid.*, 13.
107. Zakariyya, "al-'Ilmāniyyah darūrah ḥadāriyyah."
108. Quoted by Ghālī Shukrī in *Diktātoriyat al-takhalluf al-'arabī* (Cairo: al-Hay'ah al-Miṣriyyah al-'Āmmah li'l Kitāb, 1994), 43.
109. See the moving account of the recent civil war in Algeria in Nūrī al-Jarrāḥ, *al-firdaws al-dāmī: wāhid wa thalathīn yawman fī'l jazā'ir* [*The Bleeding Paradise: 31 Days in Algeria*] (London: Riad El-Rayyes Books, 2000).
110. François Burgat, ed., *L'Islamisme au Maghreb: La Voix du sud* (Paris: Karthala, 1988).
111. See the writings of al-'Azm, Adonis, Abdallah Laroui, and al-Hāfiz.
112. See Ghālī Shukrī, "Miṣr: firdaws khayru al-umam." *Qaḍayah Fikriyyah*, volumes 13–14, 199 and Yusra Muṣṭafa, "Azmat al-muthaqaf al-'aqlānī," in Maḥmūd Amīn al-'Ālim, *Qaḍayah Fikriyyah, al-Fikr al-'Arabī 'ala mashārif al-qarn al-wāḥid wa'l 'ishrūn* (Cairo: Dār Qaḍayah Fikriyyah, 1995), 219–28.
113. See Ṭāriq al-Bishrī, *al-Ḥiwār al-islāmī al-'ilmānī* (Cairo: Dār al-Shurūq, 1996).
114. Muḥammad 'Imārah, *al-Dawlah al-islāmiyyah bayna al-'ilmāniyyah wa'l sulṭah al-madaniyyah* (Cairo: Dār al-Shurūq, 1988).
115. In his preface to his major book on public freedoms in Islam, al-Ghannūshī says, "I present this book to the city Damascus that witnessed my second birth with the help of the unknown soldier, the pharmacist Muḥammad Amīn al-Mujtahid." Rāshid al-Ghannūshī, *al-Ḥuriyyāt al-'āmmah fī'l dawlah al-islāmiyya*h (Markaz Dirāsāt al-Wiḥdah al-'Arabīyyah, 1993), 5.
116. See Munīr Shafīq, *Fī al-ḥadāthah wa'l khiṭāb al-ḥadāthīi* (Casablanca: al-Markaz al-Thaqāfī al-'Arabī, 1999).
117. al-Ghannūshī, *al-Ḥuriyyāt al-'āmmah*, 310.
118. See Ibrahim M. Abu-Rabi', *Intellectual Origins of Islamic Resurgence in the Modern Arab World* (Albany: State University of New York Press, 1996).
119. Zakariyya, "al-'Ilmāniyyah darūrah hadāriyyah."

120. Shukrī, *Diktātoriat al-takhalluf*, 114.
121. See Nazih Ayubi, *Political Islam* (London: Routledge, 1994).
122. Fahmī Huwaydī, *al-Maqālāt al-maḥdhūrah* (Cairo: Dār al-Shurūq, 1998), 17.
123. According to Edward Said, Islamist discourse has a mass following in the Arab world, "Countries like Egypt and Tunisia, which have long been ruled since independence by secular nationalist parties that have now degenerated into coteries and cliques, are suddenly rent by Islamic groups whose mandate, they say with considerable justice, is granted them by the oppressed, the urban poor, the landless peasants of the countryside, all those with no hope except a restored or reconstructed Islamic past. Many people are willing to fight to the death for these ideas." Edward Said, *Representations of the Intellectual* (New York: Vintage Books, 1994), 39.
124. Muḥammad ʻĀbid al-Jābirī, "al-Mujtamaʻ al-madanī: tasā'ulāt wa āfāq," in Abdallah Ḥammūdī, *Wa'y al-mujtama' bī dhātihī: 'an al-mujtama' al-madanī fi'l maghrib al-'arabī* (Casablanca: Dār Ṭobqāl, 1998), 43.
125. ʻAlī al-Kenz, "al-Islām wa'l hawiyyah: mulāḥadhāt li'l baḥth," in Markaz Dirāsāt al-Wiḥdah al-ʻArabīyyah, *al-Dīn fi'l mujtama' al-'arabī* (Beirut: Markaz Dirāsāt al-Wiḥdah al-ʻArabīyyah, 1990), 105.
126. See Ramzī Zakī, *Waḍā'an li'l ṭabaqah al-mutawaṣitah* (Cairo: Dār al-Mustaqbal al-ʻArabī, 1998).
127. Harold J. Laski, *Liberty in the Modern State* (Harmondsworth: Penguin, 1938), 49. Laski further notes that, "Liberty always demands a limitation of political authority, and it is never attained unless the rulers of the state can, where necessary, be called to account." *Ibid.*, 50.
128. See L. Carl Brown, *Tunisia: The Politics of Modernization* (New York: Praeger, 1964).
129. ʻAbd al-Ḥamīd al-Ibrāhīmī, *al-Maghreb al-'arabī fī muftaraq al-ṭuruq fī dhil al-taḥawwulāt al-duwaliyyah* (Beirut: Markaz Dirāsāt al-Wiḥdah al-ʻArabīyyah, 1996), 112–13.
130. Abdelwahab Bouhdiba, "Place et fonction de l'imaginaire dans la société arabo-musulmane." In *Culture et société* (Tunis: Université de Tunis, 1978), 45, and Munaṣṣif Wannās, "al-Dīn wa'l dawla fī Tūnis: 1956–1987," in Markaz Dirāsāt al-Wiḥdah al-ʻArabīyyah, *al-Dīn fi'l mujtama' al-'arabī* (Beirut: Markaz Dirāsāt al-Wiḥdah al-ʻArabīyyah, 1990), 475.
131. On Bourguiba, see al-Ṣāfī Sa'īd, *Bourquiba: sīra shibh muḥarammah* (London: Riad El-Rayyes Books, 2000), and S. Bessis and S. Belhassen, *Bourguiba: un si long regne, 1975–1987* (Paris: Jeune Afrique Livre, 1988).
132. Ibrāhīmī, *al-Maghreb al-'Arabī*, 461. See also Abdelhamid Brahimi, *Stratégie de développement pour l'Algérie* (Paris: Economica, 1991).
133. A. Zghal, "Le retour de sacré et la nouvelle demande idéologique de jeunes scolarises: Le cas de la Tunisie." *Le Maghreb Musulman*, 1979.
134. Abdelkader Zghal, "al-Istrātijiyya al-jadīdah li harakat al-itijāh al-islāmī: munāwara an al-ta'bīr 'an al-thaqāfah al-siyāsiyyah al-tūnisiyyah," in Markaz Dirāsāt al-Wiḥdah al-ʻArabīyyah, *al-Dīn fi'l mujtama' al-'arabī* (Beirut: Markaz Dirāsāt al-Wiḥdah al-ʻArabīyyah, 1990), 341.
135. Ali El-Kenz, *Algerian Reflections on Arab Crises*, trans Robert W. Stooky (Texas: University of Texas Press, 1991), 26.
136. Faraj Fūda, *al-Nadhīr* (Cairo: al-Hay'ah al-Miṣriyyah, 1992), 28.
137. Burhān Ghalyūn, "al-Islām wa azmat al-ʻalāqāt al-ijtimāʻiyyah," in Markaz Dirāsāt al-Wiḥdah al-ʻArabīyyah, *al-Dīn fi'l mujtama' al-'Arabī* (Beirut: Markaz Dirāsāt al-Wiḥdah al-ʻArabīyyah, 1990), 310.
138. See al-ʻAẓm, *Naqd al-fikr al-dīnī.*
139. Samir Amin, "Etat, nation, éthique et minorité dans la crise." *Bulletin du forum du tiers-monde*, no. 6, April 1986, and Ghalyūn, "al-Islām wa azmat," 311.
140. Ayubi, *Political Islam*, 5.
141. Al-ʻAzm, "Sur l'islam," 16.

4 CONTEMPORARY ARAB PHILOSOPHICAL VIEWS OF SECULARISM

1. For a comparative study of secularism, see Nur Yalman, "On Secularism and its Critics: Notes on Turkey, India, and Iran." *Contributions to Indian Sociology*, volume 25, 1991.

2. Ernest Gellner, *Postmodernism, Reason and Religion* (London: Routledge, 1992), 5.
3. A recent Festschrift has been devoted to Fu'ād Zakariyya by his students from Kuwait University. See 'Abdallah al-'Umar, ed., *al-Duktūr Fu'ād Zakariyya Bāḥithan wā muthaqaffan wā nāqidan: kitāb tidhkārī* (Kuwait: University of Kuwait Press, 1998).
4. See Galāl Amīn, "Ḥawla mafhūm al-tanwīr: nadhrah naqdiyyah lī tayyār assāssī min tayyārāt al-thaqāfah al-'arabiyyah al-mu'ūṣirah." *Al-Mustaqbal al-'Arabī*, volume 20(7), 1997, 35–51. In an insightful article on the "secularism debate in contemporary Egypt," Fauzi Najjar mentions that the *tanwīrī* movement in Egypt is supported in the main by the Egyptian Ministry of Culture and that their books are printed by the General Egyptian Book Organization, which is a government organ. See the following by Fauzi M. Najjar, "The Debate on Islam and Secularism in Egypt." *Arab Studies Quarterly*, volume 18(2), Spring 1996, 1–22, and "Book Banning in Contemporary Egypt." *The Muslim World*, volume 91(3 and 4), Fall 2001, 399–424.
5. See al-Bukhārī Hamānī, "Makānat Zakī Najīb Maḥmūd fī'l falsafah al-'arabiyyah al-mu'āṣirah." *Al-Mustaqbal al-'Arabī*, volume 20(8), 1997, 48–55, and Ṣalāh Qunṣuwwa, "al-'Aql al-'Arabī wa'l thaqāfah al-'arabiyyah: ḥiwār ma' Zakī Najīb Maḥmūd." *Al-Mustaqbal al-'Arabī*, volume 11(8), 1988, 121–33.
6. Galāl Amīn, *al-Tanwīr al-zā'if* (Cairo: Dār al-Ma'ārif, 1999), 28.
7. This thesis is highlighted mainly by Burhān Ghalyūn in *Ightiyāl al-'aql: mihnat al-thaqāfah al-'arabiyya bayna al-salafī yya wa'l taba'iyyah* (Cairo: Madbūlī, 1990).
8. Zakariyya, *al-Ṣahwah al-islāmiyyah fī mīzān al-'aql* (Beirut: Dār al-Tanwīr, 1995), 73. Ḥassan Ḥanafī of Cairo University more or less argues the same point: "In essence, Islam is a secular religion. What this means in effect is that there is no room in Islam for an additional kind of secularism, especially the Western one." Ḥassan Ḥanafī, *al-Dīn wa'l thawrah fī miṣr*, volume 8 (Cairo: Madbūlī, 1989), 105.
9. "Nous autres musulmans avons grand besoin de quelqu'un qui nous dise, comme les philosophes de la Renaissance: 'Si vous avez devant vous la nature et les problèmes des hommes, pourquoi faut-il que toujours vous reveniez aux textes des ancèstres?' Pourquoi faites-vous de la pensée heritée une autorité inniscutable? Pourquoi ne pas affronter les situations nouvelles avec vôtre raison? Selon moi, cette incapacité du monde arabe à historiciser sa relation au passé constitue la cause première de son sous-développement intellectuel." ("We Muslims have a great need of someone who would tell us, as the philosophers of the Renaissance did, 'If you have in front of you the nature and problems of humanity, why must you always return to the ancestors' texts?' Why do you make traditional thought an infallible authority? Why not confront new situations with your own reasoning? To my mind, this inability of the Arab world to historicize its relationship to the past constitutes the main cause of its intellectual underdevelopment." Translation by Abu-Rabi') Fu'ād Zakariyya, *Laïcité ou Islamisme. Les Arabes à l'heure du choix* (Paris: La Découverte, 1989), 38. Quoted by Massimo Campanini, "Egypt," in Seyyed Hossein Nasr and Oliver Leaman, eds., *History of Islamic Philosophy*, volume 2 (London: Routledge, 1996), 1120.
10. Fu'ād Zakariyya, *al-Ḥaqīqa wa'l khayāl fī 'l ḥarakah al-islāmiyyah al-mu'āṣirah* [*Reality and Myth in the Contemporary Islamic Movement*] (Cairo: Dār Sīna, 1988). Zakariyya has this to say about secularism: "The European secular movement was not a reaction against religion but against a method of thinking. Europeans were advancing in science and industrialization. They aimed to expand and dominate the entire world. The biggest obstacle to these advances was the closed religious thinking of the church. The secularists opposed intellectual rigidity while remaining committed to their own faith." Quoted by Nancy E. Gallagher, "Islam v. Secularism in Cairo: An Account of the Dār al-Hikma Debate." *Middle Eastern Studies*, volume, 25(2), April 1989, 210.
11. Zakariyya, *al-Ḥaqīqah wa'l khayāl*, 7.
12. Fu'ād Zakariyya, *Khiṭāb ila al-'aql al-'arabī* (Cairo: Maktabat Miṣr, 1990), 21.
13. See Mohammed Arkoun, *Essais sur la pensée islamique* (Paris: Editions Maisonneuve et Larose, 1977) and *Pour une critique de la raison islamique* (Paris: Editions Maisonneuve et Larose, 1984). See also Naṣr Hāmid Abū Zayd, *Mafhūm al-naṣṣ: dirāsah fī 'ulūm al-Qur'ān* (Cairo: al-Hay'ah al-Miṣriyyah, 1990).
14. Zakariyya, *al-Ḥaqīqah wa'l khayāl*, 10.
15. *Ibid.*, 11.
16. *Ibid.*,15. In another place Zakariyya comments on extremism: "The true reason surrounding these extreme phenomena is, in my view, the political use made of Islam. The young extremists are part

of a huge bureaucracy which continues to grow and swell since the early seventies. Its aim is to exploit Islam in order to achieve political goals. Like any small part of a huge bureaucracy, it knows its aim well and marches to execute its mission relentlessly. Since these youngsters were taught that the commandments of religion bid them to lead society and since they heard from their counselors that society will not be set right unless it places itself under their tutelage, they, therefore, allow themselves to take the law into their own hands according to their law and methods...Just imagine how society could attain perfection if every individual within it has the right to be a lawgiver, judge and a policeman at one and the same time." Fu'ād Zakariyya, *Al-Ahrām*, March 1988, translated and quoted by David Sagiv, "Judge Ashmawi and Militant Islam in Egypt." *Middle Eastern Studies*, volume 28(3), July 1992, 541.

17. Zakariyya, *al-Ḥaqīqah wa'l khayāl*, 17.
18. *Ibid.*, 19.
19. *Ibid.*, 22.
20. *Ibid.*, 22.
21. Samir Amin proposes the same argument. See Samir Amin, *The Arab Nation: Nationalism and Class Struggle* (London: Zed Books, 1987).
22. Zakariyya, *al-Ḥaqīqah wa'l khayāl*, 23. See also Fu'ād Zakariyya, "People Direct Islam in any Direction they Wish." *Middle East Times*, May 28–June 3, 1991, 15.
23. *Ibid.*, 24.
24. *Ibid.*
25. *Ibid.*, 25.
26. *Ibid.*, 25–6.
27. For more details, see Fu'ād Zakariyya, *al-'Arab wa'l namudhaj al-amerīkī* (Cairo: Maktabat Miṣr, 1990).
28. "The religious criticism described in his chapter is undeniably a vigorous expression of political opposition to the Saudi ruling elite. That criticism is not merely a one-sided assault, it invites argumentative exchange." Talal Asad, *Genealogies of Religion: Discipline and Reasons of Power in Christianity and Islam* (Baltimore: Johns Hopkins University Press, 1993), 232. On protest movements in Saudi Arabia, see Mamoun Fandy, *Saudi Arabia and the Politics of Dissent* (London: Palgrave, 1999). On the larger context of the alliance between Wahabiyyah and the state in Saudi Arabia, see Alexei Vassiliev, *The History of Saudi Arabia* (New York: New York University Press, 2000).
29. Nihilism is summarized by the death of God thesis uttered by Nietzsche; in that sense, nihilism means the devaluation of the highest value; the highest value being God. For more details, see G. Vattimo, *The End of Modernity: Nihilism and Hermeneutics in Postmodern Culture* (Baltimore: Johns Hopkins University Press, 1988), especially chapter 1.
30. "Ultimate Concern is the abstract translation of the great commandment: 'The Lord, our God, the Lord is one; and you shall love the Lord your God with all your heart, and with all your soul and with all your mind, and with all your strength'." Paul Tillich, *Systematic Theology*, volume 1 (Chicago: University of Chicago Press, 1953), 12.
31. Charles Taylor, *The Ethics of Authenticity* (Cambridge, MA: Harvard University Press, 1991).
32. L. Binder, *Islamic Liberalism: A Critique of Development Ideologies* (Chicago: University of Chicago Press, 1988), 80–1.
33. Leo Strauss, *What is Political Philosophy?* (Chicago: University of Chicago Press, 1988), 13.
34. Karl Popper, *The Open Society and its Enemies*, 2 volumes (Princeton: Princeton University Press, 1962).
35. See Peter Gay, *The Enlightenment: An Interpretation* (London: Weidenfeld & Nicolson, 1966).
36. Amīn, *al-Tanwīr al-ẓā'if*, 45.
37. *Ibid.*, 56–7.
38. Ghalyūn, *Ightiyāl al-'aql*, 247.
39. In speaking of the differences between fundamentalism and modernity, Albert Memmi, a French thinker of Tunisian Jewish background, has this to say: "L'integrisme correspond à une conception complète de l'existence, émotionnelle et systématique...Cette conception, que l'on pourrait appeler totalitaire, n'est pas seulement le fait d'esprits religieux: il existe des totalitarismes en politique comme en philosophie. Ils reposent sur deux postulats. Le premier est que la vérité,

évidemment leur propre conception de la vérité, est absolue. Intégrisme signifie intégrité de la tradition, évidemment interprétée à leur manière. Elle ne supporte donc aucune autre restriction, sans être elle-même en danger. Ce qui prouve, à mon sens, que, malgré les apparences, les totalitaristes ne sont ni tellement sûrs d'eux-mêmes ni sûrs de leur vérité, sinon ils n'auraient pas besoin de la défendre si âprement. Ils ont besoin de mettre Dieu dans leur jeu. Le second postulat, qui découle du premier, est que les individus et les peuples qui s'opposent à cette conception unitaire doivent être mis dans l'impossibilité de nuire, par la coercition, par la destruction s'il le faut. L'idéologie se clôt par une action radicale, sans quoi elle ne serait pas totale." ("Fundamentalism corresponds to a complete conception of existence, emotional and systematic. This conception, which one can call totalitarian, is not only the product of religious minds. Types of totalitarianism exist in politics as in philosophy. They depend on two postulates. The first is that truth, obviously their conception of truth, is absolute. Fundamentalism signifies integrity of tradition, of course, interpreted their way. Fundamentalism cannot support any other restriction without being compromised. That proves, to my mind, that in spite of appearances, totalitarians are neither so sure of themselves nor so sure of their truth; otherwise they would not need to defend it so bitterly. They need to bring God into their camp. The second postulate, which derives from the former, is that individuals and peoples who oppose this monolithic conception must be neutralized by coercion and destruction, if necessary. Ideology is cemented by a radical action; otherwise, it would not be total." Translation by Abu-Rabi'.) Albert Memmi, "Integrisme et laïcité." *Le Monde Diplomatique*, March 1989, 3.

40. Burhān Ghalyūn, *Naqd al-siyāssa: al-dawla wa'l dīn* (Beirut: Dār al-Ṭalī'ah, 1991), 192.
41. Eickelman notes that, "The prevailing secularist bias of many current theories of society has alternately marginalized and demonized religious forces and religious intellectuals." Dale Eickelman, "Islam and the Languages of Modernity." *Daedalus: Journal of the American Academy of Arts and Sciences*, Winter 2000, 132.
42. Ghalyūn, *Naqd al-siyāssa*, 239–40. See also Burhān Ghalyūn, "al-Islām wa azmat 'alāqāt al-sulṭah al-ijtimā'iyyah," in Markaz Dirāsāt al-Wiḥdah al-'Arabīyyah, *al-Din fi 'l mujtam' al-'arabī* (Beirut: Markaz Dirāsāt al-Wiḥdah al-'Arabīyyah, 1990), 303.
43. *Ibid.*, 262.
44. Ghalyūn, *Naqd al-siyāssah*, 262.
45. Amartya Sen, "The Threats to Secular India." *New York Review of Books*, volume 40(7), April 8, 1993, 28.
46. Bernard Lewis, *The Jews of Islam* (Princeton: Princeton University Press, 1987), 3.
47. For an interesting view, see Nurcholis Madjid, "Islamic Roots of Modern Pluralism: Indonesian Experiences." *Studia Islamika: Indonesian Journal for Islamic Studies*, volume 1(1), 1994, 55–77.
48. Charles Taylor, *Sources of the Self: The Making of the Modern Identity* (Cambridge, MA: Harvard University Press, 1989).
49. Jamāl al-Ghīṭānī, one of the best known novelists in contemporary Egypt, makes the point that, "In the battle between a religious extremism and terrorism seeking to bring down a corrupt and basically repressive government, the choice for many of us, lamentable though it may be, is to side with the army and regime." Quoted by Edward Said, "The Other Arab Muslims," in his *The Politics of Dispossession* (New York: Vintage, 1994), 400.

5 FORMATION OF CONTEMPORARY IDENTITIES: NATIONALISM AND ISLAMISM IN CONTEMPORARY ARAB THOUGHT

1. Many Arab thinkers have attempted to write such a history. See Adonis, *al-Thābit wa'l mutahawwil*, 3 volumes (Beirut: Dār al-'Awdah, 1983), and Ḥussain Muruwwa, *al-Naza'āt al-mādiyyah fi'l falsafah al-'arabīyyah al-islāmiyyah*, 2 volumes (Beirut: Dār al-Fārābī, 1979). In French see Hichem Djaït, *La Grande Discorde, religion et politique dans l'islam des origines* (Paris: Gallimard, 1989).
2. The concept of civil society is rather a modern one. On the development of the term see John Keane, "Despotism and Democracy: The Origins and Development of the Distinction between

Civil Society and the State 1750–1850," in John Keane, ed., *Civil Society and the State* (London: University of Westminster Press, 1998), 35–71.

3. Quoted by Malcolm Kerr in *Islamic Reform: The Political and Legal Theories of Muḥammad 'Abduh and Rashid Rida* (Berkeley: University of California Press, 1966), 110.
4. Some argue that Islamic reform, *per se*, preceded the advent of colonialism into the Muslim world. See Charles Adams, *Islam and Modernism in Egypt* (London: Oxford University Press, 1933); Albert Hourani, *Arabic Thought in the Liberal Age* (London: Oxford University Press, 1962); Malcolm Kerr, *Islamic Reform.*
5. Kerr is not very much impressed with Islamic reform, especially with the ideas of Muḥammad 'Abduh. He argues, quite erroneously to my mind, that "The difficulty is that the teachings of 'Abduh and his circle rested on intellectual foundations that were, on the whole, vague and unsystematic." Kerr, *Islamic Reform*, 15. See the important introduction by Muḥammad 'Imārah to the ideas of Muḥammad 'Abduh, in Muḥammad 'Imārah, ed., *al-A'māl al-kāmilah li'l imām Muḥammad 'Abduh*, volume 1 (Cairo: Dār al-Shurūq, 1995).
6. Talal Asad, "Europe Against Islam: Islam in Europe." *The Muslim World*, volume 87(2), April 1997, 189. Asad goes on to argue that, "I refer here not simply to intellectual traditions, to philosophy, theology, history, etc., which (so we are continually told by critics of Islam) are in a state of decay. I am thinking in the first place of ways of living that are articulated, in diverse conditions, by Islamic tradition. But in order to be viable we should not take it for granted that the tradition needs to be remade in the image of liberal Protestant Christianity." *Ibid.*
7. Aḥmad Kamāl Abū'l Majd, "Sūrat al-ḥālah al-islāmiyyah 'ala mashārif alfiyyah jadīdah." *Wijhāt Nadhar*, volume 1(11), 1999, 5. See also Aḥmad Kamāl Abū'l Majd, *Ru'yah islāmiyyah mu'āṣirah* (Cairo: Dār al-Shurūq, 1992).
8. Ṭāriq al-Bishrī, "Ḥawla al-'urūbbah wa'l islām," in Markaz Dirāsāt al-Wiḥdah al-'Arabīyyah, *al-Ḥiwār al-qawmī al-dīnī* (Beirut: Markaz Dirāsāt al-Wiḥdah al-'Arabīyyah, 1989), 2.
9. See the recent interesting study by Ralph Coury, *The Making of an Egyptian Arab Nationalist: The Early Years of Azzam Pasha, 1893–1936* (London: Ithaca Press, 1998); Philip Koury, *Syria and the French Mandate: The Politics of Arab Nationalism, 1920–1945* (Princeton: Princeton University Press, 1987); Rashid Khalidi, Lisa Anderson, Muḥammad Muslih and Reeva S. Simon, eds., *The Origins of Arab Nationalism* (New York: New York University Press, 1991).
10. See Coury, *The Making of an Egyptian Arab Nationalist*, and Bashir M. Nafi, *Arabism, Islamism, and the Palestine Question, 1908–1941: A Political History* (London: Ithaca Press, 1998).
11. Coury, *The Making of an Egyptian Arab Nationalist*, 451.
12. Benedict Anderson, *The Spectre of Comparisons: Nationalism, Southeast Asia and the World* (London: Verso, 1998), 2.
13. See James Jankowski and Israel Gershoni, eds., *Rethinking Nationalism in the Arab Middle East* (New York: Columbia University Press, 1997).
14. "[Nationalism] is an imagined political community – and imagined as both inherently limited and sovereign." Benedict Anderson, *Imagined Communities: Reflections on the Origin and Spread of Nationalism* (New York: Verso, 1992), 6. For another definition of nationalism, Indian political theorist Achin Vanaik argues, "Nations (and nationalisms) are not intrinsically secular categories. They can rest on exclusivist racial, tribal or religious claims. Indeed, in India religious groups have been among the strongest candidates for nationhood." Achin Vanaik, *The Furies of Indian Communalism: Religion, Modernity and Secularization* (London: Verso, 1997), 31.
15. Franz Fanon, *The Wretched of the Earth* (New York: Grove Press, 1968), 210. The *locus classicus* on Fanon is Lewis Gordon, *Fanon and the Crisis of European Man: An Essay on Philosophy and the Human Sciences* (New York: Routledge, 1995). See also his "Tragic Dimensions of our Neocolonial 'Postcolonial' World," in Emmanuel C. Eze, ed., *Postcolonial African Philosophy: A Critical Reader* (Oxford: Blackwell, 1997), 241–51.
16. Ṭāriq al-Bishrī, *Bayna al-jāmi'ah al-dīnīyyah wa'l jāmi'ah al-wataniyyah fi'l fikr al-siyāsī* (Cairo: Dār al-Shurūq, 1998), 86.
17. See the writings of Muḥammad H. Haykal on the subject, especially his major work, *Ḥarb al-thalāthīn sanah: 1967 al-infijār* (Cairo: Markaz al-Ahrām li'l Tijārah wa'l Nashr, 1990).
18. *Ibid.*, 641. Haykal uses the English term "to unleash Israel" in this major volume of 1,089 pages. Noam Chomsky says that the US policy since 1945 has been wary of nationalist regimes, "These

themes are constantly reiterated in the internal record and high-level planning documents and, more important, implemented in practice: so, ten years after the hemispheric conference, the National Security Council – the highest planning body – identified the main threat to US interests as 'nationalist regimes maintained in large part by appeals to the masses of the population' in response to the increasing 'popular demand for immediate improvement in the low living standards of the masses'. That conflicted with 'a climate conducive to private investment of both domestic and foreign capital,' and the 'opportunity to earn and in case of foreign capital to repatriate a reasonable return,' as well as with what Kennan called 'the protection of our raw materials'." Noam Chomsky, "Power in the Global Arena." *New Left Review*, number 230, July–August 1998, 6–7.

19. Arthur L. Lowrie, ed., *Islam, Democracy, the State and the West: A Round Table with Dr. Ḥasan Turabi* (Tampa: World and Studies Enterprise, 1993), 17.
20. Fanon, *The Wretched of the Earth*, 166. Fanon goes on to say that, "Before independence, the leader generally emodies the aspirations of the people for independence, political liberty and national integrity. But as soon as independence is declared...the leader will reveal his inner purpose: to become the general president of that company of profiteers impatient for their returns which constitutes the national bourgeoisie." *Ibid.*, 166.
21. Ranajit Guha argues that "The historiography of Indian nationalism has for long been dominated by elitism – colonialism elitism and bourgeois-nationalist elitism." R. Guha, ed., "His Article: Consult America." *Subaltern Studies 1: Writings on South Asian History and Society* (New Delhi: Oxford University Press, 1982), 1.
22. See Ali Rattansi, "Postcolonialism and its Discontents." *Economy and Society*, volume 26(4), November 1997, 480–500.
23. See the brilliant analysis on the formation of the modern Saudi state in Waddāh Sharārah, *al-Ahl wa'l ghanīmah: muqawimmāt al-siyāsah fī'l mamlakah al-'arabīyyah al-sa'ūdiyyah* (Beirut: Dār al-Ṭalī'ah, 1981).
24. See J. S. Habib, *Ibn Sa'ūd's Warriors of Islam: The Ikhwān of Najd and Their Role in the Creation of the Sa'udi Kingdom, 1910–1930* (Leiden: Brill, 1978), and Alexi Vassiliev, *The History of Saudi Arabia* (New York: New York University Press, 2000). See also Sami Zubaida, "Is There a Muslim Society? Ernest Gellner's Sociology of Islam." *Economy and Society*, volume 24(2), May 1995, 151–88, especially 175–7.
25. Abdelkebir Khatibi, "Double Criticism: The Decolonization of Arab Sociology," in Halim Barakat, ed., *Contemporary North Africa: Issues of Development and Integration* (Washington, D.C.: Center for Contemporary Arab Studies, 1985), 12.
26. Some Arab leftist thinkers go as far as saying that "Islamic fundamentalism" is an imperialist plot which aims at fragmenting Arab society. See Riḍwān al-Sayyid, "al-Qawmiyyūn wa'l islāmiyyūn fī'l watan al-'arabī wā ḍarūrat al-hiwār wa'l talāqī," in Markaz Dirāsāt al-Wiḥdah al-'Arabīyyah, *al-Ḥiwār al-qawmī al-dīnī* (Beirut: Markaz Dirāsāt al-Wiḥdah al-'Arabīyyah, 1989), 77.
27. On the struggle between the Islamist movement and the regime in Syria, see Patrick Seale, *Asad and the Struggle for the Middle East* (Berkeley: University of California Press, 1988). In the case of Iraq, see Tarik Hamdi al-Azami, "The Emergence of the Contemporary Islamic Revival in Iraq." *Middle East Affairs Journal*, volume 3(1–2), Winter/Spring 1997, 123–41.
28. Burhān Ghalyūn, *Ightiyāl al-'aql: mihnat al-thaqāfah al-'arabīyyah bayna al-salafīyyah wa'l taba 'iyyah* (Cairo: Maktabat Madbūlī, 1990), 9.
29. S. J. al-'Azm, *al-Naqd al-dhātī ba'da al-hazīmah* (Beirut: Dār al-Ṭalī'ah, 1969).
30. See Khurshid Ahmad's thought on the matter in Ibrahim M. Abu-Rabi', ed., *Islamic Resurgence: Challenges, Directions, and Future Perspectives: A Roundtable with Khurshid Ahmad* (Tampa: WISE, 1994).
31. On the notion of the Sharī'ah, see Joseph Schacht, "Sharī'ah," in H. Gibb and M. Karammer, eds., *Shorter Encyclopedia of Islam* (London: Stacy International, 1974).
32. See Talal Asad's masterful analysis of the thought of the Saudi Islamist thinker, Safar al-Hawwali in his *Genealogies of Religion: Discipline and Reasons for Power in Christianity and Islam* (Baltimore: Johns Hopkins University Press, 1993).
33. No serious work has appeard on Malik Bennabi in English. For a poorly-written book on his life and thought, see Fawzia Bariun, *Malik Bennabi: His Life and Theory of Civilization*

(Kuala Lumpur: Muslim Youth Movement of Malaysia, 1993). See also Malik Bennabi, *Islam in History and Society*, trans. Asma Rashid (Islamabad: Islamic Research Institute, 1987), and *On the Origins of Human Society*, trans. Muḥammad Taher al-Mesawi (Kuala Lumpur: Open Press, 1998).

34. 'Allāl al-Fāsī, *Maqāṣid al-sharī'ah al-islāmiyyah wā makārimuhah* (Casablanca: al-Najāḥ, 1963).
35. See Yūsuf al-Qaraḍāwī, *Priorities of the Islamic Movement in the Coming Phase*, trans. S. M. Hassan al-Banna (London: Awakening Publications, 2000).
36. Ahmad K. Abū'l Majd, *Ḥiwār lā muwajahah* (Cairo: Dār al-Shurūq, 1989).
37. Abdelwahab El-Affendi, *Turabi's Revolution: Islam and Power in Sudan* (London: Grey Seal Books, 1991). It should be noted that Turābī has been placed under house arrest since February 2001.
38. Sayyid Quṭb, *Dirāsāt islāmiyyah* (Cairo: Dār al-Shurūq, 1976).
39. On Qaraḍāwī, see Barbara Stowasser, "Old Shaykhs, Young Women, and the Internet: The Rewriting of Women's Political Rights in Islam." *The Muslim World*, volume 91(1 and 2), Spring 2001, 99–120.
40. Yūsuf al-Qaraḍāwī, *Limādha al-islām?* (Beirut: Mu'asasat al-Risālah, 1993), 14.
41. Yūsuf al-Qaraḍāwī, *al-Sahwah al-islāmiyyah wa humūm al-watan al-'arabī wa'l islāmī* (Beirut: Mu'asasat al-Risālah, 1997), 35.
42. Yūsuf al-Qaraḍāwī, *al-Ḥulūl al-mustawrada wā kayfa janat 'alā ummatina* [1971] (Beirut: Mu'asasat al-Risālah, 1995); *al-Ḥall al-islāmī farīdah wā ḍarūrah* [1974] (Beirut: Mu'asasat al-Risālah, 1993); and *Bayināt al-ḥall al-islāmī wā shubuhāt al-'ilmaniyyīn wa'l mutagharibīn* [1987] (Beirut: Mu'asasat al-Risālah, 1993). Although Qaraḍāwī devotes his attention in the above books to the Arab "progressive" regimes in Egypt, Syria, and Iraq, he implicitly states the rest of the Arab and Muslim world suffers from the same dilemmas. He states at the beginning that only three solutions are available to the predicaments of the Arab world: first, the Qur'ānic solution; second, the democratic/liberal solution, and the third is the radical/socialist solution. Following in the footsteps of the Arab and Muslim thinkers of the nineteenth and twentieth centuries, such as Muḥammad 'Abduh, Jamāl al-Dīn al-Afghānī, Rashīd Riḍa, Muḥammad al-Bahiy, Malik Bennabi, and Muḥammad al-Ghazālī, Qaraḍāwī argues that the Muslim world was forced to forgo the Sharī'ah and the Qur'ānic solution under the intellectual and religious pressure of an advanced Western and secular civilization. He refers to the classical formula of the Nahḍah movement to explain the reasons behind the success of the Western other and the stagnation of the Muslim self. On the eve of the Western invasion, the Muslim world was suffering from a debilitating stagnation and a loss of moral and religious direction. Qaraḍāwī does not analyze the underlying reasons for decline but he seems to say that they preceded the Western intrusion into the Muslim world. However, the nineteenth century Western invasion of the Muslim world was more pernicious than the crusades in that it followed two courses of action: on the one hand, it tended to supplant the Muslim worldview, as represented by both the Qur'ān and the Sunnah, with a Western philosophy of life that takes man, and not God, as the measure of progress and prosperity. On the other hand, the West took care to produce a new class of Muslim intelligentsia that spoke its language and fulfilled its commands. This new class of intelligentsia was placed at the forefront of the Islamic affairs, and achieving this end "has been the most successful victory in the battle between the West and the Muslim world." Qaraḍāwī, *al-Ḥulūl al-mustawrada*, 20.
43. Fred Halliday notes correctly that monarchy in the Arab world, just like Islamism, "benefited from the failure of the secular nationalist project. Significantly, after this point there began to be a certain nostalgic talk of monarchy and discussion of the uses of the monarchical system." Fred Halliday, *Nation and Religion in the Middle East* (Boulder: Lynne Rienner, 2000), 93.
44. Abdullahi Ahmed An-Na'im, *Toward Islamic Reformation: Civil Liberties, Human Rights, and International Law* (Syracuse: Syracuse University Press, 1990), 1–4.
45. Ann Elizabeth Mayer, *Islam and Human Rights: Tradition and Politics* (Boulder: Westview Press, 1991).
46. Katarina Dalacoura, *Islam, Liberalism, and Human Rights* (London: I. B. Tauris, 1998).
47. "For a Muslim country, as for all complex state societies, the most pressing human rights issue is not local cultural preferences or religious-cultural authenticity; it is the protection of the individuals from a state that violates human rights, regardless of its cultural-ideological facade." Reza Afshari, *Human Rights Quarterly*, volume 16(4), 1994, 249.

48. Muḥammad H. Haykal has written a number of interesting articles on Qaddāfī and the Libyan experience. See M. H. Haykal, "Ḥiwārāt ma' al-Qaddāfī." *Wijhāt Nadhar*, volume 1(4), May 1999, 4–14. See also M. H. Haykal, *'Ām min al-azamāt: 2000–2001* (Cairo: al-Miṣriyyah li'l Nashr al-'Arabī wa'l Duwalī, 2001), and *al-'Arabī al-tā'ih* (Cairo: al-Miṣriyyah li'l Nashr al-'Arabī wa'l Duwalī, 2001).
49. A good overview of Qaddāfī and his comrades is to be found in John Cooley, *Libyan Sandstorm* (New York: Holt, Rinehart & Winston, 1982).
50. "Islamism is based on the notion of the implementation of the Sharī'ah, while taking into account that the Qur'ān and the Sunnah are the major reference for the organization of life and the source of legitimacy and government in society. And this is the main difference between Islamism and secularism." Al-Bishrī, *Bayna al-jāmi'ah al-dīnīyyah*, 91.
51. Ayman Zawāhīrī, *al-Ḥiṣād al-murr: al-ikhwān al-muslimūn fī sittīnā 'āman* (no publication information). Zawāhīrī argues that issues of governance, such as democracy and international relations are not secondary from the perspective of Islamic law, but an essential part of the main principle of Islam, which is the doctrine of oneness or *tawḥīd*. See <www.aljazeera.net/books/2002/11/11–2–1.html>
52. See Basheer Nafi, "The Arab Nationalists and the Arab Islamists: Shadows of the Past, Glimpses of the Future." *Middle East Affairs Journal*, volume 6(1–2) Winter/Spring 2000, 109–28. In January 2000, the third meeting of Arabists and Islamists was held in Beirut, Lebanon. According to Nafi, this umbrella organization, The Arab-Nationalist Islamic Conference is the only one of its kind in the Arab world that brings Muslim and Arab activists and intellectuals together to reestablish the Arab consensus on a number of significant matters.
53. See Aḥmad Ṣudqī al-Dajānī, " 'An al-'urūbbah wa'l islām wā qadāyah al-mustaqbal," in Markaz Dirāsāt al-Wiḥdah al-'Arabīyyah, *al-Ḥiwār al-qawmī al-dīnī* (Beirut: Markaz Dirāsāt al-Wiḥdah al-'Arabīyyah, 1989), 55–68.
54. See 'Abdul Mun'im Sa'īd, *al-'Arab wa mustaqbal al-niẓām al-'ālamī* (Beirut: Markaz Dirāsāt al-Wiḥdah al-'Arabīyyah, 1987).
55. See Markaz Dirāsāt al-Wiḥdah al-'Arabīyyah, *al-Ḥiwār al-qawmī al-dīnī* (Beirut: Markaz Dirāsāt al-Wiḥdah al-'Arabīyyah, 1989), and Markaz Dirāsāt al-Wiḥdah al-'Arabīyyah, *al-Mu'tamar al-qawmī al-islamī al-awwal* (Beirut: Markaz Dirāsāt al-Wiḥdah al-'Arabīyyah, 1995). See also Sohail H. Hashmi, ed., *Islamic Politics Ethics: Civil Society, Pluralism, and Conflict* (Princeton: Princeton University Press, 2002). On the notion of "civil society" in the contemporary Arab discourse, see Ḥassan Ḥanafī, "Alternative Conceptions of Civil Society: A Reflective Islamic Approach," in Sohail H. Hashmi, ed., *Islamic Politics and Ethics: Civil Society, Pluralism, and Conflict* (Princeton: Princeton University Press, 2002), 56–76.
56. See for example the powerful writings of the Egypt Islamist Muḥammad Jalāl Kishk on the subject, especially *Qirā'ah fī fikr al-taba'iyyah* (Cairo: Maktabat al-Turāth al-Islāmī, 1994). He argues that due to rampant bureaucratic corruption in the Arab world, civil society is trying to be independent of the state, which is governed by a military oligarchy. *Ibid.*, 13.
57. Fahmī Huwaydī, "al-Khiṭāb al-islāmī fī 'ālam mutajaddid," in Sayyid Yāssin, ed., *al-'Arab wā taḥadiyyāt al-qarn al-ḥādī wa'l 'ishrīn* (Amman: Mu'assassat 'Abdul Ḥamīd Shūmān, 2000), 259–63.
58. Al-Bishrī, *Bayna al-'urūba wa'l islām*, 14.
59. On Ibn Khaldūn, see Y. Lacoste, *Ibn Khaldoun, naissance de l'histoire, passé du tiers-monde* (Paris: PUF, 1966) and Aziz al-Azmeh, *Ibn Khaldun* (London: Routledge, 1982).
60. Ibn Khaldūn, *The Muqaddimah: An Introduction to History*, volume 2 (New York: Pantheon, 1958), 430. "The Institution of scientific instruction has disappeared among the inhabitants of Spain. Their former concern with the sciences is gone, because Muslim civilization in Spain has been decreasing for hundreds of years. The only scholarly discipline remaining there is Arabic philology and literature, to which the Spanish Muslims restrict themselves...Jurisprudence is an empty institution among them and a mere shadow of its real self." *Ibid.*
61. Ibn Khaldūn calls these the "traditional, conventional sciences. There is no place for intellect in them, save that the intellect may be used in connection with them to relate problems of detail with basic principles." *Ibid.*, 436.
62. 'Abd al-Majīd al-Charfī, *Taḥdīth al-fikr al-islāmī* (Casablanca: Nashr al-Fennek, 1998), 7–16.

63. Fu'ād Zakariyya, *al-Ṣaḥwah al-islāmiyyah fī mīzān al-'aql* (Cairo: Dār al-Fikr li'l Dirāsāt wa'l Nashr wa'l Tawzī', 1989), 9.
64. For a theoretical argument on the issue of Islam in Orientalist and Marxist scholarship, see Rema Hammami and Martina Rieker, "Feminist Orientalism and Orientalist Marxism." *New Left Review*, number 170, July–August 1988, 93–106.
65. Naṣr Ḥāmid Abū Zayd, *Mafhūm al-naṣṣ: dirāsa fi 'ulūm al-Qur'ān* (Casablanca: al-Markaz al-Thaqāfī al-'Arabī, 1988).
66. Rochdy Alili, *Qu'est-ce que l'islam*? (Paris: La Découverte, 1996).
67. See Sa'd al-Dīn Ibrāhīm, "al-Mufakkir wa'l amīr: tajsīr al-fajwah bayana sāni'ī al-qarār wa'l mufakirrīn al-'arab," in al-Ṭāhir Labīb, *al-Intellijensia al-'arabīyyah* (Tunis: al-Dār al-'Arabīyyah li'l Kitāb, n.d.), 213–45.
68. "To have been an Aligarah man, I have over and over again found, a passport to the respect and confidence of both Englishmen and Indians." Sir Auckland Colvin, quoted by Khaliq Ahmad Nizami, *History of the Aligarah Muslim University* (New Delhi: IDār ah-i Adabiyat-i Delhi, 1995), xii.
69. Jamal Malik, *Colonialization of Islam: Dissolution of Traditional Institutions in Pakistan* (New Delhi: Manohar, 1996), 130.
70. "Quite a few young minds were brainwashed by these religious groups [in the Dini Madaris] into carrying forward the messianic spirit of Islam into others parts of the world. Their dogmatic approach and intolerance of others' points of view often produced fanatics who were recruited for trans-territorial missions." Kamal Matinuddin, *The Taliban Phenomenon: Afghanistan 1994–1997* (Karachi: Oxford University Press, 1999), 13.
71. "Some students spend most of their lives attending scholarly sessions. Still, one finds them silent. They do not talk and do not discuss matters. More than is necessary, they are concerned with memorization. Thus, they do not obtain much of a habit in the practice of science and scientific instruction. Some of them think that they have obtained the habit. But when they enter into a discussion or disputation, or do some teaching, their scientific habit is found to be defective. The only reason for their deficiency is lack of instruction, together with the break in the tradition of scientific instruction that affects them. Apart from that, their memorized knowledge may be more extensive than that of other scholars, because they are so much concerned with memorizing. They think that scientific habit is identical with memorized knowledge. But that is not so." Ibn Khaldūn, *The Muqaddimah*, volume 2, 429–30.
72. Contemporary American Jewish theologian Marc Ellis argues that lack of criticism is the mark of many Jewish seminaries in the United States, "Trained in the texts of the traditions and the ability to guide congregations largely ignorant of these texts, Jewish seminary students are a bridge between the Jewish tradition and their congregants who are busy pursuing life in a Christian and secular America. In public, outside of the synagogue, the new rabbis, like many of the more experiences ones, act simply to deflect critical public discussion on Israel...Dissenting Jews are also silenced. Since critical discussion on the central issues facing Jews is largely absent in the core curriculum of the seminary, how could one expect rabbis to speak intelligently on these issues? *Protection rather than critical engagement becomes the modus vivendi of the rabbinic establishment*." Marc Ellis, *Practicing Exile: The Religious Odyssey of an American Jew* (Minneapolis: Fortress Press, 2002), 120–1.
73. See L. Carl Brown, *Religion and State: The Muslim Approach to Politics* (New York: Columbia University Press, 2000), 130–1.
74. "Le clerc écarté depuis longtemps, le liberal déchu depuis peu se rabattent, dans l'Etat national, sur le champ favori des études littéraires et c'est au nom de ces études que se hisse le drapeau de la culture nationale. La culture dont it s'agit est la culture classique profane, celle de l'Adab, littérature au sense restrictif du terme et done les composants sont la poésie, la prose artistique, les manuels étiquette et de savoir-vivre." ("The clergyman long since marginalized, the liberal recently fallen in the nation-state in the favorite field of literary studies, and it is in the name of these studies that the flag of national culture is hoisted. The culture which we speak of is the classic profane one, that of *Adab*, literature in the restricted sense of the term, which is constituted of poetry, artistic prose, manuals of etiquette and good living." Translation by Abu-Rabi'.) Abdallah Laroui, *L'idéologie arabe contemporaine* (Paris: Maspero, 1970), 85.

75. Malek Bennabi, *Islam in History and Society*, trans. Asma Rashid (Islamabad: Islamic Research Institute, 1988), 27.
76. Mohammed Arkoun, "History as an Ideology of Legitimation: A Comparative Approach in Islamic and European Contexts." In Gema M. Münoz, ed., *Islam, Modernism, and the West* (London: I. B. Tauris, 1999), 27. In another article, Arkoun contends that, "In contemporary Muslim societies ethnology and anthropology are still rejected on the grounds that they continue to depend on colonial strategies. This is, of course, in itself a pure ideological posture imposed by the single party nation-states." Mohammed Arkoun, "Islamic Studies: Methodologies," in John Esposito, ed., *The Oxford Encyclopedia of the Modern Muslim World*, volume 2 (New York: Oxford University Press, 1995), 335.
77. In many Muslim countries, no preacher is allowed to mount the pulpit before his *khuṭbah* is approved by the Ministry of Religious Affairs.
78. In am indebted in the phrasing of this statement to L. Kolakowski, *Main Currents of Marxism*, volume 3 (Oxford: University of Oxford Press, 1978), 465. In speaking of post-1968 communism in East Europe, Kolakowski notes that communism "ceased being an intellectual problem and became merely a question of power." *Ibid.*
79. Ishtiaq Husain Qureshi, *Education in Pakistan* (Karachi: Ma'aref, 1975), 119, quoted by Fazlur Rahman in *Islam and Modernity: Transformation of an Intellectual Tradition* (Chicago: University of Chicago Press, 1982), 111. According to the renowned Pakistani critic Iqbal Ahmad, higher education in Pakistan has almost collapsed. There are multiple reasons for that. The first relates to the question of language; the second to the failure of the modern state to introduce an alternative system of education to the colonial; and the third concerns the different functions of education under both colonial and nationalist regimes. See David Barsamian, *Iqbal Ahmad: Confronting Empire* (Cambridge: South End Press, 2000), 19.
80. We must not underestimate the large number of women who graduate from Sharī'ah colleges in Muslim universities.
81. On the end of the Cold War and the social sciences in Europe, see Ignacio Ramonet, "Nouvel ordre, rébellions, nationalismes: Un monde à reconstruire." *Le Monde Diplomatique*, May 1992, 1.
82. Hamza Alavi, "Pakistan and Islam: Ethnicity and Ideology," in Fred Halliday and Hamza Alavi, eds., *State and Ideology in the Middle East and Pakistan* (New York: Monthly Review Press, 1998), 81.
83. Talal Asad, *Genealogies of Religion: Discipline and Reasons of Power in Christianity and Islam* (Baltimore: Johns Hopkins University Press, 1993).
84. See Fu'ād Zakariyya, "al-Falsafah wa'l dīn fī'l mujtama' al-'arabī al-mu'āṣir," in Markaz Dirāsāt al-Wiḥdah al-'Arabīyyah, *al-Falsafah fī'l watan al-'arabī al-mu'āṣir* (Beirut: Markaz Dirāsāt al-Wiḥdah al-'Arabīyyah, 1985), 43–69.
85. In a visit I made to Srinagar, Kashmir, in the summer of 1998, I was invited to give a talk in Arabic at Ahl al-Hadīth College, a Wahabi-financed Islamic school with 500 students. I was surprised to learn that all the students at that school, none of whom left Kashmir, spoke fluent Arabic. On Ahl al-Ḥadīth in the South Asia, see Bashir Ahmad Khan, "The Ahl-i-Hadīth: A Socio-Religious Reform Movement in Kashmir." *The Muslim World*, volume 90 (1 and 2), Spring 2000, 133–57.
86. In his discussion of the rise of the Islamic movement in the Sudan, al-Haj Warrāq speaks about the political exploitation of Sufi brotherhoods by the Numayri regime in the 1970s and 1980s and the rise of Islamic radicalism. In the first instance, some Sufi leaders in the Sudan cooperated with the regime in exchange for financial remuneration and political prestige, and in the second, Islamism found a big support among some university students of rural and poor backgrounds, who lacked any critical sense of education, "The reason for the rising influence of the Islamist trends amongst the students is to be explained by the nature of the dominant educational systems in the country. Curricula and methods of teaching depend to a large extent on rote memorization, which kills in the student the desire for free enquiry and open dialogue." Al-Haj Warrāq, "Ṣinā'at al-wahm: al-asbāb al-ijtimā'iyyah lī dhāhirat al-hawas al-dīnī fī'l sudān." *Qaḍāyah Fikriyyah*, volume 8, 1989, 217.
87. Rif'at al-Sa'īd, "al-Islām al-siyāsī: mina al-taṭarruf ilā mazīdan mina al-taṭarruf." *Qaḍāyah Fikriyyah*, volume 8, 1989, 19. In the opinion of the Egyptian economist Galāl Amīn, the

modernization of the Azhar by the Egyptian state in the 1950s weakened the institution, "In this fashion, this great institution was transformed, or very nearly so, into a miserable copy of the existing state universities. Instead of graduating students who were proud of their heritage but able to reinterpret it in the light of contemporary needs, it brought together students who suffered from an inferiority complex because of their inability to reconcile the old religious teachings with the modern sciences." Galāl Amīn, *Whatever Happened to the Egyptians? Changes in Egyptian Society from 1950 to the Present* (Cairo: American University of Cairo Press, 2000), 48.

88. See Michael Gilsenan, *Recognizing Islam: Religion and Society in the Modern Arab World* (New York: Pantheon, 1982).
89. See Raymond Williams, "Means of Communication as Means of Production," in his *Problems in Materialism and Culture: Selected Essays* (London: Verso, 1997), 50–63.
90. *Ibid.*, 39.
91. Edward W. Said, "The Arab Right Wing," in his *The Politics of Dispossession* (New York: Vintage, 1995), 229.
92. Islamists have begun to take the issue of democracy seriously. In the view of Khurshid Ahmad, a leading Pakistani Islamist thinker, "Islam and the Muslim Umma brook no sympathy for arbitrary and authoritarian rule. Whatever arbitrary power reigns is more a product of colonization and Westernization, and not of Muslim ideals, history or contemporary aspirations...Whatever despotic or arbitrary rule exists in the Muslim lands is part of an alien and imposed tradition, against which the forces of Islamic resurgence are struggling." Khurshid Ahmad, "Islam and Democracy: Some Conceptual and Contemporary Dimensions." *The Muslim World*, volume 90 (1 and 2), Spring 2000, 19.
93. "[T]he Catholic Church...sanctified those who were born noble, powerful, and wealthy, affluence being taken as an external sign of high social position. This was perhaps a natural stance for an ecclesiastic establishment that historically had such close family, social, and economic ties with the landed elite, though the churches also hallowed the poor and the meek." See Arno J. Mayer, *The Persistence of the Old Regime: Europe to the Great War* (New York: Pantheon, 1981), 86.

6 TRADITIONAL VALUES, SOCIAL CHANGE, AND THE CONTEMPORARY ARAB PERSONALITY

1. In his comment on contemporary immigration, American essayist Gore Vidal argues that, "A characteristic of our present chaos is the dramatic migration of tribes. They are on the move from east to west, from south to north. Liberal tradition requires that borders must always be open for those in search of safety or even the pursuit of happiness. In the case of the United States, the acquisition of new citizens from all the tribes of earth has always been thought to be a very good thing. But, eventually, with so many billions of people on the move, even the great-hearted may well become edgy once we have gobbled up all the computer-proficient immigrants." Gore Vidal, "Chaos." *New York Review of Books*, December 16, 1999, 39.
2. "Exile, far from being the fate of nearly forgotten unfortunates who are dispossessed and expatriated, becomes something closer to the norm, an experience of crossing boundaries and charting new territories in defiance of the classic canonical enclosures, however much its loss and sadness should be acknowledged and registered." Edward Said, *Culture and Imperialism* (New York: Alfred A. Knopf, 1993), 317.
3. Capitalism and consumption went hand-in-hand. See Michael Miller, *The Bon Marché: Bourgeois Culture and the Department Store, 1869–1920* (Princeton: Princeton University Press, 1994) and Rosalind Williams, *Dream Worlds: Consumption in Late Nineteenth Century France* (Berkeley: University of California Press, 1982). See also Elizabeth Wilson, *Adorned in Dreams: Fashion and Modernity* (Berkeley: University of California Press, 1985) and "The Invisible Flaneur." *New Left Review*, number 191, January/February 1992, 90–110.
4. For a moving account of this group of migrants, see the following by Judith Caesar, *Crossing Borders: An American Woman in the Middle East* (Syracuse: Syracuse University Press, 1999), and *Writing off the Beaten Track: Reflections on the Meaning of Travel and Culture in the Middle East* (Syracuse: Syracuse University Press, 2002).

5. Benedict Anderson argues that in migration, "Human bodies, though caught up in the vortex of the market, are not merely another form of commodity. As they follow in the wake of grain and gold, rubber and textiles, petrochemicals and silicon chips, they carry with them memories and customs, beliefs and eating habits, musics and sexual desires." Benedict Anderson, "The New World Disorder." *New Left Review*, number 193, May/June 1992, 8.
6. See Sayyid 'Uways, *al-Tārīkh al-ladhī aḥmiluhu 'alā dhahrī*, 3 volumes (Cairo: Dār al-Hilāl, 1987). See also Jamāl Māḍī Abū al-'Azā'im, *Nufūs warā' al-aswār* (Cairo: al-Dār al-'Arabīyyah li'l Ṭibā'ah wa'l Nashr, 1990); and Nawal El Saadawi, *Qaḍḍiyat al-mar'ah al-siyāsiyyah wa'l jinsiyyah* (Cairo: Dār al-Thaqāfah al-Jadīdah, 1977).
7. Nadia Raḍwān, *al-Shabāb al-miṣrī al-mu'āṣir wā azmat al-qiyam* (Cairo: al-Hay'ah al-Miṣriyyah al-'Āmmah li'l Kitāb, 1997).
8. Yāsser Ayūb, *Warā' kull bāb: al-infijār al-jinsīfi miṣr* (Cairo: Dār Sphynix, 1995).
9. On the resurgence of Nasserism in the post-Sadat era, see Joel Gordon, "Secular and Religious Memory in Egypt: Recalling Nasserist Civics." *The Muslim World*, volume 87(2), April 1997, 94–110.
10. Galāl Amīn, *Whatever Happened to the Egyptians? Changes in Egyptian Society from 1950 to the Present* (Cairo: American University of Cairo Press, 2000), 9.
11. Ayūb, *Warā' kull bāb*, 111.
12. Muḥammad H. Haykal, "Ḥadīth mustadrad 'an al-siyāsah al-dākhiliyyah." *Wijhāt Nadhar*, volume 2(17), June 2000, 11.
13. In a fascinating new study on the political economy of contemporary Egypt, Egyptian scholar Amira Sonbol argues that the 1952 Free Officers' revolution, directed against the old regime, created a new business elite that was bound with the military establishment: "The officer class generally gained in power, prestige, and wealth, but the families and acquaintances of officers gained even more...One of the most interesting means of access to power became the government secret service, *mukhābārāt*...Membership in this service, however, gave people access to knowledge and funds that allowed them to wield great power over others and to control extensive resources as well." Amira El-Azhry Sonbol, *The New Mamluks: Egyptian Society and Modern Feudalism* (Syracuse: Syracuse University Press, 2000), 131, 133.
14. *Ibid.*, 159.
15. Ahmad Anwar, *al-Infitāhḥ wa taghayyur al-qiyam fī miṣr* (Cairo: Miṣr al-'Arabīyyah li'l Nashr wa'l Tawzī', 1993).
16. Raḍwān, *al-Shabāb al-miṣrī al-mu'āṣir wā azmat al-qiyam*, 125.
17. On the contemporary state of Egyptian economy, see Ḥāzim al-Bablāwī, *Miḥnat al-iqtiṣād wa'l iqtāṣidiyyīn* (Cairo: al-Hay'ah al-Miṣriyyah al-'Āmmah li'l Kitāb, 2000).
18. For a detailed analysis of this point and others, see René Girard, *Violence and the Sacred* (Baltimore: Johns Hopkins University Press, 1979) and *Things Hidden Since the Foundation of the World* (Stanford: Stanford University Press, 1987).
19. For an analysis of this phenomenon, see Hanna Batatu, *Syria's Peasantry, the Descendants of its Lesser Rural Notables and their Politics* (Princeton: Princeton University Press, 1999).
20. On the political context of Egyptian development in the 1970s, see Raymond Hinnebusch, *Egyptian Politics Under Sadat: The Post-Populist Development of an Authoritarian-Modernizing State* (London and Boulder, CO: Lynne Rienner Publishers, 1988).
21. In the opinion of Galāl Amīn, the rank and file of the Islamic movement in Egypt no longer belong to a narrow circle of urban and educated elite, and religious fanaticism is the product of severe "frustration of earlier hopes of social advancement." Amīn, *Whatever Happened to the Egyptians?*, 37.
22. See Abdelhadi Boutaleb, *Le monde islamique et le projet du nouvel ordre mondial* (Paris: PUF, 1995).
23. See Jack Hayward and R. N. Berki, eds., *State and Society in Contemporary Europe* (Oxford: Oxford University Press, 1979).
24. Muḥammad 'Ābid al-Jābīrī, "al-Mujtama' al-madanī: tasā'ulāt wā āfāaq," in 'Abdallah Hamūdī, *Wa'y al-mujtama' bī dhātihī: 'an al-mujtama' al-madanī fī'l maghrib al-'arabī* (Casablanca: Dār Ṭobqāl, 1998), 49.
25. Burhān Ghalyūn, "Binā' al-mujtama' al-madanī al-'arabī: dawr al-'awāmil al-dākhiliyyah wa'l khārijiyyah," in Markaz Dirāsāt al-Wiḥdah al-'Arabīyyah, *al-Mujtama' al-madanī fī'l waṭan al-'arabī* (Beirut: Markaz Dirāsāt al-Wiḥdah al-'Arabīyyah, 1992), 742.

26. *Ibid.*, 744.
27. See Nazih Ayubi, *Political Islam: Religion and Politics in the Arab World* (London: Routledge, 1991); Rif'at al-Sa'īd, "al-Islām al-siyāsī: minā al-taṭarruf ila al-mazīd minā al-taṭarruf." *Qaḍāyah Fikriyyah* (Special Issue on Political Islam), volume 8, 1989, 15–33.
28. On the Islamic movement in the contemporary Arab world, see Joel Beinin and Joe Stork, *Political Islam, Essays from The Middle East Report* (Berkeley: University of California Press, 1996), and Laura Guazzone, *The Islamist Dilemma: The Political Role of Islamist Movements in the Contemporary Arab World* (London: Ithaca Press, 1995).
29. For a general introduction on Islamism in North Africa, see F. Burgat and W. Dowell, *The Islamic Movement in North Africa* (Austin: University of Texas Press, 1993). Mohamed Tozy, *Monarchie et islam politique au Maroc* (Paris: Presses de Sciences-Politiques, 1999), and "Qui sont les islamistes au Maroc?" *Le Monde Diplomatique*, August 1999, 20. See also Abderahim Lamchichi, "Incertitudes politiques et sociales: L'islamisme s'enracine au Maroc." *Le Monde Diplomatique*, May 1996, 10–11.
30. 'Arūs al-Zubayr, "al-Dīn wa'l siyāsa fī'l Jazā'ir." *Qaḍāyah Fikriyyah*, 1989, 187–99.
31. Yadh Ben Achour, *Politique, religion et droit dans le monde arabe* (Tunis: CERP, 1992); Jacques de Barrin, "Les différentes réponses des pays maghrébins à la menace islamiste." *Le Monde*, October 5, 1995, Roula Khalaf and James Whittington, "Tunis lashes out at Islamist phantom." *Financial Times*, October 17, 1995.
32. Ṭāriq al-Bishrī, "al-Waḍ' al-dīnī fī misr bayna al-manṭūq bihī wa'l maskūt 'anhū." *Wijhāt Nadhar (Egyptian Review of Books)*, volume 1(4), May 1999, 7.
33. The best representatives of this trend are: T. J. al-'Alwānī in *al-judhūr al-tārikhiyah li'l azmah al-fikriyyah* (Cairo: IIIT, 1989), and A. H. Abu-Sulayman, *Crisis in the Muslim Mind* (Herndon: International Institute of Islamic Thought, 1986).
34. Turābī argues, perhaps a bit contentiously, that the Islamic movements represent a threat to the New World Order, "We are a threat to most Islamic governments, unfortunately...And I admit that we are a threat to the present World Order. I have to admit it, but what threat and how far? It is not a threat in the sense of a belligerent. Bellicose subversion of all world order and all peace and tranquility in the world. We just seek to correct the World Order." Arthur L. Lowrie, ed., *Islam, Democracy, the State and the West: A Round Table with Dr. Ḥasan Turabi* (Tampa: World and Studies Enterprise, 1993), 60.
35. See M. 'Abduh's analysis of *jumūd* or stagnation as a reason for crisis: M. 'Abduh, *al-A'māl al-Kāmilah lī Shaykh Muḥammad 'Abduh*, volume 3, ed. Muḥammad 'Imārah (Cairo: Dār al-Shurūq, 1993), 335–68. 'Abduh argues that the main reason behind stagnation in Islamic history was that Muslims did not perceive the "faculty of reason as the spring of certainty and belief in God, His knowledge and ability." *Ibid.*, 342.
36. See mainly Banna's work *Mudhakarāt al-da'wah wa'l dā'iyyahh* (Beirut: al-Maktab al-Islāmī, 1971); S. Quṭb, *Ma'ālim fī'l ṭarīq* (Beirut: Dār al-Shurūq, 1973); Y. Qaraḍāwī, *Islamic Awakening Between Rejection and Extremism* (Herndon: IIIT, 1991), and M. al-Ghazālī, *al-Ghazw al-thaqāfī yamtadu fī farāghina [Cultural Invasion Expands through our Vacuum]* (Amman: Mu'assassat al-Sharq, 1985).
37. Ghannūshī, *Maqālāt: harakat al-itijāh al-islāmī bī tūnis* (Paris: Dār al-Karawān, 1984), 29.
38. A. H. Nadwi, *What has the World Lost as a Result of the Decline of Muslims?* English translation, A. H. al-Nadwi, *Islam and the World*, trans. M. Kidawi (Kuwait: IIFSO, 1977). Nadwi follows the Orientalist method in tracing "Muslim decline" to the pre-modern era. In fact, he tells us, decline started in the wake of the reign of the four Rightly Guided caliphs, and its first symptoms were seen in the *de facto* separation between religion and state as practiced by the Ummayyads and Abbasids. The religious establishment was unable to prevent this cleavage between state and religion, and some ulama were actually guilty of justifying and propagating secular activities and tendencies. Nadwi elaborates on the theme of ulama and power in modern Muslim societies, and accuses a great number of ulama of "intellectual prostitution." He argues that the intellectual core of Islam, as represented by its theological class, has disintegrated because of the willingness of that class to play into the hands of politicians. The ulama, who are supposed to take the general welfare (*maṣlaḥah*) of the community into account, have neglected their traditional duties and, "are even open to purchase by the highest bidder. They have

put themselves up for auction" (*ibid.*, 169). The religion–state dichotomy has had far reaching consequences on the morality, mental aptitude, and religious thinking of Muslims. Nadwi argues that far from allowing moral degeneration to direct their lives, Muslims adopted Greek and foreign doctrines, methods, and ways of thought that were incompatible with the intellectual and theological orientation of the Qur'ān and, as a result, revealed and man-made law became confused. "If the Divine Law becomes tainted by human intervention," Nadwi maintains, "it will cease to be what it should – a guarantee for success in this world and the next. Neither will the human intellect submit to it, nor will the mind of man be won over" (*ibid.*, 95–6). Colonialism is an integral part of the modern Muslim consciousness, in spite of the fact that it is not of the making of Muslims. In other words, al Bahiy begins with the thesis that the "colonial fact" must be the basis of any discussion about modern Islamic thought. The primary goal of colonialism, he argues, is the weakening of Muslim doctrine, and consequently the weakening of Muslims themselves.

39. Abdallah Laroui, *The Crisis of the Arab Intelligentsia* (Berkeley: University of California Press, 1976).
40. S. J. al-'Azm, *al-Naqd al-dhātī ba'd al-hazīmah* (Beirut: Dār al-Ṭalī'ah, 1969).
41. F. Fūda, *Qabla al-ṣuqūt* (Cairo: n.p., 1985).
42. See Ghālī Shukrī, *Aqwās al-hazīmah: wa'y al-nukhbah bayna al-ma'rifah wa'l sulṭah* (Cairo: Dār al-Fikr, 1990). Shukrī thinks that the main reason behind the crisis of the Arab world is the failure of the Arab ruling classes to devise a new system after the loss of Palestine in 1948.
43. F. Zakariyya, *al-Ḥaqīqah wa'l khayāl fi'l harakah al-islāmiyyah al mu'āṣirah* (Cairo: Sīnā, 1988).
44. Consult the following works: Robert Brunschvig, "Problème de la décadence." In G. E. von Grunebaum and R. Brunschvig, eds., *Classicisme et déclin culturel dans l'histoire de l'islam* (Paris: Maisonneuve, 1957); W. Smith, *Islam in Modern History* (New York: New American Library, 1957); Hamilton Gibb, *Modern Trends in Islam* (Chicago: University of Chicago Press, 1947); G. E. von Grunebaum, *Modern Islam: The Search for Cultural Identity* (Berkeley: University of California Press, 1962).
45. Ḥassan Ḥanafī, *Muqadimah fī 'ilm al-istighrāb* (Cairo: al-Dār al-Faniyyah li'l Nashr wa'l Tawzī', 1991).
46. For many years, 'Alwānī was associated with the International Institute of Islamic Thought established in the United States in 1981. For a critical assessment of this movement, see 'Azīz 'Azmeh, "Aslamat al-ma'rifha wā jumūh allā 'aqlāniyyah al-siyāsiyyah." *Qaḍāyah Fikriyyah*, volumes 13 and 14, 1993, 407–19. Azmeh argues that the "Islamization of knowledge" trend was principally an ideological trend, logistically and financially made possible by money coming from the Gulf, for the purpose of co-opting certain Islamic elements in both the Arab world and the West. One must see this trend within the larger ideological and religious context of the Arab world in the 1970s and 1980s.
47. Ṭāhā 'Alwānī, "The Islamization of Methodology of Behavioral Sciences." *American Journal of the Islamic Social Sciences*, volume 6(2), December 1989, 234.
48. S. al-Khaṭīb, *Dawr al-manāhij al-gharbiyah fī siyādat manāhij al-taghrīb* (Cairo: IIIT, n.d.).
49. M. 'Imārah, *al-Jadīd fī mukhaṭaṭ al-'ālam al-gharbī tijāh al-muslimīn* (Cairo: IIIT, 1983), 7.
50. 'Imārah, *al-Ghazw al-fikrī: wahm am ḥaqīqhah* (International Institute of Islamic Thought: Cairo, 1988), 5.
51. 'Imārah agrees with Costantine Zurayk's thesis about cultural borrowing. See Zurayk, *Tensions in Islamic Civilization* (Georgetown: Center for Contemporary Arab Studies, 1978).
52. Marx says, "The production of ideas, of conceptions, of consciousness, is at first directly interwoven with the material activity and the material intercourse of men – the language of real life. Conceiving, thinking, the mental intercourse of men at this stage still appear[s] as the direct efflux of their material behavior. The same applies to mental production as expressed in the language of the politics, laws, morality, religion, metaphysics, etc., of a people. Men are the producers of their conceptions, ideas, etc., that is, real, active men, as they are conditioned by a definite development of their productive forces." Karl Marx and Frederick Engels, *Collected Works*, volume 5 (New York: International Publishers, 1976), 36.
53. 'Imārah, *al-Jadīd fī'l al-mukhaṭaṭ*, 1.

54. On Islamization perspective, see Ḥassan E. Ali, "The New World Order and the Islamic World." *American Journal of the Islamic Social Sciences*, volume 8(3), 1991, 461–72.
55. *Ibid.*, 7. A major representative of the civilizational conflict is Munīr Shafīq in *al-Islām fi ma'rakat al-ḥaḍārah* (Beirut: al-Nāsher, 1991), and *Qaḍāyah al-tanmiyyah wa'l istiqlāl fi'l ṣirā' al-ḥaḍārī* (Beirut: al-Nāsher, 1992).
56. M. 'Imārah, *Fikr al-tanwīr bayna al-'ilmāniyyīn wa'l islāmiyyīn* (Cairo: International Institute of Islamic Thought, 1993), 33.
57. 'Imārah, *al-Jadīd fi'l mukhataṭ*, 11.
58. See the analysis of this trend by both Qaraḍāwī and Lemu. Y. Qaraḍāwī, *The Islamic Awakening: Between Rejection and Extremism* (Herndon: IIIT, 1991), and A. Lemu, *Laxity, Moderation, and Extremism in Islam* (Herndon: International Institute of Islamic Thought, 1993).

7 GLOBALIZATION: A CONTEMPORARY ISLAMIC RESPONSE?

1. Giddens defines globalization "as the intensification of worldwide social relations which link distant localities in such a way that local happenings are shaped by events occuring many miles away and vice versa." Anthony Giddens, *The Consequences of Modernity* (Stanford: Stanford University Press, 1990), 64.
2. Of the few articles on globalization from an Islamic perspective, consult Zaki al-Milad, "Islamic Thought and the Issue of Globalization." *Middle East Affairs Journal*, volume 5(1–2), Winter–Spring 1999, 13–32.
3. See Ibrahim M. Abu-Rabi', *Intellectual Origins of Islamic Resurgence in the Modern Arab World* (Albany: State University of New York Press, 1996), chapter 1.
4. "The administration is yet to move beyond vague generalities regarding its concept of the post-war Middle East. Yet considerable anxiety is justified that subsequent to the war the United States might not be able to extricate itself from the Middle Eastern cauldron, especially if in the mean-time the Arab masses have become radicalized and hostile to the Arab regimes that endorsed the U.S. military action." Zbigniew Brzezinski, "The Effects of War." *New York Review of Books*, January 17, 1991, 8.
5. "With much of the Anglo-American media in the hands of the guardians of approved truths, the new imperialism, and the fate of faraway peoples, is reported and debated on the strict premise that the United States and British governments are opposed to violence as a means of resolving international disputes, and of course terrorism. The issue invariably is how best 'we' can deal with the problem of 'them'." John Pilger, *The New Rulers of the World* (London: Verso, 2002).
6. Indonesia has received a lot of coverage in the West lately. Consult the following: George Kahin, *Nationalism and Revolution in Indonesia* (Ithaca: Cornell University Press, 1952); Adam Schwarz, *A Nation in Waiting: Indonesia's Search for Stability* (St. Leonards, Australia: Allen & Unwin, 1999); Robert Hefner, *Civil Society: Muslims and Democratization in Indonesia* (Princeton: Princeton University Press, 2000); Michael Maher, *Indonesia: An Eyewitness Account* (Ringwood, Australia: Viking, 2000); V. S. Naipul, "Indonesia: The Man of the Moment." *New York Review of Books*, June 11, 1998, 40–5, and Noam Chomsky, "L'Indonésie, atout maitre du jeu américain." *Le Monde Diplomatique*, June 1998. Indonesia and several East Asian countries experienced economic collapse in 1998. According to one author, "The output losses from the East Asian Financial crisis from 1998 to 2000 were estimated at nearly $2 trillion (an amount double the income of the poorest fifth of the world's population). It was paid in loss of livelihood for tens of millions, dramatically rising poverty, small business bankruptcy, reduced health care and schooling for families under stress, and ineffectual governments who were suddenly unable to meet the modest obligations they had assumed." William K. Tapp, *The Amoral Elephant: Globalization and the Struggle for Social Justice in the Twenty-First Century* (New York: Monthly Review Press, 2001), 101.
7. See Gerard De Selys, *Tableau noir, appel à la résistance contre la privatisation de l'enseignement* (Brussels: EPO, 1998).
8. Helena Norberg-Hodge, "The Pressure to Modernize and Globalize," in Jerry Mander and Edward Goldsmith, eds., *The Case Against the Global Economy: And for a Turn Toward the Local* (San Francisco: Sierra Club Books, 1996), 36.

9. See Theodore Roszak, *The Cult of Information: The Folklore of Computers and the True Art of Thinking* (New York: Pantheon, 1986) and Vandana Shiva, *Monocultures of the Mind: Biodiversity, Biotechnology, and the Third World* (Penang, Malaysia: Third World Network, 1993).
10. One must understand the term "mode of production" in its dynamic sense. Eric Wolf argues that the utility of this concept "does not lie in the classification but in its capacity to underline the strategic relationships involved in the deployment of social labor by organized human pluralities...The concept of mode of production aims, rather, at revealing the political-economic relationships that underlie, orient, and constrain interaction." Eric Wolf, *Europe and the People Without History* (Berkeley: University of California Press, 1982), 76. Marx postulated that the bourgeoisie will always revolutionize the means of production and thus accelerate the expansion of the mode of production worldwide: "Marx's writing is famous for its endings. But if we see him as a modernist, we will notice the dialectical motion that underlies and animates his thought, a motion that is open-ended, and that flows against the current of his own concepts and desires. Thus, in *The Communist Manifesto*, we see that the revolutionary dynamic that will overthrow the modern bourgeoisie springs from that bourgeoisie's own deepest impulses and needs: The bourgeoisie cannot exist without constantly revolutionizing the instruments of production." Marshall Berman, *All That Is Solid Melts Into Air: The Experience of Modernity* (New York: Penguin books, 1982), 20. According to Immanuel Wallerstein, on the other hand, "Capitalism, emerging in the 16th century, became a world economic system only in the 19th century. It took the bourgeois revolutions 300 years to put an end to the power of the feudal elite." Immanuel Wallerstein, *The Capitalist World Economy* (Cambridge: Cambridge University Press, 1979), 13.
11. David Harvey, *Spaces of Hope* (Berkeley: University of California Press, 2000), 13.
12. See Samir Amin, *Unequal Development: An Essay on the Social Formations of Peripheral Capitalism* (New York: Monthly Review Press, 1976), and Wolf, *Europe and the People Without History*. Wolf argues that "The economic history of the Muslim world is still poorly known, but it is possible to outline some of its major aspects. Beginning with the eighth century, the Islamic countries underwent agricultural revolution that entailed changes in plants and plant strains, in farming practices, and in hydraulic technology...All this increased enormously the scale of Muslim trade relations and craft production, both for internal elites and for external consumers of luxury products." *Ibid.*, 103.
13. The exploitative nature of capitalism is based on the severance between the laborers and the means of production, "For labor power to be offered for sale, the tie between producers and the means of production has to be severed for good. Thus, holders of wealth must be able to acquire the means of production and deny access, except on their own terms, to all who want to operate them." Wolf, *Europe and the People Without History*, 77.
14. See V. I. Lenin, *Imperialism: The Highest Stage of Capitalism* (New York: International Publishers, 1939), and Ernest Mandel, *Late Capitalism* (London: Verso, 1978).
15. Andre Gunder Frank, *The Development of Underdevelopment* (New York: Monthly Review Press, 1969).
16. Wolf, *Europe and the People Without History*, 296.
17. See Ian Clark, *Globalization and Fragmentation: International Relations in the Twentieth Century* (Oxford: Oxford University Press, 1997), and in the case of India, for example, see R. Mukhrjee, *The Rise and Fall of the East India Company* (Berlin: Veb Deutscher Verlag der Wissenschaften, 1958).
18. See Edward Shils, *The Intellectuals and the Powers and Other Essays* (Chicago: University of Chicago Press, 1972), especially chapter 3, "Intellectuals in Underdeveloped Countries."
19. See chapter 6, "The Cold War and Globalization," in Clark, *Globalization and Fragmentation*, 122–47.
20. See H. Kissinger, *Years of Upheaval* (Boston: Little, Brown & Co., 1982), and *White House Years* (Boston: Little, Brown & Co., 1979).
21. On the domestic effects of the Cold War in the United States, see James T. Patterson, *Grand Expectations: The United States, 1945–1974* (New York: Oxford University Press, 1996).
22. Eric Hobsbawm contends that the world that "went to pieces at the end of the 1980s was the world shaped by the impact of the Russian revolution of 1917." Eric Hobsbawm, *The Age of Extremes: The Short Twentieth Century 1914–1991* (New York: Vintage, 1994), 4.

23. See J. Decornoyn, "Capital privé, développement du sud et solidarité mondiale: Les multinationales, omniprésentes et...impuissantes." *Le Monde Diplomatique*, November 1988, 8–9; M. Horsman and A. Marshall, *After the Nation State* (London: HarperCollins, 1994); K. Ohmae, *The Borderless World* (London: HarperCollins, 1990) and R. Reich, *The Work of Nations* (New York: Knopf, 1991). According to Samir Amin, "Although the new globalization [of the 1990s] has inhibited the ability of the nation-state to manage its domestic economy, it has not cancelled out the presence of the state." Samir Amin, *Fī muwājahatī azmatī 'aṣrinah* [*Face to Face With the Crisis of Our Age*] (Cairo: Sīnā Li'l Nashr, 1997), 71.
24. B. Karlin, "Space: New Frontier for US Entrepreneurs." *International Herald Tribune*, September 14, 1988.
25. Wealth has been transferred not just from the Periphery to the Center but also from the poor to the wealthy in the Center. On this see Simon Head, "The New, Ruthless Economy." *New York Review of Books*, February 29, 1996, 47–52.
26. Decornoyn, "Capital privé," 9.
27. Amin, *Fī muwājahatī*, 20–1.
28. Anthony G. McGrew, "Superpower Rivalry and US Hegemony in Central America," in Anthony G. McGrew and Paul G. Lewis, eds., *Global Politics: Globalization and the Nation-State* (Cambridge: Polity Press, 1992), 61–80.
29. See Z. Laidi *et al.*, *L'ordre mondial relâche* (Paris: Presses de la Fondation Nationale des Sciences, 1994). See also Paul Hirst and Grahame Thompson, "Globalization and the Future of the Nation State." *Economy and Society*, volume 24(3), August 1995, 408–42. They argue that the state has not lost its functions but that these functions have shifted to accommodate new realities.
30. See S. Strange, *The Retreat of the State: The Diffusion of Power in the World Economy* (Cambridge: Cambridge University Press, 1998).
31. See S. Amin, *Les défis de la mondialisation* (Paris: L'Harmattan/Forum du tiers-monde, 1996).
32. Amin, *Fī muwājahatī*, 133.
33. Immanuel Wallerstein, *After Liberalism* (New York: The New Press, 1995), 15.
34. See Daniel T. Griswold, "Blessings and Burdens of Globalization." *The World and I*, April 1998, 30–5.
35. See P. Bairoch and E. Helleiner, *States Against Markets: The Limits of Globalization* (London: Routledge, 1996).
36. See Peter Martin, "La mondialisation est-elle inévitable? Une obligation morale." *Le Monde Diplomatique*, June 1997, 14. The author claims the following: "Les débats sur la mondialisation se polarisent généralement sur ses enjeux économiques. Je voudrais, pour ma part, mettre en avant les arguments profondément moraux qui plaident en sa faveur, et que l'on peut résumer en une phrase: l'intégration accélérée de sociétés autrefois marginalisées est la meilleure chose qui soit arrivée du vivant de la génération d'après-guerre. La mondialisation constitue une authentique collaboration par-delà les frontières, des sociétés et des cultures, contrairement aux collaborations factices des dialogues Nord–Sud et des élites bureaucratiques." ("The debates over globalization are generally polarized around economic stakes. I would like to put forward the profoundly moral arguments which plead in its favor and that one can summarize in one phrase: the accelerated integration of previously marginalized societies is the best thing that has happened during the life of the post-war generation. Globalization consitutes an authentic collaboration beyond frontiers of societies and cultures contrary to fictitious collaborations of the North–South dialogues and the bureaucratic elite." Translation by Abu-Rabi'.) *Ibid.*, 14.
37. Ignacio Ramonet, "Régimes globalitaires." *Le Monde Diplomatique*, January 1997, 1. According to Ramonet, "On appelait 'régimes totalitaires' ces régimes à parti unique qui n'admettaient aucune opposition organisée, qui subordonnaient les droits de la personne à la raison d'Etat, et dans lesquels le pouvoir politique dirigeait souverainement la totalité des activités de la société dominée. A ces systèmes succède, en cette fin de siècle, un autre type de totalitarisme, celui des 'régimes globalitaires'. Reposant sur les dogmes de la globalization et de la pensée unique, ils n'admettent aucune autre politique économique, subordonnent les droits sociaux du citoyen à la raison compétitive, et abandonnent aux marchés financiers la direction totale des activités de la société dominée." ("We use to call 'totalitarian regimes' those single-party regimes who brook no organized opposition, and who subordinate the rights of the individuals to the needs of the state

and in whom the political power directed supremely the totality of the activities of the dominated society. To these systems one must add, at the end of this century, a different type of totalitarianism, that of 'global regimes.' Supported by the dogmas of globalization and unique thought, they accept no other political economy and subordinate the social rights of the citizens to the competitive needs and abandon to the final market the total direction of the activities of the dominated society." Translation by Abu-Rabi'.) *Ibid.*

38. See Paul Hirst and Graham Thompson, *Globalization in Question: The International Economy and the Possibilities of Government* (Cambridge: Polity Press, 1996) and Joseph E. Stiglitz, *Globalization and its Discontents* (New York: W. W. Norton & Co., 2002). According to Stiglitz, the IMF has global power without being accountable to the poor nations.
39. Charlene Spretnak, *The Resurgence of the Real: Body, Nature and Place in a Hypermodern World* (New York: Addison-Wesley, 1997), 34.
40. See C. de Brie, "Le couple Etat-nation en instance de divorce." *Le Monde Diplomatique*, May 1989.
41. See Nancy Birdsall, "Life is Unfair: Inequality in the World." *Foreign Policy*, Summer 1998, 95–113.
42. Benedict Anderson, *Imagined Communities: Reflections on the Origin and Spread of Nationalism* (London: Routledge, 1991), 140.
43. Pierre Bourdieu, "L'essence du néolibéralisme." *Le Monde Diplomatique*, March 1998, 3.
44. According to Frederic Jameson, most people in the world do not consider English to be a language of high culture, "it is the lingua franca of money and power, which you have to learn and use for practical but scarcely for aesthetic reasons." Frederic Jameson, "Notes on Globalization as Philosophical Issue," in Frederic Jameson and Masao Miyoshi, eds., *The Cultures of Globalization* (Durham: Duke University Press, 1999), 59.
45. Terry Eagleton, "The Crisis of Contemporary Culture." *New Left Review*, number 196, November–December 1992, 31.
46. According to Cohn, "The process of state building in Great Britain, seen as a cultural project, was closely linked with its emergence as an imperial power, and India was its largest and most important colony." Bernard S. Cohn, *Colonialism and its Forms of Knowledge: The British in India* (Princeton: Princeton University Press, 1996), 3.
47. Walter D. Mignolo, "Globalization, Civilization Processes, and the Relocation of Languages and Cultures," in Jameson and Miyoshi, *The Cultures of Globalization,* 37.
48. H. L. Mencken, *The American English: An Inquiry into the Development of English in the United States* (New York: Alfred A. Knopf, 1955), 25.
49. Richard Ohman, "English and the Cold War," in Noam Chomsky *et al., The Cold War and the University: Toward an Intellectual History of the Cold War Years* (New York: The New Press, 1997), 73.
50. Mignolo, "Globalization," 41. The author observes that although more people speak Spanish than French and German, it has been displaced by the European Center as a language of modernity.
51. Joseph S. Nye, Jr., *The Paradox of American Power: Why the World's Only Superpower Can't Go it Alone* (New York: Oxford University Press, 2002), 95.
52. See E. J. Perkins, *The World Economy in the Twentieth Century* (Cambridge: Schenkman, 1983).
53. M. Beaud, "Jamais tant de richesses, jamais tant de misère...sur les causes de la pauvreté des nations et des hommes dans le monde contemporain." *Le Monde Diplomatique*, November 1997, 11.
54. See Charles William Maynes, "The Perils of an Imperial America." *Foreign Policy*, Summer 1998, 36–49.
55. One must note that even some European, most notably French, intellectuals, are discussing ways to respond to what they see as the American cultural menace to Europe, and are seeking ways to protect cultural diversity and reviving their cultural independence vis-à-vis the United States of America. See Paul-Marie de la Gorce, *Le Dernier Empire* (Paris: Grasset, 1996), and Ignacio Ramonet, "L'empire américain." *Le Monde Diplomatique*, February 1997, 1. Henry Kissinger reflects the American view on this matter, "A united Europe is likely to insist on a specifically European view of world affairs – which is another way of saying that it will challenge American hegemony in Atlantic policy. This may well be a price worth paying for European unity, but

American policy has suffered from an unwillingness to recognize that there is a price to be paid." Kissinger, *White House Years*, 82. Another architect of contemporary American policy argues that the strategic task of the United States is to prevent the emergence of a dominant and antagonistic Eurasian power and to create a stable continental equilibrium with the United States as political arbiter. See Zbigniew Brzezinski, *The Grand Chessboard: American Primacy and its Geostrategic Imperatives* (New York: Basic Books, 1997), especially chapter 2.

56. A. Ahmad, *Islamic Modernism in India and Pakistan* (London: Oxford University Press, 1967).
57. For a detailed discussion, see Abu-Rabi', *Intellectual Origins*, especially chapter 1.
58. What happens to the arms industry after the end of the Cold War? According to Anderson, "Up to a point, it is plausible to argue that the end of the Cold War and the implosion of the Soviet Union may to some extent reduce the flow of munitions around the world. But Moscow's contribution to the flow was always substantially smaller than that of Washington, let alone the West as a whole. Furthermore, it was largely state-directed and outside the market. At the same time, half a century of Cold War has created huge military-industrial complexes in the West, which will powerfully resist attempts to curb their reach, and for which the world arms market...remains an irresistible magnet. Arms production itself has spread quite rapidly outside the old cores – to Brazil and Argentina, Israel, India, China, even places like Thailand and Indonesia." Benedict Anderson, "The New World Disorder." *New Left Review*, number 193, May–June 1992, 11.
59. 'Abd al-Ilāh Bilqazīz, "al-'Awlamah wa'l hawiyyah al-thaqāfiyyah" [Globalization and Cultural Identity], *Al-Mustaqbal al-'Arabī*, March 1998, 92.
60. "Le post-colonialisme est un phénomène très récent qui date du début des années 1990, comme suite à la chute des régimes communistes, la Guerre du Golfe et l'effritement du peu d'unité que le Tiers Monde était parvenu à construire...Le post-colonialisme est, avant tout, le produit du 'nouvel ordre mondial'." ("Post-colonialism is a recent phenomenon dating from the beginning of the 1990s, effected by the fall of the communist regimes, the Gulf War, and the unraveling of the small amount of unity the Third World had managed to build...Post-colonialism is, above all, the product of the 'new world order'." Translation by Abu-Rabi'.) Mahdi Elmandjra, *La décolonisation culturelle: Défi majeur du 21ème siècle* (Marrakech [Morocco]: Editions Walili, and Paris: Futuribles, 1996), 208.
61. Pierre Bourdieu notes that in its urge to control world markets, imperialism drapes itself in the legitimacy of international bodies. It uses rationalization as a means to coerce and control. That is why it is normal for the people of the Third World to revolt against this type of exploitative rationalism, "One is still defending reason when one fights those who mask their abuses of power under the appearances of reason or who use the weapons of reason to consolidate or justify an arbitrary empire." Pierre Bourdieu, *Acts of Resistance: Against the Market* (New York: The New Press, 1998), 20.
62. See for example Muḥammad 'Ābid al-Jābīrī, *Introduction à la critique de la raison arabe* (Casablanca: Editions le Fennec, 1995) and *al-Mashrū' al-nahḍawi al-'arabī* [*The Project of Arab Renaissance*] (Beirut: Markaz Dirāsāt al-Wiḥdah al-'Arabīyyah, 1996).
63. De la Gorce, *Le Dernier Empire*, 16.
64. Claude Julien, *L'empire américain* (Paris: Grasset, 1968), 25. The same ideas are presented by Jean-Jacques Servan-Schreiber, *Le défi américain* (Paris: Denoël, 1967).
65. On this phenomenon, see the following: Antonio Gramsci, "Americanism and Fordism," in *The Prison Notebooks* (New York: International Publishers, 1971), 279–316; M. Aglietta, *A Theory of Capitalist Regulation: The US Experience* (London: Verso, 1979) and "World Capitalism in the Eighties." *New Left Review*, number 136, November/December 1982; Michael Rustin, "The Politics of New Fordism or the Trouble with 'New Times'." *New Left Review*, number 175, May/June 1989, 54–78.
66. Robert J. Antonio and Alessandro Bonanno, "Post-Fordism in the United States: The Poverty of Market-Centered Democracy." *Current Perspectives in Social Theory*, volume 16, 1996, 4.
67. It must be noted that the economic system of the United States began to crystallize by the end of the nineteenth century. From the fifteenth to the eighteenth centuries, an Atlantic capitalist class was in power, "With an Atlantic class united around the defense of property in general, and slave-holding in particular, and with the 'middle classes' effectively co-opted as junior partners in the hegemonic bloc, there was no space for successful general slave uprisings...Meanwhile, the white

population – which constituted one great militia, fully and extravagantly armed, was united around defending the privileges that came from slaveholding or racism or both." Beverly J. Silver and Eric Slater, "The Social Origins of World Hegemonies," in Giovanni Arrighi and Beverly J. Silver, eds., *Chaos and Governance in the Modern World System* (Minneapolis: Minnesota University Press, 1999), 158–9.

68. Noam Chomsky, "Power in the Global Arena." *New Left Review*, number 230, July–August 1998, 4. David Harvey elaborates on the history of modernism and post-modernism in the West and how these phenomena were appropriated by Americanism directly after World War Two. He says that around 1945, "What was distinctively American had to be celebrated as the essence of Western culture. And so it was with abstract expressionism, along with liberalism, Coca-Cola and Chevrolets, and suburban houses full of consumer durables. Avant-garde artists...now political 'neutral' individualists, articulated in their works values that were subsequently assimilated, utilized and co-opted by politicians, with the result that artistic rebellion was transformed into aggressive liberal ideology." David Harvey, *The Condition of Postmodernity* (Oxford: Blackwell, 1989), 37.
69. Harvey, *The Condition of Postmodernity*, 129, 136, 137.
70. *Ibid.*, 139.
71. "U.S. hegemony has been based on efforts to win consent on a deeper (class) basis – reaching out to core working classes with promises of mass consumption." Silver and Slater, "The Social Origins of World Hegemonies," 207.
72. Michael Rustin, "The Politics of New Fordism," 55.
73. Edmund Wilson, *The American Earthquake: A Chronicle of the Roaring Twenties, the Great Depression and the Dawn of the New Deal* (New York: Da Capo Press, 1996), 569.
74. "In other words, because of the interconnection of the whole world and the potential automation of most standard production and management functions, the generation and control of knowledge, information and technology is a necessary and sufficient condition to organize the overall social structure around the interests of the information holders. Information becomes the critical raw material of which all social processes and social organizations are made." Manuel Castells, "European Cities, the Information Society, and the Global Economy." *New Left Review*, number 204, March–April 1994, 21.
75. Robert J. Antonio and Alessandro Bonanno, "Post-Fordism in the United States: The Poverty of Market-Centered Democracy." *Current Perspectives in Social Theory*, volume 16, 1996, 8–12.
76. Immanuel Wallerstein, *The Capitalist World Economy* (Cambridge: Cambridge University Press, 1979), 31–2, italics added.
77. Antonio and Bonanno, "Post-Fordism in the United States," 13.
78. Muḥammad 'Ābid al-Jābirī, "al-'Awlamah, niẓām wa aydiyūlūjiyyah," in al-Majlis al-Qawmī li'l Thaqāfah al-'Arabīyyah, *al-'Arab wa taḥādiyāt al-'awlamah* (Rabat: al-Majlis al-Qawmī li'l Thaqāfah al-'Arabīyyah, 1997), 15. A number of Islamist and Arab nationalist thinkers share the above views. For example, Egyptian Islamist Muḥammad Ibrāhīm Mabrūk contends in a very controversial book that the United States encourages pragmatism in the Muslim world as a means of colonizing this world in a new way. See Mabrūk, *Amerika wa'l islām al-nafi'ī* [*America and Pragmatic Islam*] (Cairo: Dār al-Tawzī' wa'l Nashr al-Islāmiyah, 1989), 191–211. See also 'Ādil Ḥussein, *al-Iqtiṣād al-miṣrī: minā al-istiqlāl ilā al-taba'iyyah* [*The Egyptian Economy: From Autonomy to Dependency*] (Cairo: Dār al-Mustaqbal al-'Arabī, 1986), and Ramzī Zakī, *Mushkilāt miṣr al-iqtiṣādiyyah* [*Egypt's Economic Problems*] (Cairo: Dār al-Fata al-'Arabī, 1982).
79. On an important aspect of the defense industry in the United States, see A. Ernest Fitgerald, *The Pentagonists: An Insider's View of Waste, Mismanagement, and Fraud in Defense Spending* (New York: Houghton Mifflin, 1989), and Thomas McNaugher, *New Weapons, Old Politics: America's Military Procurement Muddle* (Washington, D.C.: Hoover Institution, 1989). In criticizing American foriegn policy, American essayist Lewis Lapham notes, "Elsewhere in the world, the record of American diplomatic achievement over the last thirty years doesn't inspire a similar degree of confidence. We're good with slogans, but we don't have much talent for fostering the construction of exemplary democracies; we tend to betray our allies, dishonor our treaties, and avoid the waging of difficult or expensive wars." Lewis Lapham, "The Road to Babylon: Searching for Targets in Iraq." *Harper's Magazine*, October 2002, 38–9.

80. Ramonet, "L'empire américain," 1. See also Paul Sālem, "al-'Arab wa'l 'awlamah." *al-Mustaqabal al-'Arabī*, March, 1998, 78–90.
81. Muḥammad 'Ābid al-Jābīrī, *Mas'alt al-hawiyah: al-'urūbah, al-islām wa'l gharb* [*The Issue of Identity: Arabism, Islam, and the Occident*] (Beirut: Markaz Dirāsāt al-Wiḥdah al-'Arabīyyah, 1995), 16.
82. Noam Chomsky, *World Orders Old and New* (New York: Columbia University Press, 1994), 74–5. See also Noam Chomsky, *Profit Over People: Neoliberalism and Global Order* (New York: Seven Stories Press, 1999), 21.
83. "Mais la libération du Sud passe d'abord par une décolonisation culturelle car un des principaux objectifs du post-colonialisme est l'hégémonie culturelle et la propagation des valeurs occidentales. Les conflits à venir seront des conflits de valeurs et il y a une très grande urgence à développer une communication culturelle entre le Nord et le Sud." ("But the liberation of the South passes first by a process of cultural decolonization because one of the main objectives of post-colonialism is cultural hegemony and the propagation of Western values. The coming conflicts will be those of values and there is a great urgency to develop a cultural dialogue between North and South." Translation by Abu-Rabi'.) Elmandjra, *La décolonisation culturelle*, 214.
84. "Le Nord à deployé jusqu'à présent très peu d'efforts pour comprendre et encore moins pour parler le langage du Sud. Il faut accorder une priorité aux systèmes de valeurs pour se rendre compte que la crise actuelle entre le Nord et le Sud est une crise du système total." ("Until now, the North has made precious little effort to understand and even less to speak the language of the South. We have to assign a priority to the value systems in order to realize that the current crisis between North and South is a crisis of the entire system." Translation by Abu-Rabi'.) Mahdi Elmandjra, *Rétrospectif des futurs* (Casablanca: Ouyoun, 1992), 164.
85. Elmandjra, *La décolonisation culturelle*, 215.
86. Elmandjra, *al-Harb al-hadariyyah al-ulah* [*The First Civilizational War*] (Casablanca: 'Uyun, 1994), 21–2.
87. Samuel Huntington, *The Clash of Civilizations and the Remaking of World Order* (New York: Simon & Schuster, 1996).
88. Brian Goodwin, *How the Leopard Changed its Spots: The Evolution of Complexity* (New York: Charles Scribner's Sons, 1994), and Mitchell M. Waldrop, *Complexity: The Emerging Science at the Edge of Order and Chaos* (New York: Simon & Schuster, 1992).
89. Manuel Castells, "European Cities, the Informational Society, and the Global Economy." *New Left Review*, number 204, March/April 1994, 21. "The generation and control of knowledge, information and technology is a necessary and sufficient condition to organize the overall social structure around the interests of the information holders. Information becomes the critical raw material of which all social processes and social organizations are made." *Ibid.*
90. Richard Falk, "Vers une domination mondiale de nouveau type." *Le Monde Diplomatique*, May 1996, 16.
91. See Joseph Nye and William Owens, "America's Information Edge." *Foreign Affairs*, March–April 1996.
92. S. Sassen, *Losing Control? Sovereignty in an Age of Globalization* (New York: Columbia University Press, 1996).
93. See the interesting article by Le Sous-Commandant Marcos, "La 4e guerre mondiale a commencé." *Le Monde Diplomatique*, August 1997.

8 CONTEMPORARY ARAB THOUGHT AND GLOBALIZATION

1. Paul Sālem, "al-Wilāyāt al-mutahiddah wa'l 'awlamah: ma'ālim al-haymanah fī maṭla' al-qarn al-ḥādī wa'l 'ishrīn," in Markaz Dirāsāt al-Wiḥdah al-'Arabīyyah, *al-'Arab wa'l 'Awlamah* (Beirut: Markaz Dirāsāt al-Wiḥdah al-'Arabīyyah, 1998), 209–52.
2. Ismā'īl Ṣabrī 'Abdallah, "al-Kawkabah: al-ra'smāliyyah al-'ālamiyyah fī marḥalatī mā ba'da al-imberiāliyyah." *Al-Ṭarīq*, volume 56(4), July–August 1997, 45–69. According to Tapp, "In what has been called the Third World, local elites no longer pursue protectionist national development strategies but welcome openness and their role as regional agents of international capital. They

work to integrate their economies into globalized networks, typically not seeking the best deal for their country's workers and taxpayer." William K. Tapp, *The Amoral Elephant: Globalization and the Struggle for Social Justice in the Twenty-First Century* (New York: Monthly Review Press, 2001), 182.

3. A. 'Azmī Bishāra. "Isrā'īl wa'l 'awlamah: b'ad jawānib jadaliyat al-'awlamah isrā'īliyan," in Markaz Dirāsāt al-Wiḥdah al-'Arabīyyah, *al-'Arab wa'l 'Awlamah*, 281–96.
4. See Maḥmūd Amīn al-'Ālim, ed., *al-Fikr al-'arabī bayna al-'awlamah wa'l ḥadāthah wā mā ba'da al-hadātha. Qaḍāya Fikriyya*, volumes 19–20, 1999. Contributors to this volume include, among many others, Maḥmūd Amīn al-'Ālim, Samīr Amīn, 'Iṣṣām Khafājī, Fāris Abī Ṣa'b, Amīna Rashīd, Muḥammad Ḥāfiẓ Diyāb, 'Arūs al-Zubayrī, Ṭāher Labīb, and Feriāl Ghazoul.
5. Maḥmūd Amīn al-'Ālim, "al-'Awlamah wā khiyārāt al-mustaqbal," *Qaḍāyah Fikriyyah*, volumes 19–20, 1999, 11.
6. *Ibid*., 9–11.
7. On Indonesia, see the classic work by George Kahin, *Nationalism and Revolution in Indonesia* (Ithaca: Cornell University Press, 1952). According to Benedict Anderson, the renowned South Asianist of Cornell University, the West took turns at exploiting the Third World, "Furthermore, mottled imperialism came not in the late nineteenth-century rush, as happened to most of Africa, but stretched across the centuries: the Portuguese and Spaniards arrived in the late feudal sixteenth century, the Dutch in the mercantilist seventeenth, the British in the enlightened eighteenth, the French in the industrial nineteenth, and the Americans in the motorized twentieth." Benedict Anderson, *The Spectre of Comparisons: Nationalism, Southeast Asia and the World* (London: Verso, 1998), 5.
8. Compare al-'Ālim's position on civilization to the following statement: "Civilization then has a double edge: the ideological justification of European economic expansion and the foundation of a field of study that located Europe as the the locus of enunciation and other civilizations of the planet as the locus of the enunciated." Walter D. Mignolo, "Globalization, Civilization Processes, and the Relocation of Languages and Cultures," in Frederic Jameson and Masao Miyoshi, eds., *The Cultures of Globalization* (Durham: Duke University Press, 1999), 33.
9. Samuel Huntington, *The Clash of Civilizations and the Remaking of the World Order* (New York: Simon & Schuster, 1996).
10. Al-'Ālim, "al-'Awlamah," 25.
11. According to Noam Chomsky, American capitalism is the most dominant in the world for various reasons, one of which is the great support the American state grants private capital, "The word 'capitalist' doesn't mean capitalist. Rather, what it refers to is state-subsidized and protected private power-centers – 'collective legal entities', as they are called by legal historians – internally tyrannical, unaccountable to the public, granted extraordinary rights by U.S. courts in radical violation of classical liberal ideals." Noam Chomsky, "Power in the Global Arena." *New Left Review*, number 230, July–August 1998, 4.
12. Compare al-'Ālim's views on American capitalism to the following: "American capitalism, after the triumph of the North in the Civil War, became an industrial power of a kind still unknown in Europe, geared to constant technological innovation and fed by a steady flow of immigrant labor, offering vast opportunities for a business class in command of a state devoted to its unlimited expansion." Peter Gowan, "A Calculus of Power." *New Left Review*, number 16, July–August 2002, 63.
13. Al-'Ālim, "al-'Awlamah," 25.
14. Al-'Ālim, *Mafāhīm wā Qaḍāya ishkālīya* (Cairo: Dār al-Thaqāfah al-Jadīdah, 1989), 18.
15. Al-'Ālim agrees, more or less, with the central thesis of British sociologist Anthony Giddens that globalization is a consequence of modernity. Giddens says that globalization means the "intensification of worldwide social relations which link distinct localities in such a way that local happenings are shaped by events occuring miles away and vice versa." Anthony Giddens, *The Consequences of Modernity* (Stanford: Stanford University Press, 1990), 64.
16. Al-'Ālim, *Mafāhīm wā Qaḍāya ishkālīya*, 28–9.
17. *Ibid*., 19.
18. Al-'Azm is a pioneer thinker in the contemporary Arab world. In the late 1960s, he authored two major studies around the critique of Arab "religious reason" and the Arab defeat. See *Naqd*

al-fikr al-dīnī (Beirut: Dār al-Ṭalī'ah, 1969) and *al-Naqd al-dhātī ba'da al-hazīmah* (Beirut: Dār al-Ṭalī'ah, 1969). He also wrote a major commentary on Edward Said's Orientalism entitled "Orientalism and Orientalism in Reverse." *Forbidden Agendas* (London: al-Saqi Books, 1984). Lately, he has written two books on the Salman Rushdie controversy. See *Dhihniyat al-taḥrīm: Salmān Rushdī wā ḥaqīqat al-adab* (Damascus: Dār al-Mada, 1997), and *Mā ba'da dhihniyat al-taḥrīm: qirā'at al-āyāt al-shayṭāniyyah* (Damascus: Dār al-Mada, 1997). See also his article "The Importance of Being Earnest about Salman Rushdie," in D. M. Fletcher, ed., *Reading Rushdie* (Amsterdam: Redopi, 1994).

19. Both Samir Amin and Immanuel Wallerstein propose such an argument.
20. Ṣādiq Jalāl al-'Azm, "Ma hiya al-'awlamah?" *Al-Ṭariq*, volume 56(4), July–August 1997, 31. See V. I. Lenin, *Imperialism: The Highest Stage of Capitalism* (New York: International Publishers, 1939). For a general overview of imperialism, consult Harry Magdoff, *Imperialism: From the Colonial Age to the Present* (New York: Monthly Review Press, 1978).
21. Al-'Azm, "Ma hiya al-'awlamah?," 34.
22. In the words of Egyptian Marxist economist Fu'ād Mursī, "Capitalism is undergoing a new phase in its current evolution, which can best be described as post-industrialization, and which has come on the heels of its mecantilist, industrial, and investment phases." Fu'ād Mursī, *al-Ra'smāliyyah tujaddid nafsahah* (Kuwait: 'Ālam al-Ma'rifah, 1990), 7.
23. See Karl Kautsky, "Ultra-imperialism." *New Left Review*, number 59, 1970, 41–6.
24. Al-'Azm, "Mā hiya al-'awlamah?," in Haṣṣan Ḥanafī and Ṣādiq Jalāl al-'Azm, *Mā al-'awlamah*? (Damascus: Dār al-Fikr, 1999), 167.
25. Al-'Azm echoes Noam Chomsky's ideas on the matter. Chomsky argues that even after the Cold War, "the Pentagon budget remains at normal Cold War levels and is now increasing." Noam Chomsky, "Free Trade and Free Market: Pretense and Practice," in Jameson and Miyoshi, *The Cultures of Globalization*, 359.
26. Galāl Amīn, *al-'Awlamah* (Cairo: Dār al-Ma'ārif, 1998), 66–9.
27. See Galāl Amīn, *The Modernization of Poverty: A Study in the Political Economy of Growth in Nine Arab Countries* (Leiden: Brill, 1974).
28. Amīn, *Whatever Happened to the Egyptians? Changes in Egyptian Society from 1950 to the Present* (Cairo: American University Press, 2000), 9.
29. Amīn, *Miṣr fī muftaraq al-ṭuruq: bayna iflās al-yamīn, wa miḥnati al-yasār wā azmati al-tayyār al-dīnī* (Cairo: Dār al-Mustaqbal al-'Arabī, 1990), 9–13.
30. Amīn, *al-'Awlamah* (Cairo: Dār al-Ma'ārif, 1998), 28.
31. See Amīn, *Whatever Happened to the Egyptians?*. Amīn observes that one of the main consequences of globalization in Egyptian society in the 1980s and 1990s has been the rise in religious fanaticism, "All of this may bring us closer to understanding the growth of religious fanaticism. A natural tendency toward the stricter observance of religious teachings in the rising sections of the population with very modest social backgrounds, can easily turn into religious fanaticism if associated with severe frustration of earlier hopes of social advancement." *Ibid.*, 37.
32. Amīn, *al-'Awlamah*, 28–9.
33. Thomas L. Friedman, *The Lexus and the Olive Tree* (New York: Anchor Books, 2000). Friedman envisions the Israeli role in globalization as follows: "Israel will be a high-tech locomotive that will pull Jordan and the Palestinians with it. Already Siemens has linked up its Israeli factory...near Haifa, and a Siemens team of Palestinian systems engineers in the West Bank town of Ramallah, with Siemens headquarters back in Germany. It's just the beginning." *Ibid.*, 264.
34. Amīn, "Mab'ūth al-'awlamah aw Thomas Friedman wal' muthaqaffūn al-miṣriyyūn." *Wijhāt Nadhar*, volume 2(14), March 2000, 41.
35. Jābīrī, "al-'Arab wa'l 'awlamah: al-'awlamah wa'l hawiyyah al-thaqāfiyyah," in Markaz Dirāsāt al-Wiḥdah al-'Arabīyyah, *al-'Arab wa'l 'awlamah* (Beirut: Markaz Dirāsāt al-Wiḥdah al-'Arabīyyah, 1998), 298.
36. *Ibid.*, 300.
37. According to the Lebanese thinker Paul Sālem, the United States has exported "low culture" to the world since "high culture" has a limited market overseas. See Paul Sālem, "al-Wilāyāt al-mutahiddah," 221.
38. See 'Abd al-Bāsit 'Abd al-Mu'ṭī, *al-I'lām wa tazyīf al-wa'y* (Cairo: Dār al-Thaqāfah al-Jadīdah, 1979).

39. Frederic Jameson, "Notes on Globalization as Philosophical Issue," in Jameson and Miyoshi, *The Cultures of Globalization,* 64. Jameson also notes that, "We do not here sufficiently notice...the significance, in the Gatt and Nafta negotiations and agreements, of the cultural clauses, and of the struggle between immense U.S. cultural interests, who want to open up foreign borders to American films, television, music, and the like, and foreign nation-states who still place a premium on the preservation and development of their national languages and cultures and attempt to limit the damages – both material and social – caused by the leveling power of American mass culture: material on account of the enormous financial interests involved; social because of the very change in values likely to be wrought by what used to be called – when it was a far limited phenomenon – Americanization." *Ibid.*, 59.
40. Jābīrī, "al-'Arab wa'l 'awlamah," 303.
41. *Ibid.*, 305.
42. The following article gives a partial idea about the Islamist discussion of globalization: Zaki al-Milad, "Islamic Thought and the Issue of Globalization." *Middle East Affairs Journal*, volume 5(1–2), Winter–Spring 1999. Of the many Islamist thinkers who have written on globalization, mention should be made of 'Abdul Wahāb al-Masīrī, Jamāl al-Banna, Muḥammad Ibrāhīm Mabrūk, and Yūsuf al-Qaraḍāwī.
43. Al-Qaraḍāwī, *al-Muslimūn wa'l 'awlamah* (Cairo: Dār al-Tawzī' wa'l Nashr al-Islāmiyyah, 2000), 13, and Muḥammad Quṭb, *al-Muslimūn wa'l 'awlamah* (Cairo: Dār al-Shurūq, 2000), 10. See also Sa'īd Ḥarib, *al-Thaqāfah wa'l 'awlamah* (al-'Ayn [U.A.E.]: Dār al-Kitāb al-Jāmi'ī, 2000).
44. Qaraḍāwī, *al-Muslimūn wa'l 'awlamah*, 16.
45. *Ibid.*, 132.
46. Massignon thinks this is a *ḥadīth qudsī*. See Louis Massignon, *Essay on the Technical Language of Islamic Mysticism*, trans. Benjamin Clark (Notre Dame: University of Notre Dame Press, 1997), 165. See Muḥammad Quṭb, *al-Muslimūn wa'l 'awlamah*, 46. Another Ḥadīth stipulates, "Be in this world as if you were a stranger or an *'ābir sabil* or passer-by." The Persian mystic Abu Ḥamza al-KhurasāNī was asked once: "Who is a stranger (*gharīb*)? He replied, 'he who shuns society,' because the dervish has no home or society either in this world or the next, and when he is dissociated from phenomenal existence, he shuns everything, and then he is a stranger; and this is a very lofty degree." 'Alī bin Uthmān al-Hujwīrī, *The Kashf al-Maḥjūb: The Oldest Persian Treatise on Sufism*, trans. Reynold A. Nicholson (Bombay: Tāj Company, 1999), 146.
47. Muḥammad Ibrāhīm Mabrūk, an Islamist thinker, argues that globalization means the domination of consumerism in society and the use of military, political, and propagandist means to enforce this way of life. Pragmatism is the ideological rationale behind American globalization today. See Mabrūk, ed., *al-Islām wa'l 'awlamah* (Cairo: al-Dār al-Qawmiyyah al-'Arabīyyah, 1999), 84–5.
48. Roland Robertson, *Globalization: Social Theory and Global Culture* (London: Sage, 1996), 8.
49. See al-'Ālim, *al-Wa'y wa'l wa'y al-zā'if fi'l fikr al-'arabī al-mu'āṣir* (Cairo: Dār al-Thaqāfah al-Jadīdah, 1986), 242.
50. *Ibid.*, 123.
51. Ismā'īl Ṣabrī 'Abdallah, an Egyptian Leftist economist, spends a great deal of time worrying about the viability of the state in the Arab world. He argues that a combination of political and economic factors has weakened the state in a number of Arab countries, most notably in Yemen, Somalia, Algeria, and Lebanon. In some Third World countries, the state authority has disappeared completely for a while. See Ismā'īl Ṣabrī 'Abdallah, "al-'Arab wa'l 'awlamah: al-'awlamah wa'l iqtiṣād wa'l tanmiyyah al-'arabīyyah," in Markaz Dirāsāt al-Wiḥdah al-'Arabīyyah, *al-'Arab wa'l 'Awlamah*, 371.
52. See Muḥammad Ḥāfiẓ Diyāb, "Ta'rīb al-'awlamah: musā'alah naẓariyyah," in Maḥmūd Amīn al-'Ālim, ed., *al-Fikr al-'arabī bayna al-'awlamah wa'l ḥadāthah wā mā ba'da al-hadāthah. Qaḍāyah Fikriyyah*, volumes 19–20, 1999, 151.
53. Robertson advocates the moral acceptance of the complexity of the contemporary world. See Robertson, *Globalization*, 28.
54. 'Abdallah, "al-'Arab wa'l 'awlamah," 382–6.
55. See Charles Adams, *Islam and Modernism in Egypt* (New York: Oxford University Press, 1933).

56. Enrique Dussel, "Beyond Eurocentrism: The World-System and the Limits of Modernity," in Jameson and Miyoshi, *The Cultures of Globalization*, 13.
57. Mignolo, "Globalization," 36–7.
58. See K. N. Chaudhuri, *Trade and Civilization in the Indian Ocean: An Economic History from the Rise of Islam to 1750* (Cambridge: Cambridge University Press, 1985).
59. Enrique Dussel, *The Invention of the Americas: Eclipse of the "Other" and the Myth of Modernity* (New York: Continuum, 1995), 123–4.
60. See Ibrahim M. Abu-Rabi', "Beyond the Post-Modern Mind." *American Journal of the Islamic Social Sciences* 7, September 1990, 235–56.
61. See Jean-Marie Domenach, *Enquête sur les idées contemporaines* (Paris: Points, 1987).
62. Charlene Spretnak, *The Resurgence of the Real: Body, Nature and Place in a Hypermodern World* (New York: Addison-Wesley, 1997), 2.
63. Hannah Arendt, *The Origins of Totalitarianism* (Cleveland: Meridian Books, 1963), 143. "Imperialism, the product of superfluous money and superfluous men, began its startling career by producing the most superfluous and unreal goods." *Ibid.*, 151.
64. Richard Falk, *Explorations at the Edge of Time: The Prospects for World Order* (Philadelphia: Temple University Press, 1992), 48.
65. See David R. Griffin and Huston Smith, *Primordial Truth and Postmodern Theology* (Albany: State University of New York Press, 1989). One must note that Christian thinkers and theologians were quicker than their Muslim counterparts in providing ethical answers to the challenges of globalization. Consult Hans Kung, *A Global Ethic for Global Politics and Economics* (New York: Oxford University Press, 1998), especially chapter 2.
66. See Akbar S. Ahmed, *Postmodernism and Islam: Predicament and Promise* (London: Routledge, 1992), and Akbar S. Ahmed and Donnan Hastings, eds., *Islam, Globalization and Postmodernity* (London: Routledge, 1994). See also Walden Bello, *New Third World: Strategies for Survival in the Global Economy* (London: Earthscan, 1990).

9 RĀSHID AL-GHANNŪSHĪ AND THE QUESTIONS OF SHARĪ'AH AND CIVIL SOCIETY

1. Popular Western attitude towards Islamism is negative, to say the least. According to a French author, "L'Intégrisme musulman est une menace très grave dans notre pays, et il faut le combattre. Selon un sondage récent, 78% des Français partageaient ce point de vue, cette proportion grimpant à 92% pour les sympathisants de M. Jean-Marie Le Pen. Faut-il vraiment s'en étonner, alors que les médias présentent de l'islam une image simplificatrice et totalisante, l'identifient à la violence et à l'obscurantisme? Mais il faut sûrement s'en inquiéter, à l'heure où certains évoquent la 'guerre des civilisations,' car cette approche crée les conditions de l'affrontement avec les peuples du sud de la Méditerranée et avec une partie non négligeable de citoyens de confession musulmane en Europe." ("Islamic fundamentalism is a grave threat to our country and we must fight it. According to a recent poll, 78 percent of the French share this point of view, this proportion climbing to 92 percent for the supporters of M. Jean-Marie Le Pen. Is it surprising when the media present a simplified version of Islam identifying it to violence and obscurantism? But we should be concerned in an hour when certain people evoke the clash of civilizations. For this approach creates the conditions for a clash with the populations south of the Mediterranean and with not a negligible party of Muslim citizens in Europe." Translation by Abu-Rabi'.) Alain Gresh, "Pour un dialogue des civilisations." *Le Monde Diplomatique*, June 1995, 4.
2. Olivier Roy, *L'échec de l'Islam politique* (Paris: Le Seuil, 1992).
3. The Egyptian judge Muḥammad Sa'id al-'Ashmawi argues that religion is the wish of God, whereas politics is the wish of human beings. See his *al-Islam al-siyassi* (Cairo: Dar Sina, 1993). French translation by Richard Jacquemond as *L'Islamisme contre l'islam* (Paris: La Découverte, 1989).
4. See Fazlur Rahman, *Major Themes of the Qur'an* (Indianapolis: Bibliotheca Islamica, 1982).
5. See M. Gilsenan, *Recognizing Islam: Religion and Society in the Modern Arab World* (New York: Pantheon, 1982); H. Sharābi, *Neopatriarchy: A Theory of Distorted Change in Arab Society*

(New York: Oxford University Press, 1988), and J. Waardenburg, "Official and Popular Religion in Islam." *Social Compass*, 1978, volume 25(3–4), 315–41.

6. See the treatment of Ḥasan al-Banna in the following: Ishak M. Husaini, *The Moslem Brethren: The Greatest of Modern Islamic Movements* (Beirut: Khayat's College Book Cooperative, 1956); Richard Mitchell, *The Society of the Muslim Brothers*, new edition (New York: Oxford University Press, 1993).
7. See A. Q. 'Awdah, *Islam Between Ignorant Followers and Incapable Scholars* (Riyadh: International Islamic Publishing House, 1991).
8. See Ibrāhīm M. Abu-Rabi', *Intellectual Origins of Islamic Resurgence in the Modern Arab World* (Albany: State University of New York Press, 1996).
9. See Sa'īd Hawwa, *al-Madkhal ilā da'wat al-ikhwān al-muslimīn* (Amman: al-Matba'ah al-Ta'āwuniyyah, 1979), and *Hādhihī tajribatī wā hadhihī shahādatī* (Cairo: Mu'assassat al-Khalīj al-'Arabī, 1988).
10. See Abdelwahab El-Affendi, *Turabi's Revolution: Islam and Power in Sudan* (London: Grey Seal Books, 1991), and Arthur Lowrie, ed., *Islam, Democracy, the State and the West: A Round Table Discussion with Dr. Ḥasan al-Turabi* (Tampa: World and Islam Studies Enterprise, 1993).
11. See Rudolph Peters, "Ijtihad and Taqlid in 18th and 19th Century Islam." *Die Welt des Islams*, volume 20, 1980, 131–45.
12. Muḥammad Rida, *Sharh al-manār* (Beirut: Dār al-Turāth, 1982), volume 13, 41.
13. 'Abd al-Razzāq al-Sanhūrī, *al-Wasīt fī sharh al-qanūn al-madanī* (Cairo: Dār al-Nahḍah al-'Arabiyyah, 1964), 60–1.
14. M. Shaltūt, *al-Islām: 'aqīdah wa Sharī'ah* (Cairo: Dār al-Shurūq, 1986).
15. T. J. al-'Alwānī, *Adab al-ikhtilāf fī'l islām* (Qatar: Kitāb al-Umma, 1978).
16. Rashād Salām, *Tatbīq al-Sharī'ah bayna al-qubūl wa'l rafd* (Cairo: Dār Sīna, 1997).
17. See the excellent bibliography provided by Masud in Muḥammad Khalid Masud, *Islamic Legal Philosophy: A Study of Abu Ishaq al-Shātibī's Life and Thought* (Islamabad: Islamic Research Institute, 1977), 327–41, and by Hallaq in Wael B. Hallaq, *A History of Islamic Legal Theories: An Introduction to Sunni Usul al-Fiqh* (New York: Cambridge University Press, 1997), 263–87.
18. Abū Hāmid al-Ghazālī, *al-Mustasfa min 'ilm al-usūl*, volume 1 (Baghdad: Matba'at Muthanna, 1970), 286–7, quoted in Muḥammad Khalid Masud, *Islamic Legal Philosophy: A Study of Abu Ishaq al-Shātibī's Life and Thought* (Islamabad: Islamic Research Institute, 1977), 153.
19. M. Shaltūt, *al-Islām: 'aqīdah wā Sharī'ah* (Cairo: Dār al-Shurūq, 1986), 10.
20. On Ghannūshī's early life and education, see Azzam S. Tamimi, *Rachid Ghannouci: A Democrat within Islamism* (New York: Oxford University Press, 2001), especially chapters 1 and 2.
21. On various assessments of Ghannūshī's thought, consult the following: Mustafa al-Tawātī, "al-Harakah al-islāmiyyah fī Tūnus." *Qaḍāyah Fikriyyah*, 1989, 200–11; Mohamed E. Hamdi, *The Politicization of Islam: A Case Study of Tunisia* (Colorado: Westview Press, 1998), and Tamimi, *Rachid Ghannouchi*.
22. The author interviewed Shaykh Ghannūshī in his office in London in May 1999.
23. Rāshid Ghannūshī, *al-Huriyyāt al-'āmmah fī'l dawlah al-islāmiyyah* (Beirut: Markaz Dirāsāt al-Wiḥdah al-'Arabīyah, 1993).
24. Ghannūshī says that, "Had we rebelled against [the Islamic] frame of reference, nothing would have been left for us to refer to for guidance. Modernity, whether Tunisian or Western, has to be viewed through the Islamic [sacred] text; stringent controls have to be maintained." Ghannūshī, *al-Ḥuriyyāt al-'āmmah*, 75, quoted in Tamimi, *Rachid Ghannouchi*, 45.
25. Rāshid al-Ghannūshī, "Islamic Movements: Self-Criticism and Reconsideration." *Middle East Affairs Journal*, volume 3(1–2), Winter/Spring 1997, 14–15.
26. Ghannūshī argues that the secular state in the Arab world "has lost its ability to defend itself except through violence." *Ibid.*, 12.
27. *Ibid.*, 19.
28. *Ibid.*, 18.
29. See Tamimi, *Rachid Ghannouchi*, 14–15.
30. Mohamed E. Hamdi, *The Politicization of Islam: A Case Study of Tunisia* (Colorado: Westview Press, 1998), 17.
31. Ghannūshī, *Maqālāt: Ḥarakat al-itijāh al-islāmī fī Tūnus* (Paris: Dār al-Karawān, 1984), 13–14.

32. "In the Third World today, more often than not we see dual societies and patchwork practices that seek to accommodate seemingly irreconcilable old and new ways. Rather than the persistence of traditional culture in the face of modern intrusions, or even the development of syncretic cultures and values, we usually see instead a disruptive and incomplete westernization, cultural confusion, or the enthusiastic embrace of 'modern' practices and values." Jack Donnelly, "Cultural Relativism and Universal Human Rights." *Human Rights Quarterly*, volume 6, 1984, 411, quoted in A. E. Mayer, in *Islam and Human Rights: Tradition and Politics* (Boulder: Westview Press, 1991), 17.
33. Rāshid al-Ghannūshī, *Muqārabāt fī'l 'ilmāniyyah wa'l mujtama' al-madanī* (London: al-Markaz al-Maghāribī li'l buhūth wa'l Tarjamah, 1999), 149.
34. Ghannūshī, "The Battle Against Islam." *Middle East Affairs Journal*, volume 1(2), Winter 1993, 39.
35. Ghannūshī, *Muqārabāt*, 147–8.
36. *Ibid.*, 151. "Due to semantic inadequacies, gross errors in judgement are made when either modernism or democracy is deemed incompatible with political Islam. The modernist-secular *modus operandi*, which entails personal and political liberation, does not exist in the [contemporary] Muslim world." Ghannūshī, "The Battle Against Islam," 36.
37. Rāshid al-Ghannūshī, "Ayatu hadāthah? Laysa mushkiluna ma' al-hadāthah." *Qira'āt Siyāsiyyah*, volume 2(4), 1992, 125–35. Burhān Ghalyūn agrees with Ghannūshī's main contentions. He argues that in most Arab countries, the ruling elites have attacked the foundations of civil society in the hope of creating an absolute and permanent form of authority that is not questioned by the masses. See Ghalyūn, *Ightiyāl al-'aql*, 112.
38. Rāshid al-Ghannūshī, "Secularism in the Arab Maghreb," in John L. Esposito and Azzam Tamimi, eds., *Islam and Secularism in the Middle East* (New York: New York University Press, 2000), 99.
39. Ghannūshī, *al-Huriyyāt al-'āmmah*, 20.
40. *Ibid.*, 19.
41. Ghannūshī, "Secularism in the Arab Maghreb," 123.
42. Shāṭibī, *al-Muwafaqāt* (Beirut: Dār Ihyā' al-Turāth al-'Arabī, 1995), volume 2, 7, and Masud, *Islamic Legal Philosophy*, 226.
43. Shāṭibī, *al-Muwafaqāt*, volume 2, 8.
44. Shāṭibī, *al-Muwafaqāt*, 9–10, and Masud, *Islamic Legal Philosophy*, 226–7.
45. Ghannūshī, *al-Ḥuriyyāt*, 44–68.
46. Nasr Hāmid Abū Zayd, "al-Khitāb al-dīnī al-mu'āsir: āliyatuhū wa muntalaqātuhū al-fikriyyah." *Qaḍāyah Fikriyyah*, volume 8, 1989, 45.
47. Hādī al-'Ulwī, "Nahwa ta'sīl 'aqlaniyyah ijtimā'iyyah." *Al-Nahj*, volume 7, 1996, 6.
48. Salām, *Tatbīq al-Sharī'ah*, 26.
49. *Ibid.*, 86.
50. *Ibid.*, 126.
51. Ḥ. Ḥanafī, "Mata tamūt al-falsafah." *'Ālam al-Fikr*, volume 15, 1996, 224.
52. M. S. 'Ashmāwī, *al-Islām al-siyāssī* (Cairo: Dār Sīna, 1993), 94.
53. See Rahman, *Major Themes of the Qur'an*.
54. The two major studies in English are Abdullahi A. An-Na'im, *Toward an Islamic Reformation: Civil Liberties, Human Rights, and International Law* (Syracuse: Syracuse University Press, 1990), and Ann Elizabeth Mayer, *Islam and Human Rights: Tradition and Politics* (Boulder: Westview Press, 1991). See also Ridwan al-Sayyid, "Contemporary Muslim Thought and Human Rights." *Islamochristiana*, volume 21, 1995, 27–41, and also the special issue of *Minbar al-Hiwār* (in Arabic) on human rights and Islam (Spring 1988).
55. "A man and a woman, having reached the age of marriage, have the right to marry and form a family unrestricted by race or religion. And they have equal rights at marriage, during marriage, and upon its dissolution." Article 16 of the Universal Declaration of Human Rights.
56. See Mayer, *Islam and Human Rights*, 45, and also chapters 2 and 3.
57. An-Na'im, *Toward an Islamic Reformation*, 1.
58. Ghannūshī, *Muqārabāt*, 67.
59. Mayer, *Islam and Human Rights*, 47.
60. Ghannūshī, *Muqārabāt*, 14.

61. See ‘Abd al-Karīm Zaydān, *Ahl al-dhimmah* (Beirut: Mu’sasat al-Risālah, n.d.); and Yūsuf al-Qaraḍāwī, *Ghayr al-muslimīn fī’l mujtama‘ al-islāmī* (Cairo: Maktabat Wahba, 1977).
62. An-Na‘im, *Toward an Islamic Reformation*, 52.
63. Ghannūshī, *Muqārabāt*, 17.
64. *Ibid.*, 16.
65. ‘Allāl al-Fāsī, *Maqāṣid al-sharī‘ah al-islāmiyyah*, 8.
66. Ahmad Ḥasan, *The Doctrine of ijmā‘ in Islam: A Study of the Juridical Principle of Consensus* (Islamabad: Islamic Research Institute, 1978), 23.
67. Norberto Bobbio, “Gramsci and the Concept of Civil Society,” in John Keane, ed., *Civil Society and the State: New European Perspectives* (London: University of Westminster, 1998), 75–6.
68. See G. Hegel, *Lectures on the History of Religion* (Berkeley: University of California Press, 1987).
69. For a good bibliography on Islamic political thought consult Nasr M. ‘Ārif, *Fī maṣādir al-turāth al-siyāsī al-islāmī* (Herndon: International Institute of Islamic Thought, 1994).
70. Ghannūshī, *al-Ḥuriyyāt*, 93.
71. Abū Hāmid al-Ghazālī, *Ihyā’ ‘ulūm al-dīn* (Beirut: Dār Iḥyā’ al-Turāth al-‘Arabī, 1993), volume 1, 16.
72. Sayyid Quṭb, *Dirāsāt islāmiyyah* (Cairo: Dār al-Shurūq, 1976).
73. Ḥ. Turābī, *Nadharat f’l fiqh al-siyāssi* (Umm al-Faḥm: Markaz al-Dirāsāt al-Mu‘āṣirah, 1997), 16.
74. Ghannūshī, *al-Ḥuriyyāt*, 103.
75. *Ibid.*, 101.
76. Ahmad Kamāl Abū’l Majd, *Hiwār lā muwājaha: dirāsāt hawla al-islām wa’l ‘asr* (Cairo: Dār al-Shurūq, 1988), 105.
77. See ‘Allāl al-Fāsī, *Maqāsid*, 80.
78. Abū’l Majd, *Hiwār lā muwājaha*, 135–46.
79. Hamilton Gibb, *Modern Trends in Islam* (Chicago: University of Chicago Press, 1949), 11.
80. On Muḥammad ‘Abduh and *ijmā‘*, see Ḥasan, *The Doctrine of Ijmā‘ in Islam*, 244–50, and Malcolm Kerr, *Islamic Reform: The Political and Legal Theories of Muḥammad ‘Abduh and Rashid Rida* (Berkeley: University of California press, 1966), 132–7.
81. ‘Allāl al-Fāsī, *Maqāsid al-Sharī‘ah al-islāmiyyah*, 7–8.
82. Ghannūshī, *Muqārabāt*, 41.
83. *Ibid.*, 25–7.
84. See *ibid.*, 47, and ‘Abd al-Karīm Zaydān, *Ahl al-dhimmah* (Beirut: Mu’asasat al-Risālah, 1984).
85. Ghannūshī, *Muqārabāt*, 87.
86. *Ibid.*, 58–60.
87. “Thus states can be considered legitimate or “civilized” only when they have been formed through the explicit consent of individuals and when this active consent is formulated constitutionally and articulated continuously through parliamentary, representative mechanisms.” John Keane, “Despotism and Democracy: The Origins and Development of the Distinction Between Civil Society and the State 1750–1850,” in John Keane, ed., *Civil Society and the State: New European Perspectives* (London: University of Westminster Press, 1998), 47.
88. For more elaboration on Ghannūshī’s thought on civil society, consult John Keane, *Civil Society: Old Images, New Visions* (London: Polity Press, 1998), 28–31.
89. Ghannūshī, *Maqālāt*, 91–6.
90. Fāsī, *Maqāṣid al-Sharī‘ah*, 80.
91. Samir Amin, *Delinking: Towards a Polycentric World* (London: Zed Books, 1990), 177.
92. Ghannūshī, *al-Ḥuriyyāt*, 123.
93. S. Quṭb, *Hādha al-dīn* (Cairo: Dār al-Shurūq, 1987).
94. Ghannūshī, *al-Ḥuriyyāt*, 124.
95. ‘Abd al-Qādir ‘Awda, *al-Islām wa awdā‘unah al-qānuniyah* (Cairo: Dār al-Kitāb al-‘Arabī, 1951), 103–4.
96. A. R. Sanhūrī, *Le califat* (Paris: Gunther, 1936). See also Diyā’ al-Dīn al-Rayyis, *al-Nadhariyāt al-siyāsiyyah al-islāmiyyah* (Cairo: Dār al-Ma‘ārif, 1966), and Fathī Othmān, *Usūl al-fikr al-siyāsī al-islāmī* (Beirut: Mu’asasat al-Risālah, 1984).

97. Ghannūshī, *al-Ḥuriyyāt*, 141.
98. *Ibid.*, 162.
99. On Gramsci and his notion of civil society, consult the highly-valuable article: Norberto Bobbio, "Gramsci and the Concept of Civil Society," in Keane, *Civil Society and the State*, 73–99. According to Bobbio, "for Gramsci, civil society in the Middle Ages is the Church understood as 'the hegemonic apparatus of the ruling group, which did not have its apparatus, i.e. did not have its own cultural and intellectual organization, but regarded the universal, ecclesiastical organization as being that'." *Ibid.*, 83.
100. Ghannūshī, *al-Ḥuriyyāt*, 197.
101. *Ibid.*, 199.
102. *Ibid.*, 310.
103. Azzam Tamimi, "Democracy: The Religious and the Political in Contemporary Islamic Debate." *Encounters: Journal of Inter-Cultural Perspectives*, volume 4(1), March 1998, 38.
104. Ridwan al-Sayyid, "Contemporary Muslim Thought and Human Rights." *Islamochristiana*, volume 21, 1995, 30.
105. See Muḥammad N. Farhāt, *al-Mujtama' wa'l Sharī'ah wa'l qānūn* (Cairo: Dār al-Hilāl, 1986).

10 MUSLIM SELF-CRITICISM IN CONTEMPORARY ARAB THOUGHT: THE CASE OF SHAYKH MUḤAMMAD AL-GHAZĀLĪ

1. Ghazālī says that, "What I like most about Sayyid Jamāl al-Dīn al-Afghānī is his revolutionary fervor against authoritarianism (*istibdād*) and Muḥammad 'Abduh is his deep comprehension of the wisdom of Islam and his espousal of a conscious Muslim intelligentsia, and Rashīd Riḍa his combination of the teachings of the classical Salafīyyah of Ibn Taymiyya and Ibn Qayyim al-Jawziyya and the modern rational Salafīyyah of Jamāl al-Dīn al-Afghānī and Muḥammad 'Abduh." Personal interview with the author. Cairo, March 1995.
2. The most complete account of Ghazālī's life is rendered by Yūsuf Qaraḍāwī in *al-Shaykh al-Ghazālī kama 'araftuhu: rihlat nisf qarn* (al-Manṣūrah: Dār al-Wafā', 1997). See also Nazih N. Ayubi, "Muḥammad al-Ghazālī," in John L. Esposito, ed., *The Oxford Encyclopedia of the Modern Muslim World*, volume 2 (New York: Oxford University Press, 1993), 63–4. For a full bibliography of his work, see Fathī H. Malkāwī, ed., *al-'Atā' al-fikrī li'l Shaykh Muḥammad al-Ghazālī* (Amman: al-Ma'had al-'Ālami li'l Fikr al-Islāmī, 1996), 228–60.
3. See Qaraḍāwī, *al-Shaykh al-Ghazālī kama 'araftuhu,* 274.
4. According to Qaraḍāwī, although Ghazālī gained so much status and prestige in the Muslim world, he remained indebted to the intellectual and religious legacy of Banna. Banna had the most impact on the thought of Ghazālī. See *ibid.*, 25.
5. In his biography of Ghazālī, Qaraḍāwī, exiled by the Nasser regime to Qatar in the early 1960s, glosses over the strong relationship between Ghazālī and the Nasser regime. See *ibid.*, 39–43.
6. According to 'Alā' Muḥammad al-Ghazālī, Ghazālī's son, the Algerian president Shādhili bin Jadīd invited Ghazālī to come to Algeria to preach in the early 1980s when Ghazālī was teaching at Qatar. 'Alā' Muḥammad al-Ghazālī quotes the Algerian president as saying: "The Islamic movement has made an indelible presence in Algeria and it needs guidance. I know your salary is quite big in Qatar; however, Algeria needs to be exposed to correct Islam without any corruption, and I would like to establish an Islamic university in Algeria along the lines of the Azhar in Cairo." 'Alā' Muḥammad al-Ghazālī, "al-Sirah al-shakhsiyyah li'l Shaykh Muḥammad al-Ghazālī," in Malkāwī, *al-'Aṭā' al-fikrī li'l Shaykh Muḥammad al-Ghazālī*, 193. 'Alā' Muḥammad al-Ghazālī quotes his father as saying that, in the 1980s, "Algeria was prey to discord, the Islamic principles had been made absent purposively, and the Arabic language was not used even by the nomads. In addition, the values of European civilization had been dominant in Algerian society." *Ibid.* On Ghazālī's religious role in Algeria, see Kate Zebiri, "Islamic Revival in Algeria: An Overview." *The Muslim World*, volume 83(1), January 1993, especially 221–3.
7. On the origins of the Islamic movement in Algeria, see 'Arūs al-Zubayr, "al-Dīn wa'l siyāsah fī'l jazā'ir." *Qaḍāyah Fikriyyah*, volume 8, 1989, 187–99. Al-Zubayr discusses at length the impact

Malik Bennabi (d. 1972) exerted on the university students in Algeria. Ghazālī played a similar role in Algeria in the 1980s. See also Boumadyan Bouzayd, "Khiṭāb al-ḥarakah al-islāmiyyah fi'l jazā'ir," in *Qaḍāyah Fikriyyah*, volumes 13 and 14, 1993, 277–88.

8. Ghazālī, *Kayfa nata'āmalū ma' al-Qur'ān* (Herndon: IIIT, 1991), 29.
9. A number of contemporary Arab and Muslim thinkers use this term in their critical writings. See Burhan Ghalyūn, *Ightiyāl al-'aql: Miḥnat al-thaqāfah al-'Arabīyya bayna al-Salafiyya wa'l taba'iyyah* (Cairo: Madbūlī, 1990).
10. Ghazālī, *Kayfa nata'āmalū*, 37–8.
11. Ghazālī, *Ma'rakat al-miṣḥaf fi al-'ālam al-islāmī*, 3rd edition (Cairo: Dār al-Kutub al-Ḥadīthah, 1971), 14.
12. Ghazālī, *Naẓarāt fi al-'Qur'ān*, 5th edition (Cairo: Dār al-Kutub al-Ḥadīthah, n.d.), 179–82.
13. Ghazālī, *Ma'rakat*, 37–40.
14. Ghazālī, *al-Jānib al-'āṭifī min al-islām* (Cairo: Dār al-Kutub al-Ḥadithah, 1961).
15. *Ibid.*, 22.
16. *Ibid.*, 166.
17. It is doubtful that Ghazālī was aware of systematic theology in modern Christian thought. On the meaning and importance of systematic theology in modern Christian thought, consult Paul Tillich, *Systematic Theology*, 3 volumes (Chicago: University of Chicago Press, 1952–62).
18. Ghazālī, *Ma'rakat al-miṣḥaf*, 66.
19. Ghazālī, *Kayfa natā'āmalū*, 76.
20. Ghazālī, *al-Da'wah al-islāmiyah tastaqbil qarnaha al-khāmis 'ashar* (Cairo: Dhāt al-Satāsil, 1980), 31.
21. Ghazālī, *Kayfā nafhamū al-islām?*, 3rd edition (Cairo: Dār al-Kutub al-Islāmiyah, 1983), 74.
22. *Ibid.*, 76–7.
23. Ghazālī, *Ma'rakat al-miṣḥaf*, 70.
24. Ibn Khaldūn, *The Muqaddimah: An Introduction to History*, volume 1, trans. Franz Rosenthal (New York: Pantheon, 1958), 386.
25. *Ibid.*, 388.
26. *Ibid.*, 400.
27. *Ibid.*
28. In his critique of modern Islamism, Egyptian thinker Naṣr Ḥāmid Abū Zayd concludes that, "Islamist discourse stipulates that Islam was dismissed from the plane of reality, and on the basis of such a proposition, accepted as a certain reality, the Islamists launch their explanation of the ethical, cultural, political, economic, and social problems of life. They argue that the only way to reach a solution is by returning to Islam and implementing the Sharī'ah. This issue and the solution to it are taken for granted by the Islamists. However, they do not bother to raise the question of how and why Islam was removed from reality." Naṣr Ḥāmid Abū Zayd, "al-Khiṭāb al-dīnī al-mu'āshir: āliyatuhu wa muntalaqātuhu al-fikiriyyah." *Qaḍāyah Fikriyyah*, volume 8, 1989, 55.
29. Ghazālī, *Kayfā nafhamū*, 188.
30. *Ibid.*, 190.
31. See Imām Abū Ḥāmid al-Ghazālī, *Iḥyā' 'ulūm al-dīn* (Beirut: Dār Iḥyā' al-Turāth, 1984).
32. Ghazālī, *Kayfā nafhamū*, 198.
33. *Ibid.*, 286.
34. *Ibid.*, 118.
35. *Ibid.*, 181.
36. Ghazālī, *Turāthuna al-fikrī fi mīzān al-shar' wa al-'aql* (Herndon: IIIT, 1991), 7.
37. *Ibid.*, 10.
38. Literally it means the people who loosen and bind, or the people who are reliable in their knowledge.
39. Ghazālī, *Turāthuna al-fikrī fi mīzān al-shar' wa'l 'aql*, 27.
40. 'Abd al-Qādir 'Awda, *al-Islām wā awḍā'unah al-qānūniyyah* (Cairo: Dār al-Kitāb al-'Arabī, 1951).
41. Ghazālī, *al-Islām wa'l awḍā' al-iqtisādiyya*, 7th edition (Cairo: Dār al-Ṣaḥwah, 1987).
42. See my analysis in *Intellectual Origins of Islamic Resurgence in the Modern Arab World* (Albany: State University of New York Press, 1996).

43. Ghazālī claims that Sayyid Quṭb 'summarized his [Ghazālī's] main theses on social and economic justice in his book *Social Justice in Islam'*. Personal interview with the author. Cairo 1995.
44. Ghazālī, *al-Islām wa'l awḍā'*, 28.
45. Ghazālī antedates contemporary Western social criticism in his condemnation of the privation of education.
46. Ghazālī, *al-Islām wa'l awḍā'*, 51.
47. *Ibid.*, 53.
48. For an excellent analysis of the *naṣṣ* or people in the Qur'anic terminology, see 'Alī Shari'ati, *On the Sociology of Islam* (Berkeley: Mizan Press, 1979).
49. Ghazālī, *al-Islām wa'l awḍā'*, 54.
50. *Ibid.*, 62–3.
51. *Ibid.*, 65.
52. *Ibid.*, 104.
53. *Ibid.*, 189.
54. The term "liberal Islam" has lately been in vogue. It is used by some Western thinkers to refer to such people as Muḥammad Sa'īd 'Ashmāwī, Naṣr Ḥāmid Abū Zayd and Muḥammad Shaḥrūr.
55. "Ḥasan al-Banna was one of the most creative leaders of the Muslim world in the twentieth century. Although he did not believe in the power of the book (ideas) to change society, he encouraged his followers to be learned in the matters of both religion and the world and pursue political action in order to secure the desired change. However, one of the main characteristics of al-Banna is that he was a Sufi and remained a Sufi until his assassination in 1949." Muḥammad al-Ghazālī in a personal interview with the author. Cairo, March 1995.
56. 'Alī 'Abd al-Rāziq, *al-Islām wa uṣūl al-ḥukm* (Beirut: Dār Maktabat al-Ḥayāh, 1978). I have also consulted the following: Ali Abdelrazik, *L'Islam et les fondements du pouvoir*, trans. Abdou Filali-Ansary (Paris: La Découverte, 1994); Muḥammad 'Imārah, *al-Islām wa uṣūl al-ḥukm lī 'Alī 'Abd al-Rāziq: Dirāsah wa wathā'iq* (Beirut: Dār Maktabat al-Ḥayāh, 1978).
57. According to Ghālī Shukrī, 'Alī 'Abd al-Rāziq was not a secularist in a European sense. His Azharite learning led him to argue that the Islamic caliphate, in its Ottoman definition and formation, was not Islamic. See Ghālī Shukrī, *al-Khurūj 'ala al-naṣṣ: taḥadiyyāt al-thaqāfah wa'l dimūqraṭiyyah* (Cairo: Dār Sīna, 1994), 10.
58. Consult Bernard Lewis, *The Political Language of Islam* (Chicago: University of Chicago Press, 1987).
59. Al-Rāziq, *al-Islām wa uṣūl al-ḥukm*, 39.
60. *Ibid.*, 67.
61. *Ibid.*, 73.
62. *Ibid.*, 83.
63. *Ibid.*, 136.
64. These words are echoed several decades later by another "Muslim liberal." Khālid M. Khālid maintains that: "The Prophet...was crystal-clear about his prophetic mission; its essence never left his mind. He knew very well that he was simply a guide and messenger, not head of a government or an emperor on earth...The Prophet did not care to become a ruler and sovereign in this world, it is because prophecy is far nobler and superior." Khālid M. Khālid, *From Here We Start*, trans. Ismā'il R. el-Faruqi (Washington, D.C.: American Council of Learned Societies, 1953), 123.
65. 'Alī 'Abd al-Rāziq, *al-Islām wa uṣūl al-ḥukm*, 172–4.
66. *Ibid.*, 184.
67. *Ibid.*, 200.
68. Rif'at al-Sa'īd, *Ḥassan al-Banna, kayfa wa limādha?* (Cairo: Dār Maktabat al-Ḥayāh, 1984), 87.
69. On the thought of Khālid, consult Shākir al-Nābulsī, *Thawrat al-turāth: Dirāsa fī fikr Khālid Muḥammad Khālid* (Beirut: Dār al-Turāth, 1991).
70. See L. Binder, *Islamic Liberalism: A Critique of Development Ideologies* (Chicago: University of Chicago Press, 1988).
71. Khālid, *From Here We Start.*
72. *Ibid.*, 32.
73. Compare Khālid's ideas to the following from Hegel's *Phenomenology*, "That mental sphere [insight] is the victim of the deception of a Priesthood, which carries out its envious vain conceit

of being alone in possession of insight, and carries out its other selfish ends as well. At the same time this priesthood conspires with despotism, which takes up the attitude of being the synthetic crude unity of the real and this ideal kingdom – a singularly amorphous and inconsistent type of being – and stands above the bad insight of the multitude, and the bad intentions of the priests, and even combines both of these within itself. As the result of the stupidity and confusion produced amongst the people by the agents of priestly deception, despotism despises both and draws for itself the advantage of undisturbed control and the fulfillment of its lusts, its humors, and its whims. Yet at the same time it is itself in this same state of murky insight, is equally superstition and error." G. W. F. Hegel, *The Phenomenology of Mind*, trans. George Lichtheim (New York: Philosophical Library, 1967), 562.

74. I borrow this statement from Pauline M. Rosenau, *Post-Modernism and the Social Sciences: Insights, Inroads, and Intrusions* (Princeton: Princeton University Press, 1992), 78.
75. Khālid, *From Here We Start*, 33.
76. *Ibid.*, 36. Many a nationalist and secularist Arab intellectual has commented on the role of the Muslim religious establishment in upholding the *status quo*. For instance, the Syrian historian, Shakir Mustafa, in the course of analyzing what he views as the reasons for the modern cultural crisis in the Arab world, argues that the "ulama" fulfilled the function of providing "values and ideas which would make the exploited classes submissive, and legitimize[d] the rule of the military with their feudal-bourgeois allies: ideas of resignation, fatalism, being content with little. Of the *hadīth* (oral tradition) they chose to emphasize sayings like, 'obey those amongst you who retain power'. Their impact is felt indirectly in popular proverbs such as 'If you cannot overcome a hand, kiss it and pray that it shall be broken', or 'He who marries my mother becomes my uncle'." Shakir Mustafa, "Arab Cultural Crisis and the Impact of the Past." *Jerusalem Quarterly*, number 11, Spring 1979, 46.
77. Ghazālī, *al-Islām al-muftara 'alyhī bayna al-shuyū'iyyīn wa'l ra'smāliyyīn* (Cairo: Dār al-Turāth, 1952), 27.
78. Ghazālī, *Our Beginning in Wisdom*, trans. Ismā'īl R. al-Faruqi (Washington, D.C.: American Council of Learned Societies, 1953), 69–70.
79. Ishaq Musa al-Husaini, *The Moslem Brethren: The Greatest of Modern Islamic Movements* (Beirut: Khayat, 1956).
80. Al-Sayyid Walad Abāh, "Hal Zala lī maqūlat al-yasār ma'nah?" *al-Sharq al-Awsat*, number 6067, Sunday, September 7, 1995, 8.
81. In the eyes of many Ikhwān thinkers, Khālid M. Khālid, an Azharite by training, deviated from the "true" teachings of Islam in his liberal phase. See Qaraḍāwī, *al-Shaykh al-Ghazālī kama 'araftuhu*, 65.
82. Khālid M. Khālid, *Muwāṭinūn lā ra'āyah*, 7th edition (Beirut: Dār al-Fikr, 1974).
83. Khālid M. Khālid, *al-Dimūqraṭiyah abadan*, 4th edition (Beirut: Dār al-Fikr, 1974).
84. Khālid M. Khālid, *Azmat al-ḥuriyyah fī 'ālamina* (Cairo: Angelo, 1972).
85. Khālid, *From Here We Start*, 32.
86. *Ibid.*, 41.
87. Khālid M. Khālid, *Naḥnu al-bashar* (Cairo: Angelo, 1959), 23.
88. *From Here We Start*, 117. One must note that Khālid M. Khālid rebelled against many of his liberal ideas as he became older.
89. Ghazālī, *Kayfā nafhamū*.
90. *Ibid.*, 71.
91. *Ibid.*, 22.
92. *Ibid.*, 22–3.
93. *Ibid.*
94. Ghazālī, *al-Sunnah al-nabawiyah bayna ahl al-fiqh wa ahl al-ḥadīth* (Cairo: Dār al-Shurūq, 1989).
95. Ghazālī, *Humūm Dā'iyah* (Cairo: Dār Thābit, 1983), 31.
96. Ghazālī uses such terms as *al-ṣulṭāṭ al-mustabiddah* (oppressive authorities) or *ḥukkām al-jūr* (rulers of oppression) to refer to the current governments in the Muslim world. See Ghazālī, *al-Sunnah al-nabawiya*, 9.
97. *Ibid.*, 11.

98. *Ibid.*, 18–19.
99. Ghazālī, *Dustūr al-wiḥdah al-thaqāfiyah* baynd al-muslimīn (Cairo: Dār al-Anṣār, 1981), 250.
100. Ghazālī, *al-Sunnah al-nabawiyah,* 43.
101. See Bashir Ahmad Khan, "The Ahl-i-Hadīth: A Socio-Religious Reform Movement in Kashmir." *The Muslim World*, volume 90 (1 and 2), Spring 2000, 133–57.
102. Ghazālī, *al-Sunnah al-nabawiyah*, 45.
103. *Ibid.*, 75.
104. Ghazālī, *Turāthuna fi mīzān al-shar' wa'l 'aql*, 10.

11 ISLAM AND MUSLIMS IN CRISIS

1. Ghazālī, *Dustūr al-wiḥdah al-thaqāfiyah bayna al-muslimīn* (Cairo: Dār al-Anṣār, 1981), 4.
2. *Ibid.*, 7.
3. *Ibid.*, 17.
4. *Ibid.*, 34.
5. *Ibid.*, 85. The leaders of this school are: Maḥmūd Shaltūt, Muḥammad 'Abdallah Dārāz, Muḥammad al-Bahiy, Muḥammad al-Madanī, Muḥammad Abū Zahra, and Muḥammad al-Khuḍārī.
6. Ghazālī, *Dustūr al-wiḥdah*, 85–6.
7. *Ibid.*, 121.
8. Ghazālī, *Turāthuna al-fikrī fi mīzān al-shar' wa'l 'aql* (Herndon: IIIT, 1991), 152.
9. Ghazālī, *Dustūr al-wiḥdah*, 187.
10. See Sayyid Quṭb, *Milestones* (Karachi: International Islamic Publishers, 1981), and Muḥammad Quṭb, *Jāhiliyat al-qarn al-'ishrīn* (Beirut: Dār al-Kitāb, 1976).
11. Ghazālī, *Dustūr al-wiḥdah*, 211.
12. *Ibid.*
13. Ghazālī, *al-Sunnah al-nabawiyah bayna ahl al-fiqh Wā ahl al-ḥadīth* (Cairo: Dār al-Shurūq, 1989), 136.
14. See Michael Gilsenan, *Recognizing Islam: Religion and Society in the Modern Arab World* (New York: Pantheon, 1982).
15. Ghazālī, *Ma' Allah: Dirāsāt fi'l da'wah wa'l du 'āh* (Cairo: Dār al-Kutub al-Ḥadīthah, 1965), 41.
16. *Ibid.*, 42–4.
17. *Ibid.*, 188–96.
18. Ghazālī, *Laysa minā al-islām* (Cairo: Dār al-Kutub al-Islāmiyyah, 1983), 129.
19. *Ibid.*, 129–30.
20. G. E. von Grunebaum and R. Brunschvig, eds., *Classicisme et déclin culturel dans l'histoire de l'islam* (Paris: Maisonneuve, 1957).
21. Ghazālī, *Laysa minā al-islām*, 159.
22. Ghazālī, *'Aqīdat al-muslim* (Cairo: Dār al-Kutub al-Ḥadīthah, 1965), 8.
23. *Ibid.*, 12–14.
24. *Ibid.*, 53. See also the interesting analysis of this point in 'Abd al-Majīd al-Najjār, *Khilāfat al-insān bayna al-wahy wa'l 'aql* (Herndon: IIIT, 1993), especially 40–59.
25. Ghazālī, *Hādha dīnunah* (Cairo: Dār al-Kutub al-Ḥadīthah, 1965), 36–40. Also, Ghazālī, *Sayhat tahzīr min du āt al-tansīr* (Cairo: Dār al-Ṣahwah, 1991), 24.
26. Ghazālī, *Ẓalām minā al-gharb*, 2nd edition, (Cairo: Dār al-Kutub al-Ḥadīthah, 1965), 56.
27. Ghazālī, *'Aqīdat al-muslim*, 126.
28. *Ibid.*
29. *Ibid.*, 215.
30. On Muslim images of the West, see Susan Miller, ed., *Disorienting Encounters, Travels of a Moroccan Scholar in France in 1845–1846: The Voyage of Muḥammad As-Saffar* (Berkeley: University of California Press, 1992).
31. Ibrahim M. Abu-Rabi', *Intellectual Origins of Islamic Resurgence in the Modern Arab World* (Albany: State University of New York Press, 1995), especially chapter 3.

32. See Ibrahim M. Abu-Rabi‘, "The Concept of the Other in Modern Arab Thought: From Muḥammad ‘Abduh to Abdallah Laroui." *Islam and Christian-Muslim Relations*, volume 8(1), 1997, 85–97.
33. Ghazālī, *Kayfa nata‘āmalu ma‘ al-sunnah* (Cairo: Dār al-Turāth, 1986), 46.
34. *Ibid.*, 58.
35. Ghazālī, *Kayfa nafhamū al-islām?*, 3rd edition (Cairo: Dā al-Kutub al-Islāmiyah, 1983), 119–22.
36. Ghazālī, *Humūm dā‘iya* (Cairo: Dār Thābit, 1983), 152–3.
37. Ghazzali, *al-Ghazw al-thaqāfī yamtadu fī farāghina* (Amman: Mu'assassat al-Sharq, 1985), 6.
38. *Ibid.*, 7.
39. *Ibid.*, 40.
40. Ghazālī, *al-Ghazw al-thaqāfī yamtadu*, 44.
41. *Ibid.*, 49.
42. *Ibid.*, 51.
43. Ghazālī, *al-Islām wa'l ṭāqāt al-mu‘aṭallah* (Cairo: Dār al-Kutub al-Ḥadīthah, 1964), 34–35.
44. Ghazālī, *Our Beginning in Wisdom*, trans. Ismā‘īl R. al-Faruqi (Washington, D.C.: American Council of Learned Societies, 1953), 5–6.
45. Ghazālī, *Turāthuna al-fikrī*, 36.
46. *Ibid.*, 37–8.
47. *Ibid.*, 46.
48. *Ibid.*, 47.
49. *Ibid.*, 48.
50. Ghazālī, *Dustūr al-wiḥdah al-thaqāfiyyah*, 250–2.
51. Ghazālī, *Ẓalām mina al-gharb*, 3.
52. *Ibid.*, 31.
53. *Ibid.*, 82.
54. Jubrān Shāmiyah, *al-Dīn wa'l dawlah al-waṭaniyyah*. Quoted by al-Ghazālī in *Ẓalām mina al-gharb*, 84–7.
55. Ghazālī, *Ẓalām mina al-gharb*, 151.
56. *Ibid.*, 288.
57. *Ibid.*, 72–5.
58. Ghazālī, *Ma‘rakat al-misḥaf fī al-‘ālam al-islāmī*, 3rd edition (Cairo: Dār al-Kutub al Ḥadīthah, 1971), 216.
59. *Ibid.*, 218–20.
60. Ghazālī, *Kifāh dīn* (Cairo: Dār al-Kutub al-Ḥadithāh, 1965), 7.
61. "Al-Ghazālī was dismissed from his position in the *hay'ah ta'sīsiyah* (constituent body) of the Ikhwān in December 1953, reportedly after attempting, with two other prominent members, to unseat the organization's leader, Ḥassan al-Huḍaybī (with the approval, some Muslim Brothers suspected, of Gamal Abdel Nasser and the Free Officers." Many feel that he still remains an Ikhwani in all but name, and he certainly favors the formation of an Islamic party in Egypt today." Nazih N. Ayubi, "Muḥammad al-Ghazālī," in John L. Esposito, ed., *The Oxford Encyclopedia of the Modern Muslim World*, volume 2 (New York: Oxford University Press, 1993), 63–4.
62. Ghazālī, *'Ilal wa adwiyyah* (Cairo: Dhāt al-Salāsil, 1980), 88.
63. *Ibid.* For their commitment to revive critical Muslim reason, both ‘Abduh and Afghānī were subject to severe criticism from the side of Arab and Orientalist thinkers. Afghānī was adamant in trying to reform conditions, remind rulers that their power must depend on *shūrah*, try to wake up the ummah from stagnation, and discovered the spirit of crusaderism in the modern West. The school of Afghānī and ‘Abduh stressed two important things: (1) being committed to studying the modern sciences is an Islamic duty, and (2) being aware of the differences existing between normative Islam or revelational Islam and actual Islamic history. Many mistakes were committed throughout Islamic history. "The Manār school [of Muḥammad Rashīd Riḍa] is the only refuge for the present Islamic revivalist movement." *Ibid.* ‘Abduh, after his exile, did not withdraw from public life. He faced the enormous task of bypassing the British domination and the stagnation of the Shaykhs, the enmity of the Palace.
64. Egyptian thinker Ghālī Shukrī faults Shaykh al-Gazālī on two major counts toward the end of his life: first, his support for the killers of the writer Faraj Fūda, and second his "training of new

cadres of political Islam" in Algeria in the 1980s. See Ghālī Shukrī, "Man lā yakhāf al-Shaykh al-Ghazālī?," in his *Thaqāfāt al-niẓām al-'ashwā'ī: takfīr al-'aql wa 'aql al-takfīr* (Cairo: Kitāb al-Ahālī, 1994), 231–9.

65. One of the most important disciples of Shaykh Muḥammad al-Ghazālī is the famous Egyptian journalist Fahmī Huwaydī, who writes a weekly column in the famous daily, *Al-Ahrām*.

12 TOWARDS A CRITICAL ARAB REASON: THE CONTRIBUTIONS OF MUḤAMMAD 'ĀBID AL-JĀBIRĪ

1. Fanon says that, "decolonization is always a violent phenomenon…To tell the truth, the proof of success [of decolonization] lies in a whole structure being changed from the bottom up." Franz Fanon, *The Wretched of the Earth* (New York: Grove Press, 1968), 35.
2. On this point, see the following: Jacques Cagne, *Nation et nationalisme au Maroc* (Rabat: L'Institut Universitaire de la Recherche Scientifique, 1988); Bernard Lugan, *Histoire du Maroc des origines a nos jours* (Paris: Perrin, 2000), and Henry Munson, Jr., *Religion and Power in Morocco* (New Haven: Yale University Press, 1993).
3. See Musṭafa al-'Alawī, *Muḥammad al-Khāmis* (Casablanca: Maṭba'at al-Najāḥ al-Jadīdah, 1997), and Abdellah Hammoudi, *Master and Disciple: The Cultural Foundations of Moroccan Authoritarianism* (Chicago: University of Chicago Press, 1997).
4. On culture, post-coloniality, and the writer in post-independence North Africa, see the following: Belinda Jack, *Francophone Literatures: An Introductory Survey* (New York: Oxford University Press, 1996); Winifred Woodhull, *Transfigurations of the Maghreb* (Minneapolis: University of Minnesota Press, 1993); and Anne Armitage, "The Debate over Literary Writing in a Foreign Language: An Overview of Francophonie in the Maghreb." *Alif: Journal of Comparative Poetics*, number 20, 2000, 39–67.
5. On this point see Philip G. Altbach, "Education and Neocolonialism," in Bill Ashcroft, Gareth Griffiths, and Helen Tiffin, eds., *The Post-Colonial Studies Reader* (London: Routledge, 1999), 452–6.
6. Fanon argues that "The peasantry is systematically disregarded for the most part by the propaganda put out by the nationalist parties. And it is clear that in the colonial countries the peasants alone are revolutionary, for they have nothing to lose and everything to gain." Fanon, *The Wretched of the Earth*, 61.
7. "Moroccan salafīyyah was not only militant in the sense of playing an active role against corrupt Islam; it was also militant in its resistance to the colonizer...Religion and nationalism in Morocco went hand in hand." Mohamed El-Mansour, "Salafīs and Modernists in the Moroccan Nationalist Movement," in John Ruedy, ed., *Islamism and Secularism in North Africa* (New York: St. Martin's Press, 1996), 60.
8. Mohamed Abed Jabri, "Evolution of the Maghrib Concept: Facts and Perspectives," in Halim Barakat, ed., *Contemporary North Africa: Issues of Development and Integration* (Washington: D.C.: Center for Contemporary Arab Studies, 1985), 69.
9. For a select bibliography of Jābirī's work, see "Hiwar ma' Muḥammad 'Abid al-Jābirī," in *Prologues: Revue maghrebine du livre*, number 10, 1997, 55–8.
10. See Jābirī, *al-'Aql al-akhlāqī al-'arabī* (Casablanca: al-Markaz al-Thaqāfī al-'Arabī, 2001).
11. 'Allāl al-Fāsī, *The Independence Movements in Arab North Africa* (Washington, D.C.: American Council of Learned Societies, 1954), and *al-Naqd al-dhātī* (Rabat: Maṭb'at al-Risālah, 1979), and *Ḥadīth maghrib wa'l mashriq* (Cairo: al-Maṭba'ah al-'Ālamiyyah, 1956).
12. See the following books of Mohammed Arkoun, *Pour une critique de la raison islamique* (Paris: Editions Maisonneuve et Larose, 1984); *Arab Thought*, trans. Jasmere Singh (New Delhi: S. Chand & Co., 1988), and *The Unthought in Contemporary Islamic Thought* (London: Saqi Books, 2002).
13. M. al-Kettānī, *Jadal al-'aql wa'l naql fī manāhij al-tafkīr al-islāmī: al-fikr al-qadīm* (Casablanca: Dār al-Thaqāfah, 1992).
14. Rabeh Torki, *Le Cheikh Abdel Hamid Ben Badis: le leader de la réformation et de l'éducation en Algérie* (Algier: La Société Nationale du Livre, 1984).

15. Moḥamad Talbi, *Plaidoyer pour un islam moderne* (Casablanca: Editions Le Fennec, 1996), and *Réflexion sur le Coran* (Paris: Seghers, 1989).
16. Ali Merad, *Le réformisme musulman en Algérie de 1925 à 1940: Essai d'histoire religieuse et sociale* (Paris: Mouton, 1967).
17. For a useful survey see, M. Y. Retnani, ed., *Penseurs maghrebins contemporains* (Casablanca: Editions Eddif, 1997).
18. Both Djaït and Jābīrī have been criticized recently for their "salafī" orientation. See Hakīm bin Ḥamūda, "Ba'ḍ al-farḍiyāt al-awaliyyah ḥawla quṣūr al-fikr al-maghārībī." In Maḥmūd Amīn al-'Ālim, ed., *al-Fikr al-'arabī 'alā mashārif al-qarn al-ḥādī wa'l 'ishrīn* (Cairo: Dār Qaḍāyah Fikriyyah, 1995), 125–36; and Ṭayyib Tizīnī, *Mina al-istishrāq al-gharbī ila al-istighrāb al-maghribī: bahth fī al-qirā'ah al-Jābīrīyah li'l fikr al-'arabī wā fī afāqihī al-tārīkhīyyāh* (Ḥoms: Dār al-Dhākirah, 1996).
19. "[Ibn Khaldūn] remarks that at certain exceptional moments in history, the upheavals are such that one has the impression of being present at a new creation (ka'annahū khalq jadīd), at an actual renaissance (*nash'a mustaḥdath*), and [the emergence of] a new world (*wā 'ālam muḥdath*). It is so at present. Thus the need is felt for someone to make a record of the situation of humanity and of the world." Moḥammad Talbi, "Ibn Khaldūn." *The Encyclopaedia of Islam*, new edition, volume 3 (Leiden: Brill, 1986), 830. A large number of modern Arab thinkers have been influenced by Ibn Khaldūn's thought, and a good number devoted some of their writings to the treatment of his thought.
20. See Kamāl 'Abd al-Laṭīf, *al-Fikr al-falsafī fī'l maghrib: qira'āt fī a'amāl al-Jābīrī wal' 'Urwī* (Casablanca: Ifrīqyyah al-Sharq, 2001) and Kamāl 'Abd al-Laṭīf, "al-'Urwī fī mira'āt al-Jābīrī; al-Jābīrī fī Mira'āt al-'Urwī." *Al-Tarīq*, volume 61(2), April 2002, 10–15.
21. Jābīrī, "al-Falsafah: fann siyāghat al-mafāhīm." *Al-Sharq al-Awṣat*, number 6619, January 11, 1997, 10.
22. Jābīrī, *al-Khiṭāb al-'arabī al-mu'āṣir* (Beirut: Markaz Dirāsāt al Wiḥdah al-'Arabīyyah, 1982), 191.
23. The contemporary Arab treatment of *turāth* is quite extensive. See the following sources: Sayyid Yāssīn *et al.*, *al-Turāth wā taḥadiyāt al-'aṣr* (Beirut: Markaz Dirāsāt al-Wiḥdah al-'Arabīyyah, 1985); Hādī al-'Ulwī, *Fī'l dīn wa'l turāth* (*On Religion and Tradition*) (Jerusalem: Ṣalāḥ al-Dīn, 1975); Mohammed Arkoun, *Essais sur la pensée islamique* (Paris: Editions Maisonneuve et Larose, 1977); 'Abdelsalām Bin'abd al-'Ālī, *al-Turāth wa'l hawiyah: Dirāsāt fī 'l fikr al-falsafī fī'l maghrib* (Casablanca: Dār Ṭobqāl, 1987); Hichem Djaït, *Europe and Islam: Cultures and Modernity* (Berkeley: University of California Press, 1975); Zakī Najīb Maḥmūd, *Tajdīd al-fikr al-'arabī* (Cairo: Dār al-Shurūq, 1976); Maḥmūd Amīn al-'Ālim, *al-Wa'y wa'l wa'y al-mafqūd fī'l fikr al-'arabī al-mu'āṣir* (Cairo: Dār al-Thaqāfah al-Jadīdah, 1986), and Ḥassan Ḥanafī, *al-Turāth wa'l tajdīd: mawqifunā min al-Turāth al-qadīm* (Cairo: al-Markaz al-'Arabī, 1982).
24. See Ali Merad, *Le Réformisme*, and Hichem Djaït, *La personnalité et le devenir arabo-islamique* (Paris: Seuil, 1974).
25. Moris Godelier, *Writing and Difference* (Chicago: University of Chicago Press, 1978).
26. On this point, consult the following: Abdallah Saaf, *Politique et savoir au Maroc* (Casablanca: Nouvelle Collection Atlas, 1991); Kamāl 'Abd al-Laṭīf, *Qira'āt fī'l falsafah al-'arabiyyah al-mu'āṣirah* (Beirut: Dār al-Ṭalī'ah, 1994); and Sālim Yafūt, *al-Manāhij al-jadīdah li'l fikr al-falsafī al-mu'āsir* (Beirut: Dār al-Ṭalī'ah, 1999).
27. This is one of the main theses of Teshahiro Izutso, *Ethico-Religious Concepts of the Qur'an* (Montreal: McGill University Press, 1966).
28. See Mary M. Jones, *Gaston Bachelard, Subversive Humanist: Texts and Readings* (Madison: University of Wisconsin Press, 1991).
29. See the following by Georges Canguilhem: *La connaissance de la vie* (Paris: Vrin, 1965); *Etudes d'histoire et de philosophie des sciences* (Paris: Vrin, 1968); *On the Normal and the Pathological* (Dordrecht: Reidel, 1978), and *A Vital Rationalist: Selected Writings*, ed. F. Dealporte (New York: Zone, 1994). See also the special issue of *Economy and Society* devoted to his thought: Thomas Osborne and Nikolas Rose, eds., *Economy and Society*, volume 27, May 1998.
30. See Michel Foucault, *The Order of Things: An Archeology of the Human Sciences* (New York: Vintage Books, 1970), and *The Archeology of Knowledge and the Discourse on Language*

(New York: Pantheon, 1972). See also Dominique Lecourt, *Marxism and Epistemology: Bachelard, Canguilhem, and Foucault* (London: New Left Books, 1975).
31. Quoted by Jones, *Gaston Bachelard*, 5.
32. Foucault, *The Archeology of Knowledge*, 4.
33. Jābīrī, *Naḥnu wa'l turāth* (Casablanca: al-Markaz al-Thaqāfī al-'Arabī, 1993), 24.
34. Paul Tillich, *Systematic Theology*, volume 1 (Chicago: University Chicago Press, 1953), 108.
35. See M. Plessner, "Hirmis." *The Encylopedia of Islam*, volume 3, 463–5, and A. E. Affīfī, "The Influence of Hermitic Literature on Muslim Thought." *BSOAS*, xiii, 1950, 840–55.
36. For more detail on all of these philosophers, see Majid Fakhry, *A History of Islamic Philosophy*, 2nd edition (New York: Columbia University Press, 1983) and Seyyed Hossein Nasr and Oliver Leaman, eds., *History of Islamic Philosophy*, 2 volumes (London: Routledge, 1996).
37. "Hermeticism is the outlook associated with the Hermetic writings, a literature in Greek which developed in the early centuries after Christ under the name 'Hermes Trismegistus'. Much of it is concerned with astrology, alchemy, and other occult sciences, but there is also a philosophical Hermetic literature." Frances Yates, "Hermeticism," in *The Encyclopedia of Philosophy*, volume 3 (New York: Macmillan, 1967), 489. See also Garth Fowden, *The Egyptian Hermes: A Historical Approach to the Late Pagan Mind* (Princeton: Princeton University Press, 1986).
38. Seyyed Hossein Nasr, "The Meaning and Concept of Philosophy in Islam," in Nasr and Leaman, eds., *History of Islamic Philosophy*, volume 1, 30.
39. See the following: Iysa A. Bello, *The Medieval Islamic Controversy Between Philosophy and Orthodoxy: Ijmā' and Ta'wīl in the Conflict between al-Ghazālī and Ibn Rushd* (Leiden: Brill, 1989); Charles Genequand, *Ibn Rushd's Metaphysics: A Translation with Introduction of Ibn Rushd's Commentary on Aristotle's Metaphysics, Book Lam* (Leiden: Brill, 1986).
40. M. Mouaqit, "Mohamed Abed Al-Jabri: Rationalisme et laïcisme." In M. Y. Retnani, ed., *Penseurs maghrébins contemporains* (Casablanca: Editions Eddif, 1997), 166.
41. Fakhry, *A History of Islamic Philosophy*, xv.
42. One can locate the Tadwīn Age in the context of the great philosophical activity launched by the caliph al-Ma'mūn in the ninth century, "None of the patrons of Greek learning mentioned hitherto could match in zeal, liberality, or intellectual distinction the great 'Abbasid caliph al-Ma'mūn, whose reign marks a turning point in the development of philosophical and theological thought in Islam." Fakhry, *A History of Islamic Philosophy*, 10.
43. Jābīrī, *Naḥnu wa'l turāth*, 35.
44. *Ibid.*, 36.
45. Compare what Jābīrī says to the following: "It is known that many dualist texts written within the early Islamic empire had attacked some of the basic tenets of Islam such as prophecy and revelation; effectively, this constituted an attack both on the Prophet and on the Qur'ān." Syed Nomanul Haq, "The Indian and Persian Background," in Nasr and Leaman, eds., *History of Islamic Philosophy*, volume 1, 57. Majid Fakhry gives a slightly different assessment, "The philosophical awakening that followed in the wake of the introduction of Greek philosophy and was attended by the rise of a hitherto unknown spirit of free inquiry could not fail eventually to place in jeopardy some of the fundamental tenets of Islamic belief." Fakhry, *A History of Islamic Philosophy*, 94.
46. Jābīrī, *Naḥnu wa'l turāth*, 37–9.
47. Haq, "The Indian and Persian Background," 62–3.
48. See Anke von Kugelgen, "A Call for Rationalism: 'Arab Averroists' in the Twentieth Century." *Alif: Journal of Comparative Poetics*, number 16, 1996, 97–132.
49. Jābīrī, *Naḥnu wa'l turāth*, 242.
50. *Ibid.*, 53.
51. Jābīrī, *Takwīn al-'aql al-'arabī* (Casablanca: al-Markaz al-Thaqāfī al-'Arabī, 1991), 70–1.
52. *Ibid.*, 45.
53. *Ibid.*, 47.
54. Ḥassan Ḥanafī, *al-Turāth wa'l tajdīd* (Beirut: Dār al-Tanwīr, 1981), 64–5.
55. Jābīrī, *Takwīn al-'aql al-'arabī*, 67.
56. *Ibid.*, 68.

57. See Maḥmūd Amīn al-'Ālim, "Naqd al-Jābīrī li'l 'aql al-'arabī," in Maḥmūd Amīn al-'Ālim, *Mafāhīm wā qadāyah ishkāliyyah* (Cairo: Dār al-Thaqāfah al-Jadīdah, 1989), 143–63.
58. Jābīrī, *Takwīn al-'aql al-'arabī*, 131. See also *Naḥnu wa'l Turāth*, 228–35.
59. Jābīrī, *Naḥnu wa'l turāth*, 229.
60. Jābīrī, *Takwīn al-'aql al-'arabī*, 140–1.
61. *Ibid.*, 254.
62. Ibn Khaldūn has a similar view about the relationship between Sufīsm and Shī'īsm, "The Sufīs thus became saturated with Shī'ah theories. Shī'ah theories entered so deeply into their religious ideas that they based their practice of using the cloak (*khirqah*) on the alleged fact that 'Alī clothed al-Ḥassan al-Baṣrī in such a cloak and caused him to agree solemnly that he would adhere to the mystic path. The tradition thus inaugurated by 'Alī was continued, according to the Sufīs, through al-Junayd, one of the Sufī shaykhs." Ibn Khaldūn, *The Muqaddimah: An Introduction to History*, volume 2, trans. Franz Rosenthal (New York: Pantheon, 1958), 187.
63. Jābīrī, *Takwīn al-'aql al-'arabī*, 290.
64. Jābīrī, *Bunyat al-'aql al-'arabī* (Casablanca: al-Markaz al-Thaqāfī al'Arbaī, 1992), 486–7.
65. See Ṭāhā Ḥussain, *The Future of Culture in Egypt*, trans. S. Glazer (New York: Octagon Books, 1975).
66. Jābīrī, *Takwīn al-'aql al-'arabī*, 347.
67. See Albert Hourani, *Arabic Thought in the Liberal Age* (Cambridge: Cambridge University Press, 1970).
68. Hichem Djaït, *al-Kūfa: Naissance de la ville islamique* (Paris: Editions Maisonneuve, 1991).
69. See Ḥakīm bin Ḥamūda, "Ba'ḍ al-faraḍiyāt al-awaliyyah ḥawla quṣūr al-fikr al-maghārībī," in Maḥmūd Amīn al-'Ālim, *al-Fikr al-'arabī*, 134.
70. Jābīrī, *al-'Aql al-siyāsī al-'arabī* (Casablanca: al-Markaz al-Thaqāfī al-'Arabī, 1991), 57.
71. *Ibid.*, 75.
72. *Ibid.*, 88.
73. *Ibid.*, 113.
74. *Ibid.*, 140.
75. *Ibid.*, 206.
76. *Ibid.*, 228.
77. *Ibid.*, 232–3.
78. *Ibid.*, 233–7.
79. *Ibid.*, 259.
80. *Ibid.*, 350.
81. On this notion see Abdul Hamid el-Zein, "Beyond Ideology and Theology: The Search for the Anthropology of Islam." *Annual Review of Anthropology*, volume 6, 1977, 227–54.
82. Ernest Gellner, *Muslim Society* (Cambridge: Cambridge University Press, 1983), 56.
83. *Ibid.*, 1. "Islam is the blueprint of a social order. It holds that a set of rules exists, eternal, divinely ordained and independent of the will of men, which defines the proper ordering of society. This model is available in writing; it is equally and symmetrically available to all literate men, and to all those willing to heed literate men. Those rules are to be implemented throughout social life...Judaism and Christianity are also blueprints of a social order, but rather less so than Islam." *Ibid.*
84. Jābīrī, *al-'Aql al-siyāsī al-'arabī*, 365.
85. *Ibid.*
86. Jābīrī, *al-Dīn wa'l dawlah wa taṭbīq al-Sharī'ah* (Beirut: Markaz Dirāsāt al-Wiḥdah al- 'Arabīyyah, 1996), 21.
87. *Ibid.*, 24–30.
88. *Ibid.*, 52–3.

13 TOWARDS MODERN ARAB REASON

1. See Aramandon Salvatore, *Islam and the Political Discourse of Modernity* (London: Ithaca, 1997) 224–30, and "The Rational Articulation of Turath in Contempoary Arab Thought: The

Contributions of Muḥammad 'Abid al-Jābīrī and Ḥasan Ḥanafī." *The Muslim World*, volume 95 (3 and 4), 1995, 191–214.

2. For an analysis of the ideas of some of these thinkers, see Ibrahim M. Abu-Rabi', "The Arab World," in Seyyed Hossein Nasr and Oliver Leaman, eds., *History of Islamic Philosophy* (London: Routledge, 1996), 1082–114, and Massimo Campanini, "Egypt," in *ibid.*, 1115–28.
3. Jābīrī, *Bunyat al-'aql al-'arabī* (Casablanca: al-Markaz al-Thaqāfī al-'Arabī, 1992), 567.
4. Jābīrī, *al-Turāth wa'l ḥadāthah* (Casablanca: al-Markaz al-Thaqāfī al-'Arabī, 1991), 25.
5. Jābīrī, *al-Khiṭāb al 'arabī al-mu'āṣir* (Beirut: Markaz Dirāsāt al-Wiḥdah al-'Arabīyyah, 1982), 23.
6. See Salāma Mūsa, *Mā hiya al-nahḍah*? (Cairo: Mu'assassat Salāma Mūsa, n.d.).
7. Jābīrī, *al-Khiṭāb al-'arabī al-mu'āṣir*, 37.
8. *Ibid.*, 40.
9. Jābīrī, *al-Turāth wa'l ḥadāthah*, 248.
10. Jābīrī, *al-Khiṭāb al-'arabī al-mu'āṣir*, 59.
11. *Ibid.*, 61.
12. *Ibid.*, 197.
13. *Ibid.*, 198.
14. *Ibid.*, 201.
15. *Ibid.*
16. *Ibid.*, 205.
17. *Ibid.* 20.
18. In this regard, Jābīrī quotes the best representative of modern Islamic revivalism in the Arab world, Sayyid Quṭb who maintains today's Muslims, "are also surrounded by *jāhiliyyah*, which is of the same nature as confronted during the first period of Islam, perhaps a little deeper. It also appears that our entire environment is seized in the clutches of *jāhiliyyah*. The spirit of *jāhiliyyah* has permeated our beliefs and ideas, our habits and manners, our culture and its sources, literature and art, and current rules and laws, to the extent that what we consider Islamic culture, Islamic sources, Islamic philosophy and Islamic thought are all the products of *jāhiliyyah*." Sayyid Quṭb, *Milestones* (Karachi: International Islamic Publishers, 1981), 61.
19. Jābīrī, *Takwīn al-'aql al-'arabī* (Casablanca: al-Markaz al-Thaqāfī al-'Arabī, 1991), 338.
20. *Ibid.*, 345.
21. See al-Ḥabīb al-Janḥānī, "al-Mufakkir wa'l sultah fī'l turāth al-'arabī al-islāmī," in al-Tāhir Labīb, ed., *al-Intillejensia al-'arabīyyah* (Tunis: al-Dār al-'Arabīyyah li'l Kitāb, n.d.), 193–211.
22. Fahmī 'Abd al-Razzāq Sa'd, *al-'Āmmah fī Baghdād fī'l qarnayn al-thālith wa'l rabi' al-hijriyayn* (Beirut: al-Dār al-Ahliyyah li'l Nashr wa'l Tawzī', 1983), 65.
23. Jābīrī, *al-Muthaqafūn al-'arab fī'l hadārah al-'arabīyyah* (Beirut: Markaz Dirāsāt al-Wiḥdah al-'Arabīyyah, 1995), 36.
24. *Ibid.*, 52–3.
25. See al-Ḥabīb al-Janḥānī, *al-Tahawwul al-iqtisādī wa'l ijtimā'ī fī mujtama' sadr al-islām* (Beirut: Dār al-Gharb al-Islāmī, 1985).
26. Jābīrī, *al-Muthaqafūn al-'arab*, 52–3.
27. *Ibid.*, 115.
28. John Esposito and John Voll, *Islam and Democracy* (New York: Oxford University Press, 1996), 41.
29. Fakhry contends that, "Moreover, since throughout Muslim history the Shī'ites had been forced into the position of a disgruntled minority whose political ambitions were repeatedly thwarted, it was natural that they should rebel intellectually against the facts of religio-political reality and seek in the realm of abstract constructions a spiritual haven to which they could turn in adversity." M. Fakhry, *A History of Islamic Philosophy*, 2nd edition (New York: Columbia University Press, 1983), 41.
30. Jābīrī, *al-Masa'lah al-thaqāfiyyah* (Beirut: Markaz Dirāsāt al-Wiḥdah al-'Arabīyyah, 1994), 25.
31. *Ibid.*
32. 'Abdul Raḥmān Munīf, "al-Thaqāfah wa'l muthaqqaf fī'l mujtama' al-'arabī" in Sayyid Yāssīn, ed., *al-'Arab wa tahadiyyāt al-qarn al-hādī wa'l 'ishrīn* (Amman: Mu'assassat 'Abdul Hamīd Shūmān, 2000), 134–5.

33. Jābīrī, *al-Masa'alah al-thaqāfiyyah*, 42.
34. Jābīrī, *al-Dīn wa'l dawla wa tatbīq al-sharī'ah* (Beirut: Markaz Dirāsāt al-Wiḥdah al-'Arabīyyah, 1995), 12–22.
35. George Tarābīshī, "Ishkāliyāt al-dimūqratiyyah fī'l watan al-'arabī," in Yāssīn, *al-'Arab wa tahadiyyāt*, 531–45. Tarābīshī argues that he and his "Marxist generation" of the 1950s and 1960s were a victim of a deceitful theory which stipulated that democracy was a capitalist ploy which camouflaged class conflict in society. Now, he believes that, "as a matter of fact, democracy is an advanced product of advanced industrial societies." *Ibid.*, 533.
36. Jābīrī, *al-Dimūqraṭiyah wā huqūq al-insān* (Beirut: Markaz Dirāsāt al-Wiḥdah al-'Arabīyyah, 1994), 51.
37. *Ibid.*, 49.
38. See Ḥassan Hanafī and Muḥammad 'Ābid al-Jābīrī, *Hiwār al-mashriq wa'l maghrib* (Cairo: Madbūlī, 1990), 48. See also "Fī qadāya al-dīn wa'l fikr: hiwār ma' Muḥammad 'Ābid al-Jābīrī." *Prologues: Revue maghrebine du livre*, number 10, 1997, 48.
39. Abdou Filali-Ansari, "Can Modern Rationality Shape a New Religiosity? Mohamed Abed Jabri and the Paradox of Islam and Modernity," in John Cooper, Ronald Nettler, and Mohamed Mahmoud, eds., *Islam and Modernity: Muslim Intellectuals Respond* (London: I. B. Tauris, 1998), 158.
40. Tayyib Tizīnī, *Min al-istishrāq ilā al-istighrāb al-maghribī: bahth fi'l qirā'ah al-Jābīrīyyah li'l fikr al-'arabī* (Ḥoms: Dār al-Dhākirah, 1996), 97.
41. John Waterbury, "From Social Contracts to Extraction Contracts: The Political Economy of Authoritarianism and Democracy," in John P. Entelis, ed., *Islam: Democracy and the State in North Africa* (Bloomington: Indiana University Press, 1997), 141–2.
42. Jābīrī, "al-Mujtam' al-madanī: tasā'ulāt wā āfāq," in 'Abdalla Hamūda, ed., *Wa'y al-mujtama' bī dhātihī: 'an al-mujtama' al-madanī fi'l maghrib al-'arabī* (Casablanca: Dār Tubqāl, 1998), 49. See also Mark Tessler, "The Origins of Popular Support for Islamist Movements: A Political Economy Analysis," in Entelis, *Islam*, 93–126.
43. Jābīrī, *al-Dimūqraṭiya wā huqūq al-insān*, 35.
44. *Ibid.*, 43.
45. *Ibid.*, 48.
46. *Ibid.*, 51.
47. See Filali-Ansari, "Can Modern Rationality Shape a New Religiosity?," 159.
48. Jābīrī, *al-Dimūqraṭiyah wā huqūq al-insān*, 52–3.
49. *Ibid.*, 61.
50. *Ibid.*, 86.
51. Jābīrī, *al-Mas'alah al-thaqāfiyyah*, 175.
52. Jābīrī, *al-Dimūqraṭiyah wā huqūq al-insān*, 191.
53. *Ibid.*, 60.
54. *Ibid.*, 94.

14 COSTANTINE ZURAYK AND THE SEARCH FOR ARAB NATIONALISM

1. Zurayk was born in Damascus in 1909. He obtained a scholarship to study at the American University in Beirut in 1923, where he spent five years as a student. In 1930, he obtained his Ph.D. in philosophy from Princeton University. He died in 2000. On his life, see Zurayk, "Muqadimma," in *al-A'māl al-fikriyyah al-'āmmah li'l dokṭor Costantine Zurayk*, volume 1 (Beirut: Markaz Dirāsāt al-Wiḥdah al-'Arabīyyah, 1994), 13–14, and Hani A. Faris, "Costantine K. Zurayk: Advocate of Rationalism in Modern Arab Thought," in George N. Atiyeh and Ibrahim M. Oweiss, eds., *Arab Civilization: Challenges and Responses, Studies in Honor of Constantine K. Zurak* (Albany: State University of New York Press, 1988), 1–2, and Muhammad Dakrub, "Kostatine Zurayk." *Al-Ṭarīq*, volume 60(4), July–August 2001, 64–6. According to 'Azīz 'Azmeh, Zurayk was a pure Arab nationalist and liberal thinker who was marginalized in his home country. Azmeh draws comparisons between Zurayk's intellectual career and that of the Egyptian

thinkers Tāhā Ḥussain, 'Abd al-Razzāq al-Sanhūrī, and 'Alī 'Abd al-Rāziq. See 'Azīz 'Azmeh, "al-Dīn wa'l dunyah fī'l wāqi' al-'arabī." *Qaḍāyah Fikriyyah*, volumes 13 and 14, 1993, 348.

2. "Zurayk belongs to that early generation in the Arab East who received their modern education in academic institutions outside the Arab or Islamic worlds. It was only natural for Zurayk and his peers to look at themselves as members of a tiny circle differing from the rest of Arab thinkers." Hani A. Faris, "Costantine K. Zurayk", 29.
3. On Zurayk's role in establishing an Arab nationalist movement, see the following: Walid W. Kazziha, *Revolutionary Transformation in the Arab World: Habash and his Comrades from Nationalism to Marxism* (London: Charles Knight & Co., 1975); Ma'n Ziādeh, "Taqyīm tajribat harakati al-qawmiyyīn al-'arab fī marḥalatiha al-ūla." in Markaz Dirāsāt al-Wiḥdah al-'Arabīyyah, *al-Qawmiyyah al-'Arabiyyah: fī'l fikr wa'l mumārasah* (Beirut: Markaz Dirāsāt al-Wiḥdah al-'Arabīyyah, 1980), 325–44; and Saqir Abū Fakhir, "Costantine Zurayk: lamahāt min al-tārīkh al-sirrī lī nidālihī fī lubnān wa filastīn wa'l 'irāq." *Al-Ṭarīq*, volume 60(4), July–August 2001, 139–49.
4. See Zurayk, "Muqadimma," volume 1, 11–49.
5. Zurayk, "The Essence of Arab Civilization," in *al-A'māl al-fikriyyah*, volume 1, 9.
6. Tāhā Ḥussain, *Mustaqbal al-thaqāfa fī miṣr*, 2 volumes (Cairo: Matba'at Dār al-Ma'ārif, 1938).
7. Khālid M. Khālid, *From Here We Start*, trans. Ismā'īl R. al-Faruqi (Washington, D.C.: American Council for Learned Societies, 1953).
8. F. Zakariyya, *al-Ḥaqīqah wa'l khayal fī'l ḥaraka al-islāmiyyah al-mu'āṣirah* (Cairo: Dār al-Fikr, 1988).
9. On this movement, see the author's *Intellectual Origins of Islamic Resurgence in the Modern Arab World* (Albany: State University of New York Press, 1996), chapter 1, and George N. Atiyeh, "Humanism and Secularism in the Modern Arab Heritage: The Ideas of al-Kawakibi and Zurayk," in Atiyeh and Oweiss, *Arab Civilization*, 42–59.
10. Edward Said, *Orientalism* (New York: Pantheon, 1978).
11. Zurayk, *Naḥnū wa'l tārīkh*, in *al-A'māl al-fikriyyah*, volume 1, 65.
12. Zurayk, "Muqadimmah," volume 1.
13. M. Bennabi, *Islam in History and Society*, trans. Asma Rashid (Islamabad: Islamic Research Institute, 1988), and also G. E. von Grunebaum, *Modern Islam: The Search for Cultural Identity* (Berkeley: University of California Press, 1962).
14. Franz Fanon, *The Wretched of the Earth* (Harmondsworth: Penguin, 1967), and *Black Skins, White Masks*, trans. C. L. Markman (New York: Grove Press, 1967); Aime Cesaire, *Discourse on Colonialism*, trans. Joan Pinkham (New York: Monthly Review Press, 1972).
15. Zurayk, *al-Wa'y al-Qawmī: nazarāt fī'l hayāt al-qawmiyah al-mutafatihah fī'l sharq al-'arabī* (originally published in 1939), in *al-A'māl al-fikriyyah*, volume 1, 21.
16. *Ibid.*
17. See Maxime Rodinson, "*Al-Wa'y al-Qawmī* et sa place dans l'évolution de la pensée nationaliste arabe," in Hisham Nashabe, ed., *Studia Palestinia: Studies in Honour of Constantine K. Zurayk* (Beirut: Institute for Palestine Studies, 1988), 3–11.
18. Zurayk, *al-Wa'y al-Qawmī*, 25.
19. *Ibid.*, 70. This passage is translated by Sylvia Haim in Sylvia G. Haim, ed., *Arab Nationalism: An Anthology* (Berkeley: University of California Press, 1976), 168.
20. *Ibid.*, 71.
21. *Ibid.*, 77.
22. *Ibid.*, 90.
23. *Ibid.*, 95–7.
24. *Ibid.*, 82–4.
25. *Ibid.*, 105.
26. In the words of Faris, Zurayk considers the Arab nation to be "responsible for its period of decline because of its persecution of lively minds." Faris, "Costantine K. Zurayk," 13.
27. Zurayk, *al-Wa'y al-Qawmī*, 26–8.
28. Zurayk, "The Essence of Arab Civilization," volume 4, 13.
29. M. Berman, *All That Is Solid Melts Into Air: The Experience of Modernity* (New York: Penguin Books, 1982), 15.

30. R. Rorty, *Philosophy and the Mirror of Nature* (Princeton: Princeton University Press, 1979), 132.
31. J. Habermas, *The Philosophical Discourse of Modernity* (Cambridge: MIT Press, 1987), 2.
32. Zurayk, *Ma'nah al-nakbah*, in *al-A'māl al-fikriyyah*, first published in 1948 and *Ma'nah al-nakbah mujaddadan*, in *ibid.*, first published in 1967.
33. On modern Judaism and modernity, see Arthur Hertzberg, *Jewish Polemics* (New York: Columbia University Press, 1992), and John M. Cuddihy, *The Ordeal of Civility: Freud, Marx, Levi-Strauss, and the Jewish Struggle with Modernity* (New York: Basic Books, 1974).
34. Zurayk, *Ma'nah al-nakbah*, 18.
35. *Ibid.*, 23–7.
36. See Ṣalāḥ al-Dīn al-Munajjid, *A'midat al-nakbah* (Beirut: Dār al-Kitāb al-Jadīd, 1969).
37. Zurayk, *Ma'nah al-nakbah*, 37.
38. *Ibid.*, 38.
39. Zurayk, " 'Ilm al-nakbah," in *al-A'māl al-fikriyyah*, volume 4, 39.
40. Zurayk, *Ma'nah al-nakbah*, 40–1. For an elaboration see 'Aziz al-'Azmeh, "al-Tārīkh wa'l qawmiyyah al-'arabiyyah wa'l 'ilmāniyyah: Costantine Zurayk 'aks al-tayyār." *Majallat al-Dirāsāt al-Filasṭīniyyah*, number 35, Summer 1998, 3–22.
41. Zurayk, *Ma'nah al-nakbah mujaddadan*, 15.
42. *Ibid.*, 18.
43. *Ibid.*, 23–4.
44. Zurayk, "Ta'athur al-qawmiyyah al-'arabiyyah," in *al-A'mal al-fikriyyah* volume 4, 152.
45. *Ibid.*, 23.
46. Ḥassan Ṣa'b, *al-Insān al-'arabī wā taḥaddī al-thawra al-'ilmiyyah al-tiknolūjiyyah* (Beirut 1981), 12.
47. Zurayk, "Ta'athur al-qawmiyyah al-'arabiyyah," 28.
48. *Ibid.*, 31–5.
49. Fritz Steppat, "Re-Reading 'The Meaning of Disaster' in 1985," in Nashabe, *Studia Palestinia*, 14. Compare the preceding to this statement by an Israeli sociologist: "Israel was founded as an immigrant settler frontier state and is still an active immigrant society, engaged in a settlement and territorial expansion process down to the present day. Despite the constant rapid transformation of Israel, institutionally and culturally, it remains a settler society, *living by the sword* because it needs to make space for itself in limited terrain." Baruch Kimmerling, *The Invention and Decline of Israeliness: State, Society, and the Military* (Berkeley: University of California Press, 2001), 185.
50. Zurayk, "Ta'athur al-qawmiyyah al-'arabiyyah," 34.
51. Zurayk, *Ayyū ghad*? (first published in 1957), in *al-A'māl al-fikriyyah*, volume 1.
52. *Ibid.*, 20.
53. *Ibid.*
54. A number of contemporary Arab thinkers agree with many of these points. See Ahmad Kamāl Abū'l Majd, *Ḥiwār lā muwājahah* (Cairo: Dār al-Shurūq, 1988). Abū'l Majd argues that since the renaissance, the West has discovered unlimited possiblities in science and technology. The spirit of renaissance included the belief in the unlimited innate ability of human reason. Thus, in French philosophy, Descartes manages to conceive of man in terms of thought and nature in terms of mechanism. I think it is necessary for Muslims (a) to study European social history – the social history of capitalism and the middle class and the idea of progress; and (b) to study Western intellectual history with a focus on individuality. The bourgeois revolution inaugurated the concept of the bourgouis individual, individual happiness and utilitarianism. This leads to the concept of progress, a leading nineteenth and twentieth century term. American theologian and philosopher Reinhold Niebuhr defines progress in the following terms: "A further consequence of modern optimism is a philosophy of history expressed in the idea of progress. Either by a force immanent in nature itself, or by the gradual extension of rationality, or by the elimination of specific sources of evil, such as priesthoods, tyrannical government and class divisions in society, modern man expects to move toward some kind of perfect society. The idea of progress is compounded of many elements. It is particularly important to consider one element of which modern culture is itself completely oblivious." R. Niebuhr, *The Nature and Destiny of Man*, volume 1 (New York: Scribner's, 1964), 24.

55. Huston Smith, *Beyond The Post-Modern Mind* (Wheaton: The Theosophical Publication House, 1989).
56. Zurayk, *Naḥnū wa'l tārīkh*, 32.
57. *Ibid.*, 33–6.
58. *Ibid.*, 156–7. In the view of Samir Amin, "While in Europe, liberal thought was the banner of the industrial bourgeoisie, in Latin America it was the banner of landowners and traders." S. Amin, *Unequal Development: An Essay on the Social Formations of Peripheral Capitalism* (New York: Monthly Review Press, 1976), 297.
59. Zurayk, *Fī ma'rakatī al-ḥaḍārah*, in *al-A'māl al-fikriyyah,* volume 2.
60. *Ibid.*, 18.
61. See Marie Jean Condorcet, *Esquisse d'un tableau historique des progrès de l'esprit humain* (Paris: Agasse, 1795); August Comte, *Cours de philosophie positive* (Paris: Bachelier, 1830–42), and Pitrim Sorokin, *Social and Cultural Dynamics*, 4 volumes, and *Social Philosophies of an Age of Crisis* (Boston: Beacon Press, 1950).
62. Zurayk, *Fī m'arakat al-ḥaḍārah*, 243.
63. *Ibid.*
64. *Ibid.*, 251.
65. *Ibid.*, 258.
66. *Ibid.*
67. *Ibid.*, 248.
68. *Ibid.*, 290.
69. *Ibid.*, 295.
70. Zurayk, *Hādha al-'aṣr al-mutafajjir: nadharāt fī wāqi'īnah wā wāqī' al-insāniyyah*, in *al-A'māl al-fikriyyah*, volume 2, 48.
71. Zurayk, *Matālīb al-mustaqbal al-'arabī: humūm wa tasā'ulāt*, in *al-A'māl al-fikriyyah*, volume 3, 44.
72. Zurayk, *Naḥnū wa'l mustaqbal*, 23–4.
73. Zurayk frequently cites, Dennis Meadows *et al., The Limits of Growth: A Report for the Club of Rome's Project on the Predicament of Mankind* (New York: Universe Books, 1972).
74. Zurayk, *Naḥnū wa'l mustaqbal*, 126–36.
75. *Ibid.*, 185.
76. *Ibid.*, 209–30.
77. Zurayk, "Cultural Change and Transformation of Arab Society," in *al-A'māl al-fikriyyah*, volume 4, 101.
78. Zurayk, *Naḥnū wa'l mustaqbal*, 274–5.
79. Zurayk, "al-Jarīmah wa'l khaṭa'," in *al-A'māl al-fikriyyah*, volume 4, 250.
80. Some radical Marxists accused Zurayk of being a reactionary thinker because of his advocacy of Western ideas. See Bassām Tibī, "al-Fikr wa'l hazīmah: Arā' Costantine Zurayk fī hazīmati ḥuzayran." *Mawāqif*, volume 2(8), March 1970, 160–5.
81. Maḥmūd Suwayd, "al-'urūba wa'l islām: ḥiwār shāmil ma' Costantine Zurayk." *Majallat al-Dirāsāt al-Filasṭīniyyah*, 1996, 38–42.
82. See Māhir al-Sharīf, "Costantine Zurayk: tahawwulāt 'alā tafkīr qawmī 'arabī." *Al-Ṭarīq*, volume 60(4), July–August 2001, 67–80, and Anīs Sāyigh, ed., *Costantine Zuryak: 65 sanat min al-'aṭā'* (Beirut: Maktabat Beisān, 1996).
83. Suwayd, "al-'urūba wa'l islām," 42.

15 MAHDĪ 'ĀMIL AND THE UNFINISHED PROJECT OF ARAB MARXIST PHILOSOPHY

1. Ḥussain Muruwwa, *al-Naza'āt al-mādiyyah fī'l falsafah al-'arabīyyah al-islāmiyyah*, 2 volumes (Beirut: Dār al-Fārābī, 1979).
2. Among other Arab thinkers who applied Marxist criticism to Islamic philosophy and history one should mention the following: Hādī al-'Ulwī, *Fī'l dīn wa'l turāth* (Jerusalem: Ṣalāḥ al-Dīn, 1975); Adonis, *al-Thābit wa'l mutaḥawwil*, 3 volumes (Beirut: Dār al-'Awdah, 1983); Samir Amin, *Eurocentrism* (New York: Monthly Review Press, 1989).

3. It is known that Althusser (d. 1990) had suffered from a long period of mental instability. See his autobiography, *The Future Lasts a Long Time* (London: Chatto & Windus, 1993). The best book in English on Althusser remains Gregory Elliott, *Althusser: The Detour of Theory* (London: Verso: 1987). For a critical refutation of Althusser's main arguments, see E. P. Thompson, *The Poverty of Theory* (London: Merlin, 1978). One author comments on the legacy of Althusserianism by saying that it "seems very dated and irresistibly evokes, like the Beatles' music or Godard's fish film, a recent but vanguished past." Luc Ferry and Alain Renaut, *La Pensée: Essai sur l'Anti-Humanisme Contemporain* (Paris: Gallimard, 1985), 200. However, Elliott maintains that "Althusser is among the most significant Marxist thinkers this century; that his return to Marx has strong claims to be considered the most original enterprise in Communist, if not Marxist, philosophy since Lukacs' *History and Class Consciousness* (and superior to it), and the most fruitful development of historical materialism since Gramsci's *Prison Notebooks*." Elliott, *Althusser*, 10.
4. See Nicos Poulantzas, *Fascism and Dictatorship* (London: Verso, 1979); *State, Power, Socialism* (London: Verso, 1980). See also Bob Jessop, *Nicos Poulantzas: Marxist Theory and Political Strategy* (New York: St. Martin's Press, 1985).
5. Fawwāz Ṭarābulsī, one of Mahdī 'Āmil's closest friends, speaks of Althusser's impact on the Arab Leftist intelligentsia in his recently-released autobiography, *Sūrat al-fata bi'l aḥmar: ayyām fī'l silm wa'l ḥarb* [*A Portrait of the Young Man in Red: Chronicles of Peace and War*] (London: Riad El-Rayyes Books, 1997), 56–7.
6. On Althusser's impact on Mahdī 'Āmil's thought, see Muḥammad Boujnāl, *Mahdī 'Āmil wa ba'ḍ anṣār al-taghyiīr* (Casablanca: al-Markaz al-Thaqāfī al-'Arabī, 1998).
7. E. P. Thompson, *The Poverty of Theory and Other Essays* (New York: Monthly Review Press, 1978), 12.
8. See Keith Nield and John Seed, "Theoretical Poverty and the Poverty of Theory: British Marxist Historiography and the Althusserians." *Economy and Society*, volume 8(4), November 1979, 383–416. Also Simon Clarke *et al.*, *One-Dimensional Marxism: Althusser and the Politics of Culture* (London: Allison & Busby, 1980). Clarke maintains that "As the years went by it became clear that Althusserianism was not the passing fancy of a few avantgarde intellectuals, but that it was rapidly becoming a major intellectual current, indeed the dominant form of Marxism among the generation of students and academics who encounterd Marxism after 1968." *Ibid.*, 7. In his autobiography, Althusser confesses that he had never read systematically philosophical texts, "In fact my philosophical knowledge of texts was rather limited. I was very familiar with Descartes and Malebranche, knew a little Spinoza, nothing about Aristotle, the Sophists and the Stoics, quite a lot about Plato and Pascal, nothing about Kant, a bit about Hegel, and finally a few passages of Marx which I had studied closely." Althusser, *The Future Lasts a Long Time*, 165–6. See the essays by Althusser's trusted disciple, Etienne Balibar, *Ecrits pour Althusser* (Paris: La Découverte, 1991). For a discussion of Althusserianism's impact on the French Left, see the following: Sunil Khilnani, *Arguing the Revolution: The Intellectual Left in Postwar France* (New Haven: Yale University Press); Tony Judt, *Marxism and the French Left* (Oxford: Oxford University Press, 1986); and François Furet, *Interpreting the French Revolution* (Cambridge: Cambridge University Press, 1981).
9. On the history of Lebanese communism, see the following: Malik Abisaab, "Syrian-Lebanese Communism and the National Question, 1924–1968." Master's Thesis. City University of New York, 1992; S. Ayūb, *al-Ḥizb al-shuyū'ī fī suriyya wā lubnān* (Beirut: Dār al-Ḥuriyyah, 1960); Muḥammad Dakrūb, *Judhūr al-sindyanah al-ḥamrā': ḥikāyat nushū' al-ḥizb al-shuyū'ī al-lubnānī, 1921–1931* (Beirut: Dār al-Fārābī, 1984); Tareq Y. Ismael and Jacqueline S. Ismael, *The Communist Movement in Syria and Lebanon* (Gainesville: University Press of Florida, 1998); Ilyās Murquṣ, *Tārīkh al-aḥzāb al-shuyū'īyyah fī'l waṭan al-'arabī* (Beirut: Dār al-Ṭalī'ah, 1964); and Michael Suleiman, "The Lebanese Communist Party." *Middle Eastern Studies*, volume 3(2), January 1967, 134–59.
10. See the special section of the *Al-Ṭarīq* monthly on the life and thought of Mahdī 'Āmil: *Al-Ṭarīq*, volume 56(4), July 1997, 108–204. See also Markaz al-Buḥūth al-'Arabīyyah, *al-Nadhariyyah wa'l mumārasah fī fikr Mahdī 'Āmil: Nadwah Fikriyyah* (Beirut: Dār al-Fārābī, 1989).
11. Karl Marx and Frederick Engels, *Collected Works*, volume 5 (New York: International Publishers, 1976), 36–7.

12. Karl Marx, *The Poverty of Philosophy*, in Marx and Engels, *Collected Works*, volume 6, 166.
13. Comparing 'Āmil's work to Althusser's, one sees astonishing similarities. Althusser, according to Gregory Elliott, "dissected 'society' into four main practices: economic, political, ideological and theoretical, the ensemble of which constituted the complex unity of 'social practice'." Elliott, *Althusser*, 95. 'Āmil follows the above analysis.
14. Maḥmūd Amīn al-'Ālim, "Nadhariyat al-thawrah 'inda Mahdī 'Āmil wa adawātihah al-m'arifiyyah," in Markaz al-Buḥūth al-'Arabīyyah, *al-Nadhariyyah wa'l mumārasah fī fikr Mahdī 'Āmil: Nadwah Fikriyyah* (Beirut: Dār al-Fārābī, 1989), 50.
15. 'Āmil, *Muqadimmāt, nadhariyya Li dirāsat āthār al-fikr al-ishtirākī fī ḥarakat al-taḥarrur al-waṭanī* (Beirut: Dār al-Fārābī, 1986), 7.
16. Eric Wolf dates the beginning of capitalism to the nineteenth century when the British textile industry came under the influence of the capitalist mode of production. See Eric Wolf, *Europe and the People Without History*, 2nd edition (Berkeley: University of California Press, 1997), chapter 10.
17. Tom Nairn, "The Modern Janus." *New Left Review*, number 94, November–December 1975, 3. Quoted by Benedict Anderson, *Imagined Communites: Reflections on the Origin and Spread of Nationalism* (New York: Verso, 1992), 3.
18. "The Lebanese Communist party was slow to address the issue of Arab unity, a potent emotional force among the masses...By the mid 1960s, the Lebanese communists concluded that no Arab unitary state could long endure without an underlying unity among progressive forces." Tareq Y. Ismael and Jacqueline S. Ismael, *The Communist Movement in Syria and Lebanon* (Gainsville: University Press of Florida, 1998), 90.
19. I have referred to the following Mahdī 'Āmil's books and articles: "Nizām al-ta'līm fī lubnān." *Al-Ṭarīq*, numbers 10–11, 1970; *Madkhal ilā naqd al-fikr al-ṭā'ifī: al-qaḍiyyah al-filasṭiniyya fī aydūlūjiyyat al-burjuwāziyyah al-lubnāniyyah* (Beirut: Dār al-Fārābī, 1985); *Muqaddimāt; Fī al-dawla al-ṭā'ifiyyah* (Beirut: Dār al-Fārābī, 1986); *Azmat al-ḥadārah al-'Arabīyyah am azmat al-burjuwaziyāt al-'Arabīyyah* (Beirut: Dār al-Fārābī, 1986); *Naqd al-fikr al-yawmī* (Beirut: Dār al-Fārābī, 1988); *al-Nadhariyya fī'l mumārasa al-siyāsiyyah: baḥth fī asbāb al-ḥarb al-ahliyyah* (Beirut: Dār al-Fārābī, 1989); *Hal al-qalb li'l sharq wa'l 'aql li'l gharb?* (Beirut: Dār al-Fārābī, 1990); *Fī 'amaliyat al-fikr al-khladūnī* (Beirut: Dār al-Fārābī, 1990); *Munāqāshāt wā aḥādith fī qaḍāya ḥarakat al-taḥarrur al-waṭanī wā tamayyuz almafāhīm al-marksiyya 'Arabīyyah* (Beirut: Dār al-Fārābī, 1990).
20. This article is published as an appendix in 'Āmil, *Muqaddimāt*, 369–457.
21. He uses the term *takhalluf* in Arabic which is basically a pejorative one; it means backwardness or stagnation.
22. 'Āmil says that to develop a Marxist theory of underdevelopment, one must test Marxist doctrines against the changing economic structure of modern Arab societies. See *Muqaddimāt*, 196.
23. Ṣādiq Aḥmad Sa'd, Ibrahim Amer, *al-arḍ wa'l fallāḥ: al-mas'alah al-zirā'iyyah fī miṣr* (Cairo: Dār Misr, 1959), and Fawaz Girgis, *Dirāsāt fī tārīkh miṣr al-siyāsī mundhu al-'aṣr al-mamlūkī* (Cairo: Markaz al-Buhūth, 1968).
24. Aḥmad Ṣādiq Sa'd, *Taḥawwul al-takwīn al-miṣrī min al-namaṭ al-asyawī ilā al-namaṭ al-ra's-mālī* (Beirut: Dār al-Ḥadāthah, 1980).
25. Compare this to the following statement: "The process of creating strategic bases of the capitalist mode and dependent zones of support went on in the capitalist homelands as well as abroad. This point must be stressed because it is often obscured by an uncritical use of such terms as core and periphery. Capitalist development created peripheries within its very core." Eric Wolf, *Europe and the People Without History*, 2nd edition (Berkeley: University of California Press, 1997), 296.
26. Immanuel Wallerstein, *Historical Capitalism* (London: Verso, 1983), 13.
27. *Ibid.*, 15. Wallerstein maintains the genesis of capitalism as a historical system, "is located in late-fifteenth century Europe, that the system expanded in space over time to cover the entire globe by the late nineteenth century, and that it still today covers the entire globe." *Ibid.*, 19.
28. 'Āmil, *Muqaddimāt*, 74–5.
29. S. Amin, *The Arab Nation: Nationalism and Class Struggles* (London: Zed Books, 1983), 8.
30. See a different type of analysis offered by the Lebanese Communist Party in Ismael and Ismael, *The Communist Movement in Syria and Lebanon*, 90–2.

31. 'Āmil, *Muqaddimāt*, 375.
32. *Ibid.*, 250.
33. Immanuel Wallerstein, *The Capitalist World Economy* (London: Cambridge University Press, 1979).
34. Giovanni Arrighi, *The Geometry of Imperialism: The Limits of Hobson's Paradigm* (London: Verso, 1983), and *The Long Twentieth Century* (London: Verso, 1999).
35. See Andre Gunder Frank, *Capitalism and Underdevelopment in Latin America* (New York: Monthly Review Press, 1969); *Dependent Accumulation and Underdevelopment* (London: Macmillan, 1978); *World Accumulation, 1492–1789* (London: Macmillan, 1989).
36. 'Āmil, *Muqaddimāt*, 377.
37. Charles Bettelheim, *L'Inde indépendante* (Paris: Colin, 1962), 45, 63, 125.
38. On this concept, see L. Althusser and Etienne Balibar, *Reading Capital* (London: Verso, 1997), especially part one, and E. Balibar, "Structual Casuality, Overdetermination, and Antagonism," in Antonio Callari and David Ruccio, eds., *Postmodern Liberalism and the Future of Marxist Theory: Essays in the Althusserian Tradition* (Hanover: Wesleyan University Press, 1996), 109–19.
39. See Karl Marx, *Capital*, volume 1 (Harmondsworth, 1976–1981), 101.
40. 'Āmil, *Muqaddimāt*, 391–5.
41. For more elaboration on this point see Roger Owen, *The Middle East in the World Economy, 1800–1914* (London: Methuen & Co., 1981), especially chapter 6.
42. Yves Lacost, *Geographie du sous-développement* (Paris: PUF, 1965), 220.
43. See Malik Bennabi, *The Problem of Ideas in the Muslim World*, trans. Mohamed El-Mesawi (Beach, CA: Dār al-Ḥaḍāra, 1994).
44. Yves Lacoste, *Les pays sous-developped* (Paris: PUF, 1960), 56.
45. 'Āmil, *Muqaddimāt*, 423.
46. *Ibid*, 261.
47. For critical remarks on 'Āmil's understanding of the social history of the modern Arab world, see 'Iṣṣām Khafājī, "Musāhamah fī'l baḥth 'an hawiyatinah: ḥawla namaṭ al-intāj al-kolonyālī." In Markaz al-Buḥuth al-'Arabīyyah, *al-Nadhariyyah wa'l mumārasah fī fikr Mahdī 'Āmil: Nadwah Fikriyyah* (Beirut: Dār al-Fārābī, 1989), 199–275.
48. See Robert Vitalis, *When Capitalists Collide* (Berkeley: University of California Press). In the Indian case, see Bipan Chandra, "The Indian Capitalist Class and Imperialism Before 1947," In R. S. Sharma, ed., *Indian Society: Historical Probings* (New Delhi: Indian Council of Historical Research, 1993), 390–420. Chandra says that, "From the middle of the 19th century and especially after 1914 an independent capitalist class developed in India. From the beginning it possessed one important characteristic: in the main, it did not develop an organic link with British capitalism; it was not integrated with foreign capital in India." *Ibid.*, 392.
49. 'Āmil, *Muqaddimāt*, 25–6.
50. Marx and Engels, *Collected Works*, volume 5, 36.
51. First published in *La Pensée*, number 151, June 1970 and in English in Louis Althusser, *Essays on Ideology* (London: Verso, 1984).
52. *Ibid.*, 20.
53. *Ibid.*, 31.
54. *Ibid.*, 28.
55. 'Āmil, *Muqaddimāt*, 169.
56. 'Āmil, "Niẓām al-ta'līm fiī lubnān." *Al-Ṭarīq*, numbers 10–11, 1970, 26.
57. *Ibid.*, 29.
58. *Ibid.*, 28.
59. See Khayriyyah Qaddūḥ, "al-Fikr al-tarbawī 'indā Mahdī 'Āmil," in Markaz al-Buḥūth al-'Arabīyyah, *al-Nadhariyyah wa'l mumārasah fī fikr Mahdī 'Āmil: nadwah fikriyyah* (Beirut: Dār al-Fārābī, 1989), 99–132.
60. 'Āmil, *Muqaddimāt*, 71.
61. *Ibid.*, 267.
62. *Ibid.*, 70.
63. See the insightful article by Saad Eddin Ibrahim, "Egypt's Landed Bourgeoisie," in Saad Eddin Ibrahim, *Egypt, Islam, and Democracy: Twelve Critical Essays* (Cairo: American University in Cairo Press, 1996), 109–34.

64. 'Āmil, *Muqaddimāt*, 73.
65. *Ibid.*, 178–9.
66. See Muḥsin Ibrāhīm, *al-Yasār al-ḥaqīqī wa'l yasār al-mughāmir* (Beirut: Dār al-Fārābī, 1969).
67. Āmil, *Muqaddimāt*, 207.
68. See Farid el-Khazen, *The Breakdown of the State in Lebanon, 1967–1976* (Cambridge, MA: Harvard University Press, 2000).
69. For an elaboration of this point from a political perspective see Michael Hudson, *The Precarious Republic: Political Modernization in Lebanon* (New York: Random House, 1968).
70. 'Āmil, *Madkhal ilā naqd al-fikr al-ṭā'ifī*.
71. See Fawwāz al-Ṭarābulsī, *Ṣilat bilā waṣl: Michel Shīḥa wa'l aydiūlūjiyya al-lubāniniyyah* (Beirut: Dār al-Rayyis, 1998).
72. For more details see Roger Owen, *The Middle East in the World Economy* (London: Methuen, 1981), and Charles Issawi, *An Economic History of the Middle East and North Africa* (New York: Columbia University Press, 1982).
73. 'Āmil, *Madkhal ilā naqd al-fikr al-ṭā'ifī*, 15.
74. Michel Chiha, *Visage et présence du Liban* (Beirut: Les Conférences du Cenacle, 1964), 148.
75. *Ibid.*, 152.
76. 'Āmil, *Madkhal ilā naqd al-fikr al-ṭā'ifī*, 96–7. "Lebanon is...the expression and concrete model of a historical dream: an intercommunal coexistence which is – despite some degree of conflict (such as any complex reality is) – essentially democratic in an environment that aspires to freedom." Antoine N. Messarra, *The Challenge of Coexistence* (Oxford: Center for Lebanese Studies, 1988), 3.
77. "Chiha was under no illusion about the nature of Lebanon's democratic system. Indeed he saw communal solidarity and confessional interaction as a reflection of Lebanon's unique historical development – as a land of last resort. Democracy thus became a pragmatic response to Lebanon's 'accidental situation', to borrow the phrase Tocqueville uses in reference to the United States." El-Khazen, *The Breakdown of the State in Lebanon*, 389–90.
78. 'Āmil, *Madkhal ilā naqd al-fikr al-ṭā'ifī*, 102.
79. *Ibid.*, 125.
80. Charles Malik, *Lubnān fī dhātihī* (Beirut: Mu'assassat Badrān, 1974), 53–64. See also Michel Shīḥa, *Lubnān fī shakhṣiyatihī wā ḥudūrihī* (Beirut: Manshūrā al-Nadwah al-Lubnāniyyah, 1962).
81. Michel Chiha, *Liban d'aujourd'hui* (Beirut: Editions du Trident, 1949), 13.
82. For more on Shīḥa's ideas consult Michel Chiha, *Palestin*e (Beirut: Trident Publications, 1969).
83. 'Āmil, *Madkhal ilā naqd al-fikr al-ṭā'ifī*, 159.
84. *Ibid.*, 162–3.
85. See Kamal Salibi, *A House of Many Mansions: The History of Lebanon Reconsidered* (Berkeley: University of California Press, 1988), especially chapter 12.
86. 'Āmil, *Madkhal ilā naqd al-fikr al-ṭā'ifī*, 156–7.
87. *Ibid.*, 159.
88. *Ibid.*, 165.
89. *Ibid.*, 198.
90. On the intellectuals and the masses, see Julian Benda, *The Betrayal of the Intellectuals* (Boston: Beacon Press, 1955) and John Carey, *The Intellectuals and the Masses: Pride and Prejudice Among the Literary Intelligentsia, 1880–1939* (London: Faber & Faber, 1992).
91. 'Āmil, *Azmat al-ḥaḍārah al-'arabīyyah am azmat al-bourjūwāziyāt al-'arabīyyah?* (Beirut: Dār al-Fārābī, 1987).
92. Marx, *The Poverty of Philosophy*, 165.
93. 'Āmil, *Azmat al-ḥaḍārah*, 14.
94. *Ibid.*, 40–1.
95. *Ibid.*, 64.
96. *Ibid.*, 184.
97. Douglas Johnson, "Introduction," in Louis Althusser, *The Future Lasts a Long Time* (London: Chatto & Windus, 1993), xii.
98. See Ṭayyib Tizīnī, "Mahdī 'Āmil: mā alladhī tabaqqa minhū?" *Al-Ṭarīq*, number 4, July–August 1997, 123.

99. See Karīm Muruwwa, *Ḥiwārāt: Mufakirūn 'Arab* (Beirut: Dār al-Fārābī, 1992), 156.
100. For more analysis on 'Āmil and the Arab intelligentsia, see Kamāl 'Abdul Laṭīf, "Ḥudūd wa maḥdūdiyat al-sijāl al-aydiyolūjī." *Al-Ṭarīq*, number 4, July–August 1997, 141–55.
101. 'Āmil, *Naqd al-fikr al-yawmī*, 15.
102. Marx and Engels, *Collected Works*, volume 5, 59.
103. 'Āmil, *Naqd al-fikr al-yawmī*, 37.
104. See Ṣādiq Jalāl al-'Azm, *Naqd al-fikr al-dīnī* [*Criticism of Religious Thinking*] (Beirut: Dār al-Ṭalī'ah, 1969), and *al-Naqd al-dhātī ba'dā al-hazīmah* [*Autocriticism After Defeat*] (Beirut: Dār al-Ṭalī'ah, 1969).
105. See Aḥmad Ṣadiq Sa'd, "Ḥawla al-'alāqah bayna namaṭay al-intāj al-kolonyālī wa'l asyawī," in Markaz al-Buḥūth al-'Arabīyyah, *al-Nadhariyyah wa'l mumārasah fī fikr Mahdī 'Āmil: Nadwah Fikriyyah* (Beirut: Dār al-Fārābī, 1989), 140.
106. Adonis, *al-Thābit wa'l mutaḥawwil*, volume 1, 3.
107. Quoted by 'Āmil in *Naqd al-fikr al-yawmī*, 107.
108. *Ibid.*, 83.
109. *Ibid.*, 84–6.
110. *Ibid.*, 91. 'Āmil refers to the writings of such important Arab authors as Adonis, Yasin al-Hafiz, and Burhān Ghalyūn. Many of these thinkers are influenced by Jacques Berque's ideas on the Arab self. See Jacques Berque, *Dépossession du monde* (Paris: Editions le Seuil, 1964).
111. 'Āmil, *Naqd al-fikr al-yawmī*, 246–52.
112. See Marx and Engels, *Collected Works*, volume 5. On Althusser's periodization of Marx's work, see Louis Althusser, *Pour Marx* (Paris: Maspero, 1965). English translation: *For Marx* (London: Allen Lane, 1969).
113. Marx and Engels, *Collected Works*, volume 3.
114. Marx says that, "Alienated labor has resolved itself for us into two components which depend on one another, or which are but different expressions of one and the same relationship. Appropriation appears as estrangement, as alienation; and alienation appears as appropriation, estrangement as truly becoming a citizen." *Ibid.*, 281.
115. Michel Foucault, *L'Ordre du Discours* (Paris: Gallimard, 1971), 74.
116. 'Āmil, *Naqd al-fikr al-yawmī*, 136.

16 ABDALLAH LAROUI: FROM OBJECTIVE MARXISM TO LIBERAL ETATISM

1. See Mahdi Elmandjra, *La décolonisation culturelle: Défi majeur du 21ème siècle* (Marrakech: Editions Walili, 1996).
2. For a biography of Fanon, see David Macey, *Franz Fanon: A Biography* (New York: Picador USA, 2001). In some European and American circles, Fanon is described as a terrorist: "As Third Worldism declined, former Leftists found themselves in agreement with the author of *The Closing of the American Mind*, who, speaking at Harvard in 1988, described Fanon as 'an ephemeral writer once promoted by Sartre because of his murderous hatred of Europeans and his espousal of terrorism'." *Ibid.*, 21.
3. For a complete account of North Africa in the first half of the twentieth century, see Jacques Berque, *Le Maghréb entre deux guerres* (Paris: Le Seuil, 1962).
4. On Laroui's life and education, see Nancy E. Gallagher, "The Life and Times of a Moroccan Historian: An Interview," in Bassam el-Kurdi, ed., *Autour de la pensée de Abdallah Laroui* (Casablanca: Le Centre Culturel Arabe, 2000), 75–95.
5. Laroui, *Awrāq* (Casablanca: al-Markaz al-Thaqāfī al-'Arabī, 1996).
6. Eliās Murquṣ is a Syrian Marxist thinker who withdrew from the Communist Party and devoted his time to elaborating on Marxist notions in relation to the Arab world and with the help of Laroui's work. See E. Murquṣ, *al-Mārkisiyah fī 'aṣrina* (Beirut: Dār al-Ṭalī'ah, 1969) and *al-Mārkisiyah wa'l sharq* (Beirut: Dār al-Ṭalī'ah, 1968).
7. Abdallah Saaf, *Politique et savoir au Maroc* (Casablanca: Nouvelle Collections Atlas, 1991), 34.
8. For a good analysis of Laroui's ideas, see A. Labdaoui, *Les nouveaux intellectuels arabes* (Paris: Maspero, 1993), especially chapter 6, 211–56.

9. Laroui, "al-Taḥdīth wa'l dimūkrātiyyah." *Āfāq: Majallat Itiḥad Kuttāb al-Maghrib*, numbers 3–4, 1992, 168.
10. 'Allāl al-Fāsī, *al-Naqd al-dhātī* (Teṭwān: Maṭba'at Kremādis, n.d.).
11. Laroui, *L'idéologie arabe contemporaine* (Paris: Maspero, 1967), 4.
12. Laroui, *Islam et modernité* (Paris: Le Découverte, 1987), 80.
13. Samir Amin, *Eurocentrism* (New York: Monthly Review Press, 1989).
14. Laroui, *L'idéologie arabe contemporaine*, 3. This is deleted from the Arabic edition. In a recent work, Laroui defines Morocco as follows: "Le Maghreb, c'est aussi la décolonisation et le sous-développement économique, la dépendance et la rupture désirées et difficilement réalisable avec le marché capitaliste mondial, le biculturalisme et le retour à soi, la déchirure des consciences et l'éxigence de récupérer les valeurs perdues." ("North Africa is also decolonization and economic underdevelopment, dependence and desired rupture and realizable with difficulty with the global capitalist market, biculturalism and return to the self, rupture of conscience and the demand to recuperate the lost values." Translation by Abu-Rabi'.) *Islam et modernité*, 65.
15. Laroui, *L'idéologie arabe contemporaine*, 6.
16. Albert Hourani, "Ottoman Reform and the Politics of Notables," in Albert Hourani, Philip Khouri and Mary Wilson, eds., *The Modern Middle East* (Berkeley: University of California Press, 1993), 83.
17. Laroui, *L'idéologie arabe contemporaine*, 9.
18. *Ibid.*, 9.
19. Ḥassan Ḥanafī, *Muqadimah fī 'ilm al-istighrāb* (Cairo: al-Dār al-Faniyyah li'l Nashr wa'l Tawzi', 1991).
20. Ṣādiq Jalāl al-'Azm, *Naqd al-fikr al-dīnī* (Beirut: Dār al-Ṭalī'ah, 1969).
21. Laroui, *L'idéologie arabe contemporaine*, 39.
22. *Ibid.*, 26.
23. *Ibid.*, 27.
24. *Ibid.*
25. On Fanon's influence on Edward Said, for example, see Edward Said, *Reflections on Exile and Other Essays* (Cambridge, MA: Harvard University Press, 2000).
26. Laroui, *L'idéologie arabe contemporaine*, 51.
27. *Ibid.*, 56.
28. For more analysis, see Mark N. Katz, "The Embourgeoisement of Revolutionary Regimes: Reflections on Abdallah Laroui." *Studies in Conflict and Terrorism*, volume 21(3), 1998, 261–75.
29. *Ibid.*, 8.
30. Laroui, *Mafhūm al-aydiyūlūjiyyah*, 123.
31. *Ibid.*
32. "De la même manière, le marxisme est actuelement pour nous le résumé méthodique de l'histoire occidentale." ("Similarly, Maxiṣm is now for us the systematic resumption of Western history." Translation by Abu-Rabi'.) Laroui, *L'idéologie arabe contemporaine*, 153.
33. *Ibid.* 141.
34. B. Hindess and P. Q. Hirst, *Pre-Capitalist Modes of Production* (London: Routledge & Kegan Paul, 1975), 310.
35. Laroui argues, incorrectly to my mind, that "Le livre de Franz Fanon qui visait à être la Bible de toute l'humanité sous-développée est malgré tout prisonnier d'une expérience unique. ("The book of Franz Fanon which aimed to be the Bible of all underdeveloped humanity remains in spite of all prisoner of a unique experience." Translation by Abu-Rabi'.) Laroui, *L'idéologie arabe contemporaine*, 5.
36. Laroui, *The Crisis of the Arab Intelligentsia: Traditionalism or Historicism?* (Berkeley: Univerṣity of California Press, 1976), 83.
37. Laroui, *L'idéologie arabe contemporaine*, 29.
38. *Ibid.*, 32.
39. *Ibid.*, 33.
40. *Ibid.*, 44.
41. *Ibid.*, 37.
42. *Ibid.*, 47.

43. Laroui, *Islam et modernité*, 36.
44. *Ibid.*, 43.
45. Laroui, *Mafhūm al-dawla*, 170.
46. *Ibid.*, 51.
47. *Ibid.*, 52.
48. *Ibid.*, 58.
49. M. H. Heikel, *Cutting the Lion's Tail: Suez Through Egyptian Eyes* (London: Andre Deutsch, 1986).
50. Laroui, *L'idéologie arabe contemporaine*, 123–4.
51. Laroui, "al-Taḥdīth wa'l dimūkrātiyya." *Āfāq: Majallat Itiḥād Kuttāb al-Maghrib*, numbers 3–4, 1992, 16.
52. 'Urwi, *al-'Arab wa'l fikr al-tārīkhī* (Casablanca: al-Markaz al-Thaqāfī al-'Arabī, n.d.), 7.
53. *Ibid.*, 13.
54. *Ibid.*, 16.
55. *Ibid.*, 21.
56. "Il ne se passe pas de mois sans qu'on signale dans tel ou tel pays arabe une colloque sur le thème bien usé du citoyen face à la modernité et l'authenticité...Le philosophe-théologien pense que cette scission est non seulement éternelle, mais qu'elle se présentera toujours sous la même forme." ("It occurs no less without noticing in this or that Arab country on the well-used theme of modernism and authenticity. The theologian-philosopher thinks that this schism is not only eternal but that it will always surface in the same form." Translation by Abu-Rabi'.) *Laroui, Islam et modernité*, 75.
57. *Ibid.*, 23.
58. Laroui, *The Crisis of the Arab Intellectual*, viii.
59. Laroui, *al-'Arab wa'l fikr al-tārīkhī*, 45.
60. *Ibid.*, 56.
61. *Ibid.*, 63.
62. Laroui, *The Crisis of the Arab Intellectual*, 153–4.
63. *Ibid.*, 154.
64. A. Hourani, *A History of the Arab People* (Cambridge, MA: Harvard University Press, 1991), 445.
65. Abdallah Saaf, *Politique et savoir au Maroc* (Casablanca: Nouvelle Collections Atlas, 1991), 38–9.
66. Laroui, *Mafhūm al-aydiyūlūjiyyah*, 125.
67. Quoted by Laroui in *Islam et modernité*, 47–8.
68. 'Urwi, *Mafhūm al-ḥuriyyah*, 17.
69. Laroui, *Islam et modernité*, 54.
70. *Ibid.*, 54–60.
71. Laroui argues that, "Etat et liberté individuelle sont totalement contradictoires dans la société arabe traditionnelle." ("State and individual liberty are mutually exclusive in traditional Arab society." Translation by Abu-Rabi'.) *Ibid.*, 61.
72. *Ibid.*
73. Laroui contends erroneously that Islamism, "est plus une idéologie politico-sociale qu'une théologie ou une pratique sociale." ("is more of a political-social ideology than a theology or social practice." Translation by Abu-Rabi'.) *Ibid.*, 83.
74. Laroui, *Mafhūm al-dawlah*, 168.
75. Laroui, *Mafhūm al-'aql* (Casablanca: al-Markaz al-Thaqāfī al 'Arabī, 1996), chapter 1.
76. *Ibid.*, 25.
77. *Ibid.*, 45.
78. Laroui, *Awrāq*, 123–4.
79. "Crise de la pensée arabe signifie pour nous, au début de cette enquête, incapacité des intellectuels arabes à donner un diagnostic et, partant, une thérapeutique à l'ensemble des difficultés que connait leur société." ("The crisis of Arab thought signifies for us at the start of this search the inability of Arab intellectuals to present a diagnostic and suggest a cure for the difficulties of their society." Translation by Abu-Rabi'.) *Islam et modernité*, 81.

80. *Ibid.*, 85.
81. "The Marxist tendencies in Laroui's early works, still clear and unambigious, for example, in *La crise des intellectuelles arabes: traditionalism ou historicisme* (1974), became less pronounced in his later writings. In a lecture delivered in 1986 on the problem of methodology, he appeared to distance himself from both Marxists and poststructuralists, accusing the latter of the same 'metaphysical' and 'mystical positions' they attributed to traditional Western philosophy. Indirectly, he criticized his poststructuralist Moroccan colleagues for excessive preoccupation with epistemology and literature." Hishām Sharābī, ed., *Theory, Politics, and the Arab World* (New York: Routledge, 1990), 26.
82. Laroui, "al-Taḥdīth wa'l dimūkrāṭiyyah," 159.

17 CONCLUSIONS

1. "Israel is still an active immigrant settler society, domestically and externally a relatively strong state (even if less stable than in the past), *based on two deep cultural codes, common at least to its Jewish citizens – militarism and 'Jewishness.'*" Baruch Kimmerling, *The Invention and Decline of Israeliness: State, Society, and the Military* (Berkeley: University of California Press, 2001), 1.
2. "To be more specific, domination will thus mean the situation in which the manifested will (command) of the ruler or rulers is meant to influence the conduct of one or more others (the ruled)." Max Weber, *Economy and Society*, volume 2 (Berkeley: University of California Press, 1978), 946.
3. *Ibid.*, volume 1, 215.
4. Bryan S. Turner, *Orientalism, Postmodernism and Globalism* (London: Routledge, 1994), 9.

Bibliography

Abāh, S. W. "Hal ẓallā lī maqūlat al-yasār ma'nah?" *al-Sharq al-Awṣat*, number 6067, Sunday, September 7, 1995.

'Abd al-Fattāḥ, N. *Khitāb al-zamān al-ramādī: ru'ah fī azmati al-thaqāfah al-miṣriyyah* (Cairo: Yāfa li'l Nashr, 1990).

——, ed. *The State of Religion in Egypt Report* (Cairo: Al-Ahrām Center for Political and Strategic Studies, 1996).

——. *Taqrīr al-ḥalah al-dīnīyyah: al-taqrīr al-awwal* (Cairo: Markaz al-Dirāsāt al-Siyāsiyyah wa'l Istrātijiyyah fī'l Ahrām, 1997).

——. *Taqrīr al-ḥalah al-dīnīyyah: al-taqrīr al-thānī* (Cairo: Markaz al-Dirāsāt al-Siyāsiyyah wa'l Istrātijiyyah fī'l Ahrām, 1998).

'Abd al-Karīm, A. *Tārīkh al-ta'līm fī miṣr min nihayat hukm Muḥammad 'Alī ila awā'il ḥukm Tawfīq*, 1848–1882 (Cairo: Wazārat al-Mā'arif al-Ḥukūmiyyah, 1945).

'Abd al-Laṭīf, K. *Salāma Mūsa wā ishkāliyat al-nahḍah* (Beirut: Dār al-Ṭalī'ah, 1982).

——. *Mafāhīm multabasah fī'l fikr al-'arabī al-mu'āṣir* (Beirut: Dār al-Ṭalī'ah, 1992).

——. *Qirā'āt fī'l falsafah al-'arabīyyah al-mu'āṣirah* (Beirut: Dār al-Ṭalī'ah, 1994).

——. "Ḥudūd wa maḥdūdiyat al-sijāl al-aydiyūlūjī." *Al-Ṭarīq*, number 4 July–August 1997, 141–55.

——. *al-Fikr al-falsafī fī'l maghrib: qirā'āt fī a'māl al-Jābirī wa'l 'Urwī* (Casablanca: Ifrīqyyah al-Sharq, 2001).

——. "al-'Urwī fī mirā'at al-Jabīrī; al-Jabīrī fī mirā'at al-'Urwī." *Al-Ṭarīq*, volume 61(2), April 2002.

'Abd al-Malik, A. *Dirāsāt fī'l thaqāfah al-waṭaniyyah* (Beirut: Dār al-Ṭalī'ah, 1967).

'Abd al-Mu'ṭī, A. *al-I'lām wa tazyīf al-wa'y* (Cairo: Dār al-Thaqāfah al-Jadīdah, 1979).

'Abd al-Nūr, M. "Nāqūs al-khaṭar yadduq." *Wijhāt Nadhar*, volume 2(13), February 2000.

'Abd al-Rāziq, A. *al-Islām wā uṣūl al-ḥukm* (Beirut: Dār Maktabat al-Ḥayāh, 1978).

'Abd al-Razzāq Sa'd, F. *al-'Āmmah fī Baghdād fī'l qarnayn al-thālith wa'l rābi' al-hijriyayn* (Beirut: al-Dār al-Ahliyyah li'l Nashr wa'l Tawzī', 1983).

'Abdallah, I. S. "al-Kawkabah: al-ra'smāliyyah al-'ālamiyyah fī marḥalatī mā ba'da al-imberiāliyyah." *Al-Ṭarīq*, volume 56(4), July–August 1997.

——. "al-'Arab wa'l 'awlamah: al-'awlamah wa'l iqtiṣād wa'l tanmiyyah al-'arabiyyah," in Markaz Dirāsāt al-Wiḥdah al-'Arabīyyah, *al-'Arab wa'l 'Awlamah* (Beirut: Markaz Dirāsāt al-Wiḥdah al-'Arabīyyah, 1998).

Abdel-Malek, A. "The Occultation of Egypt." *Arab Studies Quarterly*, volume 1(3), Summer 1979.

Abdel-Malek, A. *La pensée politique arabe contemporaine* (Paris: Seuil, 1970).

Abdelrazik, A. *L'Islam et les fondements du pouvoir*, trans. Abdou Filali-Ansary (Paris: La Découverte, 1994).

Abisaab, M. "Syrian-Lebanese Communism and the National Question, 1924–1968." MA Thesis. City University of New York, 1992.

Abou Nasr, M. "L'idéologie nationale arabe dans le discours de Gamal Abd-El Nasser, 1952–1970." Thesis. Paris: Université de Paris, 1979.

Abū al-'Azā'im, J. *Nufūs warā' al-aswār* (Cairo: al-Dār al-'Arabīyyah li'l Ṭibā'ah wa'l Nashr, 1990).

Abū Fakhir, S. "Costantine Zurayk: lamaḥāt min al-tārīkh al-sirrī lī niḍālihi fī lubnān wā filasṭīn wa'l 'irāq." *Al-Ṭarīq*, volume 60(4), July–August 2001: 139–49.

Abū'l Majd, A. K. *Ḥiwār lā muwājaha: dirāsāt ḥawla al-islām wa'l 'aṣr* (Cairo: Dār al-Shurūq, 1988).

——. "Ḥawla nadwat al-ḥiwār al-qawmī al-dīnī," in Markaz Dirāsāt al-Wiḥdah al-'Arabīyyah, *al-Ḥiwār al-qawmī al-dīnī* (Beirut: Markaz Dirāsāt al-Wiḥdah al-'Arabīyyah, 1989).

——. *Ru'yah islāmiyyah mu'āṣirah* (Cairo: Dār al-Shurūq, 1992).

——. "Ṣūrat al-ḥālah al-islāmiyyah 'ala mashārif alfiyyah Jadīdah." *Wijhāt Nadhar*, volume 1(11), December 1999.

——. "Min ajl wiḥdah thaqāfiyyah 'Arabīyyah," in S. Yāssīn, ed., *al-'Arab wa taḥadiyyāt al-qarn al-ḥādī wa'l 'ishrīn* (Amman: Mu'asasat 'Abdul Ḥamīd Shūmān, 2000).

Abū Zayd, N. "al-Khiṭāb al-dīnī al-mu'āṣīir: āliyātuhu wa munṭalaqātuhū al-fikriyyah." *Qaḍāyah Fikriyyah*, volume 8, 1989.
——. *Mafhūm al-naṣṣ: Dirasah fī 'ulūm al-Qur'ān* (Cairo: al-Hay'ah al-Miṣriyyah, 1990).
——. *al-Tafkīr fī zaman al-takfīr* (Cairo: Dār Sīnā, 1995).
Abu-Deeb, K. "Cultural Creation in a Fragmented Society," in H. Hisham Sharabi, ed., *The Next Arab Decade: Alternative Futures* (Boulder: Westview Press, 1988).
Abu-Rabi', I. "Beyond the Post-Modern Mind." *American Journal of the Islamic Social Sciences* September 7, 1990, 235–56.
——. *Intellectual Origins of Islamic Resurgence in the Modern Arab World* (Albany: State University of New York Press, 1996).
——. "The Concept of the 'Other' in Modern Arab Thought: From Muḥammad 'Abduh to Abdallah Laroui." *Islam and Christian-Muslim Relations*, volume 8(1), 1997, 85–97.
——. "The Islamic Movement Inside the Green Line: The Contributions of Shaykh Rā'ed Ṣalāh." *Middle East Affairs Journal*, volume 5(1–2), Winter/Spring 1999.
Abu-Rabi', I., ed. *Islamic Resurgence: Challenges, Directions, and Future Perspectives: A Roundtable with Khurshid Ahmad* (Tampa: WISE, 1994).
Abū-Sulayman, A. *Crisis in the Muslim Mind* (Herndon: International Institute of Islamic Thought, 1995).
Adams, C. *Islam and Modernism in Egypt* (New York: Oxford University Press, 1933).
Adonis. "Reflections on the Manifestations of Intellectual Backwardness in Arab Society." In *CEMAM Reports* (Beirut: St. Joseph's University Press, 1974).
——. *al-Thābit wa'l mutaḥawwil*, 3 volumes (Beirut: Dār al-'Awdah, 1983).
Affifi, A. E. "The Influence of Hermitic Literature on Muslim Thought." *BSOAS*, xiii 1950, 840–55.
'Aflaq, M. *Fī sabīl al-ba'th* (Beirut: Dār al-Ṭalī'ah, 1959).
Aglietta, M. *A Theory of Capitalist Regulation: The US Experience* (London: Verso, 1979).
——. "World Capitalism in the Eighties." *New Left Review*, number 136, November/December 1982.
Ahmad, A. *In Theory: Classes, Nations, and Literatures* (New Delhi: Oxford University Press, 1994).
——. *Islamic Modernism in India and Pakistan* (London: Oxford University Press, 1967).
Ahmad, K. "Islam and Democracy: Some Conceptual and Contemporary Dimensions." *The Muslim World*, volume 90(1 and 2), Spring 2000, 1–21.
Ahmad, Z. "Developmental Changes in Islamic-Arab Movements." *Middle East Affairs Journal*, volume 3(1–2), Winter–Spring 1997, 3–11.
Ahmed, A. S. *Postmodernism and Islam: Predicament and Promise* (London: Routledge, 1992).
Ahmed, A. S. and D. Hastings, eds. *Islam, Globalization and Postmodernity* (London: Routledge, 1994).
Akhḍar, A. "Min naqd al-samā' ilā naqd al-ard." In F. Lenin, *Nuṣūṣ ḥawla al-mawqif mina al-dīn*, trans. M. al-Kabbe (Beirut: Dār al-Ṭalī'ah, 1972).
Alavi, H. "Pakistan and Islam: Ethnicity and Ideology." In F. Halliday and H. Alavi, eds., *State and Ideology in the Middle East and Pakistan* (New York: Monthly Review Press, 1998).
'Alawī, M. *Muḥammad al-Khāmis* (Casablanca: Maṭba'at al-Najāḥ al-Jadīdah, 1997).
Alexander, J. *Fin de Siècle Social Theory: Relativism, Reductionism, and the Problem of Reason* (London: Verso, 1995).
'Alī, H. "al-Usus al-ijtimā'iyyah li'l dhāhirah al-dīnīyyah: mulāḥadhāt fī 'ilm al-ijtimā' al-dīnī," in Markaz Dirāsāt al-Wiḥdah al-'Arabīyyah, *al-Dīn fi'l mujtama' al-'arabī* (Beirut: Markaz Dirāsāt al-Wiḥdah al-'Arabīyyah, 1990).
——. "al-Itijāh al-salafī." *'Ālam al-Fikr*, volume 26, January–April 1998.
Ali, H. "The New World Order and the Islamic World." *American Journal of the Islamic Social Sciences*, volume 8(3), 1991.
Ali, T. "Literature and Market Realism." *New Left Review*, number 199, May–June 1993.
——. "The Color Khaki." *New Left Review*, number 19, January–February 2003, 5–28.
Alili, R. *Qu'est-ce que l'islam*? (Paris: La Découverte, 1996).
'Ālim, M. A. *al-Wa'y wa'l wa'y al-zā'if fi'l fikr al-'arabī al-mu'āṣir* (Cairo: Dār al-Thaqāfah al-Jadīdah, 1986).
——. "Nadhariyat al-thawrah 'indā Mahdī 'Āmil wa adawātīhah al-ma'arifiyyah," in M. al-Buḥūth al-'Arabīyyah, *al-Nadhariyyah wa'l mumārasah fī fikr Mahdī 'Āmil: Nadwah Fikriyyah* (Beirut: Dār al-Fārābī, 1989).

——."Naqd al-Jābīrī li'l 'aql al-'arabī," in M. Amīn al-'Ālīm, *Mafāhim wā qaḍāyah ishkāliyyah* (Cairo: Dār al-Thaqāfah al-Jadīdah, 1989).

——. *Mafāhīm wā Qaḍāya ishkālīya* (Cairo: Dār al-Thaqāfah al-Jadīdah, 1989).

——. "al-Hashāshah al-nadhariyyah fī'l fikr al-'arabī al-mu'āṣir," in *al-Fikr al-'arabī bayna al-khuṣūṣiyyah wa'l kawniyyah* (Cairo: Dār al-Mustaqbal al-'Arabī, 1996).

——. "al-Fikr al-'arabī bayna al-nadhariyyah wa'l taṭbīq." *'Ālam al-Fikr*, volume 26, January–April 1998.

'Ālīm, M. A., ed. *al-Fikr al-'arabī 'alā mashārif al-qarn al-ḥādī wa'l 'ishrīn* (Cairo: Qaḍāyah Fikriyyah, 1995).

——. *al-Fikr al-'arabī bayna al-'awlamah wa'l ḥadāthah wā mā ba'da al-hadātha*, in *Qaḍāya Fikriyya*, volumes 19–20, 1999.

Altbach, P. "Education and Neocolonialism," in B. Ashcroft, G. Griffiths, and H. Tiffin, eds., *The Post-Colonial Studies Reader* (London: Routledge, 1999).

Althusser, L. *Pour Marx* (Paris: Maspero, 1965).

——. *Essays on Ideology* (London: Verso, 1984).

——. *The Future Lasts a Long Time* (London: Chatto & Windus, 1993).

Althusser, L. and Etienne Balibar. *Reading Capital* (London: Verso, 1997).

'Alwānī, T. J. *Adab al-ikhtilāf fī'l islām* (Qatar: Kitāb al-Umma, 1978).

——. "The Islamization of Methodology of Behavioral Sciences." *American Journal of the Islamic Social Sciences*, volume 6(2), December 1989.

——. *al-Judhūr al-tārikhiyah li'l azmah al-fikriyyah* (Cairo: IIIT, 1989).

Amato, P. "African Philosophy and Modernity." In E. C. Eze, ed., *Postcolonial African Philosophy: A Critical Reader* (Oxford: Blackwell, 1997).

'Āmil, M. "Niẓām al-ta'līm fī lubnān." *Al-Ṭarīq*, numbers 10–11, 1970.

——. *Madkhal ilā naqd al-fikr al-ṭā'ifī: al-qaḍiyyah al-filasṭiniyyah fī aydūlūjiyyat al-burjuwāziyyah al-lubnāniyyah* (Beirut: Dār al-Fārābī, 1985).

——. *Muqaddimāt nadhariyya li dirāsat āthār al-fikr al-ishtirākī fī ḥarakat al-taḥarrur al-waṭanī* (Beirut: Dār al-Fārābī, 1986).

——. *Fī al-dawla al-ṭā'ifiyyah* (Beirut: Dār al-Fārābī, 1986).

——. *Azmat al-ḥadārah al-'Arabiyyah am azmat al-burjuwāziyāt al-'Arabiyyah* (Beirut: Dār al-Fārābī, 1986).

——. *Naqd al-fikr al-yawmī* (Beirut: Dār al-Fārābī, 1988).

——. *al-Nadhariyya fī'l mumārasa al-siyāsiyyah: bahth fī asbāb al-ḥarb al-ahliyyah* (Beirut: Dār al-Fārābī, 1989).

——. *Hal al-qalb li'l sharq wa'l 'aql li'l gharb?* (Beirut: Dār al-Fārābī, 1990).

——. *Fī 'amaliyat al-fikr al-khaldūnī* (Beirut: Dār al-Fārābī, 1990).

——. *Munāqāshāt wā aḥādith fī qaḍāya ḥarakat al-taḥarrur al-waṭanī wā tamayyuz almāfāhim al-marksiyyah 'Arabīyyah* (Beirut: Dār al-Fārābī, 1990).

Amīn, G. *The Modernization of Poverty: A Study in the Political Economy of Growth in Nine Arab Countries* (Leiden: Brill, 1974).

——. *Miṣr fī muftaraq al-ṭuruq: bayna iflās al-yamīn, wa miḥnati al-yasār wā azmati al-tayyār al-dīnī* (Cairo: Dār al-Mustaqbal al-'Arabī, 1990).

——. "Ḥawla mafhūm al-tanwīr: nadhrah naqdiyyah li tayyār asāsī min tayārāt al-thaqāfah al-'Arabīyyah al-mu'āṣirah." *Al-Mustaqbal al-'Arabī*, volume 20(7), July 1997.

——. *al-'Awlamah* (Cairo: Dār al-Ma'ārif, 1998).

——. *al-Tanwīr al-zā'if* (Cairo: Dār al-Ma'ārif, 1999).

——. *Whatever Happened to the Egyptians? Changes in Egyptian Society from 1950 to the Present* (Cairo: American University of Cairo Press, 2000).

——. "Mab'ūth al-'awlamah aw Thomas Friedman wal' muthaqaffūn al-miṣriyyūn." *Wijhāt Nadhar*, volume 2(14), March 2000.

Amin, S. *Unequal Development: An Essay on the Social Formations of Peripheral Capitalism* (New York: Monthly Review Press, 1976).

——. *The Arab Nation: Nationalism and Class Struggles* (London: Zed Books, 1983).

——. "Etat, nation, éthique et minorité dans la crise." *Bulletin du forum du tiers-monde*, number 6, April 1986.

Amin, S. *Eurocentrism* (New York: Monthly Review Press, 1989).
——. *Empire of Chaos* (New York: Monthly Review Press, 1992).
——. "al-Thaqāfah wa'l aydiyūlūjiyyah fi'l 'ālam al-'arabī al-mu'āṣir." *Al-Ṭarīq*, volume 52(1), May 1993.
——. "Présentation," in F. Charaffeddine, *Culture et idéologie dans le monde arabe* (Paris: L'Harmattan, 1994).
——. *Re-Reading the Postwar Period: An Intellectual Itinerary* (New York: Monthly Review Press, 1994).
——. *Les défis de la mondialisation* (Paris: L'Harmattan/Forum du tiers-monde, 1996).
——. *Fī muwājahatī azmatī 'asṣrinah* (Cairo: Sīnā Li'l Nashr, 1997).
——. *Capitalism in the Age of Globalization* (London: Zed Books, 1998).
——. *Delinking: Towards a Polycentric World* (London: Zed Books, 1990).
Amin, S. and Burhān Ghalyūn, *Ḥiwār al-dīn wa'l dawlah* (Casablanca: al-Markaz al-Thaqāfī al-'Arabī, 1996).
Anderson, A. and D. Bark, eds. *Thinking About America: The United States in the 1990s* (Washington, D.C.: Hoover Institution Press, 1988).
Anderson, B. "The New World Disorder." *New Left Review*, number 193, May/June 1992.
——. *Imagined Communities: Reflections on the Origin and Spread of Nationalism* (New York: Verso, 1992).
——. *The Spectre of Comparisons: Nationalism, Southeast Asia and the World* (London: Verso, 1998).
Anderson, P. "The Affinities of Norberto Bobbio." *New Left Review*, number 170, July–August 1988.
——. "Renewals." *New Left Review*, number 1, January–February 2000.
——. "Force and Consent." *New Left Review*, number 17, September–October 2002.
An-Na'im, A. *Toward an Islamic Reformation: Civil Liberties, Human Rights, and International Law* (Syracuse: Syracuse University Press, 1990).
Anṣārī, M. *Taḥawwulāt al-fikr wa'l siyāsah fi'l sharq al-'arabī: 1930-1970* (Kuwait: 'Ālam al-Ma'rifah, 1980).
Antonio, R. J. and A. Bonanno, "Post-Fordism in the United States: The Poverty of Market-Centered Democracy." *Current Perspectives in Social Theory*, volume 16, 1999.
Anṭūn, F. *Ibn Rushd wa falsafatuhu*h (Beirut: Dār al-Ṭalī'ah, 1981).
Anwar, A. *al-Infitāḥ wa taghayyur al-qiyam fi miṣr* (Cairo: Miṣr al-'Arabīyyah li'l Nashr wa'l Tawzī', 1993).
Apple, M. W. *Education and Power* (New York: Routledge, 1995).
Arblaster, A. *Democracy* (London: Open University Press, 1994).
Arendt, H. *The Origins of Totalitarianism* (New York: Meridian Books, 1963).
'Ārif, N. M. *Fī maṣādir al-turāth al-siyāsī al-islāmī* (Herndon: International Institute of Islamic Thought, 1994).
Arkoun, M. *Essais sur la pensée islamique* (Paris: Editions Maisonneuve et Larose, 1977).
——. "The Adequacy of Contemporary Islam to the Political, Social, and Economic Development of Northern Africa." *Arab Studies Quarterly*, volume 5(1 and 2), Spring 1982: 34–53.
——. *Pour une critique de la raison islamique* (Paris: Editions Maisonneuve et Larose, 1984).
——. *Arab Thought*, trans. J. Singh (New Delhi: S. Chand and Company, 1988).
——. "Islamic Studies: Methodologies," in J. L. Esposito, ed., *The Oxford Encyclopedia of the Modern Muslim World*, volume 2 (New York: Oxford University Press, 1995).
——. "History as an Ideology of Legitimation: A Comparative Approach in Islamic and European Contexts," in G. M. Munoz, ed., *Islam, Modernism, and the West* (London: I. B. Tauris, 1999).
——. *The Unthought in Contemporary Islamic Thought* (London: Saqi Books, 2002).
Armitage, A. "The Debate Over Literary Writing in a Foreign Language: An Overview of Francophonie in the Maghreb." *Alif: Journal of Comparative Poetics*, number 20, 2000.
Aron, R. *L'opium des intellectuels* (Paris: Gallimard, 1968).
Arrighi, G. *The Geometry of Imperialism: The Limits of Hobson's Paradigm* (London: Verso, 1983).
——. *The Long Twentieth Century* (London: Verso, 1999).
Aruri, N. "The Recolonization of the Arab World." *Arab Studies Quarterly*, volume 11(2 and 3), Spring/Summer 1989.

Asad, T. *Genealogies of Religion: Discipline and Reasons of Power in Christianity and Islam* (Baltimore: Johns Hopkins University Press, 1993).
——. "Europe Against Islam: Islam in Europe." *The Muslim World*, volume 87(2), April 1997.
'Aṣfūr, J. *Hawāmish 'alā daftar al-tanwīr* (Cairo: Dār Su'ād al-Ṣabāh, 1994).
'Ashmāwī, M. S. *al-Islām al-siyāssī* (Cairo: Dār Sīnā, 1993).
Attas, S. *Islam and Secularism* (Kuala Lumpur: International Institute of Islamic Thought and Civilization, 1993).
'Awda, A. Q. *al-Islām wā awḍā'unah al-qānūniyyah* (Cairo: Dār al-Kitāb al-'Arabī, 1951).
——. *Islam Between Ignorant Followers and Incapable Scholars* (Riyadh: International Islamic Publishing House, 1991).
Ayūb, S. *al-Ḥizb al-shuyū'ī fī sūriyya wā lubnān* (Beirut: Dār al-Ḥuriyyah, 1960).
Ayubi, N. *Political Islam: Religion and Politics in the Arab World* (London: Routledge, 1991).
——. "Muḥammad al-Ghazālī," in J. L. Esposito, ed., *The Oxford Encyclopedia of the Modern Muslim World*, volume 2 (New York: Oxford University Press, 1993).
Azami, T. "The Emergence of the Contemporary Islamic Revival in Iraq." *Middle East Affairs Journal*, volume 3(1–2), Winter/Spring 1997.
'Azm, S. J. *al-Naqd al-dhātī ba dah al-hazīmah* (Beirut: Dār al-Ṭalī'ah, 1969).
——. *Naqd al-fikr al-dīnī* (Beirut: Dār al-Ṭalī'ah, 1969).
——. "The Importance of Being Earnest about Salman Rushdie," in D. M. Fletcher (ed.), *Reading Rushdi* (Amsterdam: Redopi, 1994).
——. "Mā hiya al-'awlamah?" *Al-Ṭarīq*, volume 56(4), July–August 1997.
——. *Dhihniyat al-taḥrīm: Salmān Rushdī wā ḥaqīqat al-adab* (Damascus: Dār al-Mada, 1997).
——. *Mā ba'da dhihniyat al-taḥrīm: qirā'at al-āyāt al-shayṭāniyyah* (Damascus: Dār al-Mada, 1997).
——. "Sur l'islam, la laïcité et l'Occident." *Le Monde Diplomatique*, September 1999.
——. "Mā hiya al-'awlamah?," in H. Ḥanafī and Ṣ. Jalāl al-'Azm, *Mā al-'awlamah?* (Damascus: Dār al-Fikr, 1999).
'Azmeh, A. *al-'Ilmāniyyah min mandhūr mukhtalif* (Beirut: Markaz Dirāsāt al-Wiḥdah al-'Arabīyyah, 1992).
——. "Aslamat al-ma'rifha wā jumūḥ allā 'aqlāniyyah al-siyāsiyyah." *Qaḍāyah Fikriyyah*, volumes 13 and 14, 1993: 407–19.
——. "al-Dīn wa'l dunyah fī'l wāqi' al-'arabī." *Qaḍāyah Fikriyyah*, volumes 13 and 14, 1993.
——. "Nationalism and the Arabs." *Arab Studies Quarterly*, volume 17(1 and 2), Winter and Spring 1995.
Bablāwī, H. *Miḥnat al-iqtisād wa'l iqtiṣādiyyīn* (Cairo: al-Hay'ah al-Miṣriyyah al-'Āmmah lil Kitāb, 2000).
Bahā' al-Dīn, A. "Mādha yurād bī miṣr?," in Markaz Dirāsāt al-Wiḥdah al-'Arabīyyah, *Min ḥamalat mashā'il al-taqaddum al-'arabī: Aḥmad Bahā' al-Dīn* (Beirut: Markaz Dirāsāt al-Wiḥdah al-'Arabīyyah, 1994).
Bailey, C. *Bedouin Poetry* (Oxford: Clarendon Press, 1991).
Bairoch, T. and E. Helleiner. *States Against Markets: The Limits of Globalization* (London: Routledge, 1996).
Balibar, E. *Ecrits pour Althusser* (Paris: La Découverte, 1991).
——. "Structual Casualty, Overdetermination, and Antagonism," in Antonio Callari and David Ruccio, eds., *Postmodern Liberalism and the Future of Marxist Theory: Essays in the Althusserian Tradition* (Hanover: Wesleyan University Press, 1996).
Banna, H. "Bayna al-dīn wa'l siyāsah." *Al-Ikhwān al-Muslimūn* (Weekly), March 4, 1945.
——. *Mudhakārāt al-Da'wah wa'l dā'iyah* (Beirut: al-Maktab al-Islāmī, 1971).
Barakat, H. *The Arab World: Society, Culture, and Change* (Berkeley: University of California Press, 1993).
Bariun, F. *Malik Bennabi: His Life and Theory of Civilization* (Kuala Lumpur: Muslim Youth Movement of Malaysia, 1993).
Barlow, M. and H. J. Robertson. "Homogenization of Education," in J. Mander and E. Goldsmith, eds., *The Case Against the Global Economy: And for a Turn Toward the Local* (San Francisco: Sierra Club Books, 1996).

Barnet, R. and J. Cavanagh, *Global Dreams: Imperial Corporations and the New World Order* (New York: Simon & Schuster, 1994).

Barrin, J. "Les différentes réponses des pays maghrébins à la menace islamiste." *Le Monde*, October 5, 1995.

Barsamian, D. *Iqbal Ahmad: Confronting Empire* (Cambridge: South End Press, 2000).

Basyūnī, M. *al-Ḥaqīqhah al-ghā'ibah bayna Khālid Muḥammad Khālid wā Muḥammad al-Ghazālī* (Cairo: n.p., 1997).

Batatu, H. *Syria's Peasantry, the Descendants of its Lesser Rural Notables and their Politics* (Princeton: Princeton University Press, 1999).

——. *The Old Social Classes and the Revolutionary Movements in Iraq* (Princeton: Princeton University Press, 1978).

Baumer, F. *Religion and the Rise of Scepticism* (New York: Harcourt, Brace, 1960).

Bebaeir, A. "Intellectual Currents in Contemporary Islam." *The Muslim World*, volume 81, July–October 1991, 231–44.

Beinin, J. and J. Stork. *Political Islam, Essays from The Middle East Report* (Berkeley: University of California Press, 1996).

Bellamy, R. *Liberalism and Modern Society* (Cambridge: Polity Press, 1992).

Bello, I. *The Medieval Islamic Controversy Between Philosophy and Orthodoxy: Ijmā' and Ta'wīl in the Conflict between al-Ghazālī and Ibn Rushd* (Leiden: Brill, 1989).

Bello, W. *New Third World: Strategies for Survival in the Global Economy* (London: Earthscan, 1990).

Ben Achour, Y. *Politique, religion et droit dans le monde arabe* (Tunis: CERP, 1992).

——. "Islam et laïcité: propos sur la recomposition d'un système de normativité." *Pouvoir*, 62 (1992).

Benda, J. *The Betrayal of the Intellectuals* (Boston: Beacon Press, 1955).

Bennabi, M. *Islam in History and Society*, trans. A. Rashid (Islamabad: Islamic Research Institute, 1988).

——. *The Problem of Ideas in the Muslim World*, trans. M. El-Mesawi (Beach, CA: Dār al-Ḥaḍāra, 1994).

——. *On the Origins of Human Society*, trans. M. Taher al-Mesawi (Kuala Lumpur: Open Press, 1998).

Berger, P. *The Social Reality of Religion* (London: Faber & Faber, 1973).

Berkes, N. *The Development of Secularism in Turkey*, 2nd edition (London: Hurst & Co., 1998).

Berki, R. N., ed. *State and Society in Contemporary Europe* (Oxford: Oxford University Press, 1979).

Berman, M. *All That Is Solid Melts Into Air: The Experience of Modernity* (New York: Penguin Books, 1982).

Berque, J. *Le Maghreb entre deux guerres* (Paris: Editions Le Seuil, 1962).

——. *Dépossession du monde* (Paris: Editions Le Seuil, 1964).

——. "Laïcité ou islamisme: Refuser la tentation de l'insularité." *Le Monde Diplomatique*, March 1991.

Bessis, S. and S. Belhassen. *Bourguiba: un si long regne, 1975–1987* (Paris: Jeune Afrique Livre, 1988).

Bettelheim, C. *L'Inde indépendante* (Paris: Colin, 1962).

Bilqazīz, A. "al-'Awlamah wa'l hawiyyah al-thaqāfiyyah." *Al-Mustaqbal al-'Arabī*, March 1998.

Bin'abd al-'Ālī, A. *al-Turāth wa'l hawiyah: dirāsāt fī 'l fikr al-falsafī fī'l maghrib* (Casablanca: Dār Ṭobqāl, 1987).

Binder, L. *Islamic Liberalism: A Critique of Development Ideologies* (Chicago: University of Chicago Press, 1988).

Birdsall, N. "Life is Unfair: Inequality in the World." *Foreign Policy*, Summer 1998, 95–113.

Bishāra, A. "Isrā'īl wa'l 'awlamah: b'aḍ jawānib jadaliyat al-'awlamah isrā'īliyan," in Markaz Dirāsāt al-Wiḥdah al-'Arabīyyah, *al-'Arab wa'l 'Awlamah* (Beirut: Markaz Dirāsāt al-Wiḥdah al-'Arabīyyah, 1998).

——. *al-'Arab fī Isrā'īl: r'uyah mina'l dākhil* (Beirut: Markaz Dirāsāt al-Wiḥdah al-'Arabīyyah, 2003).

Bishrī, Ṭ. *Bayna al-'urūba wa'l islām* (Cairo: Dār al-Shurūq, 1968).

——. "Ḥawla al-'urūbbah wa'l islām," in Markaz Dirāsāt al-Wiḥdah al-'Arabīyyah, *al-Ḥiwār al-qawmī al-dīnī* (Beirut: Markaz Dirāsāt al-Wiḥdah al-'Arabīyyah, 1989).

——. *Al-Ḥiwār al-islāmī al-'ilmānī* (Cairo: Dār al-Shurūq, 1996).
——. *Bayna al-jāmi'ah al-dīnīyyah wa'l jāmi'ah al-waṭaniyyah fi'l fikr al-siyāsī* (Cairo: Dār al-Shurūq, 1998).
——. "Al-Waḍ' al-dīnī fī miṣr bayna al-manṭūq bihī wa'l maskūt 'anhū." *Wijhāt Nadhar*, volume 1(4), May 1999.
Blackburn, R. *After the Fall: The Failure of Communism and the Future of Socialism* (London: Verso, 1991).
Bloom, A. *Prodigal Sons: The New York Intellectuals and Their World* (New York: Oxford University Press, 1986).
Boas, G. "Some Problems in Intellectual History." In A. O. Lovejoy, ed., *Studies in Intellectual History* (Baltimore: Johns Hopkins University Press, 1953).
Bobbio, N. *Left and Right: The Significance of a Political Distinction* (Chicago: University of Chicago Press, 1997).
——. "Gramsci and the Concept of Civil Society," in J. Keane, ed., *Civil Society and the State: New European Perspectives* (London: University of Westminster Press, 1998).
Botman, S. *The Rise of Egyptian Communism, 1939–1970* (New York: Syracuse University Press, 1993).
Bouguerra, M. L. *La recherche contre le Tiers-Monde* (Paris: PUF, 1993).
Bouhdiba, A. "Place et fonction de l'imaginaire dans la société arabo-musulmane," in *Culture et société* (Tunis: Université de Tunis, 1978).
Boujnāl, M. *Mahdī 'Āmil wā ba'd anṣār al-taghyīr* (Casablanca: al-Markaz al-Thaqāfī al-'Arabī, 1998).
Boullata, I. *Trends and Issues in Contemporary Arab Thought* (Albany: State University of New York Press, 1990).
Bourdieu, P. *Distinction: A Social Critique of the Judgement of Taste* (Cambridge, MA: Harvard University Press, 1984).
——. "L'essence du néolibéralisme." *Le Monde Diplomatique*, March 1998.
——. *Acts of Resistance: Against the Tyranny of the Market* (New York: The New Press, 1998).
——. *The State Nobility: Elite Schools in the Field of Power* (Stanford: Stanford University Press, 1996).
Boutaleb, A. *Le monde islamique et le projet du nouvel ordre mondial* (Paris: PUF, 1995).
Bouzayd, B. "Khiṭāb al-ḥarakah al-islāmiyyah fī'l jazā'ir." *Qaḍāyah Fikriyyah*, volumes 13 and 14, 1993, 277–88.
Brahimi, A. *Stratégie de développement pour l'Algérie* (Paris: Economica, 1991).
Brie, C. "Le couple Etat-nation en instance de divorce." *Le Monde Diplomatique*, May 1989.
Brinkly, A. *Liberalism and its Discontents* (Cambridge, MA: Harvard University Press, 1997).
Brown, L. C. *Tunisia: The Politics of Modernization* (New York: Praeger, 1964).
——. *Religion and State: The Muslim Approach to Politics* (New York: Columbia University Press, 2000).
Brzezinski, Z. "The Effects of War." *New York Review of Books*, January 17, 1991.
——. *The Grand Chessboard: American Primacy and its Geostrategic Imperatives* (New York: Basic Books, 1997).
Burgat, F. *L'Islamisme au Maghreb: La Voix du sud* (Paris: Karthala, 1988).
——. *L'islamisme en face* (Paris: La Découverte, 1995).
Burgat, F. and W. Dowell. *The Islamic Movement in North Africa* (Austin: University of Texas Press, 1993).
Caesar, J. *Crossing Borders: An American Woman in the Middle East* (Syracuse: Syracuse University Press, 1999).
——. *Writing off the Beaten Track: Reflections on the Meaning of Travel and Culture in the Middle East* (Syracuse: Syracuse University Press, 2002).
Cagne, J. *Nation et nationalisme au Maroc* (Rabat: L'Institut Universitaire de la Recherche Scientifique, 1988).
Calleo, D. P. *Rethinking Europe's Future* (Princeton: Princeton University Press, 2001).
Callinicos, A. "Social Theory Put to the Test of Politics: Pierre Bourdieu and Anthony Giddens." *New Left Review*, number 236, July–August 1999.

Campanini, Q. "Egypt," in S. H. Nasr and O. Leaman, eds., *History of Islamic Philosophy*, volume 2 (London: Routledge, 1996).
Canguilhem, G. *La connaissance de la vie* (Paris: Vrin, 1965).
——. *Etudes d'histoire et de philosophie des sciences* (Paris: Vrin, 1968).
——. *On the Normal and the Pathological* (Dordrecht: Reidel, 1978).
——. *A Vital Rationalist: Selected Writings*, ed. F. Dealporte (New York: Zone, 1994).
Carey, J. *The Intellectuals and the Masses: Pride and Prejudice Among the Literary Intelligentsia, 1880–1939* (London: Faber & Faber, 1992).
Caspar, R. "Un aspect de la pensée musulmane moderne: Le renouveau du Mo'tazilisme." *Mélanges*, volume 4, 1957.
Castells, M. "European Cities, the Information Society, and the Global Economy." *New Left Review*, number 204, March–April 1994.
Cavalcanti, P. and P. Piccone, eds., *History, Philosophy and Culture in the Young Gramsci* (Saint Louis: Telos Press, 1975).
Cesaire, A. *Discourse on Colonialism*, trans. J. Pinkham (New York: Monthly Review Press, 1972).
Chachour, E. *Blood Brothers* (Tarrytown: Chosen Books, 1984).
——. *We Belong to the Land* (Notre Dame: University of Notre Dame Press, 2001).
Chadwick, O. *The Secularization of the European Mind in the Nineteenth Century* (Cambridge: Cambridge University Press, 1975).
Chandra, B. "The Indian Capitalist Class and Imperialism Before 1947," in R. S. Sharma, ed., *Indian Society: Historical Probings* (New Delhi: Indian Council of Historical Research, 1993).
Charaffeddine, F. *Culture et idéologie dans le monde arabe* (Paris: L'Harmattan, 1994).
Charfi, A. "La sécularisation dans les sociétés arabo-musulmanes modernes." *Islamochristiana*, volume 8, 1982.
——. *Taḥdīth al-fikr al-islāmī* (Casablanca: Nashr al-Fennek, 1998).
Chatterjee, P. *Nationalist Thought and the Colonial World* (London: Zed Books, 1986).
——. *The Nation and its Fragments: Colonial and Postcolonial Histories*, in *The Partha Chatterjee Omnibus* (New Delhi: Oxford University Press, 1999).
Chaudhuri, K. N. *Trade and Civilization in the Indian Ocean: An Economic History from the Rise of Islam to 1750* (Cambridge: Cambridge University Press, 1985).
Chiha, M. *Liban d'aujourd'hui* (Beirut: Editions du Trident, 1949).
——. *Visage et présence du Liban* (Beirut: Les Conférences du Cenacle, 1967).
——. *Palestine* (Beirut: Trident Publications, 1969).
Chomsky, N. *World Orders Old and New* (New York: Columbia University Press, 1994).
——. "L'Indonésie, atout maitre du jeu américain." *Le Monde Diplomatique*, June 1998.
——. "Power in the Global Arena." *New Left Review*, number 230, July–August 1998.
——. *Profit Over People: Neoliberalism and Global Order* (New York: Seven Stories Press, 1999).
——. "Free Trade and Free Market: Pretense and Practice." In F. Jameson and M. Miyoshi, eds., *The Cultures of Globalization* (Durham: Duke University Press, 1999).
Clark, I. *Globalization and Fragmentation: International Relations in the Twentieth Century* (Oxford: Oxford University Press, 1997).
Clarke, S. *One-Dimensional Marxism: Althusser and the Politics of Culture* (London: Allison & Busby, 1980).
Cohn, B. *An Anthropologist Among the Historians and Other Essays* (New Delhi: Oxford University Press, 1987).
Collins, I. *Liberalism in Nineteenth-Century Europe* (London: Historical Association, 1957).
Commins, B. "'Abd al-Qādir al-Jazā'irī and Islamic Reform." *The Muslim World*, volume 78, April 1988, 121–31.
Comte, A. *Cours de philosophie positive* (Paris: Bachelier, 1830–42).
Condorcet, M. J. *Esquisse d'un tableau historique des progrès de l'esprit humain* (Paris: Agasse, 1795).
Cookson, P. Jr, and C. Persell. *Preparing for Power: America's Elite Boarding Schools* (New York: Basic Books, 1985).
Cooley, J. *Libyan Sandstorm* (New York: Holt, Rinehart & Winston, 1982).

——. *Unholy Wars: Afghanistan, America and International Terrorism* (London: Pluto Press, 2000).

Coury, R. *The Making of an Egyptian Arab Nationalist: The Early Years of Azzam Pasha, 1893–1936* (London: Ithaca Press, 1998).

Cox, H. *The Secular City: Secularization and Urbanization in Theological Perspective* (New York: Macmillan Co., 1966).

Cox, R. *Production, Power, and World Order: Social Forces in the Making of History* (New York: Columbia University Press, 1987).

Crabbs, J. "Politics, History, and Culture in Nasser's Egypt." *International Journal of Middle East Studies*, volume 6(4), 1975.

Cromer, Earl of. *Modern Egypt*, volume 1 (New York: Macmillan Co., 1908).

Cuddihy, J. M. *The Ordeal of Civility: Freud, Marx, Levi-Strauss, and the Jewish Struggle with Modernity* (New York: Basic Books, 1974).

D'Souza, D. "Solving America's Multicultural Dilemma." *The World and I*, January 1996.

Dāgher, K. "al-Ummah wa'l ummah al-'arabīyyah fī fikri Samīr Amīn." *Al-Tarīq*, volume 55(2), April 1996.

Daher, A. *Current Trends in Arab Intellectual Thought* (Washington, D.C.: Rand, 1969).

Dajānī, A. " 'An al-'urūbbah wa'l islām wā qaḍāya al-mustaqbal," in Markaz Dirāsāt al-Wiḥdah al-'Arabīyyah, *al-Ḥiwār al-qawmī al-dīnī* (Beirut: Markaz Dirāsāt al-Wiḥdah al-'Arabīyyah, 1989).

Dakrūb, M. *Judhūr al-sindyānah al-ḥamrā': ḥikāyat nushū' al-ḥizb al-shuyū'ī al-lubnānī, 1921–1931* (Beirut: Dār al-Fārābī, 1984).

——. "Costantine Zurayk." *Al-Ṭarīq*, volume 60(4), July–August 2001.

Dalacoura, E. *Islam, Liberalism, and Human Rights* (London: I. B. Tauris, 1998).

Dallal, A. "Islamic Revivalist Thought, 1750–1850." *Journal of the American Oriental Society*, volume 113(3), July–September 1993.

Darnton, R. "Intellectual and Cultural History," in M. Kammen, ed., *The Past Before Us: Contemporary Historical Writing in the United States* (Ithaca: Cornell University Press, 1980).

Darwaza, M. *al-Wiḥdah al-'Arabiyyah: Mabāḥith fi ma'ālim al-waṭan al-'arabī al-kabīr wā muqawimmāt wiḥdatihī wa'l 'aqabāt allatī taqif fi ṭarīqihā wā mu'ālajatiha wa'l marāḥil allatī yajib an yusārū fīhā ilā taḥqīqihā* (Cairo: n.p.; n.d.).

Darwish, M. *Memory for Forgetfulness: August, Beirut, 1982*, trans. I. Muhawi (Berkeley: University of California Press, 1995).

Davidson, A. *Antonio Gramsci: The Man, His Ideas* (Sydney: Australian Left Review Publications, 1968).

Dawisha, A. *Arab Nationalism in the Twentieth Century: From Triumph to Despair* (Princeton: Princeton University Press, 2003).

De Selys, G. *Tableau noir, appel à la résistance contre la privatisation de l'enseignement* (Brussels: EPO, 1998).

Decornoyn, J. "Capital privé, développement du sud et solidarité mondiale: Les multinationales, omniprésentes et…impuissantes." *Le Monde Diplomatique*. November 1988.

Devlin, J. F. *The Ba'th Party: A History from its Origins to 1966* (Stanford: Stanford University Press, 1976).

Dewey, J. *Liberalism and Social Action: The Later Works, 1925–1953* (Carbondale: Edwardsville, 1987).

Diyāb, M. H. "Ta'rīb al-'awlamah: musā'alah naẓariyyah," in M. Amīn al-'Ālim, ed., *al-Fikr al-'arabī bayna al-'awlamah wa'l ḥaḍāthah wā mā ba'da al-ḥadātha*. In *Qaḍāya Fikriyya*, volumes 19–20, 1999.

Djaït, H. *La personnalité et le devenir arabo-islamique* (Paris: Seuil, 1974).

——. *Europe and Islam: Cultures and Modernity* (Berkeley: University of California Press, 1975).

——. *La Grande Discorde, religion et politique dans l'islam des origines* (Paris: Gallimard, 1989).

——. *al-Kūfa: Naissance de la ville islamique* (Paris: Editions Maisonneuve, 1991).

Domenach, J. *Enquête sur les idées contemporaines* (Paris: Points, 1987).

Domhoff, G. W. *The Power Elite and the State* (New York: Aldine, 1989).

Donnelly, J. "Cultural Relativism and Universal Human Rights." *Human Rights Quarterly*, volume 6, 1984.

Duquoc, C. *Ambiguïté des théologies de la sécularisation* (Paris: Duculot, 1972).

Dussel, E. *The Invention of the Americas: Eclipse of the "Other" and the Myth of Modernity* (New York: Continuum, 1995).

——. "Beyond Eurocentrism: The World-System and the Limits of Modernity," in F. Jameson and M. Miyoshi, eds., *The Cultures of Globalization* (Durham: Duke University Press, 1999).

Eagleton, T. "The Crisis of Contemporary Culture." *New Left Review*, number 196, November–December 1992.

Edwards, B. M. *Islamic Politics in Palestine* (London: I. B. Tauris, 1996).

Eickelman, D. "Islam and the Languages of Modernity." *Daedalus: Journal of the American Academy of Arts and Sciences*, Winter 2000.

El-Affendi, A. *Turābī's Revolution: Islam and Power in Sudan* (London: Grey Seal Books, 1991).

El-Kenz, A. "al-Islām wa'l hawiyyah: mulāḥādhāt lī'l baḥth," in Markaz Dirāsāt al-Wiḥdah al-'Arabīyyah, *al-Dīn fī'l mujtama' al-'arabī* (Beirut: Markaz Dirāsāt al-Wiḥdah al-'Arabīyyah, 1990).

——. *Algerian Reflections on Arab Crises*, trans R. W. Stooky (Texas: University of Texas Press, 1991).

Elliott, G. *Althusser: The Detour of Theory* (London: Verso, 1987).

Ellis, M. *Practicing Exile: The Religious Odyssey of an American Jew* (Minneapolis: Fortress Press, 2002).

Elmandjra, H. *Rétrospectif des futurs* (Casablanca: Ouyoun, 1992).

——. *al-Ḥarb al-ḥaḍāriyyah al-ūlah* (Casablanca: 'Uyūn, 1994).

——. *La décolonisation culturelle: Défi majeur du 21ème siècle* (Marrakech: Editions Walīlī, 1996).

El-Mansour, M. "Salafis and Modernists in the Moroccan Nationalist Movement," in J. Ruedy, ed., *Islamism and Secularism in North Africa* (New York: St. Martin's Press, 1996).

Elon, A. "Crumbling Cairo." *New York Review of Books*, volume 42(6), April 6, 1995.

Escobar, A. *Encountering Development: The Making and Unmaking of the Third World* (Princeton: Princeton University Press, 1995).

Esposito, J. L. *Unholy War: Terror in the Name of Islam* (New York: Oxford University Press, 2002).

Esposito, J. and J. Voll. *Islam and Democracy* (New York: Oxford University Press, 1996).

Fakhry, M. *A History of Islamic Philosophy*, 2nd edition (New York: Columbia University Press, 1983).

Falk, R. *Explorations at the Edge of Time: The Prospects for World Order* (Philadelphia: Temple University Press, 1992).

——. "Vers une domination mondiale de nouveau type." *Le Monde Diplomatique*, May 1996.

Fandy, M. *Saudi Arabia and the Politics of Dissent* (London: Palgrave, 1999).

Fanon, F. *The Wretched of the Earth* (Harmondsworth: Penguin, 1967).

——. *Black Skins, White Masks*, trans. C. L. Markman (New York: Grove Press, 1967).

Farḥāt, M. N. *al-Mujtama' wa'l sharī'ah wa'l qanūn* (Cairo: Dār al-Hilāl, 1986).

Faris, H. A. "Constantine K. Zurayk: Advocate of Rationalism in Modern Arab Thought," in G. N. Atiyeh and I. M. Oweiss, eds., *Arab Civilization: Challenges and Responses, Studies in Honor of Constantine K. Zurayk* (Albany: State University of New York Press, 1988).

Fāsī, A. *The Independence Movements in Arab North Africa* (Washington, D.C.: American Council of Learned Societies, 1954).

——. *Ḥadīth maghrib wa'l mashriq* (Cairo: al-Maṭba'ah al-'Ālamiyyah, 1956).

——. *Maqāṣid al-sharī'ah al-islāmiyyah wa makārimuhah* (Casablanca: al-Najāḥ, 1963).

——. *al-Naqd al-dhātī* (Teṭwān: Maṭba'at Kremadis, n.d.).

Ferry, L. and A. Renaut. *La Pensée: Essai sur l'Anti-Humanisme Contemporain* (Paris: Gallimard, 1985).

Filali-Ansari, A. "Islam and Secularism," in G. Martin Munoz, ed., *Islam, Modernism, and the West* (London: I. B. Tauris, 1999).

——. "Can Modern Rationality Shape a New Religiosity? Mohamed Abed Jabri and the Paradox of Islam and Modernity," in J. Cooper, R. Nettler, and M. Mahmoud, eds., *Islam and Modernity: Muslim Intellectuals Respond* (London: I. B. Tauris, 1998).

Fitgerald, A. E. *The Pentagonists: An Insider's View of Waste, Mismanagement, and Fraud in Defense Spendīng* (New York: Houghton Mifflin, 1989).

FitzGerald, F. "George Bush and the World." *The New York Review of Books*, volume XLIX, September 26, 2002.

Foote, G. *Secularism Restated with a Review of Several Expositions* (London: W. J. Ramsey, 1874).

Forcey, C. *The Crossroads of Liberalism* (Oxford: Oxford University Press, 1961).

Foucault, M. *The Order of Things: An Archeology of the Human Sciences* (New York: Vintage, 1970).

———. *L'Ordre du Discours* (Paris: Gallimard, 1971).

———. *The Archeology of Knowledge and the Discourse on Language* (New York: Pantheon, 1972).

Fowden, G. *The Egyptian Hermes: A Historical Approach to the Late Pagan Mind* (Princeton: Princeton University Press, 1986).

Frank, A. G. *The Development of Underdevelopment* (New York: Monthly Review Press, 1969).

———. *Dependent Accumulation and Underdevelopment* (London: Macmillan, 1978).

———. *World Accumulation, 1492–1789* (London: Macmillan, 1989).

Freire, P. *Pedagogy of the Oppressed* (New York: Continuum, 1988).

Friedman, T. L. *The Lexus and the Olive Tree* (New York: Anchor Books, 2000).

Fūda, F. *Qabla al-suqūṭ* (Cairo: n.p., 1985).

———. *al-Nadhīr* (Cairo: al-Hay'ah al-Miṣriyyah, 1992).

Fukuyuma, F. "The End of History?" *The National Interest*, volume 16, Summer 1989: 3–18.

———. *The End of History and the Last Man* (New York: Free Press, 1992).

Furet, F. *Interpreting the French Revolution* (Cambridge: Cambridge University Press, 1981).

Gaddis, J. L. *We Now Know: Rethinking Cold War History* (New York: Oxford University Press, 1998).

———. *The United States and the Origins of the Cold War* (New York: Columbia University Press, 2000).

Galeano, E. *Days and Nights of Love and War*, trans. S. Cisneros (New York: Monthly Review Press, 2000).

Gallagher, N. "Islam v. Secularism in Cairo: An Account of the Dar Hikma Debate." *Middle East Studies*, volume 25(2), April 1989.

———. "The Life and Times of a Moroccan Historian: An Interview," in B. el-Kurdi, ed., *Autour de la pensée de Abdallah Laroui* (Casablanca: Le Centre Culturel Arabe, 2000).

Gay, P. *The Enlightenment: An Interpretation* (London: Weidenfeld & Nicolson, 1966).

Gellner, E. *Muslim Society* (Cambridge: Cambridge University Press, 1983).

———. *Nation and Nationalism* (Ithaca: Cornell University Press, 1983).

———. *Postmodernism, Reason and Religion* (London: Routledge, 1992).

Genequand, C. *Ibn Rushd's Metaphysics: A Translation with Introduction of Ibn Rushd's Commentary on Aristotle's Metaphysics, Book Lam* (Leiden: Brill, 1986).

Gerth, H. H. and C. W. Mills, eds. *From Max Weber: Essays in Sociology* (Routledge & Kegan Paul, 1948).

Ghalyūn, B. "al-Islām wa azmat 'alāqāt al-ṣulṭah al-ijtimā'iyyah," in Markaz Dirāsāt al-Wiḥdah al-'Arabīyyah, *al-Dīn fī'l mujtam' al-'arabī* (Beirut: Markaz Dirāsāt al-Wiḥdah al-'Arabīyyah, 1990).

———. *Ightiyāl al-'aql: miḥnat al-thaqāfah al-'Arabīyya bayna al-salafiyya wa'l taba'iyyah* (Cairo: Madbūlī, 1990).

———. *Le malaise arabe: l'Etat contre la nation* (Paris: La Découverte, 1991).

———. *Naqd al-siyāssa: al-dawla wa'l dīn* (Beirut, 1991).

———. "Binā' al-mujtama' al-madanī al-'arabī: dawr al-'awāmil al-dākhiliyyah wa'l khārijiyyah," in Markaz Dirāsāt al-Wiḥdah al-'Arabīyyah, *al-Mujtama' al-madanī fī'l waṭan al-'arabī* (Beirut: Markaz Dirāsāt al-Wiḥdah al-'Arabīyyah, 1992).

———. "La fin de la stratégie nationale: Stratégie et nouvel ordre mondial." *Jusoor: The Arab American Journal of Cultural Exchange and Thought for the Future*, Spring–Summer 1993.

Ghannūshī, R. *Maqālāt: ḥarakat al-itijāh al-islāmi bī tūnis* (Paris: Dār al-Karawān, 1984).

———. "Ayatū hadāthah? Laysa mushkiluna ma' al-hadāthah." *Qirā'āt Siyāsiyyah*, volume 2(4), 1992.

———. "The Battle Against Islam." *Middle East Affairs Journal*, volume 1(2), Winter 1993.

———. *al-Ḥuriyyāt al-'āmmah fī'l dawlah al-islāmiyyah* (Beirut: Markaz Dirāsāt al-Wiḥdah al-'Arabīyyah, 1993).

———. "Islamic Movements: Self-Criticism and Reconsideration." *Middle East Affairs Journal*, volume 3(1–2), Winter/Spring 1997.

Ghannūshī, R. *Muqārābāt fī'l 'ilmāniyyah wa'l mujtama' al-madanī* (London: al-Markaz al-Maghārībī li'l buḥūth wa'l Tarjamah, 1999).

———. "Secularism in the Arab Maghreb," in J. L. Esposito and A. Tamimi, eds., *Islam and Secularism in the Middle East* (New York: New York University Press, 2000).

Ghazālī, A. H. *al-Mustasfa min 'ilm al-uṣūl* , volume 1 (Baghdād: Matba'at Muthanna, 1970).
Ghazālī, M. *al-Islām al-muftara 'alyhī bayna al-shuyū'iyyīn wa'l ra'smāliyyīn* (Cairo: Dār al-Turāth, 1952).
——. *Our Beginning in Wisdom*, trans. I. R. al-Faruqi (Washington, D.C.: American Council of Learned Societies, 1953).
——. *al-Jānib al-'āṭifī fī'l islām* (Cairo: Dār al-Kutub al-Ḥadīthah, 1961).
——. *al-Islām wa al-ṭāqāt al-mu'aṭallah* (Cairo: Dār al-Kutub al-Ḥadīthah, 1964).
——. *Kifāḥ dīn* (Cairo: Dār al-Kutub al-Ḥadīthah, 1965).
——. *'Aqīdat al-muslim* (Cairo: Dār al-Kutub al-Ḥadīthah, 1965).
——. *Ẓalām mina al-gharb*, 2nd edition (Cairo: Dār al-Kutub al-Ḥadīthah, 1965).
——. *Hādha dīnunah* (Cairo: Dār al-Kutub al-Ḥadīthah, 1965).
——. *Ma' Allah: Dirāsāt fī al-da'wah wa'l d'ūah* (Cairo: Dār al-Kutub al-Ḥadīthah, 1965).
——. *Ma'rakat al-misḥaf fī al-'ālam al-islāmī*, 3rd edition (Cairo: Dār al-Kutub al-Ḥadīthah, 1971).
——. *Khuluq al-muslim* (Cairo: Dār al-Kutub al-Ḥadīthah, 1974).
——. *al-Da'wah al-islāmiyah tastaqbil qarnaha al-khāmis 'ashar* (Cairo: Dhāt al-Salāsil, 1980).
——. *Dustūr al-wiḥdah al-thaqāfiyah bayna al-muslimīn* (Cairo: Dār al-Anṣār, 1981).
——. *Humūm Dā'iyah* (Cairo: Dār Thābit, 1983).
——. *Kayfā nafhamū al-islām?* 3rd edition (Cairo: Dār al-Kutub al-Islāmiyyah, 1983).
——. *Laysā minā al-islām* (Cairo: Dār al-Kutub al-Islāmiyyah, 1983).
——. *al-Ghazw al-thaqāfī yamtadu fī farāghina* (Amman: Mu'assassat al-Sharq, 1985).
——. *al-Islām wa'l awḍā' al-qānūniyyah*, 7th edition (Cairo: Dār al-Ṣaḥwah, 1987).
——. *al-Sunnah al-nabawiyah bayna ahl al-fiqh wā ahl al-ḥadīth* (Cairo: Dār al-Shurūq, 1989).
——. *Jihād al-Da'wah: bayna 'ajz al-dākhil wa kayd al-khārij* (Damascus: Dār al-Qalam, 1991).
——. *Turāthuna al-fikrī fī mīzān al-shar' wa'l 'aql* (Herndon: International Institute of Islamic Thought, 1991).
——. *Kayfa nata'āmalū ma' al-Qur'ān* (Herndon: International Institute of Islamic Thought, 1991).
——. *Ṣayhat tahzīr min du'āt al-tanṣīr* (Cairo: Dār al-Ṣahwah, 1991).
——. *Naẓarāt fī al-Qur'ān*, 5th edition (Cairo: Dār al-Kutub al-Ḥadīthah, n.d.).
Gheissari, A. *Iranian Intellectuals in the 20th Century* (Austin: University of Texas Press, 1998).
Gibb, H. *Modern Trends in Islam* (Chicago: University of Chicago Press, 1947).
——. *The Travels of Ibn Battuta*, 3 volumes (New Delhi: Munshiram, 1993).
Gibran, G. K. *The Treasured Writings of Khalil Gibran* (Secaucus, N.J.: Castle Books, 1985).
Giddens, A. *The Consequences of Modernity* (Stanford: Stanford University Press, 1990).
——. *The Third Way: The Renewal of Social Democracy* (Cambridge: Polity Press, 1998).
Gilbert, F. "Intellectual History: Its Aims and Methods." *Daedalus*, volume 100(1), Winter 1971.
Gill, S. *American Hegemony and the Trilateral Commission* (New York: Cambridge University Press, 1990).
Gilmour, D. "Desert Ruritania." *New York Review of Books*, March 26, 1992.
Gilsenan, G. *Recognizing Islam: Religion and Society in the Modern Arab World* (New York: Pantheon, 1982).
Ginsberg, A. "After the Big Parade." *Cosmopolitan Greetings: Poems 1986–1992* (New York: Harper Perennial, 1995).
Girard, R. *Violence and the Sacred* (Baltimore: Johns Hopkins University Press, 1979).
——. *Things Hidden Since the Foundation of the World* (Stanford: Stanford University Press, 1987).
Godelier, M. *Writing and Difference* (Chicago: University of Chicago Press, 1978).
Goodwin, B. *How the Leopard Changed its Spots: The Evolution of Complexity* (New York: Charles Scribner's Sons, 1994).
Gorce, P. *Le Dernier Empire* (Paris: Grasset, 1996).
Gordon, J. "Secular and Religious Memory in Egypt: Recalling Nasserist Civics." *The Muslim World*, volume 87(2), April 1997, 94–110.
Gordon, L. *Fanon and the Crisis of European Man: An Essay on Philosophy and the Human Sciences* (New York: Routledge, 1995).
——. "Tragic Dimensions of our Neocolonial 'Postcolonial' World," in E. C. Eze, ed., *Postcolonial African Philosophy: A Critical Reader* (Oxford: Blackwell, 1997).

Gowan, P. "The Gulf War, Iraq and Western Liberalism." *New Left Review*, number 187, May/June 1991.
——. "A Calculus of Power." *New Left Review*, number 16, July–August 2002.
Gramsci, A. "Americanism and Fordism," in *The Prison Notebooks* (New York: International Publishers, 1971).
——. *Selections from the Prison Notebooks* (New York: International Publishers, 1978).
——. *The Modern Prince and Other Writings* (New York: International Publishers, 1978).
Gran, P. *Islamic Roots of Capitalism* (Austin: University of Texas Press, 1979).
——. "Political Economy as a Paradigm for the Study of Islamic History." *International Journal of Middle East Studies*, volume 11(4), July 1980, 511–26.
Gray, J. *Enlightenment's Wake: Politics and Culture at the End of the Modern Age* (London: Routledge, 1995).
Green, A. *The Tunisian Ulama, 1873–1915: Social Structure and Response to Ideological Currents* (Leiden: Brill, 1978).
Greider, W. *One World, Ready or Not: The Manic Logic of Global Capitalism* (New York: Simon & Schuster, 1997).
Gresh, A. "Pour un dialogue des civilisations." *Le Monde Diplomatique*, June 1995.
——. "Les aléas de l'internationalisme." *Le Monde Diplomatique*, May 1998.
Griffin, D. R. and H. Smith. *Primordial Truth and Postmodern Theology* (Albany: State University of New York Press, 1989).
Griswold, D. T. "Blessings and Burdens of Globalization." *The World and I*, April 1998, 30–5.
Grunebaum, G. E. *Modern Islam: The Search for Cultural Identity* (Berkeley: University of California Press, 1962).
Guazzone, L. *The Islamist Dilemma: The Political Role of Islamist Movements in the Contemporary Arab World* (London: Ithaca Press, 1995).
Guha, R. *Dominance without Hegemony: History and Power in Colonial India* (New Delhi: Oxford University Press, 1998).
Habermas, J. *The Philosophical Discourse of Modernity* (Cambridge, MA: MIT Press, 1987).
Habib, *Ibn Sa'ud's Warriors of Islam: The Ikhwan of Najd and Their Role in the Creation of the Sa'udi Kingdom, 1910–1930* (Leiden: Brill, 1978).
Habiby, E. *The Secret Life of Saeed, the Ill-Fated Pessoptimist: A Palestinian Who Became a Citizen of Israel*, trans. S. K. Jayyusi and T. LeGassick (London: Zed Books, 1985).
Haddad, Y. "Muslim Revivalist Thought in the Arab World: An Overview." *The Muslim World*, volume 76, July–October 1986.
Haddad, Y. and J. Smith, eds., *Muslim Communities in North America* (Albany: State University of New York Press, 1995).
Hafez, Y. "The Novel, Politics and Islam: Haydar Haydar's Banquest for Seaweed." *New Left Review*, number 5, September–October 2000.
Ḥāfiz, Y. *al-Hazīmah wa'l idiūlūjiyyah al-mahzūmah* (Beirut: Dār al-Ṭalī'ah, 1979).
Haj, S. *The Making of Iraq, 1900–1963* (Albany: State University of New York Press, 1997).
Hallaq, W. *A History of Islamic Legal Theories: An Introduction to Sunni Usūl al-Fiqh* (New York: Cambridge University Press, 1997).
Halliday, F. "An Encounter with Fukuyama." *New Left Review*, number 193, May–June 1992.
——. *Islam and the Myth of Confrontation: Religion and Politics in the Middle East* (London: I. B. Tauris, 1995).
——. *Nation and Religion in the Middle East* (Boulder: Lynne Rienner, 2000).
Ḥamānī, B. "Makānat Zakī Najīb Maḥmūd fī'l falsafah al-'Arabīyyah al-mu'āṣirah." *Al-Mustaqbal al-'Arabī*, volume 20(8), 1997.
Hamdi, M. *The Politicization of Islam: A Case Study of Tunisia* (Boulder: Westview Press, 1998).
Hammami, R. and Martina Rieker, "Feminist Orientalism and Orientalist Marxism." *New Left Review*, number 170, July–August 1988, 93–106.
Hammoudi, A. *Master and Disciple: The Cultural Foundations of Moroccan Authoritarianism* (Chicago: University of Chicago Press, 1997).
Ḥanafī, H. *al-Turāth wa'l tajdīd* (Beirut: Dār al-Tanwīr, 1981).
——. *al-Turāth wa'l tajdīd: mawqifunā min al-turāth al-qadīm* (Cairo: al-Markaz al-'Arabī, 1982).

——. *al-Dīn wa'l thawrah fī miṣr*, volume 8 (Cairo: Madbūlī, 1989).
——. *Muqadimah fī 'ilm al-istighrāb* (Cairo: al-Dār al-Faniyyah li'l Nashr wa'l Tawzī', 1991).
——. "al-Fikr al-'arabī al-mu'āṣir." In Maḥmūd Amīn al-'Ālim, ed., *al-Fikr al-'arabī 'alā mashārif al-qarn al-ḥādī wa'l 'ishrīn* (Cairo: Qaḍāyah Fikriyyah, 1995).
——. "al-Yasār al-islāmī: turāth al-sulṭah wa turāth al-mu'āraḍah." *Al-Qāhirah*, number 164, July 1996.
Ḥanafī, H. and M. 'Ābid al-Jābīrī. *Ḥiwār al-mashriq wa'l maghrib* (Cairo: Madbūlī, 1990).
Haq, S. N. "The Indian and Persian Background," in S. H. Nasr and O. Leaman, eds., *History of Islamic Philosophy*, volume 1 (London: Routledge, 1996).
Ḥarib, S. *al-Thaqāfah wa'l 'awlamah* (al-'Ayn, U.A.E.: Dār al-Kitāb al-Jāmi'ī, 2000).
Harvey, D. *The Condition of Postmodernity* (Oxford: Blackwell, 1989).
——. *Spaces of Hope* (Berkeley: University of California Press, 2000).
Ḥasan, A. *The Doctrine of Ijmā' in Islam: A Study of the Juridical Principle of Consensus* (Islamabad: Islamic Research Institute, 1978).
Ḥasan, M. *Legacy of a Divided Nation: India's Muslims Since Independence* (Boulder: Westview Press, 1997).
Hashmi, S., ed. *Islamic Politics and Ethics: Civil Society, Pluralism, and Conflict* (Princeton: Princeton University Press, 2002).
Hawrānī, A. *Mudhakarrāt Akram al-Ḥawrānī*, 4 volumes (Cairo: Madbūlī, 1999).
Ḥawwā, S. *al-Madkhal ilā da'wat al-ikhwān al-muslimīn* (Amman: al-Maṭba'ah al-Ta'āwuniyyah, 1979).
——. *Hādhihī tajribatī wa hādhihī shahādatī* (Cairo: Mu'assassat al-Khalīj al-'Arabī, 1988).
Haykal, M. H. *Ḥarb al-thalāthīn sanah: 1967 al-infijār* (Cairo: Markaz al-Ahrām li'l Tijārah wa'l Nashr, 1990).
——. "Ḥiwārāt ma' al-Qaddāfī." *Wijhāt Nadhar*, volume 1(4), May 1999: 4–14.
——. "Ḥadīth mustadrad 'an al-siyāsah al-dākhiliyyah." *Wijhāt Nadhar*, volume 2(17), June 2000.
——. *'Ām min al-azamāt: 2000-2001* (Cairo: al-Miṣriyyah li'l Nashr al-'Arabī wa'l Duwalī, 2001).
——. *al-'arabī al-tā'ih* (Cairo: al-Miṣriyyah li'l Nashr al-'Arabī wa'l Duwalī, 2001).
Head, S. "The New, Ruthless Economy." *New York Review of Books*, February 29, 1996.
Hefner, R. *Civil Society: Muslims and Democratization in Indonesia* (Princeton: Princeton University Press, 2000).
Heikel, M. H. *Cutting the Lion's Tail: Suez Through Egyptian Eyes* (London: Andre Deutsch, 1986).
Henrickson, D. *The Future of American Strategy* (New York: Holmes & Meier, 1988).
Hertzberg, A. *Jewish Polemics* (New York: Columbia University Press, 1992).
Heykal, M. *L'Autonome de la colère: L'assassinat de Sadate* (Paris: Editions Ramsay, 1983).
Ḥijāzī, M., ed. *Naḥwa 'ilm ijtimā' 'arabī: 'ilm al-ijtimā' wa'l mushkilāt al-'Arabīyyah al-rāhina* (Beirut: Markaz Dirāsāt al-Wiḥdah al-'Arabīyyah, 1986).
Hilāl, A. "Azmat al-fikr al-liberalī fī'l waṭan al-'arabī." *'Ālam al-Fikr*, volume 26(3–4), January–June 1998.
Hindess, B. and P. Q. Hirst. *Pre-Capitalist Modes of Production* (London: Routledge & Kegan Paul, 1975).
Hinnebusch, R. *Egyptian Politics under Sadat: The Post-Populist Development of an Authoritarian-Modernizing State* (London and Boulder, CO: Lynne Rienner, 1988).
——. *Authoritarian Power and State Formation in Ba'thist Syria: Army, Party, and Peasant* (Boulder: Westview Press, 1989).
Hirst, P. and G. Thompson. "Globalization and the Future of the Nation State." *Economy and Society*, volume 24(3), August 1995: 408–42.
Hobsbawm, E. *Nations and Nationalism Since 1780* (Cambridge: Cambridge University Press, 1994).
——. *The Age of Extremes: The Short Twentieth Century, 1914–1991* (New York: Vintage, 1994).
Hogan, M. *The Marshall Plan* (Cambridge: Cambridge University Press, 1987).
Holyoake, G. *The Principles of Secularism* (London: Austin & Co., 1870).
Horsman, M. and A. Marshall. *After the Nation State* (London: HarperCollins, 1994).
Hourani, A. *Arabic Thought in the Liberal Age, 1798–1939* (Cambridge: Cambridge University Press, 1970).
——. "The Arab Awakening Forty Years After," in D. Hopwood, ed., *Studies in Arab History: The Antonious Lectures, 1978–87* (London: Macmillan, 1990).

——. *A History of the Arab People* (Cambridge, MA: Harvard University Press, 1991).

——. "How Should We Write the History of the Middle East?" *International Journal of Middle East Studies*, volume 23(2), May 1991.

——. "Ottoman Reform and the Politics of Notables." In A. Hourani, P. S. Khoury, and M. C. Wilson, eds., *The Modern Middle East: A Reader* (Berkeley: University of California Press, 1993).

Hsu, I. *The Rise of Modern China* (London: Oxford University Press, 2000).

Hudson, M. *The Precarious Republic: Political Modernization in Lebanon* (New York: Random House, 1968).

Hujwiri, A. *The Kashf al-Maḥjūb: The Oldest Persian Treatise on Sufism*, trans. R. A. Nicholson (Bombay: Tāj Company, 1999).

Humphreys, R. *Between Memory and Desire: The Middle East in a Troubled Age* (Berkeley: University of California Press, 1999).

Huntington, S. *The Clash of Civilizations and the Remaking of World Order* (New York: Simon & Schuster, 1996).

Husaini, I. M. *The Moslem Brethren: The Greatest of Modern Islamic Movements* (Beirut: Khayat's College Book Cooperative, 1956).

Ḥussain, Ṭ. *fī al-shi'ral-jāhilī* (Cairo: Angelo, 1926).

——. *The Future of Culture in Egypt*, trans. S. Glazer (New York: Octagon Books, 1975).

Ḥussein, A. *al-Iqtiṣād al-miṣrī: mina al-istiqlāl ila al-taba'iyyah* (Cairo: Dār al-Mustaqbal al-'Arabī, 1986).

Huwaydī, F. *al-Qur'ān wa'l sulṭān* (Cairo: Dār al-Shurūq, 1982).

——." 'An al-'ilmāniyyah wa tajaliyātihah." *Al-Maqālāt al-maḥdhūrah* (Cairo: Dār al-Shurūq, 1998).

——. "al-Khiṭāb al-islāmī fī 'ālam mutajaddid," in S. Yāssīn, ed., *al-'Arab wa taḥadiyyāt al-qarn al-ḥādī wa'l 'ishrīn* (Amman: Mu'assassat 'Abdul Ḥamīd Shūmān, 2000).

Ibn Khaldūn, *The Muqaddimah: An Introduction to History*, volume 1, trans. F. Rosenthal (New York: Pantheon, 1958).

Ibrahim, I. "Tāha Ḥusayn: The Critical Spirit," in J. Spagnolo, ed., *Problems of the Modern Middle East in Historical Perspective* (London: Ithaca Press, 1992).

Ibrāhīm, M. *al-Yasār al-ḥaqīqī wa'l yasār al-mughāmir* (Beirut: Dār al-Fārābī, 1969).

Ibrāhīm, S. "al-Mufakkir wa'l amīr: tajsīr al-fajwah bayna ṣāni'ī al-qarār wa'l mufakirrīn al-'arab," in al-Ṭāhir Labīb, *al-Intellijensia al-'Arabīyyah* (Tunis: al-Dār al-'Arabīyyah li'l Kitāb, n.d.).

Ibrahim, S. E. "Egypt's Landed Bourgeoisie," in S. E. Ibrahim, *Egypt, Islam, and Democracy: Twelve Critical Essays* (Cairo: American University in Cairo Press, 1996).

Ibrahimi, A. *al-Maghrib al-'arabī fī muftaraq al-ṭuruq fī dhil al-taḥāwwulāt al-duwaliyyah* (Beirut: Markaz Dirāsāt al-Wiḥdah al-'Arabīyyah, 1996).

Idrīs, S. *al-Muthaqaf al-'arabī wa'l ṣultah: bahth fī riwāyat al-tajribah al-nāṣṣiriyyah* (Beirut: Dār al-Adab, 1993).

Iiauzu, C. *Race et civilisation: L'Autre dans la culture occidentale* (Paris: Syros, 1992).

Imārah, M. *al-A'māl al-kāmilah li 'Abd al-Raḥmān al-Kawākībī* (Cairo: al-Hay'ah al-Miṣriyyah al-'Āmmah li'l Ta'līf wa'l Nashr, 1970).

——. "Mawqi' al-fikr al-islāmī al-ḥadīth min al-itijāh al-liberalī." *Al-Ṭalī'ah*, volume 8(8), August 1972.

——. *al-Jadīd fī mukhaṭaṭ al-'ālam al-gharbī tijāh al-muslimīn* (Cairo: IIIT, 1983).

——. *al-Dawlah al-islāmiyyah bayna al-'ilmāniyyah wa'l sulṭah al-madaniyyah* (Cairo: Dār al-Shurūq, 1988).

——. *al-Ghazw al-fikrī: wahm am ḥaqīqhah* (International Institute of Islamic Thought: Cairo, 1988).

——. *Fikr al-tanwīr bayna al-'ilmāniyin wa'l islāmiyyin* (Cairo: International Institute of Islamic Thought, 1993).

——. *al-Islām wā uṣūl al-ḥukm lī 'Alī 'Abd al-Rāziq: Dirāsah wā wathā'iq* (Beirut: Mu'assassat al-Dirāsāt, 1994).

'Imārah, M. *al-A'māl al-kāmilah li'l Imām Muḥammad 'Abduh*, 5 volumes (Cairo: Dār al-Shurūq, 1995).

Iqbal, M. *The Reconstruction of Religious Thought in Islām* (Lahore: Sh. Muhammad Ashraf, 1988).

'Īsa, S. *Muthaqaffūn wa 'askar* (Cairo: Madbūlī, 1986).

Ismael, T. R. and J. S. Ismael. *The Communist Movement in Syria and Lebanon* (Gainesville: University Press of Florida, 1998).

Issawi, C. *An Economic History of the Middle East and North Africa* (New York: Columbia University Press, 1982).

Izutso, T. *Ethico-Religious Concepts of the Qur'ān* (Montreal: McGill University Press, 1966).

Jabbur, J. *The Bedouins and the Desert: Aspects of Nomadic Life in the Arab East* (Albany: State University of New York Press, 1995).

Jābir, H. "Min ajl i'ādat waṣl mā inqaṭa' aw niqāsh fī afkār Karīm Murruwwa." *Al-Ṭarīq*, volume 49(4), July–August 1990.

Jābīrī, M. Ā. *al-Khiṭāb al-'arabī al-mu'āṣir* (Beirut: Markaz Dirāsāt al-Wiḥdah al-'Arabīyyah, 1982).

——. *Naḥnu wa'l turāth* (Casablanca: al-Markaz al-Thaqāfī al-'Arabī, 1993).

——. *al-Dimūqraṭiya wa ḥuqūq al-insān* (Beirut: Markaz Dirāsāt al-Wiḥdah al-'Arabīyyah, 1994).

——. *al-Masa'alah al-thaqāfiyyah* (Beirut: Markaz Dirāsāt al-Wiḥdah al-'Arabīyyah, 1994).

——. *al-Muthaqafūn al-'arab fi'l ḥadārah al-'Arabīyyah* (Beirut: Markaz Dirāsāt al-Wiḥdah al-'Arabīyyah, 1995).

——. *Mas'alat al-hawiyah: al-'urūbah, al-islām wa'l gharb* (Beirut: Markaz Dirāsāt al-Wiḥdah al-'Arabīyyah, 1995).

——. *al-Dīn wa'l dawlah wā taṭbīq al-sharī'ah* (Beirut: Markaz Dirāsāt al-Wiḥdah al-'Arabīyyah, 1996).

——. "al-'Awlamah, niẓām wa aydiyūlūjiyyah," in al-Majlis al-Qawmī li'l Thaqāfah al-'Arabīyyah, *al-'Arab wa taḥadiyāt al-'awlamah* (Rabat al-Majlis al-Qawmī li'l Thaqāfah al-'Arabīyyah, 1997).

——. "al-Falsafah: fann siyāghat al-mafāhīm." *Al-Sharq al-Awṣat*, number 6619, January 11, 1997.

——. *Qaḍāyah fi al-fikr al-mu'āsiir* (Beirut: Markaz Dirāsāt al-Wiḥdah al-'Arabīyyah, 1997).

——. "al-Mujtam' al-madanī: tasā'ulāt wā āfāq," in 'Abdalla Ḥamūda, ed., *Wa'y al-mujtama' bī dhātihī: 'an al-mujtama' al-madanī fi'l maghrib al-'arabī* (Casablanca: Dār Ṭubqāl, 1998).

——. "al-'Arab wa'l 'awlamah: al-'awlamah wa'l hawiyyah al-thaqāfiyyah," in Markaz Dirāsāt al-Wiḥdah al-'Arabīyyah, *al-'Arab wa'l 'awlamah* (Beirut: Markaz Dirāsāt al-Wihdah al-'Arabīyyah, 1998).

——. *al-'Aql al-akhlāqī al-'arabī* (Casablanca: al-Markaz al-Thaqāfī al-'Arabī, 2001).

Jabri, M. A. "Evolution of the Maghrib Concept: Facts and Perspectives," in H. Barakat, ed., *Contemporary North Africa: Issues of Development and Integration* (Washington, D.C.: Center for Contemporary Arab Studies, 1985).

Jack, B. *Francophone Literatures: An Introductory Survey* (New York: Oxford University Press, 1996).

Jacquemond, R. "Retour à Nasser des intellectuels égyptiens." *Le Monde Diplomatique*, July 1997.

Jad'ān, F. "al-Salafīyyah: ḥudūduhah wa taḥawulātuhah." *'Ālam al-Fikr*, volume 26, January–April 1998.

Jalāl, S. "al-Yasār al-'arabī wa sosiolojiyat al-fashal." *'Ālam al-Fikr*, volume 26, January–April 1998.

Jameson, F. "Notes on Globalization as Philosophical Issue," in F. Jameson and M. Miyoshi, eds., *The Cultures of Globalization* (Durham: Duke University Press, 1999).

Jameson, F. and M. Miyoshi, eds. *The Cultures of Globalization* (Durham: Duke University Press, 1999).

Janḥānī, H. *al-Taḥawwul al-iqtiṣādī wa'l ijtimā'ī fi mujtama' ṣadr al-islām* (Beirut: Dār al-Gharb al-Islāmī, 1985).

——. "al-Mufakkir wa'l sulṭah fī'l turāth al-'arabī al-islāmi," in al-Tāhir Labīb, ed., *al-Intillejensia al-'Arabiyyah* (Tunis: al-Dār al-'Arabiyyah li'l Kitāb, n.d.).

Jankowski, J. and I. Gershoni, eds. *Rethinking Nationalism in the Arab Middle East* (New York: Columbia University Press, 1997).

Jarrāḥ, N. *al-firdaws al-dāmī: wāḥid wa thalathīn yawman fi'l jazā'ir* (London: Riad al-Rayyes Books, 2000).

Jessop, B. *Nicos Poulantzas: Marxist Theory and Political Strategy* (New York: St. Martin's Press, 1985).

Johnson, D. "Introduction," in L. Althusser, *The Future Lasts a Long Time* (London: Chatto & Windus, 1993).

Jones, M. M. *Gaston Bachelard, Subversive Humanist: Texts and Readings* (Madison: University of Wisconsin Press, 1991).

Judt, J. *Marxism and the French Left* (Oxford: Oxford University Press, 1986).

Julien, C. *L'empire américaine* (Paris: Grasset, 1968).

Jumonville, N. *Critical Crossings: The New York Intellectuals in Postwar America* (Berkeley: University of California Press, 1991).

Kahin, G. *Nationalism and Revolution in Indonesia* (Ithaca: Cornell University Press, 1952).

Kanaaneh, R. A. *Birthing the Nation: Strategies of Palestinian Women in Israel* (Berkeley: University of California Press, 2002).

Kanafani, G. "Thoughts on Change and the 'Blind Language'," in F. J. Ghazoul and B. Harlow, eds., *The View from Within: Writers and Critics on Contemporary Arabic Literature* (Cairo: American University of Cairo Press, 1994).

Kant, I. "What is Enlightenment?," in Hans Reiss, ed. *Kant: Political Writings* (Cambridge: Cambridge University Press, 1991).

Kaplan, A. *The Anarchy of Empire in the Making of U.S. Culture* (Cambridge, MA: Harvard University Press, 2002).

Karīm, K. "Min āfāt al-fikr al-'arabī al-mu'āṣirah: dirāsah naqdiyyah mujmalah li Kitāb al-ḥall al-islāmī: farīḍah wā ḍarūrah lī faḍīlat al-Shaykh Yūsuf al-Qaraḍāwī," in M. A. al-'Ālim, ed., *al-Fikr al-'arabī 'alā mashārif al-qarn al-ḥādī wa'l 'ishrīn* (Cairo: Qaḍāyah Fikriyyah, 1995).

Karlin, B. "Space: New Frontier for US Entrepreneurs." *International Herald Tribune*, September 14, 1988.

Katz, M. N. "The Embourgeoisement of Revolutionary Regimes: Reflections on Abdallah Laroui." *Studies in Conflict and Terrorism*, volume 21(3), 1998.

Katznelson, I. and Margaret Weir. *Schooling for All: Race, Class, and the Decline of the Democratic Ideal* (New York: Basic Books, 1987).

Kautsky, K. "Ultra-imperialism." *New Left Review*, number 59, 1970, 41–6.

Kazziha, W. *Revolutionary Transformation in the Arab World: Habash and His Comrades from Nationalism to Marxim* (London: Charles Knight & Co., 1975).

Keane, J. "Despotism and Democracy: The Origins and Development of the Distinction Between Civil Society and the State 1750–1850," in J. Keane, ed., *Civil Society and the State: New European Perspectives* (London: University of Westminster Press, 1998).

——. *Civil Society: Old Images, New Visions* (London: Polity Press, 1998).

Keddi, N. "Is There a Middle East?" *International Journal of the Middle East*, volume 4(3), July 1973.

——. *An Islamic Response to Imperialism: Political and Religious Writings of Sayyid Jamāl al-Dīn al-Afghānī* (Berkeley: University of California Press, 1983).

Kelley, D., ed. *The History of Ideas: Canon and Variations* (Rochester: University of Rochester Press, 1990).

Kerr, M. *Islamic Reform: The Political and Legal Theories of Muḥammad 'Abduh and Rashid Rida* (Berkeley: University of California Press, 1966).

Kettānī, M. *Jadal al-'aql wa'l naql fī manāhij al-tafkīr al-islāmī: al-fikr al-qadīm* (Casablanca: Dār al-Thaqāfah, 1992).

Khalaf, R. and James Whittington. "Tunis Lashes Out at Islamist Phantom." *Financial Times*, October 17, 1995.

Khālid, K. M. *From Here We Start*, trans. I. R. el-Faruqi (Washington, D.C.: American Council of Learned Societies, 1953).

——. *Naḥnu al-bashar* (Cairo: Angelo, 1959).

——. *Azmat al-huriyyah fī 'ālam*ina (Cairo: Angelo, 1972).

——. *al-Dimūqratiyah abadan*, 4th edition (Beirut: Dār al-Fikr, 1974).

——. *Muwāṭinūn lā ra'āyah*, 7th edition (Beirut: Dār al-Fikr, 1974).

Khalidi, R., L. Anderson, M. Muslih and R. S. Simon, eds., *The Origins of Arab Nationalism* (New York: New York University Press, 1991).

Khan, B. "The Ahl-i-Hadīth: A Socio-Religious Reform Movement in Kashmir." *The Muslim World*, volume 90(1 and 2), Spring 2000: 133–57.

Khaṭīb, M. "An al-liberāliyyah wa'l 'ālamiyyah: muḥāwalah fī'l tafkīr." *Al-Ṭarīq*, volume 52(2), July 1993.

Khaṭīb, S. *Dawr al-manāhij al-gharbiyah fī siyādat manāhij al-taghrīb* (Cairo: IIIT, n.d.).

Khatibi, A. "Double Criticism: The Decolonization of Arab Sociology," in H. Barakat, ed., *Contemporary North Africa: Issues of Development and Integration* (Washington, D.C.: Center for Contemporary Arab Studies, 1985).

Khazen, F. *The Breakdown of the State in Lebanon, 1967–1976* (Cambridge, MA: Harvard University Press, 2000).
Khilnani, S. *Arguing Revolution: The Intellectual Left in Postwar France* (New Haven: Yale University Press, 1993).
Khoury, P. *Syria and the French Mandate: The Politics of Arab Nationalism, 1920–1945* (Princeton: Princeton University Press, 1987).
Khoury, P. *Traditions et modernité: thèmes et tendances de la pensée arabe actuelle* (Beirut: n.p., 1983).
Khuri, R. *Modern Arab Thought: Channels of the French Revolution to the Arab East*, trans. I. ʻAbbās (Princeton: Princeton University Press, 1983).
Khūry, E. "al-Nakbah wa'l sirāʻ ʻalā al-kalimāt." *Al-Ṭarīq*, volume 57(3), May–June 1998.
Kīlānī, S. *Maṣīr al-jamāʻah al-ʻarabiyyah: naqd fikr Samīr Amīn* (Damascus: Dār ʻAshtarūt li'l Nashr, 1997).
Kimmerling, B. *The Invention and Decline of Israeliness: State, Society, and the Military* (Berkeley: University of California Press, 2001).
Kishik, M. *Suqūṭ al-ʻilmāniyyah* (Cairo: Dār al-I'tiṣām, 1994).
——. *Qirā'ah fī fikr al-tabaʻiyyah* (Cairo: Maktabat al-Turāth al-Islāmī, 1994).
Kissinger, H. *White House Years* (Boston: Little, Brown & Co., 1979).
——. *Years of Upheaval* (Boston: Little, Brown & Co., 1982).
——. *Diplomacy* (New York: Touchstone Books, 1995).
Kolakowski, L. *Main Currents of Marxism*, volume 3 (Oxford: Oxford University Press, 1978).
Krieger, L. "The Autonomy of Intellectual History," in D. Kelley, ed., *The History of Ideas: Canon and Variations* (Rochester: University of Rochester Press, 1990).
Kugelgen, A. V. "A Call for Rationalism: 'Arab Averroists' in the Twentieth Century." *Alif: Journal of Comparative Poetics*, number 16, 1996, 97–132.
Kung, H. *A Global Ethic for Global Politics and Economics* (New York: Oxford University Press, 1998).
Labdaoui, A. *Les nouveaux intellectuels arabes* (Paris: Maspero, 1993).
Labib, F. and N. Salem, eds. *Clash of Civilizations or Dialogue of Cultures* (Cairo: Afro-Asian Peoples' Solidarity Organization, 1997).
Labīb, Ṭ. "Gramsci nel mondo arabo." *GI Informatziori*, number 4, Instituto Gramsci, Roma, 1989.
——. "Gramsci al-ʻarab." *Al-Ṭarīq*, volume 57(3), 1998.
Lacoste, Y. *Les pays sous-développed* (Paris: PUF, 1960).
——. *Géographie du sous-développement* (Paris: PUF, 1965).
——. *Ibn Khaldoun, naissance de l'histoire, passé du tiers-monde* (Paris: PUF, 1966).
Lahbabi, M. *De l'être à la personne: Essai de personnalisme réaliste* (Paris: PUF, 1954).
——. *Le personnalisme musulman* (Paris: PUF, 1964).
——. *Le monde de demian: Le Tiers-monde accuse* (Casablanca: Sherbrooke, 1980).
Laidi, Z. *L'ordre mondial relache* (Paris: Presses de la Fondation Nationale des Sciences, 1994).
Lamchichi, A. "Incertitudes politiques et sociales: L'islamisme s'enracine au Maroc." *Le Monde Diplomatique*, May 1996.
Lapham, L. "The Road to Babylon: Searching for Targets in Iraq." *Harper's Magazine*, October 2002.
Lapidus, I. "The Separation of State and Religion in the Development of Early Islamic Society." *International Journal of Middle Eastern Studies*, volume 6(4), 1975.
Laroui, A. *L'idéologie arabe contemporaine* (Paris: Maspero 1970).
——. *The Crisis of the Arab Intelligentsia: Traditionalism or Historicism?* (Berkeley: University of California Press, 1976).
——. *Les origines du nationalisme marocain, 1830–1912* (Paris: Maspero, 1977).
Laski, H. *The Rise of European Liberalism: An Essay in Interpretation* (London: George Allen & Unwin Ltd., 1936).
——. *Liberty in the Modern State* (Harmondsworth: Penguin, 1938).
Laṭīfī, M. "Nihāyat al-dawlah al-dīnīyah fī'l islām." *Qaḍāyah Fikriyyah*, October 1993.
Lawrence, T. E. *Seven Pillars of Wisdom* (New York: Garden City, 1938).
Lazar, M. *Maisons rouges: Les Partis communistes français et italien, de la Libération à nos jours* (Paris: Aubier, 1992).

Lecourt, D. *Marxism and Epistemology: Bachelard, Canguilhem, and Foucault* (London: New Left Books, 1975).

Lefebvre, H. *Le manifeste différentialiste* (Paris: Gallimard, 1970).

Lemu, A. *Laxity, Moderation, and Extremism in Islam* (Herndon: International Institute of Islamic Thought, 1993).

Lenin, V. I. *Imperialism: The Highest Stage of Capitalism* (New York: International Publishers, 1939).

Levitt, W. K. "Islamistes palestiniens, la nouvelle génération." *Le Monde diplomatique*, June 1995.

——. "L'introuvable stratégie du pouvoir palestinien face aux islamistes." *Le Monde diplomatique*, April 1996.

Lewis, A. "Bush and Iraq." *New York Review of Books*, November 7, 2002.

——. "Bush at War." *New York Review of Books*, February 13, 2003.

Lewis, B. *The Jews of Islam* (Princeton: Princeton University Press, 1987).

——. *The Political Language of Islam* (Chicago: University of Chicago Press, 1988).

Lilla, M. "The New Age of Tyranny." *The New York Review of Books*, October 24, 2002, 28–9.

Lovejoy, A. O. *Essays in the History of Ideas* (New York: George Braziller, 1955).

Lovell, M. *A Rage to Live: A Biography of Richard and Isabelle Burton* (London: Abacus, 1998).

Lowrie, A. L., ed. *Islam, Democracy, the State and the West: A Round Table with Dr. Ḥasan Turabi* (Tampa: World and Studies Enterprise, 1993).

Lugan, B. *Histoire du Maroc des origines à nos jours* (Paris: Perrin, 2000).

Lukacs, G. *History and Class Consciousness: Studies in Marxist Dialectics*, trans. Rodney Livingstone (Cambridge, MA: MIT Press, 1971).

Lustick, I. *Arabs in a Jewish State: Israel's Control of a National Minority* (Austin: University of Texas Press, 1980).

Lyotard, J. *The Post-Modern Condition: A Report on Knowledge* (Minneapolis: University of Minnesota Press, 1991).

Mabrūk, M. I. *Amerika wa'l islām al-nafi'ī* (Cairo: Dār al-Tawzī' wa'l Nashr al-Islāmiyyah, 1989).

Mabrūk, M. I., ed. *al-Islām wa'l 'awlamah* (Cairo: al-Dār al-Qawmiyyah al-'Arabīyyah, 1999).

McCormack, G. "Breaking the Iron Triangle." *New Left Review*, number 13, January/February 2002.

Macey, D. *Franz Fanon: A Biography* (New York: Picador, 2001).

McGrew, A. G. "Superpower Rivalry and US Hgemony in Central America," in A. G. McGrew and P. G. Lewis, eds., *Global Politics: Globalization and the Nation-State* (Cambridge: Polity Press, 1992).

McNaugher, T. *New Weapons, Old Politics: America's Military Procurement Muddle* (Washington, D.C.: Hoover Institution, 1989).

Macpherson, C. B. *The Political Theory of Possessive Individualism: Hobbes to Locke* (New York: Oxford University Press, 1962).

——. *The Life and Times of Liberal Democracy* (Oxford: Oxford University Press, 1977).

Madan, T. "Secularism in its Place," in Rajeev Bhargava, ed. *Secularism and its Critics* (New Delhi: Oxford University Press, 1998).

——. *Secularism and Fundamentalism in India: Modern Myths, Locked Minds* (New Delhi: Oxford University Press, 1998).

Māḍī, A. "Salāma Mūsa wa'l falsafah." In Markaz Dirāsāt al-Wiḥdah al-'Arabīyyah, *al-Falsafah al-'Arabīyyah al-mu'āṣirah* (Beirut: Markaz Dirāsāt al-Wiḥdah al-'Arabīyyah, 1988).

——. *Jamā'at al-'unf al-miṣriyyah al-murṭabitah bi'l islām: al-judhūr al-tārikhiyyah wa'l usus al-fikriyyah wa'l mustaqbal* (Cairo: al-Markaz al-Duwalī li'l Dirāsāt, 1997).

Madjid, N. "Islamic Roots of Modern Pluralism: Indonesian Experiences." *Studia Islamika: Indonesian Journal for Islamic Studies*, volume 1(1), 1994, 55–77.

Magdoff, H. *Imperialism: From the Colonial Age to the Present* (New York: Monthly Review Press, 1978).

Maher, M. *Indonesia: An Eyewitness Account* (Ringwood: Viking, 2000).

Maḥmūd, Z. *Tajdīd al-fikr al-'arabī* (Cairo: Dār al-Shurūq, 1980).

Mālik, C. *Lubnān fī dhātihī* (Beirut: Mu'asasat Badrān, 1974).

Malik, J. *Colonization of Islam: Dissolution of Traditional Institutions in Pakistan* (New Delhi: Manohar, 1996).

Malkāwī, F., ed. *al-'Aṭā' al-fikrī li'l Shaykh Muḥammad al-Ghazālī* (Amman: al-Ma'had al-'Ālamī li'l Fikr al-Islāmī, 1996).

Mallaby, S. "The Reluctant Imperialist." *Foreign Affairs*, March–April 2002.

Mandel, E. *Late Capitalism* (London: Verso, 1978).

Marcos, S. "La 4e guerre mondiale a commencé." *Le Monde Diplomatique*, August 1997.

Marcuse, H. *One-Dimensional Man* (Boston: Beacon Press, 1964).

Mardin, Ş. *The Genesis of Young Ottoman Thought: A Study in the Modernization of Turkish Political Ideas* (Princeton: Princeton University Press, 1962).

Markaz al-Buḥūth al-'Arabīyyah, *al-Nadhariyyah wa'l mumārasah fī fikr Mahdī 'Āmil: Nadwah Fikriyyah* (Beirut: Dār al-Fārābī, 1989).

Markaz Dirāsāt al-Wiḥdah al-'Arabīyyah, *al-Qawmiyyah al-'Arabīyyah fi'l fikr wa'l mumārasah* (Beirut: Markaz Dirāsāt al-Wiḥdah al-'Arabīyyah, 1980).

——. *al-Ḥiwār al-qawmī al-dīnī* (Beirut: Markaz Dirāsāt al-Wiḥdah al-'Arabīyyah, 1989).

——. *al-Mu'tamar al-qawmī al-islāmī al-awwal* (Beirut: Markaz Dirāsāt al-Wiḥdah al-'Arabīyyah, 1995).

——. *al-'Arab wa'l 'Awlamah* (Beirut: Markaz Dirāsāt al-Wiḥdah al-'Arabīyyah, 1998).

——. *al-'Arab wa'l 'alam ba'da 11 Aylūl* (Beirut: Markaz Dirāsāt al-Wiḥdah al-'Arabīyyah, 2002).

Martin, P. "La mondialisation est-elle inévitable? Une obligation morale." *Le Monde Diplomatique*, June 1997.

Marx, K. "Theses on Feuerbach," in K. Marx and F. Engels, *On Religion* (New York: Schocken Books, 1965).

——. *The Poverty of Philosophy*, in Karl Marx and Frederick Engels, *Collected Works*, volume 6 (New York: International Publishers, 1976).

——. *Capital*, volume 1 (Harmondsworth, 1976–81).

Marx, K. and F. Engels. *Collected Works*, volume 5 (New York: International Publishers, 1976).

Masīrī, A. "al-Ru'yah al-ma'rifiyyah al-imberialiyyah." *Qirā'āt Siyāsiyyah*, volume 2(4), 1992, 137–59.

——. "The Imperialist Epistemological Vision." *The American Journal of the Islamic Social Sciences*, volume 11(3), Fall 1994, 403–15.

——. *al-Insāklubīdyyah al-ṣuhyūniyyah*, 7 volumes (Cairo: Dār al-Shurūq, 1999).

Massignon, L. *Essay on the Technical Language of Islamic Mysticism*, trans. Benjamin Clark (Notre Dame: University of Notre Dame Press, 1997).

Masud, M. K. *Islamic Legal Philosophy: A Study of Abū Ishāq al-Shāṭibī's Life and Thought* (Islamabad: Islamic Research Institute, 1977).

Matinuddin, K. *The Taliban Phenomenon: Afghanistan 1994–1997* (Karachi: Oxford University Press, 1999).

Mayer, A. *The Persistence of the Old Regime: Europe to the Great War* (New York: Pantheon, 1981).

Mayer, A. E. *Islam and Human Rights: Tradition and Politics* (Boulder: Westview Press, 1991).

Maynes, C. W. "The Perils of an Imperial America." *Foreign Policy*, Summer 1998, 36–49.

Meadows, D. *The Limits of Growth: A Report for the Club of Rome's Project on the Predicament of Mankind* (New York: Universe Books, 1972).

Mearsheimer, J. L. *The Tragedy of Great Power Politics* (New York: W. W. Norton, 2002).

Memmi, A. "Integrisme et laïcité." *Le Monde Diplomatique*, March 1989.

Mencken, H. *The American English: An Inquiry into the Development of English in the United States* (New York: Alfred A. Knopf, 1955).

Merad, A. *Le réformisme musulman en Algérie de 1925 à 1940: Essai d'histoire religieuse et sociale* (Paris: Mouton, 1967).

Messarra, A. *The Challenge of Coexistence* (Oxford: Center for Lebanese Studies, 1988).

Mignolo, W. D. "Globalization, Civilization Processes, and the Relocation of Languages and Cultures," in F. Jameson and M. Miyoshi, eds., *The Cultures of Globalization* (Durham: Duke University Press, 1999).

Milad, Z. "Islamic Thought and the Issue of Globalization." *Middle East Affairs Journal*, volume 5(1–2), Winter–Spring 1999.

Miller, M. *The Bon Marché: Bourgeois Culture and the Department Store, 1869–1920* (Princeton: Princeton University Press, 1994).

Miller, S., ed. *Disorienting Encounters, Travels of a Moroccan Scholar in France in 1845–1846: The Voyage of Muḥammad As-Saffar* (Berkeley: University of California Press, 1992).

Mirsepassi, A., A. Basu, and F. Weaver, eds., *Localizing Knowledge in a Globalizing World* (Syracuse: Syracuse University Press, 2003).

Mitchell, R. *The Society of the Muslim Brothers*, new edition (New York: Oxford University Press, 1993).

Mouaqit, M. "Mohamed Abed Al-Jabri: Rationalisme et laïcisme," in M. Y. Retnani, ed., *Penseurs maghrébins contemporains* (Casablanca: Editions Eddif, 1997).

Moughrabi, M. "The Arabic Basic Personality: A Critical Survey of the Literature." *International Journal of Middle East Studies*, volume 9(1), February 1978.

Mudimbe, V. Y. *The Invention of Africa: Gnosis, Philosophy, and the Order of Knowledge* (Bloomington: Indiana University Press, 1988).

Mukhrjee, M. *The Rise and Fall of the East India Company* (Berlin: Veb Deutscher Verlag der Wissenschaften, 1958).

Munajjid, S. D. *A'midat al-nakbah* (Beirut: Dār al-Kitāb al-Jadīd, 1969).

Munīf, A. *The Trench* (New York: Pantheon, 1990).

——. *Cities of Salt* (New York: Vintage, 1991).

——. "al-Thaqāfah wa'l muthaqqaf fī'l mujtama' al-'arabī," in S. Yāssīn, ed., *al-'Arab wa taḥadiyyāt al-qarn al-ḥādī wa'l 'ishrīn* (Amman: Mu'asasat 'Abdul Ḥamīd Shūmān, 2000).

Munīr, H. "ru'yat al-yasār li mawqi' al-uṣūliyyīn al-islāmiyyīn 'alā al-kharīṭah al-ṭabaqiyyah wa'l siyāsiyyah." *Al-Yasār*, number 8, October 1990: 43–58.

Munson, H. Jr. *Religion and Power in Morocco* (New Haven: Yale University Press, 1993).

Murquṣ, E. *Tārīkh al-aḥzāb al-shuyū'īyyah fī'l waṭan al-'arabī* (Beirut: Dār al-Ṭalī'ah, 1964).

——. *al-Mārkisiyah wa'l sharq* (Beirut: Dār al-Ṭalī'ah, 1968).

——. *al-Mārkisiyah fī 'asrina* (Beirut: Dār al-Ṭalī'ah, 1969).

Mursī, F. "Ḥawla ḥall al-ḥizb al-shuyū'ī al-miṣrī." *Qaḍāyah Fikriyyah*, volumes 11 and 12, 1992.

Mursī, F. *al-Ra'smāliyyah tujaddid nafsahah* (Kuwait: 'Ālam al-Ma'rifah, 1990).

Muruwwa, H. *al-Naza'āt al-mādiyyah fī'l falsafah al-'Arabīyyah al-islāmiyyah*, 2 volumes (Beirut: Dār al-Fārābī, 1979).

Muruwwa, K. "Ishkāliyat al-nahḍah wa'l fikr al-mārkisī al-'Arabī." *Al-Ṭarīq*, volume 75(6), 1998.

Mūsa, A. *al-Yawm al-ghad* (Cairo: Dār al-Mustaqbal, 1928).

Mūsa, S. *The Education of Salāma Mūsa*, trans. L. O. Schuman (Leiden: Brill, 1961).

——. *Mā hiya al-nahḍah*? (Cairo: Mu'assassat Salāma Mūsa, n.d.).

Mustafa, S. "Arab Cultural Crisis and the Impact of the Past." *Jerusalem Quarterly*, number 11, Spring 1979.

Mustafa, Y. "Azmat al-muthaqaf al-'aqlānī," in M. A. al-'Ālim, *Qaḍāyah Fikriyyah, al-Fikr al-'arabī 'ala mashārif al-qarn al-wāhīid wa'l 'ishrīn* (Cairo: Dār Qaḍāyah Fikriyyah, 1995).

Nābulsī, S. *Thawrat al-turāth: Dirāsa fī fikr Khālid Muḥammad Khālid* (Beirut: Dār al-Turāth, 1991).

Nadwi, A. *Islam and the World* (Kuwait: IIFSO, 1977).

Nafi, B. *Arabism, Islamism, and the Palestine Question, 1908–1941: A Political History* (London: Ithaca Press, 1998).

——. "The Arab Nationalists and the Arab Islamists: Shadows of the Past, Glimpses of the Future." *Middle East Affairs Journal*, volume 6(1–2) Winter/Spring 2000, 109–28.

Naipul, V. S. "Indonesia: The Man of the Moment." *New York Review of Books*, June 11, 1998.

Nairn, T. "The Modern Janus." *New Left Review*, 94, November–December 1975.

Najjār, A. M. *Khilāfat al-insān bayna al-waḥy wa'l 'aql* (Herndon: International Institute of Islamic Thought, 1993).

Najjar, F. "The Debate on Islam and Secularism in Egypt." *Arab Studies Quarterly*, volume 18(2), Spring 1996, 1–22.

——. "Islamic Fundamentalism and the Intellectuals: The Case of Nasr Hamid Abu Zayd." *British Journal of Middle Eastern Studies*, 27(2), 2000, 177–200.

Najjar, F. "Book Banning in Contemporary Egypt." *The Muslim World*, volume 91(3 and 4), Fall 2001, 399–424.

Nandy, A. "The Politics of Secularism and the Recovery of Religious Tolerance," in R. Bhargava, ed. *Secularism and its Critics* (New Delhi: Oxford University Press, 1998).

——. *The Intimate Enemy: Loss and Recovery of Self Under Colonialism* (New Delhi: Oxford University Press, 1998).

Naqqāsh, F. *Yawmiyyāt al-mudun al-maftūhah* (Cairo: Dāral-Thaqāfah al-Jadīdah, 1987).

——. *al-In'izāliyyūn fī miṣr: radd 'ala Tawfīq al-Ḥakīm wa Luwes 'Awad* (Cairo: al-Hay'ah al-Miṣriyyah al-'Āmmah li'l Kitāb, 1996).

Nasr, S. H. "The Meaning and Concept of Philosophy in Islam," in S. H. Nasr and O. Leaman, eds., *History of Islamic Philosophy* (London: Routledge, 1996).

Newman, R. P. *Owen Lattimore and the Loss of China* (Berkeley: University of California Press, 1992).

Nicholls, N., ed. *Modernity and Religion* (Waterloo: Wilfrid Laurier University Press, 1987).

Niebuhr, R. *The Nature and Destiny of Man*, volume 1 (New York: Scribner's, 1964).

Nield, K. and John Seed, "Theoretical Poverty and the Poverty of Theory: British Marxist Historiography and the Althusserians." *Economy and Society*, volume 8(4), November 1979, 383–416.

Nizami, K. *History of the Aligarah Muslim University* (New Delhi: IDārah-i Adabiyat-i Delhi, 1995).

Norberg-Hodge, H. "The Pressure to Modernize and Globalize," in J. Mander and E. Goldsmith, eds., *The Case Against the Global Economy: And for a Turn Toward the Local* (San Francisco: Sierra Club Books, 1996).

Nye, J. *Bound to Lead: The Changing Nature of American Power* (New York: Basic Books, 1990).

——. "Lessons in Imperialism." *Financial Times*, June 17, 2002.

——. *The Paradox of American Power: Why the World's Only Superpower Can't Go it Alone* (New York: Oxford University Press, 2002).

Nye, J. and W. Owens, "America's Information Edge." *Foreign Affairs*, March–April 1996.

Ohmae, K. *The Borderless World* (London: HarperCollins, 1990).

Ohman, R. "English and the Cold War," in N. Chomsky et al., *The Cold War and the University: Toward an Intellectual History of the Cold War Years* (New York: The New Press, 1997).

Omar, S. "Arab Nationalism: A Retrospective Evaluation." *Arab Studies Quarterly*, volume 14(4), Fall 1992.

Oren, M. B. *Six Days of War: June 1967 and the Making of the Modern Middle East* (New York: Oxford Univeristy Press, 2002).

Othmān, F. *Uṣūl al-fikr al-siyāsī al-islāmi* (Beirut: Mu'asasat al-Risāla, 1984).

Owen, R. *The Middle East in the World Economy, 1800–1914* (London: Methuen & Co., 1981).

——. *State, Power, and Politics in the Making of the Modern Middle East* (London: Routledge, 1992).

Panikkar, K. M. *Asia and Western Dominance* (New Delhi: Somaiya Publications, 1999).

Parry, B. *Delusions and Discoveries: India in British Imagination, 1880–1930* (London: Verso Press, 1998).

Patterson, J. T. *Grand Expectations: The United States, 1945–1974* (New York: Oxford University Press, 1996).

Peled, A. R. *Debating Islam in the Jewish State: The Development of Policy Toward Islamic Institutions in Israel* (Albany: State University of New York Press, 2001).

Perkins, E. J. *The World Economy in the Twentieth Century* (Cambridge: Schenkman, 1983).

Peters, R. "Ijtihād and Taqlīd in 18th and 19th Century Islam." *Die Welt des Islams*, volume 20, 1980, 131–45.

Petras, J. "The U.S. and the Middle East: Recolonization or Decolonization?" *Arab Studies Quarterly*, volume 2(2), Spring 1980.

Pilger, J. *The New Rulers of the World* (London: Verso, 2002).

Plessner, M. "Hirmis." *The Encyclopedia of Islam*, volume 3 (Leiden: Brill, 1986), 463–5.

Polyani, K. *The Great Transformation: Political and Economic Origins of Our Time* (Boston: Beacon Press, 1957).

Popper, K. *The Open Society and its Enemies*, 2 volumes (Princeton: Princeton University Press, 1962).

Poulantzas, N. *Fascism and Dictatorship* (London: Verso, 1979).

——. *State, Power, Socialism* (London: Verso, 1980).

Powell, W. and L. Lewis, eds. *High Status Track: Studies of Elite Schools and Stratification* (Albany: State University of New York Press, 1990).

Qaddūḥ, K. "al-Fikr al-tarbawī 'inda Mahdī 'Āmil." In Markaz al-Buḥūth al-'Arabīyyah, *al-Nadhariyyah wa'l mumārasah fī fikr Mahdī 'Āmil: Nadwah Fikriyyah* (Beirut: Dār al-Fārābī, 1989).

Qaraḍāwī, Y. *Ghayr al-muslimīn fī'l mujtama' al-islāmī* (Cairo: Maktabat Wahba, 1977).
——. *al-Islām wa'l 'ilmāniyyah wajhan lī wajh: rad 'ilmī 'ala Fu'ād Zakariyya wa jamā'at al-'ilmaniyyīn* (Cairo: Dār al-Ṣahwah, 1978).
——. *al-Ḥall al-islāmī, farīḍah wa ḍarūrah* (Beirut: Mu'asasat al-Risālah, 1989).
——. *The Islamic Awakening: Between Rejection and Extremism* (Herndon: International Institute of Islamic Thought, 1991).
——. *Limādha al-islām?* (Beirut: Mu'asasat al-Risālah, 1993).
——. *al-Ḥulūl al-mustawrada wa kayfa janat 'alā ummatina* (Beirut: Mu'asasat al-Risālah, 1995).
——. *al-Ṣahwah al-islāmiyyah wa humūm al-watan al-'arabī wa'l islāmī* (Beirut: Mu'asasat al-Risālah, 1997).
——. *al-Shaykh al-Ghazālī kamā 'araftuhū: rihlat nisf qarn* (al-Manṣūrah: Dār al-Wafā', 1997).
——. *al-Muslimūn wa'l 'awlamah* (Cairo: Dār al-Tawzī' wa'l Nashr al-Islāmiyyah, 2000).
——. *Priorities of the Islamic Movement in the Coming Phase*, trans. S. M. Ḥassan al-Banna (London: Awakening Publications, 2000).
Qunṣuwwa, S. "Ḥawla al-'aql wa'l thaqāfah al-'Arabiyyah: ḥiwār ma' Zakī Najīb Maḥmūd." *Al-Mustaqbal al-'Arabī*, volume 11(8), August 1988.
Qureshi, I. *Education in Pakistan* (Karachi: Ma'aref, 1975).
Quṭb, M. *Jāhiliyat al-qarn al-'ishrīn* (Beirut: Dār al-Kitāb, 1976).
——. *al-Muslimūn wa'l 'awlamah* (Cairo: Dār al-Shurūq, 2000).
Quṭb, S. *Ma'ālim fī'l ṭarīq* (Beirut: Dār al-Shurūq, 1973).
——. *Dirāsāt islāmiyyah* (Cairo: Dār al-Shurūq, 1976).
Raḍwān, N. *al-Shabāb al-miṣrī al-mu'āṣir wa azmat al-qiyam* (Cairo: al-Hay'ah al-Miṣriyyah al-'Āmmah li'l Kitāb, 1997).
Rahman, F. "Islamic Modernism: Its Scope, Method, and Alternative." *International Journal of Middle East Studies*, volume 1, 1970, 317–33.
——. *Islam and Modernity: Transformation of an Intellectual Tradition* (Chicago: University of Chicago Press, 1982).
——. *Major Themes of the Qur'ān* (Indianapolis: Bibliotheca Islamica, 1988).
Ramadan, T. *Islam, the West and the Challenges of Modernity* (Leicester: Islamic Foundation, 2001).
Ramonet, I. "Nouvel ordre, rébellions, nationalismes: Un monde à reconstruire." *Le Monde Diplomatique*, May 1992.
——. "L'empire américain." *Le Monde Diplomatique*, February 1997.
——. "Régimes globalitaires." *Le Monde Diplomatique*, January 1997.
Rattansi, A. "Postcolonialism and its Discontents." *Economy and Society*, volume 26(4), November 1997, 480–500.
Rayyis, D. D. *al-Nadhariyāt al-siyāsiyah al-islāmiyyah* (Cairo: Dār al-Ma'ārif, 1966).
Rayyis, R. "al-Khalīj al-'Arabī: 'awdat al-isti'mār," in R. N. Al-Rayyis, ed., *'Awdat al-isti'mār: min al-ghazw al-thaqāfī ilā ḥarb al-khallīj* (London: Riad El-Rayyes Books, 1991).
Reich, R. *The Work of Nations* (New York: Knopf, 1991).
Reid, D. "*Arabic Thought in the Liberal Age Twenty Five Years After*." *International Journal of Middle East Studies*, volume 14(4), November 1982: 541–57.
Retnani, M. Y., ed. *Penseurs maghrébins contemporains* (Casablanca: Editions Eddif, 1997).
Reynolds, D. *One World Divisible: A Global History since 1945* (Boston: Norton, 1999).
Rice, E. *Captain Sir Richard Francis Burton* (New York: Harper Perennial, 1990).
Riḍa, M. *Sharḥ al-manār* (Beirut: Dār al-Turāth, 1982).
Rifā'ī, G. "Mulāḥadhāt ḥawla al-manhajiyyah fī ba'd turūhāt al-tajdīd al-fikrī." *Al-Ṭarīq*, volume 52(3), April–September 1993.
Roberts, H. *The Battlefield: Algeria 1988–2002* (London: Verso, 2003).
Roberts, J. M. *Twentieth Century: The History of the World, 1901 to 2000* (London: Viking, 2000).
Robertson, R. *Globalization: Social Theory and Global Culture* (London: Sage, 1996).
Robinson, W. *Promoting Polyarchy: Globalization, U.S. Intervention, and Hegemony* (New York: Cambridge University Press, 1996).
Rodinson, M. *Marxisme et monde musulman* (Paris: Editions Du Seuil, 1972).
——. *Marxism and the Muslim World* (New York: Monthly Review Press, 1981).

——. "*Al-W'y al-Qawmī* et sa place dans l'évolution de la pensée nationaliste arabe," in H. Nashabe, ed., *Studia Palestinia: Studies in Honour of Constantine K. Zurayk* (Beirut: Institute for Palestine Studies, 1988).

Roethke, T. "The Far Field," in *The Collected Poems of Theodore Roethke* (New York: Doubleday, 1975).

Rorty, R. *Philosophy and the Mirror of Nature* (Princeton: Princeton University Press, 1979).

——. *Essays on Heidegger and Others: Philosophical Papers*, volume 2 (Cambridge: Cambridge University Press, 1991).

Rosenthal, F. "The Stranger in Medieval Islam." *Arabica: Journal of Arabic and Islamic Studies*, volume 44(1), January 1997.

Roszak, T. *The Cult of Information: The Folklore of Computers and the True Art of Thinking* (New York: Pantheon, 1986).

Roy, O. *L'échec de l'Islam politique* (Paris: Le Seuil, 1992).

Rushdie, S. *Imagined Homelands* (New York: Granta, 1990).

Russell, B. *The Autobiography of Bertrand Russell, 1872–1914* (Boston: Little, Brown & Co., 1967).

Rustin, M. "The Politics of New Fordism or the Trouble with 'New Times'." *New Left Review*, number 175, May/June 1989, 54–78.

Sa'd, A. Ṣ. *Ṣafaḥāt mina al-yasār al-miṣrī: 1945–1946* (Cairo: Madbūlī, 1976).

——. *Taḥawwul al-takwīn al-miṣrī min al-namaṭ al-asyawī ila al-namaṭ al-ra'smālī* (Beirut: Dār al-Ḥadāthah, 1980).

——. "Ḥawla al-'ālaqah bayna namaṭay al-intāj al-koloniālī wa'l asyawī," in Markaz al-Buḥūth al-'Arabīyyah, *al-Nadhariyyah wa'l mumārasah fī fikr Mahdi 'Āmil: Nadwah Fikriyyah* (Beirut: Dār al-Fārābī, 1989).

Sa'dāwī, N. *Qaḍḍiyat al-mar'ah al-siyāsiyyah wa'l jinsiyyah* (Cairo: Dār al-Thaqāfah al-Jadīdah, 1977).

——. *Mudhakārātī fī sijni al-nisā'* (Cairo: Dār al-Mustaqbal al-'Arabī, 1986).

——. *A Daughter of Isis: The Autobiography of Nawal El Saadawi* (London: Zed Books, 1999).

Sadri, M. and A. Sadri, eds., *Reason, Freedom, and Democracy in Islam: Essential Writings of Abdolkarim Soroush* (New York: Oxford University Press, 2000).

Sa'īd, A. *al-'Arab wa mustaqbal al-niẓām al-'ālamī* (Beirut: Markaz Dirāsāt al-Wiḥdah al-'Arabīyyah, 1987).

Sa'īd, R. "al-Harakah al-shuyū'iyyah al-misriyyah 'abra sab'īn 'āman." *Qaḍāyah Fikriyyah*, volumes 11 and 12, 1992.

——. "al-Islām al-siyāsī: minā al-taṭarruf ilā al-mazīd minā al-taṭarruf." *Qaḍāyah Fikriyyah* (Cairo: Dār Qaḍāyah Fikriyyah, 1995).

Sa'īd, S. *Bourquiba: sīra shibh muḥarammah* (London: Riad El-Rayyes Books, 2000).

Saaf, A. *Politique et savoir au Maroc* (Casablanca: Nouvelle Collection Atlas, 1991).

Sagiv, D. "Judge Ashmāwī and Militant Islam in Egypt." *Middle Eastern Studies*, volume 28(3), July 1992.

Said, E. *Orientalism* (New York: Vintage Books, 1978).

——. *Culture and Imperialism* (New York: Alfred A. Knopf, 1993).

——. "The Other Arab Muslims," in E. Said, *The Politics of Dispossession* (New York: Vintage, 1995).

——. *Representations of the Intellectual* (New York: Vintage, 1994).

——. "The Arab Right Wing," in E. Said, *The Politics of Dispossession* (New York: Vintage, 1995).

——. "The Formation of American Public Opinion on the Question of Palestine," in E. Said, *The Politics of Dispossession* (New York: Vintage, 1995).

——. "Ignorant Armies Clash by Night," in E. Said, *The Politics of Dispossession: The Struggle for Palestinian Self-Determination* (New York: Vintage, 1995).

——. *Reflections on Exile and Other Essays* (Cambridge, MA: Harvard University Press, 2000).

——. *The End of the Peace Process: Oslo and After* (New York: Pantheon, 2000).

——. "America's Last Taboo." *New Left Review*, volume 6, November/December 2000.

——. *The End of the Peace Process: Oslo and After* (New York: Pantheon, 2000).

Ṣalāḥ, M. "Kharīṭat ḥarakat al-'unf fī miṣr." *Wijhāt Nadhar*, volume 1(4), May 1999, 20–5.

Salām, R. *Taṭbīq al-sharī'ah bayna al-qubūl wa'l rafḍ* (Cairo: Dār Sīnā, 1997).

Ṣāleh, M. A. "al-Uṣūliyyah: hal hiyah ta'bīr 'an ikhfāq an-taḥdīth?" *Qaḍāyah Fikriyyah*, numbers 13 and 14, October 1993.

Sālem, P. "al-Wilāyāt al-mutahiddah wa'l 'awlamah: ma'ālim al-haymanah fī maṭla' al-qarn al-ḥādī wa'l 'ishrīn," in Markaz Dirāsāt al-Wiḥdah al-'Arabīyyah, *al-'Arab wa'l 'Awlamah* (Beirut: Markaz Dirāsāt al-Wiḥdah al-'Arabīyyah, 1998).

Salibi, K. *A House of Many Mansions: The History of Lebanon Reconsidered* (Berkeley: University of California Press, 1988).

Salvatore, A. "The Rational Articulation of Turāth in Contempoary Arab Thought: The Contributions of Muḥammad 'Ābid al-Jābīrī and Ḥasan Hanafī." *The Muslim World*, volume 95(3 and 4), 1995 191–214.

——. *Islam and the Political Discourse of Modernity* (London: Ithaca, 1997).

Sandal, M. "Religious Liberty: Freedom of Choice or Freedom of Conscience," in R. Bhargava, ed., *Secularism and its Critics* (New Delhi: Oxford University Press, 1998).

Sanhūrī, A. R. *al-Wasīṭ fī sharḥ al-qanūn al-madanī* (Cairo: Dār al-Nahḍah al-'Arabīyyah, 1964).

Sassen, S. *Losing Control? Sovereignty in an Age of Globalization* (New York: Columbia University Press, 1996).

Sassoon, A. S. *Gramsci's Politics* (London: Hutchinson, 1987).

Sāyigh, A., ed. *Costantine Zurayk: 65 sanat min al-'aṭā'* (Beirut: Maktabat Beisān, 1996).

Sayyid, L. *Mabādi' fī al-siyāsah wa'l adab wa'l ijtimā'* (Cairo: Dār Misr, 1963).

Sayyid, R. "Contemporary Muslim Thought and Human Rights." *Islamochristiana*, volume 21, 1995, 27–41.

Schwarz, A. *A Nation in Waiting: Indonesia's Search for Stability* (St. Leonard's: Allen & Unwin, 1999).

Seale, P. *Asad and the Struggle for the Middle East* (Berkeley: University of California Press, 1988).

Sen, A. "The Threats to Secular India." *New York Review of Books*, volume 40(7), April 8, 1993.

Servan-Schreiber, J. *Le défi américain* (Paris: Denoël, 1967).

Shafīq, M. *al-Islām fī ma'rakat al-ḥadārah* (Beirut: al-Nāsher, 1991).

——. *Qaḍāyah al-tanmiyyah wa'l istiqlāl fī'l ṣirā' al-ḥadāri* (Beirut: al-Nāsher, 1992).

——. *Fī al-ḥadāthah wa'l Khiṭāb al-ḥadāthī* (Casablanca: al-Markaz al-Thaqāfī al-'Arabī, 1999).

Shafir, G. *Land, Labor and the Origins of the Israeli-Palestinian Conflict, 1882–1914* (Berkeley: University of California Press, 1996).

Shāhīn, A. *Qiṣṣat Abū Zayd wa inḥisār al-'ilmāniyyah fī jāmi'at al-qāhirah* (Cairo: Dār al-I'tiṣām, n.d.).

Shākir, M. *Risālah fī'l ṭarīq ila thaqāfatinah* (Cairo: Dār al-Hilāl, 1991).

Shaltūt, M. *al-Islām: 'aqīdah wā sharī'ah* (Cairo: Dār al-Shurūq, 1986).

Shams al-Dīn, M. M. *Fiqh al-'unf al-musallah fī'l Islām* (Beirut: al-Mu'assassah al-Dawliyyah li'l Dirāsāt wa'l Nashr, 2001).

Sharābī, H. "Islam and Modernization in the Arab World," in J. Thompson and R. Reischauer, eds., *Modernization of the Arab World* (New York: Van Nostrand, 1966).

——. *Arab Intellectuals and the West: The Formative Years* (Baltimore: Johns Hopkins University Press, 1970).

——. *Neopatriarchy: A Theory of Distorted Change in Arab Society* (New York: Oxford University Press, 1988).

Sharābī, H., ed. *Theory, Politics, and the Arab World* (New York: Routledge, 1990).

Sharārah, W. *al-Ahl wa'l ghanīmah: muqawimmāt al-siyāsah fī'l mamlakah al-'Arabīyyah al-sa'ūdiyyah* (Beirut: Dār al-Ṭalī'ah, 1981).

Shari'āti, A. *On the Sociology of Islam* (Berkeley: Mizan Press, 1979).

Sharīf, M. "Costantine Zurayk: tahawwulāt 'ala Tafkīr qawmī 'Arabī." *Al-Ṭarīq*, volume 60(4), July–August 2001.

Sharqāwī, J. "al-Ishkāliyāt al-thalāth allatī hakamat al-'alāqah bayana al-shuyū'īyyīn wā thawrat yūlio." *Qaḍāyah Fikriyyah*, volumes 11 and 12, 1992.

Sharqāwī, M. *Salāma Mūsa: al-mufakir wa'l insān* (Cairo: Dār al-Hilāl, 1968).

Shehab, S. "Philosopher Faces Apostasy Charge." *Al-Ahram Weekly*, May 8–14, 1997.

Shīḥa, M. *Lubnān fī shakhṣiyatihī wā ḥudūriḥī* (Beirut: Manshūrāt al-Nadwah al-Lubnāniyyah, 1962).

Shils, E. *The Intellectuals and the Powers and Other Essays* (Chicago: University of Chicago Press, 1972).

Shiva, V. *Monocultures of the Mind: Biodiversity, Biotechnology, and the Third World* (Penang, Malaysia: Third World Network, 1993).

Shlaim, A. *The Politics of Partition: King Abdullah, the Zionists and Palestine, 1921–1951* (New York: Columbia University Press, 1990).

Shukrī, G. *Min al-arshīf al-sirrī li'l thaqāfah al-miṣriyyah* (Beirut: Dār al-Ṭalī'ah, 1975).

——. *Egypt: Portrait of a President* (London: Zed Books, 1981).

——. *al-Nahḍah wa'l suqūṭ fī'l fikr al-miṣrī al-ḥadīth* (Beirut: Dār al-Ṭalī'ah, 1982).

——. *Salāma Mūsa wā azmat al-ḍamīr al-'arabī* (Beirut: Dār al-Āfāq al-Jadīdah, 1983).

——. *Aqwās al-hazīmah: wa'y al-nukhbah bayna al-ma'rifah wa'l sulṭah* (Cairo: Dār al-Fikr, 1990).

——. *Aqni'at al-irhāb: al-bahth 'an 'ilmāniyyah Jadīdah* (Cairo: al-Hay'ah al-Miṣriyyah al-'Āmmah li'l Kitāb, 1992).

——. Bidāyat al-tārīkh: min zilzāl al-khalīj ilā zawāl al-soviet (Cairo: Dār Su'ād al-Sabāḥ, 1993).

——. "Man la yakhāf al-Shaykh al-Ghazālī?" In his *Thaqāfat al-niẓām al-'ashwā'ī: takfīr al-'aql wa 'aql al-takfīr* (Cairo: Kitāb al-Ahālī, 1994).

——. *al-Khurūj 'alā al-naṣṣ: tahadiyyāt al-thaqāfah wa'l dimūqratiyyah* (Cairo: Dār Sīnā, 1994).

——. *Diktātoriyat al-takhalluf al-'arabī* (Cairo: al-Hay'ah al-Miṣriyyah al-'Āmmah li'l Kitāb, 1994).

——. *Mira'āt al-manfa: asi'lah fi thaqāfat al-nafṭ wa'l harb* (Cairo: al-Hay'ah al-Miṣriyyah al-'Āmmah li'l Kitāb, 1994).

——. *Mudhakarāt thaqāfah taḥtadir* (Cairo: al-Hay'ah al-Miṣriyyah al-'Āmmah, 1995).

——. " 'Abdul Nāṣṣer wa'l muthaqaffūn," in G. Shukrī, *Mudhakārāt thaqāfah taḥtadir* (Cairo: al-Hay'ah al-Miṣriyyah al-'Āmmah li'l Kitāb, 1995).

Shumayl, S. *Falsafat al-nushū' wa'l irtiqā'* (Cairo: Dār al-Muqṭaṭif, 1910).

Silver, J. and Eric Slater, "The Social Origins of World Hegemonism," in G. Arrighi and B. J. Silver, eds., *Chaos and Governance in the Modern World System* (Minneapolis: University of Minnesota Press, 1999).

Smith, D. E. "India as a Secular State," in R. Bhargava, ed., *Secularism and its Critics* (New Delhi: Oxford University Press, 1998).

Smith, H. *Beyond the Post-Modern Mind* (Wheaton: The Theosophical Publication House, 1989).

Smith, W. *Islam in Modern History* (New York: New American Library, 1957).

Somervell, D. C. *English Thought in the Nineteenth Century* (London: Methuen & Co., 1929).

Sonbol, A. E. *The New Mamluks: Egyptian Society and Modern Feudalism* (Syracuse: Syracuse University Press, 2000).

Sonn, T. "Secularism and National Stability in Islam." *Arab Studies Quarterly*, volume 9(3), Summer 1987, 284–305.

Sorokin, P. *Social and Cultural Dynamics*, 4 volumes (Boston: Beacon Press, 1950).

——. *Social Philosophies of an Age of Crisis* (Boston: Beacon Press, 1950).

Spadafora, D. "Secularization in British Thought, 1730–1789: Some Landmarks," in W. Wagar, ed., *The Secular Mind: Transformations of Faith in Modern Europe* (New York: Holmes & Meier, 1982).

Spretnak, C. *The Resurgence of the Real: Body, Nature and Place in a Hypermodern World* (New York: Addison-Wesley, 1997).

Springborg, R. "The Arab Bourgeoisie: A Revisionist Interpretation." *Arab Studies Quarterly*, volume 15(1), Winter 1993.

Sprinker, M. *History and Ideology in Proust: A la recherche du temps perdu and the Third French Republic* (London: Verso, 1998).

Steppat, F. "Re-Reading 'The Meaning of Disaster' in 1985," in H. Nashabe, ed., *Studia Palestinia: Studies in Honour of Constantine K. Zurayk* (Beirut: Institute for Palestine Studies, 1988).

Stowasser, B. "Old Shaykhs, Young Women, and the Internet: The Rewriting of Women's Political Rights in Islam." *The Muslim World*, volume 91(1 and 2), Spring 2001, 99–120.

Strange, S. *The Retreat of the State: The Diffusion of Power in the World Economy* (Cambridge: Cambridge University Press, 1998).

Strauss, L. *What is Political Philosophy?* (Chicago: University of Chicago Press, 1988).

Suleiman, M. "The Lebanese Communist Party." *Middle Eastern Studies*, volume 3(2), January 1967, 134–59.

Suwayd, M. "al-'urūba wa'l islām: hiwār shāmil ma' Costantine Zurayk." *Majallat al-Dirāsāt al-Filasṭīniyya*, 1996.

Swartz, D. "Bridging the Study of Culture and Religion: Pierre Bourdieu's Political Economy of Symbolic Power." *Sociology of Religion*, volume 57(1), Spring 1996.

——. *Culture and Power: The Sociology of Pierre Bourdieu* (Chicago: University of Chicago Press, 1998).

Talbi, M. *Reflexion sur le Coran* (Paris: Seghers, 1989).

——. *Plaidoyer pour un islam moderne* (Casablanca: Editions Le Fennec, 1996).

Tamimi, A. "Democracy: The Religious and the Political in Contemporary Islamic Debate." *Encounters: Journal of Inter-Cultural Perspectives*, volume 4(1), March 1998: 38.

——. *Rachid Ghannouci: A Democrat within Islamism* (New York: Oxford University Press, 2001).

Tapp, W. K. *The Amoral Elephant: Globalization and the Struggle for Social Justice in the Twenty-First Century* (New York: Monthly Review Press, 2001).

Ṭarābīshī, G. "Ishkaliyat al-dimūqratiyyah fī'l waṭan al-'Arabī," in S. Yāssīn, ed., *al-'Arab wa taḥadiyyāt al-qarn al-ḥādī wa'l 'ishrīn* (Amman: Mu'assassat 'Abdul Ḥamīd Shūmān, 2000).

Ṭarābulsī, F. *Silat bila waṣl: Michāl Shīha wa'l aydiūlūjiyya al-lubnāiniyyah* (Beirut: Dār al-Rayyis, 1998).

Ṭawātī, M. "al-Harakah al-islāmiyyah fī Tūnus." *Qaḍāyah Fikriyyah*, 1989.

Taylor, C. *Sources of the Self: The Making of the Modern Identity* (Cambridge, MA: Harvard University Press, 1989).

——. *The Ethics of Authenticity* (Cambridge, MA: Harvard University Press, 1991).

——. "Modes of Secularism," in R. Bhargava, ed., *Secularism and its Critics* (New Delhi: Oxford University Press, 1998).

Tessler, M. "The Origins of Popular Support for Islamist Movements: A Political Economy Analysis," in J. P. Entelis, ed., *Islam: Democracy and the State in North Africa* (Bloomington: Indiana University Press, 1997).

Thompson, E. P. *The Poverty of Theory* (London: Merlin, 1978).

Tibī, B. "al-Fikr wa'l hazīmah: Arā' Costantine Zurayk fī hazīmatī ḥuzayrān." *Mawāqif*, volume 2(8), March 1970.

Tillich, P. *Systematic Theology*, 3 volumes (Chicago: University of Chicago Press, 1952–62).

Tizīnī, Ṭ. *Ṭarīq al-wudūḥ al-manhajī* (Beirut: Dār al-Fārābī, 1989).

——. "Naḥwa 'ilmāniyyah takūn madkhalan lī mashrū' 'arabī nahdawi jadīd." *Al-Ṭarīq*, volume 55(6), 1996.

——. *Min al-istishrāq ilā al-istighrāb al-maghribī: Baḥth fī'l qirā'ah al-Jābiriyyah li'l fikr al-'arabī* (Ḥoms: Dār al-Dhākirah, 1996).

——. "Mahdī 'Āmil: mā alladhī tabaqqā minhū?" *Al-Ṭarīq*, number 4, July–August 1997.

Toer, P. A. *The Mute's Soliloquy: A Memoir* (New York: Hyperion East, 1999).

Torki, R. *Le Cheikh Abdel Hamid Ben Badis: le leader de la réformation et de l'éducation en Algérie* (Algiers: La Société Nationale du Livre, 1984).

Toynbee, A. *Experiences* (London: Oxford University Press, 1969).

Tozy, M. *Monarchie et islam politique au Maroc* (Paris: Presses de Sciences-Politiques, 1999).

——. "Qui sont les islamistes au Maroc?" *Le Monde Diplomatique*, August 1999.

Tripp, C. *A History of Iraq*, second edition (Cambridge: Cambridge University Press, 2000).

Turābī, H. *Nadharāt fī'l fiqh al-siyāsī* (Umm al-Faḥm: Markaz al-Dirāsāt al-Mu'āṣirah, 1997).

Turner, B. *Orientalism, Postmodernism and Globalism* (London: Routledge, 1994).

'Ukāshah, T. *Mudhakarātī fī'l thaqāfah wa'l siyāsah* (Cairo: Dār al-Shurūq, 2001).

'Ulwī, H. *Fī'l dīn wa'l turāth* (Jerusalem: Salāḥ al-Dīn, 1975).

——. "Naḥwa ta'sīl 'aqlāniyyah ijtimā'iyyah." *Al-Nahj*, volume 7 (1996).

'Umar, A., ed. *al-Duktūr Fu'ād Zakariyya Bāḥithan wā muthaqaffan wā nāqidan: kitāb tidhkārī* (Kuwait: University of Kuwait Press, 1998).

'Urwī, A. "al-Taḥdīth wa'l dimūqrāṭiyyah." *Āfāq: Majallat Itihād Kuttāb al-Maghrib*, 3–4, 1992.

——. *Awrāq* (Casablanca: al-Markaz al-Thaqāfī al-'Arabī, 1996).

——. *Mafhūm al-'aql* (Casablanca: al-Markaz al-Thaqāfī al 'Arabī, 1996), chapter 1.

——. *al-'Arab wa'l fikr al-tārīkhī* (Casablanca: al-Markaz al-Thaqāfī al-'Arabī, n.d.)

'Uways, S. *al-Tārīkh al-ladhī ahmilūhu 'alā dhahrī*, 3 volumes (Cairo: Dār al-Hilāl, 1987).

Valadier, P. "Intolerance et laïcité: la religion dans le débat démocratique." *Le Monde Diplomatique*, June 1989.

Vanaik, A. *The Furies of Indian Communalism: Religion, Modernity and Secularization* (London: Verso, 1997).

Vassiliev, A. *The History of Saudi Arabia* (New York: New York University Press, 2000).

Vattimo, G. *The End of Modernity: Nihilism and Hermeneutics in Postmodern Culture* (Baltimore: Johns Hopkins University Press, 1988).

Vidal, G. "Chaos." *The New York Review of Books*, December 16, 1999.

Viswanathan, G. *Masks of Conquest: Literary Study and British Rule in India* (New York: Columbia University Press, 1989).

Von Grunebaum, G. E. and R. Brunschvig, eds. *Classicisme et déclin culturel dans l'histoire de l'islam* (Paris: Maisonneuve, 1957).

Waardenburg, J. "Official and Popular Religion in Islam." *Social Compass*, 1978, 25(3–4), 315–41.

Wahba, M. "The Meaning of Ishtirākiyyah: Arab Perceptions of Socialism in the Nineteenth Century." *Alif: Journal of Comparative Poetics*, number 10, 1990, 42–55.

Wahbah, M. "al-'Aql al-'arabī wa'l 'ilmāniyyah," in M. A. al-'Ālim, ed., *al-Fikr al-'arabī 'alā mashārif al-qarn al-ḥādī wa'l 'ishrīn* (Cairo: Qaḍāyah Fikriyyah, 1995).

Wald, A. *The New York Intellectuals: The Rise and Decline of Anti-Stalinist Left from the 1930s to the 1980s* (Chapel Hill: University of North Carolina Press, 1987).

Waldrop, M. M. *Complexity: The Emerging Science at the Edge of Order and Chaos* (New York: Simon & Schuster, 1992).

Wallerstein, I. *The Capitalist World Economy* (Cambridge: Cambridge University Press, 1979).

——. *Historical Capitalism* (London: Verso, 1983).

——. "The Bourgeoisie as Concept and Reality." *New Left Review*, number 167, January–February 1988.

——. "Eurocentrism and its Avatars: The Dilemmas of Social Science." *New Left Review*, number 226, November–December 1997.

Wannās, M. "al-Dīn wa'l dawla fī Tūnis: 1956–1987," in Markaz Dirāsāt al-Wiḥdah al-'Arabīyyah, *al-Dīn fi'l mujtama' al-'arabī* (Beirut: Markaz Dirāsāt al-Wiḥdah al-'Arabīyyah, 1990).

Waterbury, J. "From Social Contracts to Extraction Contracts: The Political Economy of Authoritarianism and Democracy," in J. P. Entelis, ed., *Islam, Democracy, and the State in North Africa* (Bloomington: Indiana University Press, 1997).

Weber, M. *Economy and Society*, 2 volumes (Berkeley: University of California Press, 1978).

William, W. A. "The Frontier Thesis and American Foreign Policy." *Pacific Historical Review* 24, November 1955.

Williams, R. "Means of Communication as Means of Production," in R. Williams, *Problems in Materialism and Culture: Selected Essays* (London: Verso, 1997).

Williams, R. *Dream Worlds: Consumption in Late Nineteenth Century France* (Berkeley: University of California Press, 1982).

Wilson, B. "Secularization: The Inherited Model," in P. E. Hammond, ed., *The Sacred in a Secular Age* (Berkeley: University of California Press, 1985).

Wilson, E. *Adorned in Dreams: Fashion and Modernity* (Berkeley: University of California Press, 1985).

——. "The Invisible Flaneur." *New Left Review*, number 191, January–February 1992, 90–110.

——. *The American Earthquake: A Chronicle of the Roaring Twenties, the Great Depression and the Dawn of the New Deal* (New York: Da Capo Press, 1996).

Wolf, E. *Europe and the People Without History* (Berkeley: University of California Press, 1982).

Wolf, M. "The Need for a New Imperialism." *Financial Times*, October 9, 2001.

Woodhull, W. *Transfigurations of the Maghreb* (Minneapolis: University of Minnesota Press, 1993).

Woolf, D. R. "The Writing of Early Modern European Intellectual History, 1945–1995," in M. Bentley, ed., *Companion to Historiography* (London: Routledge, 1997).

Wreszin, M. *A Rebel in Defense of Tradition: The Life and Politics of Dwight Macdonald* (New York: Basic Books, 1994).

Wright, R. *The Last Great Revolution: Turmoil and Transformation in Iran* (New York: Alfred A. Knopf, 2000).

Yāfūt, S. *al-Manāhij al-Jadīdah li'l fikr al-falsafī al-mu'āṣir* (Beirut: Dār al-Ṭalī'ah, 1999).

Yahya, M. *Waraqah Thaqāfiyah fi'l radd 'alā al-'ilmaniyyīn* (Cairo: al-Zahrā' li'l I'lām al-'Arabī, 1988).

Yāssīn, S. *Taḥlīl maḍmūn al-fikr al-qawmī al-'arabī* (Beirut: Markaz Dirāsāt al-Wiḥdah al-'Arabīyyah, 1980).

——. *al-Turāth wa taḥadiyāt al-'asr* (Beirut: Markaz Dirāsāt al-Wiḥdah al-'Arabīyyah, 1985).

——. *al-Shakhsīiyyah al-'Arabiyyah bayna sūrat al-dhāt wā mafhūm al-ākhar* (Cairo: Maktabat Madbūlī, 1993).

Yāssīn, S., ed. *al-'Arab wā taḥadiyyāt al-qarn al-ḥādī wa'l 'ishrīn* (Amman: Mu'assassat 'Abdul Ḥamīd Shūmān, 2000).

Yates, F. "Hermeticism," in *The Encyclopedia of Philosophy*, volume 3 (New York: Macmillan, 1967).

Yūssef, A. "al-Liberaliyyah fī nadhar al-mārkisīyyah." *Al-Ṭalī'ah*, volume 8(8), August 1972.

Zakariyya, Fareed. *From Wealth to Power: The Unusual Origins of America's World Role* (Princeton: Princeton University Press, 1998).

Zakariyya, Fu'ād. "al-Falsafah wa'l dīn fi'l mujtama' al-'arabī al-mu'āṣir," in Markaz Dirāsāt al-Wiḥdah al-'Arabīyyah, *al-Falsafah fī'l waṭan al-'arabī al-mu'āṣir* (Beirut: Markaz Dirāsāt al-Wiḥdah al-'Arabīyyah, 1985).

——. *Khiṭāb ilā al-'aql al-'arabī* (Kuwait: Kitāb al-'Arabī, 1987).

——. *al-Ḥaqīqa wa'l khayāl fī'l ḥarakah al-islāmiyyah al-mu'āṣirah* (Cairo: Sīnā, 1988).

——. "al-'Ilmāniyyah ḍarūrah ḥadāriyyah." *Qaḍāyah Fikriyyah* (1989).

——. *al-'Arab wa'l namūdhaj al-amerīkī* (Cairo: Maktabat Miṣr, 1990).

——. *Laïcité ou islamisme. Les Arabes à l'heure du choix* (Paris: La Découverte, 1991).

——. "People Direct Islam in any Direction they Wish." *Middle East Times*, May 28–June 3, 1991.

Zakī, R. *Mushkilāt misr al-iqtiṣādiyah* (Cairo: Dār al-Fata al-'Arabī, 1982).

——. *Wadā'an li'l ṭabaqah al-mutawaṣitah* (Cairo: Dār al-Mustaqbal al-'Arabī, 1998).

Zawāhīrī, A. *al-Ḥiṣād al-murr: al-Ikhwān al-Muslimūn fī sittīna 'āman* (no publication information).

Zaydān, A. K. *Ahl al-dhimmah* (Beirut: Mu'asasat al-Risālah, n.d.).

Zebiri, K. "Islamic Revival in Algeria: An Overview." *The Muslim World*, volume 83(1), January 1993.

Zein, A. H. "Beyond Ideology and Theology: The Search for the Anthropology of Islam." *Annual Review of Anthropology*, volume 6, 1977: 227–54.

Zghal, A. "Le retour de sacré et la nouvelle demande idéologique de jeunes scolarises: Le cas de la Tunisie." *Le Maghreb Musulman*, 1979.

——. "al-Istrātijiyya al-Jadīdah lī harakat al-itijāh al-islāmī: munāwara 'an al-ta'bīr 'an al-thaqāfah al-siyāsiyyah al-tūnisiyyah," in Markaz Dirāsāt al-Wiḥdah al-'Arabīyyah, *al-Dīn fi'l mujtama' al-'arabī* (Beirut: Markaz Dirāsāt al-Wiḥdah al-'Arabīyyah, 1990).

Ziadeh, M. "Taqyīm tajribat harakatī al-qawmiyyīn al-'arab fī marhalatiha al-ūla," in Markaz Dirāsāt al-Wiḥdah al-'Arabīyyah, *al-Qawmiyyah al-'Arabīyyah: fī'l fikr wa'l mumārasah* (Beirut: Markaz Dirāsāt al-Wiḥdah al-'Arabīyyah, 1980).

Zimmermann, W. *First Great Triumph: How Five Americans Made Their Country a World Power* (New York: Farrar, Straus and Giroux, 2001).

Zubaida, S. "Is There a Muslim Society? Ernest Gellner's Sociology of Islam." *Economy and Society*, volume 24(2), May 1995, 151–88.

Zubayr, A. "al-Dīn wa'l siyāsa fī'l Jazā'ir." *Qaḍāyah Fikriyyah*, 1989, 187–99.

Zurayk, C. *Tensions in Islamic Civilization* (Georgetown: Center for Contemporary Arab Studies, 1978).

——. "Abiding Truths," in *al-A'māl al-fikriyyah al-'āmmah li'l dokṭor Costantine Zurayk*, volume 4 (Beirut: Markaz Dirāsāt al-Wiḥdah al-'Arabīyyah, 1994).

Zureik, E. *The Palestinians in Israel: A Study in Internal Colonialism* (London: Routledge & Kegan Paul, 1979).

Index

'Abd al-Fattāḥ, F., 51
'Abd al-Fattaḥ, N., 23, 52
'Abd al-Rāziq, 'A., 12, 75, 95, 106, 234, 234–9, 262, 270, 271, 298, 402
Abdel Malek, A., 44, 78, 160
'Abduh, M., xii, 12, 66, 67, 68, 70, 82, 91, 105, 128, 130, 161, 168, 176, 205, 206, 218, 221, 223, 245, 249, 253, 255, 282, 283, 353, 365
Abū Ghuda, 'A., 66
Adonis, 60, 87, 88, 107, 337, 339, 341, 401
Afghānī, J., xv, 38, 55, 66, 67, 81, 91, 105, 143, 167, 178, 182, 205, 227, 256, 255, 280, 284, 376
Afghanistan, 36, 84, 143, 144, 166, 213, 225, 376
'Aflaq, M., 77, 79
Aḥmad, A., 4, 43
Aḥmad, K., 396
Aḥmad, L., 47
Alexander, J., 2
'Ālim, M. A., 51, 75, 86, 89, 160, 187–95, 205, 213, 321–6, 335
Alwani, Ṭ., 67, 160, 161, 206, 415
American pragmatism, 13–15
Americanized Islam, 13
Amīn, S., xi, 19, 25, 26, 43, 47, 67, 87, 102, 169, 172, 187–8, 221, 323, 336, 348
Anderson, B., 20, 69, 131, 132, 173
Anderson, P., 47
Arab bourgeoisie, 23, 74–98, 109, 185, 292, 319–29
Arab Christian intellectuals, 97
Arab intelligentsia, 13, 15, 55–65, 77, 81, 87, 96, 104, 116, 123, 156, 208, 221, 259–67, 282, 298, 300, 304, 300, 307, 309, 329, 337, 338, 344, 345, 350, 351, 352–67
Arab League, 5, 52, 139
Arab Left, 55, 80–7, 187, 319, 331–5, 372
Arab mind, 87, 91, 112–16, 161, 175, 189, 254, 264, 267, 281–98, 308, 316
Arab modernism, 96–9, 116, 119
Arab power elite, vii, x, 8, 9, 11–15, 16, 18, 19–25
Arab rationalism, 122, 259, 279
Arab thought xv, 7, 8, 11–14, 17, 29, 32, 42, 43–6, 49, 53, 55, 57–60, 63, 64–74, 89–92, 94–9, 116, 117, 122–7, 129, 131, 134, 145, 147, 149, 152, 161, 185, 223, 259, 261–74
Arab world, x, xi, xii–xv, 3, 22–34, 61, 66, 68, 84, 88, 103, 105, 110, 130, 138, 177
Arabization, 27, 45, 104, 134, 178, 295, 299, 385
Arendt, H., xiv, 1, 126, 185, 199, 344, 426, 456
Arkoun, M., 45, 62, 64, 117, 144, 258, 279, 385
Asad, T., 9, 35, 87, 119, 129, 377
'Aṣṣabiyyah, 38, 43, 140, 141, 185, 228, 229, 263, 365
'Attār, Ḥ., 56, 66
Authenticity, 13
'Awaḍ, L., 51, 89, 114
Azhar, 9, 32, 35, 95, 104, 144, 212, 224, 225, 232, 234, 240, 241, 366, 367, 412
'Azzām Pasha, 130

Bahā' al-Dīn, A., 51
Banna, H., 56, 57, 68, 138, 139, 150, 159, 160, 195, 204, 207, 221, 224, 230, 234, 235, 236, 238, 244, 249, 255, 256, 367, 387
Bāqūrī, Ḥ., 254
Barthes, R., 260
Bennabi, M., 137, 144, 159, 279, 300, 408
Berger, P., 102
Bishrī, Ṭ., 66, 109, 133, 159, 401
Bīṭār, S., 77
Bourdieu, P. 2, 25, 33–8, 49, 165, 173
British Mandate, 130

Capitalist mode of production, xv–xvii, 7, 26, 27, 30–3, 67, 169, 170, 188, 191, 324, 335, 336
Charaffeddine, F., 309
Chomsky, N., 4, 165, 168, 178, 179, 182
Clash of civilizations, xii, 2, 6, 188
Cold War, 83, 122, 145, 164, 165, 170, 171, 174, 176, 181, 252, 289, 293, 356
Colonialism, 44, 51–5, 60–5, 90, 96, 97, 100, 105, 114, 119, 123, 128–32, 160, 161–6, 170–8, 195, 204, 208, 215, 233, 239, 250–5
Committee of Union and Progress (CUP), 130
Committee on Social Thought, 5
Corruption, 39, 120, 146, 154, 228, 231, 232, 234, 244, 255, 366, 370
Cosmopolitan Greetings: Poems 1986–1992, 1
Coury, R., 130–40
Cromer, Earl of, 2

Dār al-Ḥadith al-Ḥassaniyah, 9
Darwaza, M., 77
Darwish, M., 43, 51, 60, 318
Defeat of 1967, 10–25
DeLeuze, J., 260